Advance in Marine Geotechnical Engineering

Advance in Marine Geotechnical Engineering

Guest Editor

Hem Bahadur Motra

MDPI

Basel • Beijing • Wuhan • Barcelona • Belgrade • Novi Sad • Cluj • Manchester

Guest Editor
Hem Bahadur Motra
Department of Geosciences
Christian-Albrechts-Universität
zu Kiel
Kiel
Germany

Editorial Office
MDPI AG
Grosspeteranlage 5
4052 Basel, Switzerland

This is a reprint of the Special Issue, published open access by the journal *Journal of Marine Science and Engineering* (ISSN 2077-1312), freely accessible at: https://www.mdpi.com/journal/jmse/special_issues/EI4WU9QL7W.

For citation purposes, cite each article independently as indicated on the article page online and as indicated below:

Lastname, A.A.; Lastname, B.B. Article Title. *Journal Name* **Year**, *Volume Number*, Page Range.

ISBN 978-3-7258-6920-6 (Hbk)
ISBN 978-3-7258-6921-3 (PDF)
https://doi.org/10.3390/books978-3-7258-6921-3

Contents

Hem Bahadur Motra
Advance in Marine Geotechnical Engineering
Reprinted from: *J. Mar. Sci. Eng.* **2025**, *13*, 2123, https://doi.org/10.3390/jmse13112123 . . . . . **1**

Weijia Ma, You Qin, Fei Gao and Qi Wu
Experimental Study of the Dynamic Shear Modulus of Saturated Coral Sand under Complex Consolidation Conditions
Reprinted from: *J. Mar. Sci. Eng.* **2023**, *11*, 214, https://doi.org/10.3390/jmse11010214 . . . . . . **5**

Qi Wu, Zifan Wang, You Qin and Wenbao Yang
Intelligent Model for Dynamic Shear Modulus and Damping Ratio of Undisturbed Marine Clay Based on Back-Propagation Neural Network
Reprinted from: *J. Mar. Sci. Eng.* **2023**, *11*, 249, https://doi.org/10.3390/jmse11020249 . . . . . . **22**

Yingtao Zhou, Xi Feng, Maoyuan Liu and Weiqun Wang
Influence of Beach Erosion during Wave Action in Designed Artificial Sandy Beach Using XBeach Model: Profiles and Shoreline
Reprinted from: *J. Mar. Sci. Eng.* **2023**, *11*, 984, https://doi.org/10.3390/jmse11050984 . . . . . . **37**

Jiayi Shen, Xinyi Wang, Qian Chen, Zhaoyi Ye, Qiaoling Gao and Jiawang Chen
Numerical Investigations of Undrained Shear Strength of Sensitive Clay Using Miniature Vane Shear Tests
Reprinted from: *J. Mar. Sci. Eng.* **2023**, *11*, 1094, https://doi.org/10.3390/jmse11051094 . . . . . **53**

Jae-Hyun Kim, Yeong-Hoon Jeong, Jeong-Gon Ha and Heon-Joon Park
Evaluation of Soil–Foundation–Structure Interaction for Large Diameter Monopile Foundation Focusing on Lateral Cyclic Loading
Reprinted from: *J. Mar. Sci. Eng.* **2023**, *11*, 1303, https://doi.org/10.3390/jmse11071303 . . . . . **67**

Mingchen Zhong and Kun Meng
Dynamic Interaction Factor of Pipe Group Piles Considering the Scattering Effect of Passive Piles
Reprinted from: *J. Mar. Sci. Eng.* **2023**, *11*, 1698, https://doi.org/10.3390/jmse11091698 . . . . . **85**

Junwei Shu, Jun Wang, Kexing Chen, Qingsong Shen and Hongyue Sun
Analysis of Factors Affecting Vacuum Formation and Drainage in the Siphon-Vacuum Drainage Method for Marine Reclamation
Reprinted from: *J. Mar. Sci. Eng.* **2024**, *12*, 430, https://doi.org/10.3390/jmse12030430 . . . . . . **100**

Yu Peng, Bolong Liu, Gang Wang and Quan Wang
Analyses of the Suction Anchor–Sandy Soil Interactions under Slidable Pulling Action Using DEM-FEM Coupling Method: The Interface Friction Effect
Reprinted from: *J. Mar. Sci. Eng.* **2024**, *12*, 535, https://doi.org/10.3390/jmse12040535 . . . . . . **117**

Miaojun Sun, Zhigang Shan, Wei Wang, Simin Xu, Xiaolei Liu, Hong Zhang and Xingsen Guo
Numerical Investigation into the Stability of Offshore Wind Power Piles Subjected to Lateral Loads in Extreme Environments
Reprinted from: *J. Mar. Sci. Eng.* **2024**, *12*, 915, https://doi.org/10.3390/jmse12060915 . . . . . . **129**

Yuan Yuan, Yian Zhao, Xiaotian Feng, Yanhua Lei and Wenbing Zhang
Spatio-Temporal Compressive Behaviors of River Pebble Concrete and Sea Pebble Concrete in Island Offshore Engineering
Reprinted from: *J. Mar. Sci. Eng.* **2024**, *12*, 1395, https://doi.org/10.3390/jmse12081395 . . . . . **153**

Ben He, Mingbao Lin, Xinran Yu, Genqiang Peng, Guoxiang Huang and Song Dai
Bearing Behavior of Large-Diameter Monopile Foundations of Offshore Wind Turbines in Weathered Residual Soil Seabeds
Reprinted from: *J. Mar. Sci. Eng.* **2024**, *12*, 1785, https://doi.org/10.3390/jmse12101785 . . . . . **167**

Ammar Alnmr and Mais Mayassah
Innovations in Offshore Wind: Reviewing Current Status and Future Prospects with a Parametric Analysis of Helical Pile Performance for Anchoring Mooring Lines
Reprinted from: *J. Mar. Sci. Eng.* **2024**, *12*, 1040, https://doi.org/10.3390/jmse12071040 . . . . . **185**

Nikolaos-Kimon Chtouris and Thomas Hasiotis
Marine Geotechnical Research in Greece: A Review of the Current Knowledge, Challenges and Prospects
Reprinted from: *J. Mar. Sci. Eng.* **2024**, *12*, 1708, https://doi.org/10.3390/jmse12101708 . . . . . **231**

Journal of
Marine Science and Engineering

MDPI

Editorial

Advance in Marine Geotechnical Engineering

Hem Bahadur Motra

Faculty of Mathematics and Natural Sciences, Institute of Geosciences, Marine and Land Geomechanics and Geotectonic, Christian-Albrechts-Universität zu Kiel, 24118 Kiel, Germany; hem.motra@ifg.uni-kiel.de

Marine geotechnical engineering is undergoing a rapid transformation driven by the increasing global demand for offshore energy, resilient coastal infrastructure, and sustainable seabed utilization. Traditionally focused on foundation design for offshore structures, the field now encompasses a wide range of challenges, including deep-sea mineral exploration, subsea cable routing, offshore wind turbine installations, and the assessment of submarine slope stability in response to climate change-induced events.

Marine geotechnical engineering involves the application of geoscientific knowledge and innovative engineering approaches to investigate and characterize seafloor materials [Contribution 1, Contribution 10]. Despite ongoing progress, the mechanical behavior of seafloor soils—particularly in response to infrastructure development—remains insufficiently understood. Tools such as cone penetration testing with pore pressure measurement, piezocone testing, and advanced geophysical surveys have enhanced the resolution of site investigations [1,2]. Furthermore, coupled hydro-mechanical modeling techniques now allow for more accurate simulations of soil behavior under cyclic and dynamic loading, which is critical for offshore wind farms and seismic-prone marine environments [Contribution 5, Contribution 6, Contribution 13, [3–6]]. Given the increasing complexity and scale of offshore structures, such as wind farms, pipelines, and subsea foundations, addressing this knowledge gap is more critical than ever.

Emerging topics such as bio-mediated soil improvement, methane hydrate-bearing sediments, and the impact of climate-driven processes like thawing permafrost and ocean acidification on soil properties are gaining prominence [Contribution 1, [4–6]]. Additionally, the integration of machine learning and data analytics into marine geotechnics is beginning to transform design optimization and risk assessment processes.

This Special Issue brings together recent research contributions that reflect the breadth and depth of innovation in marine geotechnical engineering. The selected articles highlight experimental breakthroughs, novel field techniques, and modeling strategies aimed at addressing the pressing engineering and environmental challenges facing offshore and coastal development. Furthermore, this Special Issue highlights recent theoretical, numerical, experimental, and applied contributions that enhance our understanding of seafloor behavior and improve the design, construction, and risk mitigation strategies for offshore and coastal infrastructure [Contribution 3, Contribution 4, Contribution 8]

My hope is that this collection of papers serves as a valuable reference for researchers, engineers, and policymakers working at the forefront of marine geotechnics, and that it inspires further interdisciplinary collaboration to sustainably develop and protect our ocean-based infrastructure. This Special Issue concentrates on the aforementioned problems, obtaining some interesting conclusions [Contribution 13]. The main contributions of each article are presented below.

Contribution 1: This study experimentally investigates the dynamic shear modulus behavior of saturated coral sand under complex consolidation conditions using multi-stage strain-controlled undrained cyclic shear tests. The research evaluates the influence of key consolidation parameters—effective mean principal stress (p'_0), consolidation ratio (kc), consolidation direction angle (α_0), and intermediate principal stress coefficient (b)—on the maximum shear modulus (G_0), reference shear strain (γr), and shear modulus reduction (G). New indices (μG_0 and $\mu\gamma$r) are proposed to improve predictions of G_0 and γr, and the Davidenkov model is validated for normalized shear modulus-strain relationships. The proposed model demonstrates high accuracy with deviations within $\pm 10\%$, enhancing the understanding and prediction of coral sand behavior in marine geotechnical applications.

Contribution 2: This study used resonant-column tests to analyze how the shear modulus (G) and damping ratio (D) of Chinese marine clays vary with depth (H, via σ_m) and shear strain (γ). A novel BPNN model was developed to predict G and D accurately without fitting parameters, showing robust performance across conditions.

Contribution 3: This study contributes to the design and protection of artificial sandy beaches by introducing a novel beach profile that enhances berm stability and resists erosion. Using XBeach modeling, it identifies erosion patterns under different wave conditions and evaluates both engineering and biological methods—such as plant root systems—to reduce sediment loss, offering practical insights for sustainable coastal development.

Contribution 4: This study introduces a numerical approach using the Coupled Eulerian–Lagrangian (CEL) method to evaluate the effect of confining stress on undrained shear strength in marine sediments. It proposes a new linear strength model that accounts for confining stress and corrects for vane size effects, improving the accuracy of shear strength estimation for sensitive clays in offshore engineering.

Contribution 5: This paper investigated the monotonic and cyclic behavior of a monopile-supported offshore wind turbine in sand using centrifuge testing. Under monotonic loading, the ultimate lateral capacity and bending moment distribution were assessed at different load levels. Cyclic tests revealed that rotational stiffness decreased with higher loading levels. In Fatigue Limit State (FLS) and Service Limit State (SLS) conditions, stiffness remained stable across cycles, whereas in the Ultimate Limit State (ULS), stiffness initially increased before stabilizing. The loading rate weakened monopile–soil interaction, as evidenced by bending moment trends. These findings provide critical insights for optimizing monopile design under cyclic lateral loads.

Contribution 6: In engineering applications, the formation of soil plugs within pipe piles is an inherent phenomenon that must be accounted for to enhance the accuracy of dynamic response analyses of pile group foundations. Furthermore, natural soils are typically stratified and exhibit radial heterogeneity due to sedimentary processes. Therefore, conducting dynamic response analyses of pile groups in layered and anisotropic soil conditions is essential as it offers more realistic and practically relevant insights for geotechnical design and engineering practice.

Contribution 7: This study enhances the understanding of vacuum pressure formation and drainage efficiency in SVD systems for marine reclamation. It develops a vacuum pressure model, analyzes key influencing factors, performs global sensitivity analysis, and calculates the theoretical vacuum limit, providing a foundation for optimizing SVD design and performance.

Contribution 8: This paper provides a micro-to-macro understanding of suction anchor–sandy soil interactions under slidable mooring loads, highlighting the critical role of interface friction. Using coupled DEM–FEM simulations validated by centrifuge tests, the research establishes how interface friction influences pullout resistance, displacement, rotation, and failure patterns, offering valuable insights for the design of mooring systems in marine engineering.

Contribution 9: The study of Sun et al. enhances our understanding of monopile foundation stability in offshore wind projects by incorporating the impact of submarine landslide loads, alongside traditional environmental forces such as wind, wave, and current. A validated finite element model is used to simulate complex lateral loading scenarios, revealing how landslide parameters and seabed strength influence monopile displacement, rotation, and bending. The research proposes an instability criterion, offering valuable guidance for safer foundation design in extreme marine environments.

Contribution 10: This paper investigates the mechanical performance of concrete incorporating river and sea pebbles as partial or full substitutes for traditional gravel in offshore and island construction. Using Digital Image Correlation (DIC), it reveals that increased substitution reduces compressive strength and alters failure modes due to interfacial slipping between pebbles and mortar. The findings offer critical insights into the compressive behavior and deformation characteristics of eco-friendly pebble-based concretes for marine engineering applications.

Contribution 11: He et al. investigate the mechanical behavior of weathered residual soil—the dominant seabed material in southeastern China's rocky offshore wind farm zones—and its impact on monopile foundation performance. Through dynamic triaxial tests and numerical simulations, the research reveals key insights into soil stiffness degradation and cumulative strain and evaluates monopile behavior under combined wind and wave loading. The findings offer a theoretical foundation for designing offshore wind turbine foundations in rock-based seabeds, addressing a critical gap in current practice.

Contribution 12: This review studies the feasibility of using helical piles to anchor floating offshore wind platforms in deeper waters, addressing the sector's push toward larger wind farms in complex marine environments. Through 3D numerical modeling, it identifies optimal plate positioning (Zh/Z ratios) for helical piles under varying load inclinations and shaft diameters. The results provide design guidelines for ensuring load-bearing efficiency and stability, supporting the advancement of cost-effective and resilient mooring systems in the offshore wind industry.

Contribution 13: This review highlights the urgent need for accessible geotechnical data in Greece's rapidly developing offshore energy infrastructure, including submarine cables, pipelines, and wind parks. It synthesizes current knowledge on surficial sediment behavior in the Aegean and Ionian Seas and identifies challenges in sampling and interpreting CPTu data. Emphasizing slope instability mechanisms linked to weak layers, gas presence, and seismic loading, the study advocates for the establishment of a national geological/geotechnical database to support future marine infrastructure planning and academic research.

I am pleased to present a collection of articles that reflect the interdisciplinary nature of marine geotechnical engineering. These contributions not only advance fundamental understanding but also provide practical insights that are vital for ensuring the safety, sustainability, and performance of marine infrastructure.

I extend my sincere gratitude to all the contributing authors and reviewers who have made this Special Issue possible. I hope that the findings presented here will inspire further innovation and collaboration in the evolving field of marine geotechnics.

Acknowledgments: As a Guest Editors of the Special Issue "Advances in Marine Geotechnical Engineering", I wish to extend my sincere gratitude to all the authors whose valuable contributions made the publication of this Special Issue possible.

Conflicts of Interest: The author declares no conflicts of interest.

List of Contributions:

1. Ma, W.; Qin, Y.; Gao, F.; Wu, Q. Experimental Study of the Dynamic Shear Modulus of Saturated Coral Sand under Complex Consolidation Conditions. *J. Mar. Sci. Eng.* **2023**, *11*, 214. https://doi.org/10.3390/jmse11010214.
2. Wu, Q.; Wang, Z.; Qin, Y.; Yang, W. Intelligent Model for Dynamic Shear Modulus and Damping Ratio of Undisturbed Marine Clay Based on Back-Propagation Neural Network. *J. Mar. Sci. Eng.* **2023**, *11*, 249. https://doi.org/10.3390/jmse11020249.

3. Zhou, Y.; Feng, X.; Liu, M.; Wang, W. Influence of Beach Erosion during Wave Action in Designed Artificial Sandy Beach Using XBeach Model: Profiles and Shoreline. *J. Mar. Sci. Eng.* **2023**, *11*, 984. https://doi.org/10.3390/jmse11050984.
4. Shen, J.; Wang, X.; Chen, Q.; Ye, Z.; Gao, Q.; Chen, J. Numerical Investigations of Undrained Shear Strength of Sensitive Clay Using Miniature Vane Shear Tests. *J. Mar. Sci. Eng.* **2023**, *11*, 1094. https://doi.org/10.3390/jmse11051094.
5. Kim, J.H.; Jeong, Y.H.; Ha, J.G.; Park, H.J. Evaluation of Soil–Foundation–Structure Interaction for Large Diameter Monopile Foundation Focusing on Lateral Cyclic Loading. *J. Mar. Sci. Eng.* **2023**, *11*, 1303. https://doi.org/10.3390/jmse11071303.
6. Zhong, M. and Meng, K. Dynamic Interaction Factor of Pipe Group Piles Considering the Scattering Effect of Passive Piles. *J. Mar. Sci. Eng.* **2023**, *11*, 1698. https://doi.org/10.3390/jmse11091698.
7. Shu, J.; Wang, J.; Chen, K.; Shen, Q.; Sun, H. Analysis of Factors Affecting Vacuum Formation and Drainage in the Siphon-Vacuum Drainage Method for Marine Reclamation. *J. Mar. Sci. Eng.* **2024**, *12*, 430. https://doi.org/10.3390/jmse12030430.
8. Peng, Y.; Liu, B.; Wang, G.; Wang, Q. Analyses of the Suction Anchor–Sandy Soil Interactions under Slidable Pulling Action Using DEM-FEM Coupling Method: The Interface Friction Effect. *J. Mar. Sci. Eng.* **2024**, *12*, 535. https://doi.org/10.3390/jmse12040535.
9. Sun, M.; Shan, Z.; Wang, W.; Xu, S.; Liu, X.; Zhang, H.; Guo, X. Numerical Investigation into the Stability of Offshore Wind Power Piles Subjected to Lateral Loads in Extreme Environments. *J. Mar. Sci. Eng.* **2024**, *12*, 915. https://doi.org/10.3390/jmse12060915.
10. Yuan, Y.; Zhao, Y.; Feng, X.; Lei, Y.; Zhang, W. Spatio-Temporal Compressive Behaviors of River Pebble Concrete and Sea Pebble Concrete in Island Offshore Engineering. *J. Mar. Sci. Eng.* **2024**, *12*, 1395. https://doi.org/10.3390/jmse12081395.
11. He, B.; Lin, M.; Yu, X.; Peng, G.; Huang, G.; Dai, S. Bearing Behavior of Large-Diameter Monopile Foundations of Offshore Wind Turbines in Weathered Residual Soil Seabeds. *J. Mar. Sci. Eng.* **2024**, *12*, 1785. https://doi.org/10.3390/jmse12101785.
12. Alnmr, A. and Mayassah, M. Innovations in Offshore Wind: Reviewing Current Status and Future Prospects with a Parametric Analysis of Helical Pile Performance for Anchoring Mooring Lines. *J. Mar. Sci. Eng.* **2024**, *12*, 1040. https://doi.org/10.3390/jmse12071040.
13. Chtouris, H. and Hasiotis, T. Marine Geotechnical Research in Greece: A Review of the Current Knowledge, Challenges and Prospects. *J. Mar. Sci. Eng.* **2024**, *12*, 1708. https://doi.org/10.3390/jmse12101708.

References

1. Lunne, T.; Robertson, P.K.; Powell, J.J.M. *Cone Penetration Testing in Geotechnical Practice*; Blackie Academic & Professional: London, UK, 1997.
2. Randolph, M.F. Characterisation of soft sediments for offshore applications. In Proceedings of the International Conference on Site Characterization (ISC-2), Porto, Portugal, 19–22 September 2004; pp. 209–231.
3. Andersen, K.H. Bearing capacity under cyclic loading—Offshore, along the coast, and on land. *Can. Geotech. J.* **2009**, *46*, 513–535. [CrossRef]
4. Cheng, Y.; Xu, H.; Santamarina, J.C. Hydrate-bearing sediments: Advances in experimental studies. *J. Geophys. Res. Solid Earth* **2020**, *125*, e2019JB018732.
5. Yu, X.; Li, Y.; Deng, A. Climate impacts on permafrost and subsea soil stability: A review. *Mar. Georesour. Geotechnol.* **2022**, *40*, 45–63.
6. Zhang, R.; Li, Z.; Zhou, J. Dynamic response of seabed under combined wave and current loading: A numerical study. *Ocean Eng.* **2021**, *235*, 109363.

Journal of
Marine Science
and Engineering

Article

Experimental Study of the Dynamic Shear Modulus of Saturated Coral Sand under Complex Consolidation Conditions

Weijia Ma [1], You Qin [2], Fei Gao [1] and Qi Wu [2,*]

[1] School of Mechanical Engineering, Nanjing University of Science and Technology, Nanjing 210094, China
[2] Institute of Geotechnical Engineering, Nanjing Tech University, Nanjing 210009, China
* Correspondence: qw09061801@163.com

Abstract: The shear modulus is an essential parameter that reflects the mechanical properties of the soil. However, little is known about the shear modulus of coral sand, especially under complex consolidation conditions. In this paper, we present the results of a multi-stage strain-controlled undrained cyclic shear test on saturated coral sand. The influences of several consolidation state parameters: effective mean principal stress (p'_0), consolidation ratio (k_c), consolidation direction angle (α_0), and coefficient of intermediate principal stress (b) on the maximum shear modulus (G_0), the reference shear strain (γ_r) and the reduction of shear modulus (G) have been investigated. For a specified shear strain level, G will increase with increasing p'_0 and k_c, but decrease with increasing α_0 and b. However, the difference between G for various α_0 and b can be reduced by the increase of shear strain amplitude (γ_a). G_0 shows an increasing trend with the increase of p'_0 and k_c; on the contrary, with the increase of α_0 and b, G_0 shows a decreasing trend. To quantify the effect of consolidation state parameters on G_0, a new index (μ_{G0}) with four parameters (λ_1, λ_2, λ_3, λ_4) which is related to p'_0, k_c, α_0, b is proposed to modify the prediction model of G_0 in literature. Similarly, the values of γ_r under different consolidation conditions are also evaluated comprehensively by the four parameters, and the related index ($\mu_{\gamma r}$) is used to predict γ_r for various consolidation state parameters. A new finding is that there is an identical relationship between normalized shear modulus G/G_0 and normalized shear strain γ_a/γ_r for various consolidation state parameters and the Davidenkov model can describe the G/G_0–γ_a/γ_r curves. By using the prediction model proposed in this paper, an excellent prediction of G can be obtained and the deviation between measured and predicted G is all within ±10%.

Keywords: coral sand; dynamic shear modulus; maximum shear modulus; conference shear strain; prediction model of shear modulus

1. Introduction

Carbonate soils, most commonly calcium carbonate, are usually divided into three categories based on the calcium carbonate ($CaCO_3$) content: calcareous sand (<50%), siliceous carbonate sand (50–90%), and carbonate sand (>90%) [1]. Carbonate sand, which originates mainly from coral reefs, is referred to as coral sand. Coral sand is mostly distributed in the tropical ocean [2,3] and is the common reclamation material in ocean engineering [4–6]. Due to the special formation progress of coral sand, it has the particles features of intraparticle pores, high friction angle, high compressibility, low hardness, and fragileness at high-stress levels [3,7–11], which makes the mechanical properties of coral sand quite different from those of terrigenous sand.

The marine environment is extremely complex including the complexity of coral sand deposition and the dynamic loadings on a coral sand foundation. Waves, tsunamis, and earthquakes can threaten the stability of the coral sand foundation, and then affect the safety of ocean engineering. So it is vital to explore the undrained dynamic response of saturated coral sand. The maximum shear modulus G_0 and the reduction of shear modulus (G/G_0) from small to large strain range are the essential parameters in seismic response analysis studies. Many researchers have studied the dynamic shear modulus of silica sand. The maximum shear modulus G_0 is referred to as the shear modulus at small strain ($\gamma_a < 10^{-6}$), which is a key parameter in the prediction of G. The previous researches reveal that the value of G_0 is related to the void ratio e and the effective confining pressure σ_0' [12–16]. The void ratio reflects the influence of soil property on G_0, and the effective confining pressure characterizes the effect of consolidation condition on G_0. Hara et al. [17] obtained the G_0 of cohesive soils by using shear wave velocity V_s in laboratory and in situ tests ($G_0 = \rho V_s{}^2$), and a unique correlation is established between G_0 and shear strength S_u. Hardin and Kalinski [18] investigate the shear modulus of gravelly soils including uniform and graded crushed limestone gravel, graded river gravel, standard Ottawa and crushed limestone sands, and gravel–sand–silt mixtures. The modified three-dimensional constitutive equations for the elasticity of particulate materials are used to evaluate G_0 for various types of soils. Goudarzy et al. [19,20] explored the effect of the non-plastic fines content of granular on the maximum shear modulus. The G_0 of clean Hostun sand and Hostun sand mixed with 5%, 10%, 20%, 30%, and 40% fines are analyzed. To evaluate the influence of fine content on G_0, the equivalent void ratio (e^*) is introduced to replace e in the Hardin model. The modified model has a good prediction for the Hostun sand. Yan et al. [21] investigated the small-strain shear modulus of unsaturated silty-fine sand. They find that there exists an optimum saturation $(S_r)_{opt}$ in silty-fine sand. G_0 reaches its maximum value when the silty-fine sand is in optimum saturation and an improved prediction model for G_0 is proposed for sand under different saturation degrees.

Iwasaki et al. [22] evaluated the degree of shear modulus reduction by using two types of equipment. The test results show that the shear modulus at 10^{-4} shear strain amplitude measured by different equipment is identical, and a simplified procedure for prediction G is proposed. Lanzo et al. [23] reported the test results of two reconstituted grains of sand and three laboratory-made clays. The results indicated that with the increase of σ_0' and the over-consolidation ratio (OCR), the normalized shear modulus reduction curve (G/G_0–γ_a) generally increases. Furthermore, with the increase of plasticity index (PI), the effect of σ_0', and OCR on shear modulus reduction become small. Senerakis et al. [24] found that the G/G_0–γ_a of volcanic sands were more linear than those of quartz sands. This trend was more pronounced at lower σ_0' and at higher values of the coefficient of uniformity (C_u). The parameters of σ_0' and C_u may not be used in the modified hyperbolic model to quantify the rate of modulus reduction, and it is probably due to the unique fabric of volcanic sands. Chen et al. [25] investigated the characteristics of shear modulus reduction under isotropic and anisotropic consolidations for silt. The correlations between G/G_0 and γ_a for various complex stress conditions are distinct. However, the correlation between G/G_0 and γ_a/γ_r is identical regardless of the consolidation state parameters.

In recent years, with the rise of ocean engineering, the mechanical properties of coral sand become the research focus in marine geotechnical engineering. Controlling the quality of hydraulic filling materials is the key to ensuring the construction safety of marine structures [6]. For soil mass, the shear strength is always the most critical mechanical parameter. Many studies have confirmed that the particle size and confining pressure can affect the shear strength of coral sand [26,27]. However, these researchers focused on the shear characteristics of soils under monotonic shear. Since large-scale deformation of saturated coral sand has been observed in the 1993 Mw 7.7 Guam earthquake [28], the 2006 Mw 6.7 and Mw 6.0 Hawaii earthquakes [29], and the 2010 Mw 7.0 Haiti earthquake [30], the dynamic characteristics of coral sand foundation also need further discuss, and the dynamic shear modulus of coral sand is the most essential, which can establish the constitutive relation and guide the construction of offshore engineering. In fact, engineers have long been concerned about the maximum shear modulus together with the dynamic shear modulus reduction of coral sand foundations. Giang et al. [31] found that particle shapes could affect G_0. Due to the unique particle characteristics of coral sand, the G_0 of coral sand is much higher than that of silica sand. The previous prediction model will underestimate or overestimate the G_0 of coral sand. Chen et al. [32] carried out different types of strain-controlled undrained cyclic triaxial tests, and a correlation-function-based method is proposed to calculate the secant shear modulus, which shows a good prediction of shear modulus attenuation. Wu et al. [5] studied the dynamic shear modulus of saturated marine coral sand with different fines contents (FC) and relative densities (D_r). To quantify the influence of both parameters mentioned above, the equivalent skeleton void ratio e^*_{sk} is introduced, and a unique correlation can be observed between G_0, σ'_0, and e^*_{sk}. However, most of these studies focused on the effect of soil properties such as confining pressure, relative density, void ratio, and coefficient of uniformity on the shear modulus of coral sand. The mechanism of the effect of consolidation state parameters on the shear modulus reduction is still unclear.

In this paper, we present a comprehensive experimental study of the maximum shear modulus and the reduction of the shear modulus with increasing shear strain. The influence of effective mean principal stress (p'_0), consolidation ratio (k_c), consolidation direction angle (α_0), and coefficient of intermediate principal stress (b) on the shear modulus of coral sand is systematically investigated. The cyclic deformation characteristics of the specimens are also analyzed. The cyclic deformation properties of the specimens were also analyzed. The conclusions drawn in this study can lead to a better understanding of the undrained cyclic behavior of saturated coral sand and provide some key parameters for the analysis of the seismic response of coral sand foundations.

2. Test Materials and Apparatus

2.1. Test Material

The tested coral sand material is sourced from the Nansha Islands, South China Sea. Figure 1 shows the particle distribution curve, photograph, and scanning electron microscope (SEM) picture of tested coral sand. The particle shape of the tested coral sand varies from long strips to round, and some coral and marine fragments can also be observed. From a micro perspective (the SEM picture), the tested coral sand particles have rough surfaces and are attached to fine particles. The specific gravity (G_s) of coral sand is 2.80, maximum and minimum void ratio (e_{max}, e_{min}) is 1.72 and 0.99 respectively, according to the ASTM standards of D4253-14 and D4254-14 [33,34]. Since the maximum particle size used in the specimen cannot be greater than 1/6 to 1/7 of the specimen diameter, the maximum particle size of coral sand used in this test is 2 mm. For the particle distribution curve used in this test, the mean particle size (d_{50}) is 0.31 mm, coefficient of uniformity (C_u) and curvature coefficient (C_c) is 4.67 and 0.86 respectively. Following the Unified Soil Classification System [35], the tested coral sand is classified as poorly graded sand (SP).

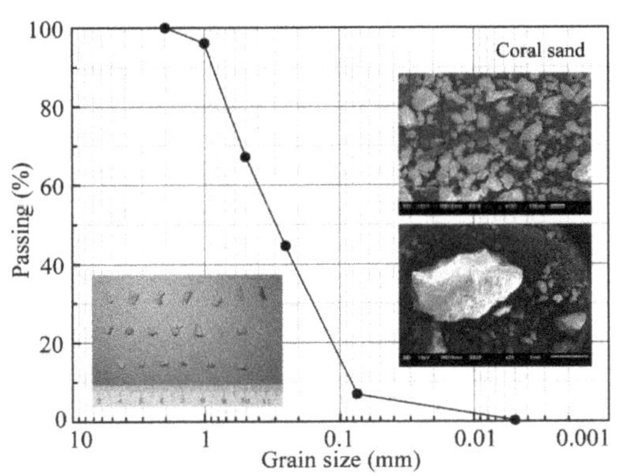

Figure 1. Particle distribution curve, photograph and scanning electron microscope picture (SEM) of tested coral sand.

2.2. Test Apparatus and Stress Distribution

An advanced hollow cylinder torsional shear apparatus manufactured by GDS Instruments (Hook, Hampshire, United Kingdom) is used in this study [Figure 2a]. The instrument is composed of four parts: pressure chamber, host, pressure controller, and data acquisition system. This apparatus can dynamically and independently control the axial load (W), torque (M_T), outer cell pressure (p_o), and inner cell pressure (p_i). The distributions of these four cyclic loadings on the specimen are shown in Figure 2b. Table 1 gives the performance parameters of the GDS apparatus including the capacity, deviation, and precision of the sensors. The four corresponding stress components (vertical stress σ_z, radial stress σ_r, circumferential stress σ_θ, and torsional shear stress $\tau_{z\theta}$) and three principal stresses (σ_1, σ_2, σ_3) are illustrated in Figure 2c,d. Table 2 gives the equations of data interpretation for all consolidation loadings, the stress components, and the consolidation state parameters. More details about this apparatus can be found in the literature [25,36,37].

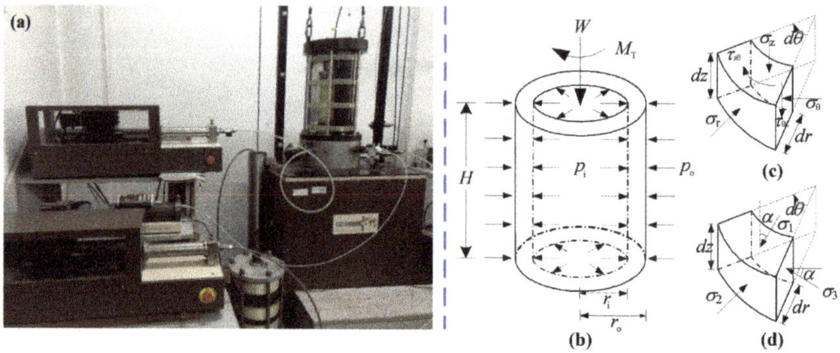

Figure 2. Hollow cylinder apparatus and illustrative stress state in a hollow cylindrical specimen subjected to axial load W, torque M_T, inner pressure p_i, and outer pressure p_o: (**a**) applied loads, (**b**) stress components, (**c**) principal stress components, and (**d**) major, intermediate, minor principal stress.

Table 1. Performance indexes of the apparatus used in this study.

Controller	Capacity	Deviation	Precision
Axial load	3 kN	0.1% F.S	3 N
Axial displacement	±40 mm	0.1% F.S	1 μm
Torque	30 Nm	0.1% F.S	0.03 Nm
Rotation displacement	360°	0.057% F.S	0.04°
Axial/Rotation frequency	≤5 Hz	-	-
Outer/inner cell pressure	1 MPa	0.1% F.S	1 kPa
Outer/inner cell volume	200 mL	0.25% F.S	0.001 mL
Back pressure	1 MPa	0.1% F.S	1 kPa
Back volume	200 mL	0.1% F.S	0.001 mL
Pore pressure	1 MPa	0.1% F.S	1 kPa

F.S = full scale.

Table 2. Equations for data interpretation.

Stress Component	Principal Stress	Stress Characteristic Parameter
Vertical $\sigma_z = \frac{W}{\pi(r_o^2-r_i^2)} + \frac{p_o r_o^2 - p_i r_i^2}{(r_o^2-r_i^2)}$	Major $\sigma_1 = \frac{\sigma_z+\sigma_\theta}{2} + \sqrt{\left(\frac{\sigma_z-\sigma_\theta}{2}\right)^2 + \tau_{z\theta}^2}$	Mean principal stress $p = \frac{\sigma_1+\sigma_2+\sigma_3}{3}$
Radial $\sigma_r = \frac{p_o r_o + p_i r_i}{r_o+r_i}$	Intermediate principal $\sigma_2 = \sigma_r$	Ratio of major and minor principal stress $k_c = \sigma_1/\sigma_3$
Circumferential $\sigma_\theta = \frac{p_o r_o - p_i r_i}{r_o-r_i}$	Minor principal $\sigma_3 = \frac{\sigma_z+\sigma_\theta}{2} - \sqrt{\left(\frac{\sigma_z-\sigma_\theta}{2}\right)^2 + \tau_{z\theta}^2}$	Coefficient of intermediate principal stress $b = (\sigma_2-\sigma_3)/(\sigma_1-\sigma_3)$
Shear $\tau_{z\theta} = \frac{3M_T}{2\pi(r_o^3-r_i^3)}$		Direction angle of principal stress $\alpha = \frac{1}{2}\arctan\left(\frac{2\tau_{z\theta}}{\sigma_z-\sigma_\theta}\right)$

3. Specimen Preparation, Saturation, and Consolidation

The hollow cylinder specimen in this study has a height of 200 mm and an inner and outer diameter of 60 mm and 100 mm. The specimen preparation method can significantly affect the mechanical properties of soil [38,39]. To ensure the uniformity of each specimen, the dry deposition method was adopted for preparing the coral sand specimens. The specimens were prepared by pouring the dried sand in seven layers into the hollow space between two molds via a funnel with a near-zero falling head. To investigate the influence of consolidation characteristic parameters on the dynamic shear modulus, the target initial relative density (D_r) of each specimen is 45%, and the corresponding void ratio is 1.355. The actual relative density after consolidation (D_{rc}) for all specimens ranged from 49.18% to 52.88% (see Table 3), and the corresponding void ratio ranged from 1.334 to 1.361. Note that the difference in the relative density before and after the consolidation is about 5%. It is probably due to the high compressibility of coral sand.

Table 3. Scheme of multi-stage strain-controlled undrained cyclic shear tests.

Test No.	End of Consolidation				Soil Property		Test Result		Fitting Parameter	
	p'_0 (kPa)	k_c	α_c/(°)	b	D_{rc} (%)	e	G_0 (MPa)	γ_r ($\times10^{-4}$)	C_1	C_2
01	50	1.0	-	-	49.18	1.361	51.6	5.464	0.46	0.92
02	100				49.45	1.359	68.1	6.056	0.48	0.98
03	200				51.64	1.343	101.1	11.844	0.48	1.02
04	300				52.47	1.337	121.7	15.264	0.48	1.01
05	100	1.5	0	0	50.96	1.348	88.1	8.758	0.52	0.98
06		2.0			51.51	1.344	91.2	12.671	0.52	1.00
07		2.5			52.88	1.334	93.7	14.613	0.52	1.01
08	100	1.5	30		51.37	1.345	82.3	9.497	0.49	1.01
09			45		51.78	1.342	75.6	9.731	0.52	1.04
10			60		51.64	1.343	74.3	10.396	0.50	1.04
11			90		51.51	1.344	66.3	11.650	0.50	1.00
12	100	1.5	0	0.25	51.78	1.342	84.2	9.315	0.47	1.02
13				0.50	51.37	1.345	81.8	9.913	0.52	0.98
14				0.75	51.64	1.343	77.5	10.582	0.49	1.05
15				1.00	51.37	1.345	75.2	11.874	0.50	0.96

After the specimen preparation was complete, the specimen was carefully set in the pressure chamber. The combination method of flushing CO_2 and de-aired water was used to make the specimen attain preliminary saturation, then applying back pressure (p_b) to 400 kPa in three steps (end of step I: p_b = 100 kPa, $p_o = p_i$ = 110 kPa; end of step II: p_b = 200 kPa, $p_o = p_i$ = 210 kPa; end of step III: p_b = 400 kPa, $p_o = p_i$ = 410 kPa); until the Skempton's B-value $\geq$ 0.97, which is a criterion indicating the specimen is completely saturated. The effective stress of the specimen always remains at 10 kPa during the saturation. After saturation, the specimens were firstly isotropically consolidated under different effective mean principal stress p'_0 (50, 100, 200, 300 kPa), and then anisotropically consolidated according to the scheme under various consolidation ratios of major and minor principal stress k_c (1.0, 1.5, 2.0, 2.5), direction angle of principal stress α_0 (0°, 30°, 45°, 60°, 90°) and coefficient of intermediate principal stress b (0, 0.25, 0.5, 0.75, 1.0). The whole consolidation process lasts for several hours. When the strain components and back pressure volume are stable, the coral sand specimen can be considered wholly consolidated. The consolidation stress paths are shown in Figure 3. The values of W, M_T, p_o, and p_i for each consolidation condition are illustrated in Table 3. The saturation and consolidation for all the tested specimens were performed following the procedures in the ASTM standard [40].

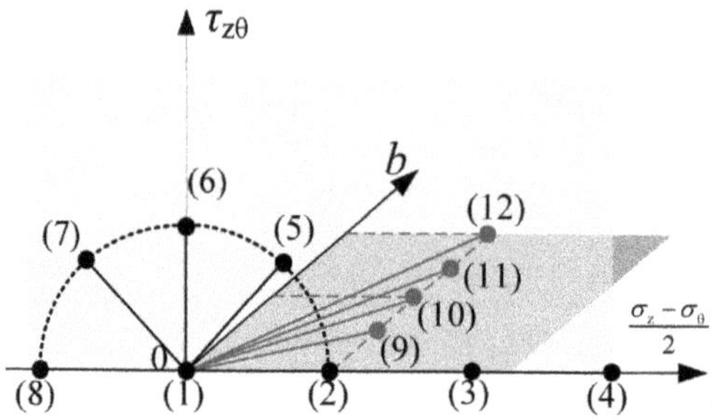

No.	k_c	α_c	b
1	1.0	-	-
2	1.5	0	0
3	2.0	0	0
4	2.5	0	0
5	1.5	30	0
6	1.5	45	0
7	1.5	60	0
8	1.0	90	0
9	1.5	0	0.25
10	1.5	0	0.50
11	1.5	0	0.75
12	1.5	0	1.0

Figure 3. Consolidation stress paths.

4. Multi-Stage Strain-Controlled Undrained Cyclic Shear Tests

It should be noted that under high-frequency seismic load, the saturated sand will generate excess pore water pressure, which will lead to the reduction of effective stress and the destruction of the foundation. In order to truly simulate the dynamic response of saturated coral sand under seismic load in the marine environment, it is more reasonable to choose the undrained test in this study. For each consolidation condition, multi-stage strain-controlled undrained cyclic torsional shear tests were performed. Table 3 lists the detailed procedure for the strain-controlled undrained cyclic shear test. 17 to 20 stages of sinusoidal cyclic strain were applied to each specimen, with ten cycles per stage. ASTM D5311/D5311M standard recommended that a range of cyclic loading frequency f = 0.1–2.0 Hz, and the frequency of 1.0 Hz is preferred [40]. Moreover, many previous studies also used a 1.0 Hz sinusoidal wave as the cyclic loading condition to observe the dynamic response of soil under earthquake events [41–43]. So, the cyclic loading frequency of 1.0 Hz was adopted for all tests in this study to simulate the seismic load. The torsional strain amplitudes change from small strain (0.001%) to large strain (0.5%). After each cyclic loading phase, the specimen was reconsolidated to the initial stress state for 10 min. This stage is intended to dissipate the excess pore water pressure (EPWP) at a large shear strain, which could affect the test result of the next stage [44]. During the drained re-consolidation stage, the volume of the specimen decreased, leading to a slight increase in D_r. However, the value of G can be less affected by density for multi-stage cyclic loading, which has been confirmed in literature [41,45]. Efforts have been made during the whole experiment process to ensure the consistency of the specimen to the greatest extent.

5. Test Results and Analysis

5.1. Typical Results of The Strain-Controlled Test

Figure 4 shows the typical test result of strain-controlled undrained cyclic torsional shear (No. 01). As the number of stages increases, the shear strain amplitude (γ_a) and shear stress amplitude (τ_a) also increase slowly, but not significantly. When γ_a reaches 1×10^{-4}, the shear stress has an observable development; when the strain reaches 2.89×10^{-4}, the EPWP (u_e) starts to develop significantly (more than 2 kPa). Note that the test is strain-controlled, τ_a for each cycle stage is constant and can eventually return to the origin. However, the cyclic shear stress may decrease during the cycle stage and produce deviation in the end. Figure 4d(I) depicts the development of the shear stress-strain relationship in the strain-controlled undrained cyclic shear test. With the increase of shear strain magnitude γ_a, the area of the hysteresis loop becomes large, indicating the gradual decrease in shear strength of the coral sand specimen. Figure 4d(II–IV) is the stress-strain relationship corresponding to the shear strain magnitude of 5×10^{-5}, 5×10^{-4}, and 5×10^{-3}, respectively. The nonlinear of the stress-strain relationship becomes obvious with the increase of γ_a, and the shear stress amplitude gradually decreases at large γ_a. This is because a large strain amplitude causes the EPWP of the coral sand specimen to rise and then increase the flow properties of the soil.

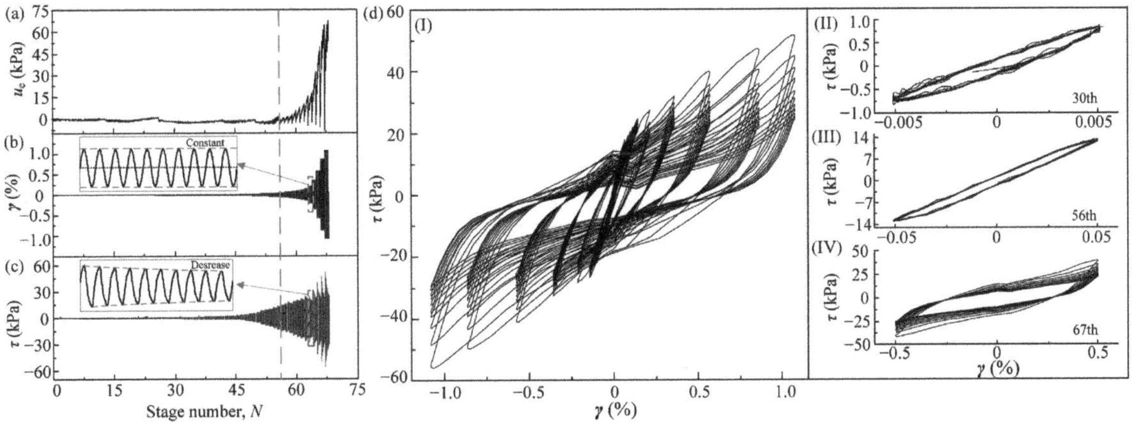

Figure 4. Typical test results of strain-controlled undrained cyclic torsional shear: (**a**) EPWP (u_e), (**b**) shear strain (γ), (**c**) torsional shear stress (τ) along with stage number (N); (**d**) stress-strain relationship of whole test period and single step.

Figure 5 demonstrates the idealized shear stress-strain response of soil under cyclic torsional shear loading. The strain-dependent secant shear modulus is used to study the modulus attenuation of coral sand in this test, which is commonly used in previous studies.

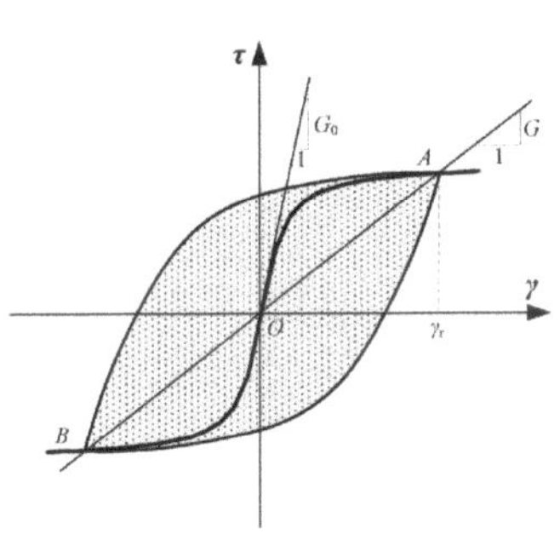

Figure 5. The idealized shear stress-strain response of soil under cyclic loading.

5.2. The Characteristics of Dynamic Shear Modulus under Various Consolidation Conditions

Figure 6 presents the relationship between G and γ_a of saturated isotropically and anisotropically consolidated coral sand for the undrained cyclic torsional shear tests. Clearly, G decreases with the increase of γ_a for all tests, and various consolidation state parameters (p'_0, k_c, α_0, b) have different effects on shear modulus reduction. Under isotropic consolidation, G increases with increasing p'_0 for a specified shear strain level, and the rates of shear modulus reduction for various p'_0 are almost the same. This is consistent with the test result of Kokusho [13] for Toyoura sand and Chen et al. [25] for Nanjing fine sand. However, under anisotropic consolidation, the effect of k_c, α_0, and b on the shear modulus reduction shows different regular. When other parameters (p'_0, α_0, b) are constant, G increases with the increase of k_c. Note that with the increase of k_c, the difference between G becomes small. This can be assumed that when k_c > 1.0, the void between coral sand particles begin to decrease gradually, which leads to the rearrangement of particles and the increase of friction between particles, making the shear modulus of coral sand increase significantly. However, when k_c continues to increase, the rearrangement between particles becomes more and more difficult, and the static shear stress only increases the friction between particles. As a result, the differences between the shear modulus for the various

k_c become small as the k_c continues to increase. Yuan et al. (2005) and Sun et al. (2013) obtained similar test results on silt, silty clay, and sludgy soil. They also proposed a prediction model to describe the trend of G_0 with the increase of k_c. [46,47] On the contrary, when α_0 and b increase, the shear modulus for a specified shear strain level shows a decreasing trend. However, this gap becomes smaller as the shear strain increases. When shear strain is over 6×10^{-4}, there is no obvious difference of G value under various α_0 or b. Figure 6 also illustrates the relationship between G and γ_a of saturated Nanjing fine sand under similar consolidation conditions, which is shown in gray symbols. The physical properties of this sandy soil can be found in Chen (2016). It is clear that the regular shear modulus reduction is quite similar for both sandy soils. However, the development trend of the shear modulus for Nanjing fine sand is significantly lower than that for coral sand under the same k_c, α_0, b. However, for the same p'_0, the modulus attenuation trend of the two sandy soils is quite close.

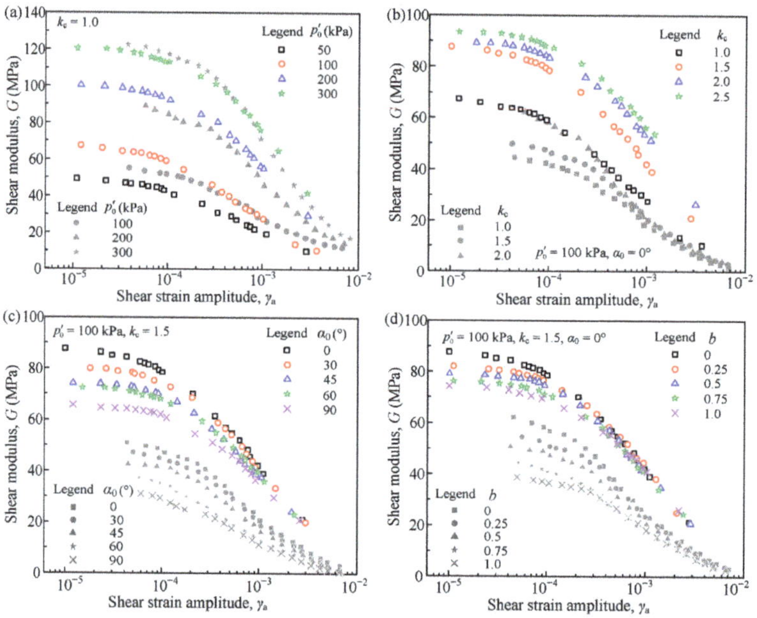

Figure 6. G versus γ_a curves of isotropically and anisotropically consolidated saturated coral sand for the undrained cyclic torsional shear tests under various (**a**) effective mean principal stress, (**b**) consolidation ratio, (**c**) consolidation direction angle, and (**d**) coefficient of intermediate principal stress.

5.3. The Maximum Dynamic Shear Modulus under Various Consolidation Conditions

The maximum dynamic shear modulus G_0 is an essential parameter in the undrained dynamic shear response of saturated sandy soils. G_0 is generally considered as the shear modulus at a small strain (less than 10^{-6}). To investigate the correlation between G_0 and various consolidation state parameters, a total of 15 strain-controlled undrained cyclic torsional shear tests were performed using the GDS hollow cylinder apparatus. Due to the limited testing accuracy of this apparatus, the dynamic shear modulus less than 1×10^{-5} is hardly measured, and G_0 cannot be obtained directly. However, according to the hyperbolic model proposed by Hardin and Drnevich [48], G_0 can be calculated by

$$G_0 = \lim_{\gamma \to 0} \frac{1}{a_1 + b_1 \gamma}, \quad (1)$$

where a_1 and b_1 are the linear fitting parameter. Hardin also gives the model to predict the G_0 of sandy soils:

$$G_0 = AF(e)\left(\frac{\sigma_0'}{P_a}\right)^n P_a, \tag{2}$$

where A and n are the material parameters, σ_0' is effective confining pressure in the triaxial test, P_a is the atmospheric pressure (P_a = 100 kPa in this study), and $F(e)$ is a function related to void ratio (e). As mentioned above, the consolidation state parameters (p_0', k_c, α_0, b) have different effects on the dynamic shear modulus, and Equation (2) cannot completely predict G_0 under complex consolidation conditions.

Figure 7 shows the correlations between G_0 and various consolidation parameters. Clearly, with the increase of mean effective principal stress and consolidation ratio, G_0 shows a gradually increasing trend. On contrary, with the increase of consolidation direction angle and coefficient of intermediate principal stress, G_0 shows a decreasing tendency.

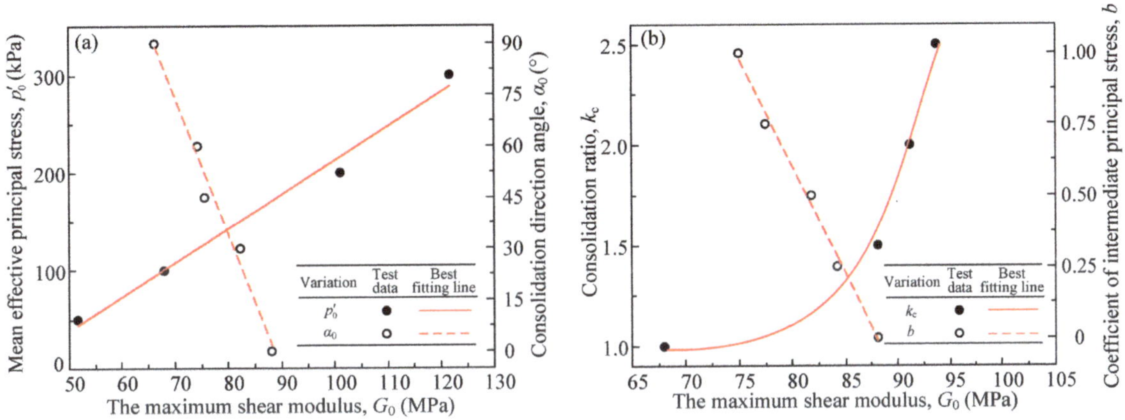

Figure 7. The correlations between the experimental G_0 and various consolidation parameters under various (**a**) effective mean principal stress and consolidation direction angle, (**b**) consolidation ratio and coefficient of intermediate principal stress.

To quantify the influence of the above parameters on G_0, a new index denoted as μ_{G0} is introduced, which can be expressed as follows:

$$\mu_{G0} = {\lambda_1}^{n_1}{\lambda_2}^{n_2}{\lambda_3}^{n_3}{\lambda_4}^{n_4}, \tag{3}$$

where

$$\lambda_1 = \frac{p_0'}{P_a},\ \lambda_2 = k_c,\ \lambda_3 = \cos(\frac{\alpha_0}{2}),\ \lambda_4 = \frac{1}{2+b}$$

and n_1, n_2, n_3, and n_4 are the weights for various parameters. Figure 8 shows the correlation between the measured G_0 and μ_{G0}. For the coral sand in this study, when n_1 = 0.527, n_2 = 0.419, n_3 = 0.760, n_4 = 0.220, there is a strong linear relationship between G_0 and μ_{G0} under complex consolidation conditions.

Furthermore, $F(e)$ in Equation (2) can be equal to e^a for simplicity according to the literature [14,16]. Thus, the prediction model of G_0 can be rewritten as:

$$G_0 = Ae^a\mu_{G0}P_a, \tag{4}$$

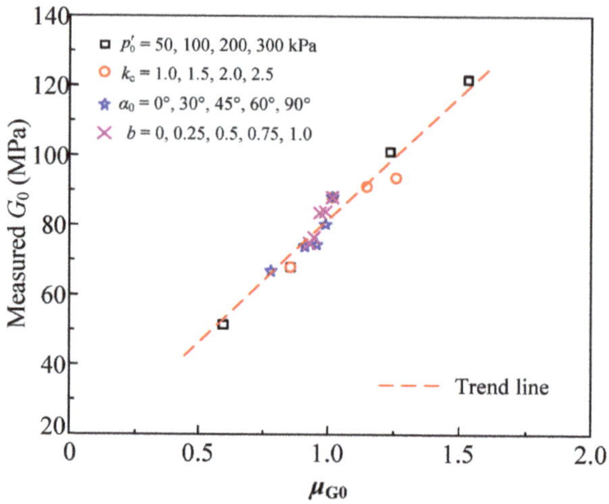

Figure 8. The correlation between the experimental G_0 versus μ_{G0}.

For the tested coral sand, the appropriate values of A and a are 0.57 and 1.25, respectively. For the isotropic condition, it is difficult to define the value of α_0 and b in hollow cylinder specimens through the calculation equations. Since the σ_2 is always equal to σ_3 in cylinder specimen for the triaxial test, it is reasonable to make $\alpha_0 = 0°$, and $b = 0$ under isotropic conditions. When $n_2 = n_3 = n_4 = 0$ (triaxial test), Equation (4) degenerates to Equation (2). The predicted G_0 for various consolidation conditions by using Equations (3) and (4) are illustrated in Table 3. Figure 9a shows the comparison between the measured and predicted G_0 of saturated coral sand. It is striking to find that all the test data are close to the line of y = x, within ±10% deviation, indicating a good prediction of the proposed model on G_0. The prediction results of Nanjing fine sand are also shown in Figure 9b. When $n_1 = 1.0$, $n_2 = 0.7$, $n_3 = 1.5$, and $n_4 = 0.2$, an acceptable prediction of G_0 within ±20% deviation can be obtained by using Equation (4).

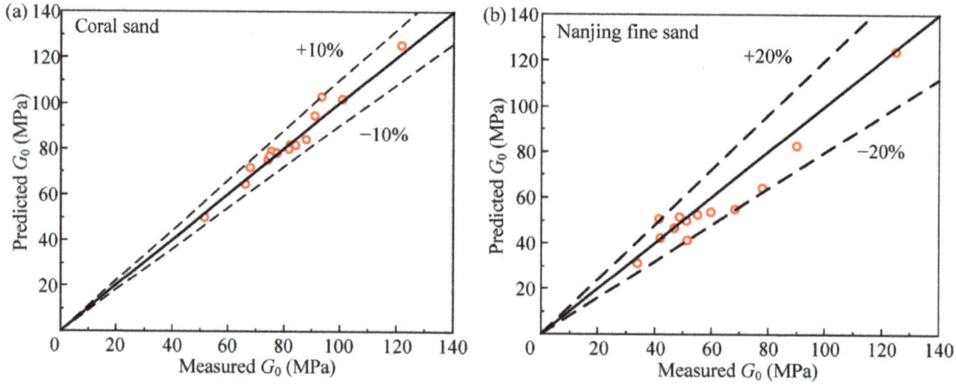

Figure 9. The comparison between the experimental G_0 versus predicted G_0 of (**a**) coral sand and (**b**) Nanjing fine sand under various consolidation conditions.

5.4. The Prediction Model of Dynamic Shear Modulus Reduction

Figure 10 shows the relationships between normalized shear modulus G/G_0 and γ_a of saturated isotropically and anisotropically consolidated coral sand. It seems that the G/G_0 versus γ_a curves shift to the right with the increase of p'_0 and k_c. However, with the increase of α_0 and b, the G/G_0–γ_a curves have little change. This implies that the feature of dynamic shear modulus reduction can be significantly affected by p_0' and k_c, rather than α_0 and b, and the consolidation state parameters of α_0 and b mainly affect the maximum shear modulus of coral sand.

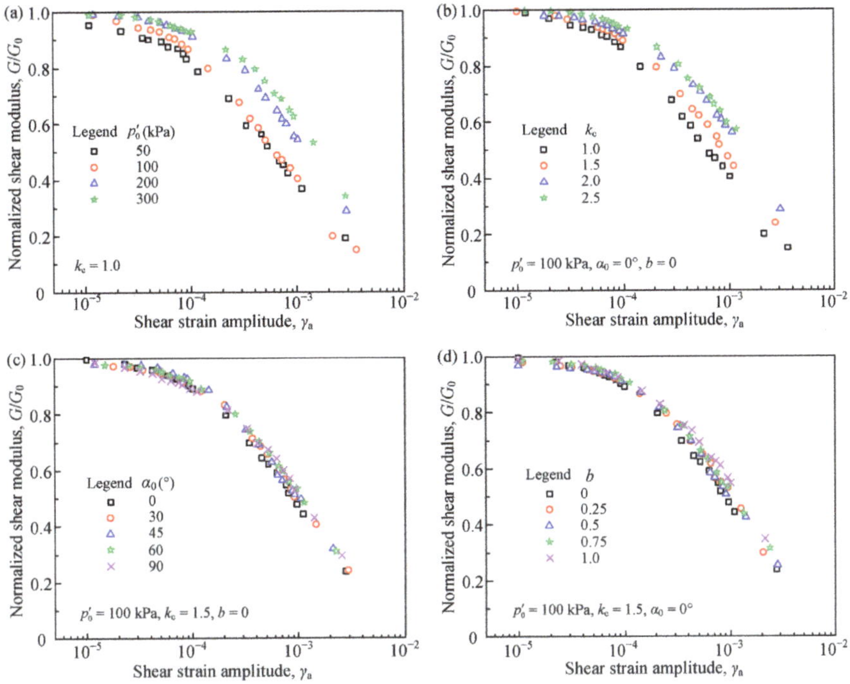

Figure 10. G_0 versus γ_a curves of isotropically and anisotropically consolidated saturated coral sand for the undrained cyclic torsional shear tests under various (**a**) effective mean principal stress, (**b**) consolidation ratio, (**c**) consolidation direction angle, and (**d**) coefficient of intermediate principal stress.

Figure 11 presents all the test data under various consolidation conditions. The boundaries of dynamic shear modulus for various silica grains of sand in literature are also shown in this figure [12,13,49,50]. The distribution of test data is slightly beyond the upper boundary given by Yuan. This indicates the differences in dynamic mechanical properties between coral sand and silica sand.

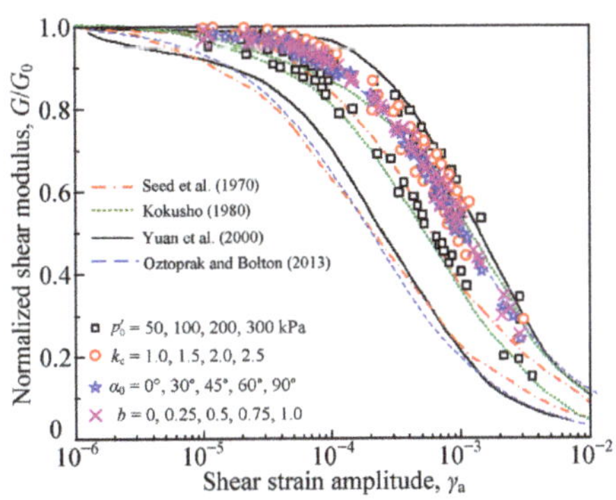

Figure 11. Shear modulus reduction curves of saturated coral sand under various consolidation conditions [12,13,49,50].

The reference shear strain γ_r refers to the value of γ_a corresponding to G/G_0 = 0.5, which is a common index to normalize the trend of dynamic shear modulus. Figure 12 plots the normalized shear modulus G/G_0, and the normalized shear strain γ_a/γ_r curves under various complex consolidation conditions. It is clear to find that the G/G_0–γ_a/γ_r curves can fall in a very narrow band, indicating the validity of γ_r in characterizing the reduction of dynamic shear modulus. In traditional triaxial tests, the strain-dependent shear modulus reduction can be described by the Davidenkov model [51], which is expressed as

$$\frac{G}{G_0} = 1 - \left[\frac{(\gamma_a/\gamma_r)^{2C_1}}{1+(\gamma_a/\gamma_r)^{2C_1}}\right]^{C_2}, \tag{5}$$

where C_1 and C_2 are the fitting parameters. The values of C_1 and C_2 for each test are illustrated in Table 3. Since the values of C_1 and C_2 for various consolidation conditions are very close, it is recommended to take the average value of C_1 (=0.5) and C_2 (=1.00) as the fitting value for all cases. Under these circumstances, Equation (5) degenerates into a hyperbolic model.

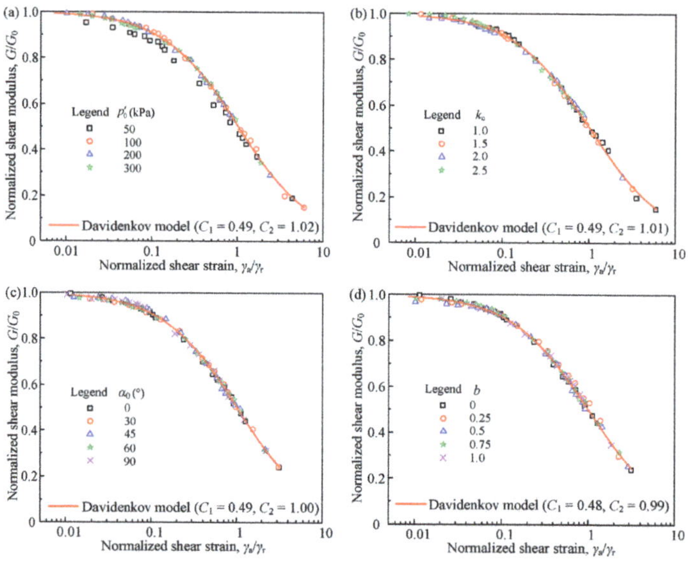

Figure 12. G/G_0 versus γ_a/γ_r curves of isotropically and anisotropically consolidated saturated coral sand for the undrained cyclic torsional shear tests under various (**a**) effective mean principal stress, (**b**) consolidation ratio, (**c**) consolidation direction angle, and (**d**) coefficient of intermediate principal stress.

It can be seen from the above results that the reference shear strain γ_r is an important parameter that evaluates the trend of shear modulus reduction. Actually, many studies have confirmed that γ_r is related to effective confining pressure σ'_0 and fine content FC. However, the influences of different consolidation state parameters under complex consolidation conditions on γ_r are rarely investigated. Figure 13 shows the correlation between γ_r and four consolidation state parameters (p'_0, k_c, α_0, b). Obviously, when the other three parameters remain constant, the values of γ_r become large with the increase of any one of those parameters. The value of γ_r ranges from 5.464 × 10^{-4} to 15.264 × 10^{-4}, and it means the consolidation state parameters affect γ_r to a certain degree. Moreover, compared with α_0 and b, p'_0, and k_c have a greater impact on γ_r.

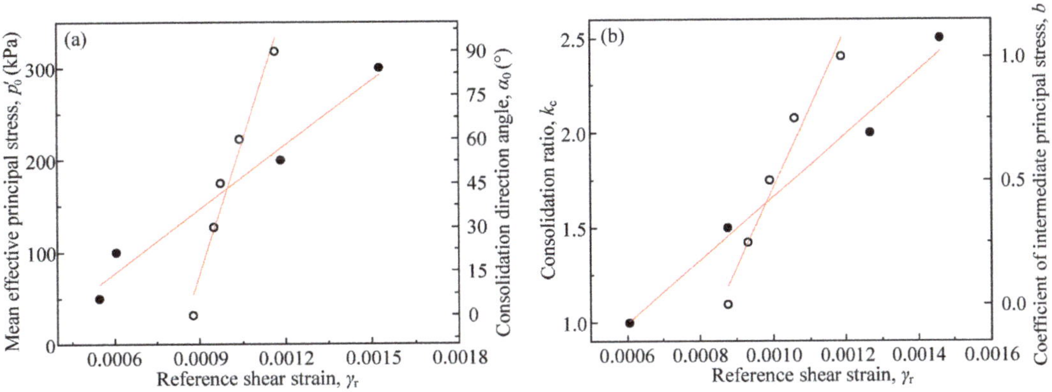

Figure 13. The correlation between γ_r and stress characteristic parameters of (**a**) effective mean principal stress and consolidation direction angle, (**b**) consolidation ratio and coefficient of intermediate principal stress.

Similarly, to quantify the influence of different consolidation state parameters on γ_r, another consolidation index $\mu_{\gamma r}$ is introduced, which can be expressed as follows:

$$\mu_{\gamma r} = (\lambda_1 \lambda_2)/(\lambda_3 \lambda_4)^m, \tag{6}$$

where λ_1, λ_2, λ_3, and λ_4 have been defined in Equation (3), and m is a calibration parameter that is determined by the correlation between consolidation state parameters and γ_r. Figure 14 shows the correlation between γ_r and $\mu_{\gamma r}$. When m = 1.0, with the increase of μ_2, γ_r also presents the increasing tendency, and a strong linear relationship can be found in this figure:

$$\gamma_r = D_1 \times \mu_{\gamma r} + D_2, \tag{7}$$

where D_1 and D_2 are the linear fitting parameters, and $D_1 = 2.1807 \times 10^{-4}$, $D_2 = 2.5403 \times 10^{-4}$ for the tested coral sand.

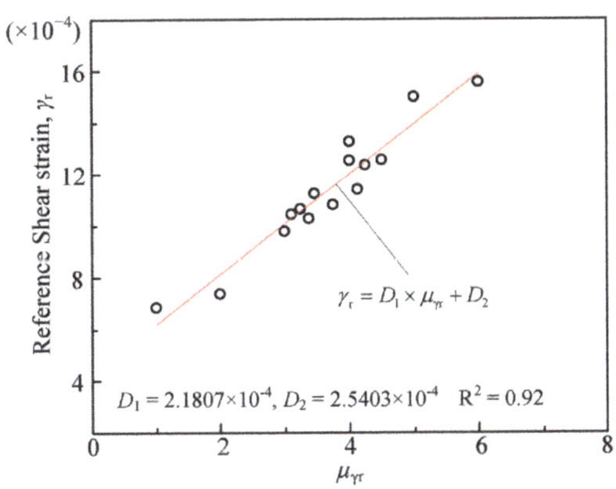

Figure 14. The correlation between reference shear strain γ_r and $\mu_{\gamma r}$.

Thus, based on the analysis of the consolidation state parameters, a prediction model of G for an undrained strain-controlled torsional shear test is established by Equations (3)–(7). This new model takes the effective mean principal stress (p_0'), consolidation ratio (k_c), consolidation direction angle (α_0), and coefficient of intermediate principal stress (b) into consideration. To verify the accuracy of the model, Figure 15a shows the correlation between the measured G in the multi-stage strain-controlled undrained cyclic shear tests and the predicted G calculated from the new model. All data are close to the line of y = x, and the deviations of measured and predicted are all within ±15%, indicating a good prediction of the proposed new model on G. Figure 15b also shows the prediction result of G for the saturated Nanjing Fine sand, when $m = -1.0$ in Equation (6), a good prediction result can be observed.

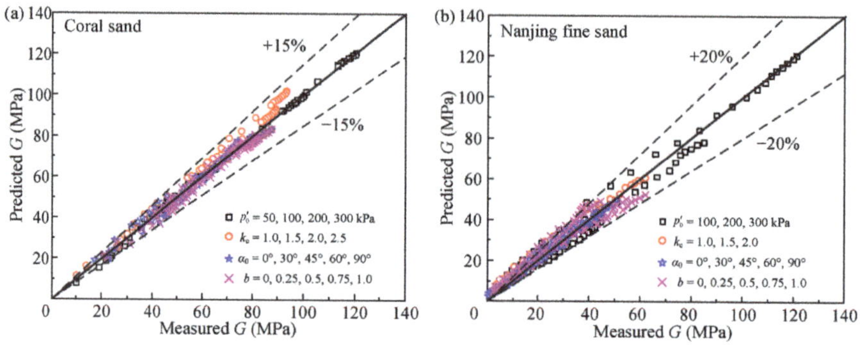

Figure 15. The correlation between the experimental G versus predicted G of (**a**) coral sand and (**b**) Nanjing fine sand under various consolidation conditions.

This study provides a comprehensive view of how the consolidation state parameters affect the dynamic shear modulus of saturated coral sand. However, the prediction model proposed in this study is still a semi-empirical formula, which is strongly related to the consolidation state parameters. Due to the lack of test data on the shear modulus under complex consolidation conditions, the correlation between fitting parameters in the formulas and physical properties also needs to be further discussed. More test data are welcomed to verify the applicability of the model and determine the physical meaning of the fitting parameters. According to the existing research results, the next step of the research will focus on determining the physical meaning of the fitting parameters and analyzing the stress state of soil elements to propose a more physical model to better predict the dynamic shear modulus of saturated sand under various consolidation conditions.

6. Conclusions

This study presented results for saturated coral sand from multi-stage strain-controlled undrained cyclic shear tests. The influences of the effective mean principal stress (p'_0), consolidation ratio (k_c), consolidation direction angle (α_0), and coefficient of intermediate principal stress (b) on dynamic shear strain reduction in saturated coral sand are investigated, and the main conclusions are as follows.

1. Shear strain modulus G decreases with the increase of γ_a for all tests, and the consolidation state parameters (p'_0, k_c, α_0, b) have a significant effect on G. For a specified shear strain level, G generally increases with increasing p'_0 and k_c, but decreases with increasing α_0 and b.
2. The consolidation state parameters can affect the maximum shear modulus G_0 severely. Specifically, G_0 has a positive correlation with p'_0 and k_c, and a negative correlation with α_0 and b. This regulation is consistent with that of G. To further analyze the influence of consolidation state parameters on G_0, a new index (μ_1) that describes the complex consolidation conditions is introduced, and the four parameters λ_1, λ_2, λ_3, λ_4 in the new index are used to quantify the effect of p'_0, k_c, α_0, b on G_0, respectively. Based on this index, a new model of G_0 is established, and the test data in this study also proves the validity of this new prediction model.

3. The reference shear strain γ_r under isotropic and anisotropic consolidations are also varied. Based on the parameters of λ_1, λ_2, λ_3, λ_4, another new index (μ_2) is also proposed, and a strong linear relationship can be observed between γ_r and μ_2. It is delighted to find that the relationships between normalized shear modulus G/G_0 and normalized shear strain γ_a/γ_r are almost identical. The Davidenkov model can be used to describe the G/G_0–γ_a/γ_r curves and for simplicity, the recommended parameters of C_1 and C_2 in this model are 0.50 and 1.00, respectively.
4. The prediction model proposed in this paper can well describe the dynamic shear modulus reduction trend of the tested coral sand under isotropic and anisotropic consolidation conditions, and the deviation between measured and predicted G are all within $\pm$10%, indicating the good prediction result of this new model. However, due to the lack of test data, more test data is needed to further confirm the effectiveness of the prediction model.
5. The test data in this study can provide important parameters for island reef engineering. Correspondingly, the prediction of dynamic shear moduli with different strains can be a reference for the seismic design of the foundation. Due to the complex consolidation conditions of soils in natural environments, the prediction model of G_0 proposed in this study can be a guideline in engineering practice.

Author Contributions: Conceptualization, W.M. and Q.W.; methodology, W.M.; validation, F.G.; investigation, W.M.; resources, W.M. and Q.W.; data curation, Y.Q.; writing—original draft preparation, W.M.; writing—review and editing, W.M. and Y.Q.; visualization, Y.Q.; supervision, Q.W.; funding acquisition, W.M.; All authors have read and agreed to the published version of the manuscript.

Funding: This research was funded by the National Natural Science Foundation of China (grant number: 52208350).

Institutional Review Board Statement: Not applicable.

Informed Consent Statement: Not applicable.

Data Availability Statement: The data used during the study are available from the first author by request.

Conflicts of Interest: The authors declare no conflict of interest.

References

1. Flores Lopez, F.A.; Taboada, V.M.; Gonzalez Ramirez, Z.X.; Cruz Roque, D.; Barrera Nabor., P.; Dantal, V.S. Normalized modulus reduction and damping ratio curves for Bay of Campeche carbonate Sand. In Proceedings of the Offshore Technology Conference, Houston, TX, USA, 30 April–3 May 2018. [CrossRef]
2. Burke, L.; Reytar, K.; Spalding, M.; Perry, A. *Reefs at Risk Revisited*; Report; World Resources Institute: Washington, DC, USA, 2011.
3. Ma, W.J.; Qin, Y.; Zhao, K.; Chen, G.X. Comparisons on liquefaction behavior of saturated coral sand and quartz sand under principal stress rotation. *Mar. Georesour. Geotechnol.* **2022**, *40*, 235–247. [CrossRef]
4. Liu, L.; Yao, X.; Ji, Z.; Gao, H.; Wang, Z.; Shen, Z. Cyclic behavior of calcareous sand from the South China Sea. *J. Mar. Sci. Eng.* **2021**, *9*, 1014. [CrossRef]
5. Wu, Q.; Liu, Q.F.; Zhuang, H.Y.; Xu, C.S.; Chen, G.X. Experimental investigation of dynamic shear modulus of saturated marine coral sand. *Ocean Eng.* **2022**, *264*, 112412. [CrossRef]
6. Wang, X.Z.; Wang, X.; Shen, J.H.; Ding, H.Z.; Wen, D.S.; Zhu, C.Q.; Lv, S.Z. Foundation filling performance of calcareous soil on coral reefs in the South China Sea. *Appl. Ocean Res.* **2022**, *129*, 103386. [CrossRef]
7. Coop, M.R. The mechanics of uncemented carbonate sands. *Géotechnique* **1990**, *40*, 607–626. [CrossRef]
8. Sharma, S.S.; Ismail, M.A. Monotonic and cyclic behavior of two calcareous soils of different origins. *J. Geotech. Geoenviron. Eng.* **2006**, *132*, 1581–1591. [CrossRef]
9. Brandes, H.G. Simple shear behavior of calcareous and quartz sands. *Geotech. Geol. Eng.* **2011**, *29*, 113–126. [CrossRef]
10. Salem, M.; Elmamlouk, H.; Agaiby, S. Static and cyclic behavior of North Coast calcareous sand in Egypt. *Soil Dyn. Earthq. Eng.* **2013**, *55*, 83–91. [CrossRef]
11. Rui, S.; Guo, Z.; Si, T.; Li, Y. Effect of particle shape on the liquefaction resistance of calcareous sands. *Soil Dyn. Earthq. Eng.* **2020**, *137*, 106302. [CrossRef]
12. Seed, H.B.; Idriss, I.M. *Soil Moduli and Damping Factors for Dynamic Response Analyses*; Report EERC 70-10; University of California: Berkeley, CA, USA, 1970.

13. Kokusho, T. Cyclic triaxial test of dynamic soil properties for wide strain range. *Soils Found.* **1980**, *20*, 45–60. [CrossRef]
14. Menq, F.Y. Dynamic Properties of Sandy and Gravelly Soils. Ph.D. Thesis, University of Texas at Austin, Austin, TX, USA, 2003.
15. Wichtmann, T.; Triantafyllidis, T. Influence of the grain-size distribution curve of quartz sand on the small strain shear modulus G_{max}. *J. Geotech. Geoenviron. Eng.* **2009**, *135*, 1404–1418. [CrossRef]
16. Senetakis, K.; Anastasiadis, A.; Pitilakis, K. The small-strain shear modulus and damping ratio of quartz and volcanic sands. *Geotech. Test. J.* **2012**, *35*, 964–980. [CrossRef]
17. Hara, A.; Ohta, T.; Niwa, M.; Tanaka, S.; Banno, T. Shear modulus and shear strength of cohesive soils. *Soils Found.* **1974**, *14*, 1–12. [CrossRef] [PubMed]
18. Hardin, B.O.; Kalinski, M.E. Estimating the Shear Modulus of Gravelly Soils. *J. Geotech. Geoenviron. Eng.* **2005**, *131*, 867–875. [CrossRef]
19. Goudarzy, M.; Rahman, M.M.; König, D.; Schanz, T. Influence of non-plastic fines content on maximum shear modulus of granular materials. *Soils Found.* **2016**, *56*, 973–983. [CrossRef]
20. Goudarzy, M.; Rahemi, N.; Rahman, M.M.; Schanz, T. Predicting the maximum shear modulus of sands containing nonplastic fines. *J. Geotech. Geoenviron. Eng.* **2017**, *143*, 0617013. [CrossRef]
21. Yan, K.; Wang, Y.; Yang, Z.; Lai, X.; Chen, C. Experimental study on small-strain shear modulus of unsaturated silty-fine sand. *Appl. Sci.* **2022**, *12*, 8743. [CrossRef]
22. Iwasaki, T.; Tatsuoka, F.; Takagi, Y. Shear moduli of sands under cyclic torsional shear loading. *Soils Found.* **1978**, *18*, 39–56. [CrossRef]
23. Lanzo, G.; Vucetic, M.; Doroudian, T.M. Reduction of shear modulus at small strains in simple shear. *J. Geotech. Geoenviron. Eng.* **1997**, *123*, 1035–1042. [CrossRef]
24. Senetakis, K.; Anastasiadis, A.; Pitilakis, K. Normalized shear modulus reduction and damping ratio curves of quartz sand and rhyolitic crushed rock. *Soils Found.* **2013**, *53*, 879–893. [CrossRef]
25. Chen, G.X.; Zhou, Z.L.; Pan, H.; Sun, T.; Li, X.J. The influence of undrained cyclic loading patterns and consolidation states on the deformation features of saturated fine sand over a wide strain range. *Eng. Geol.* **2016**, *204*, 77–93. [CrossRef]
26. Saeidaskari, J.; Alibolandi, M.; Azizkandi, A.S. Undrained monotonic and cyclic behavior of Qeshm calcareous sand. *Mar. Georesour. Geotechnol.* **2021**, *39*, 798–811. [CrossRef]
27. Wang, X.; Wang, X.Z.; Shen, J.H.; Zhu, C.Q. Particle size and confining-pressure effects of shear characteristics of coral sand: An experimental study. *Bull. Eng. Geol. Environ.* **2022**, *81*, 97. [CrossRef]
28. Vahdani, S.; Pyke, R.; Siriprusanen, U. Liquefaction of calcareous sands and lateral spreading experienced in Guam as a result of the 1993 Guam earthquake. In Proceedings of the 5th US—Japan Workshop on Earthquake Resistant Design of Lifeline Facilities and Countermeasures against Soil Liquefaction, Snowbird, UT, USA, 29 September–29 October 1994; pp. 117–134.
29. Chock, G.; Robertson, I.; Nicholson, P.; Brandes, H.; Medley, E.; Okubo, P.; Hirshorn, B.; Sumada, J.; Kindred, T.; Iinuma, G.; et al. *Compilation of Observations of the October 15, 2006 Kiholo bay (Mw 6.7) and Mahukona (Mw 6.0) Earthquakes, Hawai'I*; Report 31; Earthquake Engineering Research Institute (EERI): Oakland, CA, USA, 2006.
30. Olson, S.M.; Green, R.A.; Lasley, S.; Martin, N.; Cox, B.R.; Rathje, E.; Bachhuber, J.; French, J. Documenting liquefaction and lateral spreading triggered by the 12 January 2010 Haiti earthquake. *Earthq. Spectra* **2011**, *27*, 93–116. [CrossRef]
31. Giang, P.H.H.; Van Impe, P.O.; Van Impe, W.F.; Menge, P.; Haegeman, W. Small-strain shear modulus of calcareous sand and its dependence on particle characteristics and gradation. *Soil Dyn. Earthq. Eng.* **2017**, *100*, 371–379. [CrossRef]
32. Chen, G.X.; Liang, K.; Zhao, K.; Yang, J. Shear modulus and damping ratio of saturated coral sand under generalised cyclic loadings. *Géotechnique*, 2022; *ahead of print*. [CrossRef]
33. *ASTM D4253-14*; Standard Test Methods for Maximum Index Density and Unit Weight of Soils Using a Vibratory Table. ASTM International: West Conshohocken, PA, USA, 2006.
34. *ASTM D4254-14*; Standard Test Methods for Minimum Index Density and Unit Weight of Soils and Calculation of Relative Density. ASTM International: West Conshohocken, PA, USA, 2006.
35. *ASTM D2487*; Standard Practice for Classification of Soils for Engineering Purposes (Unified Soil Classification System). ASTM International: West Conshohocken, PA, USA, 2011.
36. Zhuang, H.Y.; Wang, R.; Chen, G.X.; Miao, Y.; Zhao, K. Shear modulus reduction of saturated sand under large liquefaction-induced deformation in cyclic torsional shear tests. *Eng. Geol.* **2018**, *240*, 110–122. [CrossRef]
37. Chen, G.X.; Ma, W.J.; Qin, Y.; Zhao, K.; Yang, J. Liquefaction susceptibility of saturated coral sand subjected to various patterns of principal stress rotation. *J. Geotech. Geoenviron. Eng.* **2021**, *147*, 04021093. [CrossRef]
38. Sze, H.Y.; Yang, J. Failure modes of sand in undrained cyclic loading: Impact of sample preparation. *J. Geotech. Geoenviron. Eng.* **2014**, *140*, 152–169. [CrossRef]
39. Huang, A.B.; Chang, W.J.; Hsu, H.H.; Huang, Y.J. A mist pluviation method for reconstituting silty sand specimens. *Eng. Geol.* **2015**, *188*, 1–9. [CrossRef]
40. *ASTM D5311D/5311M*; Standard Test Method for Load Controlled Cyclic Triaxial Strength of Soil. ASTM International: West Conshohocken, PA, USA, 2013.
41. Chen, G.X.; Zhou, Z.L.; Sun, T.; Wu, Q.; Xu, L.Y.; Sara, K.; Ling, D.S. Shear modulus and damping ratio of sand-gravel mixtures over a wide strain range. *J. Earthq. Eng.* **2019**, *23*, 1407–1440. [CrossRef]

42. Kumar, S.S.; Krishna, A.M.; Dey, A. Evaluation of dynamic properties of sandy soil at high cyclic strains. *Soil Dyn. Earthq. Eng.* **2017**, *99*, 157–167. [CrossRef]
43. Ghayoomi, M.; Suprunenko, G.; Mirshekari, M. Cyclic triaxial test to measure strain-dependent shear modulus of unsaturated sand. *Int. J. Geomech.* **2017**, *17*, 04017043. [CrossRef]
44. Wu, Q.; Hang, T.Z.; Zhao, K.; Chen, G.X. Reduction of dynamic shear modulus of saturated marine sandy silt under complex stress conditions. *Mar. Georesour. Geotech.* **2022**. [CrossRef]
45. Seed, H.B.; Wong, R.T.; Idriss, I.M.; Tokimatsu, K. Moduli and damping factors for dynamic analyses of cohesionless soils. *J. Geotech. Eng.* **1986**, *112*, 1016–1032. [CrossRef]
46. Yuan, X.M.; Sun, J.; Sun, R. Effect of Consolidation Ratios on Maximum Dynamic Shear Modulus of Sands. *Earthq. Eng. Eng. Vib.* **2005**, *4*, 59–68.
47. Sun, J.; Gong, M.S.; Tao, X.X. Dynamic shear modulus of undisturbed soil under different consolidation ratios and its effects on surface ground motion. *Earthq. Eng. Eng. Vib.* **2013**, *12*, 561–568. [CrossRef]
48. Hardin, B.O.; Drnevich, V. Shear modulus and damping in soils. *J. Soil Mech. Found. Div.* **1972**, *97*, 667–692. [CrossRef]
49. Yuan, X.M.; Sun, R.; Sun, J.; Meng, S.J.; Shi, Z.J. Laboratory experimental study on dynamic shear modulus ratio and damping ratio of soils. *Earthq. Eng. Eng. Vib.* **2000**, *20*, 133–139. [CrossRef]
50. Oztoprak, S.; Bolton, M.D. Stiffness of sands through a laboratory test database. *Geotechnique* **2013**, *63*, 54–70. [CrossRef]
51. Martin, P.P.; Seed, H.B. One-dimensional dynamic ground response analyses. *J. Geotech. Eng. Div.* **1982**, *108*, 935–952. [CrossRef]

Journal of
Marine Science and Engineering

MDPI

Article

Intelligent Model for Dynamic Shear Modulus and Damping Ratio of Undisturbed Marine Clay Based on Back-Propagation Neural Network

Qi Wu [1,2], Zifan Wang [1], You Qin [1] and Wenbao Yang [1,3,*]

1 Institute of Geotechnical Engineering, Nanjing Tech University, Nanjing 210009, China
2 Faculty of Architecture, Civil and Transportation Engineering, Beijing University of Technology, Beijing 100124, China
3 School of Civil Engineering, Chongqing University, Chongqing 400045, China
* Correspondence: yangwenbao1994@163.com

Abstract: In this study, a series of resonant-column experiments were conducted on marine clays from Bohai Bay and Hangzhou Bay, China. The characteristics of the dynamic shear modulus (G) and damping ratio (D) of these marine clays were examined. It was found that G and D not only vary with shear strain (γ), but they also have a strong connection with soil depth (H) (reflected by the mean effective confining pressure (σ_{m}) in the laboratory test conditions). With increasing H (σ_{m}) and fixed γ, the value of G gradually increases; conversely, the value of D gradually decreases, and this is accompanied by the weakening of the decay or growth rate. An intelligent model based on a back-propagation neural network (BPNN) was developed for the calculation of these parameters. Compared with existing function models, the proposed intelligent model avoids the forward propagation of data errors and the need for human intervention regarding the fitting parameters. The model can accurately predict the G and D characteristics of marine clays at different H (σ_{m}) and the corresponding γ. The prediction accuracy is universal and does not strictly depend on the number of neurons in the hidden layer of the neural network.

Keywords: marine clay; dynamic shear modulus; damping ratio; mean effective confining pressure; intelligent model; back-propagation neural network

1. Introduction

Recently, the increasing exploitation of marine resources has led to an increasing number of engineering construction projects in marine and coastal areas, including tunnels, bridges, offshore wind power facilities, and offshore oil platforms. In comparison to general engineering, marine engineering structures suffer from a greater number of technical issues concerning seismic resistance. Marine soil is the supporting layer for marine engineering, and it is also the transfer medium for seismic waves; its dynamic properties, thus, have a direct effect on the seismic responses of marine engineering structures.

The dynamic behavior of soil is principally characterized by nonlinearity and hysteresis in the dynamic stress–strain relationship. This is usually defined using two important parameters: the dynamic shear modulus G and the damping ratio D. Many previous experimental and numerical investigations have been conducted to describe the variations of G and D with the shear strain γ in different soils. The factors affecting these parameters, such as the mean effective confining pressure σ_{m}, over-consolidation ratio, plasticity index (PI), specimen size, stress anisotropy, saturation condition, grain size, mixture, and void ratio (e), have also been examined [1–11]. However, due to the technical complexity and high expense of overseas drilling, research into the variation characteristics of G and D in marine soil—particularly in cohesive marine clay—has so far been limited and inadequate.

Koutsoftas and Fisher [12] studied the effect of stress history on marine clay by means of resonant column (RC) and cyclic triaxial tests. Vrettos and Savidis [13] systematically investigated the effects of e, PI, and σ_m on marine clays in Greece by means of RC tests. Sun et al. [14,15] analyzed the effects of σ_m, PI, and the experimental apparatus on marine clay from China's Qiongzhou Strait. Banerjee and Balaji [16] investigated the effects of anisotropic consolidation (stress ratio K_c) on Chennai marine clay using a series of cyclic triaxial and RC tests. Senapati et al. [17] also used a series of cyclic triaxial and RC tests to investigate the influence of frequency on marine clay from the Ennore coast of India's Tamil Nadu saturated with various pore fluids. Li et al. [18] explored the influence of σ_m on several types of marine soil containing marine clay in China's Yellow Sea using dynamic triaxial testing.

On the other hand, geotechnical and earthquake engineering practice requires the establishment of empirical relationships that represent dynamic shear modulus degradation versus shear strain (G/G_{max}–γ) and damping ratio growth versus shear strain (D–γ). To this end, numerous researchers have analyzed this problem and proposed various functions applicable to their data. Hardin and Drnevich [19] published the first function model describing the nonlinear and hysteretic behavior of soil. They proposed a hyperbolic model to reflect the shear modulus degradation (G/G_{max}–γ), as well as an approximate model for material damping growth (D–γ), which is related to G/G_{max}. Much subsequent research was influenced by this work, and different considerations have been introduced to perfect their equations [20–24]. A summary of the representative function forms used to determine the shear modulus degradation versus shear strain γ (G/G_{max}–γ) and the damping growth versus shear strain γ (D–γ) are presented in Table 1. These models are used to depict the G/G_{max}–γ and D–γ curves under certain conditions. They commonly use a modified hyperbolic model to represent the G reduction backbone curve, and some factors (such as D_{min} or D_{max}) have been introduced to obtain the best possible fit with the target D–γ data. As a result, the existing models are empirical and were developed for specific soil types, strain ranges, and other considerations. Some are limited to the data used in the fitting, and they fail to provide a good fit for others. Furthermore, these models do not directly take into account the variation of G/G_{max}–γ and D–γ with $H(\sigma_m)$, making it impossible to construct a universal model that can be reliably applied to a variety of data sets.

Table 1. Summary of representative G/G_{max}–γ and D–γ function forms.

Function Forms	Data from	Soil Type
$G/G_{max} = 1/(1+\gamma/\gamma_r)$, $\gamma_r = \tau_{max}/G_{max}$, where G_{max} is the maximum shear modulus; γ_r is the reference strain; τ_{max} is the maximum shear stress.	Hardin and Drnevich [19]	Cohesive soil and sand
$D = D_{max}(1 - G/G_{max})$, where D_{max} is the maximum damping ratio.		
$G/G_{max} = 0.5\left[1+\tanh\left(\ln(0.000102/\gamma)^{0.492}\right)\right]{\sigma_m}^{0.272[1-\tanh(\ln(0.000556/\gamma)^{0.4})]}$,	Ishibashi and Zh-ang [20]	Sandy soil
$D = 0.333\left\{0.586(G/G_{max})^2 - 1.547(G/G_{max}) + 1\right\}$.		
$G/G_{max} = 0.5\left[1+\tanh\left(\ln((0.000102+n(\mathrm{PI}))/\gamma)^{0.492}\right)\right] \times {\sigma_m}^{0.272[1-\tanh(\ln(0.000556/\gamma)^{0.4})]e^{-0.145\mathrm{PI}^{-0.0145\mathrm{PI}^{1.3}}}}$, where n(PI) is the function related to the plasticity index of soil.		Plastic soil (Silt and Clay)
$D = 0.333/2 \times \left(1+e^{-0.0145\mathrm{PI}^{1.3}}\right) \times \left\{0.586(G/G_{max})^2 - 1.547(G/G_{max}) + 1\right\}$.		
$G/G_{max} = 1/\left(\left[1+a(\gamma)^b\right]^c\right)$, where a, b, and c are the curvature coefficient.	Borden et al. [21]	Piedmont residual soil (MH, ML, SM-ML, SM)
$D = 20.4(G/G_{max} - 1)^2 + 3.1$.		
$G/G_{max} = 1/\left[1+(\gamma/\gamma_r)^\alpha\right]$, where α is the curvature coefficient.	Stokoe et al. [22] Darendeli [23]	Undisturbed soil (CH, CL, CL-ML, MH, ML, SC, SM, SC-SM, SP, SP-SM, SW-SC, SW-SM)
$D = d \times (G/G_{max})^{0.1} \times D_{Masing} + D_{min}$, where d is the scaling coefficient, D_{min} is the small-strain damping ratio, and D_{Masing} is the modeled masing damping.	Darendeli [23]	
$G/G_{max} = 1/\left[1+(\gamma/\gamma_r)^\alpha\right] \gamma_r = \gamma_{r1}(\sigma_m/P_a)^k$, where γ_r is the reference strain corresponding to the γ value when G/G_{max} = 0.5, α is the curvature parameter, γ_{r1} is the reference strain at a mean effective confining stress σ_m of 100 kPa, P_a is the reference stress at 100 kPa, and k is a stress-correction exponent.	Zhang et al. [24]	Quaternary soil Tertiary and older soil Residual/saprolite soil

Table 1. *Cont.*

Function Forms	Data from	Soil Type
$D = D_{min} + 10.6(G/G_{max})^2 - 31.6(G/G_{max}) + 21.0$ Torsional shear test, $D = D_{min} + 9.4(G/G_{max})^2 - 26.5(G/G_{max}) + 17.1$ Resonant column test, $D_{min} = D_{min1} \times (\sigma_m/P_a)^{-k/2}$, where D_{min1} is the small-strain damping at σ_m of 100 kPa.		

In view of the special conditions of the marine environment and the relative scarcity of dynamic parameters for marine clay, the properties of G and D of marine clay still need to be further investigated. For this purpose, in this study, a series of RC tests were conducted on marine clay in Hangzhou Bay and Bohai Bay, China. The variation characteristics of G and D with soil depth H (reflected as σ_m in the laboratory test conditions) were studied and analyzed. More importantly, an intelligent prediction model based on a back-propagation neural network (BPNN) was developed. This model is universal and is not affected by differences in fitting parameters, it also takes into account the natural variations of the dynamic mechanical characteristics of soil with the value of $H(\sigma_m)$. It can not only accurately predict the values of G and D with various γ and corresponding $H(\sigma_m)$ values, but it also intelligently describes and predicts the G/G_{max}–γ and D–γ curves of marine clay. Accordingly, this study will advance the understanding of the basic dynamic properties of marine clay in Hangzhou Bay and Bohai Bay. The proposed new-intelligent model will be able to deeply excavate, learn and predict the dynamic characteristics of marine clays. Furthermore, experimental studies and proposed models will provide reliable supplementary data for the analysis of soil dynamics and seismic responses in marine engineering.

2. Experimental Measurements

2.1. Materials

This study examined undisturbed marine clay taken from the seabeds of Bohai Bay and Hangzhou Bay at depths ranging from 6.3 m to 70 m. Using an offshore drilling platform, an open thin-walled earth borrower was employed to capture the clay samples from four boreholes at the locations indicated in Figure 1. In the drilling area in Bohai Bay (BH), the seabed topography is slightly undulating, and the seawater depth varies gently with a moderate deepening trend from southwest to northeast and no obvious local undulations. The bottom terrain in the drilling area in Hangzhou Bay (HZ) is relatively flat, and the seawater depth varies widely, sloping slowly from west to east. A total of 27 marine clay samples were used for this study; 17 samples from Bohai Bay were designated BH1 to BH17, while 10 samples from Hangzhou Bay were designated HZ1 to HZ10, respectively. According to the Unified Soil Classification System [25] and laboratory assessments of basic physical qualities, the undisturbed marine clays were classified as lean clay (CL). RC tests were conducted on the marine clays at σ_m values ranging from 43 to 466 kPa, as summarized in Table 2.

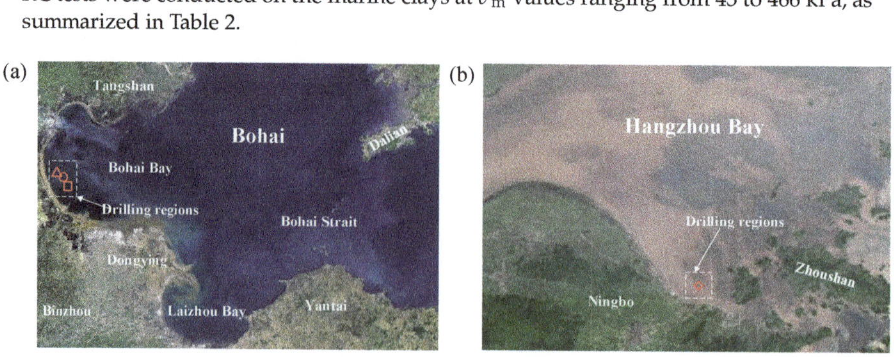

Figure 1. Geographical locations of the boreholes: (**a**) Bohai Bay and (**b**) Hangzhou Bay.

Table 2. Representative physical parameters of the marine clays.

Sample	Soil Depth H/m	Mean Effective Confining Pressure σ_m/kPa	Specific Gravity G_s	Water Content w/%	Density ρ/g·cm^{-3}	Plasticity Index PI
BH 1	6.3–6.5	43	2.67	40.72	1.9	15.99
BH 2	8.3–8.5	56	2.69	36.45	1.9	17.15
BH 3	10.8–11.0	73	2.70	38.95	1.95	16.88
BH 4	15.8–16.0	106	2.68	37.99	1.92	16.23
BH 5	23.5–23.7	157	2.67	37.87	1.97	16.98
BH 6	25.5–25.7	171	2.67	35.53	1.96	16.95
BH 7	29.8–30.0	199	2.67	38.96	1.91	15.00
BH 8	30.0–30.2	201	2.71	36.17	1.97	15.06
BH 9	31.8–32.0	213	2.67	39.04	1.92	17.12
BH 10	33.8–34.0	226	2.68	36.67	1.93	12.64
BH 11	35.2–35.4	235	2.69	36.82	1.93	17.23
BH 12	40.3–40.5	269	2.68	30.93	1.9	15.27
BH 13	43.3–43.5	289	2.70	38.17	1.94	15.95
BH 14	46.3–46.5	309	2.68	36.08	1.93	15.34
BH 15	61.8–62.0	413	2.68	33.74	2.04	13.55
BH 16	67.8–68.0	453	2.68	31.10	1.99	15.57
BH 17	69.8–70.0	466	2.67	30.84	2.01	13.14
HZ 1	18.3–18.5	123	2.68	15.52	1.81	15.52
HZ 2	23.3–25.5	156	2.67	15.64	1.94	15.64
HZ 3	28.3–28.5	190	2.70	14.37	1.97	14.37
HZ 4	33.3–33.5	233	2.67	15.07	2.06	15.07
HZ 5	40.8–41.0	273	2.71	16.57	2.07	16.57
HZ 6	48.3–48.5	323	2.70	14.76	2.07	14.76
HZ 7	53.3–53.5	356	2.69	13.35	2.04	13.35
HZ 8	58.3–58.5	390	2.70	14.76	2.06	14.76
HZ 9	63.3–63.5	423	2.70	15.97	2.06	15.97
HZ 10	68.3–68.5	456	2.69	14.08	2.03	14.08

2.2. Test Apparatus and Procedure

The specimens were tested using the TSH-100 high-precision fixed–free RC apparatus (Figure 2) from GCTS Testing Systems (Tempe, AZ, USA), which can reliably measure the G and D values of soil specimens over a wide strain range with stable and repeatable results. In the device, the confining pressure is controlled by a pneumatic servo system. A fully automatic suspension torsion drive system is used to excite the top of the soil specimen. On-specimen axial displacement can be measured by an AC deformation sensor with a range of $\pm$6 mm and 0.1% linearity, and γ can be measured by a fiber optics deformation sensor with a dual-range output: $\pm$0.1 mm low range and $\pm$5.0 mm for high range, with a 0–15 kHz flat frequency response and 0.1% linearity. The data-acquisition system has eight independent channels with a response frequency of 50 kHz, and it can record data at intervals of less than 0.2 ms.

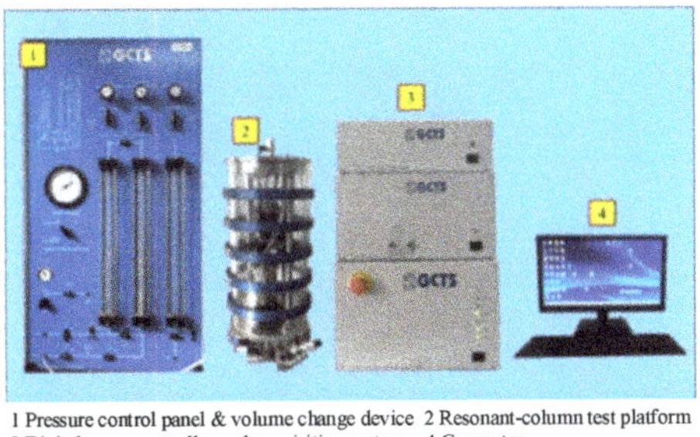

Figure 2. Schematic diagram of TSH-100 resonant column apparatus.

The test procedure can be divided into three steps. (1) A solid cylindrical specimen with a diameter of 50 mm and height of 100 mm is mounted on the device base. (2) After the specimen is installed, the top is connected to the floating torsion drive device, the displacement sensor is connected and zeroed, and the pressure chamber is closed to ensure a tight seal. (3) The specimens are uniformly consolidated according to the natural stress state based on the original marine soil depth, as summarized in Table 2. (4) When the average axial-strain rate is less than $1 \times 10^{-3}\%/\text{min}$, the consolidation is completed. The soil specimen is then excited by the automatic suspension dynamic torsion device, and the excitation frequency is steadily increased. (5) Consequently, the value of G is obtained by the theory of elastic-wave propagation once the sweep frequency reaches the resonance frequency, and the value of D is calculated by the collected free-vibration response decay curve [26,27].

$$G = \rho V_S^2 \tag{1}$$

$$\delta = \frac{1}{z}\ln\left(\frac{A_1}{A_{z+1}}\right),\ D = \sqrt{\frac{\delta^2}{4\pi^2 + \delta^2}} \times 100\%, \tag{2}$$

where V_S is the shear-wave velocity of the soil [28], δ is the logarithmic decrement of the decay curve, A_1 is the amplitude of free vibration for the first cycle after excitation switch-off, A_{z+1} is the amplitude of free vibration for the $(z + 1)$th cycle of free vibration, and z is the number of free-vibration cycles.

2.3. Experimental Results

The RC test results of the dynamic shear modulus G and damping ratio D versus shear strain γ for marine clay with changes in H (σ_m) are given in Figures 3 and 4, respectively. In line with the phenomena of previous studies, all the marine clays in Bohai Bay and Hangzhou Bay showed exhibited decreases in G and increases in D with increasing γ. Furthermore, it is noteworthy that for a given value of γ, the G value progressively increases with increasing H (σ_m), while D gradually decreases. In addition, based on the hyperbolic relationship between G and γ under small-amplitude vibrations proposed by Hardin and Drnevich [19], a linear relationship between $1/G$ and γ can be obtained, followed by the value of G_{max} for marine clay [29], as illustrated in Figure 5. The G_{max} values of the marine clays also increase with increasing H (σ_m), which is consistent with the experimental findings in Figures 3 and 4. For all the present experimental values, the overall dynamic stiffness decays with increasing γ, but it increases with increasing H (σ_m). This also indicates that the G and D values of marine clay are not only directly related to γ, but they also have an obvious and strong correlation with H (σ_m).

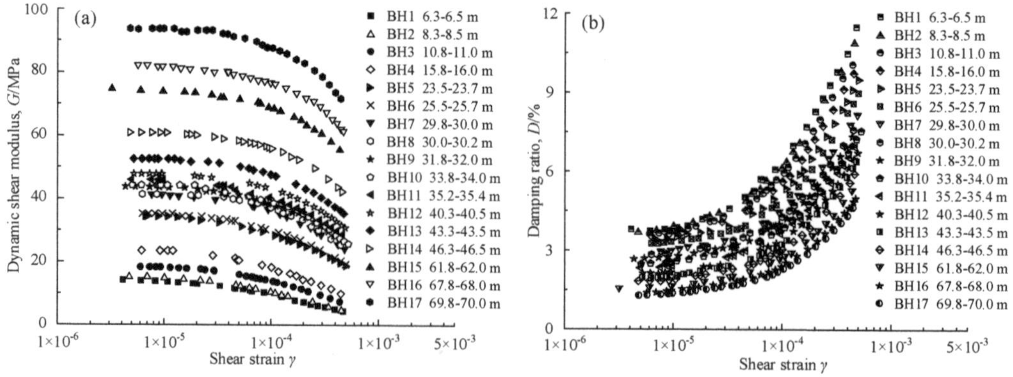

Figure 3. Experimental results of RC tests on marine clay from Bohai Bay: (**a**) variation of dynamic shear modulus with shear strain; (**b**) variation of damping ratio with shear strain.

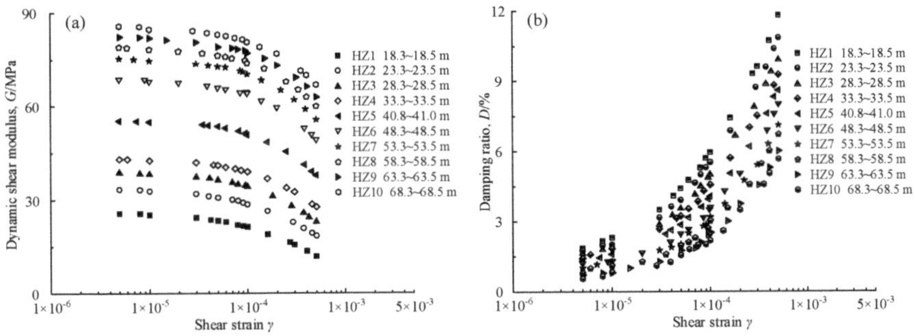

Figure 4. Experimental results of RC tests on marine clay from Hangzhou Bay: (**a**) variation of dynamic shear modulus with shear strain; (**b**) variation of damping ratio with shear strain.

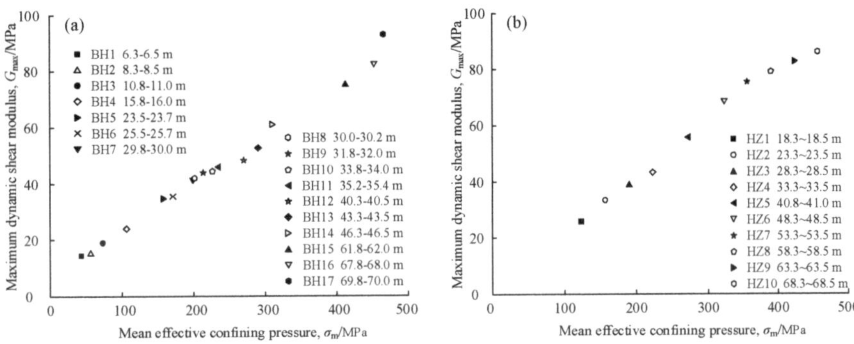

Figure 5. Maximum dynamic shear modulus of marine clays from (**a**) Bohai Bay; (**b**) Hangzhou Bay.

3. Intelligent Model

3.1. Model Framework

The representative and modified hyperbolic models of $G/G_{\max}$–γ normally have more than one curve coefficient for the best fit of the data, as shown in Table 1. In contrast, D–γ models add numerous parameters on the basis of $G/G_{\max}$–γ. In this approach, forward propagation of errors will unavoidably arise in the fitting process of the formula to the application, especially the forward propagation of errors from the $G/G_{\max}$–γ formula to the D–γ formula. To solve this problem, an intelligent model based on a BPNN is proposed. The BPNN proposed by Rumelhart et al. [30] features the forward propagation of data and the back-tpropagation of errors, and it has the ability to self-identify, learn, and model the intrinsic relationships in complex nonlinear data. This makes it particularly suitable for modeling the dynamical behaviors of soil. The intelligent BPNN model framework, which uses the information-processing characteristics of the human brain as the model reference, is shown in Figure 6. Data processing in the BPNN is performed between the input layer (I), the hidden layer (L), and the output layer (O), with each layer consisting of multiple neurons. Each neuron is connected by the weights (W_{ni}) and (W_{jn}), and the neurons (L_n) and (O_j) are controlled by the thresholds (T^{H}) and (T^{O}).

3.2. Model Settings and Procedures

The model and algorithm can be described as follows:

(1) Framework: input layer I + hidden layer L + output layer O = 2 + n + 3, as depicted in Figure 6.

(2) Initial process: normalize the data set, and initialize the connection weights and thresholds to 1.

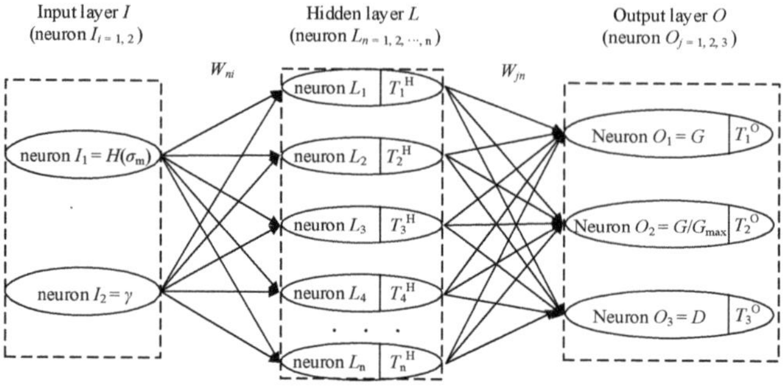

Figure 6. Technical framework for the intelligent model.

(3) Forward propagation: the input data are passed in from I_i, processed by L_n, and then reach O_j. The hyperbolic tangent sigmoid transfer function $f_{\text{Tansig}}(x)$ was chosen as the transfer function from I_i to L_n, and a linear function was chosen as the transfer function from L_n to O_j:

$$L_n = f(\sum_{i=1}^{3} w_{ni} I_i + T_n^H),\ f_{\text{Tansig}}(x) = \frac{1}{1+e^{-2x}} - 1, \tag{3}$$

where x is the input values in the function $f_{\text{Tansig}}(x)$, and

$$O_j = \sum_{n=1}^{n} w_{jn} L_n + T_j^O \tag{4}$$

(4) Back-propagation: if the output value does not match the actual value, it is transferred to the backward-propagation stage of the error. The error is apportioned to all the neurons in each layer and is used as the basis for correcting the weights and thresholds in the training and learning process.

(5) Training and learning: the weights and thresholds are continuously updated using the Bayesian regularization back-propagation and gradient-descent momentum algorithm. According to the Levenberg–Marquardt method [31], the Bayesian regularization back propagation minimizes a linear combination of squared errors and weights so that at the end of the training, the resulting network has good generalization qualities [32]. The gradient-descent momentum algorithm is used to increase the learning rate of weights and thresholds [33]. The principles of these algorithms are not repeated in this paper, and they can be implemented on multiple platforms, including Python, Octave, and MATLAB. The main process of training and learning can be expressed as follows:

$$E = \frac{1}{K}\sum_{1}^{K} |e(k)|^2,\ W_{m+1} = W_m + \eta\frac{\partial E}{\partial W_m},\ T_{m+1} = T_m + \eta\frac{\partial E}{\partial T_m} \tag{5}$$

where $e(k)$ represents the difference between each output value and the training value, E represents the total error, K represents the total number of values in the training set, and m represents the current iteration of the training process.

(6) Finally, when E is reduced to the expected training error, or the number of learning iterations reaches the pre-set maximum, the training of the intelligent model is completed. The trained model can then be applied to the prediction of the dynamic shear modulus G and damping ratio D characteristics of marine soils

3.3. Model Performance

In this study, about 70.7% of the experimental measurements from Bohai Bay and 70.0% of the experimental measurements from Hangzhou Bay were used as training data; this allowed the model to intelligently identify, excavate, and learn the intrinsic G and

D characteristics of the marine clays. The remaining data were used as a prediction set for model validation and error calculation [34]. The number of training trials was set to 1×10^6, the learning rate was set to 10^{-6}, and the training target's minimum error was set to 1×10^{-10}. The total number n of neurons in the hidden layer L was set in the range 3 to 18. No human intervention or additional curvature coefficient setting was required during the process, and machine learning was achieved entirely by the model itself.

The prediction performance of the trained, intelligent model with different n values is shown in Figure 7. It is assessed by the statistical performance indicators obtained by comparing the predicted and measured data in the prediction set. Mean absolute error (MAE), root mean square error (RMSE), and coefficient of correlation (R) were incorporated into the statistical performance indicators to analyze the prediction performance of the model better [35,36]. The MAE of G, G/G_{max}, and D for marine clays are presented in Figure 7a–c, respectively. It is evident that the MAE for marine clays is at a relatively well-desirable level for the intelligent model with different n. In particular, the MAE shows a decreasing trend with the increase in n, and a significant inflection point occurs when n is greater than 6. Subsequently, the MAE fluctuates at a lower level. Moreover, a similar phenomenon is also observed in Figure 7d–f of the RMSE values. Furthermore, the R of the predicted and measured data are presented in Figure 7g–i, where the R is greater than 0.9 for the predicted performance of the intelligent models with different n. It is worth noting that all prediction results correlate well with the measured data, despite the fact that the prediction error fluctuates with n. This further confirms that intelligent models can excavate, learn and predict the G and D values of marine clays. Therefore, the intelligent model has a good prediction performance for the G and D values of the marine clays, and the prediction accuracy does not strictly depend on n. The detailed prediction results of the intelligent model will be further evaluated and discussed in the following section.

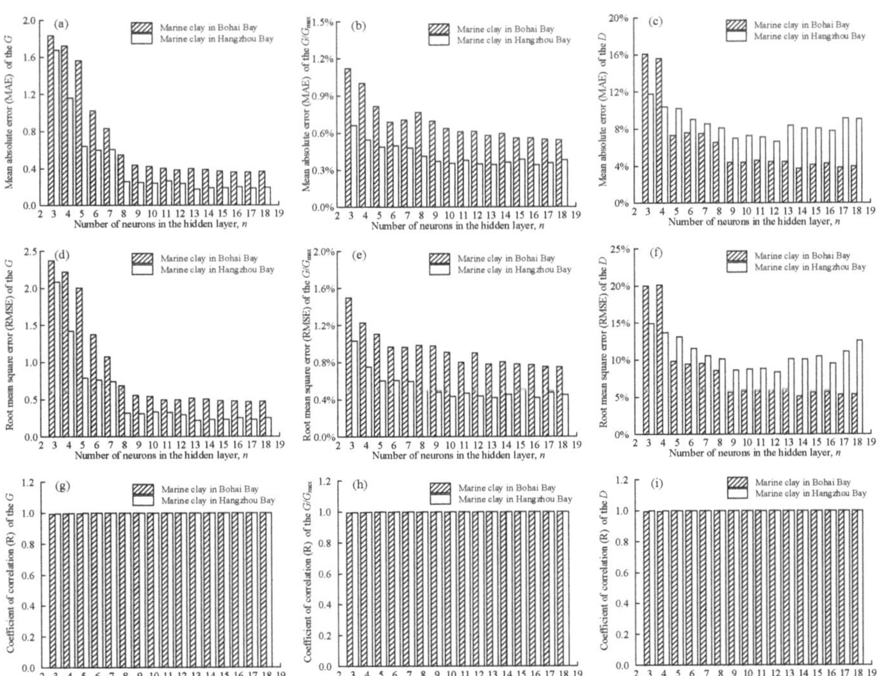

Figure 7. Prediction performance of the intelligent model with different n: (**a–c**) the MAE of G, G/G_{max}, and D for marine clays; (**d–f**) the RMSE of G, G/G_{max}, and D for marine clays; (**g–i**) the R of G, G/G_{max}, and D for marine clays.

4. Evaluation and Discussion

4.1. Evaluation of Prediction Results

To further investigate the effectiveness of the model for identifying, learning, and predicting the dynamic behaviors of marine clay, the values of the prediction set calculated using the intelligent model were compared with the measured data. That is, when both H (σ_m) and γ are known, the prediction effect can be assessed by the difference between the measured value and the predicted value. The results of this comparison are shown in Figures 8 and 9, respectively, with n = 8. It can be seen that the relative errors between the predicted and measured values of G and D are generally within ±8%. It should be noted that this error range is quite precise, considering the large uncertainties and complex internal structures of soils.

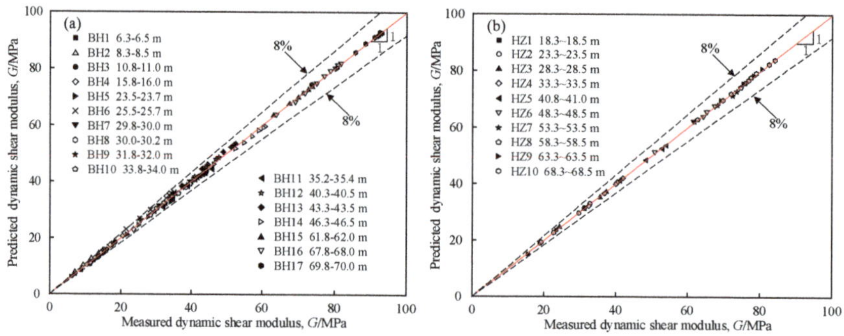

Figure 8. Comparison of predicted and measured values of the dynamic shear modulus G of marine clays from (**a**) Bohai Bay; (**b**) Hangzhou Bay.

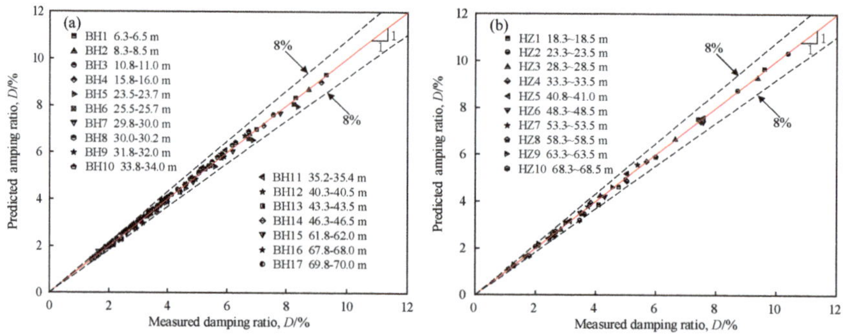

Figure 9. Comparison of predicted and measured values of the damping ratio D of marine clays from (**a**) Bohai Bay; (**b**) Hangzhou Bay.

An important difference between soils and general engineering materials is their nonlinear and hysteretic dynamic behavior. To deeply explore and evaluate the abilities of the intelligent model for prediction of the dynamic properties of marine clay, predicted curves of the normalized dynamic shear modulus G/G_{max} and damping ratio D versus shear strain γ over a wide shear strain range ($1 \times 10^{-6} \leq \gamma \leq 5 \times 10^{-4}$) are presented in Figures 10 and 11, respectively. Combining in Figures 10 and 11, it can be seen that the experimental data are largely in agreement with the predicted curves, and they are also corroborated by the predicted results of G/G_{max} and D in Figures 8 and 9. Specifically, before the line-elastic threshold shear strain ($\gamma_{LE} = 1 \times 10^{-5}$), the G/G_{max} value of marine clay decays slightly with increasing γ, while the value of D increases slightly with increasing γ; when the γ_{LE} is reached, the G/G_{max} value starts to decay at a faster rate with increasing γ, and the value of D increases at a faster rate with increasing γ. Until the nonlinear-elastic threshold shear strain ($\gamma_{NE} = 1 \times 10^{-4}$) is exceeded, the value of G/G_{max} decays rapidly with increasing γ. Meanwhile, the value of D grows rapidly with increasing γ. Furthermore, the G/G_{max} value increases with increasing H (σ_m) for a given γ value, and this is accompanied by a decreasing recession gradient. Conversely, the D value decreases with increasing H (σ_m) at a given shear strain γ, and this is followed by a decrease in the growth rate.

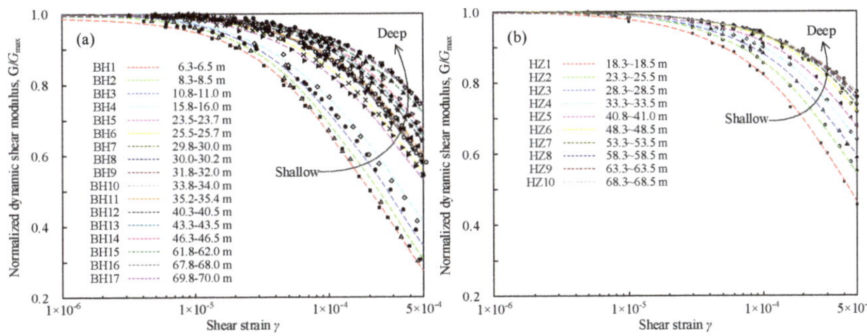

Figure 10. Comparison of measured values and predicted G/G_{max}–γ curves for marine clays from (**a**) Bohai Bay; (**b**) Hangzhou Bay.

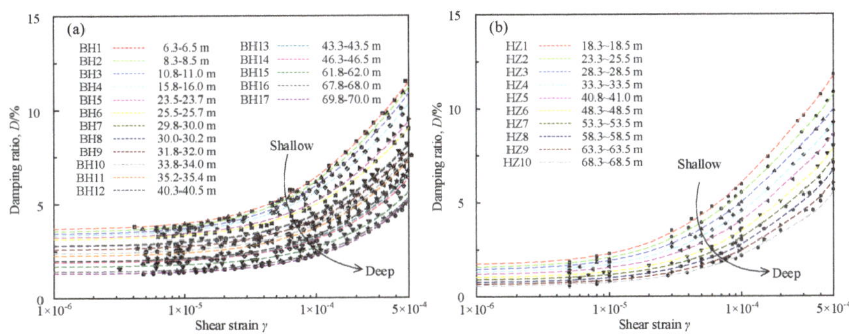

Figure 11. Comparison of measured values and predicted D–γ curves for marine clays from (**a**) Bohai Bay; (**b**) Hangzhou Bay.

In addition, The overall G/G_{max}–γ curves show a "low to high" change tendency; in contrast, the overall D–γ curves show a "high to low" trend. This means that the dynamic properties of the marine clay gradually change from non-linear to linear with increasing H (σ_m), and this is accompanied by weakening hysteresis. Thus, it can be said that the intelligent model can quite effectively describe and predict the nonlinear and hysteretic dynamic properties of marine clay. More importantly, it is not only able to accurately predict the G and D values of marine clays at different H (σ_m) and γ, but it can also intelligently predict the variation of the decay of G and the growth of D with H (σ_m). This will present a solution to a key challenge in geotechnical engineering.

4.2. Comparison with Function Models

It should be noted that most of the formulas in Table 1 do not directly consider the variation of soil dynamic characteristics with H (σ_m), which is an extremely important issue in geotechnical engineering. Hence, the proposed intelligent model was compared with representative mathematical models proposed by Ishibashi and Zhang [20] and Zhang et al. [24] to evaluate its performance. As a control, the evaluation data were used from the prediction set, and the value of n in the model was kept at 8.

Figures 12 and 13 show the performance of the three methods for G/G_{max} and D prediction using the evaluation data. Compared with the mathematical formulas proposed by Ishibashi and Zhang [20] and Zhang et al. [24], the proposed intelligent model has the best performance for the evaluated data. Ishibashi and Zhang's [20] formula overestimates the dynamic stiffness of the soil and is not applicable to marine clay; Zhang et al.'s [24] formula has satisfactory performance for G/G_{max}, but the prediction of D is relatively poor. This is mainly because, to achieve the best fit to the data, their technique normally leads to uncertainty and dispersion of the fitted parameters, and this, in turn, promotes the forward propagation of errors from G/G_{max}–γ to D–γ. Simultaneously, the intrinsic complex nonlinear dynamic characteristics of the marine clay enhance this error-propagation phenomenon. As a result, the proposed intelligent model has a very good match for the G and D properties of the marine clays. Especially for the prediction of D.

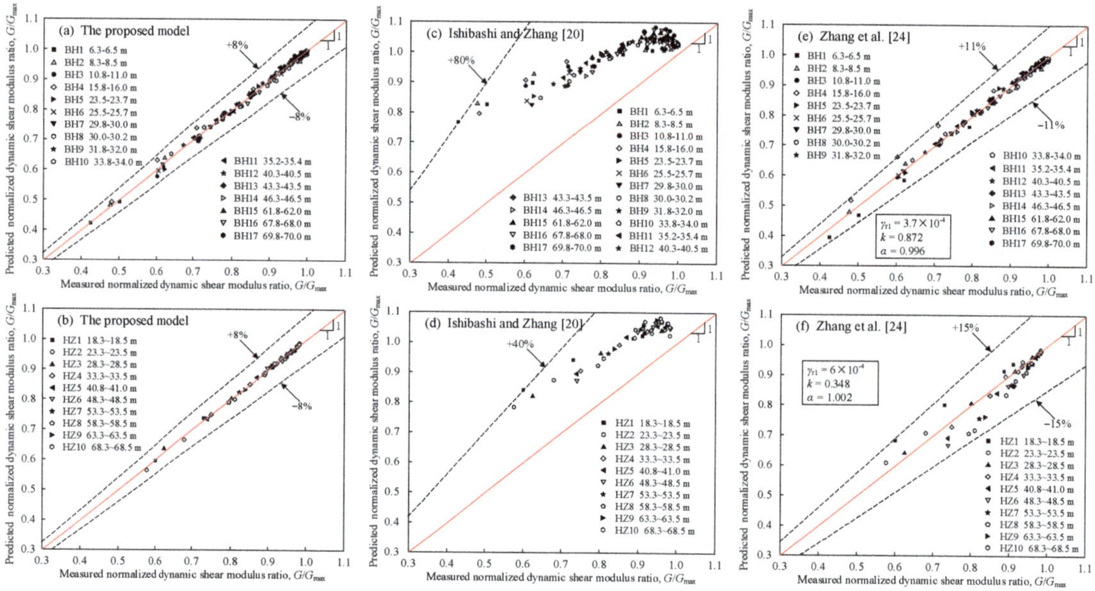

Figure 12. Comparison of the predicted performance of G/G_{max} values: (**a**,**b**) the performance of the proposed model; (**c**,**d**) the performance of the Ishibashi and Zhang's [20] model; (**e**,**f**) the performance of the Zhang et al.'s [24] model.

Thus, compared to the mathematical functions, the proposed intelligent model has very good adaptability to the dynamical characteristics of marine clay from Bohai Bay and Hangzhou Bay, China. This means that it is eminently suitable for application to geotechnical research and earthquake engineering. However, as mentioned before, sampling of the in-situ marine soil is very difficult, especially in different depths. This experimental study and the proposed model in this paper only focus on marine clay in two sea areas. Research on the dynamic properties of undisturbed marine soils is rarely available and still needs to be advanced. More types and locations of marine soils should be studied in further investigation, and an intelligent database should be constructed based on the proposed model.

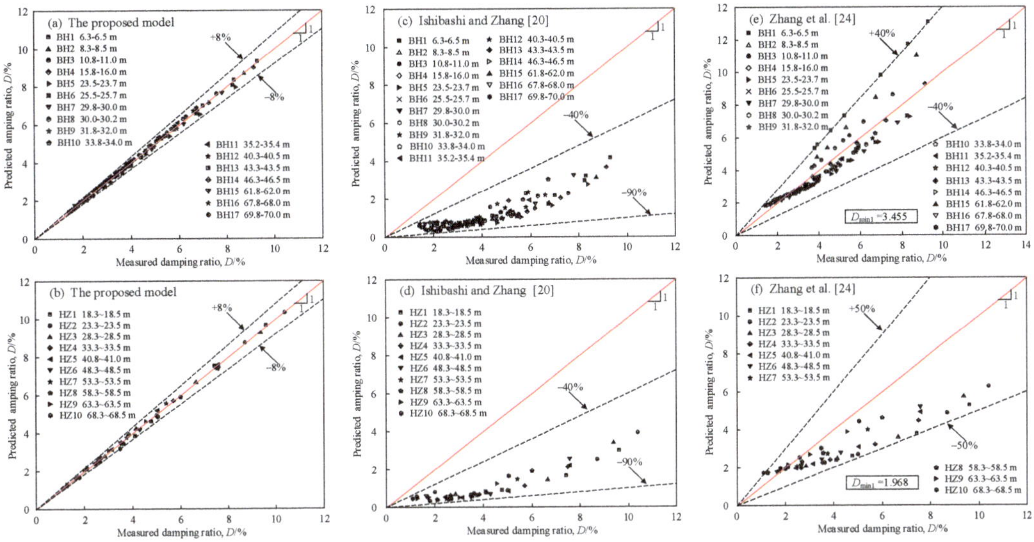

Figure 13. Comparison of the predicted performance of D values: (**a**,**b**) the performance of the proposed model; (**c**,**d**) the performance of the Ishibashi and Zhang's [20] model; (**e**,**f**) the performance of the Zhang et al.'s [24] model.

5. Conclusions

In this study, a series of RC tests were conducted to investigate the variation feature of the G and D with H (σ_m) for marine clays from Bohai Bay and Hangzhou Bay. An intelligent model was constructed that provides a great match for the G and D characteristics of marine clay. The main conclusions can be summarized as follows.

The dynamic properties of marine clays are not only directly related to the γ, but they also have a strong correlation with H (σ_m). The G decay nonlinearly with increasing shear strain γ, and D increases nonlinearly with increasing γ. Meanwhile, the G decay curve G/G_{max}–γ gradually changes from non-linear to linear with increasing H (σ_m), and this is accompanied by a weakening hysteresis in the D growth curve D–γ.

Based on a back-propagation neural network (BPNN), the proposed intelligent model can sufficiently excavate, learn and predict the G and D characteristics of marine clay. It has a good prediction performance for the G, G/G_{max}, and D values of the marine clays with various γ and H (σ_m). Moreover, it can further produce intelligent predictions of the decay of G and the growth of D.

Compared with existing mathematical functions, the intelligent model has a better prediction performance for the G and D properties of the marine clays. It avoids the forward propagation of errors and the need for human intervention regarding the fitting parameters, and the prediction accuracy does not strictly depend on n.

Author Contributions: Conceptualization, Q.W. and W.Y.; methodology, Q.W.; software, Q.W.; validation, Z.W., Y.Q. and W.Y.; investigation, Q.W.; resources, Q.W.; data curation, Z.W.; writing—original draft preparation, Q.W.; writing—review and editing, Q.W. and W.Y.; visualization, Y.Q.; supervision, W.Y.; funding acquisition, Q.W. All authors have read and agreed to the published version of the manuscript.

Funding: This research was funded by the National Natural Science Foundation of China (52008206) and the China Postdoctoral Science Foundation (2021M690279).

Institutional Review Board Statement: Not applicable.

Informed Consent Statement: Not applicable.

Data Availability Statement: The data used during the study are available from the first author by request.

Acknowledgments: Not applicable.

Conflicts of Interest: The authors declare no conflict of interest.

Nomenclature

G = dynamic shear modulus
G_{max} = maximum dynamic shear modulus
G/G_{max} = normalized dynamic shear modulus
D = damping ratio
D_{max} = maximum damping ratio
D_{min} = small-strain damping ratio
γ = shear strain
γ_r = reference strain
τ_{max} = maximum shear stress
a, b, and c = curvature coefficients
α = curvature coefficient
d = scaling coefficient
D_{Masing} = modeled masing damping
H = soil depth
σ_m = mean effective confining pressure
γ_{r1} = reference strain at σ_m of 100 kPa
P_a = reference stress of 100 kPa
k = stress correction exponent
D_{min1} = small-strain damping at σ_m of 100 kPa
w = water content of soil
ρ = density of soil
PI = plasticity index
e = void ratio
δ = logarithmic decrement of the decay curve
V_S = shear wave velocity of soil
A_1 = amplitude of free vibration for the first cycle after excitation switch-off
A_{z+1} = amplitude of free vibration for $(z + 1)^{th}$ cycle of free vibration
z = number of free-vibration cycles in resonant-column test
I = input layer
L = hidden layer
O = output layer
I_i = input layer neurons
L_n = hidden layer neurons
O_j = output layer neurons
i = the number of neurons in the input layer
n = the number of neurons in the hidden layer
j = the number of neurons in the output layer
W_{ni} = connection weights from the input layer to the hidden layer
W_{jn} = connection weights from the hidden layer to the output layer
T^H = thresholds in hidden layer neurons
T^O = output layer neurons
x = input value in function
E = total error
$e(k)$ = difference between each output value and the training value
K = total number of values in the training set
m = current number of the training process
MAE = mean-absolute-error

RMSE = root-mean-square error
R = coefficient of correlation
γ_{LE} = line-elastic threshold shear strain
γ_{NE} = nonlinear-elastic threshold shear strain

References

1. Hardin, B.O.; Drnevich, V.P. Shear modulus and damping in soils: Measurement and parameter effects (Terzaghi Leture). *J. Soil Mech. Found. Div.* **1972**, *98*, 603–624. [CrossRef]
2. Vucetic, M.; Dobry, R. Effect of Soil Plasticity on Cyclic Response. *J. Geotech. Eng.* **1991**, *117*, 89–107. [CrossRef]
3. Chen, G.X.; Zhou, Z.L.; Sun, T.; Wu, Q.; Xu, L.Y.; Khoshnevisan, S.; Ling, D.S. Shear modulus and damping ratio of sand–gravel mixtures over a wide strain range. *J. Earthq. Eng.* **2019**, *23*, 1407–1440. [CrossRef]
4. Yang, W.B.; Wu, Q.; Chen, G.X. Dynamic shear modulus prediction method of undisturbed soil in the estuary of the Yangtze River. *Rock and Soil Mech.* **2019**, *40*, 3889–3996.
5. Morsy, A.M.; Salem, M.A.; Elmamlouk, H.H. Evaluation of dynamic properties of calcareous sands in Egypt at small and medium shear strain ranges. *Soil Dynam. Earthq. Eng.* **2019**, *116*, 692–708. [CrossRef]
6. Jafarian, Y.; Javdanian, H. Small-strain dynamic properties of siliceous-carbonate sand under stress anisotropy. *Soil Dyn. Earthq. Eng.* **2020**, *131*, 106045. [CrossRef]
7. Wu, Q.; Ma, W.J.; Liu, Q.F.; Zhao, K.; Chen, G.X. Dynamic Shear Modulus and Damping Ratio of Rubber-Sand Mixtures with a Wide Range of Rubber Content. *Mater. Today Commun.* **2021**, *27*, 102341. [CrossRef]
8. Upreti, K.; Leong, E.C. Effect of mean grain size on shear modulus degradation and damping ratio curves of sands. *Géotechnique* **2021**, *71*, 205–215. [CrossRef]
9. Wu, Q.; Hang, T.Z.; Zhao, K.; Chen, G.X. Reduction of Dynamic Shear Modulus of Saturated Marine Sandy Silt under Complex Stress Conditions. *Mar. Georesour. Geotechnol.* **2022**, 1–11. [CrossRef]
10. Vrettos, C.; Banzibaganye, G. Effects of specimen size and inertia on resonant column tests applied to sands. *Soil Dyn. Earthq. Eng.* **2022**, *155*, 107136. [CrossRef]
11. Liang, K.; Chen, G.X.; Du, X.L.; Xu, C.S.; Yang, J. A Unified Formula for Small-Strain Shear Modulus of Sandy Soils Based on Extreme Void Ratios. *J. Geotech. Geoenviron. Eng.* **2023**, *149*, 04022127. [CrossRef]
12. Koutsoftas, D.C.; Fisher, J.A. Dynamic properties of two marine clays. *J. Geotech. Geoenviron. Eng.* **1980**, *106*, 645–657. [CrossRef]
13. Vrettos, C.; Savidis, S. Shear modulus and damping for Mediterranean sea clays of medium plasticity. In *Earthquakes Geotechnical Engineering*; e Pinto, P.S., Balkema, A.A., Eds.; CRC Press: Lisboa, Portugal, 1999; pp. 71–76.
14. Sun, T.; Chen, G.X.; Zhou, E.Q.; Li, X.J. Experimental study on dynamic shear modulus and damping ratio of silty clay in deep seabed. *J. Civ. Eng.* **2012**, *45*, 9–14.
15. Sun, T.; Chen, G.X.; Zhou, E.Q.; Li, X.J. Experimental study on dynamic shear modulus ratio and damping ratio of shallow marine soils over 100m in Qiongzhou Strait. *Chin. J. Geotech. Eng.* **2013**, *35*, 375–382.
16. Banerjee, S.; Balaji, P. Effect of anisotropy on cyclic properties of Chennai marine clay. *Int. J. Geosynth. Ground Eng.* **2018**, *4*, 27. [CrossRef]
17. Senapati, S.; Banerjee, S.; Thyagaraj, T. Effect of frequency on cyclic response of marine clay saturated with various pore fluids. *Int. J. Geotech. Eng.* **2021**, *15*, 1155–1164. [CrossRef]
18. Li, Y.Y.; Li, P.; Zhu, S. The study on dynamic shear modulus and damping ratio of marine soils based on dynamic triaxial test. *Mar. Georesour. Geotec.* **2022**, *40*, 473–486. [CrossRef]
19. Hardin, B.O.; Drnevich, V.P. Shear modulus and damping in soils: Design equations and curves. *J. Soil Mech. Found. Div.* **1972**, *98*, 667–692. [CrossRef]
20. Ishibashi, I.; Zhang, X. Unified dynamic shear moduli and damping ratios of sand and clay. *Soils Found.* **1993**, *33*, 182–191. [CrossRef]
21. Borden, R.H.; Shao, L.; Gupta, A. Dynamic properties of Piedmont residual soils. *J. Geotech. Eng.* **1996**, *122*, 813–821. [CrossRef]
22. Stokoe, K.H.; Darendeli, M.B.; Andrus, R.D.; Brown, L.T. Dynamic soil properties: Laboratory, field and correlation studies. In Proceedings of the 2nd International Conference on Earthquake Geotechnical Engineering, Lisbon, Portugal, 21–25 June 1999; pp. 811–845.
23. Darendeli, M. Development of a New Family of Normalized Modulus Reduction and Material Damping Curves. Ph.D. Thesis, University of Texas, Austin, TX, USA, 2001.
24. Zhang, J.; Andrus, R.D.; Juang, C.H. Normalized shear modulus and material damping ratio relationships. *J. Geotech. Geoenviron. Eng.* **2001**, *131*, 453–464. [CrossRef]
25. *ASTM D2487-17*; Standard Practice for Classification of Soils for Engineering Purposes (Unified Soil Classification System). ASTM International: West Conshohocken, PA, USA, 2017.
26. *ASTM D4015-15*; Standard Test Methods for Modulus and Damping of Soils by Fixed-Base Resonant Column Devices. ASTM International: West Conshohocken, PA, USA, 2015.
27. Senetakis, K.; Payan, M. Small strain damping ratio of sands and silty sands subjected to flexural and torsional resonant column excitation. *Soil Dyn. Earthq. Eng.* **2018**, *114*, 448–459. [CrossRef]

28. Chen, G.X.; Wu, Q.; Zhao, K.; Shen, Z.F.; Yang, J. A Binary Packing Material–Based Procedure for Evaluating Soil Liquefaction Triggering during Earthquakes. *J. Geotech. Geoenviron. Eng.* **2020**, *146*, 04020040. [CrossRef]
29. Gao, H.M.; Xia, S.S.; Chen, F.Y.; Stuedlein, A.W.; Li, X.; Wang, Z.H.; Shen, Z.F.; Chen, X.M. Dynamic shear modulus and damping of cemented and uncemented lightweight expanded clay aggregate (LECA) at low strains. *Soil Dyn. Earthq. Eng.* **2021**, *142*, 106555. [CrossRef]
30. Rumelhart, D.E.; Hinton, G.E.; Williams, R.J. Learning representations by back-propagating errors. *Nature* **1986**, *323*, 533–536. [CrossRef]
31. Marquardt, D.W. An algorithm for least-squares estimation of nonlinear parameters. *J. Soc. Ind. Appl. Math.* **1963**, *11*, 431–441. [CrossRef]
32. MacKay, D.J.C. Bayesian interpolation. *Neural Comput.* **1992**, *4*, 415–447. [CrossRef]
33. Qian, N. On the momentum term in gradient descent learning algorithms. *Neural Netw.* **1999**, *12*, 145–151. [CrossRef]
34. Mohammad, A.T.; Mat, S.B.; Sulaiman, M.Y.; Sopian, K.; Al-abidi, A.A. Implementation and Validation of an Artificial Neural Network for Predicting the Performance of a Liquid Desiccant Dehumidifier. *Energy Convers. Manag.* **2013**, *67*, 240–250. [CrossRef]
35. Alzabeebee, S.; Alshkane, Y.M.; Al-Taie, A.J.; Rashed, K.A. Soft Computing of the Recompression Index of Fine-Grained Soils. *Soft Comput.* **2021**, *25*, 15297–15312. [CrossRef]
36. Alzabeebee, S.; Mohammed, D.A.; Alshkane, Y.M. Experimental Study and Soft Computing Modeling of the Unconfined Compressive Strength of Limestone Rocks Considering Dry and Saturation Conditions. *Rock Mech. Rock Eng.* **2022**, *55*, 5535–5554. [CrossRef]

Journal of
Marine Science and Engineering

MDPI

Article

Influence of Beach Erosion during Wave Action in Designed Artificial Sandy Beach Using XBeach Model: Profiles and Shoreline

Yingtao Zhou [1,2,3,*], Xi Feng [1,2,4], Maoyuan Liu [4] and Weiqun Wang [3]

[1] Hainan Key Laboratory of Marine Geological Resources and Environment, Haikou 570206, China
[2] Key Laboratory of Marine Ecological Conservation and Restoration, Ministry of Natural Resources/Fujian Provincial Key Laboratory of Marine Ecological Conservation and Restoration, Xiamen 361005, China
[3] Shanghai Urban Construction Design & Research Institute (Group) Co., Ltd., Shanghai 200125, China
[4] College of Harbor, Coastal and Offshore Engineering, Hohai University, Nanjing 210098, China
* Correspondence: zhouyingtao@sucdri.com

Abstract: Beach width is an important factor for tourists' comfort, and the backshore is a swash zone where sediment moves quickly. Artificial sandy beaches focus on beach width stability and evolution. This paper is based on an artificial beach project in Haikou Bay, where, in view of the existing conditions, a new type of beach profile that can protect beach berm and width without being eroded by large wave action. Numerical simulation based on XBeach model were conducted to predict the morphodynamical responses of the beach, including a diagnosis of the erosion spots under storm and normal wave events, respectively. Sediment fluxes along and across the shoreline under varied scenarios, dependent on profile width and backshore slope, were discussed. It was found that normal waves with lower heights and longer periods can induce stronger erosion than storm waves due to the landform of the inner-bay in Haikou Bay. Engineering and biological methods to reduce beach erosion during wave action were discussed. Biological methods such as green-plants-root-system can retain berm surface sediment without allowing it to be transported offshore by wave action. The design concept of this artificial beach project may inspire more beach design and protection projects in coastal zones.

Keywords: artificial beach; erosion; wave action; numerical simulation

1. Introduction

Beach width is an important factor for tourist comfort, while the backshore must protected from wave erosion induced by wave run-up and nearshore currents, which have strong effects, to protect the beach volume. With the construction of artificial beaches, a better understanding of the equilibrium mechanism of the beach surface is necessary for coastal engineering designs. With the construction of artificial beaches, a better understanding of the equilibrium mechanism of the beach surface is necessary for coastal engineering designs. Artificial beaches are usually designed into arc-shaped landscape. Therefore, existing curved embankments are often re-used for the development of the artificial beach. During normal wave events, such an arc-shaped beach profile favors morpho-dynamic balance, Extreme sea states such as storm tides and high water levels (HWL) has a profound influence on wave heights in estuaries and coastal areas, as well as sand movement [1]. The evolutionary processes of underwater sandbars and nearshore slopes are well understood, and some laws have been summarized [2]. Significant efforts have been made to reveal the erosion and restoration processes of beach profiles.. Multiple methods are combined to study the coastal alongshore variation including measurements [3] physical experiments [4] and numerical experiments [5–8]. Recently, the direct application of Radar (SAR) Satellite [9] and historical multispectral Landsat images analysis [10] in studying beach erosion and shoreline retreat has also become a popular trend.

Extreme wave actions process sufficient energy to erode and rebuild coastal regions, especially those with steep slopes or beaches with coarse-grained sediments, where the profiles are almost entirely controlled by waves rather than tide currents. Increasing evidence suggests global climate change will alter wind waves and swell waves, modifying the severity and frequency of episodic coastal flooding and morphological change,which in turn exacerbated the impacts of relative sea-level-rise [11,12]. It was found that onshore bedload transport by waves is the primary cause of the onshore migration of the shoreface substances. It was observed that the shoreface development increases local wave height and strengthens wave nonlinearity through its shallow water depth. The most intense wave-breaking dissipation has been found on the crest of the shoreface, while the distribution of wave energy dissipation rates is more uniform on the quasi-equilibrium profile than that on the initial profile [13].

Anthropogenic activities, such as development and reclamation of the estuary regions also contribute to the degradation of the coastal environment and have made it lose the resilience function of the buffer zone. Traditional seawalls and check dams are constructed mostly focusing on the protection of lives and assets, but a new problem arises when coastal hydraulic constructions change the dynamic balance of the geomorphological evolution in the natural coastal zone. These will impose negative effect on landscapes, ecosystems, biodiversity, and biological interactions in the long run [14]. Coastal areas will be eroded more than before with the sediment flux from upstream decreases or sediment unable to silt under the extreme sea-states, which happens in the Mississippi River Delta and Yangtze river deltas [14,15].

Fewer datasets are based on long-term series monitoring around the world [16–18], and long-term measurement plans are extremely expensive and will probably not assist us in building artificial beaches or protecting sediment profiles from erosion. In this paper, we designed artificial beach profiles after studying the nearshore wave and current conditions, then used the open-source numerical model XBeach to analyze its morphological behavior during storms and normal wave actions. In this article, three key questions need to be answered: (1) how to design stable artificial sandy beaches in profiles and shorelines based on the local geophysical characteristics? (2) whether the beach can keep stable under wave action from storm events or normal sea-states? (3) How to choose protective measures to keep shoreline balance, in terms of engineered and biological methods ? This paper has been organized as follows. Section 2 provides brief descriptions of study sites. The numerical model and model setup are described in Section 3. Sections 4 and 5 demonstrate the project feasibility analysis, model result, and analysis. Discussion and conclusions are presented in Sections 6 and 7, respectively.

2. Study Site

The artificial beach has become one of the most popular attractions in the city of Haikou and has contributed profoundly to the city's tourism economy in recent years. The artificial beach is bounded by two newly built sand banks, which ensure the stability of water inside the bay. The sand banks are conducive to the maintenance of the artificial beach by shielding the offshore swells (Figure 1).

Haikou Bay is a semi-circular bay open to the north, from Baisha Cape in the east to Houhai in the west, across the sea from the Leizhou Peninsula in Guangdong Province, with a total coastline length of 20.5 km and water depth between 2 and 6 m. The artificial beach we built was approximately 916 m long (Figure 1a red line), based on the shallow water in front of the dam. The desilting and warping work on these sections was implemented in 2020 to clear and dredge the bed level to −2.8 m. The strip grooves on the backshore were approximately 100 m wide and 5~6 m deep.

There was a man-made island of 0.35 km^2 (Figure 1a), which was 1.5 km far away from that designed beach, and at the request of the central environmental protection and the Haikou government, the island was completely dismantled to −2.0 m.

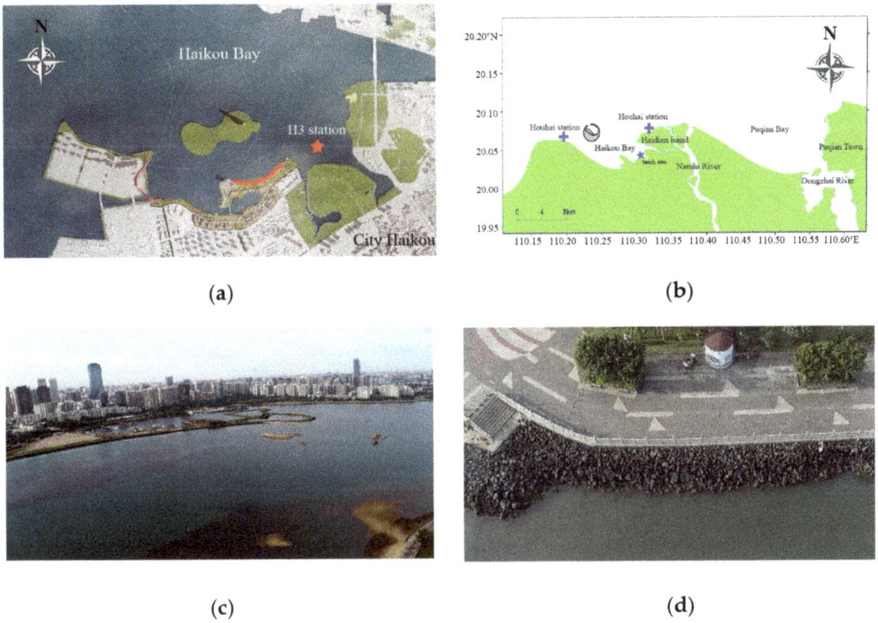

Figure 1. Haikou Bay sandy beach location. (**a**) Artificial beach location; (**b**) Wave buoy location; (**c**) Aerial of area before beach construction (I); (**d**) Aerial of area before beach construction (II).

Taking full account of the engineering planning, the depth and the nearshore hydrodynamic conditions, the artificial beach was designed with a shoreline length of 916 m. The width of the dry area (above MWL + 0.6 m) of approximately 30 m, the wet area (above ELWL + 0.6 m) of approximately 60 m, and protective stones were set the foot of the beach embankment was to reduce the loss of sand. The land boundary designed elevation was 2.20 m, and the dry beach outer boundary line was designed to have an elevation of 1.2 m. The artificial beach bottom layer within the existing breakwater was designed to fill the slag layer with the laying of a geotechnical anti-filter cloth layer. A throw pad layer of coarse sand, and a surface layer to fill 1 m thick using high-quality sand, with D50 = 0.2~0.6 mm. The total area of the sandy beach was expected to be 27,588 m^2. (Figure 2)

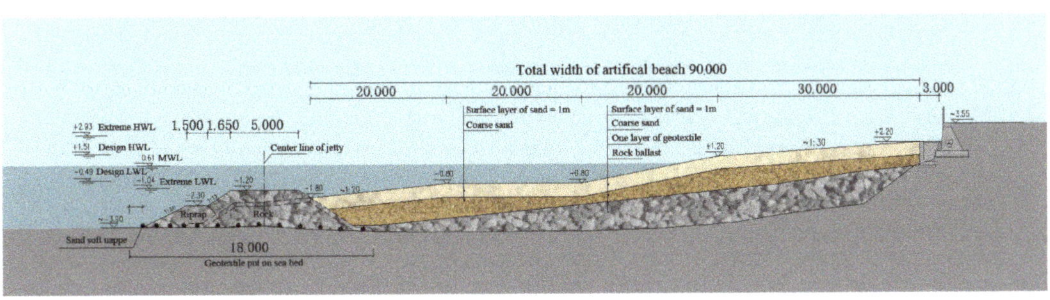

Figure 2. Rendering picture of designed sandy beach profile.

The high (HWL), mean (MWL), and low (LWL) water levels were 2.93 m, 0.61 m, and −0.49 m, respectively, based on the datum level in Haikou. The HWL and the LWL correspond to the mean high water and low water spring tides, respectively, after the analysis of the P-III type curve, and the results of the designed tide level are shown in

Figure 3. The wave conditions include both sea wind and swell waves, predominantly from the north (N-dir), NE (54%), and NNE (43%) directions. Most of the largest waves come from the north with heights exceeding 3.0 m, and with period with 6.0 s out in the bay. High energy (storm) wave conditions are generated between September and October by tropical cyclones, while waves are relatively small from October to June. The maximum wave heights induced by tropical cyclones are frequently less than 1 m in Haikou Bay.

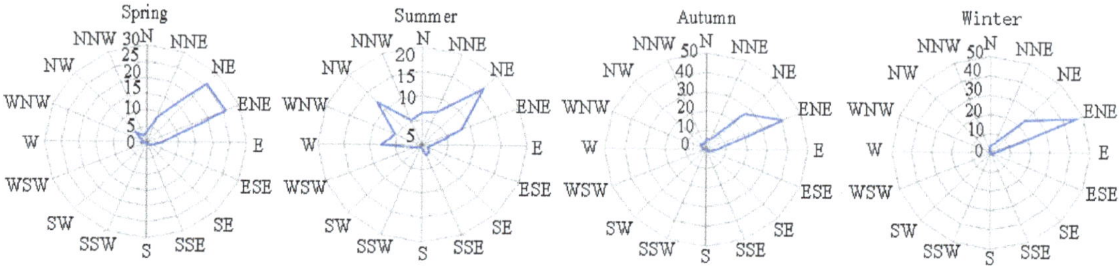

Figure 3. Wave rose chart in HOUHAI station.

3. Methods

3.1. Model Setup

XBeach is an open-source numerical model that was originally developed to simulate hydrodynamic and morphodynamic processes that impact sandy coasts with a domain size of kilometers and on the time scale of storms. Since then, the model has been applied to other types of coasts and purposes [19–22]. Using the surfbeat version of the model, the time-dependent, short wave action balance equation solves for the wave group envelope and is coupled with the non-linear shallow water equations to resolve mean currents and infragravity waves. Sediment transport is modeled using a depth-averaged advection-diffusion equation [23], and morphology change is calculated based on gradients in sediment transport at each time step. Dune erosion in Xbeach occurs directly from these transport gradients, as well as from avalanching, which is induced when a critical angle of repose is exceeded. Model formulations are described in detail in Roelvink [24,25] and are not repeated here. Xbeach has been extensively validated for dune erosion processes in numerous coastal settings [19–22].

The convective–diffusive equation to simulate sediment transport is as follows:

$$\frac{\partial hC}{\partial t} + \frac{\partial hC_u^E}{\partial x} + \frac{\partial hC_v^E}{\partial y} + \frac{\partial}{\partial x}\left[D_h h \frac{\partial C}{\partial x}\right] + \frac{\partial}{\partial y}\left[D_h h \frac{\partial C}{\partial y}\right] = \frac{hC_{eq} - hC}{T_s} \quad (1)$$

where C is the suspended sediment concentration with non-dimensional, h is bed level (m), t is time (s), u^E is Euler residual current (m/s), which is combined with wind-driven current, tidal current, infragravity waves (long period waves), offshore currents caused by nearshore breaking in the swash zone, and bottom reflux (time average velocity) (m/s). u_a is non-linear time average velocity caused by short period waves (m/s), u_a, and u_{rms} (practical water movements caused by wave) and represent the flow caused by short period waves. θ_m is mean wave direction, D_h is the sediment diffusion coefficient, C_{eq} is equilibrium concentration related to Euler residual currents and short period flows, and when the suspended sediment concentration is over this upper limit, sediment is deposited. T_s is time with dependence on the settling velocity of silt particles and the bed level.

Based on the cross-shore designed profiles and shoreline, we carried out two-dimensional simulations along the total beach. The domain of the model with two coupling grids, the big computational domain extended from coastline to 2.0 km offshore, as shown in Figure 4a,b. With a grid size of 15 m × 15 m, smaller one is 5 m. The depth data in the grids were obtained by interpolation using the 5 m × 5 m resolution bathymetry data measured on December 2020 in Figure 4c.

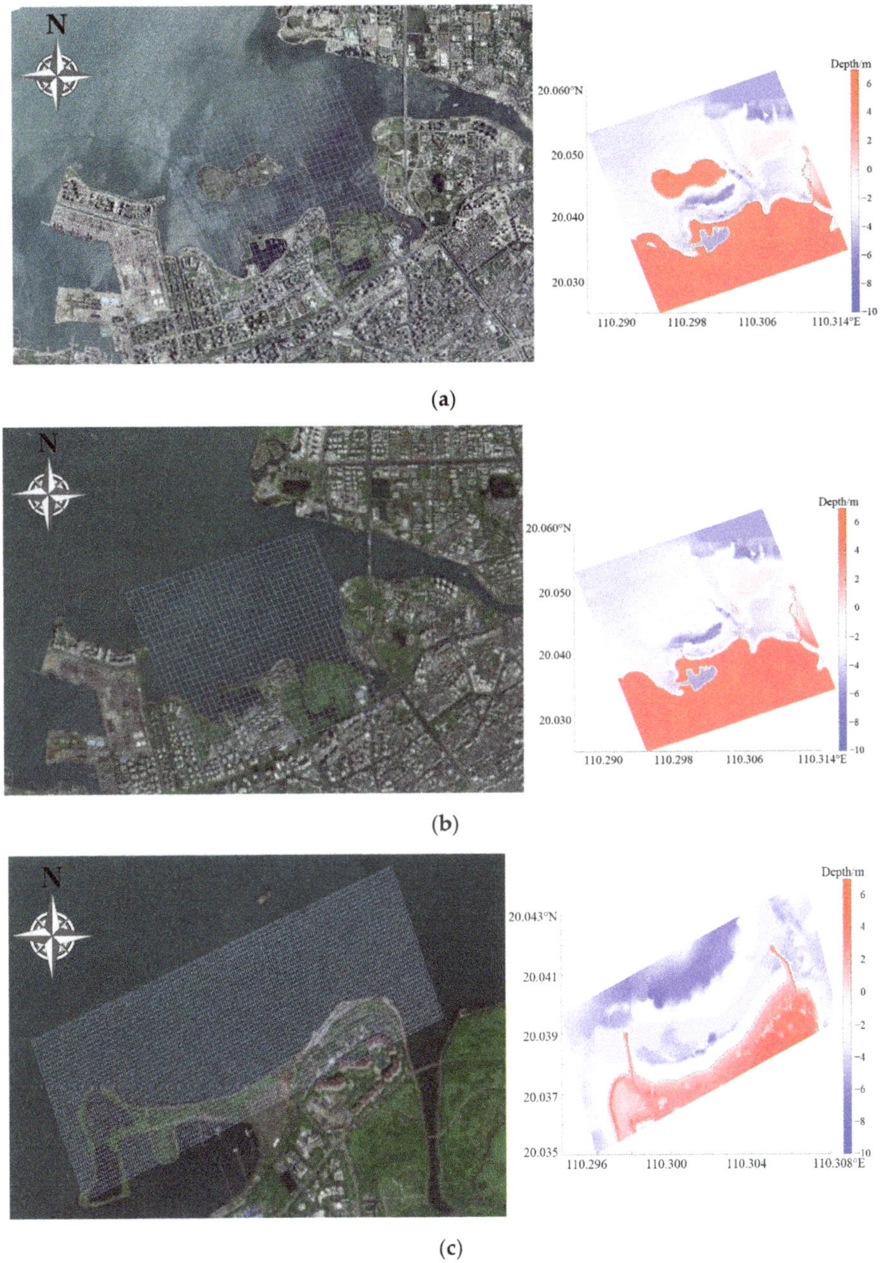

Figure 4. Model grid and depth in construction area. (**a**) model area with island; (**b**) Big model area without island; (**c**) Small model area.

The following simulation was based on the Surfbeat module in XBeach. The offshore boundary used the Neumann boundary condition and sediment transport was calculated with the Van Thiel-van Rijn equation as shown in Tables 1 and 2.

Table 1. Tidal characteristic value of Haikou (III) station.

Site	MHWL/m	MLWL/m	HWL/m	MinT/m	MeanT/m	MaxT/m	DHWL/m	DLWL/m
Xiu Ying station	1.17	−0.04	2.93	−0.86	1.21	3.79	1.51	−0.49

MHWL: mean high water level; **MLWL:** mean low water level; **HWL:** highest water level; **LWL:** lowest water level; **Min T:** minimum tidal range; **Max T:** maximum tidal range; **DHWL:** design high water level; **DLWL:** design low water level.

Table 2. Design Water level in Haikou (III) station.

Type	Mean Value	$p = 1\%$	$p = 2\%$	$p = 3.3\%$	$p = 5\%$	$p = 10\%$	$p = 20\%$
Annual maximum high tide level	2.13	3.08	2.93	2.81	2.72	2.55	2.38
Annual minimum low tide level	−0.84	−1.07	−1.04	−1.01	−0.99	−0.94	−0.90

The offshore forced conditions were provided by wave buoy data and several reports, which used the coupled wave, circulation, and sediment transport model: Delft3d [22], to simulate wave–current interaction in the Haikou Bay during the storms Haiou (T-HO), Weimaxun (T-W), and Haiyan (T-HY). The model results were modified with data measured at several measurement stations. In our Xbeach model, we used the hydrodynamic data extracted from their model results at the offshore boundary location (contains wave height Hs, wave period Tp, and wave direction Dir).

To illustrate the time period of storm and normal waves contributing different kinds of beach erosion, we superimposed modeled erosion rates for each of the three profiles we chose in the east, central, and west-most sections. The erosion rates were calculated by integrating the eroded volume per unit width over each hour. Table 3 summarizes the model parameters used in this study.

Table 3. Main parameter setting.

Parameter	Description	Value	Reference Value
CFL	Maximum Courant–Friedrichs–Lewy number	0.7	0.1~0.9
morfac	Morphological acceleration factor	5	0~1000
bedfriccoef	Bed friction coefficient/$s/m^{1/3}$	0.02	3.5×10^{-2}~0.9
wetslp	Critical avalanching slope under water	0.3	0.1~1
dryslp	Critical avalanching slope above water	1.00	0.1~2
D50	D50 grain diameter first class of sediment	0.4	-
por	Porosity	0.4	0.3~0.5
reposeangle	Angle of internal friction/°	30	0~45

3.2. Wave Scenarios

Multiple tests on storm and normal events were studied on designed beaches, with three typical storm (typhoon) events (No. 201415 T-HO; No. 201409 T-W; No. 201330 T-HY),which brought Haikou near-sea higher water levels and stronger waves causing damage and significant financial loss. The three storms had a duration of 39 h on average (defined as time when nearshore wind velocity > 3 m/s). The peak spectral wave period of the storms ranged from 1 to 1.5 s, and the direction of the waves varied throughout the storm as it passed northwest, ranging from 315 to 340 TN. The astronomical tidal range at the time of the storm was 2.80 m (mean spring tidal range in Haikou is 0.8 m).

From nearshore wave buoy data (B station and H station, Figure 1c) shows the waves during normal sea state are mostly driven by winds. Nearshore waves in the Haikou Bay area always contributed to N direction (N-dir) waves. Wind seas from NE and NNE directions, accounting for 54% and 43% in the H and B stations, respectively. During normal waves, almost all year round, waves are small and with periods between 3.0 s and 6.0 s. The largest waves come from N, with wave height over 3.0 m and wave period of 6.0 s at B station and wave height over 2.0 m with a period of 6.1 s at the H station. It can be seen from the statistical data that the average monthly wave height in the project area is 0.2~0.7 m, which is below the designed high water level of the 50-year design period. The cumulative frequency at the revetment is one percent of the characteristic wave height H1%= 1.4 m, and Tp = 6.0 s/3.0 s. Wave data of stations B and H were used to describe wave conditions for the study domain. Waves were set with Hs = 1.4 m, and Tp = 3.0 s and 6.0 s respectively for normal sea states. Wave directions were selected as NW and N (Table 4). In addition, tidal forcing were considered simultaneously with wind forcing in the model.

Table 4. Model test in storms and normal events.

Storm Number	Name	Starting Time (y/m/d)	Ending Time (y/m/d)	Fastest Wind Velocity (m/s)	Lowest Central Pressure (hPa)	Landing Location
201415	T-HO	2014.09.11	2014.09.18	40	960	WenChang
201409	T-W	2014.07.11	2014.07.21	60	910	WenChang
201330	T-HY	2013.11.03	2013.11.12	42	955	Vietnam
Model test Number	**Hs (m)**	**Tp(s)**	**Model test Number**	**Hs (m)**	**Tp (s)**	**Dir (°)**
Nom-1	1.4	6.0	Nom-2	1.4	3.0	NW
Nom-3	1.4	6.0	Nom-4	1.4	3.0	N

4. Feasibility Analysis of Engineering Construction

Sampling data collected along the beach from the Xiu-Ying Habour to the north part of HaiDian island shows that the D50 is 0.01~0.67 mm. According to the site survey in Haikou Bay, the bedload near the project area is quite silty with the percentage of clay between 10% and 20%. The spatial distribution is discontinuous, and the sand content is approximately 0.01 kg/m^3. From the perspective of sediment distribution in the artificial beach area, this is mainly sandy silt with D50 < 0.2 mm. It could be observed that the west of the beach was mostly occupied by sandy silt. Due to the mud-cleaning project taken in Haikou Bay in 2020, the original mucky layer has been removed and sea-bed has been deeply dredged, which increase the nearshore wave energy and making the bed less prone to accretion. With the improved hydrodynamic environment and the gradual stabilization of the substrate, size of bedload sediment is likely to increase.

Due to the presence of silty clay nearshore, the movement of fine-grained sludge after the construction of the project was predicted and verified. The model used the H3 site (Figure 1a) with the measured sand content data (110°18′33.63″ E; 20°02′34.37″ N) for validation, which shows that the simulation results are compared well with measurements, and it can be seen from the simulation results (Figure 5c) that the silt movement trend in the area has not been significantly enhanced after the demolition of the island, and thus the beach surface will not become muddy.

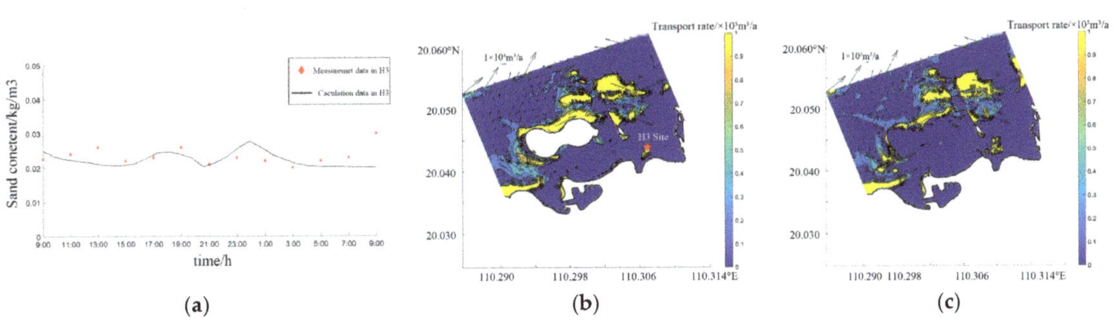

Figure 5. Sediment transport model validation and simulation. (**a**) Model validation with island. (**b**) Suspended sediment simulation with island. (**c**) Suspended sediment simulation without island.

5. Results

5.1. Profiles' Widths and Sediment Volume Change

The small area model utilizes the short-wave climb mode and can well simulate sediment movement above the MSL. Compared with Tp = 6.0 s and Tp = 3.0 s in normal wave actions (Figure 6(a1–a6)), we can see longer period waves cause greater beach erosion than shorter ones, and moving the sediment in larger scale with deeper erosion spots. With N and NW wave directions, the up limit of erosion spot caused by wave runup can reach 1.0 m above MWL. During N-dir waves, the erosion decreased from east to west due to the large shadow area of the west check dam and the beach shows alongshore variation. However, with NW-dir waves, the two sides of the check dams provide limited protection of beach volume, and the berm width displayed erosion in longshore. The nearshore volume (up volume) is nearly equal to backshore volume (down volume) in central while up volume is larger than down volume in west and opposite in east, which indicates that the sediment transport direction in the central and west parts of the beach was from east to west.

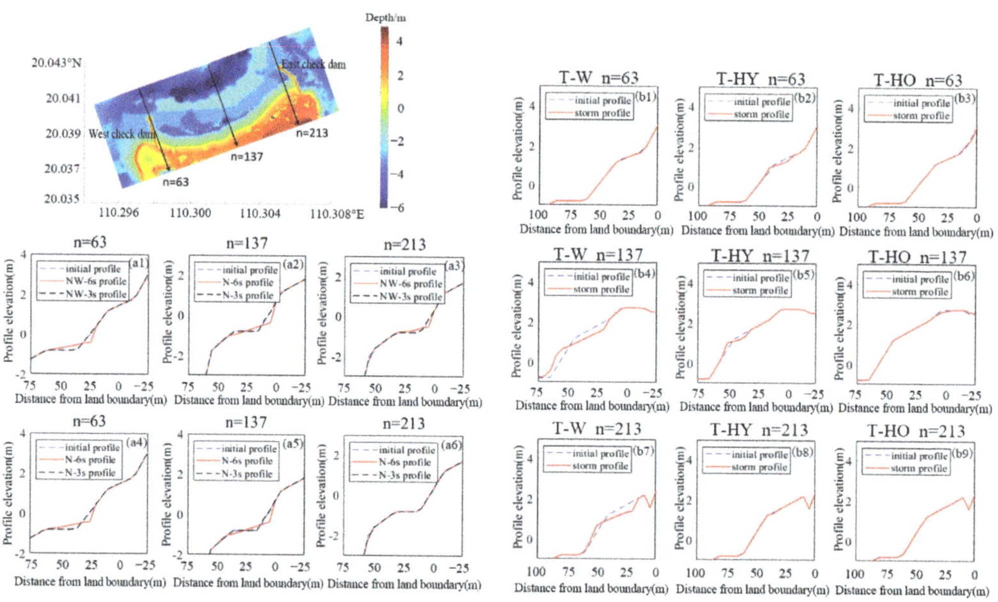

Figure 6. Comparison of profiles before and after storm event (**a1–a6**); before and after normal wave actions (**b1–b9**).

The evolution of three representative profiles (east, central and west of beach) from storm waves are shown in Figure 6(b1–b9). The width of beach is eroded and surface sediment move offshore to form sandbar under water. Wind velocity and storm duration time are main factors to induce profile erosion (Table 4). Stronger wind velocity and longer lasting time in T-W caused larger area of beach erosion than that during T-HO and T-HY events. Beach surface tends to be smooth after wave actions. T-W has caused more stronger erosion in central and west part of the beach than T-HO and T-HY, which swash zone is over 2.0 m above MWL, make more backshore erosion than T-HY and T-HO.The strongest profile volume change spot is located almost 700 m from east check dam, which illustrates great volume change between nearshore and backshore (elevation between −1.2 m and 2.0 m). Strong offshore and alongshore sediment transport in west part of the beach (Figure 7). Storm waves demonstrate no greater volume eroded than normal waves because higher height wave can not keep energy without breaking, while lower energy wave with long period can transport to nearshore easily and beach will under continuous erosion.

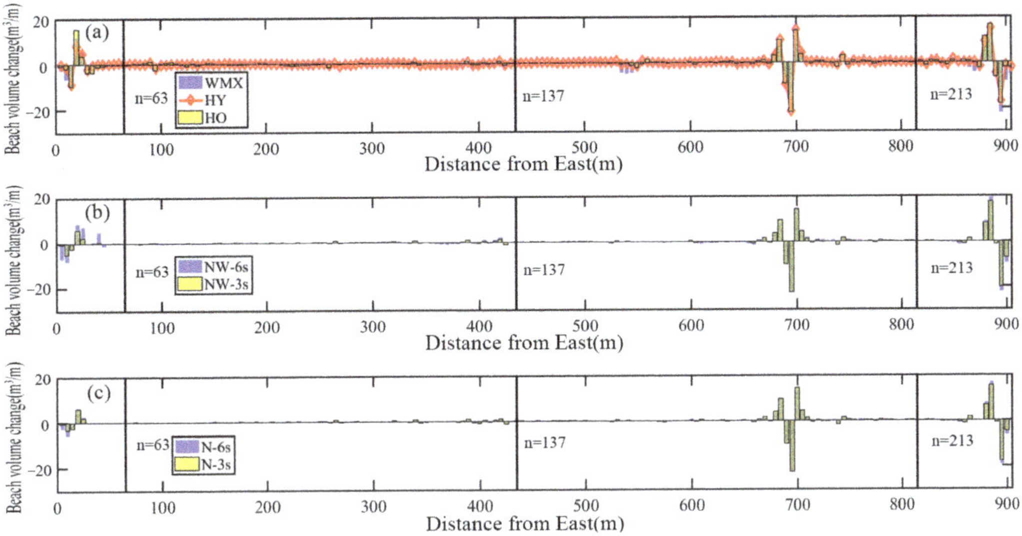

Figure 7. Beach volume change alongshore after storm and normal wave tests. (**a**). Beach volume change alongshore after storm wave events T-W, T-HY and T-HO. (**b**). Beach volume change alongshore after normal wave events Nom-1 and Nom-2. (**c**). Beach volume change alongshore after normal wave events Nom-3 and Nom-4.

During storms, the erosion of beach profiles is different from that of normal wave actions. Storm waves cause higher wave run-up and take away a large amount of sand in a few days, while recovery takes several months of normal wave actions. The width of the berm becomes narrower and the berm crest becomes lower during storms. The beach surface becomes smoother and sediment transport offshore from the berm, resulting in a reduction in beach width followed by sediment accretion below the LWL (middle profile). The east and west parts of the beach were found to be well protected on both sides by the check-dams.

5.2. Sediment Transport Alongshore and Offshore

Storm waves induced greater suspend sediment movement in beach berm between the MWL and the land boundary with concrete wall (0.61–2.2 m). Offshore is the main direction while alongshore transport is secondary. The T-W storm induced greater offshore sediment transport more than that during T-HY and T-HO, accounted for more than 5 m^3/d in the central part of the beach storm. This is because wave propagates normal to the shoreline, the two-side check dams thus functions in beach protection.

Sediment transport in the nearshore area during normal wave events is much more different from storm waves, and it can be seen that offshore sandbar reduces the wave energy and contributes more sediment transport. From the simulations, we observed that due to the landform of the inner-bay in Haikou Bay, most high-energy waves break far offshore because of the sandbar and shallow water, but lower wave heights with long periods do not break, and reach the nearshore area, which have strong effect on suspend sediment transport. Thus, the Haikou Bay artificial beach should be well protected throughout year rather than just for storm wave events (Figure 8).

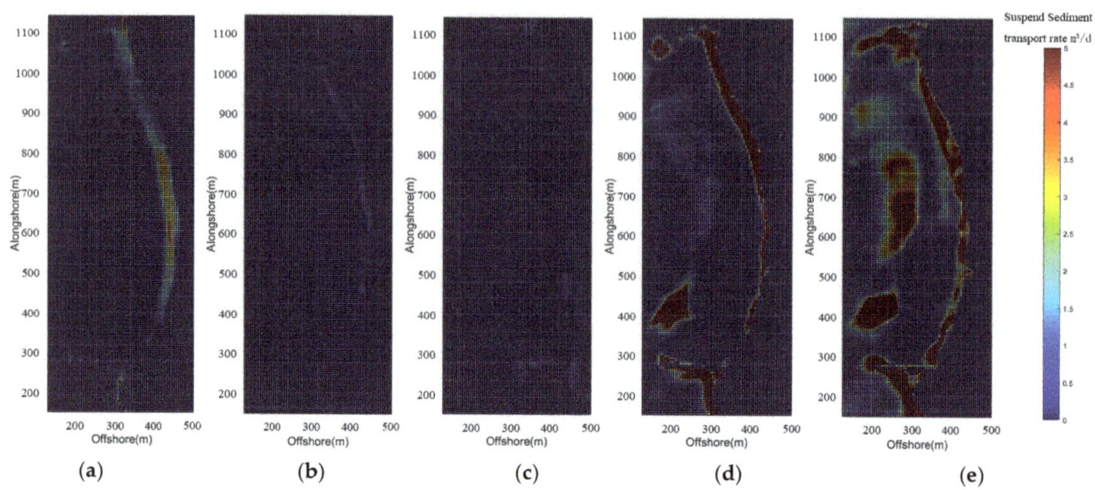

Figure 8. Suspend sediment transport due to wave actions in each model tests. (**a**) after T-W; (**b**) after T-HY; (**c**) after T-HO; (**d**) after N-6s normal waves; (**e**) after N-3s normal waves.

5.3. Shoreline Prediction

Study of beach shoreline variation during normal wave events not only provides more understanding of the wave-sediment-landform systems, but also the dynamics of sandy beaches. We used the empirical shoreline analysis tool MEPbay [26,27] to predict shoreline shape from long term wave actions. The tool presented in this paper only deals with the design shoreline and check dams. It was applicable to use wave angle and control line in two points and major physical parameters to get result of steady shoreline shapes. We are able to visually evaluate the stability of the beach by comparing the proximity of the existing shoreline with that predicted in static equilibrium.

Capes of the check dams and the central part of the beach was connected as a control line, then used NW and N as wave angle. This may be taken as the wave crest line, and is perpendicular to the incoming waves at the updrift diffraction point of the bay beach. Finally, we sketch the shoreline plane in static equilibrium. The east part of the beach was predicted to retreat due to the higher energy wave and less shadow zone in NW waves; while the west part of the beach was predicted in static equilibrium. In conclusion, the west part of the beach is predicted to become stable during normal waves, while the east part will become eroded, but the whole beach remains in dynamic-balance (Figure 9).

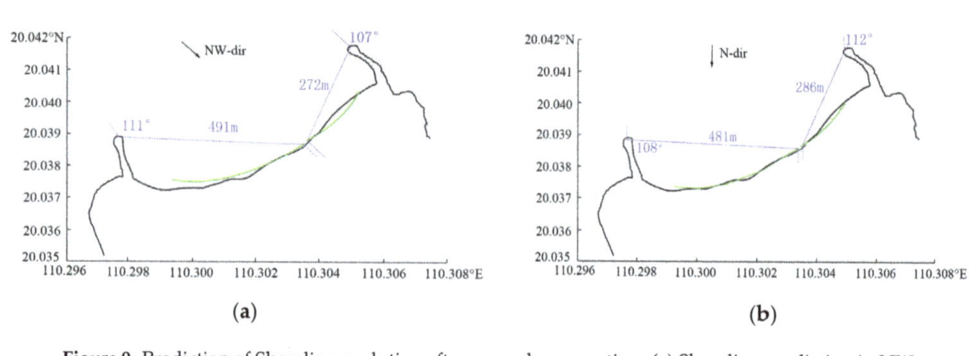

Figure 9. Prediction of Shoreline evolution after normal wave action. (**a**) Shoreline prediction in NW waves. (**b**) Shoreline prediction in N waves.

6. Discussion

6.1. Engineered Projects ("Grey Method")

Man-made constructions can increase/decrease wave energy, which induces beach erosion/deposition dramatically. Many unsuccessful engineering projects, such as the nearshore harbor construction, induced accretion of mud of the nearby beach with mud, which also shows us that changing dynamic conditions without prior assessment is dangerous and unbalances the ecosystem. It is necessary to keep the sediment without erosion and maintain the width of beach with using check dams and submerged breakwater. This constructions what we named "grey method" can make the wave breaking out of nearshore area and keep the sediment flux inside the beach area. But what we should also consider is lower wave energy do not mean better beach nourishment. Suspend sediment flux is inversely proportional to water depth, which means lower wave height will lead more suspend sediment moving to backshore and accretion on beach surface, thus the beach surface will become muddy.

6.2. Biological Methods ("Green Method")

Coastal resilience is a comprehensive indicator for coastal systems assessment. Sandy beaches are important areas for the turtles to lay their eggs, for birds migration and habitat, and for their predation. Coastal vegetation shows vertical richness from grass to shrub to trees, which provides a transition zone and has important environmental values. We emphasize coastal resilience not only enhance restoration after storm waves (i.e., the sand engine in Netherlands which was restored by natural dynamic conditions). Planting trees and grass can compensate for the loss of ecological niches and decrease abilities of sand movement which we called "soft" or "green" engineering, and we can see only minor erosion by storm waves due to the area of green plants (Figure 10) compared to concrete wall damaged without "greenery" (Figure 11). With these methods, we can build stronger and healthier coastal zone and achieve the goals of the "ocean decade plan".

(a) (b)

Figure 10. Beach berm with trees before (**a**) and after storm (**b**) in 2020 in Haikou Bay shows minor damage due to "green method" by storm waves.

(a) (b)

Figure 11. Beach berm with concert wall before (**a**) and after storm (**b**) in 2020 in Haikou Bay shows minor damage due to "grey method" by storm waves.

6.3. Offshore Infrastructure Induced Wave-Flow Field Change

From the "Results" section, we can see that normal wave action can induce more total beach erosion than storm waves. We tested normal wave events (Table 5) to illustrate how offshore infrastructure (the artificial island) caused wave refraction and flow field, although the offshore island was demolished in 2021 and the bedlevel was reduced to −2.0 m depth.

Table 5. Normal wave tests.

Model Test Number	Topography	Hs (m)	Tp (s)	Model Test Number	Hs (m)	Tp (s)	Dir (°)	Explanation
1	With island	1.4	6.0	4	1.4	3.0	NW	wave-tide coupling model
2	With island	1.4	6.0	5	1.4	3.0	N	
3	With island	1.4	6.0	6	1.4	3.0	NE	
7	Without island	1.4	6.0	10	1.4	3.0	NW	
8	Without island	1.4	6.0	11	1.4	3.0	N	
9	Without island	1.4	6.0	12	1.4	3.0	NE	

Note: **With island** means current topography (Figure 4a); **Without island** means island demolished, check dams and beach all completed (Figure 4b).

Due to the large area of shallow water, offshore waves will be dramatically reduced and well protected from the shadow zone behind the island (with island test) (Figure 12a–f). In wave current coupling model, the nearshore wave height becomes to 0.2~0.4 m. The wave from NE-dir has a closed angle with the beach shoreline, which contribute to wave height below 0.2 m nearshore. Without the island (Figure 12g–l), the artificial beach will face the open sea and wave-flow filed is improved (wave height and velocity will be greater). The predict wave height is 1.5 times higher than before and up to 0.4~0.6 m. The wave from NE-dir has a closed angle with the beach shoreline, which contribute to wave height below 0.2 m nearshore. Without the island (Figure 12g–l), the artificial beach will face the open sea and wave-flow filed is improved (wave height and velocity will be greater). The predict wave height is 1.5 times higher than before and up to 0.4~0.6 m. Wave height distribution is gradually reduced from east to west and the shadow zone remain on the sides of the two check dams. The N-dir wave is predict to shadowed in the central and western part of the beach, while NW-dir wave cannot be well defended because only a small shadow zone will provided by the check dams.

In the nearshore area, wave breaks and induces current velocity greater than 0.5 m/s. Under the conditions of NW-dir, N-dir and NE-dir waves, wave-induced currents reduce gradually from west to east. In the shadowed zone behind the island, the inshore velocity is below 0.1 m/s in all directions (Figure 13a–f). Nearshore current velocity increases after the island demolished but remains lower than 0.1 m/s, while the current at the check dams behind island area is predicted to become stronger. Without island (Figure 13g–l) velocity is predicted to be greater near the western check dam than the east, and thus contributing to significant erosion around the check dams, additional protection measurements should be considered around the western check dam.

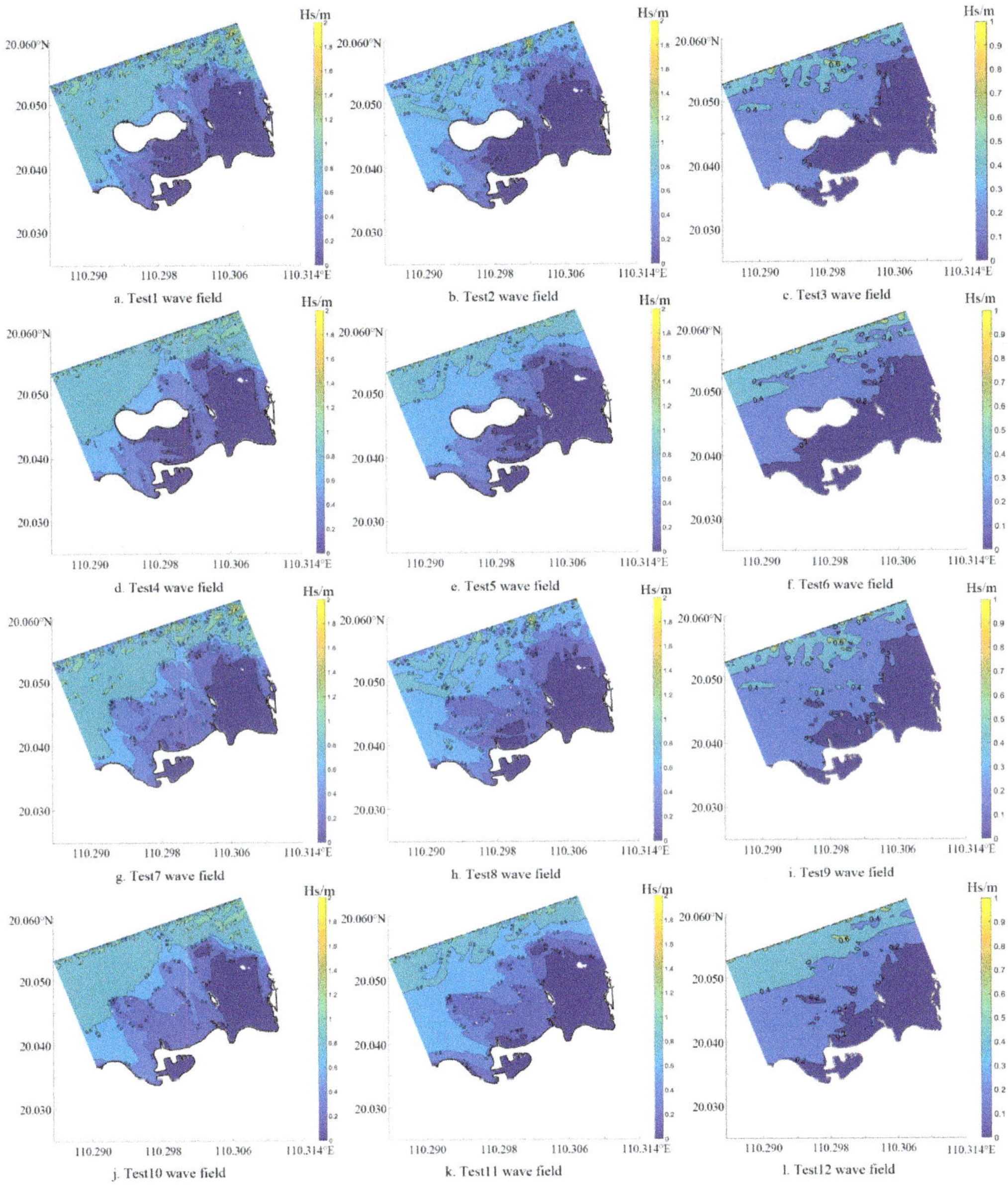

Figure 12. Wave filed in normal wave tests.

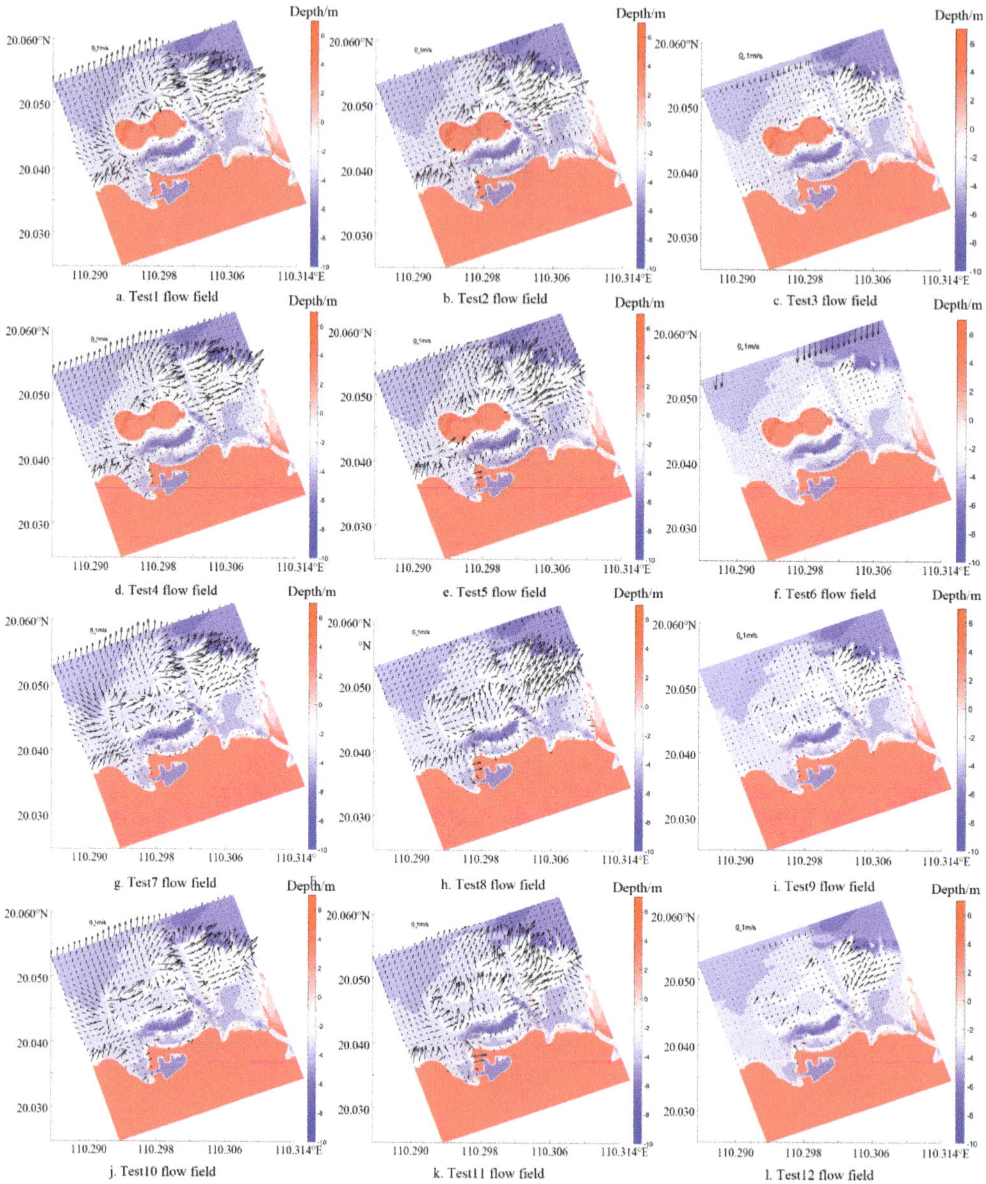

Figure 13. Flow filed in normal wave tests.

7. Conclusions

This study focuses on the beach profile evolution of an artificial sandy beach under both typical storm events and normal wave conditions, Main factors and hydrodynamics under varied sea-states associated with beach evolution were analyzed by using the Xbeach model. The main conclusions are as following:

(1) Normal waves induced greater erosion on the artificial beach than storm wave events.
(2) Waves with long wave period cause more erosion and accretion because they maintain long distance sediment transport without breaking.

(3) Sediment transport at the study site follows two main routes: offshore, and westward. It is argued that beach profiles will be eroded more in eastern portion of the beach than the western and central portion of the beach. The designed beach will maintain shoreline balance and remain in dynamic equilibrium during normal wave events.
(4) Offshore sandbars and ridges can protect the beach since wave energy can be largely reduced however they can enhance risks beach mudding and blackening in Haikou Bay.

Wave action is the main action to influence beach variation. It should be noticed that the resolved current field is vertically averaged by using this model. The physical processes are now resolved by semi-empirical functions in the XBeach model. In order to resolve more detailed physical processes in the surf zone where sediment entrainment and two phases flow could happen, more sophisticated 3D models are required.

Author Contributions: Conceptualization, Y.Z. and X.F.; methodology, Y.Z. and W.W.; software, Y.Z.; validation, Y.Z. and M.L.; writing—original draft preparation, Y.Z.; writing—review and editing, Y.Z. and M.L.; figure, M.L.; supervision, X.F. All authors have read and agreed to the published version of the manuscript.

Funding: This work was financially supported by the Fund of Hainan Key Laboratory of Marine Geological Resources and Environment (22-HNHYDZZYHJKF028) and The project was supported by the Fund of Key Laboratory of Marine Ecological Conservation and Restoration, Ministry of Natural Resources/Fujian Provincial Key Laboratory of Marine Ecological Conservation and Restoration, (EPR2023009).

Institutional Review Board Statement: Not applicable.

Informed Consent Statement: Not applicable.

Data Availability Statement: Data will be made available on request.

Acknowledgments: The authors are very much grateful to the four anonymous reviewers for their constructive comments that significantly improved the quality of this paper.

Conflicts of Interest: The authors declare no conflict of interest. The funders had no role in the design of the study; in the collection, analyses, or interpretation of data; in the writing of the manuscript, or in the decision to publish the results.

References

1. Feng, X.; Feng, H.; Li, H.; Zhang, F.; Feng, W.; Zhang, W.; Yuan, J. Tidal responses to future sea level trends on the Yellow Sea shelf. *J. Geophys. Res. Ocean.* **2019**, *124*, 7285–7306. [CrossRef]
2. Feng, H.; Feng, X.; Feng, W.; Zhang, W. Sensitivity of tides and tidal components to sea-level-rise in the Radial Sand Ridges. *Reg. Stud. Mar. Sci.* **2021**, *47*, 101918. [CrossRef]
3. Zhou, Y.; Feng, X.; Guan, W.; Feng, W. Characteristics of beach erosion in headland bays due to wave actiont: Taking the Narrabeen beach in Australia as an example. *Chin. Sci. Bull.* **2019**, *64*, 223–233. (In Chinese) [CrossRef]
4. Jiang, C.; Cao, H.; Feng, W.; Feng, X. Quasi-static balance profile Test of rigid vegetation coast under regular wave action. *Port Waterw. Eng.* **2019**, *7 11*, 30.
5. Zheng, J.; Zhang, C.; Demirbilek, Z.; Lin, L. Numerical study of sandbar migration under wave-undertow interaction. *J. Waterw. Port Coast. Ocean Eng.* **2013**, *140*, 146–159. [CrossRef]
6. Zhang, C.; Zhang, Q.; Zheng, J.; Demirbilek, Z. Parameterization of nearshore wave front slope. *Coast. Eng.* **2017**, *127*, 80–87. [CrossRef]
7. Feng, X.; Zhou, Y.; Lu, Y.; Feng, W. Characteristics of Beach Erosion in Headland Bays due to Storm-Waves. In Proceedings of the 29th International Ocean and Polar Engineering Conference, Honolulu, HI, USA, 16–21 June 2019; pp. 3821–3829.
8. Splinter, K.D.; Kearney, E.T.; Turner, I.L. Drivers of alongshore variable dune erosion during a storm event: Observations and modelling. *Coast. Eng.* **2018**, *131*, 31–41. [CrossRef]
9. Zollini, S.; Dominici, D.; Alicandro, M.; Cuevas-González, M.; Angelats, E.; Ribas, F.; Simarro, G. New Methodology for Shoreline Extraction Using Optical and Radar (SAR) Satellite Imagery. *J. Mar. Sci. Eng.* **2023**, *11*, 627. [CrossRef]
10. Vallarino Castillo, R.; Negro Valdecantos, V.; Moreno Blasco, L. Shoreline Change Analysis Using Historical Multispectral Landsat Images of the Pacific Coast of Panama. *J. Mar. Sci. Eng.* **2022**, *10*, 1801. [CrossRef]
11. O'Grady, J.G.; Hemer, M.A.; McInnes, K.L.; Trenham, C.E.; Stephenson, A.G. Projected incremental changes to extreme wind-driven wave heights for the twenty-first century. *Sci. Rep.* **2021**, *11*, 8826. [CrossRef]
12. Church, J.; Wilson, S.; Woodworth, P.; Aarup, T. Understanding sea level rise and variability. *Eos* **2007**, *88*, 43. [CrossRef]

13. Li, Y.; Zhang, C.; Cai, Y.; Xie, M.; Qi, H.; Wang, Y. Wave Dissipation and Sediment Transport Patterns during Shoreface Nourishment towards Equilibrium. *J. Mar. Sci. Eng.* **2021**, *9*, 535. [CrossRef]
14. Meade, R.H.; Moody, J.A. Causes for the decline of suspended-sediment discharge in the Mississippi River system, 1940–2007. *Hydrol. Process. Int. J.* **2010**, *24*, 35–49. [CrossRef]
15. Zhang, D.; Xie, W.; Shen, J.; Guo, L.; Chen, Y.; He, Q. Sediment dynamics in the mudbank of the Yangtze Estuary under regime shift of source and sink. *Int. J. Sediment Res.* **2022**, *37*, 97–109. [CrossRef]
16. Cristaudo, D.; Gross, B.M.; Puleo, J.A. Momentum Balance Analysis of Spherical Objects and Long-Term Field Observations of Unexploded Ordnance (UXO) in the Swash Zone. *J. Mar. Sci. Eng.* **2023**, *11*, 79. [CrossRef]
17. Kuang, C.; Ma, Y.; Han, X.; Pan, S.; Zhu, L. Experimental Observation on Beach Evolution Process with Presence of Artificial Submerged Sand Bar and Reef. *J. Mar. Sci. Eng.* **2020**, *8*, 1019. [CrossRef]
18. Yang, Z.; Yang, Z.; Deng, Z.; Chen, Y.; Yang, B.; Hou, Y.; Deng, Z.; Tong, M. Multi-Timescale Analysis of the Evolution of Sandy Coastline: A Case Study in South China. *J. Mar. Sci. Eng.* **2022**, *10*, 1609. [CrossRef]
19. Duo, E.; Sanuy, M.; Jiménez, J.A.; Ciavola, P. How good are symmetric triangular synthetic storms to represent real events for coastal hazard modelling. *Coast. Eng.* **2020**, *159*, 103728. [CrossRef]
20. van Ormondt, M.; Nelson, T.R.; Hapke, C.J.; Roelvink, D. Morphodynamic modelling of the wilderness breach, Fire Island, New York. Part I: Model set-up and validation. *Coast. Eng.* **2020**, *157*, 103621. [CrossRef]
21. Bennett, W.G.; Karunarathna, H.; Reeve, D.E.; Mori, N. Computational modelling of morphodynamic response of a macro-tidal beach to future climate variabilities. *Mar. Geol.* **2019**, *415*, 105960. [CrossRef]
22. Didier, D.; Baudry, J.; Bernatchez, P.; Dumont, D.; Sadegh, M.; Bismuth, E.; Bandet, M.; Dugas, S.; Sévigny, C. Multihazard simulation for coastal flood mapping: Bathtub versus numerical modelling in an open estuary, Eastern Canada. *J. Flood Risk Manag.* **2019**, *12* (Suppl. S1), e12505. [CrossRef]
23. Galappatti, G.; Vreugdenhil, C.B. A depth-integrated model for suspended sediment transport. *J. Hydraul. Res.* **1985**, *23*, 359–377. [CrossRef]
24. Roelvink, D.; Reniers, A.; Van Dongeren, A.; van Thiel De Vries, J.; McCall, R.; Lescinski, J. Modelling storm impacts on beaches, dunes and barrier islands. *Coast. Eng.* **2009**, *56*, 1133–1152. [CrossRef]
25. Lu, Y.; Li, S.; Zuo, L.; Liu, H.; Roelvink, J. Advances in sediment transport under combined action of waves and currents. *Int. J. Sediment Res.* **2015**, *30*, 351–360. [CrossRef]
26. Raabe, A.L.; Klein, A.H.; González, M.; Medina, R. MEPBAY and SMC: Software tools to support different operational levels of headland-bay beach in coastal engineering projects. *Coast. Eng.* **2010**, *57*, 213–226. [CrossRef]
27. Zhang, R.; Chen, L.; Liu, S.; Zhang, H.; Gong, W.; Lin, G. Shoreline evolution in an embayed beach adjacent to tidal inlet: The impact of anthropogenic activities. *Geomorphology* **2019**, *346*, 106856. [CrossRef]

Journal of
Marine Science and Engineering

MDPI

Article

Numerical Investigations of Undrained Shear Strength of Sensitive Clay Using Miniature Vane Shear Tests

Jiayi Shen [1,2], Xinyi Wang [1], Qian Chen [1], Zhaoyi Ye [1], Qiaoling Gao [3] and Jiawang Chen [3,4,*]

1 Institute of Port, Coastal and Offshore Engineering, Zhejiang University, Hangzhou 310015, China; jiayi@zju.edu.cn (J.S.); 22134161@zju.edu.cn (X.W.); 22134166@zju.edu.cn (Q.C.); 22234145@zju.edu.cn (Z.Y.)
2 Key Laboratory of Offshore Geotechnics and Material of Zhejiang Province, Zhejiang University, Hangzhou 310058, China
3 Institute of Ocean Engineering and Technology, Zhejiang University, Hangzhou 310015, China; joling@zju.edu.cn
4 Hainan Institute, Zhejiang University, Sanya 572025, China
* Correspondence: arwang@zju.edu.cn

Abstract: The laboratory miniature vane shear test (MVST) has been widely used to measure the undrained shear strength of marine sediments in offshore engineering. However, the transfer of the soil sample in tube samplers from the seabed to the laboratory releases the in situ confining stress acting on the soil and will decrease the soil strength. In this research, in order to investigate the effects of confining stress on the undrained shear strength of marine sediments, the Coupled Eulerian-Lagrangian (CEL) approach in ABAQUS is used to model the three-dimensional standard and miniature vane shear tests to estimate the undrained shear strength of sensitive clay with different sensitivities under various stress conditions. Based on the numerical simulation results, a linear strength model that not only considers confining stress effects but also can eliminate the size effects caused by vane blades of MVST is proposed. The proposed model can be used to estimate the undrained shear strength of the sensitive clay under shallow seabed surfaces.

Keywords: miniature vane shear test; CEL; undrained shear strength; confining stress; size effect

1. Introduction

Estimating the geotechnical properties of marine sediments is crucial for marine resource exploration [1–4]. The sensitive clay is a type of marine sediment and is typically composed of very fine-grained particles, such as clay and silt. These properties lead to sensitive clay having unique characteristics, including high sensitivity, high compressibility, and low shear strength; therefore, the estimation of the mechanical properties of sensitive clay is a challenging task in ocean engineering [5,6].

The vane shear test (VST) is a common method for measuring the undrained shear strength of clay in geotechnical engineering applications, such as pile capacity and slope stability [7–11]. With the expansion of offshore oil exploration in the past few decades, the VST has been widely applied in offshore engineering to measure the strength of marine sediments [12–17]. However, due to the lateral instability of the drill pipe, the VST cannot accurately estimate the shear strength of the marine sediments on seabed surfaces that are often encountered at shallow penetrations [18]. Especially for sensitive clay, the destruction of the clay structure will directly lead to a large deviation in the measurement results.

To solve this problem, the laboratory miniature vane shear test (MVST) has been proposed and used to measure the strength of the sensitive clay obtained from the shallow seabed. The procedure of the MVST involves inserting a vane into the soil sample and then rotating it at a constant rate. The shear strength of the soil can then be calculated based on the measured torque and the dimensions of the vane [19]. Hernandez et al. [20] used a fully automatic laboratory miniature vane shear device to measure the undrained shear strength of clay in different states. Zumsteg et al. [21] used the MVST to measure the undrained shear strength of different mixtures of kaolinite conditioned by foam and polymers. Arulrajah et al. [22] performed a broad range of geotechnical laboratory tests including MVSTs to evaluate the mechanical properties of the wastewater biosolids. This existing research shows that the MVST is an ideal tool to investigate the undrained shear strength of various types of soils.

It should be noted that the transfer of the soil sample in tube samplers from the seabed to the laboratory releases the in situ confining stress acting on the soils and will increase the soil void ratio and decrease the soil strength. However, the effects of such confining stress on the undrained shear strength are not considered by the existing MVST studies.

The use of the Coupled Eulerian–Lagrangian (CEL) approach has proven to be a valuable tool in studying the MVST for the measurement of sensitive clay. This method has been widely employed by researchers to investigate the MVST and the properties of sensitive clay. Ansari et al. [23] used the CEL to simulate the complete process of the MVST. Park et al. [24] developed a miniature vane shear test model to analyze the shear strength of sensitive soil samples with different water contents. Dey et al. [25] used the CEL to explore the properties of sensitive clay in submarine layers and proposed the numerical model parameters for the sensitive clay. These studies collectively demonstrate the effectiveness of the CEL method in analyzing MVSTs and simulating the properties of sensitive clay.

In this research, a three-dimensional numerical model established by the CEL approach in ABAQUS is used to conduct numerical vane shear tests. Based on the numerical simulation results, we propose a prediction model that considers the confining stress effects and can be used to estimate the undrained shear strength of sensitive clay located beneath shallow seabed surfaces.

2. CEL Modeling in ABAQUS

Numerical simulations of this research were based on the CEL approach in ABAQUS. The CEL approach combines the advantages of both the Eulerian and Lagrangian methods to simulate large deformation problems with a high computational efficiency. The large deformation of soil during the vane shear test can cause the distortion of the mesh, which may affect the accuracy of simulation results. To overcome this challenge, Eulerian analysis is used to calculate the large deformation of the soil sample during the vane shear test, while the Lagrangian analysis is employed to simulate the vane shear device. This approach effectively avoids the mesh distortion and ensures the stability of the simulation calculation results. The coupled Eulerian–Lagrangian interface treatment has been demonstrated as well suited to solve geotechnical problems involving large deformations, such as the pile penetration process [26] and static cone penetration tests [27].

2.1. Mesh Algorithm

The Lagrangian analysis employs a discretized numerical solution approach, which entails linking the material properties within the Lagrangian components to the mesh of the numerical model. As the solution process progresses, the material flow causes the mesh to undergo deformation and movement. It is important to note that although the elements undergo deformation, the mass remains constant. The governing equation for Lagrangian analysis is shown as Equation (1) [28].

$$\left.\begin{array}{l}\frac{\partial\rho}{\partial t}=0\\ \frac{\partial(\rho v)}{\partial t}=\nabla\cdot\sigma+\rho b\end{array}\right\} \tag{1}$$

where ρ is the density, t is the time, v is the velocity, σ is the stress, and b is the body force.

In the Eulerian analysis, the mesh is fixed and the material flows between the elements. The volume of fluid approach is used to monitor interfaces among materials in the multi-material mesh. When materials flow into the mesh, the Eulerian Volume Fraction (EVF) of each material is calculated. The value of the EVF is 1 as the element is filled with materials, and 0 as no material exists. If the sum of all the material volume fractions in an element is less than 1, the rest of the element is automatically packed with the "void" material, which has neither strength nor mass.

In initial calculation, the Eulerian analysis uses the EVF to describe the initial state and position of the material. In the process of numerical simulation, there can be various substances in the Eulerian element, and the material mesh is transmitted to a fixed spatial mesh as a state variable of the Eulerian element. The governing equation of Eulerian analysis is given as Equation (2):

$$\left.\begin{array}{l}\frac{\partial \rho}{\partial t}+\nabla \cdot(\rho \boldsymbol{v})=0 \\ \frac{\partial(\rho \boldsymbol{v})}{\partial t}+\nabla \cdot(\rho \boldsymbol{v} \otimes \boldsymbol{v})=\nabla \cdot \boldsymbol{\sigma}+\rho b\end{array}\right\} \quad (2)$$

where ρ is the density, t is the time, $\boldsymbol{v}$ is the velocity, $\boldsymbol{\sigma}$ is the stress, and b is the body force.

The constitutive models with strain-softening generally suffer the pathological mesh dependency of the numerical results during the development of the strain localization. However, numerical simulations of this research were based on the CEL framework. In the CEL analysis, the soil material can flow through the fixed Eulerian meshes, which means even if the soil strain in the vane shear test is very large, there will be no mesh-distortion issues [29].

2.2. The Eulerian Volume Fraction Methods

The Eulerian Volume Fraction (EVF) method is an analysis method that involves performing a Boolean comparison operation between the Eulerian object and the Lagrangian reference object, which intersects with the Eulerian object. The result is a scalar dispersion field that corresponds to the proportion of materials in the Eulerian elements. The Boolean comparison operation identifies the overlapping region between two independent objects and determines the volume fraction of each element in the Eulerian objects based on its percentage in the corresponding reference object. This dispersion field labels the region occupied by the Eulerian material in the model.

There are two methods for obtaining the discrete fields in the CEL approach, calculating the volume fraction of the external and internal regions of the Lagrangian reference object. The purpose of calculating the volume fraction of the external region is to create a corresponding material distribution characteristic based on the Lagrangian reference object. While the other method is to create material distribution characteristics in the Eulerian region excluding the Lagrangian part.

2.3. Eulerian–Lagrangian Coupling Interface Treatment

In Lagrangian analysis, the physical quantities including the coordinates, velocity, force, and mass are defined at the nodes of the elements, while the stress, strain, and density are defined at the center of the elements. In Eulerian analysis, these variables are all located at the center of the elements. The Eulerian formulation allows for the transportation of free surfaces and material interfaces on the fixed mesh, but a numerical calculation is required to track the free surface and control numerical dissipation. The coupling algorithm does not require a common node or common surface for the calculation between the Lagrangian and Eulerian mesh. Instead, the coupling surface is used for the interaction between the Lagrangian analysis and the Eulerian analysis. The coupling surface of the Lagrangian element is fixed on the mesh and receives pressure loads from the Eulerian materials from the coupling surface. The coupling surface of the Eulerian element changes in the fixed Eulerian mesh, and the finite volume method is used at each time step to obtain the position of the coupling boundary [30]. The coupling boundary bears the geometric constraints imposed by the Lagrangian element on the coupling surface. The transfer of the motion and pressure information between the Lagrangian mesh and the Eulerian mesh on the coupling surface satisfies the coordination conditions of the interface, which improves the accuracy of the coupling calculation between the Eulerian and Lagrangian objects. The coupling effect is shown in Figure 1.

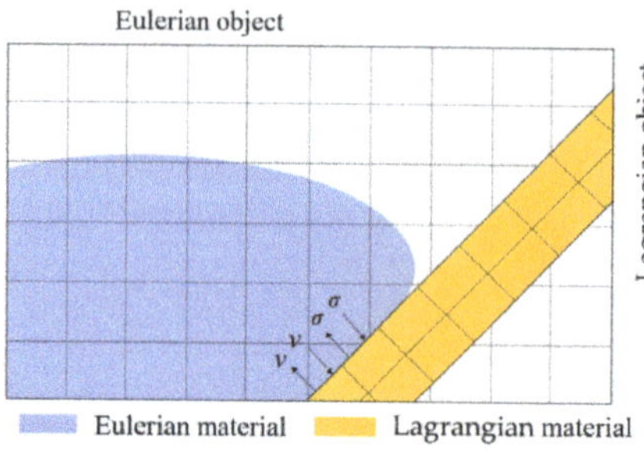

Figure 1. The Eulerian–Lagrangian coupling interface treatment.

3. CEL Modeling of Vane Shear Test

The numerical simulations of this research were based on the CEL approach in ABAQUS. The CEL approach combines the advantages of both the Eulerian and Lagrangian methods to simulate large deformation problems with a high computational efficiency.

3.1. The Mesh and Geometry of the Model

The numerical model comprises two parts, the soil and the vane shear device, as shown in Figure 2. The soil is represented as the Eulerian material with eight-node linear bricks with EC3D8R elements. The vane shear device is modeled as the Lagrangian body using S4 elements, which are fully integrated finite–membrane–strain shell elements.

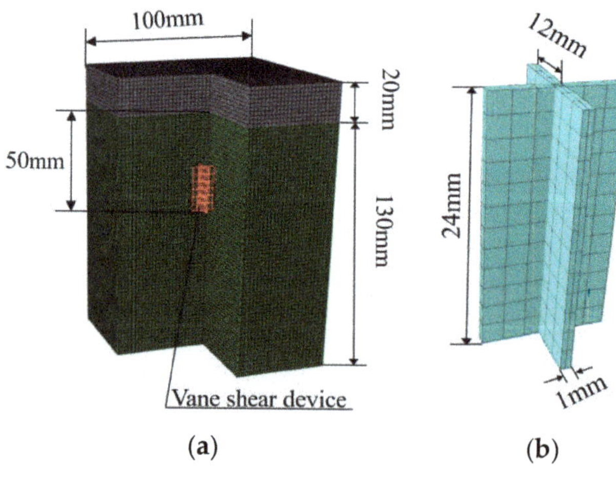

Figure 2. The numerical model of the vane shear test: (**a**) the VST model; (**b**) the vane shear device.

The VST model consists of four rectangular vanes and a soil domain as shown in Figure 2a. The soil domain is 150 mm × 100 mm × 100 mm. An additional 20 mm of empty space is added above the soil section to allow for the soil movement. We defined the soil domain size according to the ASTM standard [19] for the vane shear test to ensure the numerical results are not affected by the boundary effect. The height, diameter, and thickness of the vane shear device are 24, 12, and 1 mm, respectively, as shown in Figure 2b.

3.2. The Strain-Softening Behavior of Sensitivity Clay

Sensitive clay is widely distributed in the ocean. One of the most significant characteristics of sensitive clay is its strain-softening phenomenon. This phenomenon refers to when the sensitive clay reaches a critical state at which its ability to resist further deformation decreases sharply, leading to a rapid increase in the strain and a significant reduction in shear strength.

In this research, Scandinavian sensitive clay [31] was used in the numerical model. The linear strain-softening model of the sensitive clay is shown in Figure 3. s_u represents the undrained shear strength of the soil at the strain of γ, where s_{up} is the peak undrained shear strength before softening, and s_{uR} is the residual undrained shear strength. The pre-peak behavior is elastic until s_u reaches s_{up} and the strain γ reaches the elastic strain γ^e; this linear elastic section is specified by Young's modulus. Afterward, s_u continues to decline with the increase in strain before flattening out at the plastic strain of γ^p_{uR}. Table 1 shows the physical and mechanical parameters of the Scandinavian sensitive clay employed in this research. The unit weight, peak shear strength, residual shear strength, and plastic strain are obtained from the experimental data tested by Gylland et al. [31], and Young's modulus and Poisson's ratio are obtained from the numerical simulation data conducted by Kundu et al. [32].

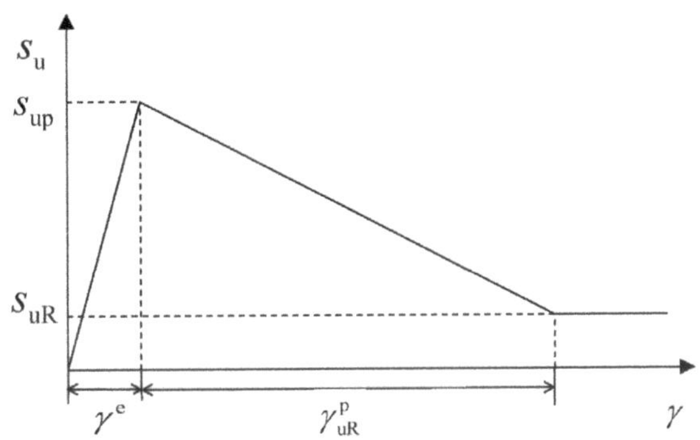

Figure 3. The strain-softening behavior of the sensitive clay.

Table 1. Input parameters for the numerical simulations.

Parameters	Values
Young's modulus, E (kPa)	300.0
Poisson's ratio, v	0.5
Unit weight, g (kN/m^3)	19.0
Peak shear strength, s_{up} (kPa)	30.0
Residual shear strength, s_{uR} (kPa)	6.0
Plastic strain, γ^p_{uR}	0.6

3.3. The Boundary Conditions

Figure 4 presents the boundary conditions of the soil domain and the vane shear device. Velocities of the elements on the soil domain's bottom were kept zero in all degrees of freedom (i.e., $v_x = v_y = v_z = 0$) and the vertical side surfaces were fixed in a horizontal displacement and free in a vertical displacement (i.e., $v_x = v_y = 0$), as shown in Figure 4a. At the center of the vane shear device, a reference point was selected and a rotation speed of 20°/s was applied [19], as shown in Figure 4b.

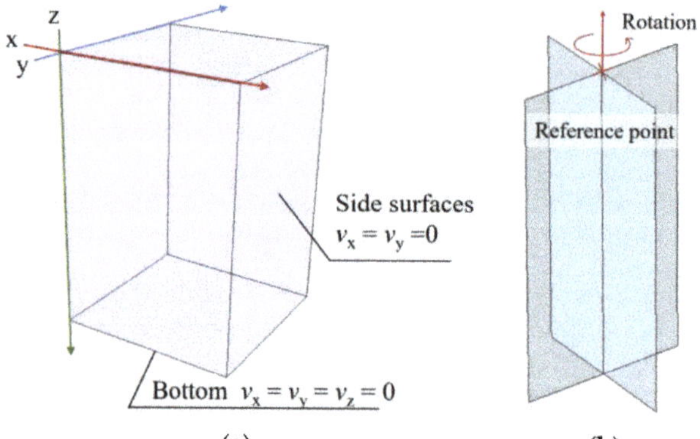

Figure 4. Boundary conditions: (**a**) the soil domain; (**b**) the vane shear device.

4. The Numerical Results of the Vane Shear Tests

4.1. Torque of the Vane Shear Test

Figure 5 presents the change of torque values and plastic strain with the increase in the rotation of the vane. It is shown that at the rotation of 5° (Point A), the soil behavior is elastic with no plastic shear strain. Then, as the torque reaches the peak value at the rotation angle of 10° (Point B), the failure occurs from the tips of the blades. During the strain-softening behavior after the torque peak, the plastic strain concentration occurs surrounding the tips and forms a squared-ring shape at the rotation of 15° (Point C), and then the plastic shear strain increases and expands further along the circle (Point D). When the rotation angle exceeds 90° (Point E), the failure spreads circumferentially, forming a full failure plane with a rounded square shape; such a phenomenon was also captured from the experiment tests by Gylland et al. [31].

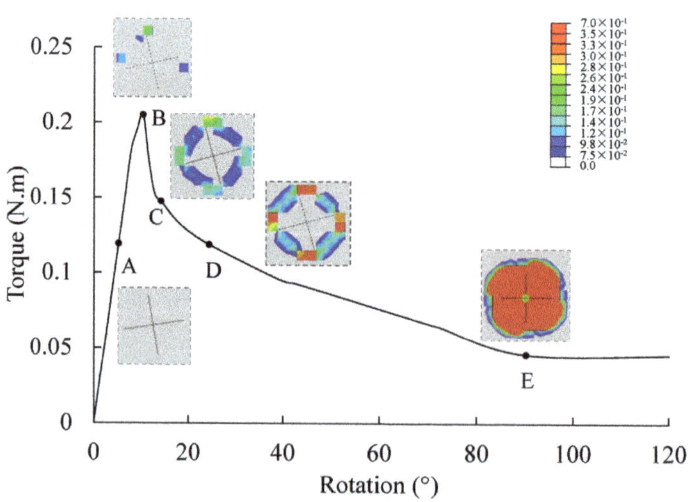

Figure 5. Changes in the torque values and plastic strain with various rotation conditions.

To test the reliability of the numerical model in Figure 5, we compared the torque generated from the numerical model with the torque obtained from the experimental data tested by Gylland et al. [31], as shown in Figure 6. Comparisons results show that the values of torque obtained from the numerical model agree well with the results obtained from the experimental tests. The peak torque obtained from the numerical model is 10.21 N·m, which is close to the experimental test with 10.42 N·m.

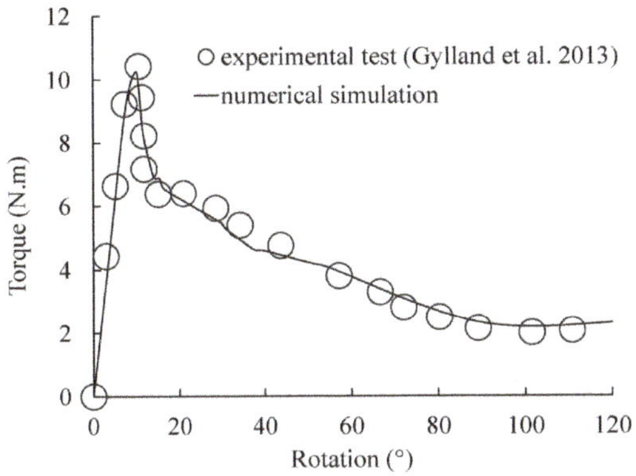

Figure 6. Comparisons of the torque obtained from the numerical simulations and experimental tests [31].

Figure 7 shows the shear stress of the soil during the VST. As the vane rotates, the shear stress gradually increases until the soil reaches its maximum shear strength at the rotation of 10°, as shown in Figure 7c. After that, the shear stress acting on the soil decreases to residual strength, as shown in Figure 7f.

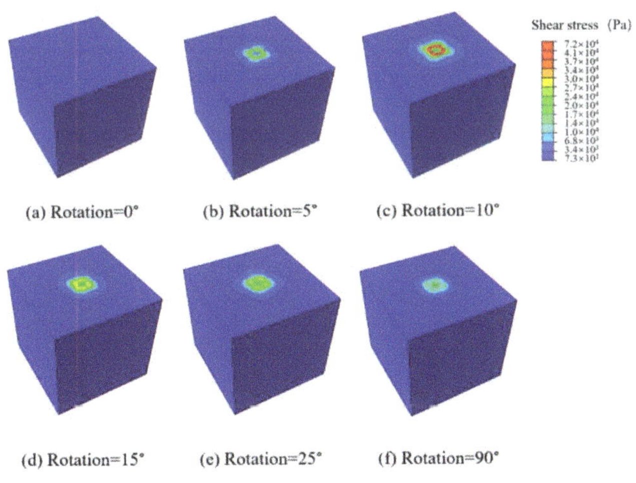

Figure 7. Shear stress during the VST.

4.2. The Undrained Shear Strength of the Clay

The undrained shear strength of the clay can be estimated from the measured torque value obtained from the vane shear tests, as shown in Equation (3) [19].

$$S_u = \frac{6T}{7\pi D^3} \tag{3}$$

where S_u is the undrained shear strength of the soil sample, T is the measured torque, and D is the diameter of the vane.

The torque obtained directly from the vane shear test was converted into the undrained shear strength, yielding the mobilized undrained shear strength of the sensitive clay during the vane shear test. The calculated peak undrained shear strength is 32.37 kPa, and the residual strength is 7.25 kPa.

4.3. The Shear Band of the Clay

The propagation of the shear zone in sensitive clay is one of the critical factors for modeling various types of failure, such as the progressive failure of embankments and submarine landslides [33].

The shear zone can be divided into three regions: the residual shear zone, the softening zone, and the non-plastic zone according to the values of equivalent plastic shear strain (PEEQVAVG) of each element in the numerical model [26]. PEEQVAVG can be calculated from the plastic strain γ^{P} of each element, as shown in Equation (4).

$$\text{PEEQVAVG} = \frac{\gamma^{P}}{\sqrt{3}} \tag{4}$$

When the undrained shear strength s_u reaches the peak during the vane shear test, the value of the PEEQVAVG is assumed to be equal to 0. When the value of s_u is up to s_{u95}, which is defined as the undrained shear strength reduced by 95% of (s_{up}-s_{uR}), the value of the PEEQVAVG = 0.35. When the PEEQVAVG falls within the range of 0–0.35, the soil has reached peak shear strength but has not yet reached residual strength, with a strength reduction of less than 95%, which indicates that the soil is in the softening stage.

In the numerical model, when the region has a PEEQVAVG $\geq$ 0.35, the region accumulates a large amount of plastic strain and is defined as the "residual shear zone "; when the region is 0 < PEEQVAVG < 0.35, the region is defined as the "softening zone "; the rest region is defined as the "non-plastic zone". The values of the PEEQVAVG of numerical models under various rotation conditions during the vane shear tests are used to calculate the types of shear zone, and the results are presented in Table 2 and plotted in Figure 8.

Table 2. Three types of shear zone under various rotation conditions.

Rotation (°)	Residual Shear Zone (%)	Softening Zone (%)	Non-Plastic Zone (%)
5	0.0	0.0	100.0
10	0.0	12.3	87.7
15	0.0	66.1	33.9
25	10.5	75.1	14.3
90	84.6	15.3	0.0

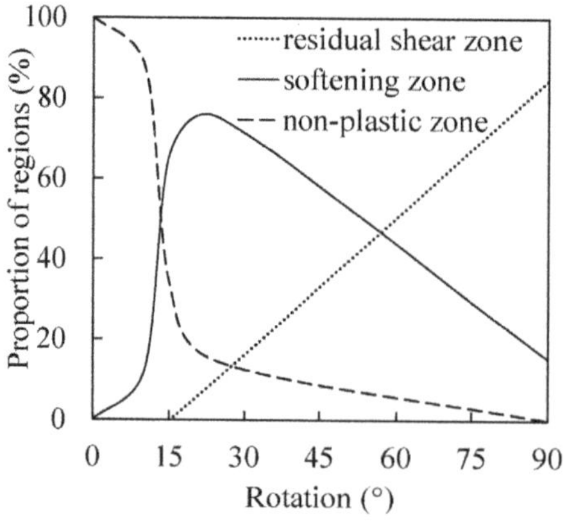

Figure 8. Variation of the shear zone in numerical simulations during the vane shear tests.

It is found that when the vane rotates to 10°, 12.3% of the soil in the shear zone transforms from the non-plastic state to the softening state. When the rotation angle increases to 15°, the proportion of softening zone reaches up to 66.1%. When the blades rotate to 25°, 10.5% of the soil in softening zone becomes completely damaged and turns into a residual stage. When the vane rotation reaches 90°, the proportion of the softening zone reduces to 15.3% and the residual shear zone increased to 84.6%.

5. Comparison Results of the Miniature and Standard Vane Shear Tests

It should be noted that the miniature vane size (H = 24 mm and D = 12 mm) presented in Figure 1 is 5.5 times smaller than that of the standard vane dimension (H = 130 mm and D = 65 mm). The larger vanes generate higher levels of torque on the soil, which could lead to an increase in soil disturbance and potential inaccuracies in measurement results. Therefore, in this research, we investigated the relations of undrained shear strength estimated from the miniature and standard vane shear tests, as shown in Figure 9.

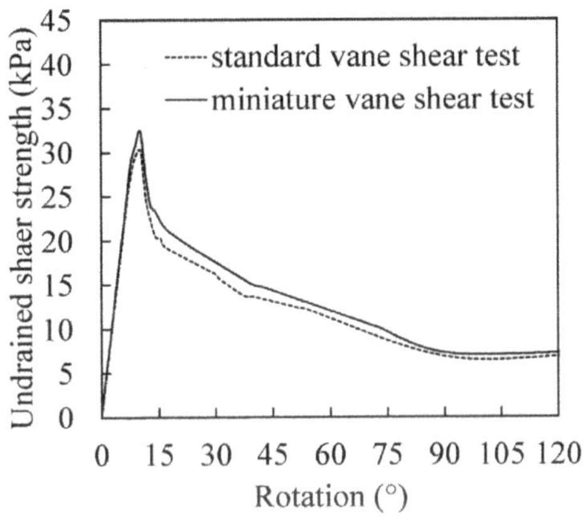

Figure 9. Comparison of the undrained shear strength obtained from the standard and miniature vane shear tests.

It can be seen that the strength measured by the MVST is higher than that measured by the standard vane shear test. The peak and residual undrained shear strength measured by the MVST are 32.38 kPa and 7.25 kPa, respectively, which are increased by 7.04% and 6.62% compared with 30.25 kPa and 6.80 kPa measured by the standard vane shear test.

The sensitivity S_t, which is defined as the ratio of the undisturbed and remolded strengths of sensitive clay, is an important index for characterizing the mechanical behavior of sensitive clay [34]. We carried out numerical simulations of the vane shear test for sensitive clay with various sensitivities. Figure 10 presents the comparison results of the undrained shear strength of the soils with an S_t from 1 to 7. It presents that, regardless of the sensitivity of the clay, the undrained shear strength measured by the miniature vane shear tests is slightly above the value measured by the standard vane shear tests.

Figure 11 shows that the peak and residual undrained shear strength of the sensitive clay obtained from the miniature vane shear tests are about 1.07 times that of the standard vane shear tests. s_{um} and s_{us} are the undrained shear strength measured by the MVST and standard VST, respectively.

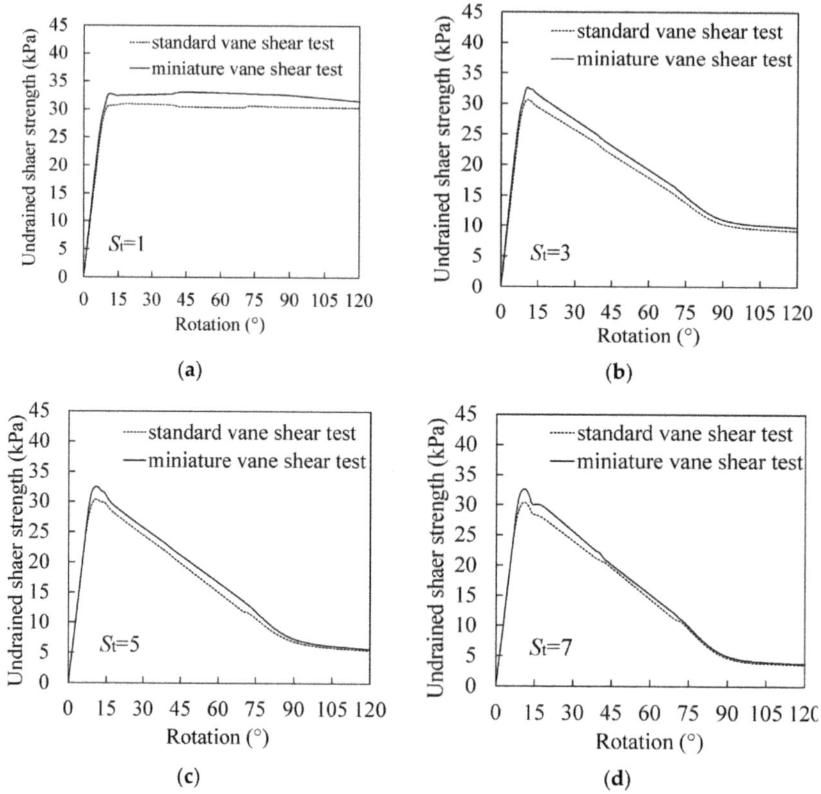

Figure 10. Comparison results of the undrained shear strength of soil samples with various S_t: (**a**) S_t = 1; (**b**) S_t =3; (**c**) S_t =5; (**d**) S_t =7.

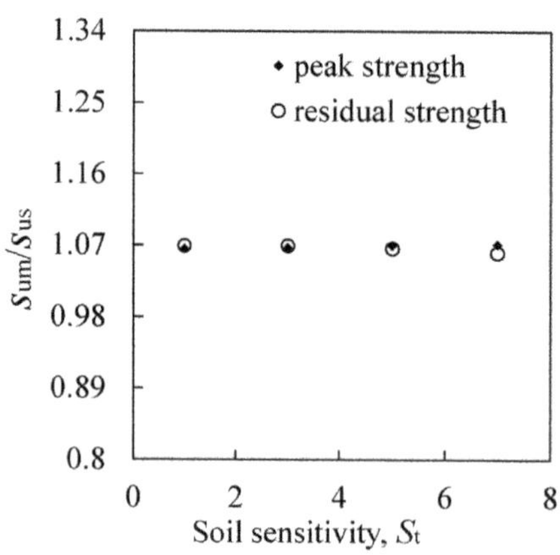

Figure 11. Relations between the miniature and standard vane shear test results.

6. Miniature Vane Shear Test under Confining Stress Conditions

The process of transferring soil samples from tube samplers on the seabed to the laboratory can release the in situ confining stress acting on the soil, which can increase the soil void ratio and decrease the soil strength. Therefore, it is necessary to investigate the influence of the confining stress on the undrained shear strength measured with the MVST. The static earth pressure σ_0 can be used to represent the confining stress acting on the soil under various depths and can be calculated from Equation (5).

$$\sigma_0 = K_0 \gamma z \tag{5}$$

where K_0 is the coefficient of static earth pressure, γ is the unit weight of the soil sample, and z is the depth.

For sensitive clay, the values of K_0 always fall within the range of 0.5–1.5, with 0.5 often serving for K_0 in the case of Norwegian sensitive clays [35]. In this research, confining stresses are applied to the soil sample during the numerical MVST to represent the in situ confining stress state of soils under shallow seabed surfaces. Figure 12 presents the undrained shear strength of soil samples under different confining stress conditions. The values of confining stress are 2 kPa, 3 kPa, and 5 kPa, representing the soil samples taken from the seabed under the depths of 24 cm, 36 cm, and 60 cm, respectively. It is shown that the undrained shear strength increases with the increase in confining stress. The values of peak strength are 32.37 kPa, 32.93 kPa, 33.79 kPa, and 34.66 kPa, and the residual strengths were 7.25 kPa, 7.44 kPa, 7.58 kPa, and 7.78 kPa when the soil samples were under the confining stress state of 0, 2 kPa, 3 kPa, and 5 kPa, respectively.

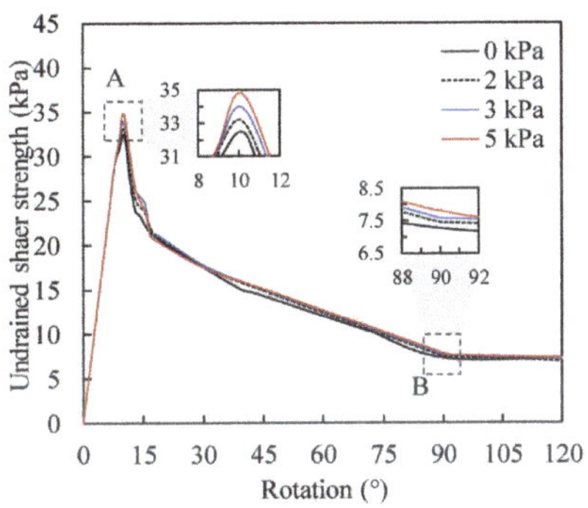

Figure 12. The undrained shear strength of the soil samples under various confining stress conditions.

Figure 13 presents the normalized undrained peak shear strength and residual strength. s'_u and s_{u0} are the undrained shear strength of soils obtained from soil samples under certain confining stress and no confining stress states, respectively.

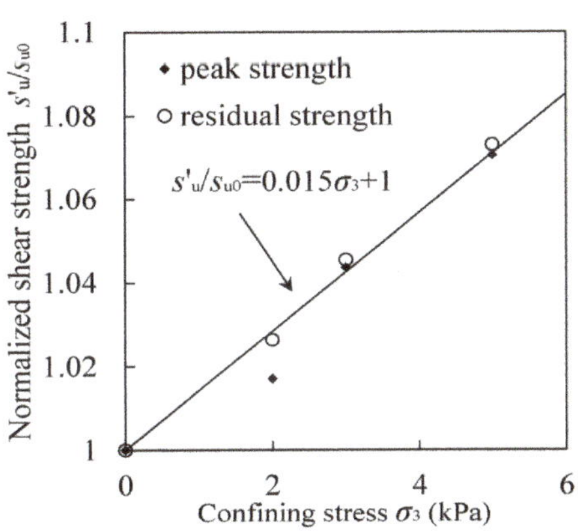

Figure 13. The undrained shear strength under various confining stress.

It is found that both the undrained peak and residual strength of the soil sample exhibit a linear increase with an increase in confining stress. A linear curve fitting method can be used to quantify the effects of confining stress on the undrained shear strength of sensitive clay, as shown in Equation (6).

$$s\prime_u = (0.015\sigma_3 + 1)s_{u0} \quad (6)$$

where s'_u is the undrained shear strength of the soil under certain confining stress, σ_3 is the confining stress, and s_{u0} is the undrained shear strength of the soil sample under no confining stress.

As the results presented in Figure 10 show, the peak and residual undrained shear strengths of the soil samples obtained from the MVST are about 1.07 times that of the standard vane shear test. Therefore, a correction factor μ = 1.07 is suggested to adjust Equation (6) to eliminate the size effect caused by blades, and the modified equation is shown in Equation (7).

$$s\prime_u = (0.014\sigma_3 + 0.93)s_{u0} \quad (7)$$

Equation (7) can not only reflect the effect of confining stress on the undrained shear strength of the soil samples obtained from the MVST but also can eliminate the size effect caused by the vane blades of MVSTs. Therefore, it can be used to estimate the undrained shear strength of the sensitive clay under shallow seabed surfaces.

7. Conclusions

In this research, three-dimensional vane shear test (VST) models were constructed using the Coupled Eulerian–Lagrangian (CEL) approach in ABAQUS to investigate the vane blade size effects and confining stress effects on the undrained shear strength of sensitive clay. The main conclusions are as follows:

1. The numerical simulations show that the failure of the soil sample initiates from the tips of the blades and propagates circumferentially. With the increase in rotation angle, the plastic shear strain extends surrounding the tips and forms a squared-ring shape. At the rotation of 90°, a complete failure plane of a rounded square shape is formed, which is consistent with the experiment results.
2. The undrained shear strength of the soil samples obtained from the miniature vane shear test (MVST) is 1.07 times that of the standard VST. Therefore, a correction factor μ = 1.07 is suggested to adjust the undrained shear strength values estimated from the MVST for engineering applications.
3. Both undrained peak and residual shear strength of the soil samples exhibit a linear increase with the increase in confining stress. Therefore, a linear prediction model that can reflect the confining stress effects on the undrained shear strength of the soil samples obtained from the MVST was proposed. It can be used to estimate the undrained shear strength of the sensitive clay under shallow seabed surfaces.

The finding of this research is based on the numerical simulation, which is open for further improvements as the miniature vane shear test apparatus considering confinement conditions is available.

Author Contributions: Conceptualization, J.S.; methodology, J.S., X.W. and Q.C.; software, X.W. and Q.C.; validation, X.W.; formal analysis, X.W. and J.S.; investigation, Q.G. and Z.Y.; resources, J.S. and J.C.; writing—original draft preparation, J.S. and X.W.; writing—review and editing, J.S., X.W., Q.C., Z.Y. and Q.G.; visualization, X.W.; supervision, J.S. and J.C.; project administration, J.S. and J.C.; funding acquisition, J.S. and J.C. All authors have read and agreed to the published version of the manuscript.

Funding: This research was funded by the Zhoushan Science and Technology Plan Project, grant number 2022C81001; the Jointed Funding Key Projects of Zhejiang Province, grant number LHZ22E090002; the Key R&D of Zhejiang Province, grant number 2021C03183; the Sanya Yazhou Bay Science and Technology City, grant number KYC-2020-01-001; the Finance Science and Technology Project of Hainan Province, grant number ZDKJ202019; and a project supported by the Scientific Research Fund of the Zhejiang Provincial Education Department, grant number Y202250867.

Institutional Review Board Statement: Not applicable.

Informed Consent Statement: Not applicable.

Data Availability Statement: The data used to support the findings and results of this study are available from the corresponding author upon request.

Conflicts of Interest: The authors declare no conflict of interest.

References

1. Zhou, P.; Chen, J.; Ruan, D.; Peng, X.; Wu, X.; Ren, Z.; Gao, Q. Design of a Marine Sediments Resistivity Measurement System Based on a Circular Permutation Electrode. *J. Mar. Sci. Eng.* **2021**, *9*, 995. [CrossRef]
2. He, S.; Peng, Y.; Jin, Y.; Wan, B.; Liu, G. Review and Analysis of Key Techniques in Marine Sediment Sampling. *Chin. J. Mech. Eng.* **2020**, *33*, 1–17. [CrossRef]
3. Sørlie, E.R.; Hartnik, L.O.; Tran, Q.A.; Eiksund, G.R.; Thakur, V.; Kjennbakken, H.; Degago, S. Physical model tests of clay-rich submarine landslides and resulting impact forces on offshore foundations. *Ocean Eng.* **2023**, *273*, 113966. [CrossRef]
4. Sun, Z.; Kong, G.; Zhou, Y.; Shen, Y.; Xiao, H. Thixotropy of a Transparent Clay Manufactured Using Carbopol to Simulate Marine Soil. *J. Mar. Sci. Eng.* **2021**, *9*, 738. [CrossRef]
5. Wang, C.; Hawlader, B.; Perret, D.; Soga, K. Effects of geometry and soil properties on type and retrogression of landslides in sensitive clays. *Géotechnique* **2022**, *72*, 322–336. [CrossRef]
6. Lin, Y.; Qin, H.; Guo, J.; Chen, J. Study on the Rheological Behavior of a Model Clay Sediment. *J. Mar. Sci. Eng.* **2021**, *9*, 81. [CrossRef]
7. Flaate, K. Factors Influencing the Results of Vane Tests. *Can. Geotech. J.* **1966**, *3*, 18–31. [CrossRef]
8. Kouretzis, G.P.; Pineda, J.; Krabbenhoft, K.; Wilson, L. Interpretation of vane shear tests for geotechnical stability calculations. *Can. Geotech. J.* **2017**, *54*, 1775–1780. [CrossRef]
9. He, C.; You, Y.; Wang, D.; Wu, H. Estimating soil failure due to torsion via vane shear test by varying vane diameter and soil properties. *Soil Tillage Res.* **2018**, *177*, 68–78. [CrossRef]
10. Jiang, S.H.; Papaioannou, I.; Straub, D. Bayesian updating of slope reliability in spatially variable soils with in-situ measure-ments. *Eng. Geol.* **2018**, *239*, 310–320. [CrossRef]
11. Saye, S.R.; Kumm, B.P.; Lutenegger, A.J. Estimating over consolidation ratio (OCR) in structured and unstructured cohesive soil with field vane tests referencing soil index properties. *Can. Geotech. J.* **2021**, *58*, 125–141. [CrossRef]
12. Zhang, H.; Jia, Y.; Liu, X.; Wei, Z.; Ji, C.; Jiao, X.; Zhu, C. Progress in in-situ measurement of sediment mechanical properties for full ocean depth. *Mar. Geol. Front.* **2019**, *35*, 1–9.
13. Lunne, T.; Andersen, K.H.; Low, H.E.; Randolph, M.F.; Sjursen, M. Guidelines for offshore in situ testing and interpretation in deepwater soft clays. *Can. Geotech. J.* **2011**, *48*, 543–556. [CrossRef]
14. Ma, W.-B.; Rao, Q.-H.; Li, P.; Guo, S.-C.; Feng, K. Shear creep parameters of simulative soil for deep-sea sediment. *J. Central South Univ.* **2014**, *21*, 4682–4689. [CrossRef]
15. Kolk, H.J.; Hooper, J.; Imms, B.W. Evaluation of offshore in situ vane test results. In *Vane Shear Strength Testing of Soils: Field and Laboratory Studies*; Richards, A.J., Ed.; ASTM STP 1014; American Society for Testing and Materials: Philadelphia, PA, USA, 1988; pp. 339–353.
16. Zhang, H.; Liu, X.; Chen, A.; Li, W.; Lu, Y.; Guo, X. Design and Application of an In Situ Test Device for Rheological Characteristic Measurements of Liquefied Submarine Sediments. *J. Mar. Sci. Eng.* **2021**, *9*, 639. [CrossRef]
17. Wang, K.; Xu, G.; Wang, J.; Wang, C. Self-boring in situ shear pressuremeter testing of clay from Dalian Bay, China. *Soils Found.* **2018**, *58*, 1212–1227. [CrossRef]
18. Young, A.G.; McClelland, B.; Quiros, G.W. In-Situ Vane Shear Testing at Sea. In *Vane Shear Strength Testing of Soils: Field and Laboratory Studies*; Richards, A.J., Ed.; ASTM STP 1014; American Society for Testing and Materials: Philadelphia, PA, USA, 1988; pp. 46–67.
19. *ASTM D 4648*; Standard Test Method for Laboratory Miniature Vane Shear Test for Saturated Fine-Grained Clayey Soil. American Society for Testing and Materials: West Conshohocken, PA, USA, 2011.
20. Alberto-Hernandez, Y.; Kang, C.; Yi, Y.; Bayat, A. Mechanical properties of clayey soil relevant for clogging potential. *Int. J. Geotech. Eng.* **2017**, *1*, 1–8. [CrossRef]
21. Zumsteg, R.; Plötze, M.; Puzrin, A. Effect of Soil Conditioners on the Pressure and Rate-Dependent Shear Strength of Different Clays. *J. Geotech. Geoenviron. Eng.* **2012**, *138*, 1138–1146. [CrossRef]

22. Arulrajah, A.; Disfani, M.M.; Suthagaran, V.; Bo, M.W. Laboratory Evaluation of the Geotechnical Characteristics of Wastewater Biosolids in Road Embankments. *J. Mater. Civ. Eng.* **2013**, *25*, 1682–1691. [CrossRef]
23. Ansari, Y.; Pineda, J.; Kouretzis, G.; Sheng, D. Experimental and numerical investigation of rate and softening effects on the undrained shear strength of Ballina clay. *Aust. Geomech.* **2014**, *49*, 51–57.
24. Park, S.-S.; Doan, N.-P.; Jeong, S.W. Numerical simulation of water content dependent undrained shear strength of clays. *Mar. Georesour. Geotechnol.* **2019**, *38*, 621–632. [CrossRef]
25. Dey, R.; Hawlader, B.; Phillips, R.; Soga, K. Large deformation finite-element modelling of progressive failure leading to spread in sensitive clay slopes. *Géotechnique* **2015**, *65*, 657–668. [CrossRef]
26. Qiu, G.; Henke, S.; Grabe, J. Application of a Coupled Eulerian–Lagrangian approach on geomechanical problems involving large deformations. *Comput. Geotech.* **2011**, *38*, 30–39. [CrossRef]
27. Gupta, T.; Chakraborty, T.; Abdel-Rahman, K.; Achmus, M. Large Deformation Finite Element Analysis of Static Cone Penetration Test. *Indian Geotech. J.* **2015**, *46*, 115–123. [CrossRef]
28. Vitali, E.; Benson, D.J. Contact with friction in multi-material arbitrary Lagrangian-Eulerian formulations using X-FEM. *Int. J. Numer. Methods Eng.* **2008**, *76*, 893–921. [CrossRef]
29. Shen, J.; Chen, Q.; Wang, L.-Z.; Wang, D. Numerical Investigations of the Failure Mechanism of Spreading Landslides. *Can. Geotech. J.* **2023**. [CrossRef]
30. Benson, D.J.; Okazawa, S. Contact in a multi-material Eulerian finite element formulation. *Comput. Methods Appl. Mech. Eng.* **2004**, *193*, 4277–4298. [CrossRef]
31. Gylland, A.; Jostad, H.; Nordal, S.; Emdal, A. Micro-level investigation of the in situ shear vane failure geometry in sensitive clay. *Geotechnique* **2013**, *63*, 1264–1270. [CrossRef]
32. Kundu, P.; Hawlader, B.; Karmaker, R. Two-dimensional finite element modelling of field vane shear test in sensitive clay. In Proceedings of the 74th Canadian Geotechnical Conference, Niagara, ON, Canada, 26–29 September 2021.
33. Quinn, P.; Diederichs, M.; Rowe, R.K.; Hutchinson, D. A new model for large landslides in sensitive clay using a fracture mechanics approach. *Can. Geotech. J.* **2011**, *48*, 1151–1162. [CrossRef]
34. Cotecchia, F.; Chandler, R.J. A general framework for the mechanical behaviour of clays. *Géotechnique* **2000**, *50*, 431–447. [CrossRef]
35. Wang, C.; Hawlader, B.; Perret, D.; Soga, K.; Chen, J. Modeling of initial stresses and seepage for large deformation fi-nite-element simulation of sensitive clay landslides. *J. Geotech. Geoenviron. Eng.* **2021**, *147*, 04021111. [CrossRef]

Journal of
Marine Science and Engineering

MDPI

Article

Evaluation of Soil–Foundation–Structure Interaction for Large Diameter Monopile Foundation Focusing on Lateral Cyclic Loading

Jae-Hyun Kim [1], Yeong-Hoon Jeong [2], Jeong-Gon Ha [3] and Heon-Joon Park [4,*]

1 Department of Civil Engineering, Kangwon National University, Chuncheon-si 24341, Republic of Korea; jaehyun2@kangwon.ac.kr
2 Civil R&D Team, Daewoo E&C, Suwon-si 16297, Republic of Korea; yeonghoon.jeong@daewooenc.com
3 Structural and Seismic Safety Research Division, Korea Atomic Energy Research Institute, Daejeon 34057, Republic of Korea; jgha@kaeri.re.kr
4 Department of Civil Engineering, Seoul National University of Science and Technology (SeoulTech), Seoul 01811, Republic of Korea
* Correspondence: heonjoon@seoultech.ac.kr

Abstract: In this study, the monotonic and cyclic behavior of an offshore wind turbine with a monopile foundation installed in a sand layer were evaluated in the centrifuge. A simplified offshore wind turbine was modeled, and the lateral load was applied to the tower under displacement control. The monotonic loading test evaluated ultimate lateral load capacity and bending moment profiles under different loading levels. During cyclic loading, variations of moment-rotation responses, cyclic stiffness, and bending moments along the pile were observed. The initial rotational stiffness of the monopile decreased as the loading level increased. In the fatigue limit state (FLS) and service limit state (SLS) loading conditions, no noticeable variation in stiffness was observed with the number of cycles. However, in the ultimate limit state (ULS), the stiffness of the monopile increased during the first few cycles, followed by a decreasing rate of increase, and reached a certain value. The loading rate had a weakening effect on the monopile–soil interaction, which was supported by the bending moments induced in the monopile.

Keywords: centrifuge modelling; offshore wind turbine; monopile; cyclic loading; loading rate; sandy soil

1. Introduction

After signing the Kyoto Protocol in 1997 by more than 160 countries, many countries have made efforts to control the environmental pollution caused by fossil fuels. Alternative reusable energy sources from water, wind, solar, and tidal power sources have been chosen to meet the environmental pollution problems. In particular, wind energy, one of the cleanest energies, was chosen to cope with the difficult pollution problems of many European countries, and offshore wind turbines have been growing up as a promising renewable energy source [1,2]. In the case of onshore wind farms, wind turbine installation is easier and faster than on offshore farms. However, it also has a lot of disadvantages, such as noise pollution and a high land acquisition price for wind turbine installation. Offshore wind turbines avoid these demerits and have an advantage due to higher wind speeds in offshore conditions.

Different foundation concepts can be chosen in order to support the offshore wind turbine. Of several types of foundations, monopiles are the most widely used for offshore wind turbines due to their proven stability and well-established design methods [3–6]. The diameter and penetration depth of the monopile depend to a large extent on the site conditions and capacity of the turbines [7]. Wind turbines with a rated power value of less than 3 MW are generally suitable for shallow water depths of less than 10 m and a pile diameter of less than 5 m. However, as large turbines with higher power generation capacity are needed to be installed at 15–30 m water depth, the demand for large diameter monopiles of 5–7 m has been growing [8,9].

In practice, the p–y curve is widely used for the prediction of the lateral behavior of monopiles. However, the original p–y curve is largely based on field tests on slender piles (i.e., long and small diameter) [3,4,10,11]. Even though applying the existing p–y method is limited to a certain condition, this approach has been broadly used to predict the lateral response of large-diameter monopiles. However, the behavior of the large-diameter piles themselves is relatively rigid compared to the small-diameter piles, so the pile rotates without noticeable deflection. Moreover, this tendency becomes extreme as the diameter increases. The problem of the application of the p–y method for large-diameter monopiles has been raised by various researchers [12–16]. In recent years, various alternative methods have been proposed to widen the applicability of the existing p–y method for monotonic lateral loads on non-slender piles [17–19].

Offshore foundations are typically exposed to complex load combinations from wind and waves in a cyclic manner, and such loads act on the foundation with different loading directions, levels, and rates during their lifetime [20]. DNV GL [6] noted that the environmental load imposed on a wind turbine should always be considered as one-way cyclic loading or two-way cyclic loading. Moreover, Bienen et al. [21] emphasized that large permanent displacements can occur when the direction of loading changes during a cycle. Meanwhile, the behaviors of the offshore foundation quite depend on the loading rate as well as the loading direction. A soil strain will gradually accumulate if the cyclic loading frequency is high enough to generate excess pore water pressure in the soil surrounding the offshore foundation. Hence, it decreases in overall strength and rigidity [22]. This implies that cyclic loads reduce the stiffness and bearing capacity of the soil, and the capacity may be lower under cyclic loading than under monotonic loading [23,24]. Byrne et al. [25] pointed out that serviceability requirements, rather than ultimate conditions, should determine the foundation design. The critical design criterion is that the permanent displacement should be lower than the service limit, typically 0.25° of accumulated rotations due to cyclic loading [6]. Moreover, the stiffness of the wind turbine system is significant, as the blade and rotor eigenfrequencies provide only a small range of frequencies suitable for design [21].

For monopile design considering the effect of cyclic loading, API [5] proposed the extended p–y method by adopting an empirical calibration factor from field cyclic loading tests, which results in a 70% degradation in the ultimate resistance of soil at seabed level. This degradation decreased linearly with depth down to $z = 2.625D$ (here, D is the monopile diameter). Below this point, the p–y curve of monotonic loading is equal to that of cyclic loading. Such a design method leads to an overall softer behavior of the foundation compared to that of the monotonic loads. However, many questions have been raised as to whether the p–y method can be fully applied to large-diameter monopiles because the lateral behavior of large-diameter monopiles is affected by the number of cycles as well as load characteristics. Recently, many researchers proposed predicting the lateral cyclic response of large-diameter monopiles, such as the high-cycle accumulation model, through numerical analysis [8,26–28] and small-scale model tests [12,16,29]. Still, a clear conclusion has not been reached, as the cyclic behavior of large-diameter monopiles is very complex.

Soil–foundation–structure interaction (SFSI) is another key issue for designing the offshore wind turbine because the system's natural frequency of the wind tower should have a safe margin from the governing loading frequencies (rotor frequency 1P and blade passing frequency 3P), including the wind and waves [30]. Several studies have been conducted to predict the dynamic performance of offshore structures. They pointed out that the cyclic stiffness between soil and foundations has a significant impact on the whole dynamic behavior of the offshore structures [31–34]. Nevertheless, there is still a lack of knowledge on the change in foundation stiffness depending on the cyclic loading level, number of cycles, cyclic loading frequency, and so on.

Therefore, in this study, a series of centrifuge model tests were performed to evaluate the cyclic behavior of the large-diameter monopile foundation in the sand layer under different cyclic loading levels and rates. In particular, the permanent displacement and stiffness variation of the soil–foundation system, which greatly affect offshore wind towers, were experimentally evaluated. In addition, soil–structure interaction behavior was investigated in the cyclic loading tests by measuring the bending moment transferred along the monopile.

2. Centrifuge Modelling

2.1. Facility

In geotechnical engineering, small-scale physical modeling is often conducted within a large centrifuge to provide correct scaling of the self-weight of structures and to simulate in situ soil stress conditions and prototype behavior accurately in a model test [35,36]. In this study, the C72–2 beam-type centrifuge model was used at the Korea Construction Engineering Development Collaboratory Program (KOCED) Geotechnical Centrifuge Testing Center installed at the Korea Advanced Institute of Science and Technology (KAIST). This model is a beam centrifuge with a radius of 5 m and a capacity of 240 g-tons. The general specifications of the centrifuge are listed in Table 1 [37].

Table 1. Specification of KAIST centrifuge.

Item	Specifications
Platform radius	5.0 m
Maximum capacity	240 g-tons
Maximum acceleration	130 g with 1300 kg payload
Maximum model payload	2400 kg up to 100 g

2.2. Modelling of Monopile

The National Renewable Energy Laboratory 5 MW wind turbine was used as a target structure for a small-scale wind turbine model because the detailed information on structural specification is open for research purposes [38]. The prototype wind turbine was first simplified to a flagpole model, which is comprised of hollow pipes and concentrated head mass, as suggested by [39]. Then, the wind turbine model was made to 1/4 the size of the simplified prototype turbine as a 'virtual model' due to the limitations of soil container size and allowable centrifugal acceleration. Iai et al. [40] presented a generalized scaling law that suggests a virtual model for modeling the large prototype model in the centrifuge tests. As described in Figure 1, in the first stage, the target structure was modeled as a simplified model by replacing a turbine blade part with a lumped mass having the same natural period as the blade part. In the second stage, the simplified model was scaled down to the 1/4 virtual model. In the final stage, the virtual model was again scaled down to a ratio of 50:1, considering the centrifuge scaling law [36]. Based on this method, the dimensions of the scaled model were further scaled without increasing the centrifugal acceleration. The details of the model simplification can be found in Seong et al. [41]. The scaling ratio of 50:1 was selected in order to minimize the rigid container boundary effect. Kim et al. [42] evaluated the rigid container boundary effect through the cone penetration test (CPT) in the centrifuge. They suggested that the boundary effect was negligible when the spacing between the rigid wall and CPT was seven times the CPT diameter or more. In this study, the boundary effect is therefore expected to be negligible because the spacing is more than ten times the monopile diameter in all experiments.

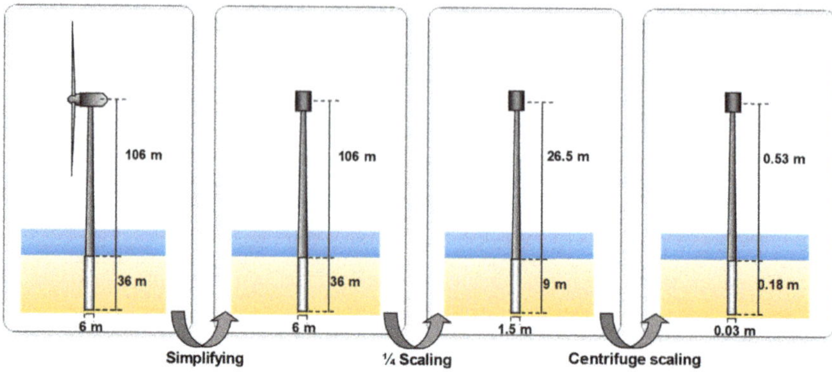

Figure 1. Schematics of monopile modeling.

The turbine model was manufactured with aluminum 7075 to ensure its stability. The turbine model was divided into three parts (lumped mass, tower, and monopile), and the bolt connections at each end of the tower part allow easy attachment to the lumped mass and the pile part. The dimensions of the turbine model are 30 mm (diameter, D), 180 mm (pile length, L_P), 508 mm (tower length, L_T), and 2.5 mm (model thickness, t), representing 1.5 m × 34.4 m × 1.25 mm in 1/4 prototype scale. The specifications of the dimensions are tabulated in Table 2. The conventional range for the ratio of wall thickness to the diameter of a pile is approximately 0.3% to 0.6%. However, recent case studies on the large-diameter monopile with a thick wall thickness ranging from 2% to 4.4% have also been reported [8,21,43,44]. In this study, due to limitations in model fabrication, the wall thickness is 2.5 mm, resulting in a ratio of wall thickness to diameter of 8.3%. Although the thickness ratio is somewhat larger than the conventional one, the results were consistently analyzed by considering the flexural rigidity, EI, of the manufactured monopile. To measure the bending load transferred from the structure–soil interaction, pairs of 11 strain gauges were attached along the tower, and each pair was installed at 180° with respect to the cross-section of the pile. All strain gauges were coated with a solvent-thinned polyurethane protective coating and insulation tape for protection purposes. Figure 2 shows a cross-section of the turbine model.

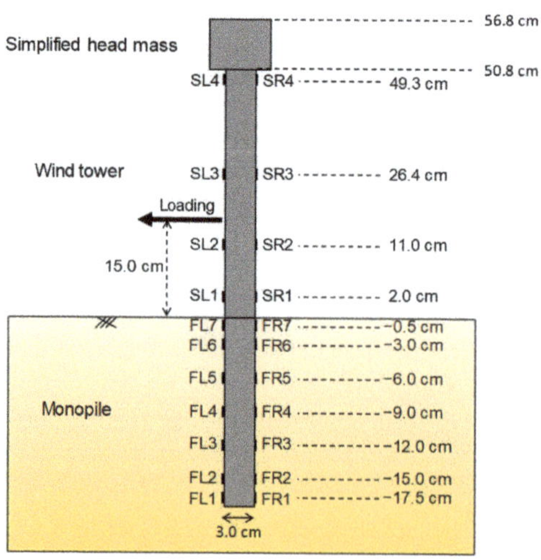

Figure 2. Cross section diagram of the monopile.

Table 2. Specific dimensions of monopile models.

Item	Offshore Wind Turbine Model	
	Prototype (m)	Model (mm) *
Pile and tower diameter, D	1.5	30
Pile length, L_P	9	180
Tower length, L_T	25.4	508
Pile and tower thickness, t	1.25	2.5

* The dimensions of the prototype were reduced to a ratio of 50:1, considering the centrifuge scaling law [35].

2.3. Soil Preparation

Silica sand artificially produced by the hammer crusher method was used in the centrifuge test. According to the Unified Soil Classification System (USCS), silica sand is classified as poorly graded sand (SP) with a mean particle size of D_{50} = 0.235 mm. The silica sand used in this study has advantages such as relatively accurate density control and uniform particle size. Moreover, the particle size effect is minimal for the centrifuge test because the mean particle size (D_{50}) is quite small, so the effect of the particle size on interfacial problems between sand particles and pile surfaces is negligible [44]. Table 3 lists the general properties of silica sand [45]. A sand-raining method was used in this study to reconstruct the ground model. This method is proven to have repeatable relative density results for the prepared model [46,47]. Using the sand raining system, the dry silica sand was poured into a cylindrical soil box with a target relative density (D_r) of 80%. The height of the ground model was 500 mm on the model scale and 25 m on the prototype scale.

Table 3. Basic soil properties of silica sand.

Items	Properties
Unified soil classification (USCS)	SP
Median particle size (D_{50}), mm	0.22
Curvature coefficient (C_c)	1.11
Uniformity coefficient (C_u)	1.96
Specific gravity (G_s)	2.65
Maximum void ratio (e_{max})	1.130
Minimum void ratio (e_{min})	0.611

2.4. Testing System

Figure 3 shows a schematic diagram of a cyclic testing system mounted in the centrifuge. A horizontal load actuator was used to apply a lateral load to the monopile under displacement control. The loading capacity and maximum loading speed of the linear actuator are 10 kN and 8.3 mm/s, respectively, in the model scale. It consists of a linear servo motor driver (Mitsubishi, MR-J2S-40A, 400W) and controller (National Instruments, NI PCI-7390, 4-axis motion controller) [44]. In all the tests performed in this study, the lateral load was subjected to a predetermined height of 150 mm (5D; here, D indicates the external diameter of the monopile) on a model scale above the sea floor due to considerable rollover moments and lateral loads.

The actuator was connected to a vertical connector, then to a hinge connection, as shown in Figure 4. With this system, the lateral loading can be transferred to the monopile, and the load is measured using a load cell installed next to the hinge connection. Three laser sensors were installed to measure the rotational and horizontal displacement of the monopile (located at 270 mm, 360 mm, and 540 mm above the ground, respectively). The data measured by the transducers were collected at a sampling rate of 10 Hz.

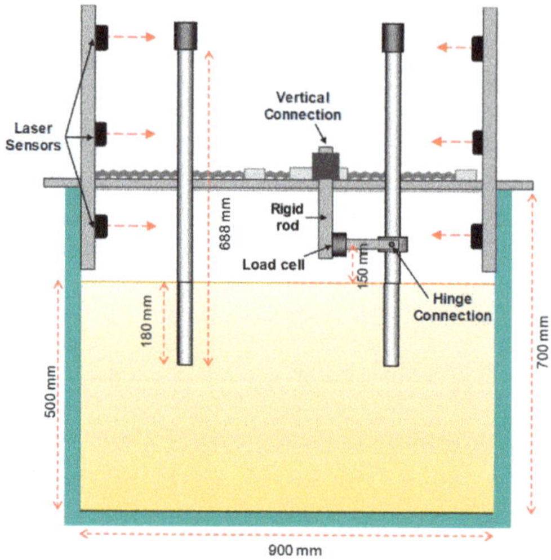

Figure 3. Cross-section diagram and photograph of the monopile.

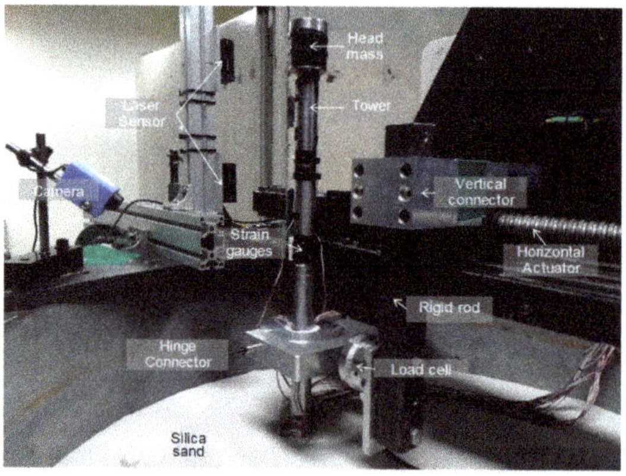

Figure 4. Photograph of the testing equipment.

3. Testing Procedure and Program

3.1. Determination of Ultimate Load Capacity

Monotonic loading tests were performed to determine the ultimate capacity of the monopile. At the target g-level, the horizontal load was applied at a given height of the monopile (5D from the seabed) by moving the horizontal actuator at a constant rate. Figure 5 shows the load-displacement curve. In the figure, straight lines were fitted to the initial stiff elastic section and the more flexible plastic section. The intersection is used to define an ultimate load following Villalobos [48], and it was approximately 2000 kN on a prototype scale. The capacity was used to define the loading levels in the cyclic tests. As a method of defining cyclic loading level, DNV GL [6] proposed the following design load states: (1) the ultimate limit state (ULS), related to the ultimate capacities (ULS: denoted by V_U); (2) the serviceability limit state (SLS), which occurs approximately 10^2 times during the lifetime of the wind turbine; and (3) the fatigue limit state (FLS), which occurs approximately 10^7 times during the lifetime of the wind turbine. The SLS is estimated at 50% of the ULS and the FLS at 30% of the ULS [6]. The limit state loads were used as the cyclic loading level, respectively. These are explained in detail in Section 4.3.

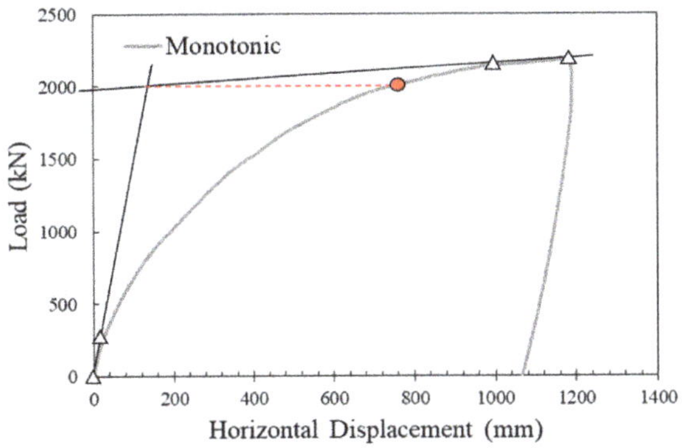

Figure 5. Determination of ultimate capacity from the monotonic load test (red circle in the figure indicates the ultimate capacity).

3.2. Testing Procedure and Program

After soil preparation, the monopile was installed into the sand by employing the jacking method at 1 g. The monopile was penetrated slowly, at 1 mm per hit, using a rubber hammer. A guiding system and two inclinometers maintain the verticality of the monopile during the installation. All monopiles in this study were penetrated using the same installation method to ensure the consistency of the experiment. The prepared soil model with monopile was carefully rested on the centrifuge basket, and the linear actuator and sensors were installed. Then, the centrifuge was ramped up to the target g-level (50 g) at 2 g/min and maintained the spinning level for 10 min after reaching the target g-level to stabilize the settlement of the soil.

Two types of centrifuge tests were conducted: monotonic and cyclic tests. The monotonic tests were performed to obtain the ultimate bearing capacity of the monopile under the lateral load. Here, two loading rates were selected to evaluate the loading rate effect: 0.2 mm/s and 2 mm/s in the model scale. In cyclic loading tests, the effects of loading level (0.3 ULS, 0.5 ULS, and ULS), number of cycles, and loading rate (0.2- and 2-mm/s) on the cyclic behavior of the monopile were evaluated. All experiments were performed at a centrifugal acceleration of 50 g with recorded values representing the prototype scale, and all testing conditions are listed in Table 4. The results of cyclic load tests were analyzed following the definitions of cyclic loading stiffness and permanent displacement illustrated in Figure 6. According to the established centrifuge scaling laws based on dimensional analyses [36], all values recorded in this study are converted to the prototype scales. This conversion was conducted using the equation $F_p = F_m \cdot N^2$, where F_p and F_m are the loads in prototype and model scale, respectively, and N is the centrifugal acceleration relative to the Earth's gravity (g).

Table 4. Testing program.

Test No.	Loading Type [1]	Load Level	Displacement [2]	Loading Rate	Cycles
1	Monotonic	-	-	0.2 mm/s	-
2	Monotonic	-	-	2 mm/s	-
3	FLS	0.24 kN	2.7 mm (11%)	0.2 mm/s	50
4	(30% ULS)			2 mm/s	
5	SLS	0.4 kN	6.4 mm (26%)	0.2 mm/s	50
6	(50% ULS)			2 mm/s	
7	ULS	0.8 kN	24 mm	0.2 mm/s	10
8				2 mm/s	

[1] All tests are loaded with a displacement control method. [2] Maximum displacement at the loading point.

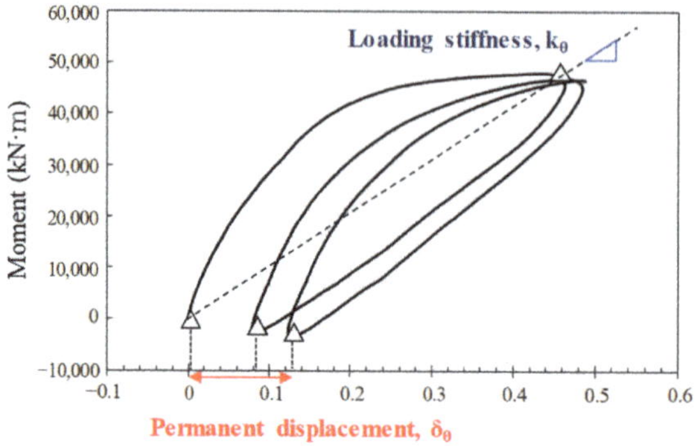

Figure 6. Definitions of cyclic loading stiffness and permanent displacement.

4. Test Results and Analysis

4.1. Criteria for Rigid and Flexible Behavior

When analyzing the soil–foundation interaction of the pile, a distinction of behavior should be considered between rigid and flexible [49]. The rigid pile rotates without significant bending, creating a "toe kick" under moments and lateral loads [50]. On the other hand, the flexible pile is characterized by structural bending without movement at the pile toe. The determination of the rigid or flexible behavior of the monopile has been proposed by various researchers (e.g., [51,52]). According to Poulos and Hull [53], the range of transition from flexible to rigid pile behavior is:

$$4.8 < \frac{E_S L^4}{E_P I_P} < 388.6 \tag{1}$$

where E_S = the elastic modulus of the soil, L = the embedded depth of the pile, E_P = the elastic modulus of the pile, and I_P = moment of inertia of the pile. Substituting the properties of the soil and the monopile model into Equation (1), the transition from rigid to flexible pile behavior becomes in the range from E_S = 19.5 MPa to E_S = 1570 MPa. The elastic modulus of the soil used in this experiment is within this range, so the behavior of the monopile tends toward the rigid and flexible cases.

4.2. Permanent Displacement and Rotational Stiffness of Monopile

The rotation of offshore wind turbines refers to the inclination of the monopile axis in relation to the horizontal plane. The rotation of the foundation has a significant impact on the performance and stability of the wind turbine. Even a small amount of accumulated rotation can greatly reduce the optimization of energy production for offshore wind turbines [1,24]. Therefore, evaluating and predicting the displacement of the foundation is of utmost importance. Accurately estimating the accumulated deformation of the structure over its design life is crucial, and serviceability requirements typically constrain it. According to DNV GL [6] and Peire et al. [54], the recommended serviceability design limits for tilt rotations of offshore wind turbines are 0.25° during installation and 0.25° during operation, respectively.

In this study, the rotational displacement of a monopile was measured based on the cyclic test results of the monopile foundation. Figure 7 presents graphs depicting the rotational displacement, referred to as a permanent rotation, which occurs when a load is applied and subsequently unloaded until the load magnitude reaches zero. In other words, the displacement values themselves do not represent the absolute displacement of the turbine but rather indicate the relative magnitude of displacement. Due to the relative displacement, it is not possible to observe the absolute tilt of the monopile. However, it can be used to analyze and predict variations in monopile displacement.

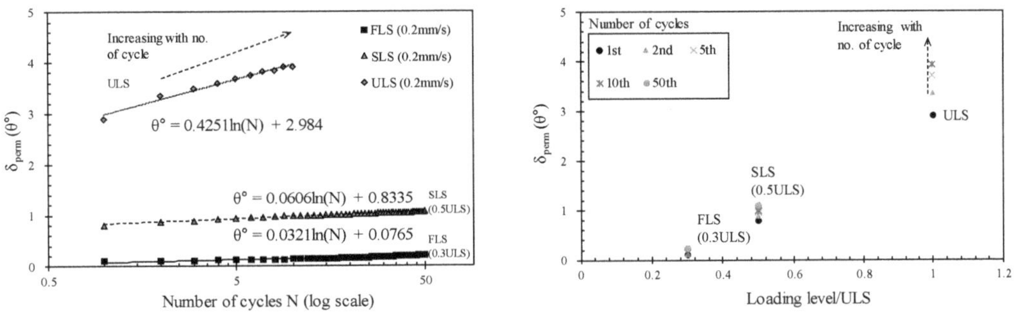

(a) (b)

Figure 7. Permanent displacement of the monopile with (**a**) number of cycles and (**b**) loading level ratio.

This graph represents the experimental results for three different magnitudes of loads under three conditions. In all three experiments, the rate of load application was 0.2 mm/s. The square markers represent the results under the FLS condition (30% of ULS), the triangle markers represent the results under the SLS condition (50% of ULS), and the diamond markers represent the results under the ULS load condition. In both graphs, the y-axis represents the permanent displacement. In graph Figure 7a, the x-axis represents the number of load cycles, while in graph Figure 7b, the x-axis represents the ratio of the load magnitude to the ultimate limit state (ULS) load value. In all three experiments, the permanent displacement increased with an increase in the number of load cycles. However, the degree of increase in displacement depends on the magnitude of the load. The slope of the trend line in Figure 7a represents the increase in permanent displacement with an increase in the number of load cycles. The slopes for the three experiments are 0.0321 (FLS experiment), 0.0606 (SLS experiment), and 0.4251 (ULS experiment).

The results of the slope values show that permanent displacement occurs to a very small extent when the load magnitude does not exceed 50% of the ultimate limit state (ULS). Moreover, the trend lines of permanent displacement in the cases of FLS and SLS are represented by a logarithmic function. This means that the majority of displacement occurs during the early stages of the number of cycles and gradually stabilizes to reach a steady state. Similar results were also observed in axial pipe–soil friction tests conducted by Boylan et al. [55], where soil densification and stabilization were observed. This implies that the occurrence of initial densification is due to the initial loading prior to long-term steady state behavior. However, when the load magnitude is at the ULS level, the permanent displacement increases significantly. In the case of the ULS load experiment, even after a few load cycles, the soil adjacent to the monopile undergoes compression, resulting in a reduction in the soil volume and subsequent loosening between the monopole and the soil. Consequently, it leads to a decrease in reaction forces.

The trends in the permanent displacements of the monopile according to the loading level and the number of cycles can also be explained by rotational stiffness graphs. Figure 8 shows the rotational stiffness of the monopile according to the loading level and the number of cycles. Generally, a smaller loading level results in a larger rotational stiffness, which aligns with the results in Figure 7. As a result, smaller permanent displacements are observed. However, the changes in stiffness with the number of cycles are different depending on the loading level. In the FLS and SLS experiments where the load magnitude does not exceed 50% of the ULS, the stiffness gradually increases during the initial cycles (within five cycles). Still, thereafter, it reaches convergence without further increases. During the initial stages of repeated loading, the monopile experiences soil densification as a result of its movement under load, leading to a gradual increase in stiffness.

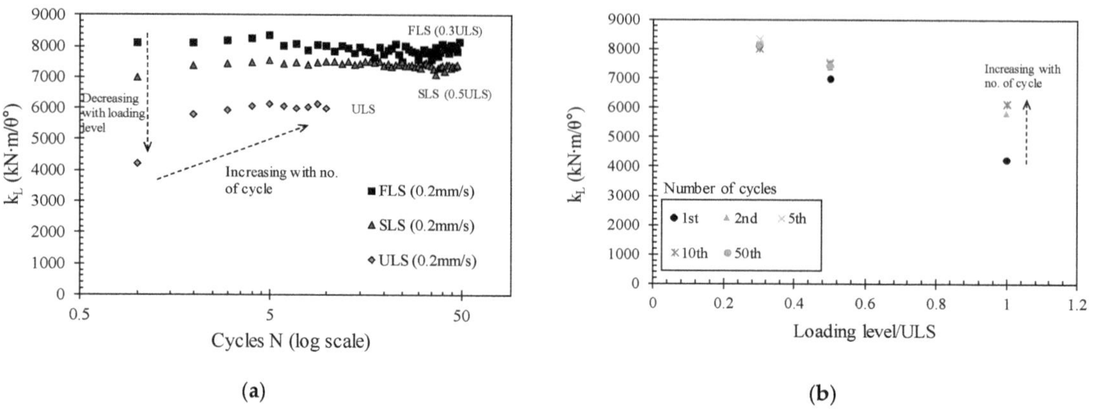

Figure 8. Cyclic rotational stiffness of monopile with (**a**) number of cycles and (**b**) loading level ratio.

However, as the relative density of the soil used in this experiment is rather large at 80%, the soil does not continue to be compacted, and the stiffness tends to converge. This observation can be explained more clearly when compared to the results of Jeong et al. [56]. In the results of the rotational stiffness of the tripod suction bucket foundation in Jeong et al. [56], the rotational stiffness gradually increases at the FLS or SLS load levels. As the number of cycles increases, the stiffness of the foundation increases continuously, although the rate of increase decreases continuously. In these tests, soil densification continues to occur because the relative density of surface soil is D_r = 40%. On the other hand, in the ULS load tests, the loading level is significantly high, resulting in a substantial increase in stiffness during the initial cycles of repeated loading. Once the number of load cycles exceeds five, a gradual increase in stiffness can be observed, and finally, it reaches a certain value.

4.3. Cyclic Loading Rate Effects on the Monopile

The variation of monopile stiffness in response to the rate of repeated loading was evaluated. Generally, the rate effects of loading are explained by the excess pore water pressure generation induced by the cyclic loading [21,24]. However, in this study, all of the tests were performed in dry soil conditions to analyze the rate effects, excluding the influence of pore pressure. Therefore, the difference in the behavior of the monopile depending on the strain rate can be identified.

Figure 9 presents the rotational stiffness results according to the differences in load rates for the FLS, SLS, and ULS experiments. Figure 9a shows the variation in stiffness for six experiments under different loading rates and load levels. The load rates were chosen to be 0.2 mm/s and 2 mm/s on a model scale under FLS, SLS, and ULS loading levels for each rate, respectively.

In all experiments, a faster loading rate resulted in lower stiffness values. This trend appears to be more prominent in experiments with smaller loads that do not exceed 50% of the ultimate limit state (ULS). Similar results were found in Jeong et al. [57] and Bienen et al. [21], where compressive cyclic loading experiments of a single bucket foundation were conducted via the centrifuge model tests. These studies demonstrated that faster loading rates were associated with lower stiffness in the case of FLS and SLS tests, which aligns with the findings of the present study and is consistent with the results of this study. Typically, faster loading rates induce an increase in pore water pressure, leading to a decrease in effective stress and ultimately resulting in a decrease in ground stiffness [21,24]. However, from the results of this experiment, it can be inferred that even in dry sand deposits, a higher load rate results in greater displacements and lower stiffness, independent of the increase in pore water pressure. It is also noted that the variation in stiffness with the number of cycles is more influenced by the loading level than the loading rate, as shown in Figure 9c–e. The faster loading rate resulted in lower soil stiffness, and this effect is more dominant when the load magnitude is smaller. However, the increase in stiffness due to repeated loading is not greatly affected by the loading speed. LeBlanc et al. [50] also emphasized that the loading rate effects are very significant in interpreting soil response under cyclic loads. Therefore, when designing the foundation for an offshore wind turbine, it is essential to consider the changes in soil stiffness caused by the loading level and the loading rate.

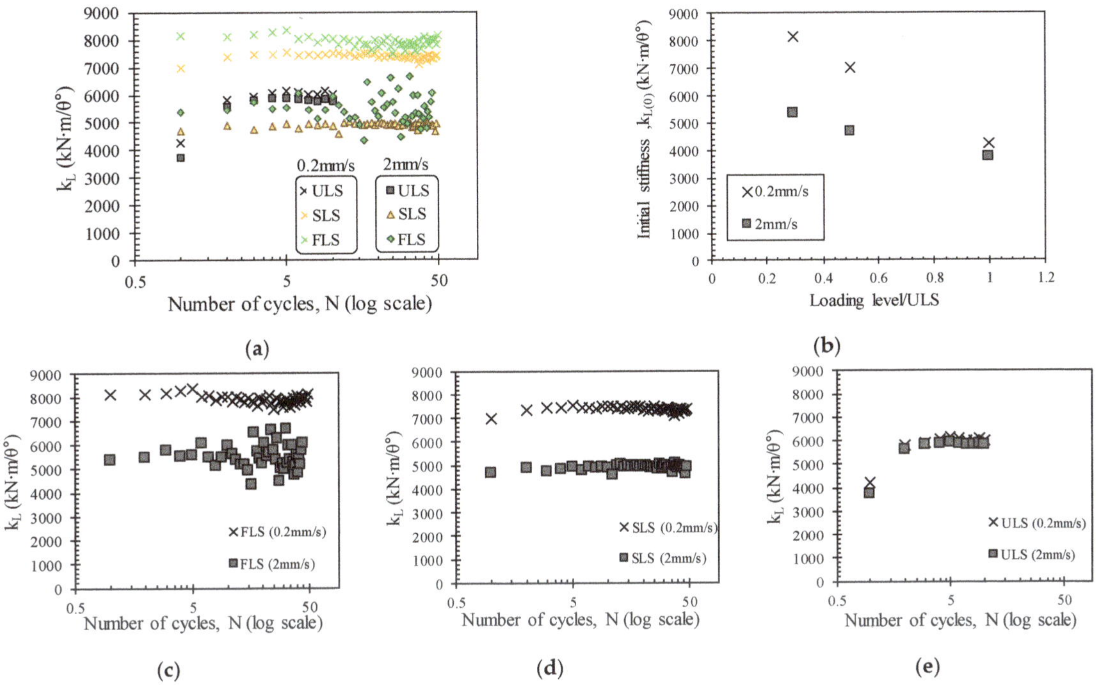

Figure 9. Cyclic rotational stiffness of monopile with loading rate with (**a**) number of cycles; (**b**) loading level ratio; and results of (**c**) FLS tests; (**d**) SLS tests; and (**e**) ULS tests.

4.4. Bending Moment Distribution of the Monotonic Load Tests

The bending moment load distributions were monitored during the monotonic load test by the strain gauges installed along the pile shaft. It should be noted that the loading was applied by the movement of the actuator at two different constant displacement rates of 0.2 mm/s (Test 1, model scale) and 2 mm/s (Test 2, model scale). Figure 10 shows the bending moment curves for the different lateral loads applied at the loading point (0.3, 0.6, 0.9, 1.2, 1.5, 1.8, 2 MN). These representative loads were selected from the load-displacement curves for each test. The bending moment measured at each location increased from the seabed with increasing depth up to 3 m and then decreased to zero at the toe of the monopile. The bending moment at a certain depth increased with increasing lateral loads until the load reached its ultimate value. In addition, the depth at which the maximum bending moment occurred was almost constant at approximately D (monopile diameter), regardless of the loading level for both tests. However, at the same loading level, the maximum bending moment of Test 1 (slow loading rate) had a 7% lower value than Test 2 (fast loading rate). It can be seen that the soil deformation induced by the pile load is dependent on the loading rate under the testing conditions, as the tests were conducted in dry sand, indicating no generation of excess pore pressure.

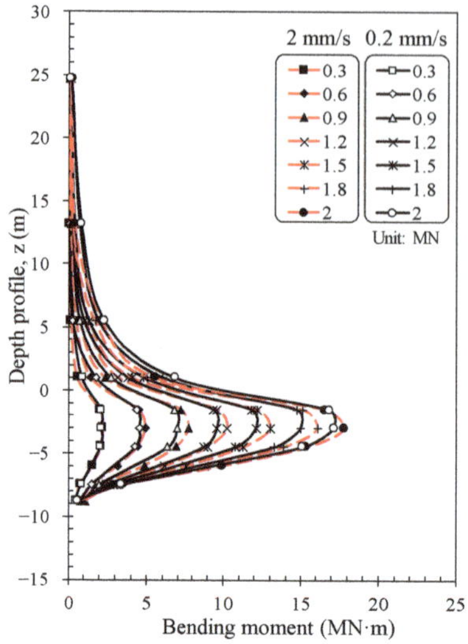

Figure 10. Bending moment profile (monotonic tests).

Based on the measured bending moment profiles, 5th polynomial fitting curves were obtained, as suggested by Wilson [58]. It provides the best mathematical estimation of the measured bending moment in the monopile [18].

$$M = f(z) = a_0z^5 + a_1z^4 + a_2z^3 + a_3z^{2.5} + a_4z + a_5 \tag{2}$$

Here, an exponent of 2.5 within Equation (2) is used to satisfy the requirement that the soil reaction pressure at the soil surface must be zero (0). For instance, the second derivative of the bending moment equals the minus of the soil pressure p (soil reaction per unit length of the monopile), and it should be zero at the soil surface ($p = -\frac{d^2M}{dz^2}$). The six coefficients can be obtained from the best-fitting curve of the 5th-order polynomial function. The pile deflection along the depth can be calculated by double integration of the bending moment profile divided by the flexural modulus of the monopile (EI, elastic modulus multiplied by the moment of inertia of the monopile cross-section area).

$$y = \int \left(\int \frac{M}{EI} dz \right) dz \tag{3}$$

where y is the lateral deflection at the depth of the monopile. Here, special care is required when double-integrating the regression of the bending moment profile with the polynomial method because significant errors can occur during the integration of a high-order function. In addition, Choo and Kim [18] described that the pile deflection calculated by the double integration of the moment profile needed to be calibrated to match the measured displacements of the exposed portion of the monopile because the rotation angle and deflection at the pile toe were not zero for the friction pile. In this study, the deflection of the pile was calculated by considering the lateral displacement of the pile and rotational angle at the soil surface (indicated as y_0 and r_0, respectively). Two laser sensors adjacent to the ground surface were used to calculate y_0 and r_0 following the suggested method proposed by Klinkvort [59].

Figure 11 presents the lateral deflection of the monopile with different loading levels. Overall, rotational behavior was dominant, but horizontal translation occurred along with rotation as the loading level increased. It is noted that the deflection of the monopile is similar to that of the short (rigid) pile under lateral load. The reasons for the rigid rotational behavior of the monopile with some translation under lateral loading are:

(1) low pile embedded depth (6D; here, D indicates external pile diameter); (2) thick pile tip thickness (D/t = 12) compared to that of the conventional monopile (D/t ≈ 40); and (3) low loading point from the ground surface (5D). Comparing the behavior of the monopile under different loading rates, it can be seen that the pile displacements under the higher loading rate condition (2 mm/s) are higher than those of the monopile under the low loading rate condition (0.2 mm/s). Moreover, the difference in displacement for both testing cases increases with increasing loading levels. The results indicated that the higher the loading rate, the more deformation is induced at the same loading level due to the rate effect of the soil, as mentioned before.

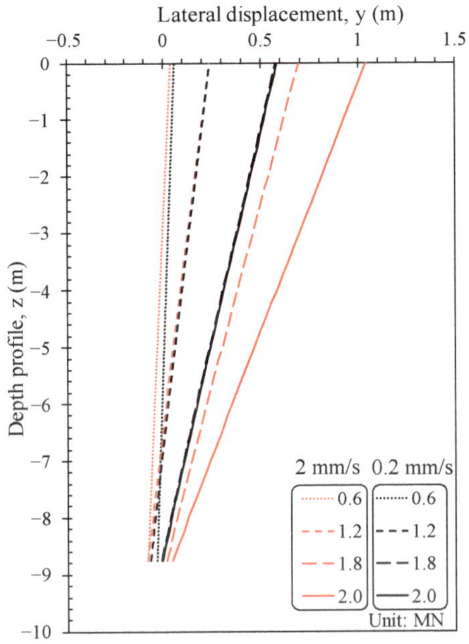

Figure 11. Distribution along the monopile shaft of lateral pile deflection.

4.5. Bending Moment Distribution of the Cyclic Load Tests

Figure 12 represents the bending moment profiles of the monopile under cyclic loading, which are induced by the 1st, 3rd, 4-, 8-, and 10-th cycles for the initial ULS loading level and the 1st, 3rd, 4-, 8-, 10-, 20-, 30-, and 50-th cycles for the initial FLS and SLS loading levels, respectively. As anticipated, the bending moment in the pile increases with the loading level (FLS, SLS, and ULS). In addition, the position where the maximum bending moment occurred was nearly constant at about 1D regardless of the loading level (FLS, SLS, and ULS). However, it is noted that the monopile bending moment decreased with the number of cycles. This is because the cyclic load was applied under displacement control at a certain loading rate, so the load acting on the pile and soil gradually decreased as the number of cyclic loads increased. In other words, accumulated soil deformation due to the cyclic load reduces the load acting on the pile and soil, resulting in a reduction in the acting load on the pile. It is also due to the fact that the soil adjacent to the pile is gradually densified as the load is repeated so that the stress acting on the pile is released, indicating the soil reaction has gradually decreased [60]. In the figure, a reduction in the maximum bending moment with the number of cycles was more prominent at the higher loading level (ULS). Again, the higher the loading level, the higher the soil densification occurs. Hence, the maximum bending moment generated by the lateral load is also greatly reduced.

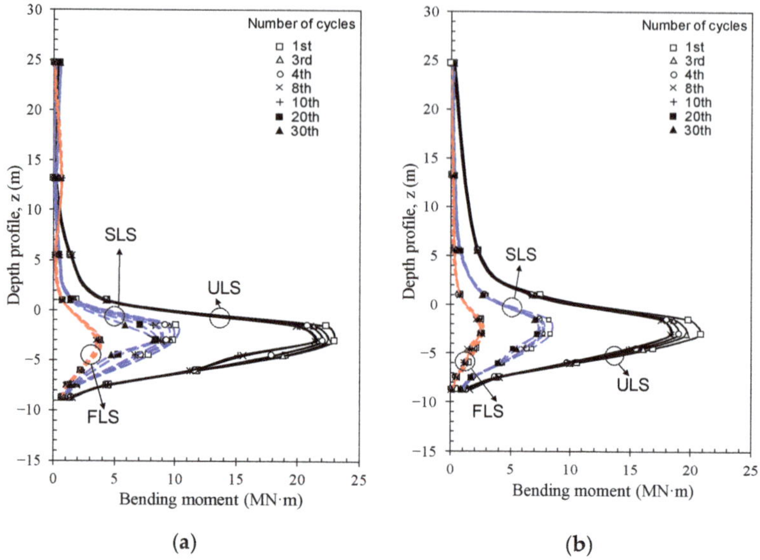

Figure 12. Bending moment profiles of the monopile during cycling with loading rate of (**a**) 0.2 mm/s and (**b**) 2 mm/s.

Figure 13 shows the ratio of maximum bending moment measured at each loading cycle to that of the initial load cycle under ULS condition $[M_{max}/(M_{max})_{int}]$. The graph clearly shows that the reduction of the maximum moment is remarkable under the condition of high cyclic loading rate. The ratio induced by 10th cycle was $M_{max}/(M_{max})_{int} = 0.88$ for fast repeated loading rate (2 mm/s in model scale) and $M_{max}/(M_{max})_{int} = 0.93$ for slow repeated loading rate (0.2 mm/s in model scale). The test conducted at the faster loading rate indicates a maximum bending moment reduction of about 5% rather than that of the slow loading test. This rate dependency behavior of the monopile was also observed in the field tests [61,62].

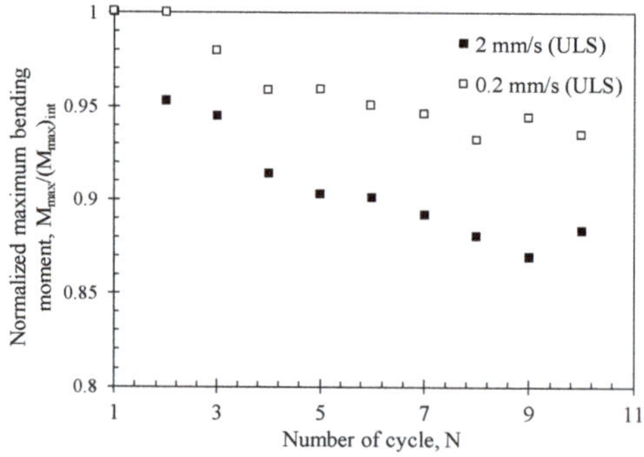

Figure 13. Normalized bending moment trend in ULS tests.

It is also noted worthy that the reduction ratio $[M_{max}/(M_{max})_{int}]$ was greatly decreased within a few number of cycles and then converged with number of cycles. The initial displacement behavior is dominant for first few number of cycles and then it reaches the plateau where it stabilizes. Similar observation was noted in suction bucket foundation for cyclic loading tests (Jeong et al. [2,56,63]) and pile-soil friction tests (Uesugi et al., Boylan et al.) [55,64].

5. Conclusions

A series of centrifuge tests were conducted to evaluate the monotonic and cyclic behavior of a large-diameter monopile installed in dry sand. The effects of loading level, number of cycles, and loading rates were investigated through the tests. Firstly, the load-displacement response and stiffness variation were assessed for monotonic and cyclic loading levels. Secondly, bending moment development under monotonic and cyclic loads was evaluated. In these tests, the wind tower and turbine were simplified as a hollow tower with a centroid head mass using 1 g and centrifuge scaling laws. The lateral load was applied by utilizing an actuator mounted on the soil container to induce a constant rated displacement on the monopile. The following conclusions were drawn based on the interpretation of the centrifuge model test:

1. As the loading level increased, the initial stiffness ($k_{\theta(0)}$) decreased with the loading level due to the nonlinearity of the soil. For the FLS and SLS tests (0.3 ULS and 0.5 ULS), the stiffness was nearly constant with the number of cycles, indicating the entire wind turbine system's behavior was almost unaffected by the cyclic load. However, for the ULS test, the stiffness of the monopile gradually increased in the initial few cycles and then converged to a certain value. The lateral loading rate affects the stiffness response of the monopile.
2. The monopile bending moment increases with the lateral loading level for monotonic tests. The position with the maximum bending moment remained consistent at about 1D depth, regardless of the loading level and loading rate. However, the larger the bending moment monitored, the higher the loading rate. This resulted in large pile deformation at the same lateral load.
3. When the monopile was subjected to cyclic loading with FLS and SLS levels, the variation of the bending moment profiles with the number of cycles was insignificant. However, for the large cyclic loading test (ULS), the maximum bending moment gradually decreased as the number of loads increased. The reduction in the maximum bending moment occurred mainly at the initial few cycles and converged.
4. The cyclic loading rate effect was prominent in the ULS state. It was confirmed that the faster the loading rate, the larger the reduction in the maximum bending moment due to the densification of the soil adjacent to the pile.

In this study, the centrifuge test was conducted on a monopile thicker than the typical wall thickness (8.3% of the monopile diameter). Moreover, the installation process was not simulated, which can significantly affect the behavior of the monopile. The number of cycles and displacement-controlled loading tests are also limited to specific conditions. Therefore, the results of this study are valid only for specific experimental conditions, and more extensive experimental studies are needed to understand the behavior of various monopiles.

Author Contributions: Conceptualization, H.-J.P., Y.-H.J. and J.-G.H.; data curation, Y.-H.J., J.-H.K. and H.-J.P.; writing—original draft preparation, J. H.K. and Y. H.J.; writing review and editing, H.-J.P. and Y.-H.J.; supervision, H.-J.P.; project administration, H.-J.P.; formal analysis, J.-H.K. and J.-G.H.; investigation, Y.-H.J. All authors have read and agreed to the published version of the manuscript.

Funding: This study was supported by the Research Program funded by SeoulTech (Seoul National University of Science and Technology).

Institutional Review Board Statement: Not applicable.

Informed Consent Statement: Not applicable.

Data Availability Statement: Not applicable.

Conflicts of Interest: The authors declare no conflict of interest.

References

1. Houlsby, G.T.; Ibsen, L.B.; Byrne, B.W. Suction caissons for wind turbines. In *Frontiers in Offshore Geotechnics: ISFOG, Perth, WA, Australia;* CRC Press: Boca Raton, FL, USA, 2005; pp. 75–93.
2. Jeong, Y.H.; Kim, J.H.; Park, H.J.; Kim, D.S. Cyclic behavior of unit bucket for tripod foundation system supporting offshore wind turbine via model tests. *Wind. Energy* **2019**, *22*, 257–268. [CrossRef]
3. Matlock, H. Correlations for design of laterally loaded piles in soft clay. In Proceedings of the 2nd Offshore Technology Conference, Richardson, TX, USA, 21–23 April 1970; pp. 577–594.
4. Reese, L.C.; Cox, W.R.; Koop, F.D. Analysis of laterally loaded piles in sand. In Proceedings of the Offshore Technology Conference, Houston, TX, USA, 5–7 May 1974; pp. 473–483.
5. American Petroleum Institute. *Recommended Practice 2GEO—Geotechnical and Foundation Design Considerations*, 22nd ed.; RP2A-WSD; American Petroleum Institute: Washington, DC, USA, 2014.
6. *DNVGL-ST-0126;* Support Structures for Wind Turbines. Det Norske Veritas: Oslo, Norway, 2018.
7. Arany, L.; Bhattacharya, S.; Macdonald, J.H.; Hogan, S.J. Closed form solution of Eigen frequency of monopile supported offshore wind turbines in deeper waters incorporating stiffness of substructure and SSI. *Soil Dyn. Earthq. Eng.* **2016**, *83*, 18–32. [CrossRef]
8. Achmus, M.; Kuo, Y.S.; Abdel-Rahman, K. Behavior of monopile foundations under cyclic lateral load. *Comput. Geotech.* **2009**, *36*, 725–735. [CrossRef]
9. LeBlanc, C.; Houlsby, G.T.; Byrne, B.W. Response of stiff piles in sand to long-term cyclic lateral loading. *Géotechnique* **2010**, *60*, 79–90. [CrossRef]
10. Murchison, J.M.; O'Neill, M.W. Evaluation of p-y relationships in cohesionless soils. In *Analysis and Design of Pile Foundations;* ASCE: Reston, VA, USA, 1984; pp. 174–191.
11. American Petroleum Institute. *Recommended Practice for Planning. Designing and Constructing Fixed Offshore Platforms—Working Stress Design. RP2A-WSD*, 20th ed.; API: Houston, TX, USA, 2000.
12. Klinkvort, R.T.; Leth, C.T.; Hededal, O. Centrifuge modelling of a laterally cyclic loaded pile. *Int. J. Phys. Model.* **2010**, *7*, 959–964.
13. Hearn, E.N.; Edgers, L. Finite element analysis of an offshore wind turbine monopile. In *GeoFlorida 2010: Advances in Analysis, Modeling & Design;* ASCE: Reston, VA, USA, 2010; pp. 1857–1865.
14. Doherty, P.; Gavin, K. Laterally loaded monopile design for offshore wind farms. *Proc. Inst. Civ. Eng. Energy* **2012**, *165*, 7–17. [CrossRef]
15. Haiderali, A.; Cilingir, U.; Madabhushi, G. Lateral and axial capacity of monopiles for offshore wind turbines. *Indian Geotech. J.* **2013**, *43*, 181–194. [CrossRef]
16. Frick, D.; Achmus, M. An experimental study on the parameters affecting the cyclic lateral response of monopiles for offshore wind turbines in sand. *Soils Found.* **2020**, *60*, 1570–1587. [CrossRef]
17. Thieken, K.; Achmus, M.; Lemke, K.; Terceros, M. Evaluation of p-y approaches for large-diameter monopiles in sand. *Int. J. Offshore Polar Eng.* **2015**, *25*, 134–144. [CrossRef]
18. Choo, Y.W.; Kim, D. Experimental development of the p-y relationship for large-diameter offshore monopiles in sands: Centrifuge tests. *J. Geotech. Geoenviron.* **2016**, *142*, 04015058. [CrossRef]
19. Djillali, A.M. Numerical investigation of large-diameter monopiles in sands: Critical review and evaluation of both API and newly proposed p-y curves. *Int. J. Geomech.* **2018**, *18*, 04018141.
20. Rudolph, C.; Bienen, B.; Grabe, J. Effect of variation of the loading direction on the displacement accumulation of large-diameter piles under cyclic lateral loading in sand. *Can. Geotech. J.* **2014**, *51*, 1196–1206. [CrossRef]
21. Bienen, B.; Klinkvort, R.T.; O'Loughlin, C.D.; Zhu, F.; Byrne, B.W. Suction caissons in dense sand, part I: Installation, limiting capacity and drainage. *Géotechnique* **2018**, *68*, 937–952. [CrossRef]
22. Zhu, B.; Ren, J.; Yuan, S.; Zhu, J.; Yang, Q.; Gao, Y.; Kong, D. Centrifuge modeling of monotonic and cyclic lateral behavior of monopiles in sand. *J. Geotech. Geoenviron.* **2021**, *147*, 04021058. [CrossRef]
23. Foglia, A.; Ibsen, L.B.; Andersen, L.V.; Roesen, H.R. Physical modelling of bucket foundation under long-term cyclic lateral loading. In Proceedings of the Twenty-Second International Offshore and Polar Engineering Conference, Rhodes, Greece, 17–22 June 2012.
24. Andersen, K.H. Bearing capacity under cyclic loading—Offshore, along the coast, and on land. *Can. Geotech. J.* **2009**, *46*, 513–535. [CrossRef]
25. Byrne, B.W.; Houlsby, G.T. Experimental investigations of the response of suction caissons to transient combined loading. *J. Geotech. Geoenviron.* **2004**, *130*, 240–253. [CrossRef]
26. Staubach, P.; Machaček, J.; Tafili, M.; Wichtmann, T. A high-cycle accumulation model for clay and its application to monopile foundations. *Acta Geotech.* **2022**, *17*, 677–698. [CrossRef]
27. Achmus, M.; Abdel-Rahman, K.; Peralta, P. *On the Design of Monopile Foundations with Respect to Static and Quasi-Static Cyclic Loading;* European Wind Energy Association: Brussels, Belgium, 2005.
28. Kuo, Y.S.; Achmus, M.; Abdel-Rahman, K. Minimum embedded length of cyclic horizontally loaded monopiles. *J. Geotech. Geoenviron.* **2012**, *138*, 357–363. [CrossRef]
29. Møller, I.F.; Christiansen, T.H. Laterally Loaded Monopile in Dry and Saturated Sand-Static and Cyclic Loading: Experimental and Numerical Studies. Master's Thesis, Aalborg University, Aalborg, Denmark, 2011.

30. Bhattacharya, S.; Adhikari, S. Experimental validation of soil–structure interaction of offshore wind turbines. *Soil Dyn. Earthq. Eng.* **2011**, *31*, 805–816. [CrossRef]
31. Scharff, R.; Siems, M. Monopile foundations for offshore wind turbines–solutions for greater water depths. *Steel Constr.* **2013**, *6*, 47–53. [CrossRef]
32. Li, Z.; Haigh, S.K.; Bolton, M.D. Centrifuge modelling of mono-pile under cyclic lateral loads. In Proceedings of the 7th International Conference of Physical Modelling in Geotechnics, Zurich, Switzerland, 27 June–2 July 2010; pp. 965–970.
33. Klinkvort, R.T.; Hededal, O. Lateral response of monopile supporting an offshore wind turbine. In Proceedings of the Institution of Civil Engineers-Geotechnical Engineering; ICE Publishing: London, UK, 2013; Volume 166, pp. 147–158.
34. Su, L.; Lu, J.; Elgamal, A.; Arulmoli, A.K. Seismic performance of a pile-supported wharf: Three-dimensional finite element simulation. *Soil Dyn. Earthq. Eng.* **2017**, *95*, 167–179. [CrossRef]
35. Schofield, A.N. Cambridge geotechnical centrifuge operations. *Geotechnique* **1980**, *30*, 227–268. [CrossRef]
36. Taylor, R.E. *Geotechnical Centrifuge Technology*; CRC Press: Boca Raton, FL, USA, 2018.
37. Kim, D.S.; Kim, N.R.; Choo, Y.W.; Cho, G.C. A newly developed state-of-the-art geotechnical centrifuge in Korea. *KSCE J. Civ. Eng.* **2013**, *17*, 77–84. [CrossRef]
38. Jonkman, J.; Butterfield, S.; Musial, W.; Scott, G. *Definition of a 5-MW Reference Wind Turbine for Offshore System Development (No. NREL/TP-500-38060)*; National Renewable Energy Lab. (NREL): Golden, CO, USA, 2009.
39. Van der Tempel, J.; Molenaar, D.P. Wind turbine structural dynamics—A review of the principles for modern power generation, onshore and offshore. *Wind. Eng.* **2002**, *26*, 211–222. [CrossRef]
40. Iai, S.; Tobita, T.; Nakahara, T. Generalised scaling relations for dynamic centrifuge tests. *Geotechnique* **2005**, *55*, 355–362. [CrossRef]
41. Seong, J.T.; Ha, J.G.; Kim, J.H.; Park, H.J.; Kim, D.S. Centrifuge modeling to evaluate natural frequency and seismic behavior of offshore wind turbine considering SFSI. *Wind. Energy* **2017**, *20*, 1787–1800. [CrossRef]
42. Kim, J.H.; Choo, Y.W.; Kim, D.J.; Kim, D.S. Miniature cone tip resistance on sand in a centrifuge. *J. Geotech. Geoenviron.* **2016**, *142*, 04015090. [CrossRef]
43. Haiderali, A.; Nakashima, M.; Madabhushi, S. Cyclic lateral loading of monopiles for offshore wind turbines. In *Frontiers in Offshore Geotechnics III*, 1st ed.; Meyer, V., Ed.; CRC Press: Oslo, Norway, 2015; pp. 711–716.
44. Choo, Y.W.; Kim, D.; Park, J.H.; Kwak, K.; Kim, J.H.; Kim, D.S. Lateral response of large-diameter monopiles for offshore wind turbines from centrifuge model tests. *Geotech. Test.* **2014**, *37*, 107–120. [CrossRef]
45. Jo, S.B.; Ha, J.G.; Yoo, M.; Choo, Y.W.; Kim, D.S. Seismic behavior of an inverted T-shape flexible retaining wall via dynamic centrifuge tests. *Bull. Earthq. Eng.* **2014**, *12*, 961–980. [CrossRef]
46. Lo Presti, D.C.F.; Pedroni, S.; Crippa, V. Maximum dry density of cohesionless soil by pluviation and by ASTM D 4253-83: A comparative study. *Geotech. Testing J.* **1992**, *15*, 180–189.
47. Tabaroei, A.; Abrishami, S.; Hosseininia, E.S. Comparison between two different pluviation setups of sand specimens. *J. Mater. Civ. Eng.* **2017**, *29*, 04017157. [CrossRef]
48. Villalobos, F.A. Model Testing of Foundations for Offshore Wind Turbines. Ph.D. Thesis, University of Oxford, Oxford, UK, 2006.
49. Briaud, J.L.; Smith, T.O.; Meyer, B.J. Using the pressuremeter curve to design laterally loaded piles. In Proceedings of the Offshore Technology Conference, Houston, TX, USA, 2–5 May 1983.
50. LeBlanc, C. Design of Offshore Wind Turbine Support Structures. Ph.D. Thesis, Technical University of Denmark, Copenhagen, Denmark, 2009.
51. Budhu, M.; Davies, T.G. Nonlinear analysis of laterality loaded piles in cohesionless soils. *Can. Geotech. J.* **1987**, *24*, 289–296. [CrossRef]
52. Carter, J.P.; Kulhawy, F.H. *Analysis and Design of Drilled Shaft Foundations Socketed into Rock*; Electric Power Research Inst.: Palo Alto, CA, USA, 1988.
53. Poulos, H.G.; Hull, T.S. The role of analytical geomechanics in foundation engineering. In Proceedings of the 1989 Foundation Engineering Conference, Evanston, IL, USA, 25–29 June 1989; pp. 1578–1606.
54. Peire, K.; Nonneman, H.; Bosschem, E. Gravity based foundations for the Thornton Bank Offshore Wind Farm. *Terra Aqua* **2009**, *115*, 19–29.
55. Boylan, N.P.; White, D.J.; Brunning, P. Seabed friction on carbonate soils: Physical modelling of axial pipe-soil friction. In Proceedings of the Offshore Technology Conference, Houston, TX, USA, 5–8 May 2014.
56. Jeong, Y.H.; Lee, S.W.; Kim, J.H. Centrifuge modeling for the evaluation of the cyclic behavior of offshore wind turbine with tripod foundation. *Appl. Sci.* **2021**, *11*, 1718. [CrossRef]
57. Jeong, Y.H.; Kim, J.H.; Manandhar, S.; Ha, J.G.; Park, H.J.; Kim, D.S. Centrifuge modelling of drained pullout and compression cyclic behaviour of suction bucket. *Int. J. Phys. Model.* **2020**, *20*, 59–70. [CrossRef]
58. Wilson, D. Soil-Pile-Superstructure Interaction in Liquefying Sand and Soft Clay. Ph.D. Thesis, University of California, Davis, Davis, CA, USA, 1998.
59. Klinkvort, R.T. *Monopile Design through Centrifuge Technology*; OSIG Evening Geoforum, OSIG-SUT: London, UK, 2018.
60. Randolph, M.; Gourvenec, S. *Offshore Geotechnical Engineering*; CRC Press: Boca Raton, FL, USA, 2017.
61. Byrne, B.W.; McAdam, R.A.; Burd, H.J.; Beuckelaers, W.J.; Gavin, K.G.; Houlsby, G.T.; Zdravković, L. Monotonic laterally loaded pile testing in a stiff glacial clay till at Cowden. *Géotechnique* **2020**, *70*, 970–985. [CrossRef]

62. McAdam, R.A.; Byrne, B.W.; Houlsby, G.T.; Beuckelaers, W.J.; Burd, H.J.; Gavin, K.G.; Zdravković, L. Monotonic laterally loaded pile testing in a dense marine sand at Dunkirk. *Géotechnique* **2020**, *70*, 986–998. [CrossRef]
63. Jeong, Y.H.; Ko, K.W.; Kim, D.S.; Kim, J.H. Studies on cyclic behavior of tripod suction bucket foundation system supporting offshore wind turbine using centrifuge model test. *Wind. Energy* **2021**, *24*, 515–529. [CrossRef]
64. Uesugi, M.; Kishida, H.; Tsubakihara, Y. Friction between sand and steel under repeated loading. *Soils Found.* **1989**, *29*, 127–137. [CrossRef]

Journal of
Marine Science and Engineering

MDPI

Article

Dynamic Interaction Factor of Pipe Group Piles Considering the Scattering Effect of Passive Piles

Mingchen Zhong and Kun Meng *

College of Transportation, Shandong University of Science and Technology, Qingdao 266000, China; 202001130327@sdust.edu.cn
* Correspondence: skd996565@sdust.edu.cn

Abstract: Based on the plane–strain assumption, a calculation model of pile–soil–pile vertical coupling vibration response considering the scattering effect of passive piles is established in this paper. Using this model, the vertical displacement expressions of pile core soil and pile surrounding soil, soil displacement attenuation function, and longitudinal complex impedance are obtained. Then, based on the strict pile–soil coupling effect, the displacement of the active pile under vertical load and scattering effect, as well as the displacement of the passive pile under incident waves, are solved separately. A new type of dynamic interaction factor for pipe group piles is derived by introducing scattering effect factors. A numerical example shows that the degenerate solution in this paper is in good agreement with the existing solution, which verifies the rationality of the solution. Considering the scattering effect is helpful in improving the accuracy of vibration response analysis of pile groups. The variation in parameters such as slenderness ratio, pile spacing, and outer diameter has significant effects on the interaction factor, and compared with the solid pile, the influence of parameter change on the pipe pile is smaller.

Keywords: passive pile; pipe pile; pile group; scattering effect; pile–pile dynamic interaction factor

1. Introduction

In recent years, with the gradual extension of human activities into the ocean, the construction demands of marine engineering have increased sharply. In order to adapt to the complex marine environment, these structures generally use pile groups as their foundation type. Under the action of dynamic loads such as wind and sea waves, the vibration of pile groups' foundation needs to consider multidimensional factors. It is necessary to consider the pile–soil interaction and the mechanical response analysis of pile–pile coupling, which has always been a hot issue in the fields of soil dynamics, geotechnical engineering, and structure foundation interaction [1–3].

Poulos [4] first fully studied pile–soil interaction and proposed the superposition principle, initially proposed the pile–pile dynamic response interaction factor to reflect the pile foundation interaction, and considered the influence of parameter changes such as Poisson's ratio on the settlement behavior of pile groups. Kaynia et al. [5] solved the dynamic equation of pile groups using the boundary integral method and continuous medium Green's function and obtained relevant solutions. Mylonakis et al. [6] preliminarily analyzed the vibration impact of the source pile on the receiving pile based on Randolph and Wroth's shear displacement model and proved that the impact of pile vibration cannot be ignored. On this basis, Mylonakis et al. [7] deduced the pile–pile dynamic interaction factor in uniform geology using the Winkler foundation model and analyzed the influence of soil layer and impedance on the interaction factor. Poulos et al. [8] proposed a double pile interaction coefficient and analyzed the relationship between settlement behavior and interaction coefficient. In addition, Nogami [9], Mylonakis [10], Chen [11], and others carried out pile group vibration research using the Winkler foundation model, taking into account the incident wave generated by the active pile vibration. Bahaa [12], Randolph [13], and others considered various effects of piles and proposed new interaction factors to better reflect the interaction between piles. Mylonakis [10], Wang [14], Wang [15], Zhang [16], and others reasonably layered the foundation, solved the interaction factor of solid pile type in layered soil, and fully analyzed the influence of parameter changes on the interaction factor. Chen et al. [17] and Cao et al. [18] broke down the problem into an extended soil mass and two fictitious piles characterized, respectively, by the Young's modulus of the soil and that of the difference between the pile and soil and solved the interaction coefficient of double piles in half space based on the model of Muki and Sternberg. Results confirmed the validity of the proposed approach and portrayed the influence of the governing parameters on the pile interaction. Luan et al. [19] considered the infrasound waves generated by passive piles, solved the vibration displacement of each part of the solid pile, and proposed an interaction factor.

Due to the fact that the core soil cannot be ignored in the calculation and analysis of pipe piles, there will inevitably be differences in the solution analysis of the pile group model mentioned above. Liu [20] extended the traditional interaction factor to the type of pipe piles on the basis of the Winkler foundation model, conducted appropriate parameter analysis, and concluded that parameter changes had a greater impact on the interaction factor. Yan [21] and Liu [22] solved the dynamic interaction factor of pipe piles in saturated soil on the basis of the previous work and conducted appropriate parameter change analysis.

In the complex and changeable working environment at sea, small-spacing pile groups are generally used in marine infrastructure construction. When the pile spacing is less than eight times the diameter of pile foundation, the interaction between pile foundation and pile foundation needs to be considered. Generally, the pile foundation with a vibration wave generated by a load is called the active pile, and the pile foundation nearby affected by the vibration wave is called the passive pile. The above study only considers the vibration impact of the active pile on the passive pile, ignoring that the vibration of the passive pile in turn will cause the secondary vibration of the active pile, which will cause large errors. At this time, it is more appropriate to consider the scattering effect of passive piles [19]. Pipe piles have been widely studied and used in engineering in recent years [23–26], but there is a lack of comparative analysis of pipe pile types and solid pile types in the current pile group vibration research. Therefore, based on the continuum theory and the superposition principle [5,27], this paper extends the solid pile type to the pipe pile type and considers the scattering wave generated by the passive pile vibration, establishes the pile groups calculation model, introduces the scattering effect factor, solves the new interaction factor, and explores the difference in dynamic response characteristics of the pipe pile and the solid pile when considering the scattering effect of passive piles. Based on the assumption of small deformation, this paper only considers the vertical deformation of pipe piles and soil and ignores the lateral deformation. In the subsequent research work, the lateral deformation will be considered for detailed theoretical improvement.

2. Physical Model Considering the Passive Piles Scattering Effect

2.1. Pile Groups Calculation Model and Basic Assumptions

Figure 1 is the calculation model of pile groups under vertical dynamic load. As shown in the figure, the pipe pile parameter symbol H is the pile foundation length, r_0 is the inner diameter, r_1 is the outer diameter, A_p is the cross-sectional area of the pile body, S is the pile spacing, ρ_p is the pile body density, and E_p is the elastic modulus. The soil parameter symbol $G_{s0}(G_{s1})$ is the shear modulus of soil, $\rho_{s0}(\rho_{s1})$ is the damping ratio, and $\delta_{s0}(\delta_{s1})$ is the density. The relevant parameters of pile core soil and pile surrounding soil are denoted by subscripts $s0$ and $s1$. The vertical harmonic load $P_G e^{i\omega t}$ acts on the top of the pile foundation, where ω is the excitation circle frequency, $\mathrm{i} = \sqrt{-1}$. The mathematical model established in this paper conforms to the following assumptions:

(1) At the pile–soil interface, the stress and displacement are continuous without relative sliding [28,29];

(2) The pile core soil and the soil around the pile are regarded as homogeneous viscoelastic bodies without anisotropy;

(3) The pile group foundation is placed on rigid bedrock;

(4) The soil around the pile is divided into infinite thin layers without interaction between layers.

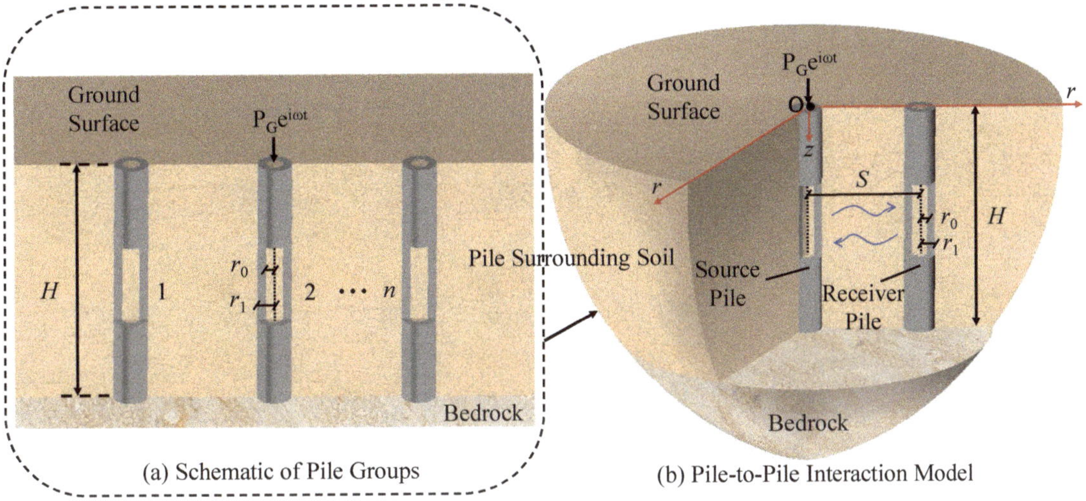

Figure 1. Pile group calculation model.

2.2. Pile Group Model Considering Scattering Effect

Most previous studies only considered the influence of active piles of the solid pile type on passive piles, ignoring the scattered waves generated by passive piles and the dynamic response of the pipe pile type. In fact, the scattered waves generated by passive piles change the original soil stress field, and the influence degree of the pile group's interaction with pipe pile type is also different; its mechanism is shown in Figure 2. Under the action of vertical dynamic load P_1, the active pile generates vertical displacement W^P_{1-1} and incident waves in the soil. When the incident wave propagates S distance in the soil around the pile, the soil displacement is W^{s1}_{2-1}, which causes the passive pile to produce displacement W^P_{2-1} and generates scattered waves in the soil. The scattered wave propagates to the position of the active pile, causing its vibration to produce vertical displacement W^P_{1-2}. Therefore, the mechanism of pile–pile dynamic interaction considering the scattering effect of passive piles in this paper is:

(1) The derivation of the displacement of the active pile under vertical dynamic load via the analytical method W^P_{1-1}.

(2) The active pile vibration produces an incident wave that propagates radially along the soil around the pile, and its displacement can be expressed as:

$$W^{s1}_{2-1} = \mu(S) W^P_{1-1} \tag{1}$$

where $\mu(S)$ is the displacement attenuation function,

$$\mu(S) = \frac{W^{s1}(S)}{W^{s1}(r_1)} \tag{2}$$

(3) The incident wave propagates to the passive pile, causing vertical vibration and displacement and generating a scattered wave. The scattered wave propagates to the active pile, causing its secondary vibration.

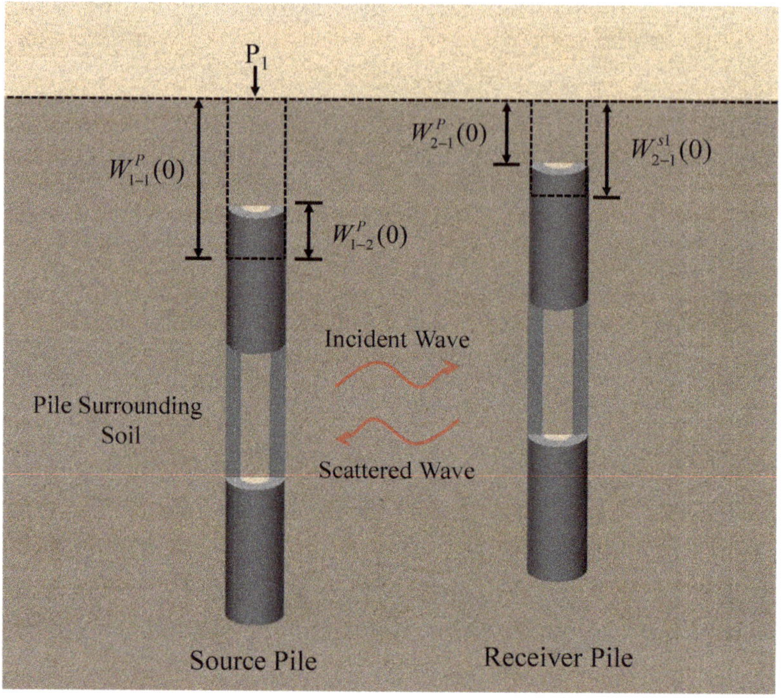

Figure 2. Action mechanism.

3. Solution of Governing Equations and Physical Models

3.1. Soil Impedance

Based on the plane strain assumption, the soil governing equation established in this section conforms to the following assumptions:

(1) It neglects the radial displacement of pile core soil and pile surrounding soil;

(2) It ignores the vertical stress gradient of pile core soil and pile-surrounding soil.

Therefore, the governing equation of soil under vertical dynamic load is:

$$\frac{d^2W^{s0}}{dr} + \frac{1}{r}\frac{dW^{s0}}{dr} + \frac{\omega^2\rho_{s0}}{G^*_{s0}}W^{s0} = 0 \tag{3}$$

$$\frac{d^2W^{s1}}{dr} + \frac{1}{r}\frac{dW^{s1}}{dr} + \frac{\omega^2\rho_{s1}}{G^*_{s1}}W^{s1} = 0 \tag{4}$$

where W^{s0} is the vertical displacement of the pile core soil and W^{s1} is the vertical displacement of the soil around the pile. ρ_{s0} is the density of soil in the pile core and ρ_{s1} is the density of soil around the pile. $G^*_{s0} = G_{s0}(1+2i\delta_{s0})$, $G^*_{s1} = G_{s1}(1+2i\delta_{s1})$ is the complex shear modulus of soil mass.

The solutions of Equations (3) and (4) are obtained as follows:

$$W^{s0} = A_0K_0(q_0r) + B_0I_0(q_0r) \tag{5}$$

$$W^{s1} = A_1K_0(q_1r) + B_1I_0(q_1r) \tag{6}$$

where $q_0 = \sqrt{\frac{-\rho_{s0}\omega^2}{G^*_{s0}}}$, $q_1 = \sqrt{\frac{-\rho_{s1}\omega^2}{G^*_{s1}}}$. $I_0(\,)$ and $K_0(\,)$ are modified Bessel functions of type I and type II, respectively, and A_0, B_0, A_1, and B_1 are the coefficients to be determined.

Consider the boundary conditions at $r = 0$ and infinity and the displacement continuity conditions of the pile–soil interface:

$$W^{s0}\big|_{r=0} = \text{Finite value},\ W^{s0}\Big|_{r=r_0} = W^P_{1-1} \tag{7}$$

$$W^{s1}\big|_{r\to\infty} = 0,\ W^{s1}\Big|_{r\to r_1} = W^P_{1-1} \tag{8}$$

The solution is as follows: $A_0 = 0$, $B_0 = \frac{W^P_{1-1}}{I_0(q_0r_0)}$, $A_1 = \frac{W^P_{1-1}}{K_0(q_1r_1)}$, $B_1 = 0$, namely:

$$W^{s0} = \frac{W^P_{1-1}}{I_0(q_0r_0)} I_0(q_0r) \tag{9}$$

$$W^{s1} = \frac{W^P_{1-1}}{K_0(q_1r_1)} K_0(q_1r) \tag{10}$$

Further, the displacement attenuation function $\mu(S)$ of the soil at position s away from the active pile can be obtained as follows:

$$\mu(S) = \frac{K_0(q_1S)}{K_0(q_1r_1)} \tag{11}$$

Based on the relationship between stress and strain, the soil shear stress can be obtained using Formulas (9) and (10):

$$\tau_{s0} = G^*_{s0}\frac{dW^{s0}}{dr} = -\frac{G^*_{s0}q_0W^P_{1-1}}{I_0(q_0r_0)} I_1(q_0r) \tag{12}$$

$$\tau_{s1} = G^*_{s1}\frac{dU}{dr} = -\frac{G^*_{s1}q_1W^P_{1-1}}{K_0(q_1r_1)} K_1(q_1r) \tag{13}$$

Thus, the soil resistance f_{s0} and f_{s1} borne by the pile foundation are:

$$f_{s0} = 2\pi r_0\tau_{s0}\Big|_{r=r_0} = -\psi_{s0}W^P_{1-1} \tag{14}$$

$$f_{s1} = -2\pi r_1\tau_{s1}\Big|_{r=r_1} = \psi_{s1}W^P_{1-1} \tag{15}$$

where $\psi_{s0} = 2\pi r_0\frac{G^*_{s0}q_0I_1(q_0r_0)}{I_0(q_0r_0)}$, $\psi_{s1} = 2\pi r_1\frac{G^*_{s1}q_1K_1(q_1r_1)}{K_0(q_1r_1)}$.

3.2. Displacement of the Active Pile under External Load

Based on the elastodynamic analysis, the governing equation of the active pile under external load can be established as follows:

$$E_pA_p\frac{d^2W^P_{1-1}}{dz^2} + \sigma\omega^2W^P_{1-1} + f_{s0} - f_{s1} = 0 \tag{16}$$

where $\sigma = \rho_pA_p$.

We substitute Formulas (14) and (15) into Formula (16):

$$E_pA_p\frac{d^2W^P_{1-1}}{dz^2} + (\sigma\omega^2 - \psi_{s0} - \psi_{s1})W^P_{1-1} = 0 \tag{17}$$

The solution is as follows:

$$W^P_{1-1} = A_{1-1}e^{\xi z} + B_{1-1}e^{-\xi z} \tag{18}$$

where $\xi^2 = \frac{\psi_{s0}+\psi_{s1}-\sigma\omega^2}{E_pA_p}$. A_{1-1}, B_{1-1} are the coefficients to be determined.

Consider the boundary conditions at $z = 0$ and $z = H$:

$$\frac{dW^P_{1-1}}{dz}|_{z=0} = -\frac{P_1}{E_pA_p} \tag{19}$$

$$W^P_{1-1}|_{z=H} = 0 \tag{20}$$

where P_1 is the external load acting on the active pile.

By introducing the pile foundation displacement expression (18) into the boundary conditions in (19) and (20), we obtain:

$$A_{1-1} = -\frac{P_1}{E_pA_p\xi(1+e^{2H\xi})} \tag{21}$$

$$B_{1-1} = \frac{e^{2H\xi}P_1}{E_pA_p\xi(1+e^{2H\xi})} \tag{22}$$

3.3. Passive Piles Displacement Caused by Incident Waves

By introducing Equations (11) and (18) into Equation (1), we can derive that the soil displacement at distance S of the incident wave is:

$$W^{s1}_{2-1} = \frac{K_0(q_1S)}{K_0(q_1r_1)}(A_{1-1}e^{\xi z} + B_{1-1}e^{-\xi z}) \tag{23}$$

The passive pile has dynamic response under the action of the incident wave. At this time, based on the elastodynamic analysis, the passive pile control equation is established:

$$E_pA_p\frac{d^2W^P_{2-1}}{dz^2} + \sigma\omega^2W^P_{2-1} - \psi_{s1}(W^P_{2-1} - W^{s1}_{2-1}) - \psi_{s0}W^P_{2-1} = 0 \tag{24}$$

The solution is as follows:

$$W^P_{2-1} = \frac{\psi_{s1}\mu(S)}{2\xi E_pA_p}z(-A_{1-1}e^{\xi z} + B_{1-1}e^{-\xi z}) + A_{2-1}e^{\xi z} + B_{2-1}e^{-\xi z} \tag{25}$$

where A_{2-1} and B_{2-1} are the coefficients to be determined.

Consider the boundary conditions at $z = 0$ and $z = H$:

$$\frac{dW^P_{2-1}}{dz}|_{z=0} = 0 \tag{26}$$

$$W^P_{2-1}|_{z=H} = 0 \tag{27}$$

Introducing Equation (25) into Equations (26) and (27), the undetermined coefficients of the governing equation are:

$$\begin{aligned} A_{2-1} &= \psi_{s1}\mu(S)\frac{A_{1-1}-B_{1-1}-B_{1-1}\xi H+A_{1-1}\xi He^{2\xi H}}{2E_pA_p\xi^2(e^{2\xi H}+1)} \\ &= -\frac{\psi_{s1}\mu(S)P_1(1+e^{2\xi H}+2\xi He^{2\xi H})}{2E_p^2A_p^2\xi^3(e^{2\xi H}+1)^2} \end{aligned} \tag{28}$$

$$\begin{aligned} B_{2-1} &= \psi_{s1}\mu(S)\frac{B_{1-1}e^{2\xi H}+A_{1-1}\xi He^{2\xi H}-B_{1-1}\xi H-A_{1-1}e^{2\xi H}}{2E_pA_p\xi^2(e^{2\xi H}+1)} \\ &= \frac{\psi_{s1}\mu(S)P_1e^{2\xi H}(1+e^{2\xi H}-2\xi H)}{2E_p^2A_p^2\xi^3(e^{2\xi H}+1)^2} \end{aligned} \tag{29}$$

3.4. Secondary Displacement of Active Piles Caused by Scattered Waves

Considering the scattered wave generated by the passive pile, the soil displacement at position S from the passive pile can be obtained by introducing Equations (11) and (25) into Equation (1) as:

$$W_{1-2}^{s1} = \mu(S)W_{2-1}^{P} = \mu(S)[\frac{\psi_{s1}\mu(S)}{2\xi E_p A_p}z(-A_{1-1}e^{\xi z} + B_{1-1}e^{-\xi z}) + A_{2-1}e^{\xi z} + B_{2-1}e^{-\xi z}] \quad (30)$$

The active pile receives the scattered wave and causes a dynamic response. Based on the elastodynamic analysis,, the control equation of the active pile is established:

$$E_p A_p \frac{d^2 W_{1-2}^{P}}{dz^2} + \sigma\omega^2 W_{1-2}^{P} - \psi_{s1}(W_{1-2}^{P} - W_{1-2}^{s1}) - \psi_{s0}W_{1-2}^{P} = 0 \quad (31)$$

The solution is:

$$\begin{aligned} W_{1-2}^{P} = {} & z[\tfrac{\psi_{s1}^2\mu(S)^2}{8\xi^2 E_p^2 A_p^2}A_{1-1}z - \tfrac{\psi_{s1}\mu(S)}{2\xi E_p A_p}A_{2-1} - \tfrac{\psi_{s1}^2\mu(S)^2}{8\xi^3 E_p^2 A_p^2}A_{1-1}]e^{\xi z} + z[\tfrac{\psi_{s1}^2\mu(S)^2}{8\xi^2 E_p^2 A_p^2}B_{1-1}z \\ & + \tfrac{\psi_{s1}\mu(S)}{2\xi E_p A_p}B_{2-1} + \tfrac{\psi_{s1}^2\mu(S)^2}{8\xi^3 E_p^2 A_p^2}B_{1-1}]e^{-\xi z} + A_{1-2}e^{\xi z} + B_{1-2}e^{-\xi z} \end{aligned} \quad (32)$$

where A_{1-2} and B_{1-2} are the coefficients to be determined.

At this time, only the scattering wave is considered. According to the superposition principle, the boundary conditions are:

$$\frac{dW_{1-2}^{P}}{dz}|_{z=0} = 0 \quad (33)$$

$$W_{1-2}^{P}|_{z=H} = 0 \quad (34)$$

Introducing Equation (32) into Equations (33) and (34), the undetermined coefficients of the governing equation are:

$$A_{1-2} = -\frac{V_1 + e^{\xi H}V_2\xi}{\xi + \xi e^{2\xi H}} \quad (35)$$

$$B_{1-2} = \frac{e^{\xi H}(e^{\xi H}V_1 - V_2\xi)}{\xi + \xi e^{2\xi H}} \quad (36)$$

where:

$$V_1 = \frac{\mu(S)^2\psi_{s1}^2(B_{1-1} - A_{1-1})}{8A_p^2E_p^2\xi^3} + \frac{\mu(S)\psi_{s1}(B_{2-1} - A_{2-1})}{2A_pE_p\xi} = \frac{\mu(S)^2\psi_{s1}^2P_1}{8A_p^3E_p^3\xi^4} + \frac{\mu(S)\psi_{s1}P_1}{2A_p^2E_p^2\xi^3} \quad (37)$$

$$\begin{aligned} V_2 = {} & H\left[\frac{\mu(S)^2\psi_{s1}^2}{8A_p^2E_p^2\xi^2}A_{1-1}H - \frac{\mu(S)\psi_{s1}}{2A_pE_p\xi}A_{2-1} - \frac{\mu(S)^2\psi_{s1}^2}{8A_p^2E_p^2\xi^3}A_{1-1}\right]e^{\xi H} \\ & + H\left[\frac{\mu(S)^2\psi_{s1}^2}{8A_p^2E_p^2\xi^2}B_{1-1}H + \frac{\mu(S)\psi_{s1}}{2A_pE_p\xi}B_{2-1} + \frac{\mu(S)^2\psi_{s1}^2}{8A_p^2E_p^2\xi^3}B_{1-1}\right]e^{-\xi H} \\ & = \frac{\mu(S)^2\psi_{s1}^2P_1He^{\xi H}(3 + 3e^{2\xi H} + 2\xi He^{2\xi H} - 2\xi H)}{4A_p^3E_p^3\xi^4(1 + e^{2\xi H})^2} \end{aligned} \quad (38)$$

3.5. A New Interaction Factor Considering Scattering Effect of Passive Piles

Mylonakis et al. [10] and Dobry et al. [30] deduced the traditional interaction factor in the previous study, which only considered the incident wave generated by the vibration of the active pile and ignored the scattering effect of the passive pile. The expression is:

$$\alpha = \frac{W_{2-1}^{P}}{W_{1-1}^{P}} \tag{39}$$

The model only quantifies the unidirectional effect of active pile vibration on passive piles. However, in the pile groups, the interaction between piles is mutual. There is not only the impact of the active pile on the passive pile, but also the impact of the passive pile on the active pile. Therefore, for pile groups with small spacing, the influence of scattered waves generated by passive piles on active piles cannot be ignored. Therefore, the scattering effect factor γ is introduced in this paper, and the scattering effect of passive piles is included in the interaction analysis between pile groups. Its mathematical expression is:

$$\gamma = \frac{W_{1-2}^{P}}{W_{1-1}^{P}} \tag{40}$$

The scattering effect factor is introduced into Equation (39), and the new double pile interaction factor is obtained:

$$\alpha = \frac{W_{2-1}^{P}}{W_{1-1}^{P} - W_{1-2}^{P}} = \frac{W_{2-1}^{P}}{(1-\gamma)W_{1-1}^{P}} \tag{41}$$

4. Example Analysis

The parameter system for the example analysis is shown in Table 1:

Table 1. Example parameters.

$E_p/E_s = 6.5 \times 10^3$	$H/d = 40$	$S/d = 2$	$\rho_p/\rho_s = 1.25$
$\nu_s = 0.4$	$\delta_s = 0.05$	$r_0 = 0.3$	$r_1 = 0.6$

4.1. Comparative Analysis

The obtained solution is reduced to a solid pile to verify the rationality of this derivation and to explore the difference between the traditional model and the model considering the scattering effect of the passive piles. The obtained dynamic interaction factors of pile groups are compared with the solutions of Mylonakis et al. [10]. It can be seen from Figure 3 that the degenerated solutions in this paper are in good agreement with the existing solutions. It can be seen from the figure that in the case of small spacing, the scattering effect has a certain impact on the pile–pile dynamic interaction factor. In the range of $a_0 < 0.75$, the real part of the solution in this paper is greater than the Mylonakis et al. [10] solution; in the range of $a_0 > 0.75$, the real part of the solution in this paper is smaller than that of the traditional result. For the imaginary part of the interaction factor, the above situation also exists, and the corresponding frequency is $a_0 = 0.5$. Therefore, considering the scattering effect in pile group analysis can improve the accuracy.

4.2. Parameter Analysis

Figure 4 shows the difference between the change in interaction factors of pipe pile type and solid pile type caused by the change in slenderness ratio when considering the scattering effect of passive piles in 1×2 pile groups, where $r_0 = 0.2$. Within the frequency range shown in the figure, the interaction factors of pipe piles and solid piles show certain oscillation characteristics. Due to the existence of pile core soil, the acting force of pipe piles consumes part of the energy, the oscillation amplitude is small, and the interaction between pile groups is smaller. As the slenderness ratio increases, the oscillation frequency decreases gradually. In the range of $a_0 < 0.6$, the real part of the interaction factor increases gradually; in the range of $a_0 < 1.1$, the amplitude of the imaginary part of the interaction factor increases gradually. This is because in the low-frequency range, the longer the pile foundation, the more difficult it is for the load to be transmitted to the bedrock, the greater the impact on the soil is around the pile, and the more obvious the interaction between piles. In the range of $a_0 > 1.2$, the amplitude level of the interaction factor of solid pile type gradually increases with the increase in slenderness ratio, but when the slenderness ratio is greater than 60, the variation amplitude decreases, because the influence of pile top load on the soil around the pile is mainly concentrated in the upper soil, and when the pile length reaches a certain value, the influence of vibration on adjacent piles does not increase significantly. At the same time, in the above change trend, the change range of pile group interaction of pipe pile type is small, because the existence and length of pile core soil increase, the force generated on the pipe pile increases, and the energy consumed increases, indicating that compared with the solid pile type, the change in slenderness ratio has less interference with the pile groups interaction of pipe pile type.

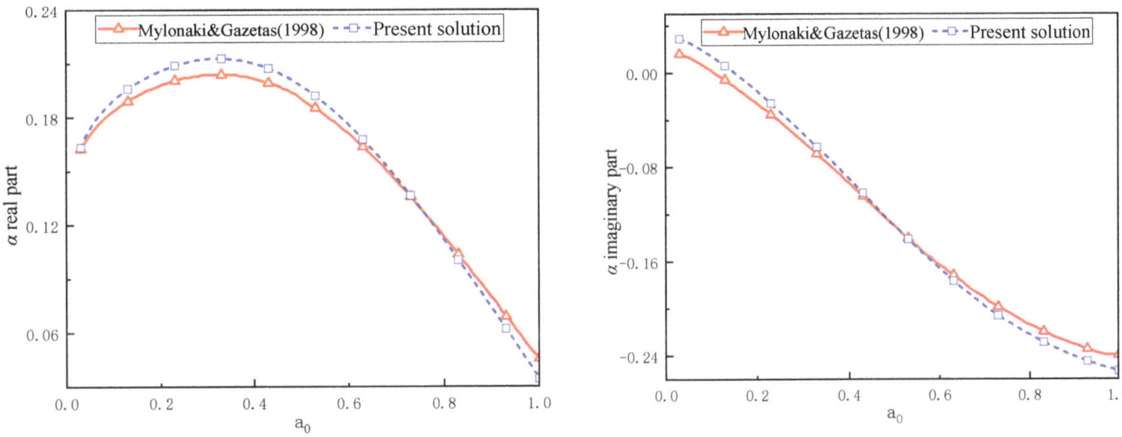

(**a**) α real part (**b**) α imaginary part

Figure 3. A comparison between the degenerate solution of this paper and the solution of Mylonakis and Gazetas (1998) [10].

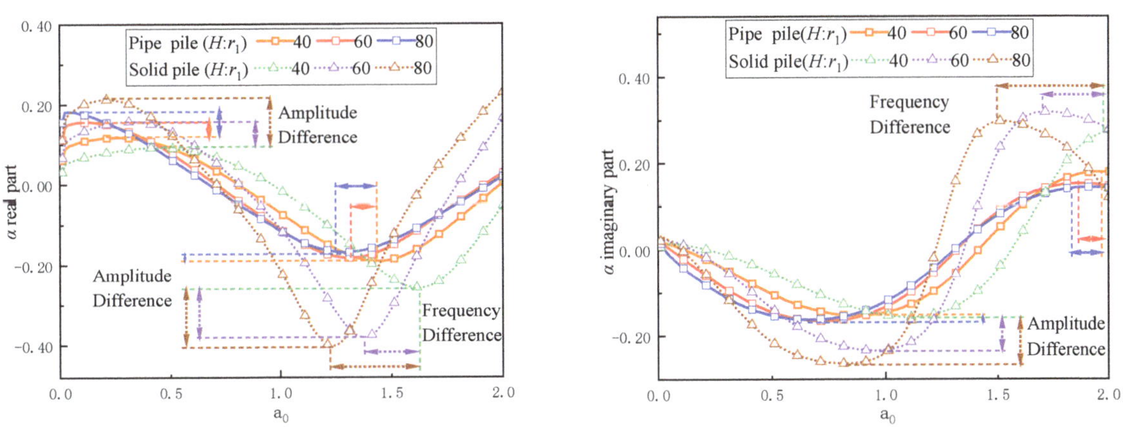

(**a**) α real part (**b**) α imaginary part

Figure 4. The difference between the changes in interaction factors of two kinds of 1 × 2 pile groups caused by the change in slenderness ratio.

Figure 5 shows the difference between the change in interaction factors of pipe pile type and solid pile type caused by the change in pile spacing when considering the scattering effect of passive piles in 1 × 2 pile groups. It can be seen from the figure that the interaction factors of pipe piles and solid piles show certain oscillation characteristics. Due to the existence of pile core soil, the acting force of pipe piles consumes part of the energy, the oscillation amplitude is small, and the interaction between pile groups is smaller. With the increase in pile spacing, the oscillation amplitude level decreases gradually, and the change in pipe pile is small. The oscillation frequency decreases gradually, and the difference between the real part and the virtual part is small. This is because when $a_0 < 1.5$, the shear wave generated by the pile foundation vibration attenuates rapidly, and its influence on the soil around the pile is small. Therefore, the greater the pile spacing, the less obvious the interaction between pile groups. At the same time, in the above change trend, the change range of pile groups interaction of pipe pile type is small because the incident wave and scattered wave generated by the vibration in the soil around the pile weaken with the increase in pile spacing, and the force of pile core soil on the pipe pile is more prominent, indicating that compared with the solid pile type, the change in pile spacing has less interference on the pile groups interaction of pipe pile type.

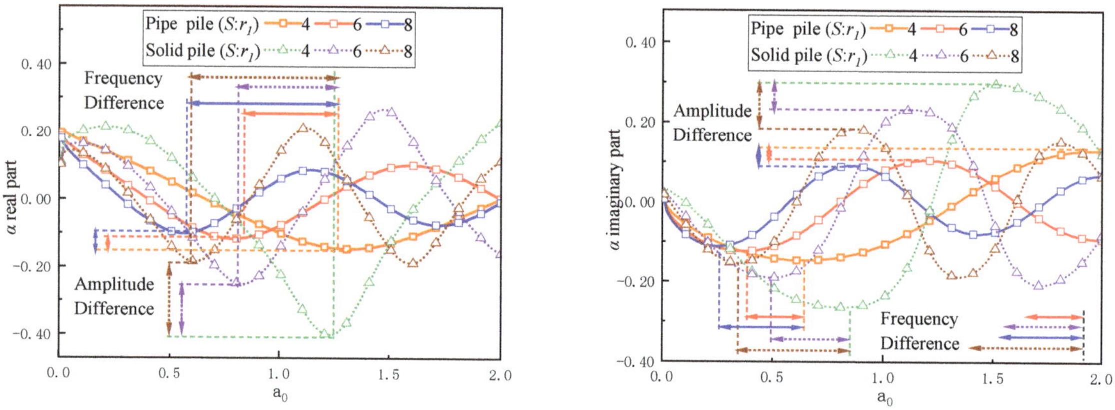

(a) α real part (b) α imaginary part

Figure 5. The difference between the changes in interaction factors of two kinds of 1 × 2 pile groups caused by the change in pile spacing.

Figure 6 shows the difference between the change in interaction factor of pipe pile type and solid pile type caused by the change in outer diameter when considering the scattering effect of passive piles in 1 × 2 pile groups. It can be seen from the figure that the interaction factors of pipe pile and solid pile show certain oscillation characteristics. Due to the existence of pile core soil, the acting force of pipe pile consumes part of energy, the oscillation amplitude is small, and the interaction between pile groups is smaller. With the increase in outer diameter, the oscillation amplitude increases gradually; the oscillation frequency increases gradually because the pile wall becomes thicker and its stiffness stronger, and the vibration effect of the pile foundation is strengthened. At the same time, in the above trends, the change range of the pile group interaction of pipe pile type is small, because the pile wall of the pipe pile is thin, and there is the effect of pile core soil on the pile, indicating that compared with the solid pile type, the change in outer diameter has less interference on the interaction of the pipe pile.

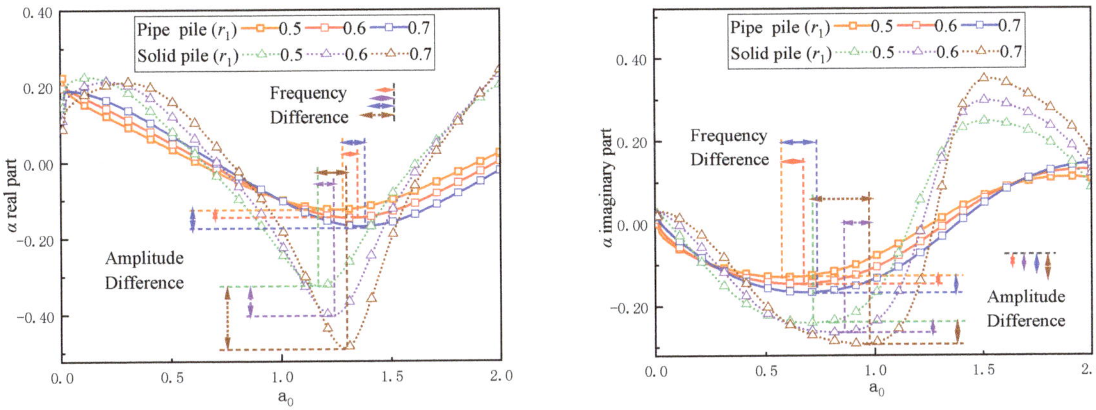

(a) α real part **(b)** α imaginary part

Figure 6. The difference in the change in interaction factor between two kinds of 1 × 2 pile groups caused by the change in outer diameter.

Figure 7 shows the difference between the change in interaction factors of pipe pile type and solid pile type caused by the change in pile–soil modulus ratio when considering the scattering effect of passive piles in 1 × 2 pile groups. Within the frequency range shown in the figure, the interaction factors of pipe piles and solid piles show certain oscillation characteristics. Due to the existence of pile core soil, the acting force of pipe piles consumes part of the energy, the oscillation amplitude is small, and the interaction between pile groups is smaller. With the increase in pile–soil modulus ratio, the oscillation frequency decreases gradually, and the change range of the pipe pile is larger. In the range of $a_0 > 1.0$, the amplitude level of the interaction factor gradually increases because the modulus of soil around the pile decreases and its constraint effect on the pile foundation decreases, so the interaction between pile groups is enhanced. In the amplitude change, the change amplitude of the pipe pile is not obvious because the existing pile core soil has a binding effect on the pile foundation, so the interaction between pile groups is not obvious, indicating that compared with the solid pile type, the change in pile–soil modulus ratio has less interference on the interaction between pile groups of pipe pile type, but has greater interference on the oscillation frequency.

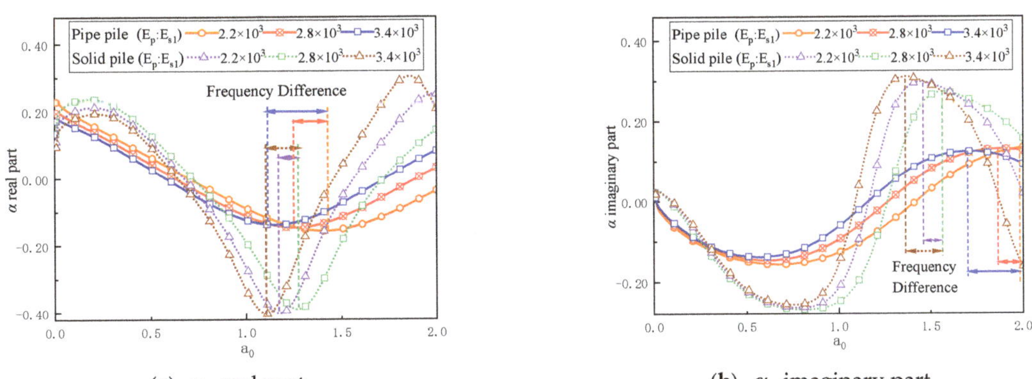

(a) α real part **(b)** α imaginary part

Figure 7. The difference between the change in interaction factors of two 1 × 2 pile groups caused by the change in pile–soil modulus ratio.

The following is the difference analysis of the change in interaction factors between pipe pile type and solid pile type caused by the change in length diameter ratio and pile spacing when considering the scattering effect of passive piles in 2 × 2 pile groups. Figure 8 shows the designed 2 × 2 pile groups model. Unless otherwise specified, the model parameters are the same as those of the 1 × 2 pile groups.

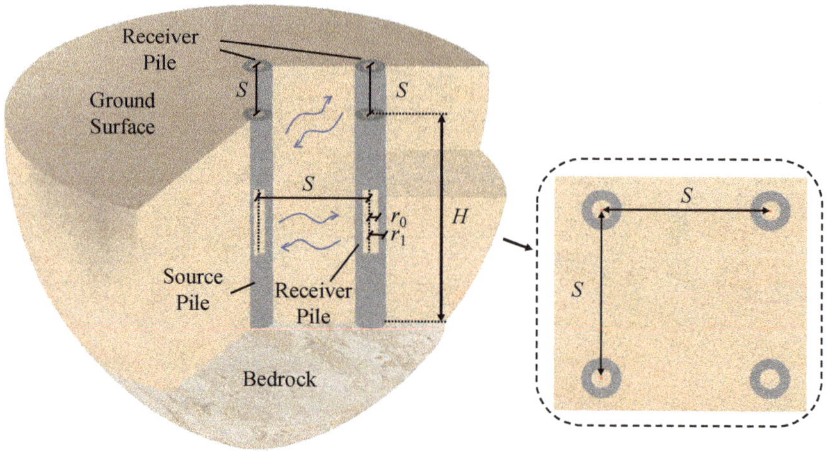

Figure 8. 2 × 2 schematic diagram of pile groups model.

Figure 9 shows the difference between the change in interaction factors of pipe pile type and solid pile type caused by the change in slenderness ratio when considering the scattering effect of passive piles in 2 × 2 pile groups. In the frequency range shown in the figure, the interaction factors of pipe pile and solid pile show certain oscillation characteristics, in which the oscillation amplitude of the pipe pile is larger in the low-frequency range, and the difference between the two amplitudes is smaller in the high-frequency range. As the slenderness ratio increases, the oscillation frequency decreases gradually. In the range of $a_0 < 1.0$, the amplitude of the imaginary part of the interaction factor increases gradually. This is because in the low-frequency range, the longer the pile foundation is, the more difficult it is for the load to be transmitted to the bedrock, the greater the impact on the soil around the pile, and the more obvious the interaction between piles. In the range of $a_0 > 1.0$, the amplitude level of the interaction factor gradually increases, but when the slenderness ratio is greater than 60, the change amplitude decreases because the influence of the pile top load on the soil around the pile is mainly concentrated in the upper soil, and when the length of the pile reaches a certain value, the influence of the vibration on the adjacent pile does not increase significantly. At the same time, in the above change trend, the change range of pile groups interaction of pipe pile type is small because the size and length of the pile core soil increase, the force generated on the pipe pile increases, and the energy consumed increases, indicating that compared with the solid pile type, the change in slenderness ratio has less interference on the pile groups interaction of pipe pile type. Among the amplitude changes caused by the slenderness ratio between the 1 × 2 and 2 × 2 pile groups, the amplitude difference between the pipe pile and the solid pile of pile group 2 × 2 is smaller because the pile–pile connection is closer.

Figure 10 shows the difference between the change in interaction factors of pipe pile type and solid pile type caused by the change in pile spacing when considering the scattering effect of passive piles in 2 × 2 pile groups. In the frequency range shown in the figure, the interaction factors of pipe pile and solid pile show certain oscillation characteristics. With the increase in pile spacing, the oscillation amplitude of the interaction factor gradually decreases, indicating that the interaction between piles is gradually weakening. The oscillation frequency of the interaction factor decreases gradually. This is because when

$a_0 < 1.5$, the shear wave generated by the pile foundation vibration attenuates rapidly, and its influence on the soil around the pile is small. Therefore, the greater the pile spacing, the less obvious the interaction between pile groups. At the same time, in the above change trend, the change range of pile groups interaction of pipe pile type is small because the incident wave and scattered wave generated by the vibration in the soil around the pile weaken with the increase in pile spacing and the force of pile core soil on the pipe pile is more prominent, indicating that compared with the solid pile type, the change in pile spacing has less interference on the pile groups interaction of pipe pile type. Among the amplitude changes caused by the pile spacing between the 1 × 2 and 2 × 2 pile groups, the amplitude difference between the pipe pile and the solid pile of pile group 2 × 2 is smaller because the pile–pile connection is closer.

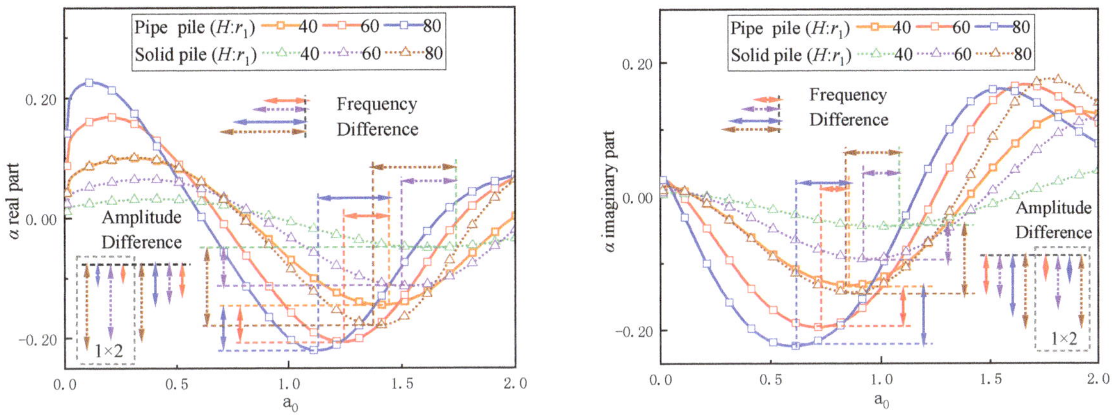

(a) α real part **(b)** α imaginary part

Figure 9. The difference between the changes in interaction factors of two kinds of 2 × 2 pile groups caused by the change in slenderness ratio.

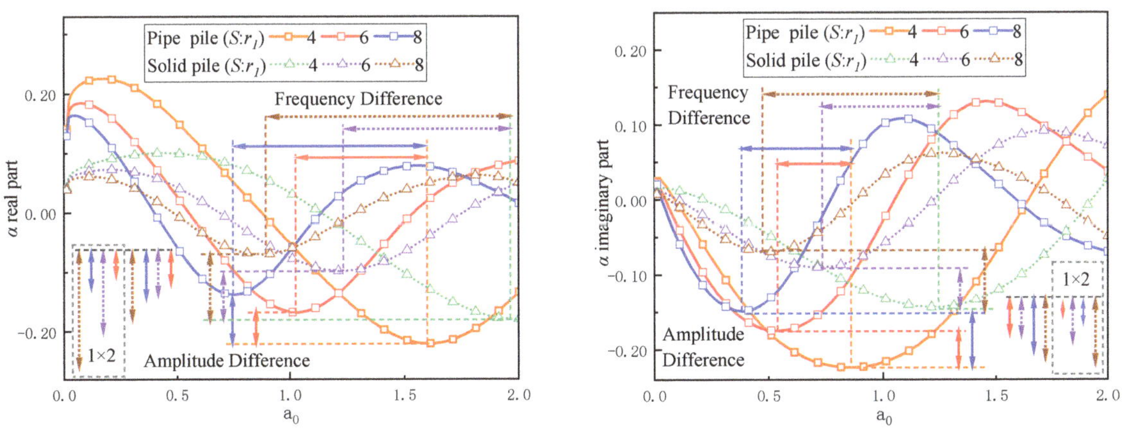

(a) α real part **(b)** α imaginary part

Figure 10. The difference between the changes in interaction factors of two kinds of 2 × 2 pile groups caused by the change in pile spacing.

5. Conclusions

Based on elastodynamic analysis, a calculation model of pile groups under vertical dynamic load is established in this paper. Considering the scattered wave generated by passive piles' vibration, the diffraction effect factor is proposed, and the traditional interaction factor is modified. In this paper, the degenerate solution is compared with the existing theoretical solution to verify the rationality of the solution in this paper. Via the analysis of calculation examples, the differences between the changes in interaction factors of 1×2, 2×2 pipe piles and solid piles caused by the changes in slenderness ratio, pile spacing, and other changes are discussed, respectively. The conclusions are as follows:

(1) As the slenderness ratio increases, the oscillation frequency decreases gradually. In the low-frequency range, the amplitude level of the interaction factor gradually increases. In the high-frequency range, the amplitude of the interaction factor of solid pile type increases, and the change amplitude of the pipe pile in the above comparison is small. The change in slenderness ratio has less interference with the interaction between pipe piles.

(2) As the pile spacing increases, the oscillation amplitude level gradually decreases, indicating that the interaction between piles is gradually weakening. The oscillation frequency also gradually decreases, and the variation amplitude of the pipe pile in the above comparison is small. The change in pile spacing has less interference with the interaction between pipe piles.

(3) As the outer diameter increases, the oscillation amplitude increases gradually, indicating that the larger the outer diameter, the more obvious the interaction. The oscillation frequency increases gradually, and the variation amplitude of the pipe pile in the above comparison is small. The change in outer diameter has less interference with the interaction between pipe piles.

(4) As the pile–soil modulus ratio increases, the oscillation frequency decreases gradually. In the high-frequency range, the amplitude level of the interaction factor gradually increases, and the amplitude change in the pipe pile is small in the comparison. The change in pile–soil modulus ratio has less interference with the interaction between pipe piles, but greater interference with oscillation frequency.

In engineering practice, the soil plug effect is inevitable in pipe piles, which needs to be considered in order to improve the solution results of the dynamic response analysis of pile groups. At the same time, most natural soil is layered, and due to sedimentation, there is radial heterogeneity, so it is necessary to carry out the dynamic response analysis of pile groups in layered soil and anisotropic soil, which will have greater practical significance for engineering practice.

Author Contributions: Conceptualization, K.M.; methodology, K.M.; software, M.Z.; validation, M.Z.; formal analysis, M.Z.; investigation, M.Z.; resources, M.Z.; data curation, M.Z.; writing—original draft preparation, M.Z.; writing—review and editing, M.Z.; visualization, M.Z.; supervision, K.M.; project administration, K.M.; funding acquisition, K.M. All authors have read and agreed to the published version of the manuscript.

Funding: This research was funded by the National Science Foundation for Young Scientists of China, grant number 52108326.

Institutional Review Board Statement: Not applicable.

Informed Consent Statement: Not applicable.

Data Availability Statement: Not applicable.

Conflicts of Interest: The authors declare no conflict of interest.

References

1. Qiu, W.; Wang, Z.; Wang, B. Study on pile cap effects of pile group foundations under linear wave action by a hybrid BEM and EEM method. *Ocean Eng.* **2022**, *266*, 112958. [CrossRef]
2. Wang, Z.; Qiu, W. Mechanical model for predicting wave loads on complex pile group foundations under linear wave action. *Eng. Anal. Bound. Elem.* **2022**, *145*, 321–334. [CrossRef]

3. Hi, Y.; Yao, W.; Yu, G. Dynamic Analysis on Pile Group Supported Offshore Wind Turbine under Wind and Wave Load. *J. Mar. Sci. Eng.* **2022**, *10*, 1024. [CrossRef]
4. Poulos, H.G. Analysis of the Settlement of Pile Groups. *Géotechnique* **1968**, *18*, 449–471. [CrossRef]
5. Kaynia, A.M.; Kausel, E. *Dvmamic Stiffess and Seismic Response of Pile Groups*; Massachusetts Institute of Technology: Cambridge, UK, 1982.
6. Mylonakis, G.; Gazetas, G. Settlement and additional internal forces of grouped piles in layered soil. *Géotechnique* **1998**, *48*, 55–72. [CrossRef]
7. Mylonakis, G.; Gazetas, G. Lateral Vibration and Internal Forces of Grouped Piles in Layered Soil. *J. Geotech. Geoenviron. Eng.* **1999**, *125*, 16–25. [CrossRef]
8. Poulos, H.G.; Davis, E.H. Settlement and load distribution analysis of pile groups. *Aust. Geomech. J.* **1971**, *GI*, 18–28.
9. Nogami, T. Dynamic Group Effect in Axial Responses of Grouped Piles. *J. Geotech. Eng.* **1983**, *109*, 228–243. [CrossRef]
10. Mylonakis, G.; Gazetas, G. Vertical Vibration and Additional Distress of Grouped Piles in Layered Soil. *Soils Found.* **1998**, *38*, 1–4. [CrossRef]
11. Chen, H.; Liang, F. Simplified boundary element method for lateral vibration response of pile groups in frequency domain. *Chin. J. Geotech. Eng.* **2014**, *36*, 1057–1063.
12. El Sharnouby, B.; Novak, M. Stiffness constants and interaction factors for vertical response of pile groups. *Can. Geotech. J.* **1990**, *27*, 813–822. [CrossRef]
13. Randolph, M.F.; Wroth, C.P. An analysis of the vertical deformation of pile groups. *Géotechnique* **1979**, *29*, 423–439. [CrossRef]
14. Wang, J.; Zhou, D.; Liu, W. Horizontal impedance of pile groups considering shear behavior of multilayered soils. *Soils Found.* **2014**, *54*, 927–937. [CrossRef]
15. Wang, L.H.; Ai, Z.Y. Vertical Vibration Analysis of a Pile Group in Multilayered Poroelastic Soils with Compressible Constituents. *Int. J. Geomech.* **2021**, *21*, 04020232. [CrossRef]
16. Zhang, S.; Cui, C.; Yang, G. Vertical dynamic impedance of pile groups partially embedded in multilayered, transversely isotropic, saturated soils. *Soil Dyn. Earthq. Eng.* **2019**, *117*, 106–115. [CrossRef]
17. Chen, S.L.; Song, C.Y.; Chen, L.Z. Two-pile interaction factor revisited. *Can. Geotech. J.* **2011**, *48*, 754–766. [CrossRef]
18. Cao, M.; Chen, L. Analysis of interaction factors between two piles. *J. Shanghai Jiaotong Univ.* **2008**, *13*, 171–176. [CrossRef]
19. Luan, L.; Zheng, C.; Kouretzis, G.; Ding, X. Dynamic analysis of pile groups subjected to horizontal loads considering coupled pile-to-pile interaction. *Comput. Geotech.* **2020**, *117*, 103276. [CrossRef]
20. Liu, L.; Niu, J.; Xiao, Q.; Yan, Q. Vertical vibration of pipe pile groups based on the principle of superposition. *Chin. J. Appl. Mech.* **2017**, *34*, 534–540+613.
21. Yan, Q.; Liu, L.; Niu, J. Study on Longitudinal Vibration of Pipe Pile Groups in Saturated Soil Based on Dynamic Interaction Factor. *J. Xinyang Norm. Univ. Nat. Sci. Ed.* **2017**, *30*, 651–657.
22. Liu, L.; Yang, X. Pile To Pile Vertical Dynamic Interaction And Vertical Vibration Of Pile Groups In Saturared Soil. *Eng. Mech.* **2011**, *28*, 124–130+137.
23. Pham, N.T.; Vuong, V.D.; Tran, T.V.; Van Le, T.; Vu, A.Q. Numerical simulation of extremely severe corrosion of the STK400 graded steel pipe pile in Southern Vietnam's brackish environment: Effects on macrocell corrosion of seawater flow and tide. *Mater. Res. Express* **2022**, *9*, 056501. [CrossRef]
24. Di, T.; Wu, W.; Zhang, Y.; Wang, Z.; Liu, X.; Xu, M.; Mei, G. Semi-analytical approach for nondestructive test for offshore pipe piles considering soil-pile slippage induced by heavy hammer impact. *Ocean Eng.* **2022**, *260*, 112080. [CrossRef]
25. Liu, H.; Fei, K.; Xu, X. Development and application of the large-diameter driven cast-in-place concrete thin-wall pipe pile. In Proceedings of the 16th International Conference on Soil Mechanics and Geotechnical Engineering 2005, Osaka, Japan, 12–16 September 2005.
26. Liu, H.L.; Chu, J.; Deng, A. Deng. Use of large-diameter, cast–in situ concrete pipe piles for embankment over soft clay. *Can. Geotech. J.* **2009**, *46*, 915–927. [CrossRef]
27. Roesset, J.M. Stiffness and damping coefficients of foundations. In Proceedings of the ASCE Geotechnical Engineering Division National Convention, New York, NY, USA, 30 October 1980; pp. 1–30.
28. Novak, M. Dynamic Stiffness and Damping of Piles. *Can. Geotech. J.* **1974**, *11*, 574–598. [CrossRef]
29. Milos, N.; Fakhry, A.; Toyoaki, N. Dynamic Soil Reactions for Plane Strain Case. *J. Eng. Mech. Div.* **1978**, *104*, 953–959.
30. Dobry, R.; Gazetas, G. Simple method for dynamic stiffness and damping of floating pile groups. *Géotechnique* **1988**, *38*, 557–574. [CrossRef]

Journal of
Marine Science and Engineering

MDPI

Article

Analysis of Factors Affecting Vacuum Formation and Drainage in the Siphon-Vacuum Drainage Method for Marine Reclamation

Junwei Shu [1,2], Jun Wang [2,3], Kexing Chen [4], Qingsong Shen [1,5] and Hongyue Sun [2,*]

1. College of Civil Engineering and Architecture, Zhejiang University, Hangzhou 310058, China; junweishu@zju.edu.cn (J.S.); shen_qs1@hdec.com (Q.S.)
2. Ocean College, Zhejiang University, Zhoushan 316021, China; nbwj8885@126.com
3. Zhejiang Seaport Engineering Construction Consultants Co., Ltd., Ningbo 315800, China
4. Zhejiang Electric Power Design Institute, Hangzhou 310012, China; kx_zepdi@126.com
5. Power China Huadong Engineering Corporation Limited, Hangzhou 311122, China

* Correspondence: shy@zju.edu.cn

Abstract: Traditional drainage methods for marine reclamation typically consume large amounts of energy and have a negative environmental impact. The siphon-vacuum drainage method (SVD) automatically forms a vacuum and drains using less energy. It has significant potential for research and application. In this study, a theoretical model is used to calculate the vacuum formation process and drainage rate. Qualitative analysis and global sensitivity analysis were conducted to investigate the effect of various factors in the SVD on vacuum formation and drainage. The qualitative analysis suggests that modifying the length and diameter of the siphon pipe and the thickness of the sealing soil column to increase the siphon rate can improve the vacuum degree and drainage efficiency. Sobol global sensitivity analysis reveals that the sealing soil column thickness is the main factor affecting the vacuum, with a first-order sensitivity index accounting for up to 79.48%. The impact of cylinder diameter and the local resistance coefficient (0.43%) can be almost neglected. A fitting equation for estimating the maximum achievable vacuum is provided. Calculations show that the vacuum formed by the SVD can reach over 80 kPa. This work can help optimize SVD design and advance environmentally friendly marine reclamation projects.

Keywords: siphon-vacuum drainage method; vacuum degree; sealing soil column thickness; sensitivity analysis; soil improvement

1. Introduction

Many developed regions are situated in coastal areas, benefiting from access to maritime resources and trade routes. The demand for land is escalating due to population growth and economic expansion in these areas. The marine reclamation method can be used to increase the land area in coastal regions [1]. Marine dredged soil, commonly utilized in reclamation, has characteristics including high compressibility, high water content, low bearing capacity, and low permeability [2–4]. The drainage consolidation method is economical and efficient, making it a prevalent choice for large-scale marine reclamation [5–8]. Techniques such as surcharge preloading, vacuum preloading, and electroosmosis are often employed for drainage [9–11]. The surcharge preloading applies an external load to the soil surface to promote water expulsion. The vacuum preloading enhances drainage by creating a vacuum under a membrane, reducing pore water pressure. Electroosmosis uses electric currents to drive water and ion movement, facilitating soil dewatering. Among them, vacuum preloading is widely used. It has been implemented in various projects, including the Tianjin Lingang Economic Zone in China [12], the expansion of Fisherman Island in Australia [13], and land reclamation in Singapore [14].

However, vacuum preloading requires a considerable amount of electricity. Traditional vacuum pumps require 75 kW for every 10,000 m^2 of soft soil, and a new water and gas separation vacuum pump demands 25 kW [15]. In most cases, vacuum preloading lasts at least 90 days. If the electricity originates from coal, this process will result in significant carbon dioxide emissions. Furthermore, the transmission and maintenance of the vacuum will consume a considerable amount of materials [16]. Taking the maintenance of the vacuum as an example, a significant amount of plastic film is required for sealing. The production and disposal of plastic film can lead to greenhouse gas emissions. Additionally, the abandonment of plastic film can lead to soil and water pollution. Today, climate change and environmental pollution have become global concerns [17,18]. Consequently, exploring low-carbon and environmentally friendly methods is an effective measure to alleviate these issues.

Siphon is a gravity-driven drainage method that operates without the need for external power [19]. However, the siphon drainage at high lift will be interrupted due to air accumulation. Cai et al. [20] found that small-diameter siphon pipes could solve this problem, allowing the siphon to work effectively for a long time. These small-diameter siphon pipes have been successfully applied in slope drainage engineering. Sun et al. [21] applied the siphon drainage method to soft soil drainage first. The pore water within the soft soil seeps into the vertical drainage wells under the action of a siphon. The model tests have shown that siphon drainage could reduce the water level in soft soil, enhance drainage efficiency, lower the pore water pressure, and thereby increase the effective stress of the soft soil. Shen et al. [22] conducted a full-scale field test on improving soft soil using the siphon drainage method. The results indicated a 2.78 m drop in groundwater levels and a settlement of 17.82 cm after 16.5 days of employing siphon. This method eliminates the necessity for vacuum pumps, sealing membranes, and sand cushions. Furthermore, it is easy to construct and maintain in engineering projects. In summary, the siphon drainage method emerges as an economical, low-carbon, and environmentally friendly method for improving marine dredged soil. However, groundwater seepage occurs due to its own weight in siphon drainage. The drainage effect of the siphon drainage method on surface soil is not as effective as vacuum preloading, which relies on vacuum pressure.

In vacuum preloading, the vacuum pressure is used to discharge pore water, thereby inducing soil consolidation [23]. In addition, the drainage rate has an impact on both project duration and costs. The increase in vacuum pressure can facilitate drainage. Therefore, the effectiveness and economy of the siphon drainage method for improving soft soils can be enhanced by the addition of vacuum pressure. The siphon-vacuum drainage method (SVD) is shown in Figure 1. This method uses a siphon to automatically create vacuum pressure innovatively in soft soil. Shu et al. [24] have studied the mechanism of vacuum formation and developed a theoretical model to calculate the vacuum pressure and drainage rate. The vacuum pressure and drainage are influenced by factors in the SVD. In order to achieve greater vacuum pressure and better drainage effectiveness, it is necessary to analyze the factors in the SVD.

This research aims to improve understanding of how SVD factors affect vacuum formation and drainage for better marine reclamation. Firstly, the model for calculating the vacuum pressure and drainage rate is summarized. Then, the qualitative effects of each factor on vacuum formation and drainage are analyzed by the calculation results. Moreover, a global sensitivity analysis was conducted to obtain the proportion that each factor affects vacuum formation. Finally, the maximum vacuum degree that can be formed theoretically by the SVD was calculated. The results of this study can serve as a basis for the optimized design of the SVD.

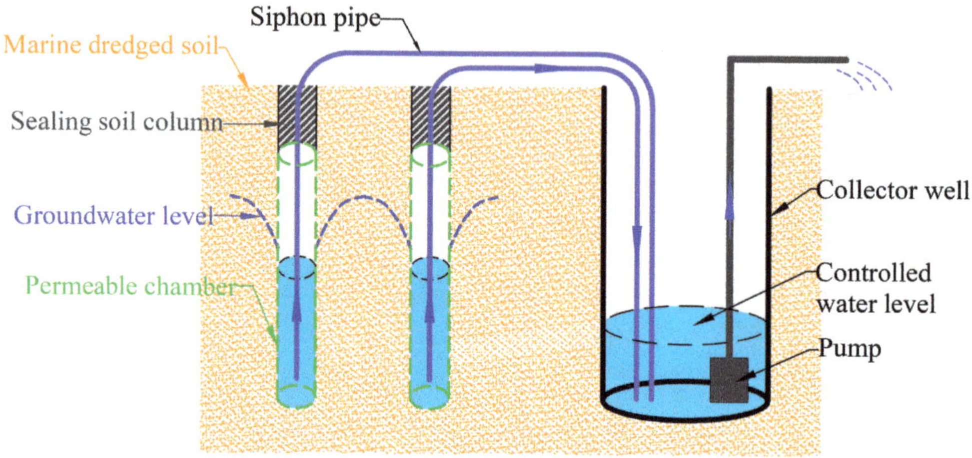

Figure 1. Schematic diagram of the SVD.

2. Qualitative Analysis of Vacuum Pressure and Drainage

2.1. Calculation Method

2.1.1. Cylindrical Model

When dealing with large-scale marine dredged soil, a large number of vertical drainage wells are typically inserted into the dredged soil. The strength of marine dredged soils is improved, as pore water flows into vertical drainage wells. The vertical drainage bodies are arranged in a certain form. As shown in Figure 2, the common forms of arrangement are square and equilateral triangles. Square and hexagonal units are obtained by uniformly dividing the soil layers. The units are simplified to a circle for ease of calculation. The conversion equations between the diameter of the circle (d_e) and the spacing of the vertical drainage wells (l) are, respectively:

$$d_e = l\sqrt{4/\pi} \tag{1}$$

$$d_e = l\sqrt{2\sqrt{3}/\pi} \tag{2}$$

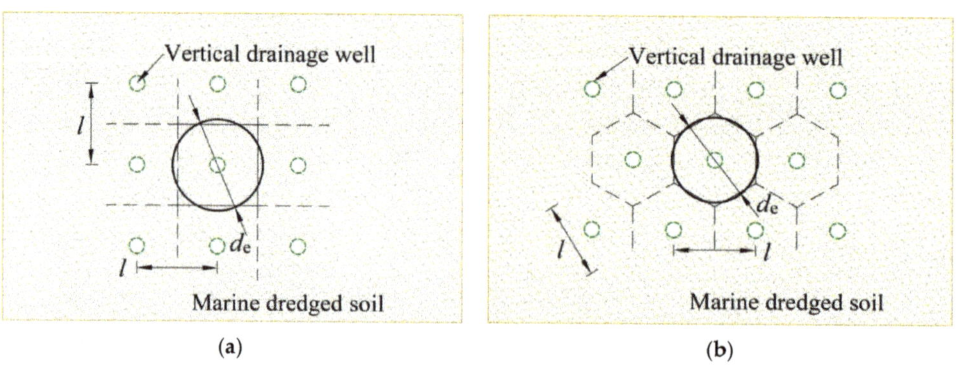

Figure 2. Form of vertical drainage wells arrangement: (**a**) square; (**b**) equilateral triangle.

When improving marine dredged soil with the SVD, the siphon pipes and permeable chambers will be inserted into the soil layer. The simplified cylindrical model of a single permeable chamber is shown in Figure 3. The bottom and sides of the cylinder are impermeable. The initial groundwater level is located at the surface of the soil layer. The bottom of the permeable chamber is situated at the bottom of the cylinder, and the permeable chamber is sealed by saturated dredged soil. The thickness of the sealing soil column above the chamber is represented by h_s. The center point at the bottom of the permeable chamber serves as the origin (0, 0) for a two-dimensional axisymmetric coordinate system.

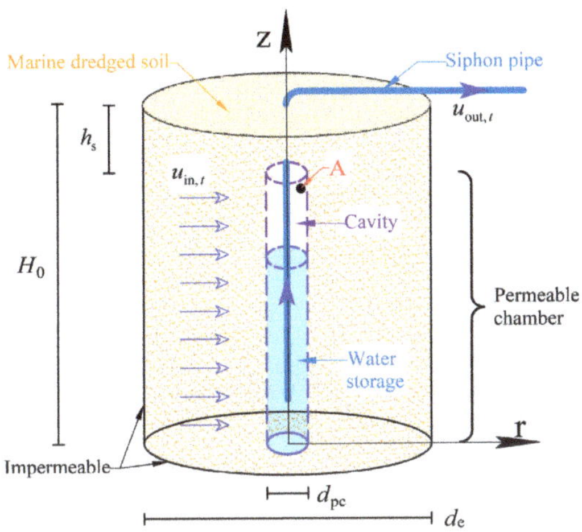

Figure 3. Schematic diagram of a cylindrical model of a single permeable chamber.

2.1.2. Calculation Equations

After the SVD starts, both the air pressure and the water level in the permeable chamber will decrease. The air pressure at point A ($p_{A,\,t}$) will become negative. The pore water in the dredged soil will seep into the permeable chamber and then be discharged through the siphon. A theoretical model of vacuum formation has been developed by Shu et al. [24]. The model involves detailed equations derivations for the three processes of siphon drainage, seepage drainage, and changes in air pressure. The calculations are based on the principle of energy conservation for siphon drainage The Dupuit assumption is used to describe the distribution of seepage velocities. The non-steady seepage process is broken down into a sequence of steady flows, which are solved iteratively. It is assumed that the gas within the permeable chamber dissolves and releases in water almost immediately.

In this study, the equations in the model are generalized and simplified. The SVD factors involved in the three processes are summarized. The flow rate of siphon drainage ($U_{out,\,t}$) and the amount of gas dissolved in it ($V_{out,\,t}$) can be expressed by Equations (3)–(5):

$$a_{out,\,t} = \left(h_{w,\,t-1} + \frac{p_{A,\,t-1}}{\gamma_w} - H_0 + \frac{p_s}{\gamma_w}\right)\frac{g}{L} - \left(1 - \frac{d^4}{d_{pc}^4} + \sum \zeta_i\right)\frac{u_{out,\,t-1}^2}{2L\pi^2 r^4} - \frac{\lambda u_{out,\,t-1}^2}{4\pi^2 r^5} \tag{3}$$

$$U_{out,\,t} = \pi r^2 \left(\sum_{i=1}^{t-1} a_{out,\,t_i}\Delta t + \frac{a_{out,\,t}\Delta t}{2}\right)\Delta t \tag{4}$$

$$V_{out,\,t} = \frac{\gamma_w(h_{w,\,t-1} - h_c) + p_{A,\,t-1} + p_s}{p_s} V_m U_{out,\,t} \tag{5}$$

where $a_{out,\,t}$ is the acceleration of siphon at time t; $h_{w,\,t-1}$ is the water level in the permeable chamber at time $t-1$; $p_{A,\,t-1}$ is the air pressure of point A at time $t-1$; $u_{out,\,t-1}$ is the siphon drainage velocity at time $t-1$; H_0 is the depth of the permeable chamber; p_s is the standard atmospheric pressure (101.3 kPa); ζ_i and λ are the local and frictional resistance coefficients of the siphon pipe, respectively; γ_w is the weight of water; d and r are the diameter and radius of the siphon pipe, respectively; d_{pc} is the diameter of the permeable chamber; Δt is the time interval; h_c is the distance between the inlet of the siphon pipe and the bottom of the permeable chamber; and V_m is the solubility of gas dissolved in water under standard atmospheric pressure. According to Equations (3)–(5), the factors L, d, d_{pc}, ζ_i, and λ in the SVD are related to the siphon drainage.

The water level ($h'_{w,\,t}$) and the total volume of gas ($V'_{all,\,t}$) in the permeable chamber after siphon drainage are as follows:

$$h'_{w,\,t} = h_{w,\,t-1} - U_{out,\,t}/\pi r_{pc}^2 \tag{6}$$

$$V'_{all,\,t} = V_{all,\,t-1} - V_{out,\,t} \tag{7}$$

where r_{pc} is the radius of the permeable chamber, and $V_{all,\,t-1}$ is the total volume of gas in the chamber at time $t-1$.

The gas in the chamber will reach a balance between dissolution and release. The relationship between the total volume of gas in the chamber ($V'_{all,\,t}$) and the air pressure at point A ($p'_{A,\,t}$) can be expressed as follows:

$$\pi\left(H_0 - h_s - h'_{w,\,t}\right)\left(p'_{A,\,t} + p_s\right)r_{pc}^2/p_s + \left(0.5\gamma_w h'_{w,\,t} + p'_{A,\,t} + p_s\right)V_m \pi h'_{w,\,t} r_{pc}^2/p_s = V'_{all,\,t} \tag{8}$$

where h_s is the thickness of the sealing soil column. The first term on the left side of the equation represents the volume of the gaseous gas in the cavity, while the second term represents the volume of the dissolved gas in the water within the chamber. According to Equations (6)–(8), the factors h_s and d_{pc} in the SVD are related to the changes in air pressure.

Due to the short time of vacuum formation, the seepage at this stage is dominated by the horizontal direction. Therefore, only seepage in the horizontal direction is considered in this model. The flow rate of the seepage ($U_{in,\,t}$) and the amount of gas dissolved in it ($V_{in,\,t}$) can be expressed by Equations (9) and (10).

$$U_{in,\,t} = \frac{2\pi K_h \Delta t}{\ln\frac{d_e}{d_{pc}}}\int_0^{H_0-h_s}\left[H_0 - H(r_{pc}, z, t)\right]dz \tag{9}$$

$$V_{in,\,t} = \frac{2\pi K_h \Delta t}{\ln\frac{d_e}{d_{pc}}}\int_0^{H_0-h_s}\frac{\gamma_w(H_0 - z) + p_s}{p_s}V_m\left[H_0 - H(r_{pc}, z, t)\right]dz \tag{10}$$

where $H(r_{pc}, z, t)$ represents the boundary conditions at the outlet of seepage, and K_h is the horizontal hydraulic conductivity. According to Equations (9) and (10), the factors K_h, h_s, d_e, and d_{pc} in the SVD are related to the seepage drainage.

2.2. *Results and Discussion of Vacuum Pressure and Drainage*

The above equations were compiled using MATLAB. Time was discretized into multiple steps, and the iterative calculation method is based on the results of the previous step to compute the results of the next step. The calculations within each step follow the sequence of siphon drainage, resulting in changes in air pressure and water level, subsequent seepage, and the corresponding variations of air pressure and water level. When the air pressure reaches its minimum value, the process of vacuum formation is considered complete.

2.2.1. Vacuum Pressure

The theoretical model has been validated by full-scale field test results [24], with one such test result depicted in Figure 4, including both measured and calculated results. Table 1 provides the parameters of the field test. In the test, permeable chambers were arranged in a square pattern with a spacing of 0.9 m. The diameter (d_e) of the cylinder was calculated to be 1.015 m according to Equation (1). As shown in Figure 4, the model calculation results are in good agreement with the measured results. At 351 s, the measured results show that the air pressure reaches its minimum value at −42.7 kPa, the model calculation result is −41.5 kPa. The air pressure rapidly decreases in the first 50 s. After 100 s, the rate of air pressure decline significantly slows down. Before 400 s, the air pressure stabilizes essentially.

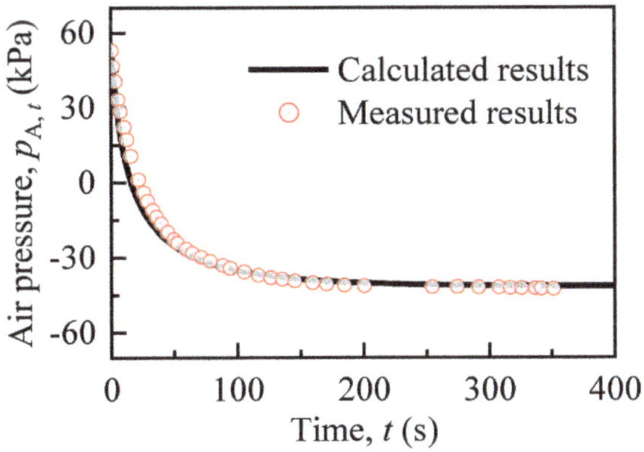

Figure 4. Test results and calculations of air pressure changes.

Table 1. The parameters and their values required for the model calculation.

Parameters	Values
Thickness of sealing soil column, h_s (m)	5.3
Length of siphon pipe, L (m)	50
Distance between the inlet of the siphon pipe and the bottom of the permeable chamber, h_c (m)	1
Depth of the permeable chamber, H_0 (m)	18
Horizontal hydraulic conductivity, K_h (m/s)	3.75×10^{-9}
Cylinder diameter, d_e (m)	1.015
Diameter of permeable chamber, d_{pc} (m)	5×10^{-2}
Diameter of siphon pipe, d (m)	5×10^{-3}
Time interval, Δt (s)	0.01
Local resistance coefficient of siphon pipe, ζ_i	0.131

Although the theoretical model disregards the time for gas dissolution and release in water, it still effectively simulates the vacuum formation process. Thus, the model can be used to analyze the impact of various factors on vacuum formation. If more accurate equations could be proposed to represent seepage and siphon drainage, the calculated results of the vacuum formation process would align more closely with the measured results.

2.2.2. Drainage

The water storage within the chamber is influenced by both siphon drainage and seepage drainage. The siphon drainage reduces the water storage within the chamber, while seepage drainage increases it. The flow rates of siphon drainage and seepage drainage are calculated based on the theoretical model described above. The model parameters are as given in Table 1. The model calculation results for the flow rate of siphon drainage and seepage drainage are given in Figure 5. The area of the shaded part is the result of the change in water storage within the chamber. The process of vacuum formation is divided into an early stage and a later stage. In the early stage, the flow rate of the siphon experiences a brief, rapid increase, and it is significantly greater than that of seepage.

Hence, siphon drainage plays a dominant role in the variability of water storage within the chamber during this early stage. Subsequently, the flow rate of the siphon decreased while the flow rate of seepage gradually increased. The impact of seepage drainage in the later stage is strengthened. At 400 s, the flow rate of seepage drainage is very similar to that of siphon drainage.

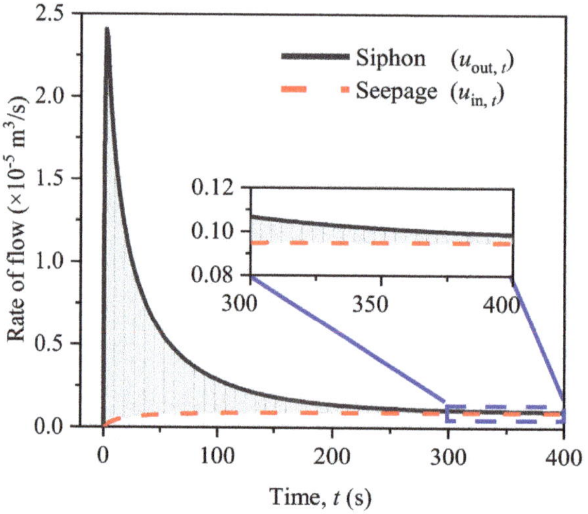

Figure 5. Drainage flow rate of siphon and seepage.

The flow change trends of siphon and seepage by calculations are consistent with theoretical analysis. Considering the agreement between the calculated and measured results of air pressure, it is believed that the model can be utilized to calculate the seepage flow rate. Thus, the calculated results can also be used to analyze the effects of various factors on seepage. However, for computational efficiency, the model uses stable well flow theory instead of actual unstable seepage, which makes it unsuitable for calculating seepage over extended periods.

The effectiveness of the SVD in improving marine dredged soil is related to the amount of pore water discharge. The pore water is discharged through seepage. Therefore, the flow rate of seepage drainage was selected to evaluate the effectiveness of the SVD in discharging pore water from marine dredged soil.

2.3. Results and Discussion on the Impact of Factors

The discharge of pore water from marine dredged soil using the SVD involves three main processes: siphoning, air pressure changes in the chamber, and seepage. Therefore, the siphon, chamber size, and seepage flow rate are the primary aspects influencing vacuum formation and drainage. Factors affecting the siphon flow rate include the siphon pipe length (L), the minor head loss coefficient of the siphon pipe (ζ), and the diameter of the siphon pipe (d). Factors influencing chamber size include the thickness of the sealing soil column (h_s) and the diameter of the permeable chamber (d_{pc}). Additionally, factors affecting the flow rate of seepage include the horizontal permeability coefficient (K_h), the diameter of the permeable chamber (d_{pc}), and the diameter of the cylindrical model (d_e).

Based on the engineering conditions and the dimensions of existing materials, different values for these factors are selected to calculate vacuum formation and drainage. Furthermore, the effects of these factors on vacuum formation and drainage were analyzed. The factor values for the reference scenario (0-0) are shown in Table 1. Fourteen scenarios have been designed to investigate the influence of seven factors. Table 2 provides the values for these fourteen scenarios.

Table 2. Factor values of each scenario.

Number	Factor	Diameter of Siphon Pipe, d (mm)	Length of Siphon Pipe, L (m)	Local Resistance Coefficient of Siphon Pipe, ζ	Thickness of Sealing Soil Column, h_s (m)	Diameter of Permeable Chamber, d_{pc} (cm)	Horizontal Hydraulic Conductivity, K_h ($\times 10^{-9}$ m/s)	Cylinder Diameter, d_e (m)
0-0	/	5	50	0.131	5.3	5	3.75	1.015
1-1	d	4	50	0.131	5.3	5	3.75	1.015
1-2		6	50	0.131	5.3	5	3.75	1.015
2-1	L	5	20	0.131	5.3	5	3.75	1.015
2-2		5	80	0.131	5.3	5	3.75	1.015
3-1	ζ	5	50	0	5.3	5	3.75	1.015
3-2		5	50	700	5.3	5	3.75	1.015
4-1	h_s	5	50	0.131	2	5	3.75	1.015
4-2		5	50	0.131	8	5	3.75	1.015
5-1	d_{pc}	5	50	0.131	5.3	3	3.75	1.015
5-2		5	50	0.131	5.3	7	3.75	1.015
6-1	K_h	5	50	0.131	5.3	5	1	1.015
6-2		5	50	0.131	5.3	5	7	1.015
7-1	d_e	5	50	0.131	5.3	5	3.75	0.7
7-2		5	50	0.131	5.3	5	3.75	1.3

2.3.1. Diameter of Siphon Pipe

Figure 6 presents the variation curves of vacuum formation and drainage rate (total seepage rate) for different diameters of siphon pipes (d). As shown in Figure 6a, there are significant differences observed in the pressure variation among the three scenarios during the early stage. In the later stage, the pressure change for all three scenarios becomes relatively gradual. The larger the diameter of the siphon pipe (d), the smaller the final air pressure formed (greater vacuum degree). The impact of the diameter (d) on the final vacuum degree is relatively small. A comparison between Figures 6b and 6a reveals that the impact of the diameter of the siphon pipe (d) on drainage is similar to its effect on vacuum formation. The effect of the siphon pipe diameter (d) on drainage and vacuum formation is similar when comparing Figure 6b with Figure 6a.

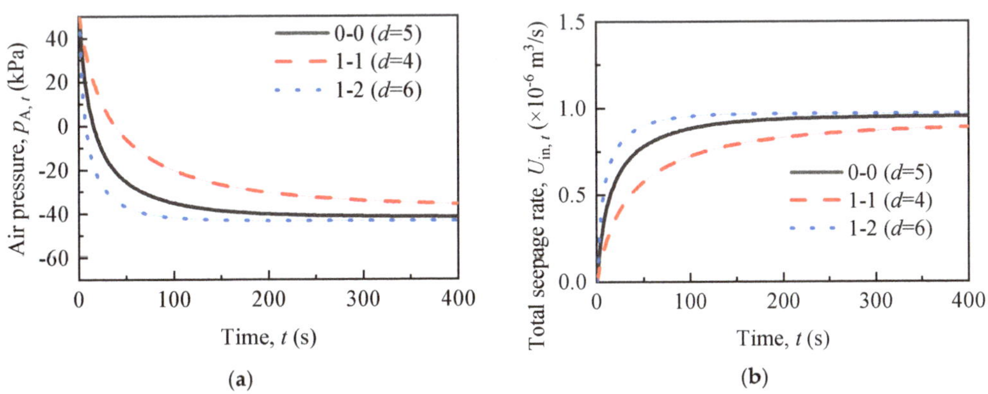

Figure 6. (**a**) Vacuum formation and (**b**) drainage rate under the influence of the siphon pipe diameter.

The diameter of the siphon pipe (d) primarily affects the siphon rate and does not directly influence seepage. A larger siphon rate results in a faster decrease in water storage and air pressure within the chamber (cavity enlargement). The seepage rate is increased by the smaller water pressure (volume of water storage) and air pressure in the chamber. Additionally, the siphon primarily impacts the early stage of drainage. Therefore, the diameter of the siphon pipe (d) mainly affects the vacuum formation and drainage in the early stages. Although the vacuum degree and drainage rate can be increased by using a larger diameter of siphon pipe (d), the increase is small.

2.3.2. Length of Siphon Pipe

As the siphon pipe length (L) increases, the resulting vacuum degree and drainage rate decrease, as shown in Figure 7. The siphon pipe length (L) affects the frictional resistance along the siphon pipe. As a result, it also only influences the early stages of vacuum formation and drainage through the siphon rate. The frictional resistance increases due to the increase in siphon pipe length (L). This resistance diminishes the siphon rate, thereby resulting in a lower vacuum degree. It is observed that the siphon pipe length (L) has a relatively minor effect on the final vacuum degree and drainage rate, according to Figure 7.

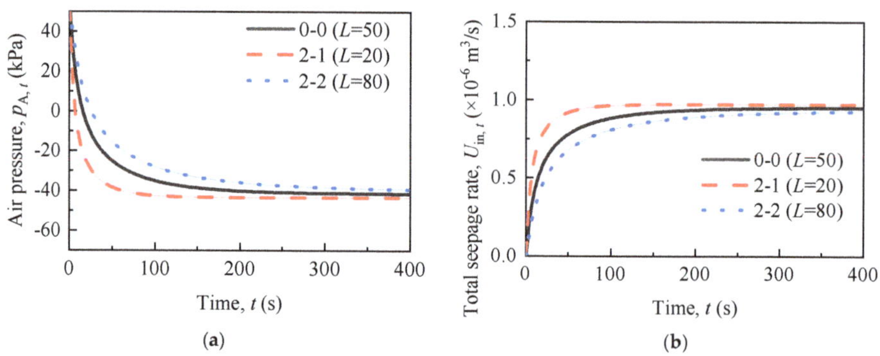

Figure 7. (**a**) Vacuum formation and (**b**) drainage rate under the influence of the siphon pipe length.

2.3.3. Local Resistance Coefficient of Siphon Pipe

The local resistance coefficient (ζ) affects vacuum formation and drainage in the same way as the siphon pipe length (L). The siphon rate can be reduced by increasing the local resistance coefficient (ζ). Figure 8 shows that the process of vacuum formation and the increase in drainage rate slows down at a local resistance coefficient of 700. However, the final vacuum degree and drainage rate are almost unaffected. A local resistance coefficient (ζ) of 700 is an unusually large value. This unusual local resistance may occur when the siphon pipe is accidentally bent. However, the local resistance hardly discounts the final vacuum degree and drainage rate formed by the SVD. It shows that the siphon pipe has some resistance to risk. The siphon pipe can effectively perform its intended function when it is neither leaking nor clogging.

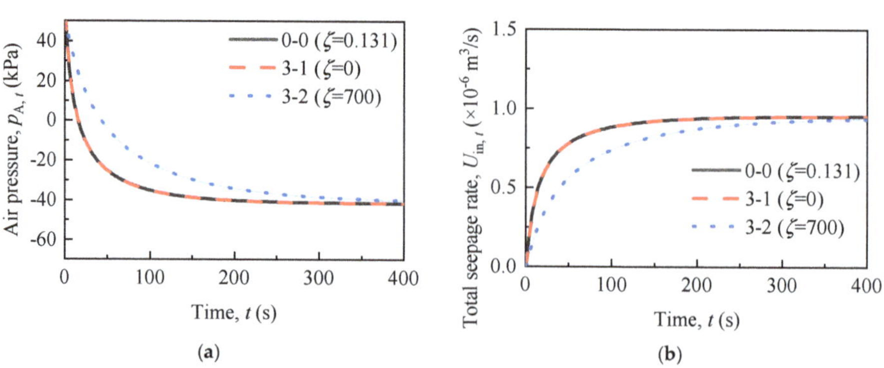

Figure 8. (**a**) Vacuum formation and (**b**) drainage rate under the influence of the minor head loss coefficient of siphon pipe.

2.3.4. Thickness of Sealing Soil Column

The thickness of the sealing soil column (h_s) determines the height of the permeable chamber. The cavity formation and air pressure changes are influenced by the volume of the permeable chamber. The surface area of the chamber determines the cross-sectional area of the seepage. As shown in Figure 9a, the thickness (h_s) has a significant impact on the early stage of vacuum formation and the final vacuum degree. A lower thickness (h_s) results in more water storage in the chamber. More time is required to discharge more water storage in order to achieve a balance between siphon and seepage rates. Hence, the process of vacuum formation will be more gradual and prolonged in scenarios where the thickness (h_s) is smaller.

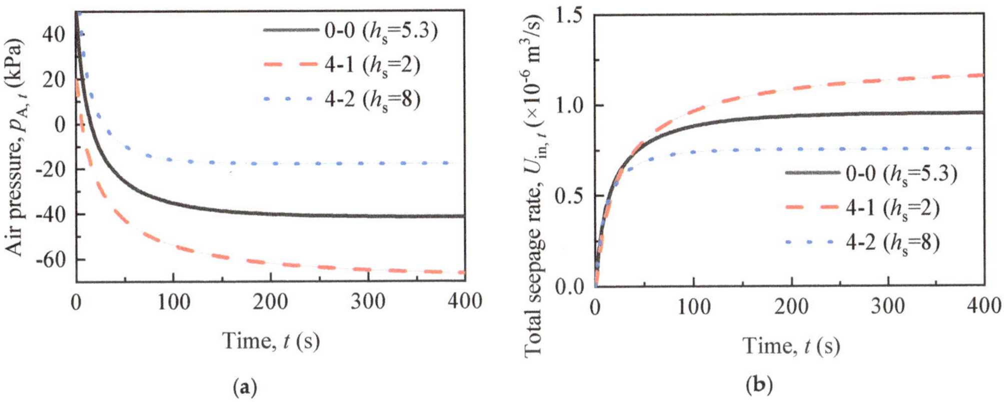

Figure 9. (**a**) Vacuum formation and (**b**) drainage rate under the influence of the thickness of sealing soil column.

The effect of the thickness of the sealing soil column (h_s) on the drainage rate is similar to its effect on the vacuum formation (Figure 9a,b). The thickness (h_s) affects both the vacuum formation and the cross-sectional area. In scenario 4-1, a greater vacuum degree results in a greater seepage velocity. Additionally, the cross-sectional area in scenario 4-1 is larger, resulting in a greater seepage rate. Consequently, the difference in seepage rates between the three scenarios gradually becomes significant in the later stages.

The effect of the sealing soil column thickness (h_s) on both vacuum formation and drainage rate is significant. Decreasing the thickness of the sealing soil column (h_s) is beneficial for increasing both the final vacuum degree and the drainage rate. Therefore, it is an important factor that requires particular attention in engineering applications.

2.3.5. Diameter of Permeable Chamber

The vacuum formation curves at different diameters of the permeable chambers (d_{pc}) are presented in Figure 10a. The diameter of the chambers (d_{pc}) affects both the permeable chamber volume and the cross-sectional area of the seepage, which is similar to the thickness of the sealing soil column (h_s). However, the effects of the two on vacuum formation are not the same. The diameter of the chamber (d_{pc}) changes the time required to achieve a stable vacuum degree but has very little effect on the final vacuum degree. This is because the increase in the diameter of the permeable chamber has a greater promoting effect on seepage, leading to the seepage flow rate approaching the siphon flow rate more quickly.

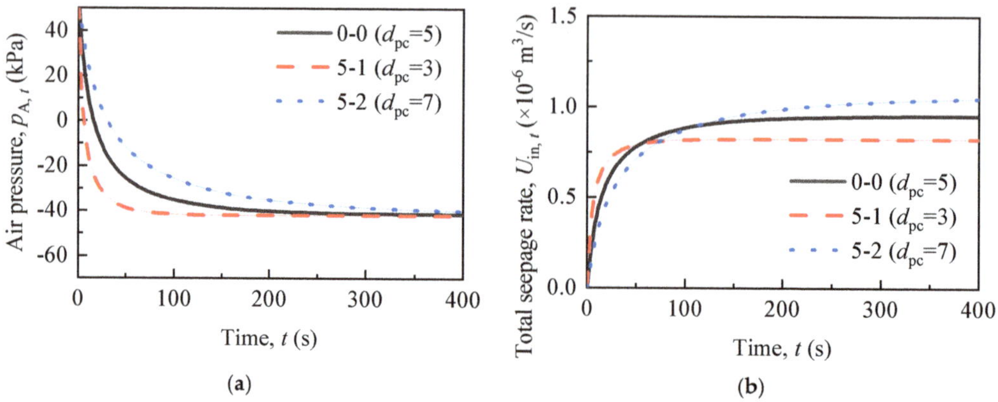

Figure 10. (**a**) Vacuum formation and (**b**) drainage rate under the influence of the permeable chamber diameter.

There is an intersection in the drainage rate curves between scenarios 5-1 and 5-2 (Figure 10b). The increase in the diameter (d_{pc}) slows down the vacuum formation, resulting in a slow growth of the seepage rate in the early stages. However, the vacuum degrees of the three scenarios are essentially similar in the later stage. A larger diameter of the chamber (d_{pc}) results in a greater cross-sectional area, enabling a higher seepage rate in the later stage. Therefore, increasing the inner diameter of the permeable chamber (d_{pc}) appropriately can expedite drainage and reduce construction time.

2.3.6. Horizontal Hydraulic Conductivity

The seepage rate is influenced directly by the horizontal hydraulic conductivity (K_h). Therefore, the horizontal hydraulic conductivity (K_h) primarily influences the later stages of vacuum formation and drainage. As shown in Figure 11, the influence of the horizontal hydraulic conductivity (K_h) on the seepage rate is significant, while its effect on the vacuum degree is minor. It shows that the vacuum formation in low-permeability soil is mainly affected by siphon drainage and permeable chamber size. The hydraulic conductivity is an inherent property of the soil and can be challenging to adjust. However, a higher hydraulic conductivity contributes to drainage.

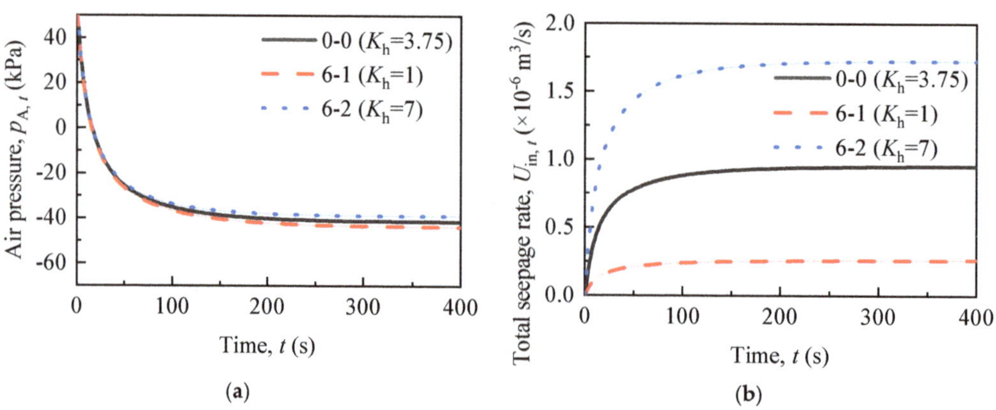

Figure 11. (**a**) Vacuum formation and (**b**) drainage rate under the influence of the horizontal permeability coefficients.

2.3.7. Cylinder Diameter

The cylinder diameter affects drainage by influencing the seepage rate. Its impact pattern is similar to that of the horizontal hydraulic conductivity (K_h). However, the effect of cylinder diameter on seepage is not as significant as the effect of the horizontal hydraulic conductivity (K_h). As shown in Figure 12, the cylinder diameter has almost no impact on vacuum formation and only a minor influence on drainage. The cylinder diameter can be determined based on the cost and duration of the project.

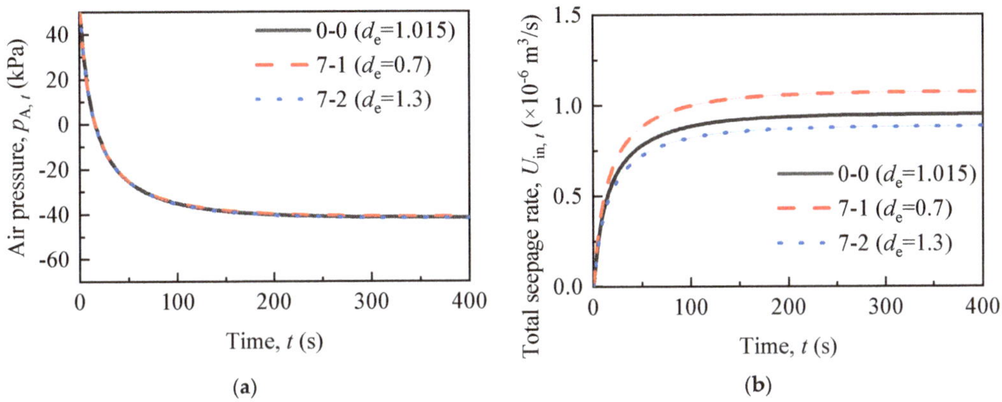

Figure 12. (**a**) Vacuum formation and (**b**) drainage rate under the influence of the cylinder diameter.

3. Global Sensitivity Analysis

3.1. Global Sensitivity Analysis Method

The global sensitivity analysis method has the ability to analyze the sensitivity of multiple factors simultaneously. It can extend the range of factor change to the entire domain while allowing each factor to have different ranges of variation and achieve simultaneous changes. Sobol is a widely applied global sensitivity analysis method. Several scholars have already employed this method in various fields such as geotechnical engineering, agriculture, materials science, and environmental studies [25–29]. The impact proportion of each factor on the final vacuum degree can be calculated using Sobol. This enables the optimization of design factors in the SVD.

The core principle of the Sobol is to decompose the function model into individual factors and their combinations. The corresponding sensitivity indices are obtained by calculating the impact of the variance of individual or multiple input factors on the total output variance. The calculation equations for Sobol are as follows [29,30]:

The function model $f(X)$ can be decomposed into a sum of 2^p increasing terms to obtain the Equation (11).

$$f(X) = f_0 + \sum_{i=1}^{p} f_i(x_i) + \sum_{\substack{i,j=1,2,\cdots,p \\ i<j}} f_{i,j}(x_i, x_j) + \cdots + f_{1,2,\cdots,p}(x_1, x_2, \cdots, x_p) \quad (11)$$

where $f(0)$ is a constant; $X = [x_1, x_2, \ldots, x_i, \ldots, x_p]$, x_i is a performance indicator or influence factor, and $i = 1, 2, \ldots, p$.

The total variance (V) and bias-variance (V_i) of Sobol are denoted as:

$$V = \int f^2(X)\mathrm{d}X - f_0{}^2 \quad (12)$$

$$V_i = \int f_i{}^2 \mathrm{d}x_i \quad (13)$$

The expression for the decomposition of the total variance into the bias-variance is:

$$V = \sum_{i=1}^{p} V_i + \sum_{\substack{i,j=1,2,\cdots,p \\ i<j}} V_{i,j} + \cdots + V_{1,2,\cdots,p} \quad (14)$$

The Sobol sensitivity indices can be obtained by dividing both sides of Equation (14) by V:

$$1 = \sum_{i=1}^{p} S_i + \sum_{\substack{i,j=1,2,\cdots,p \\ i<j}} S_{i,j} + \cdots + S_{1,2,\cdots,p} \quad (15)$$

where S_i is the first-order sensitivity index, indicating the influence of the variation of factor i on the model output; $S_{i,j}$ is the second-order sensitivity index, indicating the joint influence of simultaneous variations in factors i and j on the model output; and S_i^T is the total-order sensitivity index, indicating the sum of sensitivity indices for factor i across all orders.

The sensitivity indices can serve as indicators to evaluate the importance of various factors. Before calculating the sensitivity indices for each factor, a reasonable range of values (minimum to maximum) must be defined for the seven factors under study, as shown in Table 3. Then, the factors are sampled using the sobolset function in MATLAB. The random numbers generated by this sampling method form a low-discrepancy sequence, which is uniform and efficient. Figure 13 shows the 200 randomly collected data points for the thickness of the sealing soil column (h_s), with a uniform data distribution. The sampling dimension for this study is seven, meaning that each set of samples contains seven data points (one for each factor). To eliminate the influence of sample size on the results, a series of sample libraries were obtained by incrementing the sample size at intervals of 50 (50, 100, 150, etc.). First-order and total-order sensitivity indices were calculated for each sample library.

Table 3. Range of factor values.

Factor	Diameter of Siphon Pipe, d (mm)	Length of Siphon Pipe, L (m)	Local Resistance Coefficient of Siphon Pipe, ζ	Thickness of Sealing Soil Column, h_s (m)	Diameter of Permeable Chamber, d_{pc} (cm)	Horizontal Hydraulic Conductivity, K_h ($\times 10^{-9}$ m/s)	Cylinder Diameter, d_e (m)
Maximum value	6	200	700	9	8	10	1.5
Minimum value	4	20	0	1	3	1	0.5

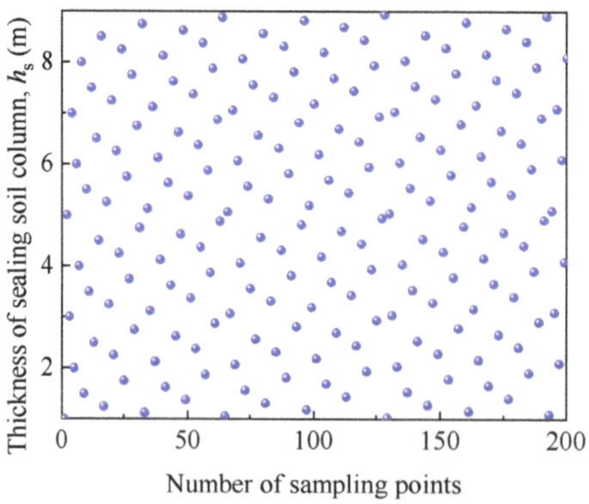

Figure 13. Distribution of randomly collected data points for sealing soil column thickness.

3.2. Results and Discussion

As shown in Figure 14, the sensitivity indices calculated in this study converge well. The first-order and total-order sensitivity indices obtained are essentially stable when the sample size exceeds 2000 sets. Table 4 provides the first-order and total-order sensitivity indices for the seven parameters when the sample size is 5000. The first-order sensitivity indices are ranked from highest to lowest as follows: 0.7772 (h_s), 0.0731 (d), 0.0618 (L), 0.0419 (K_h), 0.0196 (d_{pc}), 0.0024 (d_e), and 0.0018 (ζ). The sum of the first-order sensitivity indices has reached 0.9779. The total-order sensitivity indices are ranked from highest to lowest as follows: 0.7825 (h_s), 0.0861 (d), 0.0749 (L), 0.0483 (K_h), 0.0273 (d_{pc}), 0.0027 (d_e), and 0.0024 (ζ). The thickness of the sealing soil column (h_s) has an extremely high impact on the vacuum degree. Its first-order sensitivity index accounts for 79.48%, and the total-order sensitivity index accounts for 76.40%. This significantly exceeds the impact of other factors. Therefore, the thickness of the sealing soil column (h_s) is the factor that needs the most attention in the SVD design. The results of the global sensitivity analysis are consistent with the analysis results in Section 2.3. The diameter of the permeable chamber (d_{pc}) and the local resistance coefficient of the siphon pipe (ζ) have a very small impact on the final vacuum degree.

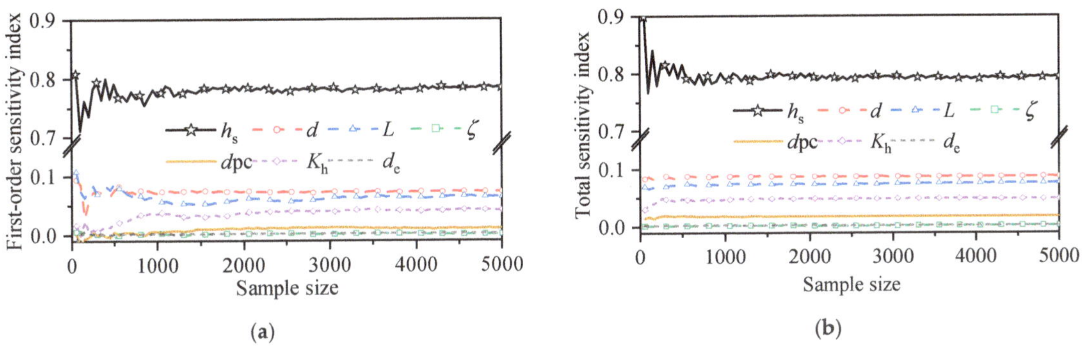

Figure 14. Sensitivity indices of various factors corresponding to different sample sizes: (**a**) first-order; (**b**) total-order.

Table 4. The first-order and total-order sensitivity indices of various factors when the sample size is 5000.

Factor	Diameter of Siphon Pipe, d (mm)	Length of Siphon Pipe, L (m)	Local Resistance Coefficient of Siphon Pipe, ζ	Thickness of Sealing Soil Column, h_s (m)	Diameter of Permeable Chamber, d_{pc} (cm)	Horizontal Hydraulic Conductivity, K_h ($\times 10^{-9}$ m/s)	Cylinder Diameter, d_e (m)
S_i	0.0731	0.0618	0.0018	0.7772	0.0196	0.0419	0.0024
ΣS_i				0.9779			
$S_i/\Sigma S_i$	7.48%	6.32%	0.18%	79.48%	2.00%	4.28%	0.25%
S_i^T	0.0861	0.0749	0.0024	0.7825	0.0273	0.0483	0.0027
ΣS_i^T				1.0242			
$S_i^T/\Sigma S_i^T$	8.41%	7.31%	0.23%	76.40%	2.67%	4.72%	0.26%

4. Calculation of Maximum Vacuum Degree

The thickness of the sealing soil column (h_s) has an impact of approximately 80% on the vacuum degree. Therefore, exploring the quantitative relationship between vacuum degree and sealing soil column thickness (h_s) is valuable for assessing the maximum vacuum degree that the SVD can form. First, the values of the remaining six factors are determined to be L = 50 m, ζ = 0.131, d = 5 mm, d_{pc} = 5 cm, K_h = 3.75 × 10^{-9} m/s, and d_e = 1.015 m.

The range of values for the thickness of the sealing soil column (h_s) is [0.1, 0.9] m. Secondly, based on the theoretical model, calculate the maximum vacuum degree (Max $|p_{A,t}|$) under different thicknesses of the sealing soil column (h_s), as shown in Figure 15. Finally, a fitting equation for the calculation results of the maximum vacuum degree is obtained:

$$\text{Max}|p_{A,\,t_k}| = 0.0164h_s^3 - 0.3979h_s^2 - 5.8132h_s + 81.08 \quad (0.1 \le h_s \le 9.9) \qquad (16)$$

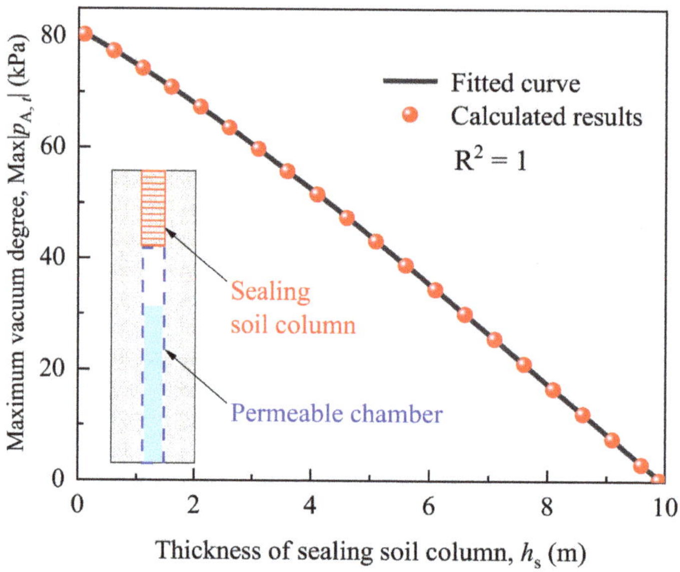

Figure 15. Maximum vacuum degree achievable with different thicknesses of sealing soil column.

The determination coefficient (R^2) of the fitting curve is 1, indicating a good fit. When h_s = 0.1 m, the vacuum degree can reach 80.49 kPa. The smaller the sealing soil column thickness (h_s), the greater the vacuum degree that can be automatically formed in the SVD. Additionally, it can shorten the path for pore water from the upper soil to seep into the vertical drainage well (permeable chamber). Thus, using smaller thicknesses of the sealing soil column (h_s) can enhance the reinforcement effect on soft soil. Naturally, this should be done while ensuring proper sealing.

5. Conclusions

Siphon-vacuum drainage is a promising method for marine reclamation, with the potential to reduce the environmental impact and operational costs. In this study, the factors influencing vacuum formation and drainage in the SVD have been comprehensively analyzed. The findings provide a basis for optimizing the design of the SVD in marine reclamation projects, leading to more sustainable and efficient land development along coastal regions. The following conclusions can be drawn:

- After the SVD is started, a vacuum gradually forms inside the permeable chamber. The duration of the vacuum formation process is generally less than 400 s. During this process, the seepage drainage rate gradually increases. The siphon rate ($U_{out,\,t}$) initially rises rapidly and then decreases slowly, gradually approaching the seepage rate ($U_{in,\,t}$). The siphon drainage plays a dominant role in the water storage change within the permeable chamber during the early stages.
- The length (L), local resistance coefficient (ζ), and diameter of the siphon pipe (d) influence the early stages of vacuum formation and drainage by affecting the siphon.

Increasing the siphon rate ($U_{\mathrm{out},\,t}$) can lead to a greater vacuum degree and drainage rate. Reducing the thickness of the sealing soil column (h_s) can create a larger vacuum degree, resulting in a larger cross-sectional area and drainage rate. The diameter of the permeable chamber (d_{pc}) primarily affects the drainage rate through the cross-sectional area.

- The first-order sensitivity indices are as follows: 0.7772 (the sealing soil column thickness, h_s), 0.0731 (the siphon pipe diameter, d), 0.0618 (the siphon pipe length, L), 0.0419 (the horizontal hydraulic conductivity, K_h), 0.0196 (the permeable chamber diameter, d_{pc}), 0.0024 (the cylinder diameter, d_e), and 0.0018 (the local resistance coefficient, ζ). The sealing soil column thickness (h_s) has an extremely high impact on the vacuum degree, accounting for 79.48%. The combined impact of the cylinder diameter (d_e) and local resistance coefficient (ζ) on the vacuum degree accounts for only 0.43%.
- A fitting curve was obtained that describes the relationship between the maximum vacuum degree ($\mathrm{Max}\,|p_{A,\,t}|$) and different sealing soil column thicknesses (h_s). Calculations indicate that the maximum vacuum degree ($\mathrm{Max}\,|p_{A,\,t}|$) can exceed 80 kPa. Reducing the sealing soil column thickness (h_s) can also shorten the path for pore water in the upper soil to seep into the vertical drainage well. Therefore, using the smallest possible sealing soil column thickness (h_s) while ensuring sealing can enhance the improvement effect.

Author Contributions: Conceptualization, J.S. and H.S.; methodology, J.S. and J.W.; software, Q.S.; validation, J.S., J.W. and Q.S.; investigation, J.S. and J.W.; resources, K.C. and H.S.; data curation, J.S.; writing—original draft preparation, J.S. and J.W.; writing—review and editing, K.C. and H.S.; visualization, J.S.; supervision, K.C. and H.S.; project administration, K.C. and H.S.; funding acquisition, K.C. and H.S. All authors have read and agreed to the published version of the manuscript.

Funding: This study was supported by the National Natural Science Foundation of China (42230702).

Institutional Review Board Statement: Not applicable.

Informed Consent Statement: Informed consent was obtained from all subjects involved in the study.

Data Availability Statement: Some or all data, models, or codes that support the findings of this study are available from the corresponding author upon reasonable request.

Conflicts of Interest: Author Kexing Chen is employed by the Zhejiang Electric Power Design Institude. The author Jun Wang is employed by Zhejiang Seaport Engineering Construction Consultants Co., Ltd. and is concurrently a on-the-job doctoral student at the Ocean College, Zhejiang University. The author Qingsong Shen has recently completed his PhD at the College of Civil Engineering and Architecture, Zhejiang University, and is now employed by Power China Huadong Engineering Corporation Limited. The remaining authors declare that the research was conducted in the absence of any commercial or financial relationships that could be construed as a potential conflict of interest.

References

1. Liu, J.J.; Li, J.K.; Lei, H.Y.; Zheng, G.; Jin, Y.W. Ground Improvement of Dredged Fills with Two Improved Vacuum Preloading Methods: Case Study. *J. Geotech. Geoenviron. Eng.* **2022**, *148*, 05022008. [CrossRef]
2. Malekzadeh, M.; Sivakugan, N. One-dimensional electrokinetic stabilization of dredged mud. *Mar. Georesources Geotechnol.* **2017**, *35*, 603–609. [CrossRef]
3. Shinsha, H.; Kumagai, T. Material properties of solidified soil grains produced from dredged marine clay. *Soils Found.* **2018**, *58*, 678–688. [CrossRef]
4. Dahal, B.K.; Zheng, J.J.; Zhang, R.J.; Song, D.B. Enhancing the mechanical properties of marine clay using cement solidification. *Mar. Georesources Geotechnol.* **2019**, *37*, 755–764. [CrossRef]
5. Karunaratne, G.P. Prefabricated and electrical vertical drains for consolidation of soft clay. *Geotext. Geomembr.* **2011**, *29*, 391–401. [CrossRef]
6. Mesri, G.; Khan, A.Q. Ground Improvement Using Vacuum Loading Together with Vertical Drains. *J. Geotech. Geoenvironmental Eng.* **2012**, *138*, 680–689. [CrossRef]
7. Li, J.F.; Chen, H.E.; Yuan, X.Q.; Shan, W.C. Analysis of the Effectiveness of the Step Vacuum Preloading Method: A Case Study on High Clay Content Dredger Fill in Tianjin, China. *J. Mar. Sci. Eng.* **2020**, *8*, 38. [CrossRef]

8. Xia, C.Q.; Deng, Y.B.; Zhu, M.; Niu, J.J.; Zheng, L.K.; Chen, X.S. One-Dimensional Solar Energy Thermal Consolidation Model Testing and Analytical Calculation for Marine Soft Clays. *J. Mar. Sci. Eng.* **2022**, *10*, 1634. [CrossRef]
9. Spross, J.; Larsson, S. Probabilistic observational method for design of surcharges on vertical drains. *Geotechnique* **2021**, *71*, 226–238. [CrossRef]
10. Ge, S.Q.; Jiang, W.H.; Zheng, L.W.; Xie, X.Y.; Xie, K.H.; Feng, G.H.; Zhang, X.L. Theoretical analysis and experimental verification of large deformation electro-osmosis consolidation treatment of dredged slurry. *Eng. Geol.* **2023**, *312*, 106924. [CrossRef]
11. Ge, S.Q.; Ma, Y.; Wang, K.; Zheng, L.W.; Xie, X.Y.; Chen, X.H.; Yu, H.S. Unsaturated hydro-mechanical-electro-chemical coupling based on mixture-coupling theory: A unified model. *Int. J. Eng. Sci.* **2023**, *191*, 103914. [CrossRef]
12. Lei, H.Y.; Feng, S.X.; Wang, L.; Jin, Y.W. Field instrumentation and settlement prediction of ground treated with straight-line vacuum preloading. *Geomech. Eng.* **2019**, *19*, 447–462. [CrossRef]
13. Indraratna, B.; Rujikiatkamjorn, C.; Baral, P.; Ameratunga, J. Performance of marine clay stabilised with vacuum pressure: Based on Queensland experience. *J. Rock Mech. Geotech. Eng.* **2019**, *11*, 598–611. [CrossRef]
14. Lam, K.P.; Wu, S.F.; Chu, J. Field trial of a membraneless vacuum preloading system for soft soil improvement. *Proc. Inst. Civ. Eng. -Ground Improv.* **2020**, *173*, 40–50. [CrossRef]
15. Zheng, G.; Liu, J.J.; Lei, H.Y.; Rahman, M.S.; Tan, Z.K. Improvement of very soft ground by a high-efficiency vacuum preloading method: A case study. *Mar. Georesources Geotechnol.* **2017**, *35*, 631–642. [CrossRef]
16. Lei, H.Y.; Lu, H.B.; Liu, J.J.; Zheng, G. Experimental Study of the Clogging of Dredger Fills under Vacuum Preloading. *Int. J. Geomech.* **2017**, *17*, 04017117. [CrossRef]
17. Orlove, B.; Lazrus, H.; Hovelsrud, G.K.; Giannini, A. Recognitions and Responsibilities On the Origins and Consequences of the Uneven Attention to Climate Change around the World. *Curr. Anthropol.* **2014**, *55*, 249–275. [CrossRef]
18. Khan, S.A.R.; Ponce, P.; Yu, Z. Technological innovation and environmental taxes toward a carbon-free economy: An empirical study in the context of COP-21. *J. Environ. Manag.* **2021**, *298*, 113418. [CrossRef]
19. Garrett, R.E. Principles of Siphons. *J. World Aquac. Soc.* **1991**, *22*, 1–9. [CrossRef]
20. Cai, Y.L.; Sun, H.Y.; Shang, Y.Q.; Xiong, X.L. An investigation of flow characteristics in slope siphon drains. *J. Zhejiang Univ. Sci. A* **2014**, *15*, 22–30. [CrossRef]
21. Sun, H.Y.; Wu, G.; Liang, X.; Yan, X.; Wang, D.F.; Wei, Z.L. Laboratory modeling of siphon drainage combined with surcharge loading consolidation for soft ground treatment. *Mar. Georesources Geotechnol.* **2018**, *36*, 940–949. [CrossRef]
22. Shen, Q.S.; Wang, J.; Sun, H.Y.; Shu, J.W.; Shang, Y.Q. Analysis of the influence of siphon hole spacing on soft-soil drainage effect. *Proc. Inst. Civ. Eng. -Geotech. Eng.* **2023**. *ahead of print*. [CrossRef]
23. Qian, J.H.; Zhao, W.B.; Cheung, Y.K.; Lee, P.K.K. The theory and practice of vacuum preloading. *Comput. Geotech.* **1992**, *13*, 103–118. [CrossRef]
24. Shu, J.W.; Sun, H.Y.; An, N. Theoretical and field investigation into the vacuum formation in the siphon-vacuum drainage system for soft ground improvement. *Can. Geotech. J.* **2024**. [CrossRef]
25. Zhang, C.; Chu, J.G.; Fu, G.T. Sobol's sensitivity analysis for a distributed hydrological model of Yichun River Basin, China. *J. Hydrol.* **2013**, *480*, 58–68. [CrossRef]
26. Rohmer, J.; Loschetter, A.; Raucoules, D.; de Michele, M.; Raffard, D.; Le Gallo, Y. Revealing the surface deformation induced by deep CO₂ injection in vegetated/agricultural areas: The combination of corner-reflectors, reservoir simulations and spatio-temporal statistics. *Eng. Geol.* **2015**, *197*, 188–197. [CrossRef]
27. Ghasemizade, M.; Baroni, G.; Abbaspour, K.; Schirmer, M. Combined analysis of time-varying sensitivity and identifiability indices to diagnose the response of a complex environmental model. *Environ. Model. Softw.* **2017**, *88*, 22–34. [CrossRef]
28. Hamdia, K.M.; Silani, M.; Zhuang, X.Y.; He, P.F.; Rabczuk, T. Stochastic analysis of the fracture toughness of polymeric nanoparticle composites using polynomial chaos expansions. *Int. J. Fract.* **2017**, *206*, 215–227. [CrossRef]
29. Ke, H.; Hu, J.; Xu, X.B.; Wu, X.W.; Li, Y.C.; Lan, J.W. Analytical solution of leachate flow to vertical wells in municipal solid waste landfills using a dual-porosity model. *Eng. Geol.* **2018**, *239*, 27–40. [CrossRef]
30. Sobol, I. *On sensitivity Estimation for Nonlinear Mathematical Models*; Keldysh Applied Mathematics Institute: Moscow, Russia, 1990; pp. 112–118.

Journal of
Marine Science and Engineering

MDPI

Article

Analyses of the Suction Anchor–Sandy Soil Interactions under Slidable Pulling Action Using DEM-FEM Coupling Method: The Interface Friction Effect

Yu Peng [1,2], Bolong Liu [1,*], Gang Wang [1] and Quan Wang [3]

1 Key Laboratory of Rock Mechanics and Geohazards of Zhejiang Province, Shaoxing University, Shaoxing 312000, China; yupeng@polyu.edu.hk (Y.P.); gangw277842@whut.edu.cn (G.W.)
2 Department of Civil and Environmental Engineering, The Hong Kong Polytechnic University, Hung Hom, Kowloon, Hong Kong, China
3 Jinghe New City of Xixian New Area Real Estate Development Co., Ltd., Xi'an 713700, China; 18142399817@163.com
* Correspondence: 2021000164@usx.edu.cn

Abstract: The microscale mechanisms underlying the suction anchor–sandy soil interaction under slidable pulling actions of mooring lines remain poorly understood. This technical note addresses this knowledge gap by investigating the suction anchor–sandy soil interaction from micro to macro, with a particular emphasis on the effect of interface friction. The discrete element method (DEM) was utilized to simulate the sandy soil, while the finite element method (FEM) was employed to model the suction anchors. The peak pulling forces in numerical simulations were verified by centrifuge test results. The research findings highlight the significant influence of interface friction on the pulling force–displacement curves, as it affects the patterns of suction anchor–sandy soil interactions. Furthermore, clear relationships were established between the magnitude of interface friction, rotation angle, and pullout displacement of suction anchors. By examining the macro-to-micro behaviors of suction anchor–sandy soil interactions, this study concludes with a comprehensive understanding of failure patterns and their key characteristics under different interface friction conditions. The findings proved that the interface friction not only influences the anti-pullout capacity but also changes the failure patterns of suction anchor–soil interactions in marine engineering.

Keywords: soil–structure interaction; sandy soil; micromechanics; DEM-FEM coupling; suction anchor; failure pattern

1. Introduction

With the rapid development in marine engineering, suction anchor foundations have gained increasing popularity for anchoring floating buildings and structures in the sea [1,2]. These anchor foundations, consisting of cylinder suction anchors and mooring line systems, are commonly connected to floating buildings and structures using the mooring lines that are attached to the annular pad eyes [3,4], as displayed in Figure 1a,b. Throughout the lifespan of floating buildings and structures, the suction anchor and the surrounding soil experience significant pulling forces from mooring lines to ensure engineering safety [5,6]. Therefore, comprehending suction anchor–soil interactions is essential for the design of suction anchor foundations in marine engineering.

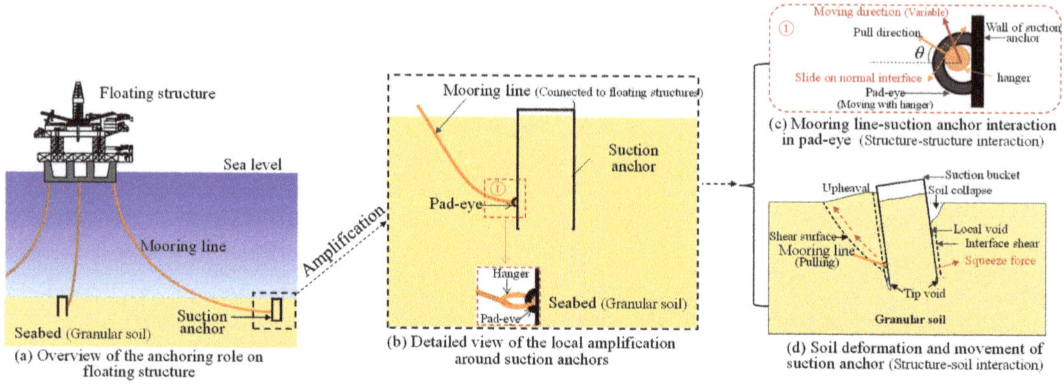

Figure 1. The interactions among mooring lines, suction anchors, and granular soil.

Suction anchor–soil interactions in marine engineering have garnered significant attention in previous studies. Researchers have carried out a sequence of experimental tests to examine the anti-pullout capacity of suction anchors and explore the correlation between pulling forces and the displacement of suction anchors in granular soil [7,8]. Experiment test results have demonstrated that various factors, including pulling directions of mooring lines, towing positions, and soil properties, affect the anti-pullout capacity of the suction anchors, while interface friction between suction anchors and surrounding soils plays a critical role in determining the behavior of interactions between suction anchors and soil [9,10]. Nevertheless, prior studies on suction anchor–soil interactions primarily focused on evaluating the resistance to pullout and the displacements of suction anchors. As a result, the microscale mechanisms of suction anchor–soil interactions under different interface friction conditions remained poorly understood.

Moreover, previous numerical studies have usually simplified the pulling actions of mooring lines on pad eyes as a constant force or fixed pulling movements [11,12], overlooking the contact sliding behaviors between hangers (tail end of mooring lines) and pad eyes, as well as the variations in force (Figure 1c). Because variable soil resistances influence the hanger sliding within pad eyes, the movement direction of the hanger cannot be predetermined and is usually in a substantial deviation from the intended pulling direction (as depicted in Figure 1c). Consequently, assuming a constant load or displacement instead of contact action between hangers and pad eyes (structure–structure interaction) is improper. Although continuous numerical methods including the finite element method (FEM) are capable of simulating the deformation of suction anchors and structure–structure interactions, these methods fall short in terms of accurately simulating large soil deformation and failure (see Figure 1d) [13,14]. Consequently, the discrete element method (DEM) is popular among many researchers, as it can analyze sandy soil behavior on a microscale and model significant soil deformations [15,16]. However, modeling the contact behaviors between hangers and suction anchors poses challenges for existing discrete element method (DEM) approaches in structure–structure interaction simulation [14]. Hence, harnessing the strengths of both DEM and FEM could offer valuable insights into the interactions between suction anchors and sandy soils under pulling action from mooring lines. To date, there have been no studies that have utilized a DEM-FEM simulation to examine the influence of interface friction on suction anchor–soil interactions under slidable pulling actions.

This technical note endeavors to investigate the underlying mechanism of the interaction between suction anchors and sandy soil under slidable pulling action from micro to macro, considering various interface friction conditions. The study initiates by analyzing pulling force–displacement curves under different interface friction conditions. Subsequently, a comprehensive analysis is carried out to evaluate the displacement features of suction anchors and soil behaviors at the particle scale. Lastly, the patterns of interaction between suction anchors and soil under varying interface friction conditions are summarized. The results of this study offer a reference for designing the suction anchor foundations used in marine engineering.

2. Numerical Research on Suction Anchor–Soil Interaction

2.1. The Centrifuge Model Tests

This study utilized the centrifuge tests carried out by Bang et al. [17] to investigate the anti-pullout capacity of model suction anchors under slidable pulling actions from mooring lines. The centrifuge tests were conducted in a tank. The foundation soil was a type of sandy soil. The specific gravity of the soil was 2.62, while the grain size was 0.1~1.0 mm. An actuator was utilized to generate the pulling action on mooring lines in the experimental tests. The model suction anchors, as shown in Figure 2b, were constructed using a smooth steel tube. The model suction anchor had an underwater weight of 40.3 g. Pulling actions during the tests were applied on the pad eye at a depth of $h = -45$ mm (75% depth), which is approximately the location with the highest anti-pullout capacity [14,18,19]. The tests were carried out at the gravitational acceleration of 100 g (981 m/m^2). Note that the model of the suction anchor (shown in Figure 2) under the gravitational acceleration of 100 g corresponds to a suction anchor with a diameter of 3.0 m and a length of 6.0 m in prototype dimensions. To prevent the suction anchor from experiencing obvious excess pore water pressure, two air holes (refer to Figure 2a) were drilled at the top. It should be emphasized that the model tests were conducted using sandy soil that was easy for the dissipation of excess pore water pressure. Similar to prior studies [20,21], excess pore water pressure was not taken into account in the experimental tests. Further information regarding the specific details can be found in the study by Bang et al. [17].

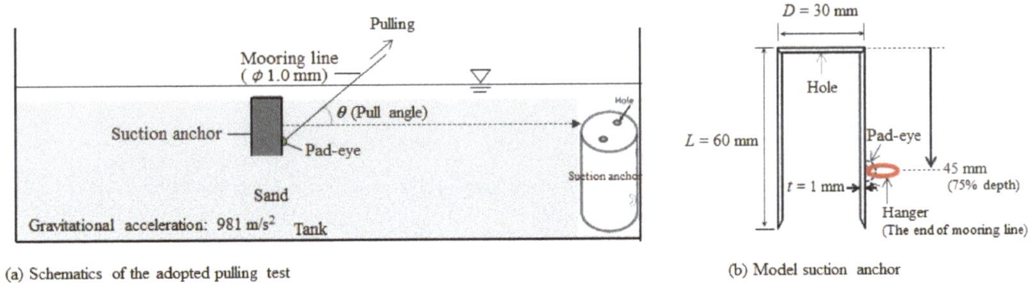

Figure 2. Experimental anti-pullout tests for suction anchors in granular soil (modified from Bang et al. [17]).

2.2. The Numerical Model in DEM-FEM Simulations

In this study, coupled DEM-FEM simulations were employed. The size of the model suction and the pulling position in the simulations were the same as that in the experimental tests carried out by Bang et al. [17]. DEM simulations are well suited for sandy soil, while FEM is commonly used for modeling solid structures [22,23]. Following the approach of previous studies [14,18,19], a DEM-FEM coupling method was adopted in this research. Balls in DEM were utilized to simulate the sandy soil, while meshes in FEM were employed to create the suction anchors. The deformation of the suction anchors in the centrifuge tests was small relative to the displacement, satisfying the criteria for employing the one-way transient coupled DEM-FEM simulations [24,25]. Similar to previous investigations [14,19,26], the one-way transient coupling method was employed in simulations. This method encompasses the analysis of boundary data, specifically particle contact forces on the structure's surfaces in the DEM simulation; then, these forces are integrated into the FEM simulation as boundary conditions at each step, without any feedback from the FEM part to the DEM part. In the computing process, the initial geometry of the suction anchor was shared between the DEM and FEM components. Firstly, the DEM part collected particle contact forces on the suction anchor's boundary, which consisted of facet elements. These loads were then transformed into vertex forces on each boundary element. Subsequently, the forces exerted on vertices were utilized for conducting transient structure analysis within the FEM component. Consistent with prior research [14,19], the buoyant unit weight of the grains (as indicated by the density of grains in Table 1) was employed to take the underwater state of sandy soil into consideration.

Table 1. Main numerical parameters for modeling suction anchor–soil interactions.

Parameters	Value	Unit
Grains		
Density (ρ)	1650	kg/m^3
Elasticity modulus (E)	1.0×10^6	N/m^2
Friction coefficient (f)	0.5	\
Restitution coefficient	0.30	\
Rolling resistance (RR)	0.20	\
Timestep	5.0×10^{-5}	s
Poisson ratio (v)	0.30	\
Acceleration of gravity (g)	981	m/s^2
Suction anchor		
Elasticity modulus (E)	2.0×10^{11}	N/m^2
Friction coefficient (f)	0.35, 0.55	\
Restitution coefficient	0.80	\
Poisson ratio (v)	0.30	\
Roller		
Elasticity modulus (E)	2.0×10^{11}	N/m^2
Friction coefficient (f)	0.0	\
Restitution coefficient	0.8	\
Poisson ratio (v)	0.3	\

Like prior investigations [14,19], the DEM-FEM simulations utilized a symmetry-based modeling method to decrease computational expenses [27,28]. A frictionless container was employed to contain 1/2 foundation soil and 1/2 the suction anchor, as depicted in Figure 3a, capitalizing on the axisymmetric characteristics in experimental tests. Additionally, a coarse-grained model [16,29,30] was implemented in this study to ensure the same macroscopic soil properties throughout different regions while selectively increasing the grain size in certain regions to decrease the simulation time. The computational model consisted of 3 different zones: Zone 1, which encompassed a small-grain region around the suction anchor, and two larger grain zones, Zone 2 and Zone 3, surrounding Zone 1, as shown in Figure 3a. In Zone 1, the grain diameters were 2~2.8 mm, with a median diameter (d_{50}) of 2.4 mm. The ratio of the suction anchor diameter to d_{50} was 12.5, which was deemed sufficient to disregard grain-scale effects [31,32]. To prevent the migration of grains from the small-grain zones into the neighboring large-grain zones, enlargement factors were applied. Consequently, in comparison to the grains in Zone 1, those in Zones 2 and 3 were amplified by amplification coefficients of 1.6 and 2.56, respectively, which was similar to previous studies [14,33]. When the pulling action was applied to the suction anchors, the particle movement primarily occurred in Zone, which confirmed the rational design of the numerical model's zoning approach. Consistent with previous DEM simulations [14,19] conducted on the same tests, the simulated sandy soil had a porosity of 0.37 in this study. Similar to prior research [14,19,34], the Hertzian spring dashpot model and the linear spring Coulomb limit model were utilized to compute the normal particle contact behaviors and the tangential particle contact behaviors, respectively. To account for the influence of grain angularity on grain contact behavior, the linear spring rolling limit model, as offered by Wensrich and Katterfeld [15] was employed.

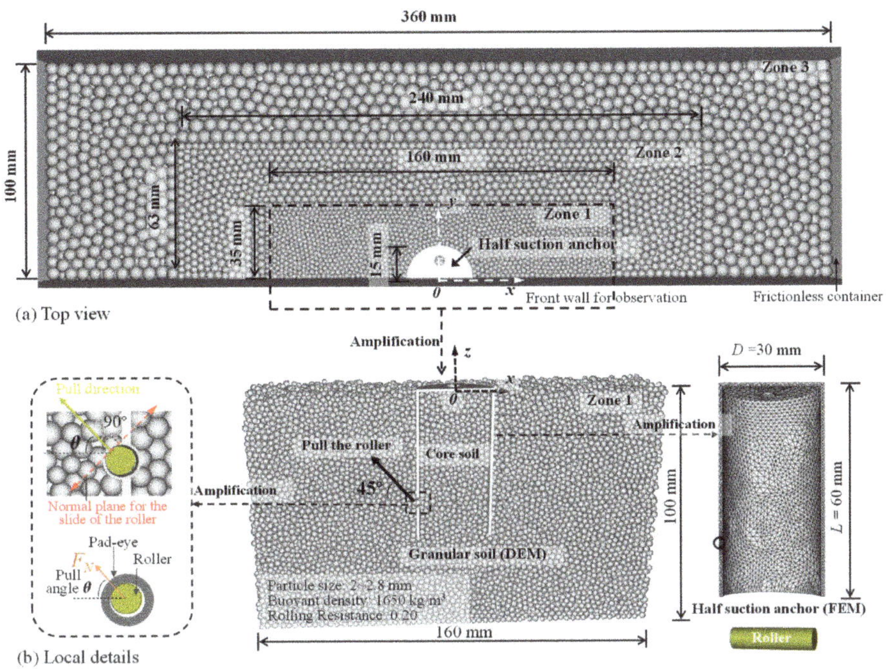

Figure 3. The DEM-FEM model of suction anchor–granular soil interaction in simulations.

In line with previous numerical simulations [19,25], finite element meshes were employed to construct suction anchors with triangular geometry, composed of 7837 vertices. The physical properties of the suction anchors were set with steel properties. As shown in Figure 3b, to replicate the pulling behavior observed in the centrifuge tests, where the hanger pulls the suction anchor (as shown in Figure 2), the pulling motion of the confined roller inside the pad eye was controlled during simulations. Consistent with the experiments, the pulling action in simulations was controlled by pulling velocity at a rate of 2 mm/s, which was in line with previous research [14,19]. Moreover, this pulling velocity matched the velocity of the movement of floating structures, as indicated by prior numerical studies [35,36]. The pull angle (θ) was maintained at a constant 45° angle, consistent with that in experimental tests. In line with previous simulations [14,19] based on the tests of Bang et al. [17], Young's modulus (E) values for the grains and suction anchors were determined as 1.0×10^6 kN/m^2 and 2×10^{11} kN/m^2, respectively.

Numerical parameters were calibrated using the peak pulling forces (refer to Figure 4) at various anchoring positions (h = 5%~95% depths) that were gained from the centrifuge tests, in line with previous DEM research on soil–structure interactions [14,37]. The calibration with forces provides a comprehensive representation of the soil–structure interaction intensity on a physical level, reflecting the action and properties of structures, along with the soil properties, as demonstrated in previous DEM-based studies [14,38,39]. The major numerical parameters utilized in DEM-FEM simulations are presented in Table 1. In the adopted tests, model suction anchors were built with smooth steel tubes, which led to a low interface friction value (f = 0.35) for the anchor surfaces in numerical simulations. After calibrating numerical parameters, a subsequent investigation was conducted to explore the impact of interface friction on suction anchor–soil interactions. Both a low interface friction condition (f = 0.35) and a high interface friction condition (f = 0.55) were considered in the simulations. Note that it is a common practice in numerical studies to conduct extension studies using validated parameters, which can save significant amounts of time and resources compared to directly conducting experimental tests [13,25]. However, it is important to emphasize that the most ideal approach is to accompany numerical analysis with corresponding experimental tests whenever sufficient time, test conditions, and funding are available.

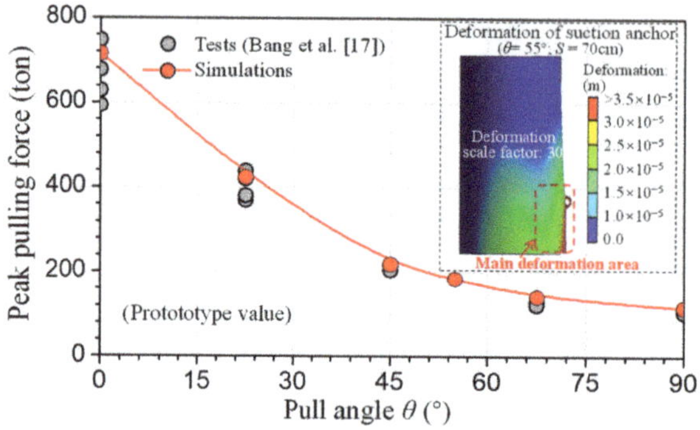

Figure 4. Comparison of peak pulling forces in centrifuge tests and numerical simulations under different pull angles [17].

It should be noted that many parameters, including grain size, grain shape, void ratio, and grain size distribution, usually have some variations between simulations and experiment tests in most DEM-based research [40,41]. Consequently, the specific numerical value derived from these investigations based on DEM may differ to a certain extent from the values in experiments. Consequently, instead of aiming for exact numerical value agreement, the primary focus should be on providing micromechanical mechanisms and the trend in soil behaviors.

3. Results and Analyses

The design of suction anchors often benefits from the data inferred from pulling force–displacement (*P-S*) curves [42,43]. Figure 5 depicts the evolution of the pulling force (T) observed in simulations under different interface friction conditions. Obviously, the pulling force in Group 2 was much larger than that in Group 1 because of the increased intensity of suction anchor–soil interactions resulting from higher interface friction. As the pulling distance increased, the pulling force first grew fast and then stabilized without peaks under the low interface friction (f = 0.35). However, under the condition of f = 0.55, as the pulling distance increased, the pulling force first grew fast and then obviously reduced, leading to an emergence of evident peaks in pulling forces. The discrepancy in the shapes of curves was in fact associated with the difference in patterns of suction anchor–soil interactions, which will be discussed in subsequent sections.

Comprehending the movement of suction anchors and soil particle behaviors is essential for accurately understanding the mechanism of suction anchor–sandy soil interactions [44]. Figure 6 illustrates the movement of suction anchors and the behavior of soil particles at the particle scale. The displacement of suction anchors was greatly different under different interface friction conditions: A large pullout displacement and small rotation angle of the suction anchor were observed under the low interface friction of f = 0.35, while a small pullout displacement and a relatively large rotation angle were found under the condition of f = 0.55. Due to the large anchor rotation angle, the soil deformation (upheaval) on two sides of the suction anchors was much larger under higher interface friction, as shown in Figure 6b. The pullout displacements demonstrated that higher interface friction between the suction anchor and soil is useful for enhancing the anti-pullout capacity in suction anchor foundations.

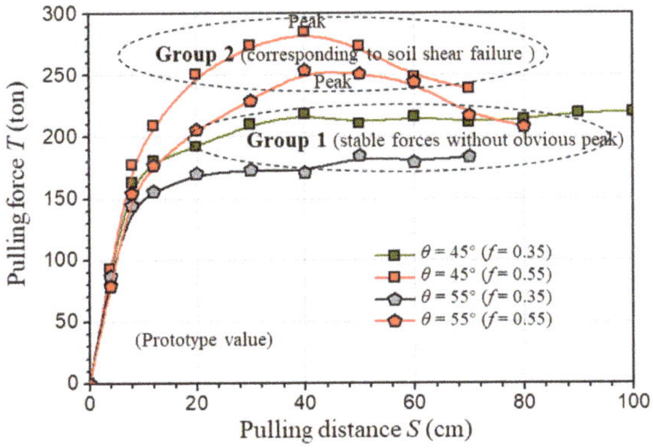

Figure 5. Pulling force–displacement curves under different interface friction conditions.

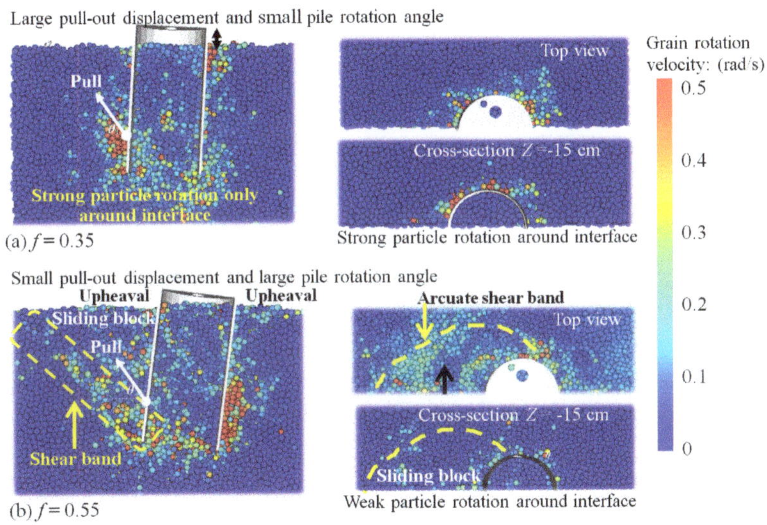

Figure 6. Comparative analysis of displacements of suction anchors and the surrounding grain rotation velocity distributions under different interface friction conditions (S = 70 cm; θ = 55°): (**a**) f = 0.35, and (**b**) f = 0.55.

The rotational velocity of grains serves as a valuable indicator of soil shear behavior [14]. As shown in Figure 6a, under the low interface friction of f = 0.35, strong particle rotation was only distributed around the suction anchor–soil interface, indicating the existence of strong interface shear behaviors between the suction anchor and soil. In contrast, under the condition of f = 0.55, an additional banded particle rotation area and a corresponding sliding block above it were observed on the pulling side (Figure 6b), indicating a typical internal soil shear failure under high interface friction. According to previous studies [14,19], the shearing out to the soil surface of shear bands typically results in a significant reduction in pulling forces (corresponding to soil resistances). This phenomenon can effectively explain the emergence of prominent peaks in pulling force–displacement curves under high interface friction.

4. Discussion

4.1. The Interface Friction Effect on Failure Patterns of Anchor–Soil Interactions

This section focuses on exploring the influence of interface friction on the failure patterns of suction anchor–soil interactions. The trajectories and translation velocities of grains play a crucial role in comprehensively understanding the soil failure behavior in the vicinity of structures [14]. Figure 7 shows the trajectories and translation velocities of grains under varying interface friction conditions in simulations. Under the low interface friction of $f = 0.35$, a short particle trajectory was only observed in limited areas, which corresponds to weak soil movement and relatively small soil disturbance areas during suction anchor–sandy soil interactions. Under the condition of $f = 0.55$, the particle trajectory was much longer and widely distributed, with a relatively flat bottom boundary on the pulling side. The flat boundary corresponding to the bottom of the shear band indicated a relatively bulk movement on the left pulling side, which can be attributed to shear failure within the soil. Moreover, violent rotation was observed in the core soil, which corresponds to the huge rotation angle of suction anchors during suction anchor–sandy soil interactions.

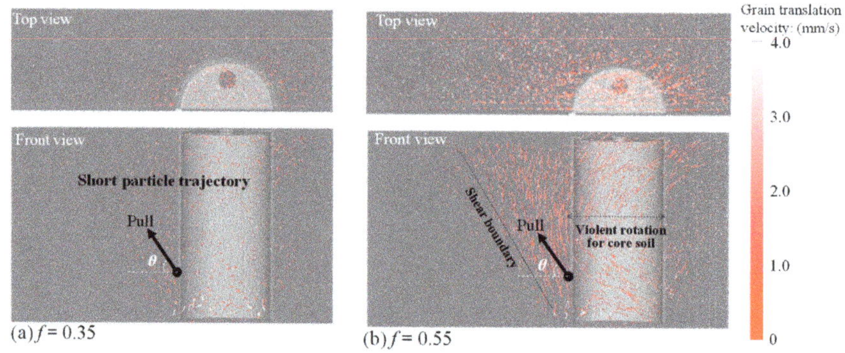

Figure 7. Comparison of trajectories and translation velocities of grains under different interface friction conditions in simulations (S = 0~70 cm; θ = 55°): (**a**) f = 0.35, and (**b**) f = 0.55.

The definitive failure patterns of suction anchor–soil interactions under different interface friction conditions are presented in Figure 8, based on the aforementioned micro-to-macro analyses. Similar to previous studies [14,19,25], the numerical simulations were conducted with a 3D model, while the failure modes of suction anchor–soil interactions (results in Figure 8) were determined in 2D format. The decision to use 2D diagrammatic representations is justified by the following reasons: Firstly, 2D representations make it easier for readers to discern the interaction modes between suction anchors and sandy soil compared to 3D views. Secondly, the loading direction (pulling direction) considered in this study is confined to the 2D vertical plane. Previous studies [14,19] have demonstrated that the most significant deformations and stresses occur within this vertical plane. Under low interface friction conditions, suction anchor–soil interactions exhibit a representative interface shear failure pattern. In such scenarios, suction anchor–soil interactions are distinguished by significant pullout displacements, small rotation angles of suction anchors, and small soil deformation. Under high interface friction conditions, suction anchor–soil interactions exhibit a representative internal soil shear failure pattern. They are distinguished by relatively small pullout displacements, large rotation angles of suction anchors, and large soil deformation around the anchors (obvious soil upheaval). To summarize, the failure pattern of suction anchor–sandy soil interactions is notably influenced by changes in interface friction. Disregarding the impact of interface friction will result in misjudgments regarding the deformation of sandy soil and the anti-pullout capacity of suction anchors, potentially compromising the safety of floating structures in marine engineering.

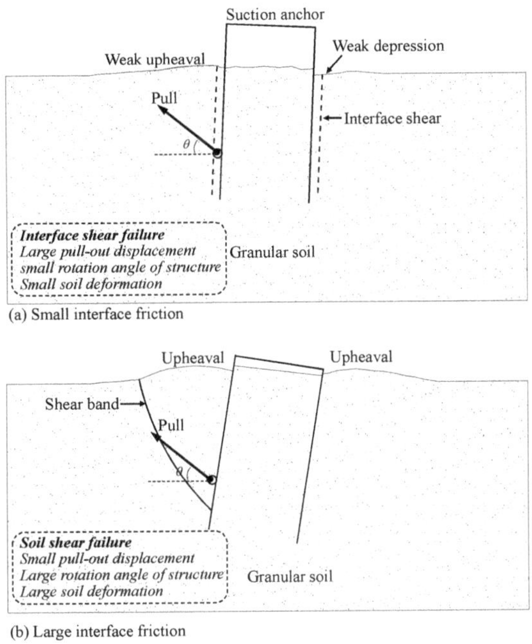

Figure 8. Diagrammatic representations of failure modes for suction anchor–sandy soil interactions under different interface friction conditions: (**a**) small interface friction, and (**b**) Large interface friction.

4.2. The Limitations of the Study and Future Research Directions

In the DEM-FEM coupled numerical study, the influence of fluid (water) in the experimental tests was simplified rather than directly modeled, taking into account well-drained conditions. Additionally, although the parameters in the DEM-based simulation were calibrated using experimental tests, real-world validation was not conducted for the analysis results of the interface friction effect on suction anchor–sandy soil interactions in the numerical study. For future studies, it is recommended to perform additional experimental tests to further validate the findings, provided that the test conditions allow for it. Furthermore, it is essential to highlight that, in this study, the mooring line was installed solely at the 75% depth position, with pull forces applied along a vertical plane. Therefore, further investigation into the interface friction effect is warranted for suction anchors moored at various depths or subjected to horizontal pull forces.

5. Conclusions

This technical note presents a series of DEM-FEM simulations aimed at examining the influence of interface friction on suction anchor–soil interactions under the slidable pulling actions of mooring lines, from micro to macro. The key findings can be outlined in the following points:

(1) Interface friction significantly influenced the shapes of pulling force–displacement curves of suction anchors due to its effect on the pattern of suction anchor–soil interactions. Under low interface friction conditions, the pulling forces increased with pulling distance first and then tended to be stable, which corresponded to the stable interface slide during suction anchor–soil interactions. However, under high interface friction conditions, a distinct peak pulling force emerged with an increase in pulling distance, corresponding to internal soil shear failure.

(2) The interface friction alters the movement of suction anchors and the surrounding soil deformation. Low interface friction leads to large pullout displacements and small rotation angles of suction anchors due to the weak impede effect on the pullout behaviors of suction anchors. In contrast, high interface friction leads to stronger suction anchor–sandy soil interaction forces, which impede the pullout of suction anchors and further result in obvious anchor rotation, larger soil deformations, and the emergence of an additional banded particle rotation area within the soil.

(3) The conclusion on the effect of interface friction on the failure patterns of suction anchor–sandy soil interactions was drawn after the analyses of macro-to-particle-scale soil behaviors. Under high interface friction, longer particle trajectories and wider soil disturbance areas corresponded well to the much larger rotation angle of suction anchors and huge soil deformation. Finally, the characteristics of the two definitive soil failure patterns, namely the interface shear failure and internal soil shear failure during suction anchor–soil interactions, were identified.

In summary, this technical note proves the effectiveness of three-dimensional DEM-FEM coupling methods in modeling suction anchor–soil interaction behaviors under the slidable pulling actions of mooring lines. The findings highlight the notable influence of interface friction on the intensity of suction anchor–soil interactions along with the failure pattern. This investigation provides valuable knowledge for analyzing the behaviors of suction anchor foundations in marine engineering.

Author Contributions: Conceptualization, Methodology, writing—original draft preparation and writing—review and editing, Y.P.; writing—review and editing, formal analysis, software, validation, resources and supervision, funding acquisition, project administration, B.L.; writing—review and editing, formal analysis, data curation, investigation, funding acquisition, project administration, G.W. and Q.W. All authors have read and agreed to the published version of the manuscript.

Funding: This work has been funded by the Natural Science Foundation of Zhejiang Province (LTGS23E040001), Shaoxing Science and Technology Plan Project (No. 2022A13003), China Post-doctoral Science Foundation (2023M732689), and National Natural Science Foundation of Zhejiang Province (No. LQ24D020012).

Institutional Review Board Statement: Not applicable.

Informed Consent Statement: Not applicable.

Data Availability Statement: The data presented in this study are available upon request from the corresponding author.

Conflicts of Interest: Author Quan Wang was employed by the Jinghe New City of Xixian New Area Real Estate Development Co. Ltd. The remaining authors declare that the research was conducted in the absence of any commercial or financial relationships that could be construed as a potential conflict of interest.

References

1. Fu, D.; Zhou, Z.; Yan, Y.; Pradhan, D.L.; Hennig, J. A method to predict the torsional resistance of suction caisson with anti-rotation fins in clay. *Mar. Struct.* **2021**, *75*, 102866. [CrossRef]
2. Wang, Y.; Zhang, S.; Ren, Y.; Xu, H.; Ren, B.; Zhang, Y.; Gaunt, P. Site investigation and soil parameters for offshore suction bucket design: A case study of Houhu wind turbine. *Ocean Eng.* **2022**, *255*, 111458. [CrossRef]
3. Wang, X.; Yang, X.; Zeng, X. Seismic centrifuge modelling of suction bucket foundation for offshore wind turbine. *Renew. Energy* **2017**, *114*, 1013–1022. [CrossRef]
4. Yang, Y.; Bao, J.; Yang, H.; Pang, Z.; Wang, Y. Microscopic analysis of the influence of soil properties on the suction bucket installation in sand based on the CFD-DEM model. *Comput. Geotech.* **2023**, *156*, 105249. [CrossRef]
5. Lai, H.; Gu, X.; Tu, W.; Lin, Y.; Xiao, J. Effects of soil small strain nonlinearity on dynamic impedance of horizontally loaded suction caisson for offshore wind turbines. *Soil Dyn. Earthq. Eng.* **2023**, *165*, 107731. [CrossRef]
6. Huang, Z.; Shi, L.; Cai, Y. Suction contribution to uplift capacity of suction buckets under serviceability conditions. *Ocean Eng.* **2023**, *283*, 115041. [CrossRef]
7. Ueda, K.; Uzuoka, R.; Iai, S.; Okamura, T. Centrifuge model tests and effective stress analyses of offshore wind turbine systems with a suction bucket foundation subject to seismic load. *Soils Found.* **2020**, *60*, 1546–1569. [CrossRef]

8. Houlsby, G.; Kelly, R.; Huxtable, J.; Byrne, B. Field trials of suction caissons in sand for offshore wind turbine foundations. *Géotechnique* **2006**, *56*, 3–10. [CrossRef]
9. Zhang, P.; Li, J.; Le, C.; Ding, H. Seismic responses of two bucket foundations for offshore wind turbines based on shaking table tests. *Renew. Energy* **2022**, *187*, 1100–1117. [CrossRef]
10. Peng, Y.; Tan, Y.; Qu, L. Micromechanical analysis of the suction bucket-granular soil interactions under the pull action of anchor lines: Embedded length effect. *Ocean Eng.* **2024**, *291*, 116443. [CrossRef]
11. Cheng, X.; Cheng, W.; Wang, P.; El Naggar, M.H.; Zhang, J.; Liu, Z. Response of offshore wind turbine tripod suction bucket foundation to seismic and environmental loading. *Ocean Eng.* **2022**, *257*, 111708. [CrossRef]
12. Tu, W.; He, Y.; Liu, L.; Liu, Z.; Zhang, X.; Ke, W. Time Domain Nonlinear Dynamic Response Analysis of Offshore Wind Turbines on Gravity Base Foundation under Wind and Wave Loads. *J. Mar. Sci. Eng.* **2022**, *10*, 1628. [CrossRef]
13. Ahmed, S.S.; Hawlader, B.C. Numerical analysis of inclined uplift capacity of suction caisson in sand. *Int. J. Offshore Polar Eng.* **2015**, *25*, 145–155. [CrossRef]
14. Peng, Y.; Yin, Z.-Y. Micromechanical analysis of suction pile-granular soil interaction under inclined pulling load: Effect of pulling angle. *Ocean Eng.* **2023**, *270*, 113615. [CrossRef]
15. Wensrich, C.M.; Katterfeld, A. Rolling friction as a technique for modelling particle shape in DEM. *Powder Technol.* **2012**, *217*, 409–417. [CrossRef]
16. Peng, Y.; Yin, Z.-Y.; Ding, X. Analysis of particle corner-breakage effect on pile penetration in coral sand: Model tests and DEM simulations. *Can. Geotech. J.* **2023**, *60*, 749–765. [CrossRef]
17. Bang, S.; Jones, K.; Kim, K.; Kim, Y.; Cho, Y. Inclined loading capacity of suction piles in sand. *Ocean Eng.* **2011**, *38*, 915–924. [CrossRef]
18. Xu, Q.; Ye, J. An adaptively coupled DEM–FEM algorithm for geometrical large deformation analysis of member structures. *Comput. Part. Mech.* **2020**, *7*, 947–959. [CrossRef]
19. Peng, Y.; Yin, Z.-Y. Micromechanical analysis of suction pile-granular soil interaction under inclined pulling load of mooring line: Mooring depth effect. *Mar. Struct.* **2023**, *92*, 103499. [CrossRef]
20. Bang, S.; Leahy, J.C.; Cho, Y.; Kwon, O. Horizontal bearing capacity of suction piles in sand. *Transp. Res. Rec.* **2006**, *1975*, 21–27. [CrossRef]
21. Kim, Y.; Kim, K.; Cho, Y.; Bang, S. *Centrifuge Model Tests on Suction Pile Pullout Loading Capacity in Sand*; CRC Press: Boca Raton, FL, USA, 2010.
22. Liu, F.; Yi, J.; Cheng, P.; Yao, K. Numerical simulation of set-up around shaft of XCC pile in clay. *Geomech. Eng.* **2020**, *21*, 489–501.
23. Qu, L.; Yang, C.; Ding, X.; Kouroussis, G.; Zheng, C. A continuum-based model on axial pile-head dynamic impedance in inhomogeneous soil. *Acta Geotech.* **2021**, *16*, 3339–3353. [CrossRef]
24. Kešner, A.; Chotěborský, R.; Linda, M.; Hromasová, M.; Katinas, E.; Sutanto, H. Stress distribution on a soil tillage machine frame segment with a chisel shank simulated using discrete element and finite element methods and validate by experiment. *Biosyst. Eng.* **2021**, *209*, 125–138. [CrossRef]
25. Peng, Y.; Yin, Z.-Y. Micromechanical analysis of suction bucket-granular soil interaction under eccentric pulling action of mooring lines: Effect of horizontal pulling angle. *Ocean Eng.* **2023**, *284*, 115217. [CrossRef]
26. Dratt, M.; Katterfeld, A. Coupling of FEM and DEM simulations to consider dynamic deformations under particle load. *Granul. Matter* **2017**, *19*, 49. [CrossRef]
27. Bernhardt, M.L.; Biscontin, G. Experimental validation study of 3D direct simple shear DEM simulations. *Soils Found.* **2016**, *56*, 336–347. [CrossRef]
28. Zheng, Z.; Zang, M.; Chen, S.; Zhao, C. An improved 3D DEM-FEM contact detection algorithm for the interaction simulations between particles and structures. *Powder Technol.* **2017**, *305*, 308–322. [CrossRef]
29. Chan, E.L.; Washino, K. Coarse grain model for DEM simulation of dense and dynamic particle flow with liquid bridge forces. *Chem. Eng. Res. Des.* **2018**, *132*, 1060–1069. [CrossRef]
30. Ahlman, B. Coarse-Graining Fields in Particle-Based Soil Models. Master's Thesis, Umeå University: 2020.
31. Kotrocz, K.; Mouazen, A.M.; Kerényi, G. Numerical simulation of soil–cone penetrometer interaction using discrete element method. *Comput. Electron. Agric.* **2016**, *125*, 63–73. [CrossRef]
32. Fu, Z.; Chen, S.; Liu, S. Discrete Element Simulations of Shallow Plate-Load Tests. *Int. J. Geomech.* **2016**, *16*, 04015077. [CrossRef]
33. Falagush, O.; McDowell, G.R.; Yu, H.-S.; de Bono, J.P. Discrete element modelling and cavity expansion analysis of cone penetration testing. *Granul. Matter* **2015**, *17*, 483–495. [CrossRef]
34. Antypov, D.; Elliott, J. On an analytical solution for the damped Hertzian spring. *Europhys. Lett.* **2011**, *94*, 50004. [CrossRef]
35. Diaz, B.D.; Rasulo, M.; Aubeny, C.P.; Fontana, C.M.; Arwade, S.R.; DeGroot, D.J.; Landon, M. Multiline anchors for floating offshore wind towers. In Proceedings of the OCEANS 2016 MTS/IEEE Monterey, Monterey, CA, USA, 19–23 September 2016; pp. 1–9.
36. Hung, L.C.; Lee, S.; Tran, N.X.; Kim, S.-R. Experimental investigation of the vertical pullout cyclic response of bucket foundations in sand. *Appl. Ocean Res.* **2017**, *68*, 325–335. [CrossRef]
37. Khanal, M.; Elmouttie, M.; Poulsen, B.; Olsson, A.; Adhikary, D. Effect of loading rate on sand pile failure: 2D DEM simulation. *Geotech. Geol. Eng.* **2017**, *35*, 889–896. [CrossRef]

38. Mondal, S.; Disfani, M.; Narsilio, G.A. Battered minipiles in fine-grained soils: Soil-structure interaction. *Comput. Geotech.* **2022**, *147*, 104762. [CrossRef]
39. Brunelli, A.; De Silva, F.; Piro, A.; Parisi, F.; Sica, S.; Silvestri, F.; Cattari, S. Numerical simulation of the seismic response and soil–structure interaction for a monitored masonry school building damaged by the 2016 Central Italy earthquake. *Bull. Earthq. Eng.* **2021**, *19*, 1181–1211. [CrossRef]
40. Qu, T.; Wang, M.; Feng, Y. Applicability of discrete element method with spherical and clumped particles for constitutive study of granular materials. *J. Rock Mech. Geotech. Eng.* **2022**, *14*, 240–251. [CrossRef]
41. Du, L.; Liu, X.; Han, Y.; Deng, Z. Generation of irregular particle packing with prescribed statistical distribution, spatial arrangement, and volume fraction. *J. Rock Mech. Geotech. Eng.* **2022**, *15*, 375–394. [CrossRef]
42. Arany, L.; Bhattacharya, S. Simplified load estimation and sizing of suction anchors for spar buoy type floating offshore wind turbines. *Ocean Eng.* **2018**, *159*, 348–357. [CrossRef]
43. Wang, X.; Zeng, X.; Li, J.; Yang, X.; Wang, H. A review on recent advancements of substructures for offshore wind turbines. *Energy Convers. Manag.* **2018**, *158*, 103–119. [CrossRef]
44. Byrne, B.; Houlsby, G.; Martin, C.; Fish, P. Suction caisson foundations for offshore wind turbines. *Wind Eng.* **2002**, *26*, 145–155. [CrossRef]

Journal of
Marine Science and Engineering

MDPI

Article

Numerical Investigation into the Stability of Offshore Wind Power Piles Subjected to Lateral Loads in Extreme Environments

Miaojun Sun [1], Zhigang Shan [1], Wei Wang [1], Simin Xu [2], Xiaolei Liu [2], Hong Zhang [3] and Xingsen Guo [2,3,4,*]

1 Zhejiang Engineering Research Center of Marine Geotechnical Investigation Technology and Equipment, Zhejiang Huadong Geotechnical Investigation & Design Institute Co., Ltd., Powerchina Huadong Engineering Co., Ltd., Hangzhou 311122, China; sun_mj2@hdec.com (M.S.); shan_zg@hdec.com (Z.S.); wang_w20@hdec.com (W.W.)

2 Shandong Provincial Key Laboratory of Marine Environment and Geological Engineering, Ocean University of China, Qingdao 266100, China; xusimin@stu.ouc.edu.cn (S.X.); xiaolei@ouc.edu.cn (X.L.)

3 College of Engineering, Ocean University of China, Qingdao 266100, China; zhanghong9645@ouc.edu.cn

4 Department of Civil, Environmental and Geomatic Engineering, University College London, London WC1E 6BT, UK

* Correspondence: xingsen.guo@ucl.ac.uk

Abstract: Monopile foundations are extensively utilized in the rapidly expanding offshore wind power industry, and the stability of these foundations has become a crucial factor for ensuring the safety of offshore wind power projects. Such foundations are subjected to a myriad of complex environmental loads during their operational lifespan. Whilst current research predominantly concentrates on the effects of wind, wave, and current loads on monopile stability in extreme environments, it is imperative to consider the potential influence of unexpected submarine landslide loads. In this study, we provide a comprehensive overview of wind, wave, current, and submarine landslide loads on monopile foundations in extreme environments. Subsequently, we establish a finite element model for analyzing the stability of monopiles under complex lateral loads, and validate the accuracy of the model by comparing it with the previous numerical findings. A case study is performed with reference to the Xiangshui Wind Farm project to analyze the effects of varying submarine landslide densities, velocities, impact heights, and seabed sediment strengths on pile head horizontal displacement, pile rotation at the mudline, and maximum bending moment. The findings indicate that the increase in submarine landslide density, velocity, and impact height leads to an increase in horizontal displacement at the pile head, pile rotation at the mudline, and maximum bending moments, and a horizontal failure mode is observed in seabed sediments. Furthermore, under the same load conditions, a decrease in seabed sediment strength and internal friction angle triggers instability in monopiles, with a noteworthy transition from horizontal failure to deep-seated seabed sediment failure. Finally, we propose a criterion for monopile instability under diverse loading conditions.

Keywords: offshore wind power; monopile foundation; environmental loads; submarine landslides; stability analysis; seabed sediment properties

1. Introduction

Wind energy is a widely adopted renewable energy source and plays a pivotal role in the development of offshore wind power resources. In recent years, offshore wind projects have been rapidly emerging as modern scientific research has paid increasing attention to sustainable development and efficient use of resources. This growth is attributed to the abundant wind energy resources and broader installation areas available in the marine environment, as well as their minimal impact on human activities [1–4]. According to the Global Offshore Wind Report 2023 [5], the global installed capacity of offshore wind power reached 64.3 GW by the end of 2022, with 8.8 GW of newly installed capacity. Mainland

China accounted for a significant share of 57.6%, followed by the United Kingdom and Taiwan. Forecasts indicate a continuous annual increase in global offshore wind power installation capacity over the next decade. It is estimated that 15.45 GW of additional offshore wind capacity will be installed globally by 2023, with a cumulative total of 60.2 GW expected to be installed in the next 10 years.

Currently, pile foundations are widely employed in offshore wind power projects due to their robust adaptability to geological conditions, simple structure, convenient design and manufacturing, and ease of construction [6]. However, damages to pile foundations during the operation of offshore wind power projects have been reported, which is attributed to the influence of complex loads [7]. Consequently, ensuring the stability of pile foundations becomes a critical prerequisite for project safety. Current research on the stability of offshore pile foundation primarily focuses on the external dynamic loads acting on the piles, including wind, waves, and currents. Zeng et al. [8] investigated the effect of breaking waves on the monopile foundation of offshore wind turbines on the slope edge by utilizing laboratory experiments and computational fluid dynamics models. It was found that, during wave breaking, the pressure acting on the monopile exhibited a wave-like distribution with a gradual decrease in the point of action. Shi et al. [9] developed a "three-stage" computational model for monopile foundation of offshore wind turbines to investigate force conditions in soil, water, and air. They derived the total dynamic impedance of the foundation to predict its dynamic response, and analyzed tower displacement under various monopile parameters. Miles et al. [10] conducted a series of laboratory experiments to analyze the coupled effects of waves and currents as well as to study the influence of these factors on the monopile foundation of offshore wind turbines. Ong et al. [11] performed dynamic analysis on offshore monopile under the influence of sea currents using a finite element model. They examined the response of monopiles under wind–wave coupling conditions in shallow water with varying parameters. Buljac et al. [12] conducted experiments on a small-scale wind turbine in a wind–wave–current tank, and investigated the combined effects of wind, waves, and currents on the monopile foundation of offshore wind turbines. It was found that, among the overall loads acting on the offshore wind turbine, the longitudinal oscillating force induced by currents dominated. Achmus et al. [13] established a calculation model for the interaction between waves, wind turbines, and seabed foundations. They simplified wind–wave loads into concentrated horizontal forces acting on the top of the tower to study the horizontal bearing characteristics of offshore wind power monopile foundations. Wu et al. [14] employed finite element analysis to study high-pile foundations for offshore wind power, and they also simulated the evolution of the load-bearing capacity of wind power foundations under varying soil strength parameters. The results indicated that improved soil, increased burial depth, and a larger pile diameter effectively enhanced the load-bearing capacity of pile foundation.

Previous studies have predominantly focused on assessing the effects of wind, waves, and currents on the stability of pile foundation. However, in recent years, given the frequent occurrence of extreme storms and geological events worldwide [15], attention has shifted towards understanding the effect of incidental loads, such as submarine landslides, on pile foundations. Submarine landslides are manifest as localized or widespread seabed instability, significant deformations, and sliding phenomena [16–18]. High-speed submarine landslides can cause considerable damage to marine structures with unidirectional impact loads [19–21]. For instance, the 1929 Grand Banks landslide in Canada travelled at a speed of up to 20 m/s, leading to the destruction of 12 seabed pipelines [22–25]. The 2006 submarine landslide in the Luzon Strait severed 11 seabed communication cables, resulting in prolonged communication interruptions [26]. Currently, research on the influence of submarine landslides on piles is primarily concentrated on the quantification of the impact loads of submarine landslides. Li et al. [27] conducted 12 experiments in a submarine landslide model trough and optimized the formula for a dimensionless resistance coefficient acting on pile foundations by adjusting variables such as the slope of the model trough and the mass fraction of kaolin clay in the landslide body. Li et al. [28]

employed computational fluid dynamics to study the impact force of submarine debris flows on the monopile and analyzed the characteristics of the drag force acting on the monopile. Li et al. [16] simulated the impact of submarine debris flows on pile foundations using computational fluid dynamics and proposed a formula for predicting impact forces. However, whilst these studies have analyzed the impact forces of submarine landslides on pile foundations, they have not explored whether pile foundations would be unstable and the instability mechanism after exposure to the impact loads of submarine landslides. Simultaneously, the stability of pile foundations under the combined effects of submarine landslides, wind, waves, currents, and other complex loads still lacks in-depth exploration, and there is an urgent need for further research in this regard.

This study develops a finite element model to investigate the interaction between piles and soil under complex lateral loading conditions. The accuracy of the model is validated through finite element simulation cases from previous studies. Subsequently, based on a quantification equation for submarine landslide impact loads established by previous researchers, the study determines the lateral loads experienced by a monopile under the coupled effects of submarine landslides, wind, waves, and currents in complex environments. Finally, the stability analysis of a monopile under complex lateral loading conditions is conducted by considering different seabed sediment strengths, and the stability of monopile foundations is discussed in detail.

2. Numerical Model

2.1. Generalization of Loads on Offshore Wind Turbine Structures in Complex Environments

In the marine environment, offshore wind turbine structures are exposed to wind, waves, and currents throughout their operational lifespan. Additionally, they may encounter sporadic loads such as landslides, as depicted in Figure 1. Specifically, the wind exerts forces on the blades and hub of the turbine, while the tower (the upper section of the monopile) is exposed to wave and current loads. Furthermore, the pile foundation may experience occasional loads from seabed landslides. Clearly, the structure of offshore wind turbines is subject to a complex interaction of forces. To facilitate analysis, current research often simplifies these dynamic loads to horizontal forces acting on individual pile foundations. Subsequently, investigations focused on the stability of monopile foundations under the combined influence of these horizontal loads [13,29,30].

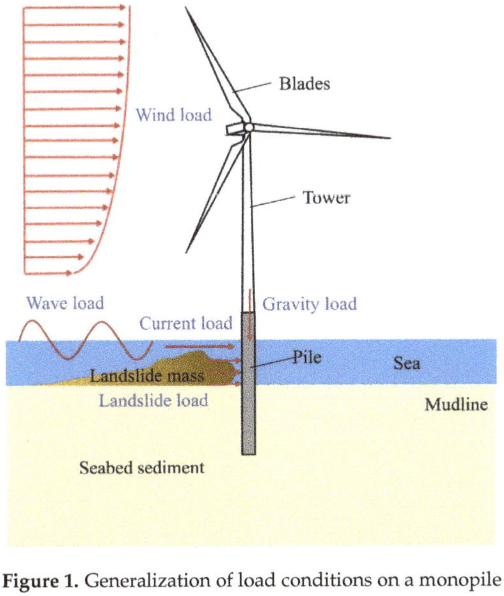

Figure 1. Generalization of load conditions on a monopile foundation of offshore wind turbines.

2.1.1. Aerodynamic Loads

The aerodynamic loads acting on offshore wind turbines can be categorized into blade wind load and tower load. Blade wind load is the wind-induced force experienced by the entire rotor blades of the turbine, constituting the primary load factor. Meanwhile, tower load represents the wind force acting on the tower structure exposed to the air. Given the relatively smaller dimensions of the tower, the magnitude of this load is comparably smaller. The blade wind load can be simplified as follows [31]:

$$F_a = \frac{1}{2}\rho_a A_R C_T U^2, \tag{1}$$

where F_a is the wind load on blades; ρ_a is the density of air, $\rho_a = 1.225\ \text{kg/m}^3$; A_R is the rotor swept area, which is calculated according to the size of the blade; C_T is the coefficient of thrust; and U is the wind speed. Considering the different ranges of wind speed, the thrust coefficient can be approximated as three different segments over the operational range of the turbine:

When cut-in wind speed (U_{in}) $\leq$ wind speed (U) $\leq$ the rated wind speed (U_R), the impeller thrust coefficient is calculated as follows [32]:

$$C_T = \frac{3.5(2U_R + 3.5)}{{U_R}^2}, \tag{2}$$

When the rated wind speed (U_R) $\leq$ wind speed (U) $\leq$ cut-out wind speed (U_{out}), the calculation formula for the impeller thrust coefficient is as follows:

$$C_T = 3.5U_R(2U_R + 3.5) \cdot \frac{1}{U^3}, \tag{3}$$

When the wind speed is low, Equation (2) will overestimate the thrust coefficient when assuming that the impeller thrust coefficient does not exceed 1, so its value is limited to 1.

The diameter of the tower structure is small relative to the wind range, and its influence on the wind flow is negligible, so the wind load acting on the tower is calculated according to the following formula [33]:

$$F_t = \frac{1}{2}\rho_a U^2(Z) C_s D, \tag{4}$$

where F_t is the wind load of the tower; C_s is the coefficient of drag force for wind, which is dimensionless and is not affected by the specific size of the object, but is only related to the shape of the structure. In engineering, it is used to represent the resistance characteristics of the movement of the object, and the tower is a cylindrical section, which can be taken as 0.5 after calculation; and D is the diameter of pile. According to the wind resistance design code [34], the exponential formula for simulating the change in average wind speed along the height is as follows:

$$\frac{U(Z)}{U(Z_1)} = \left(\frac{Z}{Z_1}\right)^{\alpha}, \tag{5}$$

where $U(Z_1)$ is the average wind speed at the standard height Z_1, which is generally 10 m, and α is the wind shear index, $\alpha = 0.143$.

2.1.2. Hydrodynamic Loads

Hydrodynamic loads that include wave and current forces are known as wave–current coupled loads. According to the Code for Design of Wind Turbine Foundations for Offshore Wind Power Projects (NB/T10105-2018) [35], a simplified approach for wave loading involves the Morison equation [36]. This equation decomposes wave forces into two components. One is proportional to acceleration and represents the inertial force, while the other one is proportional to the square of velocity and symbolizes drag force. The formulation is as follows:

$$F_W = F_D + F_I = \frac{1}{2} C_D \rho_s A \vec{U} |\vec{U}| + C_M \rho V_0 \vec{U}, \tag{6}$$

where F_W is the wave load; F_D is the drag force term; F_I is the inertial force term; A is the projected area per unit beam height perpendicular to the wave propagation direction; V_0 is the volume of drainage per unit cylinder height; ρ_s is the density of seawater and $\rho_s = 1025$ kg/m^3; C_D is the coefficient of drag force perpendicular to the axis of the cylinder, which reflects the viscous effect caused by the viscosity of the fluid; and C_M is the coefficient of inertial force. According to the Code of Hydrology for Harbour (JTJ213-98) [37], the cylinder under the action of wave and current loads can take $C_D = 1.2$ and $C_M = 2.0$. $\vec{U}$ is the wave velocity.

For current loads, the current is idealized as a uniform motion, so it does not produce acceleration at the water quality point. Only the inertial force term in the Morison's formula is omitted, and only the drag force term is calculated [38]:

$$F_C = \frac{1}{2} C_W \rho_s A \vec{U} |\vec{U}|, \tag{7}$$

where F_C is the current load; and C_W is the coefficient of drag force for current, $C_W = 0.73$.

2.1.3. Submarine Landslide Impact Loads

For the impact force of submarine landslides acting on structures, Feng et al. [39] varied the content of kaolin and silt to produce submarine debris flows with diverse rheological properties and densities. Then, they experimentally simulated the influence of these debris flows on model piles. By integrating fluid mechanics theory, they developed an expression that correlates the drag coefficient with the Reynolds number of non-Newtonian fluids.

$$F_L = \frac{1}{2} C_d \rho_L v^2 h D, \tag{8}$$

where F_L is the landslide load; C_d is the coefficient of drag force for landslide; ρ_L is the debris flow density of submarine landslides; v is the flow velocity of the landslide; h is the impact height of submarine landslides; and D is the diameter of pile.

The drag coefficient can be used to measure the magnitude of the impact force. According to the principles of fluid mechanics, the drag coefficient is closely related to the Reynolds number. The relationship between the drag coefficient and the Reynolds number was fitted [39] as follows:

$$C_d = 0.87 + \frac{4.71}{Re^{0.57}}, \tag{9}$$

The Reynolds number of non-Newtonian fluids is often expressed as follows:

$$Re = \frac{\rho_L \cdot v^2}{\mu \cdot \dot{\gamma}} = \frac{\rho_L \cdot v^2}{\tau}, \tag{10}$$

where $\dot{\gamma}$ is the shear rate of the near-pile slurry; μ is the debris flow viscosity; and τ is the shear stress. The relationship between fluid shear stress and shear rate can be described by the Herschel–Bulkley model [40]. Feng et al. [39] used the rheometer to test the rheological parameters of the slurry, and obtained the expression of the rheological curve:

$$\tau = 0.5 + 1.5 \dot{\gamma}^{0.42}, \tag{11}$$

where $\dot{\gamma} = \frac{v}{D}$.

2.1.4. Superimposition of Environmental Loads

For simplicity, this study simplifies the analysis of horizontal loads acting on offshore wind turbines, as depicted in Figure 2. The figure depicts wind load on blades, wind load on tower, wave load, current load, and landslide load, and their respective impact zones. Given the distinctive structural design of offshore wind turbines, the primary load on the foundation piles is manifested as an overturning moment. Various environmental loads can be equivalently represented as horizontal loads and moments applied at the same elevation, as illustrated in Figure 2. Submarine landslides apply loads to the sides of the pile through uniformly distributed forces.

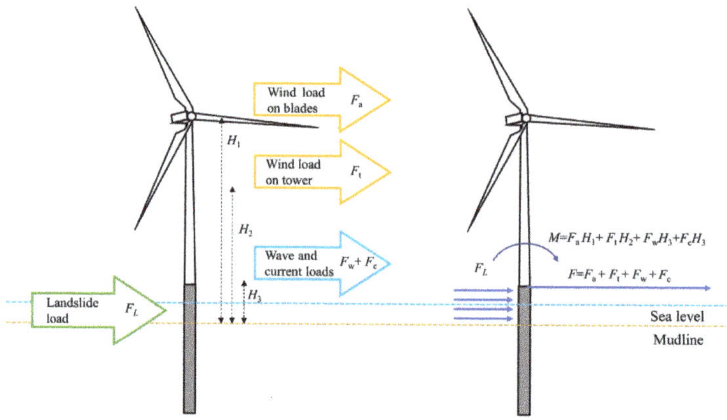

Figure 2. Schematic diagram of load simplification.

2.2. *Pile–Soil Interaction Model under Complex Horizontal Loads*

2.2.1. Monopile Model

To solve the pile body displacement and stress at the pile head under horizontal loading, based on the beam bending theory, an element analysis method is employed. Lai [41] selected a differential element of length dz along the horizontal loaded pile, and derived the following equation through the equilibrium of bending moments:

$$(M + dM) - M + P_z dy + S dz = 0, \tag{12}$$

According to the beam theory:

$$\frac{d^2M}{dz^2} = E_p I_p \frac{d^4y}{dz^4}, \tag{13}$$

The governing equations for the horizontal load of the pile can be obtained immediately by the combination of two formulas:

$$E_p I_p \frac{d^4y}{dz^4} + P_z \frac{d^2y}{dz^2} + p = 0, \tag{14}$$

where $p = \frac{dS}{dz}$ is the earth reaction force. The essence of calculating the horizontal load response of the pile foundation by the finite element method is to solve the governing equation of the horizontally loaded pile.

An isotropic elastic model is adopted for the monopile, and the stress–strain relationship of the pile material is modelled by Hooke's law. Hooke's law in three dimensions can be expressed as follows:

$$\begin{bmatrix} \sigma_{xx} \\ \sigma_{yy} \\ \sigma_{zz} \\ \sigma_{xy} \\ \sigma_{yz} \\ \sigma_{zx} \end{bmatrix} = \frac{E}{(1-2v)(1+v)} \begin{bmatrix} 1-v & v & v & 0 & 0 & 0 \\ v & 1-v & v & 0 & 0 & 0 \\ v & v & 1-v & 0 & 0 & 0 \\ 0 & 0 & 0 & \frac{1}{2}-v & 0 & 0 \\ 0 & 0 & 0 & 0 & \frac{1}{2}-v & \frac{1}{2}-v \end{bmatrix} \begin{bmatrix} \varepsilon_{xx} \\ \varepsilon_{yy} \\ \varepsilon_{zz} \\ \gamma_{xy} \\ \gamma_{yz} \\ \gamma_{zx} \end{bmatrix}, \quad (15)$$

where E is Young's modulus and v is the Poisson's ratio.

2.2.2. Soil Model

The Mohr–Coulomb model can describe the elastoplastic characteristics of soil to some extent, and is widely applied in lateral load pile models [42]. The simulation of the soil in this paper adopts the elastoplastic Mohr–Coulomb model, which can effectively assess the effect of landslide surges. The model mainly involves the following parameters, i.e., the cohesion c, the friction angle φ, Young's modulus E, Poisson's ratio v, and the dilation angle ψ. According to Johnson [43], the failure envelope only depends on the principal stress (σ_1, σ_3) and not on the medium principal stress (σ_2). When mapped to a three-dimensional stress space, the Mohr–Coulomb theory is decomposed into irregular hexagonal pyramids. This pyramid forms a destruction/yield envelope, and these determine the behavior of the soil. When the stress point is located in the envelope surface, the material undergoes elastic deformation; and when the stress reaches the yield surface, the material will undergo plastic deformation. In this study, it is assumed that the soil has a linear elastic relationship before failure.

2.2.3. Pile–Soil Contact Model

The "contact pair" algorithm is used to simulate the interaction between pile and soil through defining the normal and tangential contact. The discretization method of the surface adopts the "face-to-face contact", which allows the geometry of the master and slave surfaces to be considered simultaneously. The shear stress and normal pressure of the contact surface are calculated with high accuracy. The "hard" contact option is used for normal contact, while the Coulomb contact is used for tangential contact. The interface shear stress is calculated as follows [44]:

$$\tau_f = \sigma_n' tan\delta_{cs} \quad (16)$$

where τ_f is the shear stress of the contact surface; σ_n' is the normal effective stress; δ_{cs} is the friction angle of the pile–soil interface in the critical state. The tracking of the relative movement of the contact surface adopts "finite sliding", and the calculation accuracy is improved by continuously determining whether the master and slave surfaces are in contact.

2.2.4. Finite Element Method for Solution

Finite element method is a mathematical approximation of the actual physical system. The analyzed object is subdivided into simple and interacting tiny units, and all of which together form a mechanical system. It treats the solution domain as a composition of many small interconnected subdomains and gives an approximate solution to each subdomain. Finally, the approximate solutions of all subdomains satisfy the corresponding equilibrium conditions, leading to the final solution [45].

In this study, computational analysis is performed using the standard solver module of ABAQUS software that can simulate most of the material and geometric nonlinear problems. The Newton–Raphson method is usually used to solve the ABAQUS/standard nonlinear response, and the principle of this method is described below. The equilibrium equation for a structure or soil at a given time is as follows:

$$I(u) - P(u) = 0, \tag{17}$$

where I is the internal force of the finite element node at that moment; P is the external load on the finite element node at that time; and u is the displacement of the node at that time. Assuming that r is a displacement correction, after i iterations, there is:

$$I(u_i + r_{i+1}) - P(u_i + r_{i+1}) = 0, \tag{18}$$

where $r_{i+1} = u_{i+1} - u_i$. Expand $I(u_i + r_{i+1}) - P(u_i + r_{i+1})$ Taylor near u_i, and the higher-order terms are omitted:

$$I(u_i) - P(u_i) = (\frac{\partial P(u_i)}{\partial u} - \frac{\partial I(u_i)}{\partial u})r_{i+1}, \tag{19}$$

Similarly, the following equation can be obtained:

$$I(u_{i+1}) - P(u_{i+1}) = (\frac{\partial P(u_{i+1})}{\partial u} - \frac{\partial I(u_{i+1})}{\partial u})r_{i+2}, \tag{20}$$

The total load is expressed as follows:

$$P_T - I(u_{i+1}) = R_{i+1}, \tag{21}$$

where P_T is the total load and R_{i+1} is the residual. ABAQUS will iterate until R_{i+1} is within the set tolerance.

2.3. Numerical Model Verification

We utilize the stability analysis of large-diameter monopile foundations under horizontal load conducted by Dai et al. [46] as a case study to verify the effectiveness of the proposed numerical model. In this case, the single pile had a diameter of 5 m and a total length of 38 m, and a buried depth of 30 m. For offshore wind turbine applications, the monopile foundation is considered as a hollow steel pipe pile, which is equivalent to a solid rigid pile based on flexural stiffness assumptions. This ensures consistent load-bearing capacity and failure modes [46]. The equivalent elastic modulus of the rigid pile is 2.2×10^4 MPa, with a Poisson's ratio of 0.24. The seabed in this study comprises soft clay, which is represented by a cylinder with a radius of 50 m and a height of 60 m. Key seabed parameters include a friction angle of 18°, a Young's modulus of 3.5 MPa, a Poisson's ratio of 0.3, and a cohesive strength of 10 kPa, which are characterized by the Mohr–Coulomb yield criterion. To generate the displacement–load curve of the monopile, a displacement load of 5 m is applied at the pile head using the displacement-controlled method to simulate horizontal loading. Based on these parameters, we establish a three-dimensional finite element model of the full-scale large-diameter monopile foundation for offshore wind turbines on soft clay seabed, as depicted in Figure 3.

To ensure a balance between computational efficiency and accuracy, the mesh density is increased at the pile–soil interface and is gradually decreased from the interface to the edge of the model. A mesh sensitivity analysis is conducted on the established model to evaluate the influence of mesh size on the results. Mesh sizes at the contact surface vary from 0.8D to 0.08D. The resulting displacement–load curves of the monopile are compared. Figure 4 illustrates the horizontal load–displacement response curves at the monopile–seabed interface for different mesh sizes. It is evident that, when the mesh size at the interface is set to 0.1D, the numerical results remain stable, indicating that a mesh size of 0.1D at the interface almost does not affect the numerical results.

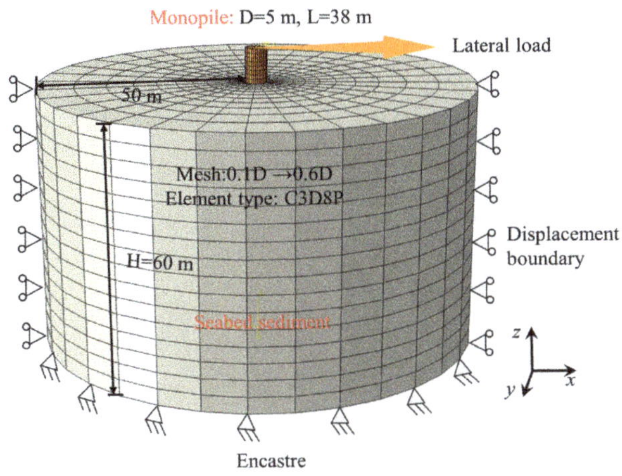

Figure 3. Pile–soil interaction finite element model.

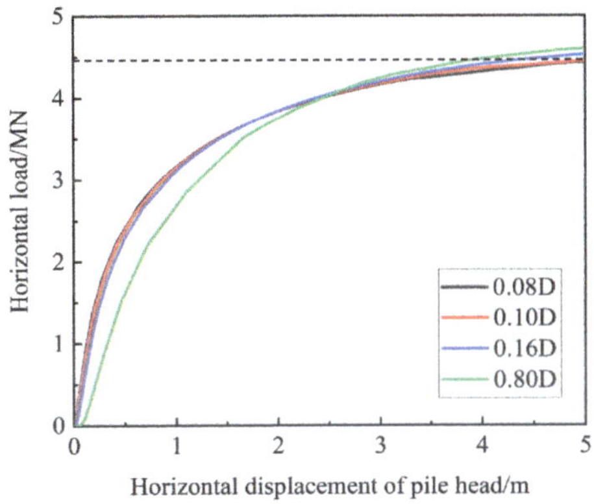

Figure 4. Effect of mesh size in pile–soil contact zone on horizontal load–displacement response curves.

Figure 5 presents a comparison between the numerical results of this study and the results of validation case, where the horizontal load–displacement response at the pile head is used as a reference for validation. As horizontal load gradually increases, the horizontal displacement undergoes three stages, i.e., elastic, plastic development, and plastic failure. Initially, at low horizontal loads, the pile head displacement increases linearly with the horizontal load, and the displacement remains below 0.1 m. As the horizontal load at the pile head increases, the relationship between horizontal displacement and load changes from linear to nonlinear, which means that the pile–soil system starts to deform plastically until the horizontal displacement reaches 1 m. Subsequently, the pile–soil system experiences plastic failure with further increase in horizontal load. When the horizontal displacement of pile head reaches 5 m, the validation error is 1.19%, indicating that the numerical model accurately simulates the interaction between the monopile and the seabed under horizontal loading conditions.

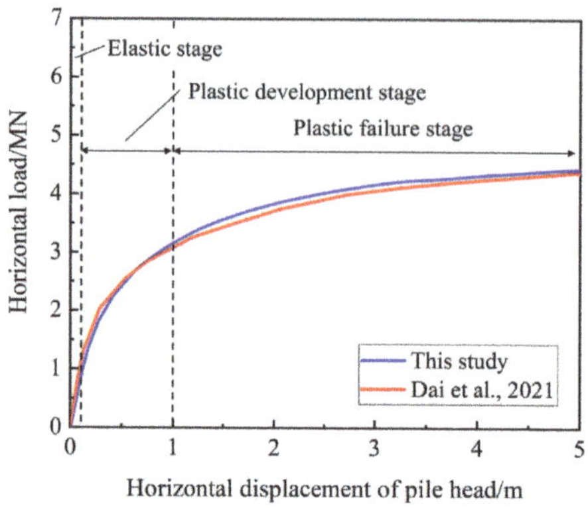

Figure 5. Comparison of horizontal load–displacement curves between previous results [46] and results of this study.

3. Results and Discussion

3.1. Case Study on Stability Analysis of Monopile under Complex Loads

This paper takes the wind power project in Xiangshui County, Yancheng City, Jiangsu Province, China, as an example [47] to establish a three-dimensional finite element model of a wind power monopile foundation and the seabed under horizontal loads. The Xiangshui Wind Farm is located in the mudflat area of Chenjiagang Town, Xiangshui County, Jiangsu Province. It consists of 134 large-scale wind turbines with a single unit capacity of 1.5 MW, totaling 201 MW in installed capacity, with an annual grid-connected power generation of approximately 440 million kWh. The wind farm employs concrete monopile foundations with a pile diameter (D) of 4.3 m and a pile length (L) of 70 m. The burial depth (L_d) of the monopile is 60 m. The three-dimensional finite element model consists of two parts: the seabed and the wind turbine monopile foundation. The monopile is modeled using a linear elastic model, with a Young's modulus (E_{pile}) of 25 $\times$ 10^6 kPa, a Poisson's ratio (υ_{pile}) of 0.20, and a density (ρ_{pile}) of 2400 kg/m^3. To eliminate boundary effects, the radius of the model domain for the seabed is set to 70 m, with a height of 140 m. The seabed soil adopts the Mohr–Coulomb yielding criteria. The contact between the monopile and the seabed is modeled by a Coulomb friction contact, where the surfaces of the monopile and seabed are considered as primary and second surfaces, respectively, with a friction coefficient of 0.39. During the calculation process, separation of the monopile–seabed interface is allowed.

In harsh marine environments, offshore monopile wind turbines are subjected to lateral loads from wind, waves, and currents, as well as occasional geological hazards such as seabed landslides. Field investigations at the Xiangshui wind farm project [47] indicate that the total gravitational load of the whole wind turbine system is 2.06 $\times$ 10^3 kN·m. Under normal operating conditions of this wind farm, the wind speed at a height of 10 m above sea level is 13.4 m/s, the water depth is 5 m, the wave height is 2.68 m, the wavelength is 74.1 m, and the current velocity is 0.88 m/s. Therefore, the wind loads on the blades, tower load, wave load, and current load can be calculated according to Formulas (1), (4), (6) and (7), as shown in Table 1. By converting and superimposing the environmental loads at different points of action, the horizontal load applied at the pile head is 307,102 N, with a clockwise moment of 10,891,482 N·m. Furthermore, the load of occasional seabed landslides can be calculated according to Formula (8). Here, seabed landslides of different densities, velocities, and impact heights are considered to analyze their effects on pile stability. The coupling of these loads can result in significant overturning moments on the monopile, leading to rotation.

Table 1. Environmental loads on a monopile.

Load Type	Force/N	Distance between the Action Point and the Pile Head/m
F_a	205,319	52.3
F_t	16,080	27.7
F_W	54,557	−2.5
F_C	31,145	−5

The design of offshore wind turbine foundations typically needs to follow the following criteria: FLS, which stands for Fatigue Limit State and primarily predicts the system's fatigue and long-term performance; SLS, which stands for Serviceability Limit State and mainly predicts characteristic frequencies and deformations during serviceability; ULS, which stands for Ultimate Limit State and mainly predicts the system's load-bearing capacity under extreme loads [31]. This paper focuses on the stability of offshore wind turbine foundations under the influence of submarine landslides during normal operation, thus employing the SLS design criteria for assessment. Current regulations specify the SLS for monopiles. The current standard defines the SLS of monopiles. According to DNV (Det Norske Veritas) [48] regulations, the permanent cumulative rotation at the mudline of a monopile is 0.25°. Therefore, in this study, a rotation angle of 0.25° at the mudline of a monopile is considered to indicate pile instability.

3.2. *The Influence of Different Types of Submarine Landslides on the Stability of Monopiles*

The effect of seabed landslides on monopiles is primarily controlled by the magnitude of the impact force and the location of action (impact height). Based on the analysis above, this section mainly investigates the influence of three main factors: landslide density, landslide velocity, and landslide impact height. The density of seabed sediment is taken as 2130 kg/m^3, with a Young's modulus of 80 $\times$ 10^3 kPa, a Poisson's ratio of 0.33, a cohesion of 10 kPa, and an internal friction angle of 10°. According to Takahashi [49], the maximum velocity of submarine landslides is approximately 20 m/s. In this study, landslide velocities (v) are set to be 10 m/s, 15 m/s, and 20 m/s, respectively. According to field geological surveys, the densities (ρ_L) of seabed landslides are taken as 1400 kg/m^3, 1600 kg/m^3, and 1800 kg/m^3, respectively [50]. The impact heights (h) of seabed landslides are taken as 5 m, 6 m, 7 m, 8 m, and 9 m, respectively [28].

3.2.1. Effect of Submarine Landslide Density

To assess the effect of different landslide densities on monopile stability, a landslide velocity of 15 m/s and a landslide impact height of 6 m are standardized for comparison. The displacement, rotation angle, and bending moment of the monopile under various densities are depicted in Figure 6. When the landslide density is 1400 kg/m^3, the resulting landslide impact force is 3,561,713 N, leading to a horizontal displacement of 0.09 m at the pile head. As the density of the seabed landslide increases to 1800 kg/m^3, the landslide impact force increases to 4,574,803 N, and the pile head horizontal displacement reaches 0.13 m. Obviously, the greater the density of submarine landslides, the greater the pile head horizontal displacement. However, the gradient of the horizontal displacement at the pile head remains basically unchanged with the increase in landslide density. For every 200 kg/m^3 increase in landslide density, the horizontal displacement of the pile head increases by 0.02 m. Similarly, the rate of increase in the pile rotation angle remains relatively constant with increasing landslide density. For every 200 kg/m^3 increase in landslide density, the maximum pile rotation angle increases by approximately 0.04°. At a landslide density of 1400 kg/m^3, the maximum rotation angle at the mudline of the pile is 0.19°, whereas it increases to 0.27° at a density of 1800 kg/m^3, indicating a state of failure. The maximum bending moment of the pile increases as the landslide density increases. At a density of 1600 kg/m^3, the maximum bending moment of the pile is 47.5 MN·m, which is 3.6 times the calculated result without landslide load. Meanwhile, at a density of 1800 kg/m^3, the maximum bending moment of the pile reaches 61.9 MN·m, which is

4.7 times the calculated result without landslide load. To analyze the stress states of the sediment and monopile under loading, the next section primarily focuses on the Mises stress nephograms of the sediment and monopile. The aforementioned results can be elucidated by comparing the Mises stress nephograms of the sediment (Figure 7) and the monopile (Figure 8) at densities of 1400 kg/m^3 and 1800 kg/m^3. When the monopile is subjected to lateral loads, the sediment experiences higher compressive stress on the pressure side due to lateral loads. With the increase in density, the lateral load intensifies, resulting in increased stress in the sediment. It can be observed that the variation in landslide density does not alter the distribution of the sediment–pile interaction (SPI) failure zones. The SPI failure zones mainly include the compression failure zone occurring at the pile head, the shear failure zone caused by pile rotation at the pile base, and the lateral failure zone of the pile. The range of the SPI pile head failure zone is 6.3 D when the density is 1400 kg/m^3, while that is 7.3 D when the density is 1800 kg/m^3. The stress nephogram of the monopile aligns with that of the sediment, showcasing that an increase in density leads to increased stress in the monopile. The maximum stress of the monopile occurs at a depth of about 10 m below the seabed surface, which is consistent with the location of the maximum bending moment of the monopile, and it increases with the increasing displacement at the pile head.

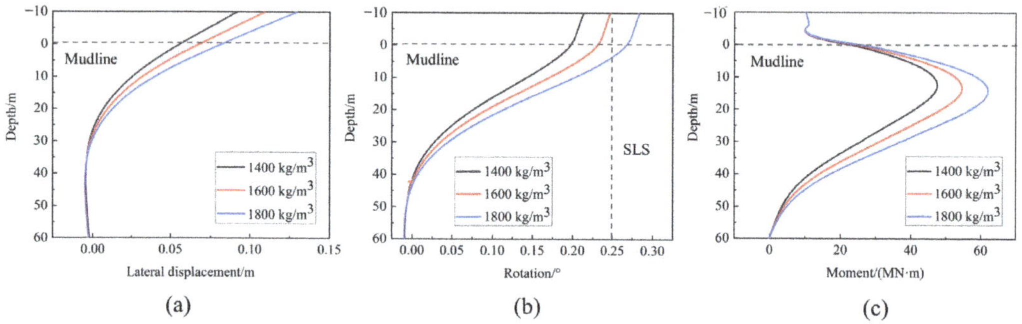

Figure 6. The effect of different landslide densities on the response of a monopile: (**a**) displacement of pile; (**b**) rotation angle of pile; (**c**) bending moment of pile.

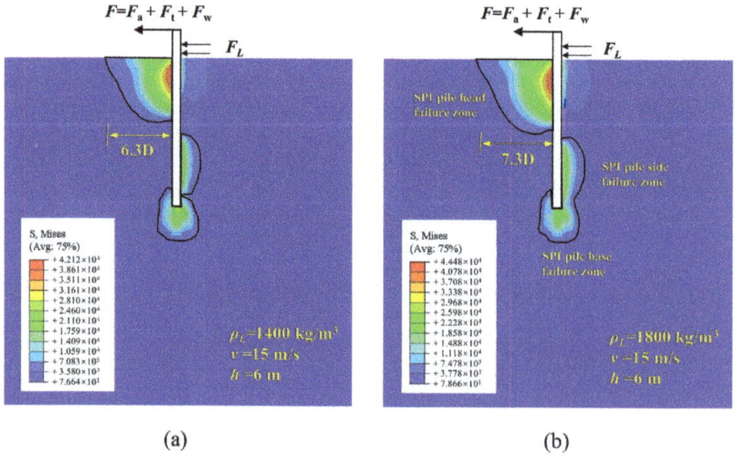

Figure 7. Stress nephograms of sediment at different submarine landslide densities: (**a**) the landslide density is 1400 kg/m^3; (**b**) the landslide density is 1800 kg/m^3.

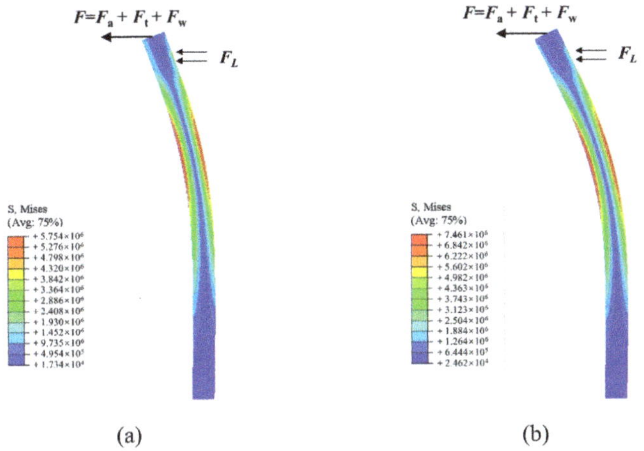

Figure 8. Stress nephograms of pile body at different submarine landslide densities (deformation coefficient of 100): (**a**) the landslide density is 1400 kg/m^3; (**b**) the landslide density is 1800 kg/m^3.

3.2.2. Effect of Submarine Landslide Velocity

The effects of different landslide velocities (10 m/s, 15 m/s, and 20 m/s) on monopile stability are analyzed, where the landslide density is 1600 kg/m^3 and the impact height is 5 m. Figure 9 illustrates the horizontal displacement response of the monopile under various submarine landslide velocities. It is evident that, at a landslide velocity of 10 m/s, the resulting landslide impact force is 1,511,617 N, causing a horizontal displacement of 0.04 m at the pile head. At 15 m/s, the impact force increases to 3,390,260 N, with a pile head horizontal displacement of 0.08 m. At 20 m/s, the impact force peaks at 6,017,307 N, with a corresponding pile head horizontal displacement of 0.19 m. Clearly, higher submarine landslide velocities lead to increased impact force and pile head horizontal displacement. Furthermore, the gradient of increase in pile head horizontal displacement is more pronounced when the landslide velocity increases from 15 m/s to 20 m/s than when it increases from 10 m/s to 15 m/s, indicating a nonlinear increase in underwater landslide impact force and a steeper gradient of increase in pile head horizontal displacement with increasing landslide velocity. Moreover, greater submarine landslide velocities result in larger pile rotation angles. At 10 m/s, the maximum pile rotation angle is only 0.09°, whereas, at 20 m/s, it can reach 0.38°, indicating monopile instability. Similarly, the gradient of increase in pile rotation angle also rises gradually with increasing landslide velocity. In addition, the maximum bending moment of the pile increases with increasing landslide velocity. At 10 m/s, it is 23.5 MN·m, which is 1.8 times the calculated result without landslide load. At 20 m/s, it can reach 82.7 MN·m, which is 6.2 times the result without landslide load. The gradient of increase in maximum bending moment of the pile also gradually grows with increasing landslide velocity. It is noteworthy that the position of the inflection point of the pile bending moment shifts downward as the incidental impact load reaches a certain threshold at larger submarine landslide velocities. Figures 10 and 11 depict the Mises stress nephograms of the sediment and pile body at velocities of 10 m/s and 20 m/s, respectively. It is observed that, with increasing landslide velocity, the impact force of submarine landslides increases, resulting in a significant increase in sediment stress. As a result, the area of the SPI failure zone at the pile head increases, with the horizontal range expanding from 5 D to 8.6 D. Additionally, the SPI failure zones at the pile base and pile side are interconnected. Stress gradually extends downward, and the stress concentration point moves accordingly. The distribution of stress in the monopile body corresponds to the stress distribution in the sediment. At 10 m/s, the maximum stress point is 9 m below the seabed surface, and, at 20 m/s, it is 16 m below the seabed surface. As the landslide velocity increases, the underwater landslide impact force grows, the upper monopile displacement increases, and the maximum pile body stress rises, but the stress at the pile head decreases.

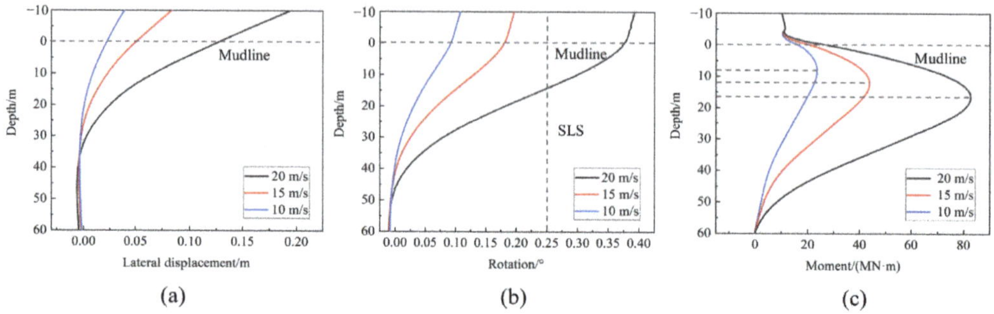

Figure 9. The effect of different landslide velocities on the response of a monopile: (**a**) displacement of pile; (**b**) rotation angle of pile; (**c**) bending moment of pile.

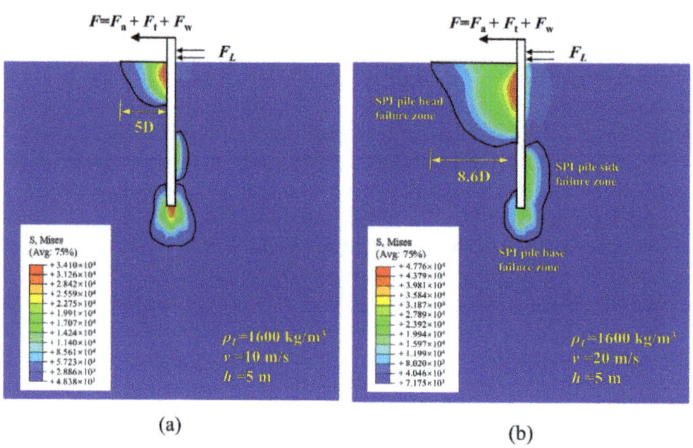

Figure 10. Stress nephograms of sediment at different submarine landslide velocities: (**a**) v = 10 m/s; (**b**) v = 20 m/s.

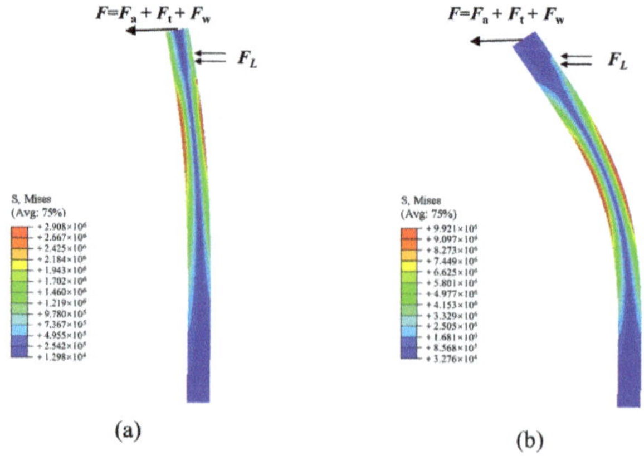

Figure 11. Stress nephograms of pile body at different submarine landslide velocities (deformation coefficient of 100): (**a**) v = 10 m/s; (**b**) v = 20 m/s.

3.2.3. Effect of Submarine Landslide Impact Height

This section explores the influence of impact heights varying from 5 m to 9 m on monopile stability, where the landslide velocity is 15 m/s and the density is 1600 kg/m^3. Figure 12 depicts the horizontal displacement response of a monopile under varying submarine landslide impact heights. At 5 m impact height, the landslide exerts a force of 3,390,260 N, resulting in a horizontal displacement of 0.08 m at the pile head. Conversely, at 9 m impact height, the force increases to 6,102,468 N, causing a displacement of 0.23 m. It is clear that higher impact heights yield greater forces and larger displacements. Moreover, as the submarine landslide impact heights increase, the rotation angle of the pile body also increases. The maximum rotation angle at 5 m impact height is 0.2°, while that at 9 m impact height is 0.46°, indicating instability and eventual failure of the pile. The gradient of rotation angle increases gradually with impact height, but is less significant compared with the influence of landslide velocity. For every 1 m increase in impact height, horizontal displacement at the pile head increases by approximately 0.05° to 0.07°. Likewise, changes in the maximum bending moment of the pile body follow a distinct trend. At 5 m impact height, it is 43.8 MN·m, which is 3.3 times the calculated result without considering landslide loads. Yet, at 9 m impact height, it reaches 95.5 MN·m, which is 7.2 times the calculated result. The maximum bending moment increases gradually with impact height, and it increases by 23 MN·m from 5 m to 7 m, and by 28.7 MN·m from 7 m to 9 m. Furthermore, the submarine landslide impact height affects the location of the inflection point of the bending moment of pile body. As the impact height increases, the inflection point shifts downward due to the increase in impact force and range. Figure 13 illustrates the sediment stress nephograms under different impact heights. The SPI failure zones under different landslide impact heights still distribute near the pile head, lower part of the pile side, and near the pile base. With the increase in landslide impact height, the evolutions of SPI failure zones at pile head and pile base exhibit opposite trends. The range of the SPI failure zone at the pile head gradually increases from 6.7 D to 9.5 D, while the range of the SPI failure zone at the pile base gradually decreases. This reflects an increased contribution of the upper soil to the resistance force as the landslide impact height increases. Figure 14 displays the distribution of the pile body stress. With increasing landslide impact height, stress increases, and the maximum stress point shifts downward, corresponding to the change in pile bending moment.

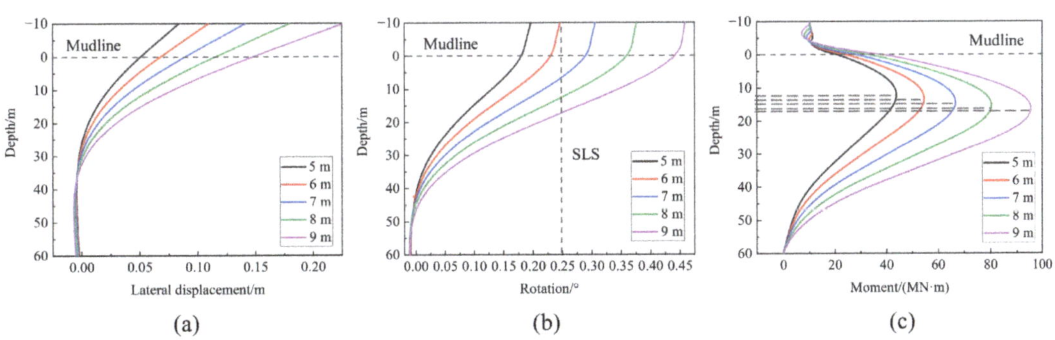

Figure 12. The effect of different submarine landslide impact heights on the response of a monopile: (**a**) displacement of pile; (**b**) rotation angle of pile; (**c**) bending moment of pile.

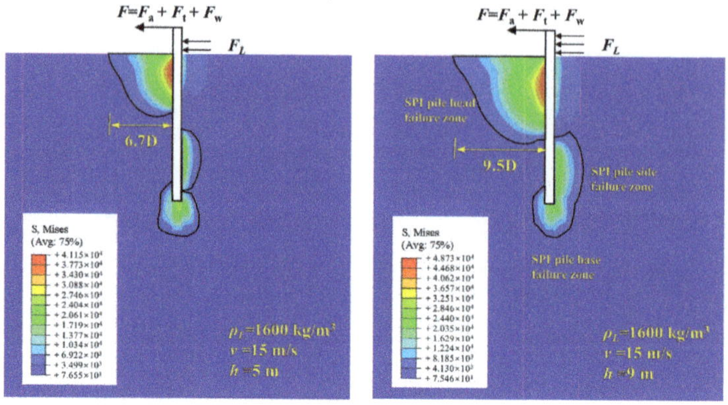

(a) (b)

Figure 13. Stress nephograms of sediment at different submarine landslide impact heights: (**a**) $h = 5$ m; (**b**) $h = 9$ m.

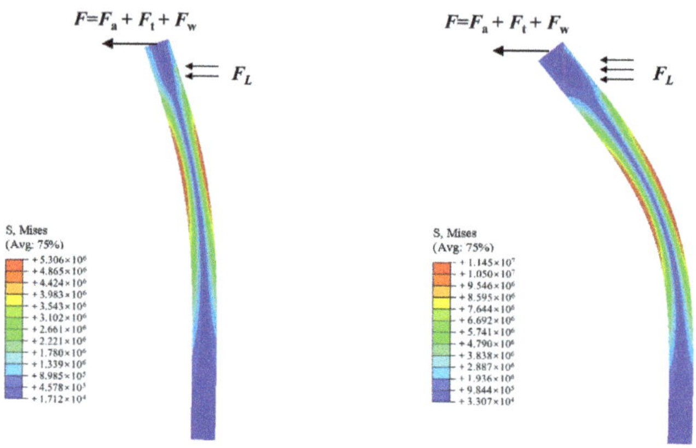

(a) (b)

Figure 14. Stress nephograms of pile body at different submarine landslide impact heights (deformation coefficient of 100): (**a**) $h = 5$ m; (**b**) $h = 9$ m.

3.3. *The Influence of Seabed Sediment Strength on the Stability of Monopiles*

This section investigates the influence of seabed sediment strength on monopile stability. Wang and Yu [51] conducted laboratory direct shear tests to evaluate the strength of marine sediments. Based on the test results, this study selects sediment cohesion values of 5 kPa, 10 kPa, 15 kPa, and 20 kPa, along with internal friction angles of 0°, 5°, 10°, and 15° for comparative analysis. The loading conditions on the monopile remain the same as before, with a landslide velocity of 15 m/s, a landslide density of 1600 kg/m^3, a landslide impact height of 7 m, and a landslide impact force of 4,746,364 N.

3.3.1. Effect of Cohesion

Figure 15 depicts the displacement and rotation at the mudline of a monopile under varying sediment cohesion, where the internal friction angle is 10°. As sediment cohesion diminishes, both horizontal displacement and rotation increase. For instance, the mudline displacement at 20 kPa cohesion is only 0.049 m with a rotation angle of 0.19°. Conversely, the mudline displacement at 5 kPa cohesion increases to 0.23 m, accompanied by a rotation angle of 0.50°, indicating instability. Notably, the decrease in sediment cohesion yields more significant increases in both the displacement and rotation at the mudline. A decrease in cohesion from 10 kPa to 5 kPa results in a displacement change of 0.13 m and a rotation angle increase of 0.22°, which implies that the horizontal load-bearing capacity of the sediment on a monopile is lost when cohesion falls below 10 kPa. Fitting a hyperbolic curve to monopile displacement and rotation for various sediment cohesion levels can yield empirical formulas correlating sediment cohesion to monopile behavior. Comparative analysis of Mises stress contour plots of sediment (Figure 16) and monopile stress distribution (Figure 17) at cohesion values of 20 kPa and 5 kPa demonstrates that, as sediment cohesion decreases, both the SPI failure zones at the pile head and pile base undergo substantial expansion due to the increased horizontal displacement of the monopile. Specifically, the horizontal span of the SPI pile head failure zone escalates from 5.9 D to 13.8 D. Meanwhile, there is a significant reduction in maximum stress, which plummets from 71.95 kPa to 28.17 kPa. This observation suggests a more pronounced dispersion of stress under these conditions. In addition, as cohesion decreases, stress concentration points shift downward, which transitions monopile damage from horizontal to depth-wise, corresponding to stress changes in the monopile with the sediment. The reduction in cohesion diminishes the load-bearing capacity of the sediment, resulting in overall tilting of the monopile.

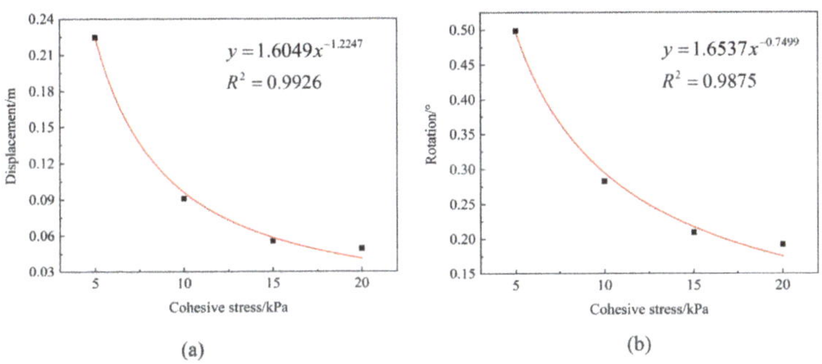

Figure 15. Displacement and rotation at the mudline of a monopile under different cohesion: (**a**) displacement at the mudline; (**b**) rotation at the mudline.

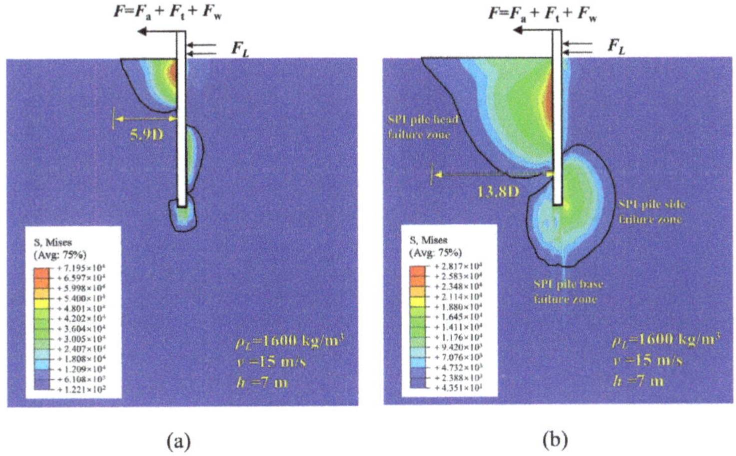

Figure 16. Stress nephograms of sediment under different cohesion: (**a**) cohesion is 20 kPa; (**b**) cohesion is 5 kPa.

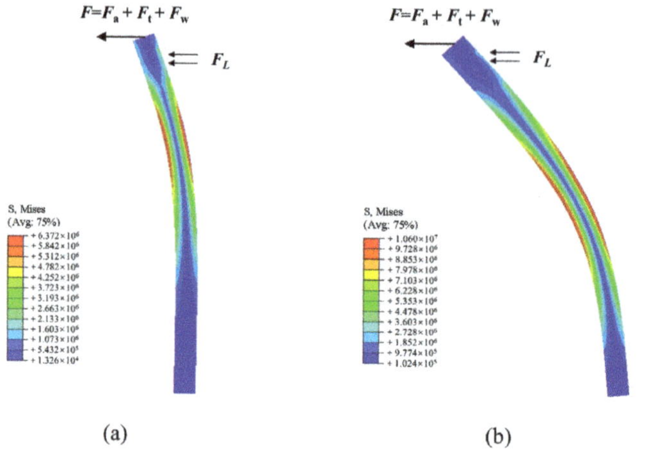

Figure 17. Stress nephograms of pile body under different cohesion (deformation coefficient of 100): (**a**) cohesion is 20 kPa; (**b**) cohesion is 5 kPa.

3.3.2. Effect of Internal Friction Angle

Figure 18 illustrates the displacement and rotation angle at the mudline of the monopile for different internal friction angles under 10 kPa cohesion. It can be observed that, as the internal friction angle decreases, the horizontal displacement and rotation angle of the monopile increase. When the internal friction angle is 15°, the pile displacement is 0.076 m and the rotation angle is 0.25°, indicating instability of the monopile. When the internal friction angle decreases to 0°, the pile displacement increases to 0.147 m and the rotation angle increases to 0.38°. It is observed that a decrease in the internal friction angle leads to a slightly larger increase in displacement and rotation angle at the mudline of the monopile. Empirical formulas relating the sediment internal friction angle to pile displacement and the rotation angle can be obtained by linearly fitting the displacement and rotation angle of the monopile at the mudline for different internal friction angles. Figures 19 and 20 show the Mises stress nephograms of sediment and the pile body when the internal friction angles are 15° and 0°, respectively. It can be observed that, when the internal friction angle decreases, the areas of both the SPI pile head failure zone and the SPI pile base influence zone significantly increase. The influence zone at the pile head increases from 6.6 D to 13.6 D and the maximum stress decreases from 62.61 kPa to 19.82 kPa. When the internal friction angle is 15°, the stress concentration zone is located on the compression side of the sediment, which is approximately 10–15 m below the seabed surface, whereas, when the internal friction angle is 0°, the stress concentration zone significantly expands. The sediment from the seabed surface to a depth of 35 m below the seabed surface undergoes compression due to the displacement of the monopile, resulting in stress concentration on the compression side. Meanwhile, when the internal friction angle is 0°, significant stress concentration also occurs at the pile base, indicating that, in this case, the impact of the landslide on the monopile base cannot be ignored in design. As the internal friction angle decreases, the stress on the pile body gradually increases, and the stress concentration zone of the pile body gradually shifts downward. However, the monopile does not undergo significant tilting, indicating that the change in the internal friction angle has a relatively small effect on pile displacement.

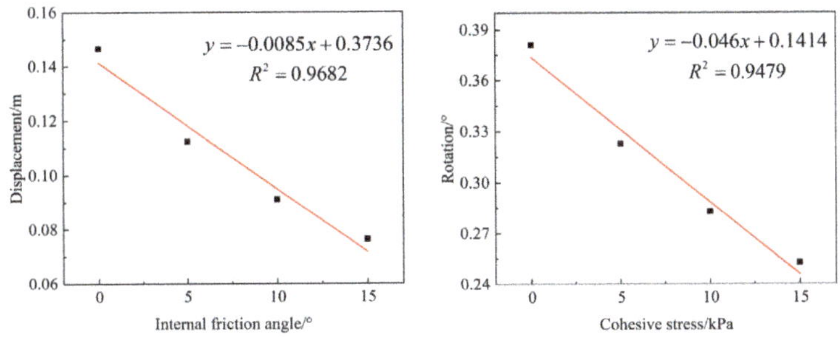

(a) (b)

Figure 18. Displacement and rotation at the mudline of a monopile under different internal friction angles: (**a**) displacement at the mudline; (**b**) rotation at the mudline.

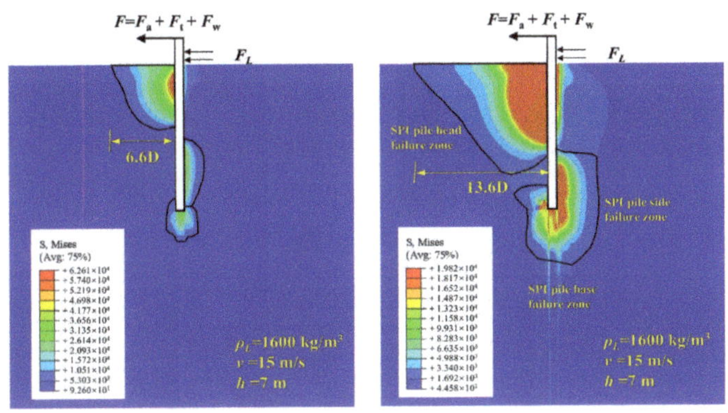

(a) (b)

Figure 19. Stress nephograms of sediment under different internal friction angles: (**a**) internal friction angle is 15°; (**b**) internal friction angle is 0°.

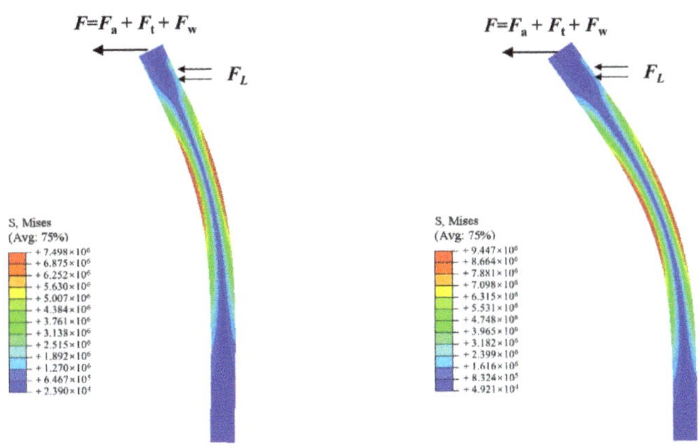

(a) (b)

Figure 20. Stress nephograms of pile body under different internal friction angles (deformation coefficient of 100): (**a**) internal friction angle is 15°; (**b**) internal friction angle is 0°.

4. Conclusions

This study quantifies the wind, wave, current loads, and seabed landslide loads acting on offshore wind turbine structures during their service life, and simplifies them into horizontal loads and moments applied to the pile head. A finite element analysis model of offshore wind turbine foundation under complex lateral loading conditions is established, and the stability of monopiles under the coupling effect of seabed landslides as well as offshore wind and wave loads is investigated.

1. As the density, velocity, and impact height of submarine landslides increase, the force on the monopile increases. Consequently, all the horizontal displacement, pile rotation angle, and maximum bending moment at the pile head increase. The escalation in submarine landslide density and impact height yields a proportional increase in the horizontal displacement, pile rotation angle, and maximum bending moment. Moreover, an increase in submarine landslide velocity leads to a hyperbolic surge in the horizontal displacement, pile rotation angle, and maximum bending moment. Once a specific lateral loading threshold is reached, three distinct SPI failure zones emerge within the seabed sediment, i.e., the compressive wedge failure zone at the pile head, the rotational shear failure zone at the pile base, and the failure zone along the pile side. Further increase in lateral loading prompts a gradual expansion of the sediment compression failure zone at the pile head, while the shear failure zone at the pile base progressively intertwines with the failure zone along the pile side. In the scenario of the designated case study, the cumulative rotation angle at the mudline of the monopile reaches 0.27° when the horizontal influence range at the pile head extends to 7.3 D, thereby triggering instability failure in accordance with DNV standards.
2. A decrease in the cohesion of the seabed sediment subjected to the same lateral load leads to a reduction of the horizontal bearing capacity of the sediment. Consequently, this triggers a hyperbolic increase in displacement and rotation angle at the mudline of the monopile. For instance, when the cohesion of the seabed sediment decreases from 20 kPa to 5 kPa, the area of sediment compression failure zone at the pile head enlarges and the horizontal influence range surges from 5.9 D to 13.8 D. It is noteworthy that the area of the full-flow failure zone on the pile side decreases, while the area of the shear failure zone at the pile base increases. The shear failure zone at the pile base extends upwards to cover the original failure zone on the pile side. In the context of the specified case study, the monopile experiences instability failure when the cohesion of the seabed sediment drops below 10 kPa.
3. Under the same lateral load, a decrease in the internal friction angle of the seabed sediment leads to a linear increase in displacement and rotation angle at the mudline of the monopile. When the internal friction angle decreases from 15° to 0°, the area of the sediment compression failure zone at the pile head enlarges, and the horizontal influence range expands from 6.6 D to 13.6 D. The failure zone on the pile side merges with the shear failure zone on the pile base. Concurrently, the area of stress concentration zones on the compression side of the pile head and on the opposite side of the pile base, where seabed sediments are distributed, increases significantly. This stress concentration renders sediment more susceptible to failure. In the conditions of the chosen case study, the monopile experiences instability failure when the internal friction angle of the sediment is below 15°.
4. This study investigates the stability of wind turbine foundations during operation by simplifying submarine landslide, wind, wave, and current loads into horizontal loads, which offers insights into the design of such foundations. However, further research should consider the distribution and instantaneous dynamic characteristics of submarine landslide, wind, wave, and flow loads, and conduct more comprehensive calculations to enhance analytical precision. In addition, future studies can integrate analysis with field-measured environmental data to better quantify environmental loads.

Author Contributions: Conceptualization, M.S., Z.S. and W.W.; methodology, M.S., Z.S. and S.X.; software, M.S. and S.X.; validation, Z.S., W.W. and S.X.; formal analysis, S.X. and X.G.; investigation, M.S., Z.S. and W.W.; resources, M.S., Z.S. and W.W.; data curation, X.G.; writing—original draft preparation, M.S., S.X. and X.G.; writing—review and editing, Z.S., W.W., H.Z. and X.L.; visualization, M.S. and S.X.; supervision, Z.S., X.L. and X.G.; project administration, M.S., Z.S. and W.W.; funding acquisition, X.G., H.Z. and X.L. All authors have read and agreed to the published version of the manuscript.

Funding: This research was financially supported by the "Pioneer" and "Leading Goose" R&D Program of Zhejiang (2022C03009), the Shandong Provincial Key Laboratory of Ocean Engineering with grant at Ocean University of China (kloe202301), the Opening Fund of the State Key Laboratory of Geohazard Prevention and Geoenvironment Protection at Chengdu University of Technology (SKLGP2023K001), the Opening Fund of the State Key Laboratory of Coastal and Offshore Engineering at Dalian University of Technology (LP2310), the Fundamental Research Funds for the Central Universities (202441003), and the National Natural Science Foundation of China (42207181).

Institutional Review Board Statement: Not applicable.

Informed Consent Statement: Not applicable.

Data Availability Statement: All data, models, and code generated or used during this study appear in this submitted article.

Conflicts of Interest: Author M.S., Z.S. and W.W. was employed by the company Zhejiang Engineering Research Center of Marine Geotechnical Investigation Technology and Equipment, Zhejiang Huadong Geotechnical Investigation & Design Institute Co., Ltd., Powerchina Huadong Engineering Co., Ltd., Hangzhou 311122, China. The remaining authors declare that the research was conducted in the absence of any commercial or financial relationships that could be construed as a potential conflict of interest.

Abbreviations and Symbols

A_R	Rotor swept area
C_D	Coefficient of drag force perpendicular to the axis of the cylinder
C_M	Coefficient of inertial force
C_T	Coefficient of thrust
C_W	Coefficient of drag force for current
C_d	Coefficient of drag force for landslide
C_s	Coefficient of drag force for wind
E_{pile}	Young's modulus of pile
E_pI_p	Flexural rigidity of pile
F_C	Current load
F_D	Drag force
F_I	Inertial force
F_L	Landslide load
F_W	Wave load
F_a	Wind load on blades
F_t	Wind load on tower
L_d	Monopile buried depth
P_T	Total load
P_Z	Vertical load
R_{i+1}	Residual
$\vec{U}$	Wave speed
U_{in}	Cut-in wind speed
U_{out}	Cut-out wind speed
V_0	Volume of drainage per unit of cylinder height
Z_1	Standard height
$\dot{\gamma}$	Shear rate of the near-pile slurry
δ_{cs}	Friction angle of the pile–soil interface in the critical state
$\varepsilon_{\text{xx}}, \varepsilon_{\text{yy}}, \varepsilon_{\text{zz}}, \gamma_{\text{xy}}, \gamma_{\text{yz}}, \gamma_{\text{zx}}$	Component of strain
ρ_{L}	Debris flow density of submarine landslides

$\rho_{\mathbf{a}}$	Density of air
$\rho_{\mathbf{pile}}$	Density of pile
$\rho_{\mathbf{s}}$	Density of seawater
σ_1, σ_3	Principal stress
σ_2	Medium principal stress
$\sigma_{\mathbf{n}}'$	Normal effective stress
$\sigma_{\mathbf{xx}}, \sigma_{\mathbf{yy}}, \sigma_{\mathbf{zz}}, \sigma_{\mathbf{xy}}, \sigma_{\mathbf{yz}}, \sigma_{\mathbf{zx}}$	Component of stress
$\tau_{\mathbf{f}}$	Shear stress of the contact surface
$v_{\mathbf{pile}}$	Poisson's ratio of pile
h	Impact height of submarine landslides
$U_{\mathbf{R}}$	Rated wind speed
A	Projected area per unit beam height perpendicular to the wave propagation direction
D	Diameter of a monopile
E	Elastic modulus
I	Internal force of the finite element node
L	Pile length
M	Moment
P	External load on the finite element node
S	Shear force
U	Wind speed
$U(\mathrm{Z}_1)$	Average wind speed
c	Cohesion intercept
i	Iteration
p	Earth reaction force
r	Displacement correction
u	Displacement of the node
v	Flow velocity of the landslide
α	Wind shear index
μ	Debris flow viscosity
τ	Shear stress
v	Poisson's ratio
φ	Internal friction angle
ψ	Dilation angle

References

1. Esteban, M.D.; Diez, J.J.; López, J.S.; Negro, V. Why offshore wind energy? *Renew. Energy* **2011**, *36*, 444–450. [CrossRef]
2. Zhang, J.H.; Hao, W. Development of offshore wind power and foundation technology for offshore wind turbines in China. *Ocean Eng.* **2022**, *266*, 113256. [CrossRef]
3. Soares-Ramos, E.P.P.; De Oliveira-Assis, L.; Sarrias-Mena, R.; Fernández-Ramírez, L.M. Current status and future trends of offshore wind power in Europe. *Energy* **2020**, *202*, 117787. [CrossRef]
4. Simoncelli, M.; Zucca, M.; Ghilardi, M. Structural health monitoring of an onshore steel wind turbine. *J. Civ. Struct. Health Monit.* **2024**, 1–15. [CrossRef]
5. Global Wind Energy Council. Global offshore Wind Report 2023. Available online: https://gwec.net/gwecs-global-offshore-wind-report-2023/ (accessed on 28 August 2023).
6. Xie, M.; Lopez-Querol, S. Numerical simulations of the monotonic and cyclic behaviour of offshore wind turbine monopile foundations in clayey soils. *J. Mar. Sci. Eng.* **2021**, *9*, 1036. [CrossRef]
7. Chen, Y.; Gu, M.; Chen, R.; Kong, L.; Zhang, Z.; Bian, X. Behavior of pile group with elevated cap subjected to cyclic lateral loads. *China Ocean Eng.* **2015**, *29*, 565–578. [CrossRef]
8. Zeng, X.; Shi, W.; Michailides, C.; Zhang, S.; Li, X. Numerical and experimental investigation of breaking wave forces on a monopile-type offshore wind turbine. *Renew. Energy* **2021**, *175*, 501–519. [CrossRef]
9. Shi, Y.; Yao, W.; Jiang, M. Dynamic analysis on monopile supported offshore wind turbine under wave and wind load. *Structures* **2023**, *47*, 520–529. [CrossRef]
10. Miles, J.; Martin, T.; Goddard, L. Current and wave effects around windfarm monopile foundations. *Coast. Eng.* **2017**, *121*, 167–178. [CrossRef]
11. Ong, M.C.; Li, H.; Leira, B.J.; Myrhaug, D. Dynamic analysis of offshore monopile wind turbine including the effects of wind-wave loading and soil properties. In Proceedings of the International Conference on Offshore Mechanics and Arctic Engineering, Nantes, France, 9–14 June 2013; Volume 55423.

12. Buljac, A.; Kozmar, H.; Yang, W.; Kareem, A. Concurrent wind, wave and current loads on a monopile-supported offshore wind turbine. *Eng. Struct.* **2022**, *255*, 113950. [CrossRef]
13. Achmus, M.; Kuo, Y.S.; Abdel-Rahman, K. Behavior of monopile foundations under cyclic lateral load. *Comput. Geotech.* **2009**, *36*, 725–735. [CrossRef]
14. Wu, T.; Lu, Z.; Dou, D. Model Tests and Finite Element Analysis of Behaviors of Ocean and Offshore Elevated Piles under Lateral Load. *Sci. Technol. Eng.* **2013**, *13*, 7697–7702. (In Chinese)
15. Guo, X.; Liu, X.; Li, M.; Lu, Y. Lateral force on buried pipelines caused by seabed slides using a CFD method with a shear interface weakening model. *Ocean. Eng.* **2023**, *280*, 114663. [CrossRef]
16. Rafiei, A.; Rahman, M.S.; Gabr, M.A.; Ghayoomi, M. Analysis of wave-induced submarine landslides in nearly saturated sediments at intermediate water depths. *Mar. Georesources Geotechnol.* **2022**, *40*, 1411–1423. [CrossRef]
17. Liu, X.; Wang, Y.; Zhang, H.; Guo, X. Susceptibility of typical marine geological disasters: An overview. *Geoenvironmental. Disasters* **2023**, *10*, 10. [CrossRef]
18. Guo, X.; Fan, N.; Liu, Y.; Liu, X.; Wang, Z.; Xie, X.; Jia, Y. Deep seabed mining: Frontiers in engineering geology and environment. *Int. J. Coal Sci. Technol.* **2023**, *10*, 23. [CrossRef]
19. Guo, X.; Liu, X.; Zheng, T.; Zhang, H.; Lu, Y.; Li, T. A mass transfer-based LES modelling methodology for analyzing the movement of submarine sediment flows with extensive shear behavior. *Coast. Eng.* **2024**, *191*, 104531. [CrossRef]
20. Guo, X.; Fan, N.; Zheng, D.; Fu, C.; Wu, H.; Zhang, Y.; Song, X.; Nian, T. Predicting impact forces on pipelines from deep-sea fluidized slides: A comprehensive review of key factors. *Int. J. Min. Sci. Technol.* **2024**, *34*, 211–225. [CrossRef]
21. Wang, Z.; Zheng, D.; Guo, X.; Gu, Z.; Shen, Y.; Nian, T. Investigation of offshore landslides impact on bucket foundations using a coupled SPH–FEM method. *Geoenvironmental. Disasters* **2024**, *11*, 2. [CrossRef]
22. Guo, X.; Stoesser, T.; Zheng, D.; Luo, Q.; Liu, X.; Nian, T. A methodology to predict the run-out distance of submarine landslides. *Comput. Geotech.* **2023**, *153*, 105073. [CrossRef]
23. Mohrig, D.; Ellis, C.; Parker, G.; Kelin, X.; Midhat, H. Hydroplaning of subaqueous debris flows. *Geol. Soc. Am. Bull.* **1998**, *110*, 387–394. [CrossRef]
24. Guo, X.; Nian, T.; Stoesser, T. Using dimpled-pipe surface to reduce submarine landslide impact forces on pipelines at different span heights. *Ocean. Eng.* **2022**, *244*, 110343. [CrossRef]
25. De Blasio, F.V.; Elverhøi, A.; Issler, D.; Harbitz, C.B.; Bryn, P.; Lien, R. Flow models of natural debris flows originating from overconsolidated clay materials. *Mar. Geol.* **2004**, *213*, 439–455. [CrossRef]
26. Hsu, S.K.; Kuo, J.; Chung-Liang, L.; Ching-Hui, T.; Doo, W.B.; Ku, C.Y.; Sibuet, J.C. Turbidity currents, submarine landslides and the 2006 Pingtung earthquake off SW Taiwan. *TAO Terr. Atmos. Ocean. Sci.* **2008**, *19*, 7. [CrossRef]
27. Li, D.L.; Yan, E.C.; Feng, B. Impact of submarine debris flow on offshore piles. *J. Zhejiang Univ. Eng. Sci.* **2019**, *53*, 2342–2347. (In Chinese)
28. Li, R.Y.; Chen, J.J.; Liao, C.C. Numerical study on interaction between submarine landslides and a monopile using CFD techniques. *J. Mar. Sci. Eng.* **2021**, *9*, 736. [CrossRef]
29. Xi, R.; Du, X.; Wang, P.; Xu, C.; Zhai, E.; Wang, S. Dynamic analysis of 10 MW monopile supported offshore wind turbine based on fully coupled model. *Ocean. Eng.* **2021**, *234*, 109346. [CrossRef]
30. Bisoi, S.; Haldar, S. Dynamic analysis of offshore wind turbine in clay considering soil–monopile–tower interaction. *Soil Dyn. Earthq. Eng.* **2014**, *63*, 19–35. [CrossRef]
31. Arany, L.; Bhattacharya, S.; Macdonald, J.; Hogan, S.J. Design of monopiles for offshore wind turbines in 10 steps. *Soil Dyn. Earthq. Eng.* **2017**, *92*, 126–152. [CrossRef]
32. Frohboese, P.; Schmuck, C.; Hassan, G.G. Thrust coefficients used for estimation of wake effects for fatigue load calculation. In Proceedings of the European Wind Energy Conference, Berlin, Germany, 23–24 November 2010; pp. 1–10.
33. Charlton, T.S.; Rouainia, M. Geotechnical fragility analysis of monopile foundations for offshore wind turbines in extreme storms. *Renew. Energy* **2022**, *182*, 1126–1140. [CrossRef]
34. *JTG/T 3360-01—2018*; Recommend Profession Standard of the People's Republic of China, Code for Wind Resistance Design of Highway Bridges. People's Communications Press: Beijing, China, 2016. Available online: https://xxgk.mot.gov.cn/2020/jigou/glj/202006/t20200623_3313096.html (accessed on 1 March 2019).
35. *NB/T 10105-2018*; Energy Industry Recommended Standard of the People's Republic of China, Code for Basic Design of Wind Turbines for Offshore Wind Farm Projects. China Water Power Press: Beijing, China, 2018. Available online: https://www.chinesestandard.net/PDF/English.aspx/NBT10105-2018 (accessed on 25 December 2018).
36. Morison, J.R.; Johnson, J.W.; Schaaf, S.A. The force exerted by surface waves on piles. *J. Pet. Technol.* **1950**, *2*, 149–154. [CrossRef]
37. *JTS 145-2015*; Profession Standard of the People's Republic of China, Code of Hydrology for Harbour. China Communications Press: Beijing, China, 1998; pp. 77–78. Available online: https://xxgk.mot.gov.cn/2020/jigou/syj/202006/t20200623_3313586.html (accessed on 31 August 2015).
38. Zhang, C.; Tang, G.; Lu, L.; Jin, Y.; An, H.; Cheng, L. Flow-induced vibration of two tandem square cylinders at low Reynolds number: Transitions among vortex-induced vibration, biased oscillation and galloping. *J. Fluid Mech.* **2024**, *986*, A10. [CrossRef]
39. Feng, B.; Sun, H.L.; Cai, Y.Q. Experimental study of submarine landslide impact on offshore wind power piles. *Ocean. Eng.* **2019**, *37*, 114–121. (In Chinese)
40. Herschel, W.H.; Bulkley, R. Konsistenzmessungen von gummi-benzollösungen. *Kolloid-Zeitschrift* **1926**, *39*, 291–300. [CrossRef]

41. Reese, L.C.; van Impe, W. Derivation of equations and methods of solution. In *Book Single Piles and Pile Groups under Lateral Loading*, 2nd ed.; Taylor and Francis: Abingdon, UK, 2001; pp. 23–24.
42. Abbas, J.M.; Chik, Z.H.; Taha, M.R. Single pile simulation and analysis subjected to lateral load. *Electron. J. Geotech. Eng.* **2008**, *13*, 1–15.
43. Johnson, K.; Lemcke, P.; Karunasena, W.; Sivakugan, N. Modelling the load–deformation response of deep foundation under oblique loading. *Environ. Model. Softw.* **2006**, *21*, 1375–1380. [CrossRef]
44. Hu, Q.; Han, F.; Prezzi, M.; Salgado, R.; Zhao, M. Lateral load response of large-diameter monopiles in sand. *Géotechnique* **2022**, *72*, 1035–1050. [CrossRef]
45. Liu, H.J.; Sun, P.P.; Geng, H.R.; Hao, R. Horizontal bearing capacity of offshore wind power pile foundation under different sea conditions and geological conditions. *Period. Ocean. Univ. China* **2019**, *8*, 51–58. (In Chinese)
46. Dai, S.; Han, B.; Wang, B.; Luo, J.; He, B. Influence of soil scour on lateral behavior of large-diameter offshore wind-turbine monopile and corresponding scour monitoring method. *Ocean. Eng.* **2021**, *239*, 109809. [CrossRef]
47. Zhang, X.L.; Liu, J.X.; Han, Y.; Du, X.L. A framework for evaluating the bearing capacity of offshore wind power foundation under complex loadings. *Appl. Ocean Res.* **2018**, *80*, 66–78. [CrossRef]
48. DNV GL, DNVGL-ST-0126 Support Structures for Wind Turbines, 2018. Edition July 2018. Available online: https://www.dnv.com/energy/standards-guidelines/dnv-st-0126-support-structures-for-wind-turbines (accessed on 1 December 2021).
49. Takahashi, T. Mechanical characteristics of debris flow. *J. Hydraul. Div.* **1978**, *104*, 1153–1169. [CrossRef]
50. Laberg, J.S.; Vorren, T.O. A late Pleistocene submarine slide on the Bear Island trough mouth fan. *Geo-Mar. Lett.* **1993**, *13*, 227–234. [CrossRef]
51. Wang, X.F.; Yu, H.G. The experience relationship between the state and the direct shear test index about marine facies clayed soil. In Proceedings of the National Engineering Geology Academic Conference and "Engineering Geology and West Coast Construction" Academic Conference, Fujian, China, 17 November 2013; Volume 5. (In Chinese)

Journal of
Marine Science and Engineering

MDPI

Article

Spatio-Temporal Compressive Behaviors of River Pebble Concrete and Sea Pebble Concrete in Island Offshore Engineering

Yuan Yuan *, Yian Zhao, Xiaotian Feng, Yanhua Lei and Wenbing Zhang

College of Ocean Science and Engineering, Shanghai Maritime University, Shanghai 201306, China; zy2621691401@163.com (Y.Z.); feng824395549@163.com (X.F.); yhlei@shmtu.edu.cn (Y.L.); zhangwb@shmtu.edu.cn (W.Z.)

* Correspondence: yuanyuan@shmtu.edu.cn; Tel.: +86-021-3828-2522

Abstract: Obtaining river or sea pebbles from local resources for concrete production is considered an economical and eco-friendly alternative, particularly in marine and island-offshore engineering. However, the resulting changes in the mechanical properties of these concrete have attracted attention. This study investigates the compressive behavior of concretes where river or sea pebbles partially (i.e., 33% and 67%) or fully (i.e., 100%) replace traditional gravel as coarse aggregate, using a noncontact full-field deformation measurement system based on digital image correlation (DIC). Compared to the traditional gravel concrete (GC), compressive strengths of the river pebble concrete (RPC) at constitution rates of 33%, 67%, and 100% decreased by 6.5%, 29.8%, and 38.9% while those values of the sea pebble concrete (SPC) decreased by 13.1%, 32.7%, and 44.3%, respectively. Meanwhile, SPC exhibited slightly lower compressive strength than RPC. The peak strains of both SPC and RPC decreased at lower substitution rates, although their stress-strain curves resembled those of GC. In contrast, RPC and SPC at higher substitution rates exhibited a noticeable stage of load hardening. Full-field deformation data and interfacial characteristics indicated that the compressive failure modes of both RPC and SPC showed significant interfacial slipping between pebbles and mortar with increasing coarse aggregate substitution rates. In comparison, fractures in coarse aggregate and mortar were observed in damaged GC. The study demonstrated that the spatio-temporal compressive deformation response and failure modes of SPC and RPC were distinct due to the introduction of pebbles, providing insights for engineering applications of river/sea pebble concrete in practical offshore or island construction projects.

Keywords: digital image correlation; pebble concrete; substitution rate; compressive strength; deformation measurement

1. Introduction

In island reef construction, the transportation of river sand, gravel, and freshwater from the mainland significantly increases project costs and fails to guarantee adherence to construction schedules [1,2]. Additionally, the extensive extraction of gravel as a raw material for coarse aggregate in concrete not only degrades natural ecological environments but also imposes significant financial burdens on engineering projects due to rising costs [3–5]. Emerging maritime and island reef constructions have increasingly explored marine resources like seawater, sea sand, sea pebbles, and coral aggregates for concrete engineering purposes [6,7]. Specifically, sea pebbles are used as a coarse aggregate (referred to hereafter as sea pebble concrete, SPC) due to their accessibility and abundant reserves. Over the years, the use of pebbles as a coarse aggregate in island reef construction engineering has proven feasible [8,9]. Because of its superior performance in fluidity, self-compaction, and pumpability, hydraulic structure codes recommend using pebbles as a coarse aggregate in large-scale concrete structures like infilled piles and foundations [10–12]. In fact, due to the influence of the shape and surface texture of aggregate on the interlocking between mortar and aggregates, the mechanical properties of these concretes with pebbles as the coarse aggregate (hereinafter referred to as pebble concrete, PC) cannot be readily inferred based on knowledge of those traditional concretes using gravel as the coarse aggregate (hereinafter referred to as gravel concrete, GC), which limits their further applications [13,14].

Current investigations into PC are mainly on river pebbles (hereinafter referred to as river pebble concrete, RPC). The shape, roughness, surface chemical composition, and mineral composition of pebbles differ significantly, resulting in notable changes in the interfacial transition zone (ITZ) and consequently distinct compressive responses [15]. Particularly, RPC demonstrates lower compressive strength but greater resistance to crack expansion under compressive loads in comparison with GC, underscoring the significant influence of local deformation characteristics and the weaker ITZ between smoother pebbles and mortar on its compressive performance [16]. On the other hand, inorganic salt ions such as chloride and sulfate concentrate diffuse into sea pebbles, potentially affecting pore content, internal stresses, and compressive strength, thereby altering the bonding properties at the ITZ in SPC [7,17,18]. Under compressive loads, the ITZ between coarse aggregates and mortar matrix is typically the weakest point, where local deformation predominantly leads to concrete failure. In practice, in order to enhance the compressive strength of PC, researchers are exploring partial or complete substitution of traditional gravel with pebbles as the coarse aggregate in concrete, which complicates their compressive deformation behaviors [9,19].

Despite growing recognition of the mechanical behaviors of PC relating to local deformation and crack development, accurately pinpointing local damage and quantifying deformation in these regions remains challenging. Traditionally, concrete compressive strength is evaluated through compressive strength tests and stress-strain curves under load conditions, providing an overall estimation of deformation in tested concrete samples [16,20,21]. Furthermore, qualitative analysis of damaged images of concrete cubes helps in assessing crack propagation paths [22–24]. However, these traditional methods offer only general estimations and are unable to locate those randomly occurring damaged areas or provide detailed insights into local deformation and crack propagation. In recent decades, a noncontact optical methodology named the digital image correlation (DIC) technique has been introduced to track the complicated and unpredictable deformation in the concrete [25–27]. By capturing the digital speckle image sequences on the concrete surface, the full-field displacement and strain data could be calculated by comparing the speckle patterns decorated on the concrete based on some image registration algorithms [26–28]. In this way, the local deformation data of any point on the tested concrete can be determined, especially in those regions near the ITZ [29,30]. Based on the DIC technique, the shear cracking and crack slipping could be quantitatively tracked based on the calculated displacement and strain fields during the whole loading process, with which the damage behavior and failure mechanism of the concretes were further analyzed [31].

In this paper, a full-field compressive deformation measurement system for RPC/SPC was established. The full-field displacement and strain of these concrete were evaluated, which were produced by partially or completely replacing traditional gravel coarse aggregates with river/sea pebbles at series substitution rates. On this basis, a quantitative analysis is conducted to examine the local characteristics and spatial distribution of deformation and cracks occurring in RPC/SPC under compressive load conditions. Furthermore, peak strain and stress on the concrete cubes as well as the interfacial characteristics of RPC/SPC at series substitution rates are evaluated and compared. This allows us to investigate the failure modes and potential failure mechanisms of different kinds of RPC/SPC employed in practical island reef constructions.

2. Materials and Methods

2.1. Raw Materials and Concrete Specimen Preparation

As illustrated in Figure 1, river pebble, sea pebble, and gravel are used as the raw materials of coarse aggregates to make concrete, and their physical parameters were characterized and listed in Table 1 [32,33]. Gravel is irregular and has a rough surface while both river pebble and sea pebble are approximately rounded and have smooth surfaces. In this study, six sets of tested RPC/SPC specimens were prepared with a certain weight proportion of river pebbles or sea pebbles replacing gravel as the coarse aggregate, respectively. Meanwhile, GC specimens with only gravels as the coarse aggregate were prepared as the control group.

Figure 1. The prepared coarse aggregates. (**a**) River pebbles, (**b**) sea pebbles, and (**c**) gravels.

Table 1. Physical parameters of coarse aggregates.

Coarse Aggregate	River Pebble	Sea Pebble	Gravel
Gradation (mm)	5~25	5~25	5~25
Apparent density (kg/m^3)	2845	2780	2603
Bulk density (kg/m^3)	1736	1694	1549
Water absorption (%)	1.3	1.1	1.05
Moisture content (%)	0.01	0.04	0.01
Crushing index (%)	12.1	11.7	9.6

In order to study the compressive properties of RPC and SPC, seven groups of pebble concrete specimens with weight substitution rates (SR) of 33%, 67%, and 100% are, respectively, prepared and compared with the GC. It should be noted that the substitution rates were determined by some preliminary experiments. According to a series of pre-conducted experiments, the proportion of compressive strength reduction was smaller if the substitution rates of pebbles were smaller than 1/3, and the compressive strength reduction significantly increased if the pebble substitution rate exceeded 2/3. Therefore, as shown in Table 2, the mix proportion of these samples is designed according to the specification for mix proportion design of ordinary concrete in the Chinese industry standard (JGJ55-2011) [28,34]. Seven groups of concrete specimens are denoted as S(R)-0, R-33, R-67, R-100, S-33, S-67, and S-100, representing the control group and tested RPC and SPC specimen with weight substitution rates of 33%, 67%, and 100%, respectively. Here, the strength grade of these concretes is set as C40 and the water-cement ratios of GC and PC are 0.49 and 0.48. Then, the cement, river sand, gravel, pebbles, mixing water, and water-reducing agent are mixed, where the cement is PO 42.5 ordinary Portland cement (Zhejiang Portan Building Materials Technology Co., Ltd., Zhejiang China) and the river sand (fineness modulus of 2.60, density of 2.70 g/cm^3) is taken the as opup fine aggregate. The gradation of the gravel is 5~25 mm while the mass ratio of pebbles with diameters of 5~10, mm:10~15 mm:15~20, and mm:20~25 mm is set as 10%:20%:65%:5%. In addition, the polycarboxylate type superplasticizer is employed as the water-reducing agent to improve the fluidity of the concrete and reduce the amount of mixing water. The same slump was designed and verified to ensure the comparability between seven groups of concrete samples.

Table 2. Mix proportion of the concrete specimen (kg/m^3).

Specimen	SR (%)	Cement	Water	Sand	Gravel	Pebble
S(R)-0	0	388	190	569	1156	0
R-33	33	370	177.5	569	774.5	381.5
R-67	67	370	177.5	569	381.5	774.5
R-100	100	370	177.5	569	0	1156.0
S-33	33	370	177.5	569	774.5	381.5
S-67	67	370	177.5	569	381.5	774.5
S-100	100	370	177.5	569	0	1156.0

As seen in Figure 2, the concretes were prepared by fully stirring and pounding materials in a mold sized of 100 mm × 100 mm × 100 mm. Then, the mixture is vibrated thoroughly by a vibrating table. After standing in a room maintained at 20 °C and about 95% relative humidity for 24 h, the cube specimens are demolded and then cured in fresh water at a room temperature of 20 °C for 28 days. In this experiment, ten specimens are prepared for each tested case, and the front surface is decorated with speckle patterns for the DIC experiment. The upper, lower, and front sides of the cube concrete are polished with sandpaper to guarantee the smoothness of the tested surface. After cleaning the dust on the surface, matte black paint is first sprayed on the front surface of the cube specimen and the white matte paint is then carefully sprayed as randomly distributed speckles on the black background.

Figure 2. Preparation of the concrete specimen. (**a**) Stirring, (**b**) pounding, (**c**) vibration, (**d**) standing, (**e**) demolding, and (**f**) curing.

2.2. Experiment and Methods

The compressive deformation measurement experiment of the concrete specimens is performed on the established noncontact DIC platform based on computer vision and mathematical computation, which is shown in Figure 3. As seen in Figure 3a, the compressive load is uniformly applied on the upper surface of the tested concrete cube. A CCD camera is positioned in front of the tested specimen with the direction of the optical axis perpendicular to the specimen surface. Digital speckle image sequences are continuously recorded during the loading process, which can be used to find the most similar region in the deformed speckle image (also called target image) for those selected subsets in the undeformed image (also called reference image) based on the DIC registration algorithm, which is shown in Figure 3b. In Figure 3c, the experimental setup of the compressive test is established. The compressive tests are developed according to the standard for test methods of mechanical properties on ordinary concrete in the Chinese industry standard (GB/T 50081-2002) [29,35]. The compression testing machine (SF-YAW-3000D, Shanghai Hualong Test Instrument Co., LTD, Shanghai, China)is adopted to apply the uniformly distributed compressive load on the cube concrete with a loading rate of 0.8 MPa/s. The imaging apparatus is equipped by placing the industrial CCD camera (Pointgrey®, GS3-PGE-91S6) with a resolution of 3376 × 2704 pixels coupled with a lens (Tokina® KCM-1216UMP5, 12 mm, F1.6–22, both from Shanghai Wuling photoelectric Technology Co., LTD, Shanghai, China) in front of the tested specimen surface. The distance from the camera to the center of the specimen is ~300 mm while the pixel number of the specimen in the digital image is ~1300. The digital speckle images are continuously recorded with an image capturing rate of 9 frames/s. The peak loads of the concrete specimens are simultaneously recorded.

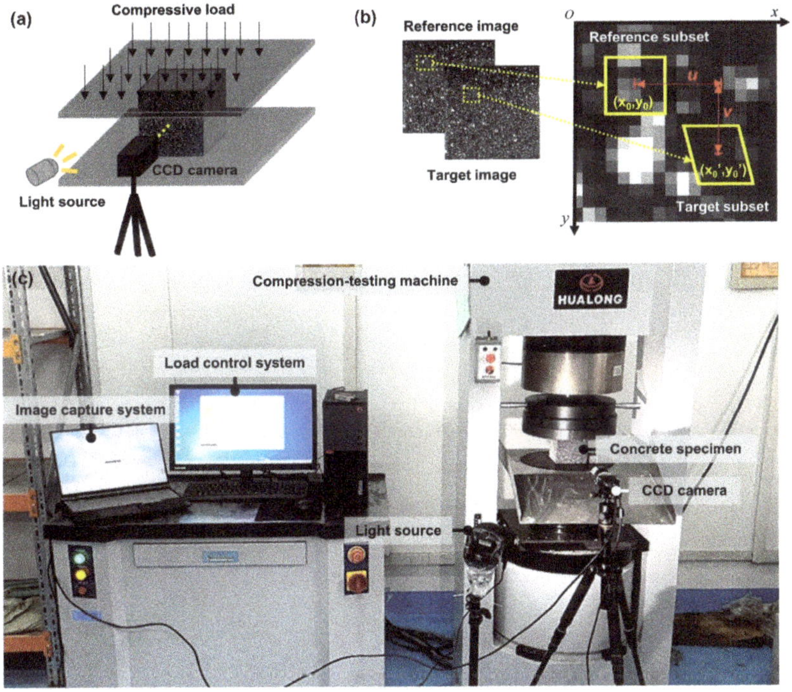

Figure 3. (**a**) Schematic diagram of the concrete compressive test based on the DIC technique. (**b**) The DIC registration algorithm. (**c**) The experimental setup of the compressive test.

Subsequently, the well-developed DIC correlation registration algorithms are employed to quantitatively obtain the deformations of concrete specimens under compressive load conditions. The sampling spacing for each point is set as 20 pixels and the typical size of the subset is 31 × 31 pixels. Based on the ZNSSD (zero normalized sum of squared differences) correlation criterion and the Newton-Raphson iterative algorithm, the full-field deformation data can be calculated by searching "the best-matched subsets" for all the sampling points chosen on the specimen surface. Then, the strain fields are constructed by the strain window method based on the measured displacement data [19]. Correlation calculations for the time-series digital speckle images are conducted to obtain the spatial-temporal deformation information of seven groups of concrete specimens (i.e., GC, RPC, and SPC) during the compressive loading process.

3. Results and Discussion

3.1. Compressive Strength

Based on the measurement data of concrete cubes included in each test case, compressive strengths and stress-strain curves of seven groups of concretes (i.e., S(R)-0, R-33, R-67, R-100, S-33, S-67, and S-100) are illustrated in Figure 4. As seen in Figure 4a, the compressive strength values of both RPC and SPC decreased with the increase in substitution rates, which is consistent with the results of a previous study [9]. Compared with S(R)-0, the peak loads of R-33, R-67, and R-100 decreased by 6.5%, 29.8%, and 38.9% while those values of S-33, S-67, and S-100 decreased by 13.1%, 32.7%, and 44.3%. On one hand, it was obvious that the compressive strengths of both the RPC and SPC presented a smaller reduction at smaller substitution rate cases (i.e., R-33 and S-33) but remarkably decreased at higher substitution rates (i.e., R-67, R-100, S-67, and S-100). On the other hand, the compressive strengths of SPCs were relatively lower than those of RPCs under the same condition of pebble substitution rate, indicating a slightly lower overall compressive strength than RPCs. If the gravels were totally replaced by pebbles, the overall compressive strengths of PC were reduced by ~40%. In fact, the compressive strength of the S(R)-0, R-33, and S-33 was larger than the expected compressive strength of 40 MPa, whereas those data of R-67, R-100, S-67, and S-100 were smaller, which was different from the results in [9]. It was because the water absorption of the employed recycled aggregates in [9] was much higher than the control group; however, the parameters in this paper are almost indistinguishable (Table 1).

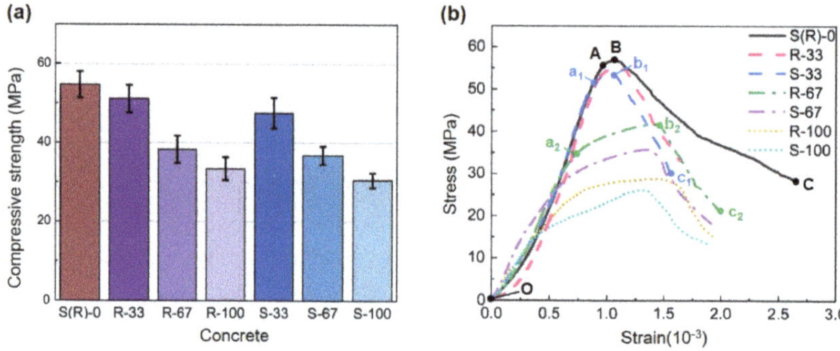

Figure 4. (**a**) Compressive strengths and (**b**) stress-strain curves of the tested concretes.

Correspondingly, the compressive stress—strain curves were presented in Figure 4b. It was found that the curves of R-33 and S-33 were similar to S(R)-0 whereas those of R-67, R-100, S-67, and S-100 were significantly different. Particularly, in the linear elastic deformation stage, the curves of PCs with lower substitution rates were relatively close to GC (e.g., Oa_1 or OA). With the increase of loads, these curves (i.e., S(R)-0, R-33, and S-33) reached the peak stress very quickly (e.g., AB or a_1b_1) before the peak stress point (e.g., A or a_1). In comparison, the linear elastic deformation periods of R-67, R-100, S-67, and S-100 were relatively shorter and then maintained a long period of slower growth (i.e., load hardening stage, a_2b_2) before peak stress (i.e., b_2). Then, in the failure stage, the descent slope of S(R)-0 (i.e., BC) in the failure stage was smaller than that of PC, implying a better ductility of GC compared with PC at all substitution rate conditions. From the viewpoint of compressive characteristics, the compressive strength of PC was closely related to the substitution rates of pebbles, and the failure stage was significantly determined by the type of coarse aggregate. It was possible that the compressive strength was associated with the crack propagation within the concrete but the concrete failure was caused by the weak bond between the aggregate and mortar. That is to say, investigations on the local deformation, crack initiation, and extension are quite necessary to clarify the distinct compressive behaviors of these newly developed PCs.

3.2. Full-Field Deformation Measurement and Crack Analysis

Displacement and strain fields of RPC and SPC at different substitution rates as well as GC were calculated to explore the mechanism of the distinct compressive failure behaviors of the concretes. According to the similar trend of the stress-strain curves between RPC and SPC at the same substitution rate as shown in Figure 4b, S(R)-0, S-33, and R-67 were selected as representatives to compare the full-field compressive deformation of RPC and SPC at different substitution rates with traditional GC. In Figures 5 and 6, the spatial-temporal displacement and strain fields of S(R)-0, S-33, and R-67 are presented.

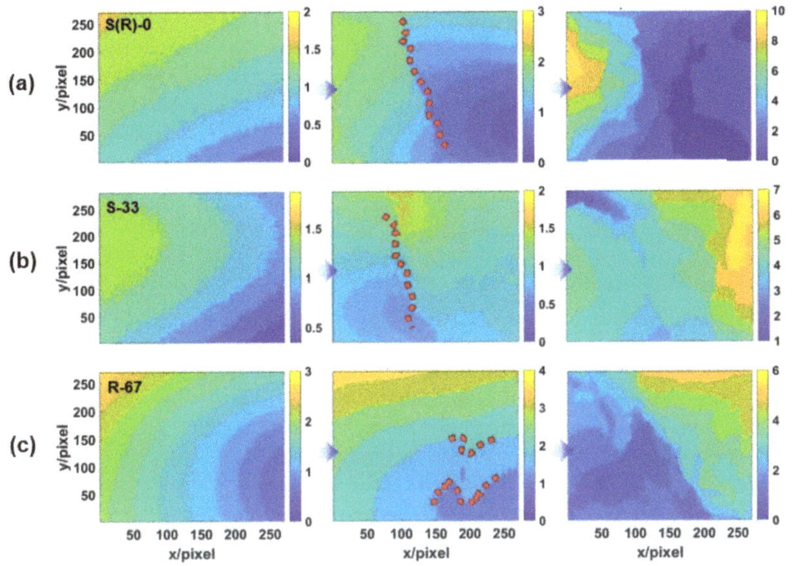

Figure 5. Displacement fields of the (**a**) S(R)-0, (**b**) S-33, and (**c**) R-67 at three typical stages with the increase of compressive loads.

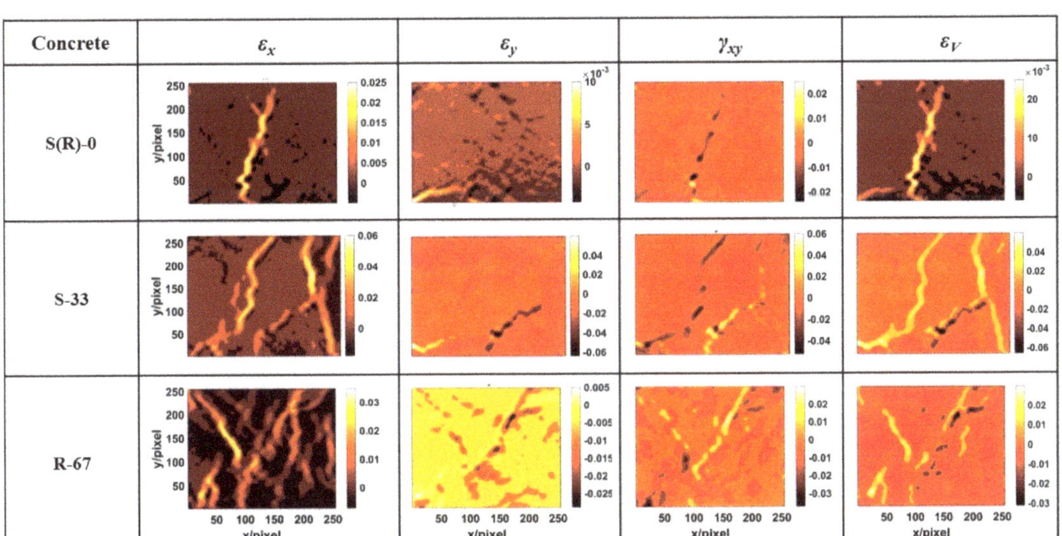

Figure 6. Strain fields of the GC (S(R) −0), SPC (S−33), and RPC (R−67).

3.2.1. Displacement Fields during the Compressive Loading Process

In Figure 5, three typical loading stages were selected to present the displacement fields of S(R)-0, S-33, and R-67. Here, three stages were determined by choosing the corresponding data at ~35% of the peak loads (denoting the linear elastic deformation state), the peak load (i.e., B, b_1, b_2 in Figure 4b), and failure (i.e., C, c_1, c_2 in Figure 4b) stage. In the linear elastic deformation stage, as shown in the first column of Figure 5, the displacement fields of the three sets of concretes are distributed with uniform gradients from the top to the bottom of the cubes. With the increase of loads, the displacement fields trended to be heterogeneous, and discontinuous regions appeared (marked by the red dotted lines in Figure 5). Obviously, a sharp division throughout the cube from the top to bottom appeared in the displacement fields of S(R)-0 and S-33 while dispersive and local inhomogeneous displacement distribution were found in R-67. The local damage continuously developed until the complete failure of concrete cubes, which was illustrated in the third column of Figure 5. The full-field deformations of S(R)-0 and S-33 were similar but were significantly different from R-67, which were consistent with the stress-strain curves illustrated in Figure 4b. The displacement distribution indicated that the local displacement gradient led to distinct local deformation development in the concrete, resulting in various forms of failure modes.

3.2.2. Strain Field Analysis at Failure Stage

In order to explore the inherent cause of concrete failure, the strain fields of S(R)-0, S-33, and R-67 at the failure stage are illustrated in Figure 6, including the normal strain ε_x, ε_y in x, y directions, shear strain γ_{xy}, and volumetric strain ε_V at point C, c_1, and c_2, as illustrated in Figure 4b. Comparing the normal strains in two directions for each individual concrete specimen, it was obvious that ε_x dominantly contributed to the failure of the concrete. In contrast, values of ε_y were relatively smaller than the corresponding ε_x. That is to say, the larger deformation in the concrete cubes under compressive conditions is perpendicular to the loading direction for both the GC and PC.

However, it should be noted that the spatial distributions of ε_x for S(R)-0 and S-33 were distinct, which exactly corresponded to the remarkably different descent slopes of two kinds of concretes detected by stress-strain curves in Figure 4b. In addition, the spatial distribution of shear deformations of S-33 and R-67 were more obvious than S(R)-0. For the volumetric strain ε_V, the values of S(R)-0 were basically positive whereas those of S-33 and R-67 were obviously positive and negative, indicating that S(R)-0 tended to expand but compression and expansion simultaneously occurred in S-33 and R-67. Moreover, the spatial distribution of volumetric strain of both the RPC and SPC were dispersion, implying that the introduced pebbles changed the local damage in the PC even if the compressive strength was not changed a lot. This also proved that the damage in the pebble concretes was closely related to the type of the coarse aggregates.

It could be found that the strain fields could be used to track the spatial-temporal distribution of cracks in the concrete. The larger the strains, the larger the difference between neighboring regions in the concrete, which suggested the potential location of the cracks. For example, as shown in Figure 6, a single penetrated crack was observed in the gravel concrete cube according to the volumetric strain ε_V. In contrast, more vertical and horizontal cracks were found in S-33 and R-67. The significant difference between S-33 and R-67 lay in that the vertical cracks in S-33 still tended to be penetrated whereas no obvious penetrated cracks could be found in R-67. Particularly, the spatial distribution of cracks in R-67 was local and statistically dispersed on the concrete. Combining the compressive properties of the concretes in Section 3.1, it was determined that the generation of cracks in the concrete cube was closely related to the development of the stress–strain curves as shown in Figure 4b. Under compression load conditions, the concrete first experienced elastic deformation, and then the penetrated cracks occurred to S(R)-0 due to the strong bonding between gravel and mortar, which finally led to a typical brittle fracture in the concrete. In contrast, the relatively weaker bonding between the smooth surface of pebbles and mortar easily resulted in a local expansion of interstice in the pebbled concrete (e.g., S-67), and thus typical load hardening stages were observed in the stress-strain curves. It was possible that the failure of the PC was dominated by the relative slip between the pebbles and the mortar due to the weaker ITZ.

3.3. Influence of Pebble Substitution Rates on Compressive Deformation Behaviors

3.3.1. Peak Strain and Peak Stress

Peak values of compressive strain and stress for traditional GC and PC at various pebble substitution rates are illustrated in Figure 7. The influence of substitution rates on the peak strain and stress is shown in Figure 7a. Interestingly, the peak strain curves of both SPC and RPC initially decreased and then increased with increasing substitution rates, with the smallest peak strains observed at the 33% substitution rate. Particularly, the peak strains of RPC at pebble substitution rates of 67% and 100% were strikingly smaller than that of GC (decreasing by approximately 69.8% and 75.3%), whereas for SPC, the decrease was only ~27.2% and ~15.5%. On the other hand, the peak stress of RPC/SPC decreased with increasing substitution rates, with the values of SPC slightly lower than RPC at equivalent substitution rates. Although PCs at lower pebble substitution rates exhibited comparable compressive strength to conventional GC, there was a significant reduction in peak strain, suggesting an enhanced plastic deformation capacity of PCs. Furthermore, comparing RPC and SPC in Figure 7b, it was noted that peak strains of SPC at higher substitution rates (e.g., 67% and 100%) were larger than those of RPC, despite their peak stresses being similar at the same substitution rates. Salt ions on the surface of sea pebbles may potentially participate in the hydration process, thereby weakening the bonding between coarse aggregates and cementing materials. Combing the strain field distribution in Figure 6, it is deduced that the generation of microcracks, as well as initiation and propagation of local cracks in PC, are primarily influenced by the shape of coarse aggregates at lower substitution rates, but become more closely related to the bonding strength in the ITZ of PC as substitution rates increase.

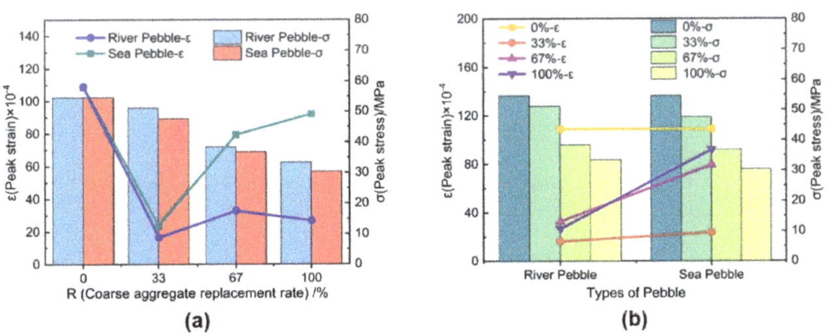

Figure 7. Peak strain and peak stress of the river/sea pebble concretes (**a**) with the increase of pebble substitution rates (i.e., 0, 33%, 67%, and 100%) (**b**).

3.3.2. Crack Distribution and Interfacial Characteristics

The strain fields of seven groups of tested cubes (i.e., S(R)-0, R-33, R-67, R-100, S-33, S-67, and S-100) at the failure stage are depicted in Figure 8 to demonstrate how river/sea pebble substitution rates influenced the spatial distribution of cracks in the PC. In Figure 8a, a penetrated crack was clearly observed running through the center of GC along the loading direction. In comparison, the crack numbers of the two kinds of PC were significantly higher than GC, where several shorter and dispersed cracks were randomly distributed in both RPC and SPC. As pebble substitution rates increased, cracks appeared to transition from vertical penetrative to local and dispersed patterns. The crack numbers increased but the length shortened, implying obvious local deformation and crack propagation characteristics in PCs. Particularly, both a dominant penetrated crack and dispersed local cracks were observed in both S-33 and R-33, potentially explaining their comparable compressive strength but significantly smaller peak stress compared to S(R)-0. Subsequently, noticeable penetrated cracks gradually diminished with increasing pebble substitution rates, significantly reducing the compressive strength of RPC/SPC. Considering Figures 6 and 7, it is noteworthy that strains in SPC were relatively larger than those in RPC at equivalent substitution rates, particularly at 67% and 100%. In the strain fields depicted in Figure 8c,d,f,g, RPC exhibited generally more cracks compared to SPC at equivalent pebble substitution rates, ranging from 33% to 100%. The interaction of cementing materials with seawater during the curing process of SPC is inferred to have reduced its ductility under compressive loading conditions [1].

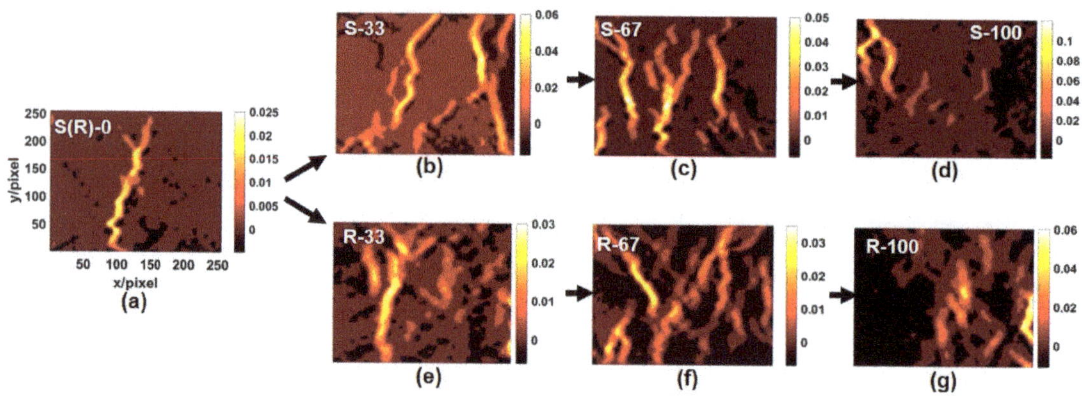

Figure 8. Development of strain fields of the RPC/SPC cubes with the increase of substitution rates at failure stage (**a–g**).

Figure 9 displays images of damaged concrete cubes showing interfacial views of S(R)-0, S-33, R-67, and S-100 to illustrate failure details in the concretes. Two types of damage were defined and labeled as aggregate damage and interfacial damage, respectively. Aggregate damage primarily resulted from the fracture of coarse aggregate (labeled as green dashed regions), while interfacial damage occurred due to slip movements between the pebble aggregate and cementing material (labeled as cyan-dotted ovals). Additionally, cracks generated in the concrete cubes were labeled with dotted yellow lines.

Accordingly, one might observe that damages in GC (i.e., S(R)-0) were mainly caused by gravel fracture, with cracks randomly distributed throughout the concrete cube, as shown in Figure 9a. In comparison, the interfacial damage began to appear around the pebble surface of S-33, which could be seen by some yellow dotted lines in Figure 9b. As the pebble substitution rate increased, it appeared that failure in the pebble concrete cubes tended to transition to interfacial damage, depicted in Figure 9c,d. In Figure 9d, damage primarily occurred at the pebble interfaces, with yellow dotted lines indicating gaps between pebbles and mortar, while cyan-dotted ovals showed traces of detached pebbles.

Combining the crack distribution in Figure 8 with Figure 9a, it is evident that the crack penetration observed in GC was closely associated with aggregate and mortar damage. In Figure 9b–d, randomly distributed cracks in RPC/SPC resulted from pebble detachment due to relative motion between pebbles and cementing materials. Essentially, the weaker bonding strength between the smoother surface of pebbles and neighboring cementing materials, compared to irregular gravel, makes the regions between pebbles and cementing materials the weakest in the concrete, eventually leading to interfacial damage in pebble concretes. As the pebble substitution rate increased, weaker bonding between pebbles and cementing materials increasingly controlled crack propagation and eventually influenced concrete failure modes.

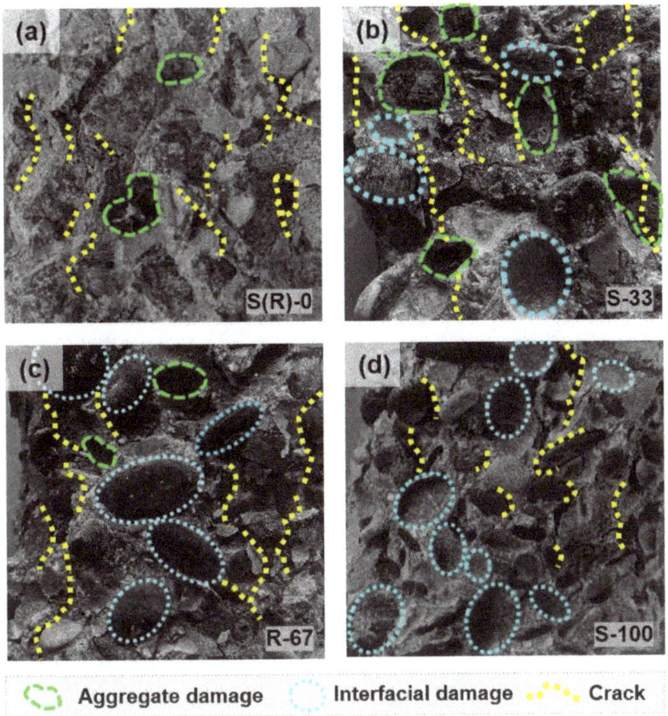

Figure 9. Interfacial views of the damaged GC and SPC cubes under compressive loads, where (**a–d**) were S(R)-0, S-33, R-67, and S-100, respectively.

3.3.3. Compressive Failure Mode

Based on the analysis of crack distribution and interfacial characteristics, diagrams illustrating three possible failure modes in the concrete are summarized in Figure 10. In this study, the failure modes of the concretes were defined as coarse aggregate fracture, pebble interfacial slipping, and mortar fracture. As shown in Figure 10a, coarse aggregate fracture was frequently observed when there was stronger bonding between the rough surface of coarse aggregate and the mortar matrix. In contrast, the weaker bonding strength between the smoother pebble and the mortar matrix facilitated the development of microcracks into macrocracks at the ITZ, illustrated as pebble interfacial slipping in Figure 10b. In fact, mortar fracture between aggregates could be observed simultaneously with either coarse aggregate damage or pebble slip fracture, as illustrated in Figure 10c.

In this sense, the failure modes of the tested concrete are summarized in Figure 10d. For GC, the bonding strength between the irregular and tough surface and the mortar matrix was stronger, resulting in failure typically as coarse aggregate and mortar fracture. If a smaller portion of gravel was replaced by river/sea pebbles (e.g., R-33 and S-33), pebble interfacial slipping would gradually occur. However, with a higher percentage of gravel, the gravel and mortar fracture remained the dominant failure mode in the concrete. Therefore, the compressive strength was only slightly reduced, but this inherently affected the strain distribution and significantly reduced the peak strain. As pebble substitution rates increased in RPC/SPC, their failure mode shifted to pebble interfacial slipping, where pebbles detached from the mortar at the ITZ. Consequently, local cracks were generated at the ITZ and distributed randomly in the concrete, consistent with the shorter and dispersed cracks observed in Figures 6 and 9. Consequently, it can be concluded that introducing pebbles into the concrete led to a transition in failure mode from coarse aggregate and mortar fracture to pebble interfacial slipping with increasing pebble substitution rates in both RPC and SPC. By comparison, the distinct bonding strengths between different types of pebbles and their neighboring mortar matrix led to different scales of pebble slipping, thereby influencing the distribution and development of local deformation and cracks in the concrete.

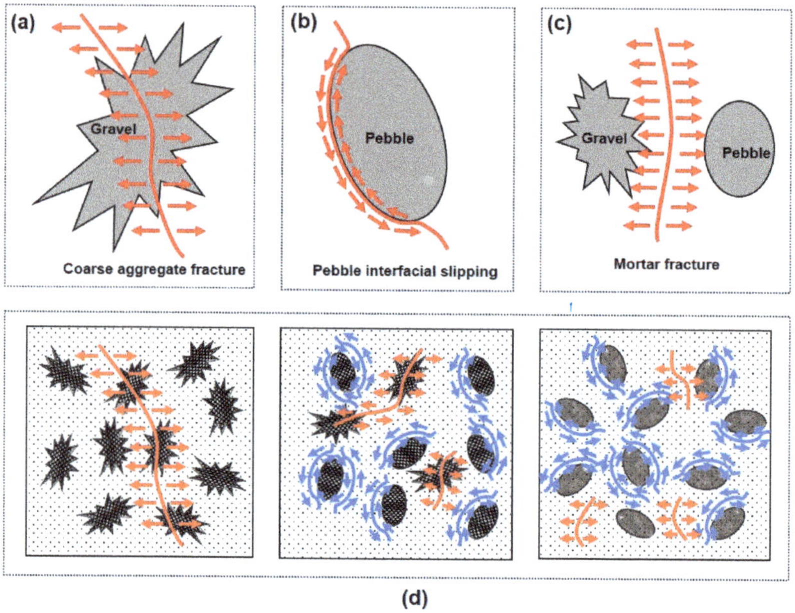

Figure 10. Failure mode diagram of the gravel and river/sea pebble concretes, where (**a**) was aggregate fracture, (**b**) was slip fracture of pebble concrete, and (**c**) was cementing material fracture. (**d**) Possible failure mode diagram of experimental concretes.

Therefore, if the compressive strength is the main consideration, both RPC and SPC at lower substitution rates can be employed to replace GC to some extent. However, it is important to note that the local deformation and failure modes of PC at higher pebble substitution rates are distinct, which will indeed influence the stability and safety of construction in practical engineering applications. It is recommended to apply these PCs to some non-bearing structures. Specifically, it was demonstrated that the compressive strength of SPC was similar to RPC, but the peak strain and deformation characteristics differed slightly. These investigations into RPC/SPC pave the way for their use as alternative solutions in offshore or island engineering projects.

4. Conclusions

The compressive behaviors of two types of pebble concrete, where river/sea pebbles partially or fully replaced traditional gravels as the coarse aggregate, were quantitatively evaluated using a noncontact full-field deformation measurement system. The compressive strength, displacement, and strain fields, as well as cracks in the tested concrete cubes (i.e., S(R)-0, R-33, R-67, R-100, S-33, S-67, and S-100), were thoroughly investigated. From this analysis, the following conclusions can be drawn:

(1) The compressive strength and peak stress of the RPC/SPC generally decreased with increasing pebble substitution rates compared to traditional GC. Particularly, peak

strains in both RPC and SPC initially decreased and then increased with higher pebble substitution rates.

(2) The elastic deformation stage in the stress-strain curves of both RPC and SPC at lower pebble substitution rates (i.e., R-33 and S-33) was similar to that of GC, but the failure stages were steeper. However, obvious load-hardening stages were observed in the stress-strain curves of RPC and SPC at higher substitution rates (i.e., R-67, R-100, S-67, and S-100).

(3) Based on the measured full-field displacement and corresponding strain fields, the spatial—temporal distribution of cracks was tracked in the concretes. It revealed a single penetrated crack in GC, whereas RPC/SPC exhibited several dispersed local shorter cracks. Correspondingly, the failure mode in GC was coarse aggregate and mortar matrix fracture, while PC showed obvious pebble interfacial slipping.

(4) Comparing RPC and SPC, their compressive deformation and failure behavior characteristics were similar, although the compressive strengths of RPC were relatively higher. Specifically, peak strains of SPC at higher substitution rates (e.g., 67% and 100%) were larger than RPC, consistent with the spatial distribution and local characteristics of strain fields and cracks. However, SPC showed increased numbers and width of generated cracks compared to RPC.

(5) In practical applications, if the feasibility of RPC has been verified, SPC could be employed in offshore or island engineering projects instead of RPC to some extent. Otherwise, strengthening solutions should be considered for RPC/SPC according to the compressive mechanical property requirements of some concrete design codes.

Author Contributions: Conceptualization, Y.Y. and Y.L.; Data curation, Y.Y., Y.Z., and X.F.; Funding acquisition, Y.Y. and W.Z.; Investigation, X.F. and Y.Z.; Methodology, Y.Y. and W.Z.; Software, Y.Z. and Y.L.; Supervision, Y.Y. and W.Z.; Validation, Y.Z. and X.F.; Visualization, X.F. and Y.Y.; Writing—original draft, Y.Y.; Writing—review and editing, Y.Y. and Y.Z. All authors have read and agreed to the published version of the manuscript.

Funding: This research was funded by the National Natural Science Foundation of China (Grant no. 12372183) and the Shanghai Sailing Program (Grant no. 23YF1416100).

Institutional Review Board Statement: Not applicable.

Informed Consent Statement: Not applicable.

Data Availability Statement: The original contributions presented in the study are included in the article, further inquiries can be directed to the corresponding author.

Conflicts of Interest: The authors declare no conflicts of interest.

References

1. Lao, J.-C.; Huang, B.-T.; Xu, L.-Y.; Khan, M.; Fang, Y.; Dai, J.-G. Seawater Sea-Sand Engineered Geopolymer Composites (EGC) with High Strength and High Ductility. *Cem. Concr. Compos.* **2023**, *138*, 104998. [CrossRef]
2. Bader, M.A. Performance of Concrete in a Coastal Environment. *Cem. Concr. Compos.* **2003**, *25*, 539–548. [CrossRef]
3. Nedeljković, M.; Visser, J.; Šavija, B.; Valcke, S.; Schlangen, E. Use of Fine Recycled Concrete Aggregates in Concrete: A Critical Review. *J. Build. Eng.* **2021**, *38*, 102196. [CrossRef]
4. Feng, W.; Tang, Y.; Yang, Y.; Cheng, Y.; Qiu, J.; Zhang, H.; Isleem, H.F.; Tayeh, B.A.; Namdar, A. Mechanical Behavior and Constitutive Model of Sustainable Concrete: Seawater and Sea-Sand Recycled Aggregate Concrete. *Constr. Build. Mater.* **2023**, *364*, 130010. [CrossRef]
5. Feng, N.Q.; Yan, J.H.; Peng, G.F. Ecological Environment and Concrete Technology in China. *KEM* **2006**, *302–303*, 12–18. [CrossRef]
6. Huang, Y.; Li, X.; Lu, Y.; Wang, H.; Wang, Q.; Sun, H.; Li, D. Effect of Mix Component on the Mechanical Properties of Coral Concrete under Axial Compression. *Constr. Build. Mater.* **2019**, *223*, 736–754. [CrossRef]
7. Huang, Y.; He, X.; Wang, Q.; Sun, Y. Mechanical Properties of Sea Sand Recycled Aggregate Concrete under Axial Compression. *Constr. Build. Mater.* **2018**, *175*, 55–63. [CrossRef]
8. Ribeiro, S.; Ribeiro, D.D.C.; Dias, M.B.D.S.; Garcia, G.C.R.; Santos, É.M.B.D. Study of the Fracture Behavior of Mortar and Concretes with Crushed Rock or Pebble Aggregates. *Mater. Res.* **2011**, *14*, 46–52. [CrossRef]
9. Zhou, C.; Chen, Z. Mechanical Properties of Recycled Concrete Made with Different Types of Coarse Aggregate. *Constr. Build. Mater.* **2017**, *134*, 497–506. [CrossRef]

10. *SL 677–2014*; Specifications for Hydraulic Concrete Construction. Ministry of Water Resources of the People's Republic of China, China Water & Power Press: Beijing, China, 2014.
11. *JTS 202–2011*; Specifications for Concrete Construction of Port and Waterway Engineering. Ministry of Transport of the People's Republic of China, People's Communications Press Co., Ltd.: Beijing, China, 2011.
12. Bayle, P.M.; Blenkinsopp, C.E.; Conley, D.; Masselink, G.; Beuzen, T.; Almar, R. Performance of a Dynamic Cobble Berm Revetment for Coastal Protection, under Increasing Water Level. *Coast. Eng.* **2020**, *159*, 103712. [CrossRef]
13. Lu, Z.; Liu, G.; Wu, Y.; Dai, M.; Jiang, M.; Xie, J. Recycled Aggregate Seawater–Sea Sand Concrete and Its Durability after Immersion in Seawater. *J. Build. Eng.* **2023**, *65*, 105780. [CrossRef]
14. Meddah, M.S.; Zitouni, S.; Belâabes, S. Effect of Content and Particle Size Distribution of Coarse Aggregate on the Compressive Strength of Concrete. *Constr. Build. Mater.* **2010**, *24*, 505–512. [CrossRef]
15. Sun, X.; Zhang, B.; Dai, Q.; Yu, X. Investigation of Internal Curing Effects on Microstructure and Permeability of Interface Transition Zones in Cement Mortar with SEM Imaging, Transport Simulation and Hydration Modeling Techniques. *Constr. Build. Mater.* **2015**, *76*, 366–379. [CrossRef]
16. Chen, Z.; Zhou, C.; Ye, P. The Compressive Strength and Flexural Strength Test of Recycled Pebble Aggregate Concrete. *Appl. Mech. Mater.* **2013**, *357–360*, 1433–1436. [CrossRef]
17. Jun, Y.; Kim, J.H.; Han, S.H.; Kim, T. Influence of Seawater on Alkali-Activated Slag Concrete. *Mater Struct* **2021**, *54*, 121. [CrossRef]
18. Mohammed, T.U.; Hamada, H.; Yamaji, T. Performance of Seawater-Mixed Concrete in the Tidal Environment. *Cem. Concr. Res.* **2004**, *34*, 593–601. [CrossRef]
19. Da Silva, M.A.; Pepe, M.; De Andrade, R.G.M.; Pfeil, M.S.; Toledo Filho, R.D. Rheological and Mechanical Behavior of High Strength Steel Fiber-River Gravel Self Compacting Concrete. *Constr. Build. Mater.* **2017**, *150*, 606–618. [CrossRef]
20. Chen, Z.; Mo, L.; Song, C.; Zhang, Y. Investigation on Compression Properties of Seawater-Sea Sand Concrete. *Adv. Concr. Constr.* **2021**, *12*, 93–103. [CrossRef]
21. Liu, H.B.; Zhou, S.; Wei, H.B.; Li, W.J.; Xiu, R.; Zhu, B. Mechanical Properties, Permeability and Freeze-Thaw Durability of Low Sand Rate Pervious Concrete. *J. Phys. Conf. Ser.* **2021**, *1765*, 012022. [CrossRef]
22. Ohtsu, M.; Watanabe, H. Quantitative Damage Estimation of Concrete by Acoustic Emission. *Constr. Build. Mater.* **2001**, *15*, 217–224. [CrossRef]
23. Ng, C.; Alengaram, U.J.; Wong, L.S.; Mo, K.H.; Jumaat, M.Z.; Ramesh, S. A Review on Microstructural Study and Compressive Strength of Geopolymer Mortar, Paste and Concrete. *Constr. Build. Mater.* **2018**, *186*, 550–576. [CrossRef]
24. Yang, S.; Zhang, X.; Yu, M.; Yao, J. An Analytical Approach to Predict Fracture Parameters of Coral Aggregate Concrete Immersed in Seawater. *Ocean Eng.* **2019**, *191*, 106508. [CrossRef]
25. Li, D.; Huang, P.; Chen, Z.; Yao, G.; Guo, X.; Zheng, X.; Yang, Y. Experimental Study on Fracture and Fatigue Crack Propagation Processes in Concrete Based on DIC Technology. *Eng. Fract. Mech.* **2020**, *235*, 107166. [CrossRef]
26. Le, D.B.; Tran, S.D.; Torero, J.L.; Dao, V.T.N. Application of Digital Image Correlation System for Reliable Deformation Measurement of Concrete Structures at High Temperatures. *Eng. Struct.* **2019**, *192*, 181–189. [CrossRef]
27. Huang, Y.; He, X.; Wang, Q.; Xiao, J. Deformation Field and Crack Analyses of Concrete Using Digital Image Correlation Method. *Front. Struct. Civ. Eng.* **2019**, *13*, 1183–1199. [CrossRef]
28. Hu, Y.; Guo, W.; Zhu, W.; Xu, Y. Local Damage Detection of Membranes Based on Bayesian Operational Modal Analysis and Three-Dimensional Digital Image Correlation. *Mech. Syst. Signal Process.* **2019**, *131*, 633–648. [CrossRef]
29. Aliabadian, Z.; Zhao, G.-F.; Russell, A.R. Crack Development in Transversely Isotropic Sandstone Discs Subjected to Brazilian Tests Observed Using Digital Image Correlation. *Int. J. Rock Mech. Min. Sci.* **2019**, *119*, 211–221. [CrossRef]
30. Bolivar, J.; Frégonèse, M.; Réthoré, J.; Duret-Thual, C.; Combrade, P. Evaluation of Multiple Stress Corrosion Crack Interactions by In-Situ Digital Image Correlation. *Corros. Sci.* **2017**, *128*, 120–129. [CrossRef]
31. Lakavath, C.; Joshi, S.S.; Prakash, S.S. Investigation of the Effect of Steel Fibers on the Shear Crack-Opening and Crack-Slip Behavior of Prestressed Concrete Beams Using Digital Image Correlation. *Eng. Struct.* **2019**, *193*, 28–42. [CrossRef]
32. *GB/T 14685–2011*; Standardization Administration of China, Pebble and Crushed Stone for Construction. General Administration of Quality Supervision, Inspection and Quarantine of the People's Republic of China: Beijing, China, 2011.
33. *JGJ52–2006*; Standard for Technical Requirements and Test Method of Sand and Crushed Stone (or Gravel) for Ordinary Concrete. Ministry of Construction of the People's Republic of China, China Architecture & Building Press: Beijing, China, 2006.
34. *JGJ55-2011*; Specification for mix proportion design of ordinary concrete. China Academy of Building Science, China Architecture & Building Press: Beijing, China, 2011.
35. *GB/T 50081-2002*; Standard for test method of mechanical properties on ordinary concrete. Ministry of Construction of the People's Republic of China, China Architecture & Building Press: Beijing, China, 2002.

Journal of
Marine Science and Engineering

MDPI

Article

Bearing Behavior of Large-Diameter Monopile Foundations of Offshore Wind Turbines in Weathered Residual Soil Seabeds

Ben He [1], Mingbao Lin [2], Xinran Yu [2], Genqiang Peng [2], Guoxiang Huang [1] and Song Dai [2,*]

1 Power China Huadong Engineering Corporation Limited—HDEC, Key Laboratory Far Shore Wind Power Technol Zhejiang Province, Hangzhou 311122, China; he_b2@ecidi.com (B.H.); huang_gx@hdec.com (G.H.)
2 School of Civil Engineering, Shandong University, Jinan 250061, China; 202435148@mail.sdu.edu.cn (M.L.); 202215034@mail.sdu.edu.cn (X.Y.); 202315069@mail.sdu.edu.cn (G.P.)
* Correspondence: dais1027@sdu.edu.cn

Abstract: The southeastern rock base sea area is the most abundant wind resource area, and it is also the mainstream construction site of offshore wind farms (OWFs) in China. The weathered residual soil is the main seabed component in the rock base area, which is the important bearing stratum of the offshore wind turbine foundation. Previous studies on the mechanical properties of seabed materials and bearing characteristics of the pile foundations in OWFs have mainly focused on the submarine soil-based seabed, resulting in a lack of direct reference for the construction of offshore wind power in the rocky seabed. Therefore, the mechanical properties of weathered residual soil and the bearing behaviors of monopile foundations are mainly investigated in this study. Firstly, dynamic triaxial tests are conducted on the weathered residual soil, and experiments analyze insight into the evolution law of the hysteresis curve, cumulative strain, and stiffness attenuation. Then, the horizontal loading behaviors of monopile foundations in residual soil are analyzed by numerical simulations; more critically, the service performances under wind and wave coupling loads are evaluated, which provide a direct theoretical basis for the construction and design of offshore wind turbine foundations in rock base seabeds.

Keywords: offshore wind farm; rock base seabed; weathered residual soil; monopile foundation; bearing behavior

1. Introduction

Wind energy is one of the most widely used renewable energy sources, and offshore wind power has the advantages of stable wind speed, abundant resources and no occupation of arable land compared with onshore wind energy [1,2]. In recent years, the rapid development of global offshore wind power has become an important means to promote industrial transformation and energy revolution [3,4]. A monopile foundation has the advantages of a simple, loaded, proven construction technology, and a high bearing capacity, and it is the most widely used foundation form on offshore wind farms [5]. Offshore wind turbine foundations last for a long time in complex marine environments, and the large-diameter monopile foundations are subjected to coupling loads combining wind, waves, current, and the overturning moment [6]. Horizontal load is an important control factor in the design of offshore wind turbine foundations [7–10]. Therefore, accurate evaluation of the horizontal bearing characteristics of large-diameter monopile foundations is necessary to ensure the safe installation and long-term normal service of offshore wind turbines [11–13].

Up until now, China has made remarkable achievements in the field of offshore wind power, with a cumulative installed capacity of 4.7 GW, which is the leading position in the world. With the rapid advancement of this field, the construction environment of offshore wind power projects is undergoing profound changes. The main construction sites of offshore wind farms have begun to shift from a sea area dominated by soft clay and silty seabed area to a weathered rock base sea area [14]. The weathered residual soil is the main component of the seabed in the rock-based area, and it is also the important stressed formation of the offshore wind turbine foundation. However, affected by sedimentation and weathering, the engineering geological properties and cyclic response of the weathering residual soil are obviously different from those of the marine soft clay and sandy soil [15]. At present, there have been abundant and systematic studies on the safety analysis and design methods of the large-diameter monopile foundation on a soil-based seabed, but hardly any research on monopile foundations on weathered rock seabeds has been carried out [16]. The design parameters of seabed materials and the *p–y* design method used for pile foundations in the existing regulations and studies are basically aimed at soft clay [17,18] and sandy seabeds [19–21] and cannot provide a direct reference and basis for the design and construction of monopile foundations in rock-based seabeds. Therefore, it is necessary to conduct a specific study on the mechanical properties of weathered residual soil materials and the horizontal bearing characteristics of large-diameter monopile pile foundations in a rock-based seabed.

The traditional analysis methods for determining the horizontal loading behavior of pile foundations can be divided into three types, i.e., the ultimate ground resistance method, the elastic ground reaction method, and the elastic–plastic composite ground reaction method (the *p–y* curve method). The *p–y* curve can simulate the pile–soil response under horizontal loads and is widely used in the horizontal loading analysis of pile foundations. In order to more accurately evaluate the horizontal bearing characteristics of large-diameter monopile foundations, many scholars have carried out many studies on the horizontal loading behavior of pile foundations through model tests [22], field tests [23], and numerical simulations [24,25], and many modified *p–y* curves for the large-diameter monopile foundation have been established. Long and Vanneste (1994) [26], Verdure et al. (2003) [27], and Peng et al. (2006) [28] have carried out some horizontal cyclic loaded in situ tests successively, and large amounts of precious data were obtained, including information on the displacement and bending moment. More studies about the horizontal loading behavior of pile foundations have been carried out through physical modeling experiments and numerical simulations. For example, Byrne et.al. (2010) conducted model tests of a rigid pile under horizontal unidirectional and bidirectional cyclic loads and analyzed the effects of cyclic load ratio and loading times on cumulative deformation [29]. Lesny and Wiemann (2005) used ABAQUS v6.14 software to simulate the horizontal loading behaviors of large-diameter monopile foundations and modified the initial reaction modulus of the traditional *p–y* curve method [30]. The above studies are of great significance to the analysis of the horizontal loading behavior of large-diameter monopile foundations in soil seabeds and also provide an important theoretical basis and method support for the study of the horizontal loading characteristics of large-diameter monopile foundations in weathered residual soil.

Therefore, weathered residual soil, as a special seabed material, is reviewed as the study object, and the mechanical properties of weathered residual soil and the bearing behaviors of pile foundations in weathered residual soil are mainly investigated by dynamic triaxial tests and numerical simulations. Firstly, dynamic triaxial tests are carried out for the weathered residual soil, and experiments analyze the evolution law of the hysteresis curve, cumulative strain, and stiffness attenuation. Then, the horizontal loading behaviors of monopile foundations in residual soil are analyzed by numerical simulation and, more critically, the service performances under wind and wave coupling loads are evaluated, which provide a direct theoretical basis for the construction and design of offshore wind turbine foundations in a rock-based seabed.

2. Soil Sample and Test Method

2.1. Residual Soil Sample

The testing soil samples were taken from an offshore wind farm in Pingtan City, Fujian Province, and the sampling depth is 2–15 m below the surface, which is mainly weathered granite residual soil. To secure the natural state and reduce additional disturbance, the static pressure sampling method of the drilling rig is used to bring the soil sample out through the bulldozer by applying pressure, which is then immediately wrapped in a plastic tube and sealed with tape and wax, and transported back to the laboratory through a wooden box with cushioned foam for proper preservation. According to the geotechnical test procedure, a series of necessary physical and mechanical properties tests were carried out on the weathered residual soil samples. The specific gravity method was used to test the specific gravity of the weathered residual soil samples, and the drying method was used to test the natural moisture content. The liquid–plastic limit combined measurement method was used to test the liquid–plastic limit index of the samples, and the sieve analysis method and the densimeter method were used to determine the particle size curve. The basic physical properties of the weathered residual soil are shown in Table 1.

Table 1. Basic physical properties of weathered residual soil.

Natural Density (g/cm^3)	Water Content (%)	Liquid Limit (%)	Plastic Limit (%)	Plasticity Index	Uniformity Coefficient Cu	Curvature Coefficient Cc
1.90	31.36	37.05	22.98	14.07	100.20	0.18

2.2. Testing Apparatus and Procedure

The instrumentation used in this paper is the GDS Dynamic Triaxial Test System (ELDyn) from the UK, as shown in Figure 1, which consists of an axial pressure loading module, a peripheral pressure loading module, a pressure chamber, a counter-pressure controller, a data acquisition module, and the GDSLab operating software (v2.5.0). Under the strain-controlled mechanism, the test system can implement a maximum axial dynamic load of ±5 kN, a maximum frequency of 20 Hz, and a maximum pressure of 1000 kPa. This test system can meet the requirements of different test conditions and test scenarios. Cylindrical soil samples were prepared with a diameter of 50 mm and a height of 100 mm. As the tested soil showed low permeability, the dynamic tests were carried out under undrained conditions. The vacuum saturation method was adopted as the only saturation method in this study, and the saturation of soil samples was up to the test requirement after 24 h vacuum saturation. The samples were submerged in a vacuum saturator after cutting and were placed on the apparatus immediately after the completion of saturation for the experiments.

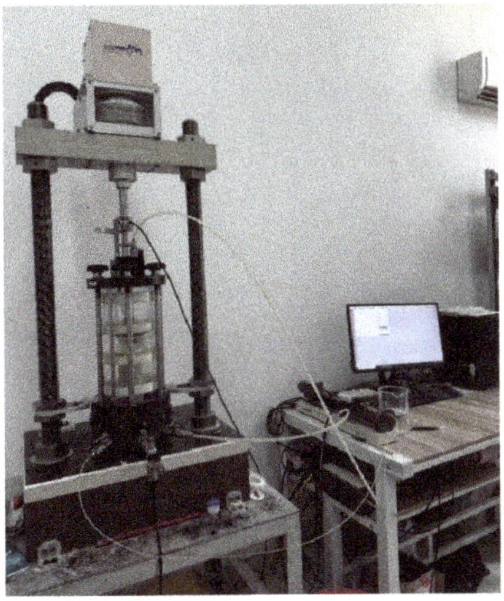

Figure 1. British GDS dynamic triaxial test system.

Static triaxial tests were carried out on the weathered residual soil under three level confining pressures 100 kPa, 200 kPa and 300 kPa. Dynamic triaxial tests were carried out on the three levels of confining pressures, i.e., 40 kPa, 55 kPa and 70 kPa. The cyclic axial load is controlled by the cyclic stress ratio (CSR), and the dynamic triaxial test schedule of weathered residual soil is illustrated in Table 2.

Table 2. Dynamic triaxial test schedule of weathered residual soil.

Test Number	Confining Pressure (kPa)	CSR
RS-1~4	40	0.4, 0.5, 0.55, 0.6
RS-5~8	55	0.4, 0.45, 0.5, 0.6
RS-9~12	70	0.4, 0.45, 0.5, 0.6

3. Mechanical Properties of Weathered Residual Soil

3.1. Static Testing Results

The effective cohesion of the weathered residual granite is 6.57 kPa and the effective internal friction angle is 34.77°. The stress–strain curves of the testing soil samples under different confining pressures are illustrated in Figure 2. The deviational stress of the soil samples accumulates continuously with the increase in axial strain, and the stress–strain curves first increase linearly, then slowly grow non-linearly, and eventually flatten out. When the axial strain is 0–3%, the soil specimen is in the elastic deformation period, and the curve increases linearly. When the axial strain is 3–6%, the sample is in the elastoplastic deformation stage, and the internal structure of the soil sample begins to fail irreversibly, and the curve grows nonlinear. The strain hardening occurs when the axial strain is greater than 6%, and the specimen gradually loses its bearing capacity and finally in the failure state.

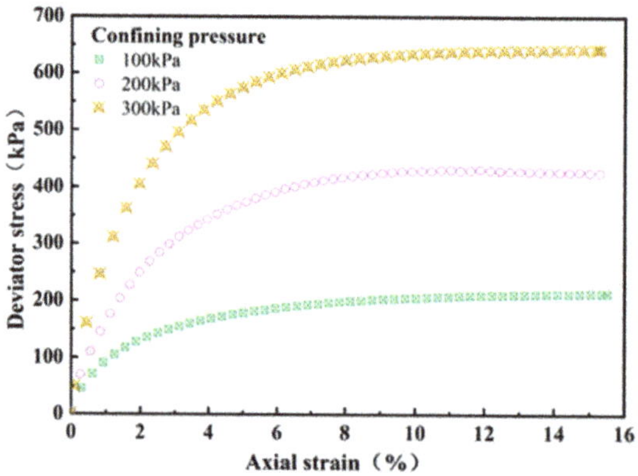

Figure 2. Stress–strain curve in the static triaxial test.

3.2. Evolution of Hysteresis Curve of Weathered Residual Soil

Figure 3 shows the hysteresis curves of weathered residual soil samples at 40 kPa confining pressure. When the cyclic stress ratio (CSR) is relatively small, the shape and position of hysteresis curves of the soil sample basically do not change significantly with the increase in the cycle numbers, and the cumulative strain is small. Under cyclic loads with small CSR, the soil sample is still in a stable state, and the morphology of the soil sample is basically unchanged, which indicates that the internal connections of soil particles do not change greatly. As shown in Figure 3a, the areas of hysteresis curves in each cycle are roughly same, which means the dissipated energy after each cycle is almost the same.

When the CSR is relatively large, the hysteresis loops gradually change with the increase in cycle numbers. The hysteretic loops rotate toward the direction of axial strain accumulation and change from a relatively regular spindle shape to other shapes. The morphology of the soil sample is crushed, and the internal positions of soil particles change obviously. Meanwhile, under the same confining pressure, the larger the CSR is, the faster the plastic deformation accumulates, as shown in Figure 3b.

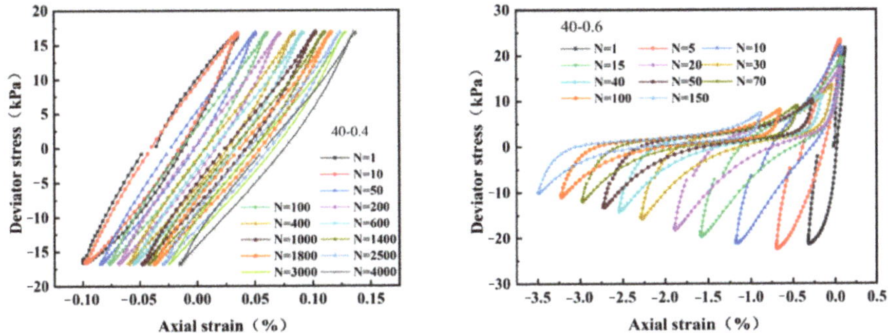

(**a**) under small CSR (**b**) under large CSR

Figure 3. Stress–strain curve of the dynamic triaxial test.

3.3. Development Law of Cumulative Strain

Figure 4 shows the relationship between the accumulative strain and the number of cyclic loads under different dynamic stress amplitudes with three levels of confining pressure. When the CSR is relatively small, the cumulative strain generated by the soil under the action of the cyclic load is small, and the cumulative strain increases slightly with the increase in the number of cycles but is at a low level as a whole. At this time, the appearance of the sample is almost unchanged and can withstand long-term low-strength cyclic loading. When the CSR is relatively large, the cumulative strain of the sample first increases slowly and then increases rapidly after a certain number of cycles. Under the action of high-strength dynamic load, the internal structure of the soil is destroyed, resulting in the axial flattening of the external shape. The larger the CSR, the faster the cumulative strain curve develops, and the more prone to deformation and failure of the sample.

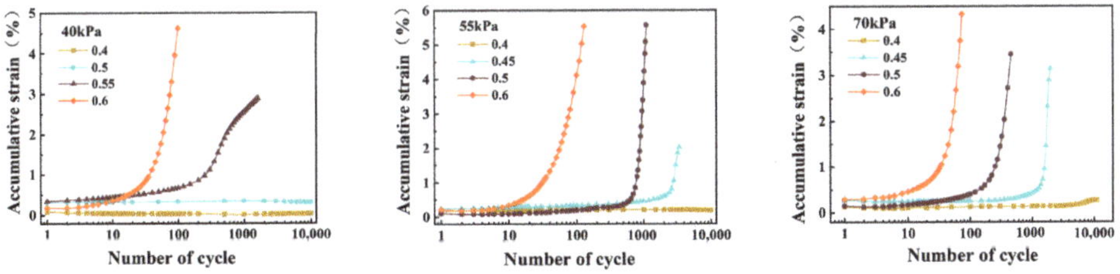

Figure 4. Development law of accumulative strain.

3.4. Development Law of Dynamic Elastic Modulus

Figure 5 shows the development law of dynamic elastic modulus of weathered residual soil under different confining pressures. It can be seen from Figure 5 that the attenuation ratio of dynamic elastic modulus under small CSR decreases slightly with the increase in the cycle number. After the number of cyclic loads reaches a certain number, the dynamic elastic modulus maintains a relatively stable level and the stiffness maintains a large value, indicating that the strength of the soil sample can resist the influence of the cyclic loads and maintain a relatively stable state.

When the CSR is relatively large, the dynamic elastic modulus ratios of the soil sample rapidly decay to near 0 with the increase in the cycle number. More critically, the greater the CSR, the more drastic the modulus decay. Under large cyclic loads, soil samples are unable to withstand high-strength cyclic loads and gradually lose the bearing capacity. The large CSR leads to the obvious attenuation of dynamic elastic modulus under the same confining pressure.

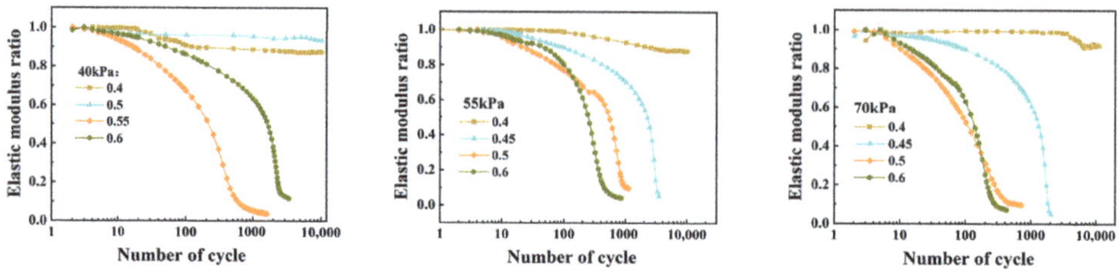

Figure 5. Development law of dynamic elastic modulus ratio.

4. Finite Element Numerical Model of Pile–Soil Interaction

There are various foundation forms for offshore wind turbines, and a monopile foundation is the most widely used in offshore wind farms. The monopile foundation is long-term in complex marine environments and is subjected to the coupling loads combining the wind and wave loads. The horizontal load is the main loaded mode of offshore wind turbine foundation. Therefore, the 3D numerical model of offshore wind turbine monopile foundation in weathered residual soil is established in the study, as shown in Figure 6, and the horizontal bearing characteristics of the monopile foundation are analyzed. The size of the seabed foundation is 100 m in diameter and 60 m in height, and the numerical model of the monopile foundation is 5 m in diameter and 38 m in length (30 m in pile depth and 8 m in pile length above the mud surface). The monopile foundation is equivalent to a solid steel pile, and the linear elastic constitutive model is adopted. The Mohr–Coulomb constitutive model is adopted for the weathered residual soil seabed, and the parameters of the monopile foundation and seabed material are illustrated in Table 3. In order to more clearly describe and compare the bearing characteristics of monopile foundations in weathered residual soil, the horizontally loaded behavior of monopile foundations in soft clay is also conducted in the study. For the convenience of comparison and description, the soft clay is recorded as soil A and the weathered residual soil is recorded as soil B.

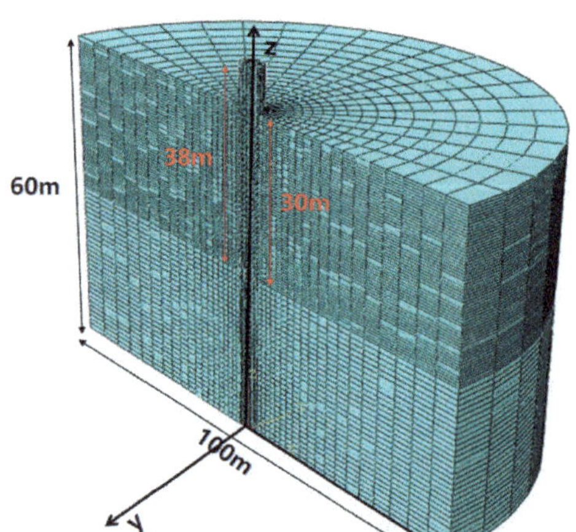

Figure 6. Finite element calculation model of pile–soil interaction.

In the numerical model, the C3D8 elements are used for foundation and monopile components, and the mesh size of the pile body and soil surrounding the pile is 0.5 m, and the mesh size of the soil under the pile bottom is 1 m. The contact mode between pile and soil is hard to contact in the normal direction and friction contact in the tangential direction. The contact friction coefficient of pile–soil interaction is determined by the formula $k = tan(0.75\varphi')$, meanwhile, the coefficient k in soft clay (soil A) is 0.42, and that in weathered residual soil (soil B) is 0.49. The displacements in the x, y and z directions of the numerical model are constrained at the bottom of the soil, the displacements in the x and y directions are constrained at the side, and no constraints are set at the top surface.

Table 3. Material parameters in the numerical model.

Assembly Unit	Elasticity Modulus (kPa)	Cohesive Force c' (kPa)	Internal Friction Angle φ' (°)	Poisson Ratio	Weight (kN/m^3)
Monopile foundation	2.1×10^8	—	—	0.24	—
Soft clay seabed	9300	11.88	30.94	0.32	16.8
Weathered residual seabed	17,500	6.57	34.77	0.3	19

5. Bearing Characteristics of Monopile Foundation

5.1. Horizontal Load–Displacement Response

Based on the above-established numerical model of pile–soil interaction, the displacement control method is used to obtain the horizontal load–displacement response curve of the pile head. A series of horizontal displacements are applied to the pile top, and the corresponding horizontal loads of the pile top are extracted. The horizontal load–displacement response curve of the pile head is illustrated in Figure 7.

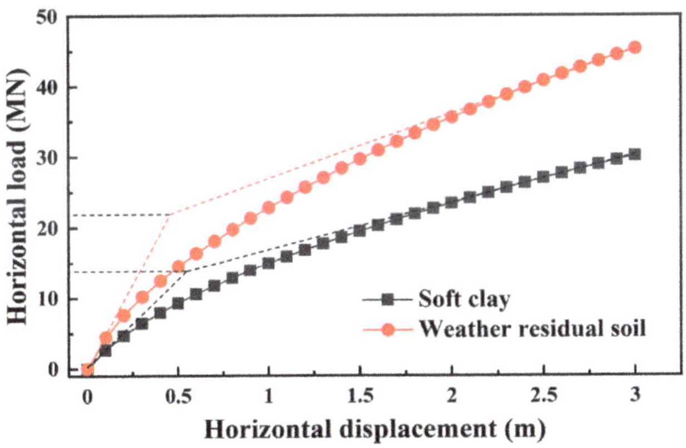

Figure 7. Horizontal load–displacement of monopile foundation.

It can be seen from Figure 7 that the horizontal load of the monopile foundation increases with the increase in horizontal displacement whether in weathered residual soil (soil B) and soft clay (soil A) and the load–displacement response curve undergoes the linear to a nonlinear relationship. At the initial loading stage of horizontal load, the pile–soil system is in the elastic deformation stage, and the relationship between horizontal load and displacement is linear. With the increase in horizontal load, plastic deformations occur on the soil around the monopile foundation, and the curvature of the load–displacement response increases slowly. The relationship between horizontal load and displacement becomes nonlinear, and the pile–soil system is in the plastic failure stage.

By comparing the bearing characteristics of monopile foundation in A and soil B seabed, the horizontal load–displacement response of pile head in soil B is always above that in soil A, and the ultimate bearing capacities of monopile foundation in weathered residual soil and soft clay seabed are 21.3 and 14.4 MN, respectively. The initial stiffness of monopile foundation in in weathered residual soil is 44.28 MN/m, and that is soft clay is

26.15 MN/m. The bearing capacities of monopile foundations in weathered residual soil are larger than those of soft clay.

5.2. Bending Moment and Shear Force Response

Figure 8 shows the response of the bending moment of the pile body with burial depth at the 3 m horizontal displacement imposed on the pile head. It can be seen that the pile bending moment firstly increases with the burial depth, then gradually decreases after reaching the peak value; meanwhile, the maximum value of bending moment occurs at the 11 m burial depth. It is also noted that the bending moment of the pile body in soil A is obviously greater than that in soil A. The maximum bending moment in soil A is 423 MN·m, and the maximum bending moment in soil B is 641 MN·m, that means that the horizontal resistance of soil B is greater than that in soil A, and greater bending moment is needed to make the pile–soil structure failure in soil B.

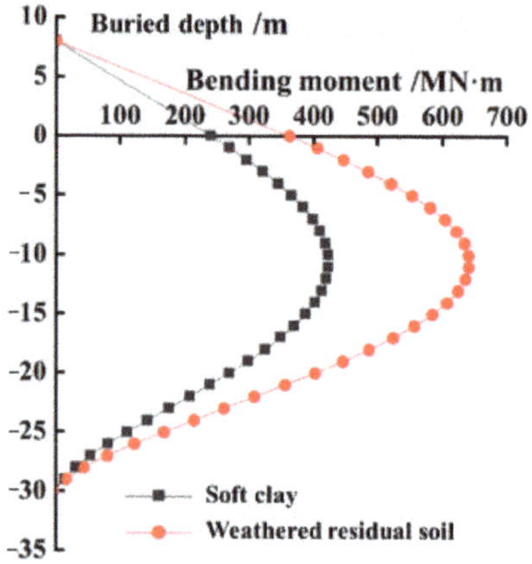

Figure 8. Bending moment with burial depth.

Figure 9 illustrates the response of the shear force with the pile burial depth at the 3 m horizontal displacement imposed on the pile head, and the negative value of shear force in the figure only represents the opposite direction. The changing trend of the shear force of monopile foundation in two soil seabeds is the same. The shear force gradually decreases from 0–11 m burial depth and changes direction at −11 m burial depth, which corresponds to the maximum bending moment of the pile. The absolute value of shear force under 11 m burial depth increases firstly and then decreases, and reaches the maximum value at 22 m burial depth, which corresponds to the rotation point of the pile. Compared with the two working conditions, the shear force value of the pile body in soil B is greater than in soil A, and greater shear force is required to make the deformation failure of the pile–soil structure in soil B.

5.3. Horizontal Displacement of Pile Body with Burial Depth

The monopile foundations in weathered residual soil and soft clay belong to the rigid pile in the study, and the horizontal displacements of the pile body at different burial depths are illustrated in Figure 10. With an imposed 3 m horizontal displacement on the pile head, the pile displacement–burial depth curves of two soil seabeds are completely consistent, as shown in Figure 10a, and the monopile foundation rotates around a point at about 22 m burial depth, which is defined as the rotation center. The pile body rotates to the right above the rotation center and rotates to the left below the rotation center. Meanwhile, the rotation center is 2/3 of burial depth (L), and this study's conclusions have been obtained in previous studies.

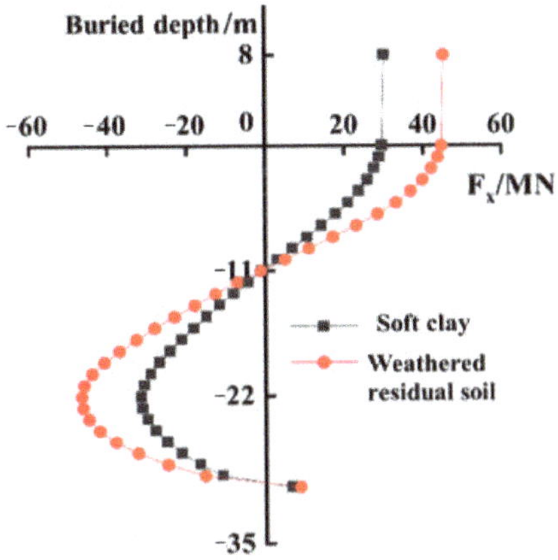

Figure 9. Shear force with burial depth.

Figure 10b shows the response of pile displacement with burial depth in two soil seabed under 25,000 kN horizontal load. It is noted that the overall horizontal displacement of the pile body in soil A is much larger than that in soil B, indicating that the bearing capacity of soil B is larger than soil B. At the same time, the monopile foundation rotates around the rotation center at about 22 m burial depth, where the pile foundation has no horizontal deformation, as characterized by the rigid pile.

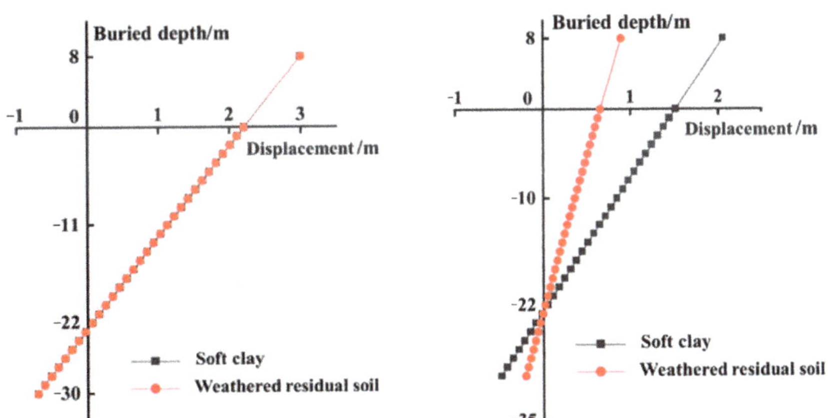

(**a**) 3 m horizontal displacement (**b**) 25,000 kN horizontal load

Figure 10. Pile horizontal displacement–burial depth curve.

5.4. *p–y Curve Response*

The soil reaction of the soil around the pile is extracted after the 3 m horizontal displacement imposed on the pile head, and Figure 11 shows the distribution curve of soil resistance with the burial depth, where the positive and negative values of soil resistance only indicate the load direction. It is noted that the seabed with a 0–22 m burial depth provides the left-directed resistance, and soil resistance gradually increases and then decreases with the increase in the burial depth. Meanwhile, the ultimate soil resistances reach the maximum at about 11 m burial depth in two soil seabed, and there is no resistance at 22 m of the burial depth, which indicates that there is no lateral displacement of the monopile foundation at a 22 m burial depth. Below a 22 m burial depth, the soil around the monopile foundation provides right-directed resistance, and the soil resistance increases with the increase in the burial depth, which corresponds to the pile displacement distribution with the burial depth in Section 5.3.

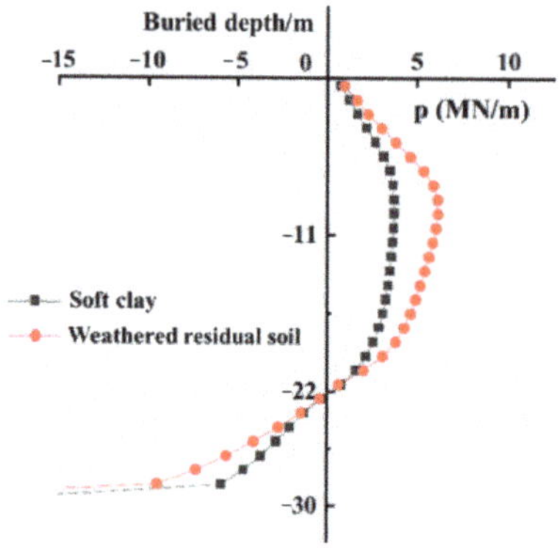

Figure 11. Distribution of soil resistance along burial depth of pile body.

Figure 12 shows p–y curves at different burial depths. The soil resistance increases with the increase in horizontal displacement, and the p–y curves increase linearly and then nonlinear slowly. Under the same load conditions, the p–y curve of soft clay seabed is below that in the weathered residual soil, indicating that weathered residual soil can produce greater resistance to prevent the deformation of the monopile foundation.

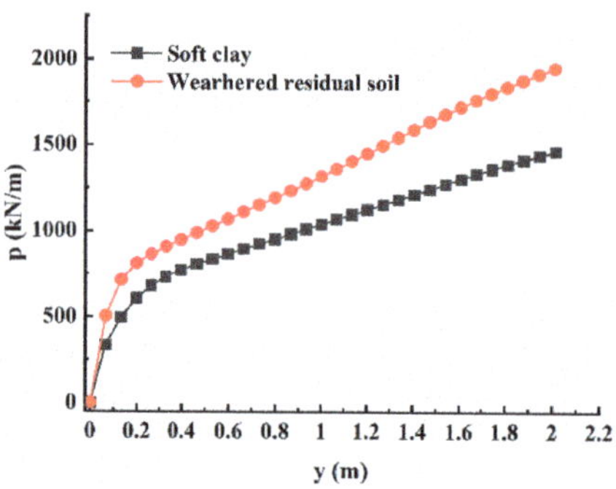

(**a**) 2 m

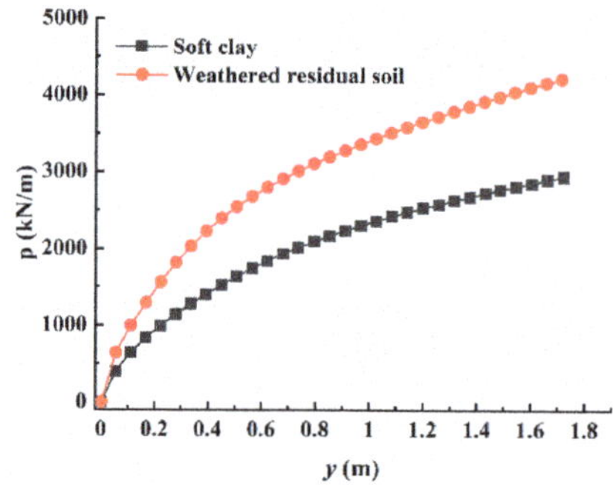

(**b**) 5 m

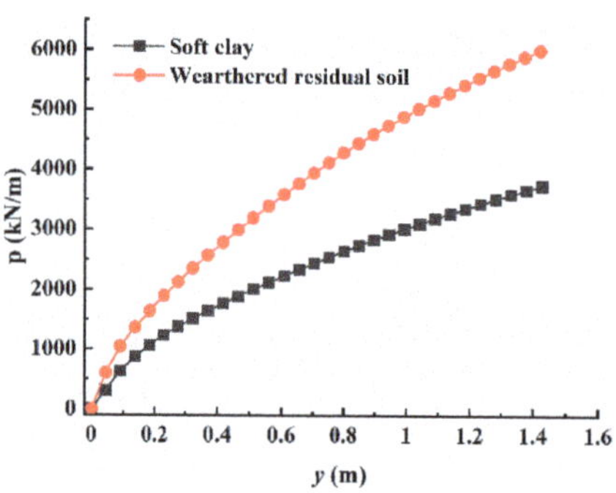

(**c**) 8 m

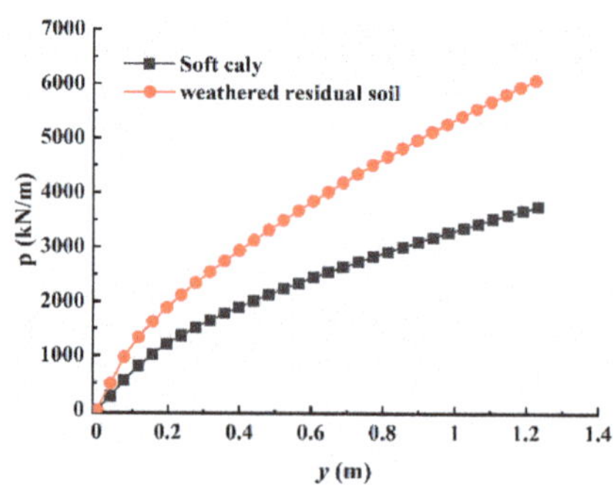

(**d**) 10 m

Figure 12. *Cont.*

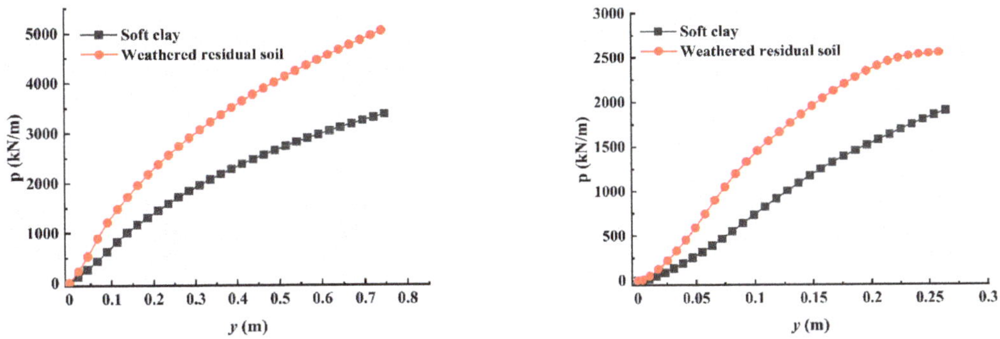

(e) 15 m (f) 20 m

Figure 12. *p–y* curves at different burial depths.

6. Long-Term Service Performance of Monopile Foundation

The monopile foundation of offshore wind turbines is subjected to the cyclic loads combining the wind and wave, and the coupling loads are imposed on the established numerical mode to investigate the long-term service performance.

6.1. Calculation and Application Method of Wind and Wave Loads

6.1.1. Wind Load Calculation

The wind loads applied to the tower and blade of offshore wind turbines can be divided into the average wind and the fluctuating wind, and the specific manifestations of wind speed acting on the structure are as follows:

$$V(z,t) = \overline{v}(z) + v(z,t) \tag{1}$$

where $\overline{v}(z)$ is the average wind speed, which does not change with time in a certain period of time. $v(z,t)$ is the fluctuating wind speed, and changes with time evolution according to random law.

Among, the change law of the average wind speed with height can be expressed by exponential function (Formula (2)), and the average wind speed at any height can be calculated according to the reference height and average wind speed in the standard.

$$\frac{\overline{v}(z)}{\overline{v_b}} = \left(\frac{z}{z_b}\right)^{\alpha} \tag{2}$$

where z and $\overline{v}(z)$ are the calculated height and the average wind speed at any height. z_b and $\overline{v_b}$ are the reference height and the corresponding average wind speed recommended in the standard. α is the ground roughness index, which is valued as 0.12, due to the surface type being offshore sea or island in the study. According to the wind energy resource report and the distribution map of wind energy resources in the coastal region, the average wind speed at a height of 10 m is 37.5 m/s in the study.

Fluctuating wind speed is characterized by a large amount of randomness, and the wind speed spectra with similar statistical characteristics are generally used for the simulation of the fluctuating wind speed. Davenport's horizontal pulsating wind spectrum is used in the study, and the computational formula is given below.

$$\begin{cases} S_v(n) = \overline{v_{10}}^2 \frac{4kx^2}{n(1+x^2)^{4/3}} \\ x = 1200n/\overline{v_{10}} \end{cases} \tag{3}$$

where $S_v(n)$ is the power spectrum of the fluctuating wind speed, n is the fluctuating wind frequency, Hz. k is the ground roughness coefficient, $\overline{v_{10}}$ is the average wind speed at 10 m height, m/s. The time history and power spectrum of the fluctuating wind speed with a 40 s period at 10 m height can be obtained by MATLAB (https://ww2.mathworks.cn/products/matlab.html?s_tid=hp_ff_p_matlab), as shown in Figure 13.

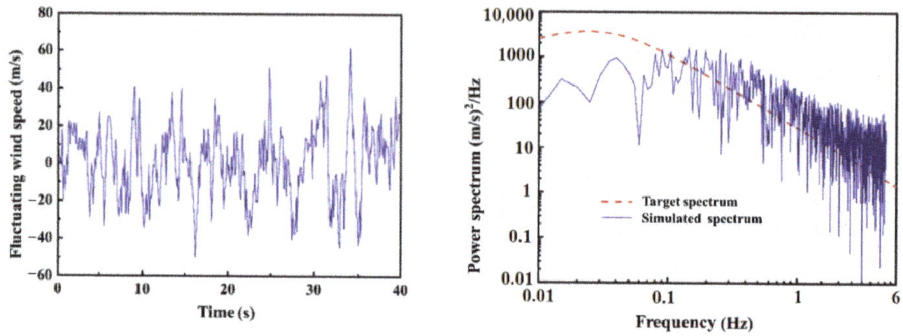

(a) (b)

Figure 13. Fluctuating wind speed time history curve and power spectrum. (**a**) Time history curve of fluctuating wind speed at 10 m height. (**b**) Power spectrum for simulating wind speed.

After the average wind speed and fluctuating wind speed are obtained, the total wind speed at each height can be calculated according to the Formulas (1) and (2), and the wind load actioning different heights of the offshore wind turbine can be calculated as Formula (4). The time history curve of total bending moment acting on the mud surface raised by the wind loads actioning on offshore wind turbines, and the shapes and dimensions of the tower and blades are determined from the basic component parameters of EN-136/4 MW turbine, which is also illustrated in Table 4.

$$F_w = 0.5\rho V(z,t)^2 cA \tag{4}$$

where F_w is wind load, ρ is the air density, 1.225 kg/m^3, $V(z,t)$ is the wind speed at Zm height above the water level, m/s, c is the shape factor, which can be 0.5. A is the projected area of the tower perpendicular to the wind direction, m^2.

Table 4. Basic component parameters of EN-136/4 MW wind turbine.

Wind Turbine Parts	Offshore Wind Turbine Size (m)				Weight (t)
	Length	Width	High	External Diameter	
Cabin	13.96	4.33	5.54	-	145
Hub	4.07	5.19	5.08	-	100
Blade	63.44	4.2	3.39	-	-
Up end of tower	-	-	29.9	3.66–4.19	62.76
Middle end of tower	-	-	27.77	4.19–4.63	90.97
Lower end of tower	-	-	18.33	4.63–5.00	83.42

6.1.2. Wave Load Calculation

The Airy wave theory has the advantages of simple principles and convenient calculation and has been widely used in marine structural engineering. Therefore, the Airy wave theory is used to calculate the wave load in the study, and calculation parameters are referenced in the study [31]. The calculation formulas of horizontal velocity u and acceleration $\frac{\partial u}{\partial t}$ in Airy wave theory are as follows.

$$u = \frac{H\omega \cosh k(d+z)}{2\sinh kd} \cos\theta \tag{5}$$

$$\frac{\partial u}{\partial t} = \frac{H\omega^2 \cosh k(d+z)}{\sinh kd} \sin\theta \tag{6}$$

where the forward direction of the wave is defined as the X-axis and the vertical upward direction of the pile center is the Z-axis. $\theta = kx - \omega t$, $k = 2\pi/L$. H is the wave height, which is 6.54 m in the study. ω is the circular frequency, Hz. d is the water depth, m. T is the wave period, which is 8 s in the study.

Wave motion parameters are determined by the Airy wave theory, and the Morison equation is used to calculate the wave load distributed on a monopile foundation, as in the formula given below.

$$df = 0.5 * \frac{\Upsilon}{g} C_D D_u |u| d_z + \frac{\Upsilon}{g} C_M A \frac{\partial u}{\partial t} d_z \tag{7}$$

where C_D is the velocity force coefficient, C_M is the mass force coefficient, D is the pile diameter, m. d_z is the unit pile length, m. A is the cross-sectional area of the monopile foundation m^2.

6.1.3. Combining Wind and Wave Loads

Wind and wave loads actioning on the monopile foundation are calculated according to the above-simplified theories and methods, and the equivalent load of wind and wave loads is applied to the pile head, as Formula (8) shows. The mechanical effects of the equivalent combined load on pile sections are the same as that before the equivalent transformation. The time history curve of the equivalent bending moment and force applied to the pile head are shown in Figure 14.

$$\begin{aligned} F_{et} &= \left(\int_0^H F_{wih} dh + \int_{-Z}^0 F_{waz} dz \right)_t \\ M_{et} &= \left(\int_0^H F_{wih} h dh + \int_{-Z}^0 F_{waz} z dz \right)_t \end{aligned} \tag{8}$$

where t is the calculated timeline time, h represents the height above the water surface of wind load, z is the depth below the water surface of wave load, F_{et} and M_{et} are the equivalent load and equivalent bending moment of the pile head, and F_{wih} and F_{waz} are wind load at hm height and wave load at zm depth.

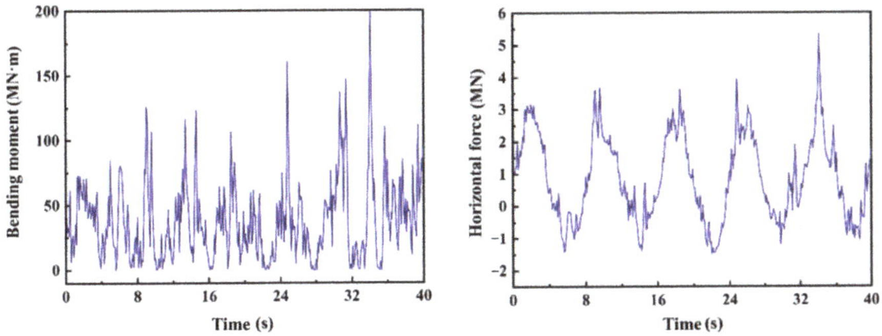

(**a**) Equivalent bending moment (**b**) Equivalent horizontal force

Figure 14. Equivalent load time history curve of wind–wave combination acting on pile head.

The central point at the pile head (8 m) and the central point of the monopile below 10 m mud surface are selected as the feature points, respectively. The change curves of horizontal displacement at different feature points of monopile foundation in two soil seabeds are shown in Figure 15. It is noted that the displacement time–history response curve fluctuates in an 8 s period, due to wave load with 8 s period actioned on monopile foundation. In general, the displacement time–history response curve of feature points at 8 m is above that of −10 m, indicating that the horizontal displacement of the pile head is greater. It can also be seen that the displacement time–history response curve of feature points of monopile foundation in soil A is above that in soil B, which indicates that the horizontal displacement of monopile foundation in weathered residual soil seabed is small and has a large bearing capacity.

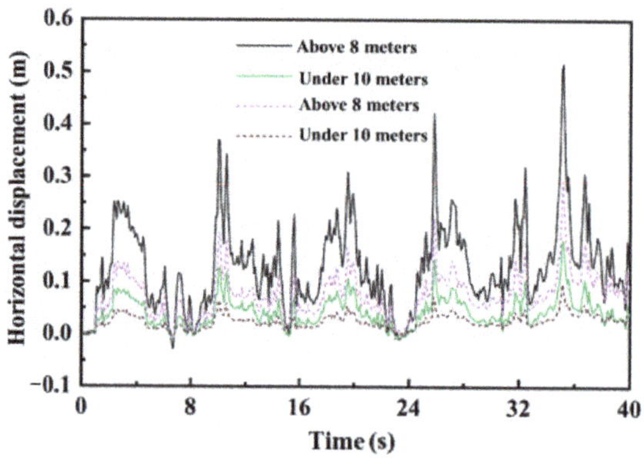

Figure 15. Displacement time history response curves of feature points.

6.2. Long-Term Bearing Performance under Cyclic Loads

The *p–y* curve is a key index in the design of the monopile foundation. Due to the special properties of seabed material and the size effect of the monopile foundation, there are great differences between numerical simulation results and *p–y* curve recommended by API.

6.2.1. The *p–y* Curve Recommended by API

The specific calculation method of *p–y* curve of soft clay is included in the API specification, and the ultimate soil resistance of soil at per unit pile length is calculated by the Formulas (9) and (10). when $x < x_r$,

$$p_u = (3 + \gamma x / C_u + 0.5x/D)C_u D \tag{9}$$

When $x \geq x_r$,

$$p_u = 9C_u D \tag{10}$$

where γ is the effective weight of soil, C_u is the soil's undrained shear strength, and D is the diameter of the monopile foundation. x is the calculated depth from the mud's surface and x_r is the critical depth of the soil layer, which is determined by the formula $x_r = 6C_u D/(\gamma D + 0.5C_u)$.

Under static loads, the *p–y* curve of soil is determined by Formulas (11) and (12); when $y < 8y_{50}$,

$$p/p_u = 0.5(y/y_{50})^{1/3} \tag{11}$$

When $y \geq 8y_{50}$,

$$p/p_u = 1 \tag{12}$$

where y is the flexural deformation of the monopile foundation and y_{50} is the flexural deformation when the soil resistance on reaching $\frac{1}{2}p_u$, which is determined by the formula $y_{50} = 2.5\ \varepsilon_{50}D$, where ε_{50} is the strain value corresponding to half of the maximum deviational stress in the triaxial undrained compression test.

Under cyclic loads, the p–y curve of soil mass is determined by Formula (13) and (14). When $y < 3y_{50}$, the cyclic p–y curve is consistent with that under static loads. When $y \geq 3y_{50}$, there are two cases: (1) When $x \geq x_r$,

$$p = 0.72p_u \tag{13}$$

(2) When $x < x_r$ and $y \geq 15y_{50}$,

$$p = 0.72p_u(x/x_r) \tag{14}$$

In this case, there is a linear transition connection during $3y_{50} < y < 15y_{50}$.

6.2.2. Comparison of p–y Curves under Different Working Conditions

Figure 16 shows the p–y curves at the −5 m burial depth under static and cyclic loads, and p–y curves calculated by API specification. The soil resistance ratios of horizontal displacement points under different working conditions are illustrated in Figure 17. The p–y curves under static loads are above that under cyclic loads in Figure 16, which indicates that the bearing capacity of the monopile foundation is weakened by the long-term cyclic loads. It is also noted from Figure 16 that the soil resistance ratios are always below 1 and decrease first and then flatten with the increase in the horizontal displacement. The soil resistance ratio under cyclic and static loads in soft clay eventually tends to 0.82, while that in weathered residual soil tends to 0.7, indicating that the monopile foundation in weathered residual soil is more susceptible to being disturbed by cyclic loads.

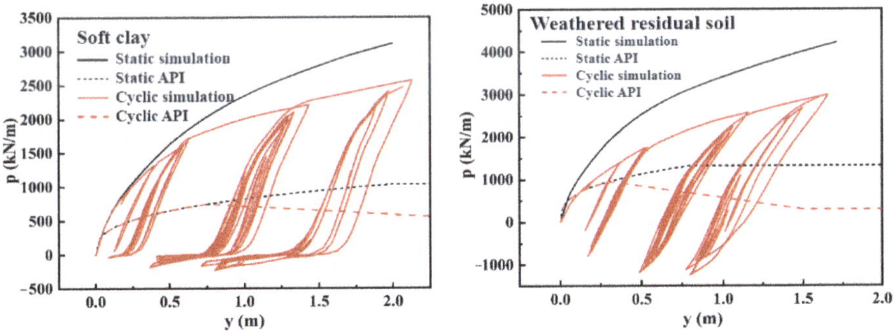

(**a**) Soft clay seabed (**b**) Weathered residual soil seabed

Figure 16. p–y curves under different working conditions and API standard at depth of −5 m.

Comparing the static p–y curve calculated by numerical simulation with the static p–y curve calculated by API specification, it is found that the p–y curve calculated by API specification is below that from numerical analysis. The ratio of static soil resistance obtained by API and numerical simulation rapidly decreases when the horizontal displacement y is small (0–0.5 m). When the horizontal displacement y is greater than 0.5 m, the soil resistance ratios decrease trend slows down, which indicates that the API specification underestimates the soil resistance to a certain extent, especially in the case of large horizontal displacement. In addition, the static soil resistance ratio of API and numerical simulation in soft clay is overall greater than that in weathered residual soil, and it is obvious that the API specification is more unsuitable for weathered residual soil.

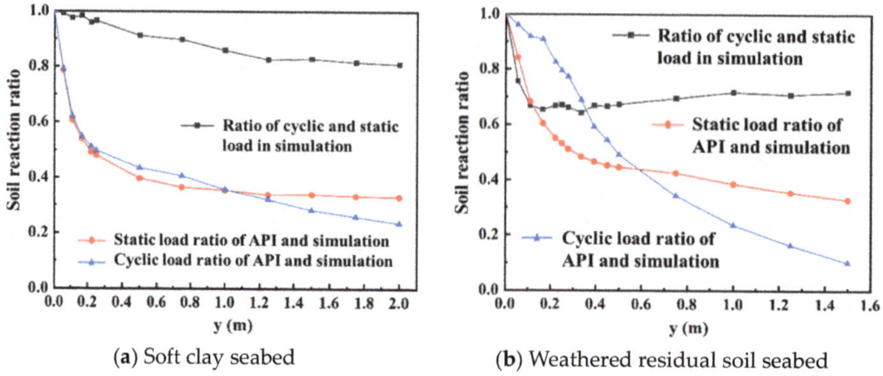

Figure 17. Soil resistance ratio under different working conditions at depth of −5 m.

The cyclic *p–y* curve method recommended by API specification also significantly underestimates the soil resistance, and the underestimation degree becomes more obvious with the increase in horizontal displacement. In soft clay seabed, the changing trend of the soil resistance ratios of API cyclic *p–y* curves and cyclic numerical simulation is the same as that under static working conditions, the cyclic soil resistance ratios decrease rapidly from 1 to 0.4 at the initial small displacement stage, and then decrease slowly trends toward 0.2. However, the changing trend of the soil resistance ratios in weathered residual soil is different. The ratio decreases slightly with the increase in horizontal displacement, and the cyclic soil resistance ratio is also higher than the static ratio in the small displacement stage, while the cyclic soil resistance ratio is lower than the static ratio in the large displacement stage and continues to decline to 0. This is because the cyclic loads have a greater influence on the weathered residual soil.

7. Conclusions and Prospect

This paper focused on the mechanical properties of weathered residual soil and the bearing behaviors of monopile foundations in weathered residual soil. Some dynamic triaxial tests were carried out for the investigation of cyclic responses of weathered residual soil, and bearing behaviors of monopile foundation in weathered residual soil were compared with those in soft clay. The main conclusions are summarized below.

(1) The effective cohesion of the weathered residual soil is 6.57 kPa, the effective internal friction angle is 34.77°, and the stress–strain response presents strain hardening under different confining pressures.

(2) Under large cyclic loads, hysteretic curves of weathered residual soil change from a shuttle shape to an inverse S shape, and strain accumulates rapidly to the failure stage.

(3) The ultimate bearing capacities of a 5 m diameter monopile foundation in weathered residual soil and soft clay seabed are 21.3 and 14.4 MN, respectively.

(4) The bearing behaviors of monopile foundation in weathered residual soil are better than that in soft clay, and the traditional *p–y* design method underestimates the bearing capacity of weathered residual soil.

The main construction sites of offshore wind farms in China have gradually shifted from the soil-based seabed area to the weathered rock-based sea area, and weathered granites with different weathering degrees differ greatly. Some studies of weathered residual soil and bearing behaviors of monopiles in weathered residual soil are carried out in this paper, which is relatively limited. In the future, different weathered granites should be tested, and the bearing characteristics and design methods of pile foundations in rock-based seabed need to be studied urgently, to provide reference and solution in the construction of offshore wind power in rock-based seabeds.

Author Contributions: Formal analysis, B.H. and X.Y.; investigation, B.H. and S.D.; methodology, G.H., B.H. and S.D.; supervision, X.Y. and M.L.; writing—original draft, B.H. and M.L.; writing—review and editing, X.Y., G.P. and S.D. All authors have read and agreed to the published version of the manuscript.

Funding: The authors wish to appreciate the financial supports provided by China Postdoctoral Science Foundation (2023M742093), Postdoctoral Innovation Project of Shandong Province (SDCX-ZG-202302004), National Natural Science Foundation of China Joint Program (U23A20663), National Natural Science Foundation of China (52409161; 52171266; 52271294), Key Lab Far Shore Wind Power Technol Zhejiang Prov (ZOE2023006).

Institutional Review Board Statement: Not applicable.

Informed Consent Statement: Not applicable.

Data Availability Statement: Data are available upon request.

Conflicts of Interest: Authors Ben He and Guoxiang Huang were employed by the company Power China Huadong Engineering Corporation Limited. The remaining authors declare that the research was conducted in the absence of any commercial or financial relationships that could be construed as a potential conflict of interest.

References

1. Alrwashdeh, S.S. Investigation of Wind Energy Production at Different Sites in Jordan Using the Site Effectiveness Method. *Energy Eng. J. Assoc. Energy Eng.* **2019**, *116*, 47–59. [CrossRef]
2. Jansen, M.; Staffell, I.; Kitzing, L.; Quoilin, S.; Wiggelinkhuizen, E.; Bulder, B.; Riepin, I.; Müsgens, F. Offshore wind competitiveness in mature markets without subsidy. *Nat. Energy* **2020**, *5*, 614–622. [CrossRef]
3. Yan, X.; Zhang, N.; Ma, K.; Wei, C.; Yang, S.; Pan, B. Overview of Current Situation and Trend of Offshore Wind Power Development in China. *Power Gener. Technol.* **2024**, *45*, 1–12. [CrossRef]
4. Liu, D.; Liu, M.; Xu, X.; Wang, J.; Fan, C.; Li, X.; Han, J. Future prospects research on offshore wind power scale in China based on signal decomposition and extreme learning machine optimized by principal component analysis. *Energy Sci. Eng.* **2020**, *8*, 3514–3530. [CrossRef]
5. Arany, L.; Bhattacharya, S.; Macdonald, J.; Hogan, S.J. Design of monopiles for offshore wind turbines in 10 steps. *Soil Dyn. Earthq. Eng.* **2017**, *92*, 126–152. [CrossRef]
6. Shi, Y.; Yao, W.; Jiang, M. Dynamic analysis on monopile supported offshore wind turbine under wave and wind load. *Structures* **2023**, *47*, 520–529. [CrossRef]
7. Kim, J.H.; Jeong, Y.H.; Ha, J.G.; Park, H.J. Evaluation of Soil–Foundation–Structure Interaction for Large Diameter Monopile Foundation Focusing on Lateral Cyclic Loading. *J. Mar. Sci. Eng.* **2023**, *11*, 1303. [CrossRef]
8. Dai, S.; Han, B.; Huang, G.; Gu, X.; Jian, L.; Liu, S. Failure mode of monopile foundation for offshore wind turbine in soft clay under complex loads. *Mar. Georesour. Geotechnol.* **2022**, *40*, 14–25. [CrossRef]
9. Alsharedah, Y.A.; Newson, T.; Naggar, M.H.; Black, J.A. Lateral Ultimate Capacity of Monopile Foundations for Offshore Wind Turbines: Effects of Monopile Geometry and Soil Stiffness Properties. *Appl. Sci.* **2023**, *13*, 12269. [CrossRef]
10. Li, F.; Tian, P.; Wang, L.; Chen, M. Investigation on lateral bearing capacity of monopile under combined vertical-lateral loads and scouring condition. *Mar. Georesour. Geotechnol.* **2021**, *39*, 505–514. [CrossRef]
11. Achmus, M.; Kuo, Y.S.; Abdel-Rahman, K. Behavior of monopile foundations under cyclic lateral load. *Comput. Geotech.* **2009**, *36*, 725–735. [CrossRef]
12. Zhang, X.-L.; Xue, J.-Y.; Han, Y.; Chen, S.-L. Model test study on horizontal bearing behavior of pile under existing vertical load. *Soil Dyn. Earthq. Eng.* **2021**, *147*, 106820. [CrossRef]
13. Dai, S.; Han, B.; Wang, B.; Luo, J.; He, B. Influence of soil scour on lateral behavior of large-diameter offshore wind-turbine monopile and corresponding scour monitoring method. *Ocean Eng.* **2021**, *239*, 109809. [CrossRef]
14. Dai, S.; Yu, X.; Han, B.; He, B. Cyclic behavior of seabed building material of offshore wind farm in rock-based sea area: Submarine completely weathered granite. *Ocean Eng.* **2024**, *296*, 117024. [CrossRef]
15. Han, B.; Wang, B.; Dai, S.; Hou, X.; He, B. Bearing failure mechanism of rock-socketed monopile foundation for offshore wind turbine in weathered-granite seabed. *Mar. Georesour. Geotechnol.* **2023**, *41*, 1026–1037. [CrossRef]
16. Wang, Y.; Zhang, S.; Yin, S.; Liu, X.; Zhang, X. Accumulated Plastic Strain Behavior of Granite Residual Soil under Cycle Loading. *Int. J. Geomech.* **2020**, *20*, 04020205. [CrossRef]
17. Zhang, X.; Zhang, X.; Xu, C.; Wu, Y. The calculation method of vertical bearing capacity of pile foundation considering cyclic weakening effect of soft clay. *Comput. Geotech.* **2024**, *172*, 106422. [CrossRef]
18. Wang, M.; Wang, M.; Cheng, X.; Lu, Q.; Lu, J. A New p–y Curve for Laterally Loaded Large-Diameter Monopiles in Soft Clays. *Sustainability* **2022**, *14*, 15102. [CrossRef]
19. Hamderi, M. Finite Element-Based p-y Curves in Sand. *Arab. J. Sci. Eng.* **2023**, *48*, 14183–14194. [CrossRef]

20. Alver, O.; Eseller-Bayat, E.E. A dynamic p–y model for piles embedded in cohesionless soils. *Bull. Earthq. Eng.* **2023**, *21*, 3297–3320. [CrossRef]
21. Lu, W.; Zhang, G. New p-y curve model considering vertical loading for piles of offshore wind turbine in sand. *Ocean Eng.* **2020**, *203*, 107228. [CrossRef]
22. Oldham, D. *Experiments with Lateral Loading of Single Piles in Sand*; Publication of: Balkema (AA); National Academies: Washington, DC, USA, 1985.
23. Byrne, B.W.; McAdam, R.A.; Burd, H.J.; Beuckelaers, W.J.A.P.; Gavin, K.G.; Houlsby, G.T.; Igoe, D.J.P.; Jardine, R.J.; Martin, C.M.; Muirwood, A.; et al. Monotonic laterally loaded pile testing in a dense marine sand at Dunkirk. *Geotechnique* **2020**, *70*, 986–998. [CrossRef]
24. Achmus, M.; Abdel-Rahman, K.; Kuo, Y.S. Numerical Modelling of Large Diameter Steel Piles under Monotonic and Cyclic Horizontal Loading. In Proceedings of the Tenth International Symposium on Numerical Models in Geomechanics, Rhodes, Greece, 25–27 April 2007.
25. Hearn, E. Finite Element Analysis of an Offshore Wind Turbine Generator Monopile Foundation. Master's Thesis, Tufts University, Medford, MA, USA, 2009.
26. Long, J.H.; Vanneste, G. Effects of Cyclic Lateral Loads on Piles in Sand. *J. Geotech. Eng.* **1994**, *120*, 225–244. [CrossRef]
27. Verdure, L.; Garnier, J.; Levacher, D. Lateral Cyclic Loading of Single Piles in Sand. *Int. J. Phys. Model. Geotech.* **2003**, *3*, 17–28. [CrossRef]
28. Peng, J.R.; Clarke, B.G.; Rouainia, M. A Device to Cyclic Lateral Loaded Model Piles. *Astm Geotech. Test. J.* **2006**, *29*, 341–347. [CrossRef]
29. Byrne, B.W.; Leblanc, C.; Houlsby, G.T. Response of stiff piles to long term cyclic loading. *Géotechnique* **2010**, *60*, 79–90.
30. Lesny, K.; Wiemann, J. *Design Aspects of Monopiles in German Offshore Wind Farms: Proceedings of the International Symposium on Frontiers in Offshore Geotechnics*; AA Balkema Publishing: Rotterdam, The Netherlands, 2005.
31. Dai, H. Analysis of Steel Pipe Pile Dynamic Characteristics under Scour Conditon. Ph.D. Thesis, Southeast University, Nanjing, China, 2017.

Journal of
Marine Science and Engineering

MDPI

Review

Innovations in Offshore Wind: Reviewing Current Status and Future Prospects with a Parametric Analysis of Helical Pile Performance for Anchoring Mooring Lines

Ammar Alnmr * and Mais Mayassah

Department of Structural and Geotechnical Engineering, Széchenyi István University, 9026 Győr, Hungary; mayassah.mais@hallgato.sze.hu
* Correspondence: alnmr.ammar@hallgato.sze.hu

Abstract: This study examines the current status and future potential of the offshore wind sector. Offshore wind is pivotal in transitioning to a low-carbon society and meeting rising energy demands, despite being capital-intensive. The industry aims to develop larger-scale wind farms in deeper ocean locations, with projections indicating significant cost reductions. To explore deeper ocean areas, specialized foundations like floating platforms moored to the seabed are required. This study proposes helical piles anchored in the seabed as a method to secure mooring lines. Using Plaxis 3D, a parametric examination was conducted on helical piles with two plates: one fixed at the pile's toe and the other varying in position between 0.5 and 13 m from the seabed surface. Load inclination angles (0, 20, 40, and 60 degrees) were used to simulate mooring line loads. Results indicate the optimal Zh/Z ratios for maintaining load-bearing capacity and stability: 0.12 (10 mm movements), 0.22 (25 mm), and 0.26 (50 mm) for small shaft diameters; and 0.34 (10 mm), 0.38 (25 mm), and 0.46 (50 mm) for large shaft diameters. These findings highlight the importance of specific load inclination angles based on shaft diameter and allowable movement for effective performance.

Keywords: offshore wind; offshore wind support structures; floating offshore wind turbine; helical piles; numerical modeling

1. Introduction

Growing worries about climate change brought on by the detrimental effects of fossil fuel consumption on the environment and human health have made the shift to renewable energy sources imperative. Since the Industrial Revolution, fossil fuels (coal, oil, and natural gas) have dominated the world's energy mix, providing most of energy for electricity, transportation, and heating. This has led to a significant increase in greenhouse gas (GHG) emissions, which are the primary cause of the ongoing climate change crisis. To achieve climate neutrality in the future, the world must decarbonize its energy mix by increasing the share of renewable energy sources.

Fossil fuels account for 81.79% of the world's energy output, with low-carbon sources, including nuclear (3.99%) and renewables (14.21%), making up the remaining sources [1]. In terms of cost and capacity, solar and wind power are viable options [2]. Regulations influencing the development of renewable energy are shaped by international accords like the Kyoto Protocol and the Paris Climate Change Agreement [3]. It is expected that these top-down tactics would spearhead international efforts, particularly in Europe, to fulfill aggressive policy-driven targets in the fight against global warming [4].

Since ancient times, wind has been used for a variety of reasons. Wind is a natural phenomenon that is caused by the sun's uneven heating and the Earth's rotation [5]. According to Poudineh et al. [6], it has been used for pumping water, grinding grain, and powering sails. Today, the main method of producing power from wind energy is through onshore or offshore turbines. Due to its resurgence as a viable electrical source in the late 20th century, onshore and offshore wind energy systems have seen substantial technological breakthroughs [5].

Compared to onshore turbines, offshore wind offers enormous resource potential as it expands into open-water areas [6,7]. The concept's potential was demonstrated by Germany's early trials in the 1930s and by the first practical installation in Sweden in 1990 [7]. A significant advancement in the production of renewable electricity was made by Denmark's 4.95 MW commercial offshore wind farm [7].

Due to restrictions on onshore locations and land use concerns, the offshore wind business has flourished [7–10]. Stronger and more consistent winds assist offshore sites, resulting in higher power output [3,11]. Although offshore projects have similar functionality, the hostile maritime environment makes them more difficult technologically, requiring larger capital investments [12–14]. The offshore wind industry's expansion has been hampered by its complexity, as well as by the small number of investors and large capital required [9,13].

In general, the convergence of significant cost reductions, continuous technological progress, and appealing subsidy programs provided by national authorities has established offshore wind energy as a reliable and economically feasible electricity source [15]. While originating in Europe, offshore wind is progressively gaining significance in global electricity decarbonization initiatives, both in the immediate and long-term perspectives [3].

Europe has emerged as the leader in offshore wind, showing a wealth of knowledge and advanced technology. The region has 25 GW of installed offshore wind power with 116 wind farms and 5402 turbines spread over 12 nations, mostly in the northwest [16]. The capacity allocation among these countries is shown in Table 1.

Table 1. Offshore wind installations in Europe by country, 2020 [16].

Country	Number of OWFs	Number of Turbines Connected	Cumulated Capacity (MW)
The UK	40	2294	10,428
Germany	29	1501	7689
Denmark	14	559	1703
Belgium	11	399	2261
The Netherlands	9	537	2611
Sweden	5	80	192
Finland	3	19	71
Ireland	1	7	25
Portugal	1	3	25
Spain	1	1	5
Norway	1	1	2
France	1	1	2
Total	116	5402	25,014

Table 1 shows how different countries have developed offshore wind to different degrees. This diversity is not just attributable to the abundance of wind resources at sea as historical factors, supportive structures, solid governmental backing, technological advancement, and grid access all play important roles.

Coastal waters in Europe have a great deal of wind potential, especially because they are shallow even when they are far from the coast. Three decades ago, this benefit propelled Europe to become a leader in offshore wind development [17]. The most-developed basin is the North Sea, which contributes about 20 GW (or 79% of Europe's total offshore wind capacity). The remaining capacity is split between the Atlantic Ocean (less than 1%), the Baltic Sea (9%), and the Irish Sea (12%), per WindEurope [16]. Table 2 details the expected installations by country from 2024 to 2027 [18].

Table 2. Projected installations by country from 2024 to 2027 [18].

Country (MW)	Year			
	2024	**2025**	**2026**	**2027**
Belgium	-	-	500	500
Denmark	190	210	800	900
France	530	990	300	800
Germany	1630	900	1420	2210
Ireland	-	-	-	560
Italy	-	-	250	520
The Netherlands	350	700	350	1000
Poland	-	-	920	1090
Spain	-	-	-	160
Norway	-	10	-	-
The UK	1670	1900	3890	3820
Total	4370	4710	8430	11,560

When viewed in a larger context, offshore wind and Power-to-X (PtX) have the potential to completely transform the way in which ambitious climate objectives are met. PtX is the process of transforming energy into a gas or liquid for storage or immediate use [19,20]. By allowing the synthesis of hydrogen—an effective, clean, and flexible energy carrier—from all or part of the generated electricity, this strategy broadens the potential applications of offshore wind power beyond the production of electricity [21]. Green hydrogen and offshore wind are seeing a rise in popularity. However, their high present costs are preventing them from being widely adopted. IRENA predicts that long-term green hydrogen costs could be reduced, driven by financial and regulatory incentives, by 85% as a result of falling costs for electrolysis facilities and renewable electricity.

This study investigates offshore wind farm infrastructure and future prospects, highlighting the need for creative solutions. With traditional foundation technologies being insufficient to meet the industry's changing demands, this study proposes using helical piles as mooring line anchors, and their design is also refined to increase bearing capacity. These innovations aim to make offshore wind energy development more sustainable. Despite its high initial cost, offshore wind energy is critical in the transition to a low-carbon society. As businesses expand to larger-scale wind farms in deeper ocean regions, specialized foundations such as floating platforms tethered to the seabed become increasingly important. This study looks into the usage of helical piles anchored to the seabed to secure mooring lines for floating offshore wind turbines. This study uses the Plaxis 3D tool to examine the efficacy of helical piles in sandy soil under varied load situations. The aim of this study is to provide realistic design guidance for optimizing helical pile foundations; hence, improving the efficiency and dependability of offshore wind energy systems.

To comprehensively explore the offshore wind sector's current status and future trajectories, we employed a mixed review technique coupled with a numerical study. This approach involved several key steps:

1. Surveying the database and selecting pertinent keywords to ensure a comprehensive coverage of the relevant literature.
2. Assembling and screening research papers to extract valuable insights and identify emerging trends in the offshore wind sector.
3. Comparing various offshore wind foundation types to discern their strengths, weaknesses, potential areas for further research and improvement, as well as determining prospects for offshore wind.
4. Applying numerical modeling techniques to investigate the efficacy of helical piles with two helices at varied loading inclinations as anchors for resisting loads from floating offshore mooring lines. These piles are installed utilizing machine-mounted hydraulic or electrically powered drilling equipment that screws them directly into the ground, thus allowing for easy installation in marine environments.

Section 4 delves into the numerical modeling approach, providing a detailed discussion of the methodology and findings.

The search encompassed a wide array of sources, including journal articles, books, conference papers, websites, and proceedings. Figure 1 illustrates the keyword network within the offshore wind domain, visualized using VOSviewer (version 1.6.20). This tool provides a distance-based representation of keyword relationships, with each node representing a keyword and links denoting connections. The distance between nodes indicates the strength of their relationship: shorter distances signify stronger links, while greater distances indicate weaker connections. The link strength of a node is determined by the sum of all its connection strengths. Additionally, different colors denote different research years, and the node size reflects the number of publications in which the keyword was initially used. Our study findings, discussed in the subsequent sections, cover various aspects of offshore wind farms and their components, the prospects for offshore wind, the recent utilization of machine learning algorithms in turbine design, and the application of helical piles for anchoring mooring lines and tendons in the seabed. Special emphasis will be placed on helical pile behavior, particularly with respect to their resistance to upward movement and pullout load, and this will be analyzed through numerical modeling.

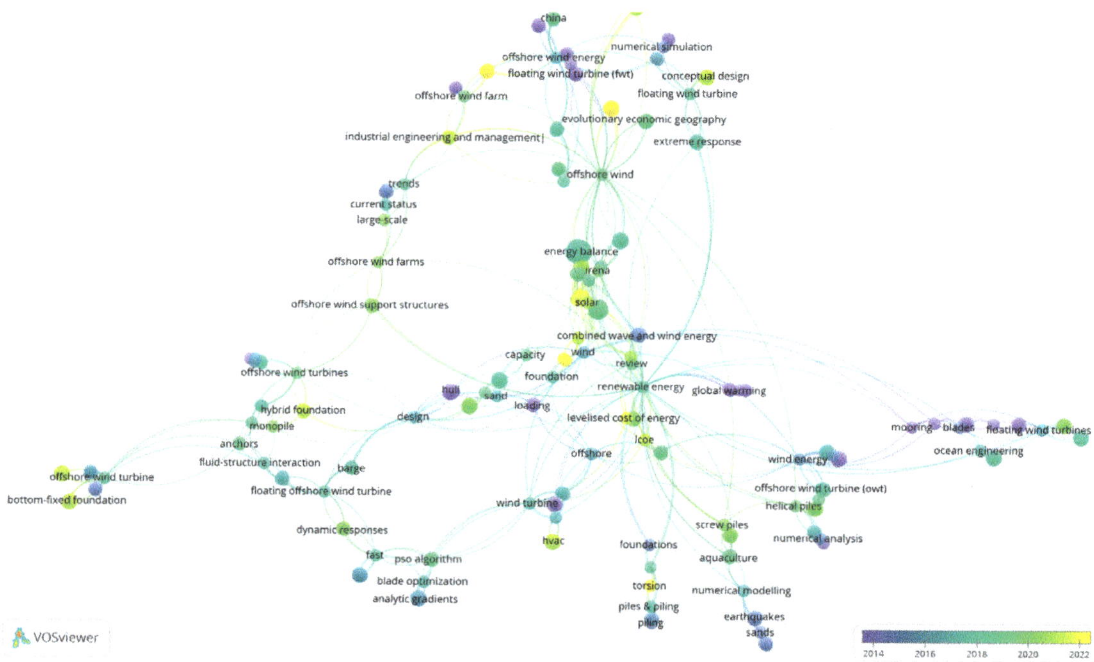

Figure 1. A network of keywords.

2. Offshore Wind Farms

The offshore wind farm (OWF), which is made up of a group of wind turbines placed in bodies of water (usually seas that are distant from the shoreline), is a crucial structural component of offshore wind energy [22]. An offshore wind farm (OWF) combines onshore wind installation ideas with offshore structures that are derived from the established practices of the oil and gas (O&G) industry [7,23].

There are five steps (Figure 2) involved in creating an OWF [24]. First, it entails deciding on an appropriate offshore location, which is achieved by evaluating the environment and wind resources, creating the OWF, and securing building permits. The manufacturing, installation, and use of maritime equipment in the operation of OWF components are covered in later phases. Over the course of its 25-year existence, routine maintenance seeks to minimize downtime. It is then either updated with new technology or safely decommissioned [24].

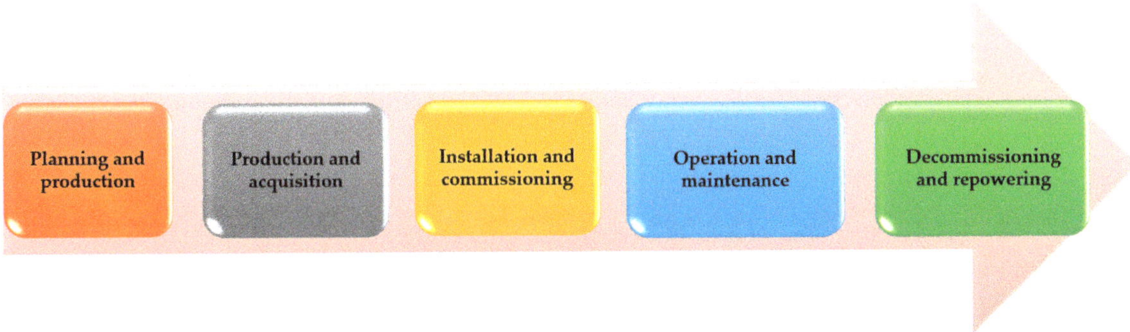

Figure 2. Five life-cycle stages of an OWF ([24], modified by authors).

The average distance to the shore and water depth, which were compiled by Díaz and Guedes Soares [3], are shown in Table 3. Advances in technology and the availability of offshore places for larger installations have led to a trend where offshore wind farms (OWFs) are relocating farther from the shore in order to obtain superior wind resources [3]. Figure 3 illustrates a distinct shift toward greater depths, as per the IRENA data [25], depicting the trajectory observed between 2000 and 2022 across Europe, China, and other regions worldwide. Notably, offshore wind farms have migrated toward deeper waters and increased distances from the shoreline. The OWF capacity (size) and delivery year (color) are indicated by the spheres on the graph.

Since 2000, offshore wind farms in Europe and China have seen significant growth. In Europe, the average farm size increased from 25 MW to 468 MW in 2022, with depths deepening from 7 to 32 m and distances from the shore extending to 35 km. In China, the average farm size reached 436 MW in 2022, with depths of 35 m and distances from the shore of 27 km (according to IRENA data) [25]. These data are consistent with the current trend of deeper water locations being chosen for offshore wind farms (OWFs). This pattern is expected to continue as water depths and distances from the coast increase.

Foundations, offshore wind turbines, connecting cables, and onshore and offshore substations make up an offshore wind farm's (OWF's) main parts, which together make up the transmission system. This OWF component structure was standard, as seen in Figure 4.

Table 3. The average water depth and distance to shore for each region until 2019 (compiled based on [3]).

Region	The Average Water Depth (m)	The Average Distance to Shore (km)
America	25.5	4.5
Europe	17.4	23.3
Asia	6.7	6.9

2.1. Offshore Wind Turbine

A key component of offshore wind farms (OWFs) is an offshore wind turbine (OWT), which is a contemporary technology that produces electricity from wind in an offshore environment. With an average installed capacity of 8.2 MW in Europe as of 2020, these turbines typically have three blades that are oriented upwind and horizontally [16]. An OWT configured in its typical manner is shown in Figure 5.

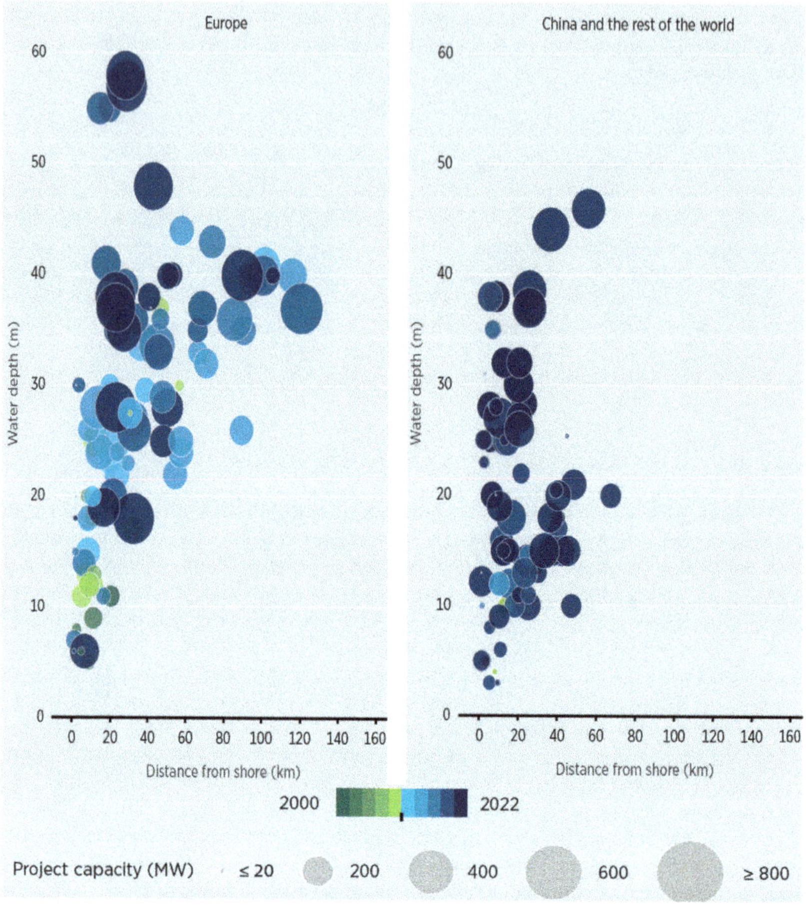

Figure 3. Water depth and average distance from shore [25].

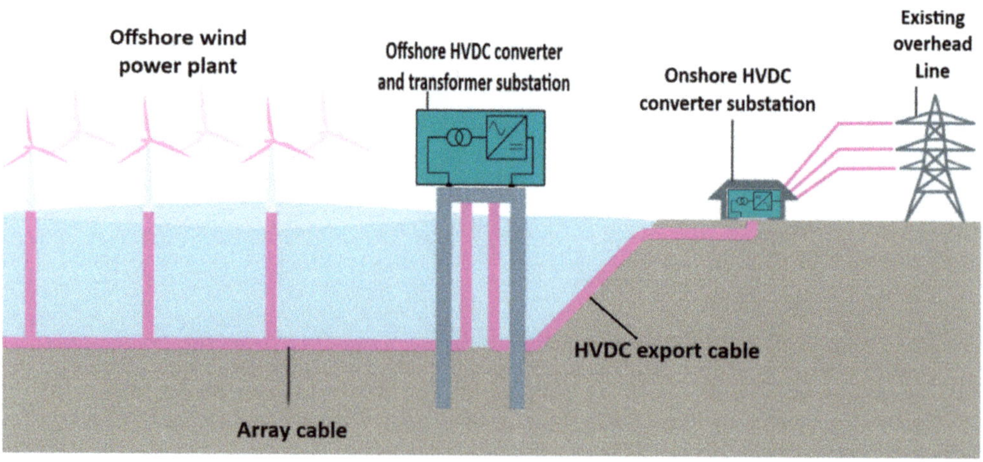

Figure 4. The components and layout of an OWF schematically represented [26].

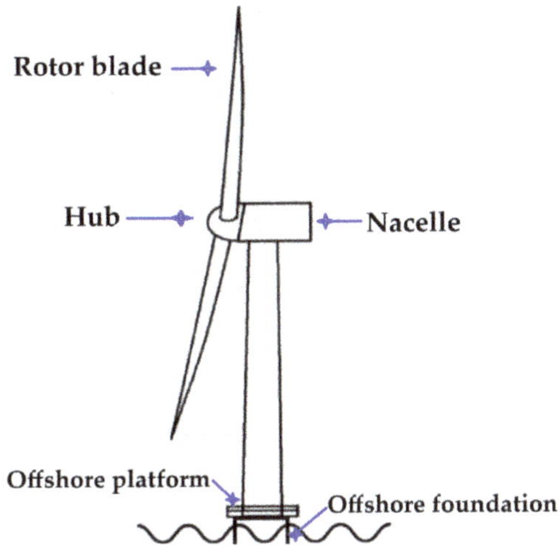

Figure 5. A typical arrangement of an OWT ([22], modified by authors).

Manufacturers are concentrating on bigger and more potent offshore wind turbines (OWTs) in order to increase electricity output while cutting costs; this is demonstrated by the rise in OWTs over the past few decades (see Figure 6) [3,27]. The upcoming generation of offshore wind turbines (OWTs), with capacities ranging between 10 and 14 MW, is expected to be utilized in projects scheduled for commissioning after 2022 [16].

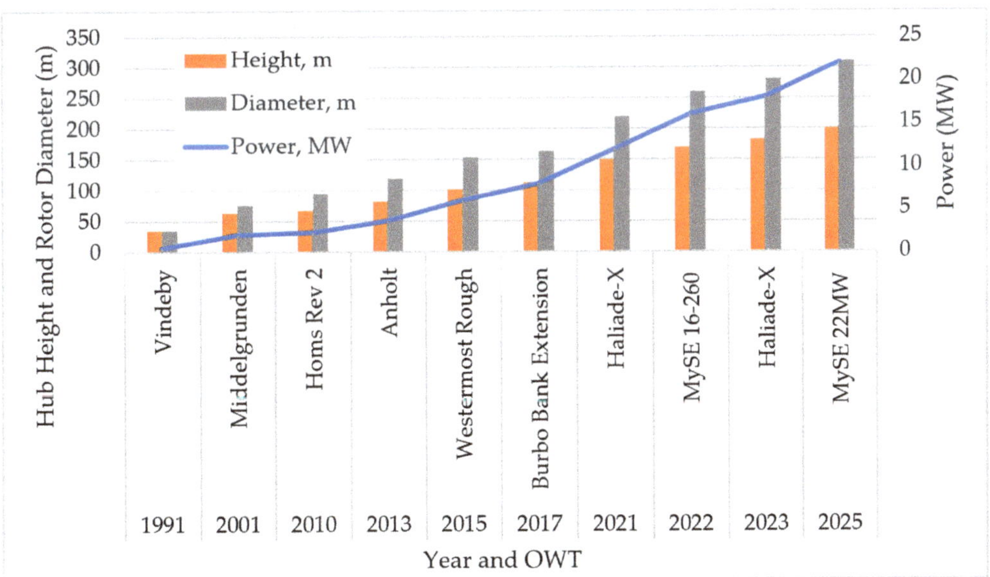

Figure 6. OWTs' increasing power and size (compiled based on [28,29]).

In 2022, a 16 MW turbine was installed offshore in the second phase of China Three Gorges (CTG)'s Zhangpu Liuao wind farm in collaboration with Goldwind. Goldwind's GWH252-16MW turbine features 123 m-long blades and a 252 m rotor diameter, covering approximately 50,000 square meters. Shortly after, Mingyang Smart Energy commissioned its MySE 16-260 offshore wind turbine in China, surpassing Goldwind's turbine as the world's largest. With a 260 m rotor diameter, the MySE 16-260 offers a swept area of 53,902 square meters. In October 2023, Mingyang announced plans for a new offshore wind turbine model with a 22 MW capacity, which is set for development between 2024 and 2025. The MySE 22 MW will have a rotor diameter exceeding 310 m, making it the most powerful globally. It will also be typhoon-resistant and suitable for fixed-bottom and floating applications [28]. Such specifications demand the foundation to be larger, and its load will be bigger. In addition, for floating foundations, the mooring line loads will be bigger and necessitate careful study on its behavior. In this study, the focus will be on studying the behavior of helical piles used as anchors to link the mooring line of floating foundations.

2.2. Foundations

The first offshore wind farm (OWF) that operated close to the coast was the Vindeby OWF in Denmark, which had eleven turbines with a combined 4.95 MW, in 1991. Located in shallow waters (2–6 m) close to the shoreline (1.5–3 km), this innovative OWF has subsequently been abandoned [4,7]. Stronger foundation structures are needed as OWFs travel deeper into windier waters and farther out to sea in order to endure shifting loads from waves, ice, winds, and marine conditions [30]. Figure 7 shows these loads.

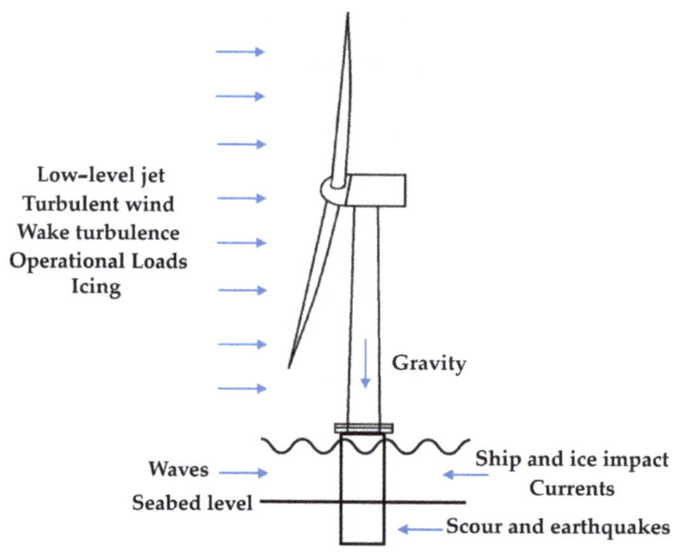

Figure 7. The impact of different loads on offshore wind turbines (OWTs) ([22], modified by authors).

Offshore wind farms (OWFs) have an average lifespan of 25 years and must survive a range of aerodynamic, hydrodynamic, and seismic loads in severe marine settings. Due to the tight foundation design specifications imposed, an OWF is generally more expensive than an onshore option [11,31]. Offshore wind foundation designs attempt to tackle these problems by leveraging technologies from the oil and gas (O&G) industry [27,32]. Using specialized vessels, foundations are laid offshore after being manufactured onshore [33]. The state of the seabed, the depth of the water, and the available funds all affect the sort of foundation that is chosen [34].

Most offshore wind turbines (OWTs) in operation today, whether in shallow waters or not, use bottom-fixed foundations—such as monopiles, jackets, and gravity bases—which are firmly fixed to the seafloor. However, bottom-fixed alternatives lose some of their cost-effectiveness after 50 m [31]. Suction bucket jackets (SBJs) are recommended by Ørsted as a practical substitute for diving down to 100 m; however, only a small number of small-scale

OWFs have used SBJs in shallow waters [35]. Interestingly, systematic studies on this kind of foundation are still rare.

Gravity base, jacket, and monopile foundations were being used by about 96.1% of offshore wind farms (OWFs) in Europe at the end of 2020, according to WindEurope's [16] report. This predominance indicates that certain foundation types require more investigation. Figure 8 illustrates the common schematic diagrams and utilization of different foundation types based on water depth. Floating foundation will be discussed in detail in Section 3.

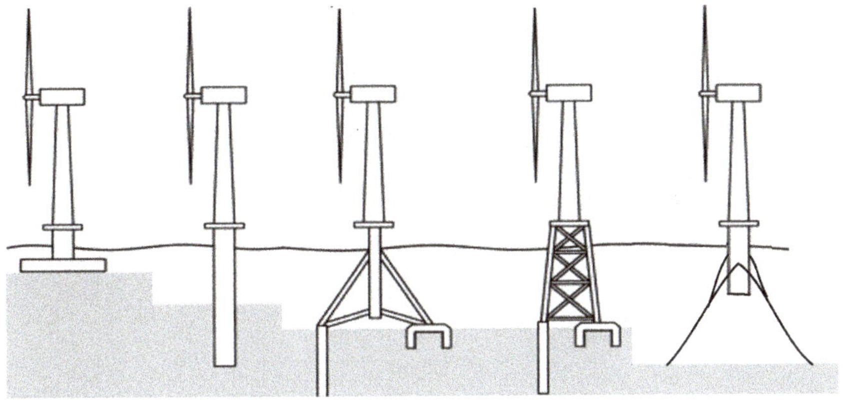

Figure 8. A schematic representation and utilization of different offshore foundation types based on water depth (compiled based on [36,37]).

Accounting for 80.5% of all new installations in 2020, monopiles continue to be the most widely used kind of foundation in Europe. In terms of providers, EEW and Sif have offered 423 monopiles in total throughout Germany, Belgium, and the Netherlands. With 19%, or 100 units, jackets are the second most common foundation type, which are provided to Morray East in the UK by Lamprell and Smulders. Kincardine and Windfloat Atlantic received three semi-subs structures (0.5%) from the Navantia-Windar Consortium, as shown in Figure 9 [16].

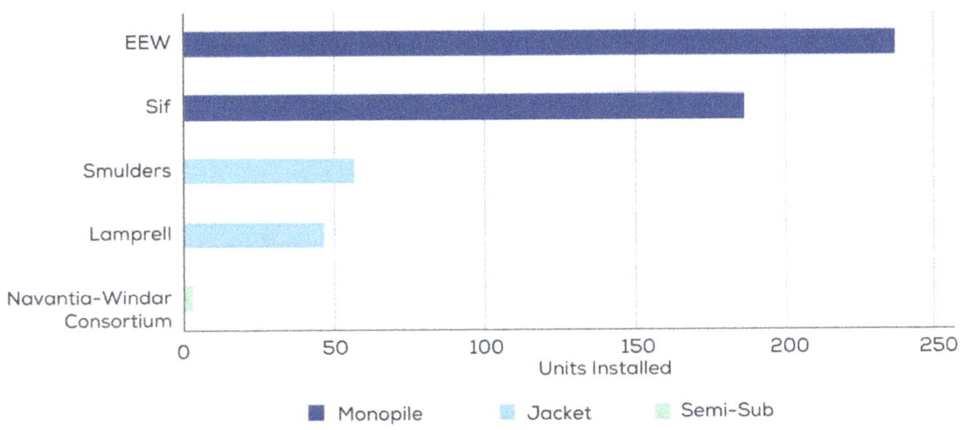

Figure 9. The manufacturing companies that erected foundations in Europe in 2020 [16].

2.2.1. Monopile

A steel tube pile is placed into the seafloor to form a monopile foundation, which is usually 20–40 m long and 3–8 m in diameter [31]. This kind works well in shallow waters that are between 0 and 30 m deep. By creating side friction with the soil, it efficiently lowers vertical loads. By shifting the weight to the surrounding soil, monopiles effectively manage horizontal stresses without bending or rotating [34,38]. This foundation is commonly utilized for offshore wind turbines (OWTs) due to its ease of installation and appropriateness [39].

The sandy and muddy seabed of the North Sea makes pile construction easier and lowers costs for owners of offshore wind farms. Furthermore, the majority of offshore farms in Europe are situated in shallow waters, where there is a maximum depth of 30 m [3]. An extra transition piece at seabed level is advised between the foundation and the tower to alleviate issues with maintaining vertical monopiles. This part allows access to the turbine and vertically aligns the foundation [11,32].

According to Burton et al. [11], the transition piece makes it easier to put the tower and turbine on top of the foundation. By 2020, 4681 monopile foundations—or 81.2% of the market—had been installed in Europe, according to WindEurope [16]. Monopiles are expected to remain the most popular foundation type in Europe. With the rapid growth in offshore wind activity and increasing turbine sizes, it is crucial to quickly scale up the manufacturing of the largest monopile segments [40].

2.2.2. Gravity Foundations

Burton et al. [11] and Esteban et al. [41] have stated that the gravity base (GBS) foundation is typically built with affordable materials such as reinforced concrete and that it has the shape of a hollow frustum. But, steel or a combination of steel and concrete are also good choices. Heavy lift cranes and huge transport vessels are not needed because these foundations are constructed onshore, frequently in drydocks, which are then transported to the site using a semi-floating technique [38].

Materials such as sand, rock, or iron ore are added as ballast into the hollow interior of the GBS once it is in position. Significant weight is produced by this addition to resist loads that are applied vertically, as well as horizontally [3,41]. Strong sea overturning movements that may cause the structure to topple over are avoided in large part due to the ballast [11,31]. The GBS foundation is a feasible substitute in regions with shallow waters, i.e., those up to 20 m deep, where it is difficult to drive monopiles into the seabed because of semi-hard and uniform conditions (like rocky soil) [3,41].

The weight of a solid concrete, ballast-filled GBS foundation is around 1500–4500 tons, which is significantly more than that of other foundation types [42]. Dredging or soil preparation is necessary to create a flat surface at the installation sites in order to guarantee sufficient support [38,41]. All the same, GBS foundations account for 5% of the European market with 289 units deployed [16].

With its solid concrete construction and ballast-filled weight, the GBS is significantly heavier than other foundation types, weighing between 1500 and 4500 tons [42]. The installation locations need to be leveled out via dredging or soil preparation in order to guarantee sufficient support [38,41]. In spite of this, GBS foundations, of which there are 289 installed units, account for 5% of the European market [16].

2.2.3. Jacket

The jacket foundation is a space frame structure with three or four legs that is anchored into the seafloor by leg piles, as described by Wu et al. [31] and Díaz and Guedes Soares [3]. Its usefulness for offshore areas with water depths ranging from 25 to 50 m has been noted by Díaz and Guedes Soares [3]. Some sites have even been known to accommodate depths of 80 m [37]. The jackets are delivered to the site by flat-top barges or other vessels after being manufactured onshore as a single frame unit. For extra mobility, they occasionally float in a manner akin to gravity bases. The jackets are dropped into the ocean and secured with leg piles after being raised vertically by enormous cranes upon arrival [38].

In deeper waters, jackets with their wide legs provide a lighter option to monopiles for handling stronger overturning motions or principal horizontal loads. Due to their reduced total member cross-sectional area, their design lessens fatigue damage from wave inertia stress. However, the requirement for significant transition sections and their intricate design has led to increased production costs. By 2020, there were 568 jacket foundation units that had been built in Europe, constituting about 9.9% of the market as a whole [16].

The selection of the suitable foundation types for an offshore wind farm is primarily driven by economic factors and is often made during the initial design phase. Hence, it is crucial to be able to generate cost estimates for various foundation designs based on limited information. Fischer [43] offered a simplified cost estimate of 2 EUR/kg for monopiles and 4–6 EUR/kg for jackets, elucidating the preference for monopiles due to their more frequent usage compared to other types. Due to the higher fabrication expenses associated with conical sections, the estimated costs of towers range from 2–3 EUR/kg. In practice, economic comparisons between foundation types necessitate more intricate cost functions. For instance, while the lower mass of jackets is advantageous for the lifting capacities needed during installation, their larger dimensions result in greater storage requirements. Additionally, it is worth considering that fabrication costs for jackets could significantly decrease with large-scale installation, potentially due to the advancement of enhanced assembly strategies. In practical terms, this means that, when estimating the cost of foundations, the actual cost might be 15% to 25% higher or lower than the initial estimate. This acknowledgment of a margin of error is common in various engineering and construction contexts, where early estimates are made based on preliminary information, and the accuracy improves as more detailed designs are developed [44].

3. Prospects for Offshore Wind

In offshore wind, floating foundations are a relatively new development. Most offshore wind resources are located at depths of more than 60 m, making them unsuitable for conventional bottom-fixed foundations. The winds are stronger and more reliable in these deeper, farther offshore locations. Higher capacity factors can be achieved by utilizing these ideal wind resources without being constrained by sea depth thanks to floating foundations [45].

Europe has plenty of wind-producing regions and shallow waters, making it the perfect place to install bottom-fixed foundations to meet the growing demand for offshore wind. However, there is limited space with comparable characteristics in places like Japan and the US West Coast. This has spurred interest in floating solutions, which could accelerate the worldwide shift to green energy by accelerating offshore wind expansion in difficult deepwater regions [46].

A construction intended to float and be supported by an anchoring mechanism is called a floating foundation. According to Xu et al. [47] the oil and gas (O&G) industry is the source of the common designs of floating foundations. An example of one of these ideas is shown in Figure 10. These styles consist of the following:

- Spar: Spar is a long, thin, and cylindrical buoy that stays above water by using ballast. The significant weight of the structure offers stability in dynamic waters deeper than 120 m, making it easier to construct than alternative floating foundations [37,47].

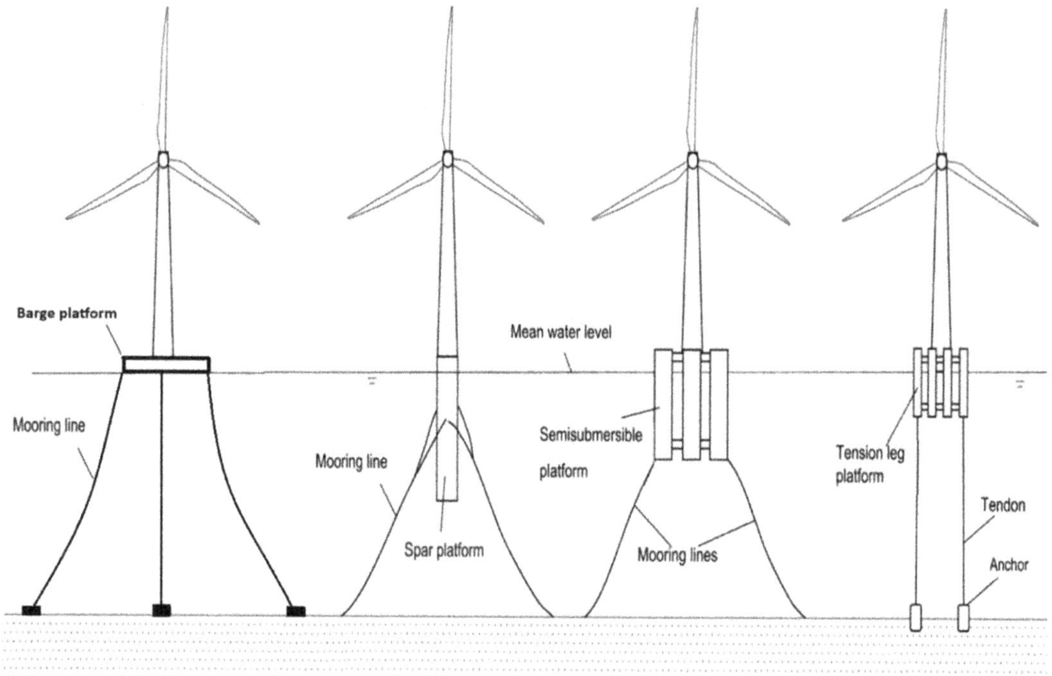

Figure 10. Schematic diagram of the barge, spar floating, SSP, and TLP foundations ([24], modified by authors).

Numerous experimental and numerical studies have been conducted to evaluate the performance of spar-type offshore wind turbines. These comprehensive investigations span various disciplines, encompassing aerodynamics, hydrodynamics, elastic multi-structure dynamics, and automated control [48,49]. The aerodynamics of floating offshore wind turbines (FOWTs) are commonly simulated using numerical methods such as BEM, GDW, and CFD [50]. Furthermore, coupled dynamics analysis and simulation tools have been developed for FOWTs [51].

The FAST platform, developed by NREL, stands out as the most frequently utilized and recognized numerical simulation software for floating offshore wind turbines (FOWTs) [52]. Moreover, experimental studies have been carried out to assess the performance of spar-type FOWTs.

The DeepCwind project validated offshore wind energy modeling methods through the testing of three prototype floating wind turbines at a 1/50th scale in a wave basin. These prototypes included a semisubmersible, a tension-leg platform, and a spar buoy [53]. Despite using the Froude number to compare wave-induced dynamics between models and prototypes, achieving aerodynamic similarity was challenging due to the Reynolds scale difference. Consequently, in numerous instances, a disk with a comparable drag force was employed to simulate the wind rotor.

The Ocean Basin Laboratory at Martinek conducted a Froude-scaled model test of the Hywind spar-type floating offshore wind turbine (FOWT) at a scale of 1:47, whereby they assessed its performance in various sea states [54]. Additionally, the State Key Laboratory of Ocean Engineering at Shanghai Jiao Tong University developed a 1:40 scale model of the OC3-Hywind spar, which was constructed in the DHI Offshore Wave Basin in Hørsholm, Denmark. A comparative study evaluated the experimental and numerical results that were obtained using the FAST code [55]. Moreover, computational research was conducted to analyze the design of the Hywind spar, which was equipped with a 5 MW turbine, in the time domain, covering aspects such as platform motions, mooring dynamics, tower elastic responses, blade–rotor dynamics, and aeroloading [56].

- Semi-Submersible Platform (SSP): This platform floats above the water's surface while remaining partially submerged. Mooring lines are used by both spar and SSP to keep a loose connection to the seafloor. Suitable for water depths up to 120 m, SSP is a flexible sort of floating foundation [37].

As the offshore wind industry expands into deeper waters (50–300 m), the semi-submersible platform is gaining popularity [57]. Compared to spars, semi-submersibles have shallower drafts, enabling quayside assembly and wet towing, which is a significant advantage. Collu [58] enhanced the support structure of the Dutch tri-floater by implementing several improvements. These included dividing the foundation's columns into three compartments with the addition of two horizontal bulkheads. Furthermore, T-/H-section and radius ring stiffeners were incorporated to augment the foundation's integrity and stiffness on both local and global scales.

Roddier et al. [59] introduced the WindFloat, another prominent semisub-type floating offshore wind turbine (FOWT). Similar to the Dutch trifloater, the WindFloat features a foundation with three columns. The wind turbine is situated in one of these columns, while the remaining columns are ballasted to uphold their vertical alignment. Each column incorporates a permanent water ballast system at its base to regulate the structure's draft to the desired level. Additionally, an active water ballast system is situated atop the permanent ballast to facilitate water transfer between columns.

The active mechanism of the floating structure dynamically adjusts the weight of each column to ensure the wind turbine maintains its vertical position amidst fluctuations in wind speed and direction.

Semisubmersible FOWTs require coupled dynamics studies for proper design. A recent study investigated the performance deviations of a floating offshore wind turbine (FOWT) with a broken mooring line, utilizing the OC4 DeepCwind semisubmersible as a benchmark [60]. Another study evaluated the overall performance of the OC4 and WindFloat semisubmersible FOWT hulls under identical environmental and control conditions. This investigation employed a fully coupled simulation program, encompassing the turbine, floater, and mooring system, as well as featuring a 5 MW wind turbine and a catenary mooring configuration [61]. Additionally, a proposal has been made for a semisubmersible floating foundation housing multiple wind turbines, along with a coupled dynamic analytical tool [62,63].

- Tension Leg Platform (TLP): TLPs are well known in the O&G sector, and they are commonly used as FOWT substructures. TLP wind turbines have significantly lower heave, roll, and pitch motions than other floating foundations. It might drastically reduce manufacturing costs in deep oceans compared to stationary platforms. A seafloor-supported underwater platform is supported vertically by tendons. TLP is a lightweight, highly stable construction that can be used in water up to 120 m deep. But, TLP is not employed much because of its complicated and expensive mooring method [37,47].

Zhao et al. [64] introduced a novel multicolumn Tension Leg Platform (TLP) foundation called Windstar TLP, which was designed specifically for the NREL offshore 5 MW reference turbine. This design mimicked the site-specific environmental conditions of the OC3-Hywind. On the other hand, Bachynski and Moan [65] conducted the design and analysis of five parametric single-column Tension Leg Platform Wind Turbines (TLPWTs) under varying wind and wave conditions. They employed Simo, Reflex, and Aerodyn numerical tools for a comprehensive coupled analysis, and they estimated the platform movements and structural loads on both turbine components and tendons.

Nihei and Fujioka [66] presented tank test findings for a 1:100 scale Tension Leg Platform-type floating offshore wind turbine (TLP-type FOWT) equipped with three revolving blades. These tests were conducted under combined wave and wind conditions.

Their results indicate that the interaction between the blades and the wind reduces the pitch motion of the floater and the vibrations in the mooring lines. However, the dynamic coupling effects between the hull or tendon and the turbine necessitate modeling, as they can induce significant shifts in the initial natural frequencies of the TLP motion due to the tower's elastic behavior. Additionally, a recent study conducted an analysis of the fatigue life of a TLP offshore wind turbine in the time domain, wherein they considered various factors such as blade–rotor dynamics, mooring dynamics, and platform motions [67].

- Barge: The barge-type FOWT uses wind turbines mounted on a shallow-draft barge frame. The barge type is stable because of its broad waterplane surface. Similar to semisubmersibles, quayside assembly and wet towing are possible. The barge-type foundation has the advantage of being simple to manufacture. Barge-type wind turbines are typically employed in calm seas, such as harbors, due to their sensitivity to wave motions.

There are limited barge-type floating offshore wind turbine (FOWT) systems in existence, including the ITI Energy Barge [68]. Among them, Floatgen, designed by the French company Ideol, stands out. Floatgen employs a concrete, ring-shaped support structure, and it features a moon pool, which is also referred to as a damping pool, to mitigate wave-induced vibrations [57].

Developed in the 1970s, floating foundations for offshore wind were put to the test in real life in 2008 in Italian waters using an 80 kW turbine mounted atop a TLP. Subsequently, a number of pilot projects [69] were undertaken in the US, Europe, and Asia.

By the end of 2020, there was only about 100 MW of floating offshore wind power in the world, mostly in the UK, Portugal, and Japan. However, the Global Wind Energy Council (GWEC [20]) predicts a notable increase, calculating that 6.5 GW might be installed by 2030. This comprises large-scale 1 GW projects in Asia and Europe [20].

The 2023 Global Offshore Wind Report [70] heralds a significant advancement in the worldwide expansion of offshore wind energy. According to their analysis, a staggering 380 GW of offshore wind capacity is forecasted to be installed across 32 markets in the next decade (2023–2032). Notably, nearly half of this growth is anticipated to originate from the APAC region, with Europe contributing 41%, North America 9%, and LATAM 1%. IRENA estimates that, between 2011 and 2024, the total installed costs of floating wind projects could potentially decrease by 70%, i.e., from 14,161 to 4310 USD/kW. Furthermore, as shown in Figure 11, by 2024, these improvements should result in a more appealing Levelized Cost of Energy (LCOE) of roughly 0.13 USD/kWh, a considerable drop from 0.88 USD/kWh in 2011 [71].

The projected development of new offshore wind capacity in the APAC region from 2023 to 2032 is poised to mitigate approximately 650 Mt CO_2 emissions annually. However, GWEC Market Intelligence predicts potential bottlenecks in all regions except China by 2026. To overcome these challenges, substantial additional investments and enhanced global cooperation will be imperative. Using floating offshore turbines (FOT) in deeper water will significantly contribute to mitigating CO_2 emissions as the stronger winds and fewer environmental constraints allow for higher power output and larger turbine sizes, thus resulting in reduced CO_2 emissions. This necessitates further study on linking the mooring lines of floating foundations to the seabed.

Delving into discussions about offshore wind farms and their intricate components, as well as the dynamic trajectory of offshore wind development, highlights the critical need for innovative solutions to meet the sector's changing demands. Traditional foundation systems are becoming increasingly ineffective as offshore wind farms grow in size, in their distance from shore, and in their water depth. In light of this, this study proposes using helical piles as mooring line anchors and presents an optimization framework that takes into account inclination angle and plate position to improve bearing capacity. These advancements not only address industry challenges, but also pave the way for sustainable and efficient offshore wind energy deployment, which aligns with the overall goals of this research project. The following section will detail this study.

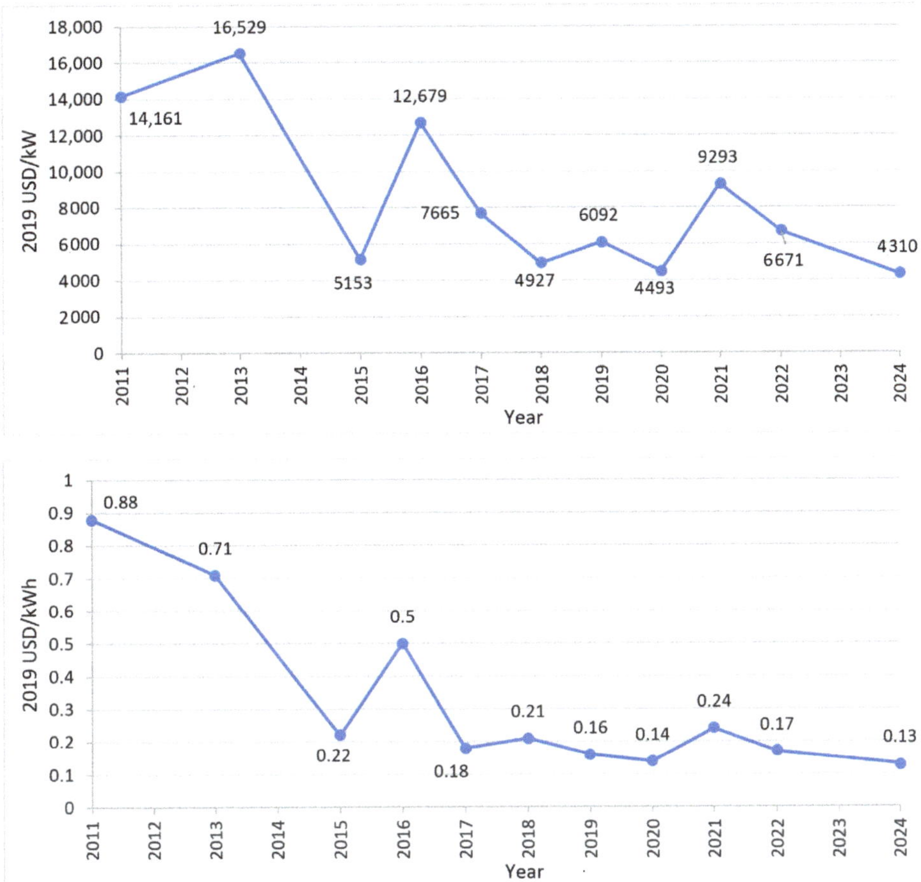

Figure 11. Lifecycle cost of energy (LCOE), installed cost, and capacity factor for floating offshore wind, worldwide trends, 2011–2024 ([71] modified by authors). (**A**) Total installed cost and (**B**) levelized cost of electricity.

4. Utilizing Helical Piles: A Solution for Anchoring Mooring Lines

4.1. Introduction

Helical piles are primarily utilized to counteract tension forces arising from overturning moments and uplift in different structures. As such, they have been proposed as a viable substitute for driven piles in offshore applications, offering substantial uplift capacity thanks to the anchoring effect of the helix. However, there are currently no established standards for evaluating the suitability of helical piles in offshore settings [72].

The direction and intensity of the load transferred to an anchor depend on the type of mooring, which is typically categorized into three types: (i) catenary, where the load inclination ranges from 75–90 degrees from the vertical line; (ii) taut (or semi-taut), with an inclination of 45–60 degrees from the vertical line; and (iii) tension leg, which has an inclination of 0–20 degrees from the vertical line [73].

Helical piles are a form of composite-type anchors that combine plate- and pile-type elements. These piles typically consist of a steel circular shaft attached to one or more helices. During installation, compressive force and torque are applied at the head to screw them into the ground, resulting in reduced underwater noise compared to traditional hammering methods. Similar to plate anchors, helical piles withstand tensile loading by utilizing the soil bearing resistance above the topmost helix [72,74,75]. When subjected to lateral loading, helical piles exhibit behavior similar to straight shafted piles, as noted by Ding et al. [76], albeit with some improvement due to the rotation of the helices. However, the complete mobilization of plate resistance may transpire if pile rotation aligns the loading direction with the shaft. One of the primary hurdles in employing helical piles offshore is the necessity to scale up from the relatively modest dimensions utilized in onshore applications thus far, as highlighted by Sharif et al. [77] and Davidson et al. [78]. Overcoming this challenge will necessitate installation tools capable of applying large torques of several MN.m. Nonetheless, this obstacle can be addressed by employing groups of smaller helical piles, as suggested by Bradshaw et al. [79].

This study utilized the PLAXIS 3D program to evaluate the efficacy of helical piles with small and large shaft diameters, and this featured two helical plates: one anchored at the base and the other situated at various positions along the shaft. The investigation focused on assessing their ability to withstand uplift loads imposed by mooring lines in sandy soil within the context of floating offshore wind systems. Given the intricacies involved and challenges associated with field and laboratory experiments, numerical analysis emerged as a compelling approach for conducting a comparative parametric study of the specified piles in this research [80].

4.2. Plaxis Validation

The primary aim of this section is to validate the precise simulation capabilities of the Plaxis 3D program in replicating the behavioral characteristics associated with pullout load and the relationship between pullout load and upward movement for piles in sandy soil. This validation process is essential to fulfill the overarching objective of obtaining results within a parametric study, thus facilitating the comparison of reliability and accuracy across the various parameters under investigation.

The numerical modeling assumptions utilized in the 3D Finite Element Method (FEM) were first validated against field case study data and centrifuge test concerning helical piles subjected to pullout loading in sand, as detailed by [79,80]. The parameters required for the HS constitutive model were deduced from the soil parameters provided in the case study. In situations where certain parameters were not directly available, they were estimated based on the in situ relative density derived from the case study, employing the correlations outlined in Table 4 [81].

Table 4. The soil material parameters utilized in the Finite Element Method (FEM) study (compiled by authors based on [81]).

Soil Parameter	Sand Parameters Corresponding to Relative Density (D_r)
Drainage type	Drained
Oedometer stiffness, E_{oed}^{ref} $(\mathrm{kN/m^2})$, at P_{ref} = 100 kPa	$60{,}000D_r$
Secant stiffness, E_{50}^{ref} $(\mathrm{kN/m^2})$, at P_{ref} = 100 kPa	$60{,}000D_r$
Unload/reload stiffness, E_{ur}^{ref} $(\mathrm{kN/m^2})$, at P_{ref} = 100 kPa	$180{,}000D_r$
Shear modulus at very small strains, G_o^{ref} $(\mathrm{kN/m^2})$	$60{,}000 + 68{,}000D_r$
Reference shear strain (at $G_s = 0.722G_0$), $\gamma_{0.7}$	$(2 - D_r)/10{,}000$
Friction angle, $\varnothing_p'$ (degrees)	$28 + 12.5D_r$
Effective cohesion intercept c'ref (kPa)	-
Angle of dilation, Ψ (degrees)	$-2 + 12.5D_r$
Failure ratio, $\mathbf{R_f}$ $(-)$	$1 - D_r/8$
Unload–reload Poisson's ratio, vur	0.2
Power of stress level dependency of stiffness, m $(-)$	$0.7 - (100D_r/320)$
Saturated unit weight, $\gamma_{\mathbf{sat}}$ $(\mathrm{kN/m^3})$	$19 + 1.6 \times D_r$
Unsaturated unit weight, $\gamma_{\mathbf{unsat}}$ $(\mathrm{kN/m^3})$	$15 + 4D_r$

Plaxis 3D (V20), a specialized finite element analysis software tailored for geotechnical engineering tasks, provides a comprehensive suite of elements, degrees of freedom, and crucial functionalities necessary for effective numerical simulations. The software leverages a variety of element types to precisely depict various aspects of geotechnical models. For instance, 10-node tetrahedral elements are utilized to represent three-dimensional soil structures accurately, while 3-node line beam elements are employed for modeling the shafts of helical and granular anchor piles. In addition to these, 6-node plate elements are adept at simulating helices and laboratory model walls, while 12-node interface elements allow for a realistic representation of the soil–structure interactions along model boundaries. Interfaces are particularly vital in Plaxis 3D as they capture the intricate interplay between helical piles and the surrounding soils. They enable the transfer of loads and deformations, thus facilitating a comprehensive examination of pile–soil interface behavior. In this study, the material model employed for the interfaces aligns with that used for the adjacent soil model. In our analysis, we implemented, for interfaces between the shaft and pile soil, a specific interface reduction factor (R_{inter}) of 0.7 for the field study of Salem and Hussein [82] and 0.51 for centrifuge test of Davidson et al. [83]. For interfaces between the pile soil and the surrounding site soil around the pile, the R_{inter} was set at 1. Additionally, we activated gap closure to enhance the accuracy of the interface behavior during numerical simulation.

Plaxis 3D offers a wide array of material models designed to accurately depict the behavior of soil. These models, including Hardening Soil, Hardening Soil Small, Mohr–Coulomb, and Soft Soil, account for elasticity, plasticity, and hardening characteristics. By incorporating these models, the software enables realistic material responses to applied loads, enhancing the fidelity of the analysis.

The Hardening Soil model was chosen for this study owing to its advanced capabilities and reliable performance. Distinguished by its ability to simulate both soft and stiff soils, this model surpasses the Mohr–Coulomb model in several aspects. It incorporates stress-dependent stiffness, accommodates stiffness reduction due to shear strain, and offers a nuanced treatment of dilatancy and yield. With a wide range of defining parameters, which can be derived from laboratory testing or field experience, the Hardening Soil model has proven efficacy in simulating soil behavior across diverse conditions. Its extensive utilization in numerous research studies attests to its effectiveness and versatility [84–88].

In the Hardening Soil model, achieving precise soil deformation modeling necessitates the integration of three distinct stiffness parameters (all of which are applied at a specific reference stress level): Triaxial Loading Stiffness (E_{50}), Triaxial Unloading–Reloading Stiffness (E_{ur}), and Oedometer Loading Modulus (E_{oed}). This combination of parameters enables users to differentiate between loading and unloading–reloading stiffnesses. Such differentiation significantly enhances the model's capacity to accurately depict the soil's response across diverse loading conditions and its intricate behavior under varying stress states [87].

The current numerical analysis comprises four distinct calculation phases. Initially, the first phase involves simulating the initial geo-stress induced solely by the weight of the soil, leading to a K_0 consolidation of the ground, where K_0 is approximated as $(1 - \sin \varphi)$. Moving to the second phase, the simulation focuses on the effect of pile installation. This phase idealizes the process of installing displacement piles as a cavity expansion problem, one that is primarily influenced by penetration resistance in sand [89]. During pile installation, the helical blade, coupled with the closed-end shaft, displaces the soil radially, forming a cavity. This process induces stress changes and densification within the soil mass, particularly in cohesionless soil. Therefore, employing cavity expansion by volumetric strain is an appropriate approach for modeling the installation effect [90]. To replicate the increase in stress around the pile, the pile cavity can be expanded before loading by applying positive volumetric strains [91,92]. In this study, cavity expansion through volumetric strain was executed before activating the pile elements. A collective volumetric strain of 2% for a case study of the Sharkia Governorate, Egypt, as well as 16% for the centrifuge test undertaken at the University of Dundee, was deemed appropriate for the outcomes. Figure 12 illustrates a cross-section of the typical displacement contours following cavity expansion when it is conducted in the second calculation phase. The disturbed soil around the shaft is activated; subsequently, the shaft, plate elements, and interface elements are activated in the third calculation phase. The final stage entails simulating the application of load on the pile head.

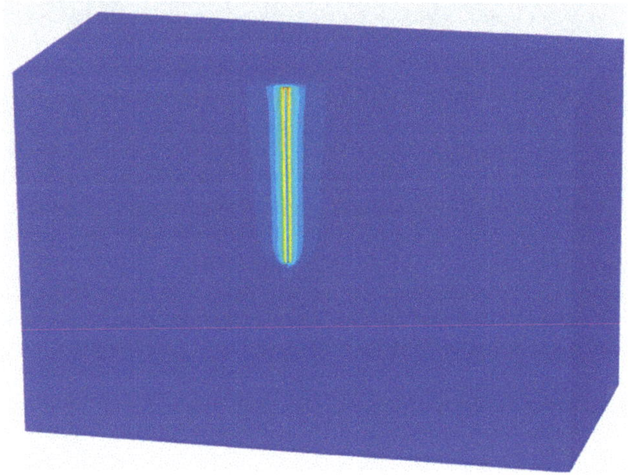

Figure 12. Cross-section displaying typical displacement contours subsequent to cavity expansion that is conducted during the second calculation phase.

4.2.1. The Case Study of Sharkia Governorate, Egypt (According to Salem and Hussein [82])

Salem and Hussein [82] documented the performance of helical piles from field trials conducted in dense sands (site 4) in Sharkia Governorate, Egypt. The helical piles were installed to depths (L) of 1.9 m, with a pile shaft diameter (Dc) of 45 mm, as well as two helical plates with diameters (Dh) of 0.2 m and thicknesses (th) of 10 mm. The spacing between the helical plates measured approximately two and a half times the diameter of the helix, which is denoted as $S/Dh = 2.50$, where S represents the helix spacing and Dh signifies the helix diameter. A summary of the helical pile configuration is presented in Table 5. The soil at the site was determined to be dense sand for modeling based on the available ground investigation data. The phreatic water level was observed at 2 m below ground level. A summary of the soil properties reported by Salem and Hussein is shown in Table 6.

Table 5. Helical pile configuration for verification of a field study [82] and centrifuge test [83].

Case Study	Load Type	Shaft	Helical Plate		Helical Plate Number, N	Depth (m)	Plate Spacing Ratio (S/Dh)
		Dc (mm)	Dh (mm)	th (mm)			
Field study [82]	Pullout	45	200	10	2	1.9	2.5
Centrifuge test [83]	Pullout	880	1700	110	2	13	2

Table 6. Soil parameters for verification of the field study of Salem and Hussein [82].

Model Parameter		HS		HS Small	
Symbol	**Soil Parameters**	**Disturbed Sand around Shaft (Drained Behavior)**	**Sand (Drained Behavior)**	**Disturbed Sand around Shaft (Drained Behavior)**	**Sand (Drained Behavior)**
γ_{sat} (kN/m^3)	Saturated unit weight	20	20	20	20
γ_{unsat} (kN/m^3)	Unsaturated unit weight	18	18	18	18
E_{50}^{ref} (kN/m^2)	Reference secant stiffness	30,000	46,700	30,000	46,700
E_{oed}^{ref} (kN/m^2)	Reference tangent stiffness	30,000	46,700	30,000	46,700
E_{ur}^{ref} (kN/m^2)	Reference unloading–reloading stiffness	90,000	140,000	90,000	140,000
C' (kN/m^2)	Cohesion	0.3	0.3	0.3	0.3
$\varnothing'$ (°)	Internal friction angle	34.25	39	34.25	39
Ψ (°)	Dilatancy angle	6	12	6	12
v_{ur} (−)	Unloading/reloading Poisson's ratio	0.2	0.2	0.2	0.2
m (−)	Exponential power	0.544	0.457	0.544	0.457
R_f (−)	Failure ratio	0.938	0.903	0.938	0.903
G_o^{ref} (kN/m^2)	Shear modulus at very small strains			94,000	112,900
$\gamma_{0.7}$ (−)	Reference shear strain (at $G_s = 0.722G_0$)			0.00015	0.00012

The average relative densities (D_r) obtained for Site 4 were approximately 78%. The load application at the pile head was executed through displacement control, thus ensuring the maximum displacement matched that of the field test. The helical pile, composed of steel, was modeled as a linear elastic material with the following properties: Modulus of Elasticity (E) = 2×10^5 MN/m^2, Unit Weight (γ) = 78.5 kN/m^3, and Poisson's ratio (ν) = 0.3. A summary of the helical pile configuration is provided in Table 5. To ensure that the boundaries had no effect on the studied problem, the model dimensions were taken as presented in Figure 13.

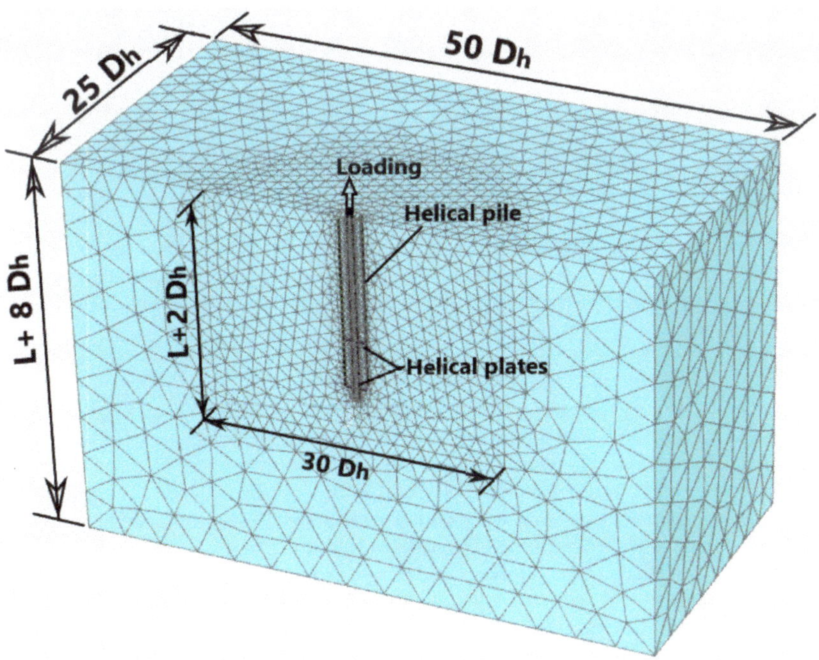

Figure 13. Typical mesh generated for helical pile modeling in 3D FEM and dimensions.

4.2.2. Centrifuge Test Undertaken at the University of Dundee (According to Davidson et al. [78,83])

The numerical results were also validated against small-scale centrifuge tests conducted at the University of Dundee (UoD), as detailed by Davidson et al. [83]. These tests involved the installation of three screw anchors in very dense sand (referred to as VD, with an average relative density (D_r) of 84%) and one in medium dense sand (MD, D_r = 57%). Conducted in dry sand at 48 g, the experiments replicated the stress field that would be obtained in saturated sand at 80 g, as justified by Li et al. [93]. Specifically, our study focused on validating numerical results against the U2VD test, which featured two helices spaced at two helix diameters in very dense sand, thus closely resembling our study conditions. Table 7 provides an overview of the soil properties. At prototype scale (a scaling factor of 80 g), the helix diameter (*Dh*) of all model anchors installed in very dense sand was 1.7 m, with a core diameter (*Dc*) of 0.88 m. A summary of the helical pile configuration is provided in Table 5. The installation process and uplift loading in the centrifuge tests were intentionally slow to simulate the drained installation and loading conditions typical of offshore environments.

Table 7. Soil parameters for verification of the centrifuge test of Davidson et al. [83].

Model Parameter		HS		HS Small	
Symbol	**Soil Parameters**	**Disturbed Sand around Shaft (Drained Behavior)**	**Sand (Drained Behavior)**	**Disturbed Sand around Shaft (Drained Behavior)**	**Sand (Drained Behavior)**
γ_{sat} (kN/m^3)	Saturated unit weight	19.24	20.3	19.24	20.3
γ_{unsat} (kN/m^3)	Unsaturated unit weight	18	18.4	18	18.4
E_{50}^{ref} (kN/m^2)	Reference secant stiffness	21,000	50,400	21,000	50,400
E_{oed}^{ref} (kN/m^2)	Reference tangent stiffness	21,000	50,400	21,000	50,400
E_{ur}^{ref} (kN/m^2)	Reference unloading–reloading stiffness	63,000	151,200	63,000	151,200
C' (kN/m^2)	Cohesion	0.3	0.3	0.3	0.3
$\varnothing'$ (°)	Internal friction angle	32	38.5	32	38.5
Ψ (°)	Dilatancy angle	0	8.5	0	8.5
υ_{ur} (−)	Unloading/reloading Poisson's ratio	0.2	0.2	0.2	0.2
m (−)	Exponential power	0.59	0.434	0.59	0.434
R_f (−)	Failure ratio	0.938	0.895	0.938	0.895
G_o^{ref} (kN/m^2)	Shear modulus at very small strains			83,800	117,120
$\gamma_{0.7}$ (−)	Reference shear strain (at $G_s = 0.722G_0$)			0.00017	0.00012

Figure 14 illustrates the outcomes of the pullout loading simulation, showing generally favorable agreement with the predictions of behavior for the HS model, albeit with minor discrepancies. These differences were attributed to the simplification of the relative density distribution employed in the simulation.

4.3. Problem Description

The objective of the present study is to investigate the performance of a helical pile with small and large shaft diameters in supporting the mooring line of floating offshore wind systems. To achieve this goal, a helical pile with a length of 15 m, a small shaft diameter of 12 cm, and a large shaft diameter of 0.88 m were considered. The pile was equipped with two helical plates: one at the bottom to support the pull-out load and one at the top, which was positioned between 0.5 and 13 m from the seabed to optimize the best location. The helical plates had a diameter of 0.6 m for a small shaft diameter and 1.7 m for a large shaft diameter, as well as a thickness of 2.54 cm for a small shaft diameter and 11 cm for a large shaft diameter. The sea water depth was assumed to be 150 m. The load was applied at different angles from the vertical line, including 0, 20, 40, and 60 degrees, thus representing various scenarios of mooring line configurations. The soil considered in this study was dense sand. The Hardening Soil (HS) model was employed to simulate the soil behavior, with its parameters presented in Table 6 for a small shaft diameter and Table 7 for a large shaft diameter.

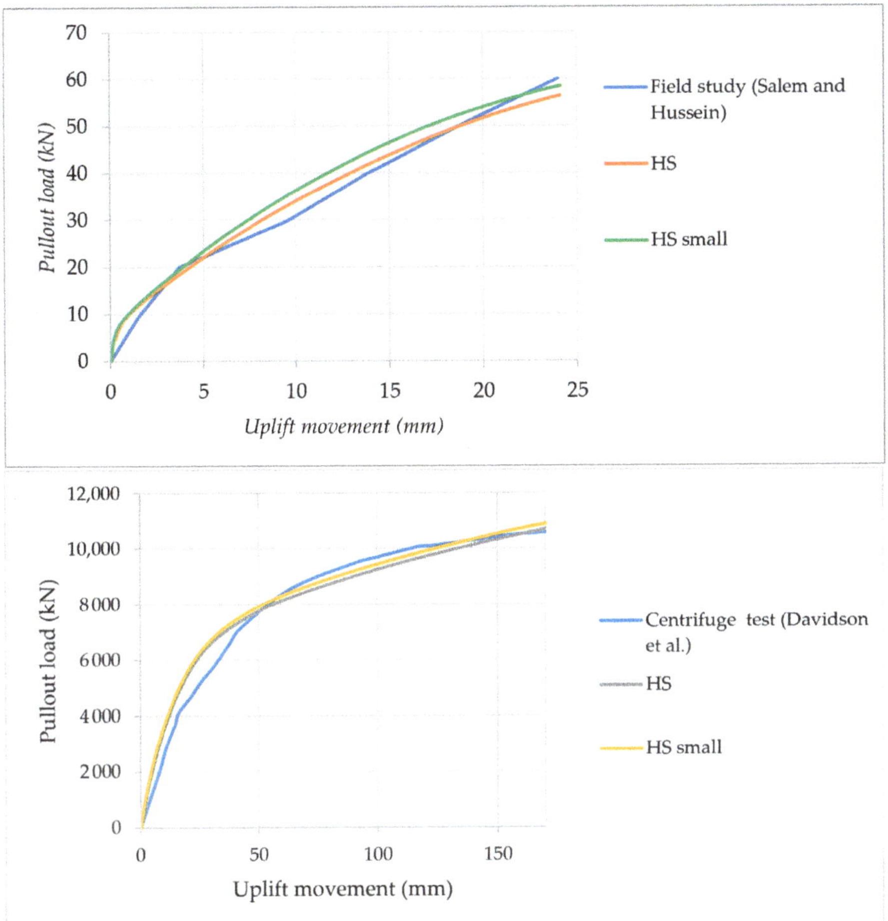

(A)

(B)

Figure 14. Load–displacement curves of the Calibrated Numerical Model using Plaxis 3D. (**A**) Field-tested pile in sand [82] and (**B**) centrifuge test [83].

4.4. Methodology

The present study follows a methodology similar to that of Alnmr et al. [94,95]. Figure 15 provides a cross-sectional view of reinforced soil featuring helical piles. The ratio of the model width to the pile diameter was designed to be around 50, as shown in Figure 13, which is considered adequate for minimizing the influence of boundary effects on the results. A 3D model is utilized to calculate the load (F) for different locations of the top plate of the helical pile (Zh) and various inclination angles (i).

The current numerical analysis consisted of four calculation phases. In the first phase, we simulated the initial geo-stress caused by the soil's weight, leading to a K_0 consolidation of the ground, where K_0 was approximated as $1 - \sin \varphi$. The second phase focused on simulating pile installation, which was idealized as a cavity expansion problem influenced by penetration resistance in sand. During this phase, the helical blade and closed-end shaft displaces the soil radially, creating a cavity and inducing stress changes and densification, particularly in cohesionless soil. Cavity expansion through volumetric strain was used to model this effect. Positive volumetric strains were applied to replicate the increased stress around the pile before loading. In this study, we used a volumetric strain of 2% for the Sharkia Governorate, Egypt case study, which represented the small shaft diameter, and 16% for the centrifuge test at the University of Dundee, which represented the large shaft diameter. The disturbed soil around the shaft was activated; subsequently, the shaft with the required diameter, plate elements in the required location, and interface elements were activated in the third calculation phase. The final stage involved simulating the application of load with the required inclination on the pile head. The soil parameters are shown in Table 6 for the small shaft diameter, as well as in Table 7 for the large shaft diameter.

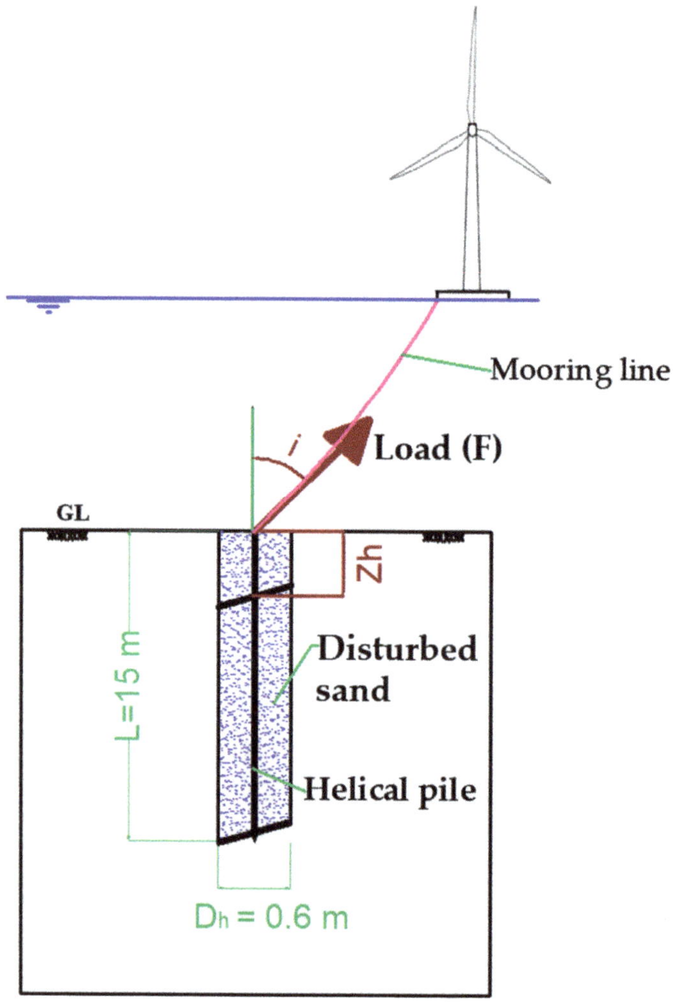

Figure 15. Cross-sectional view of reinforced soil with a helical pile.

Boundary and Initial Conditions

In the model, the lateral boundaries are considered to have zero horizontal displacements, while the bottom exhibits zero horizontal and vertical displacements. This assumption mirrors the natural soil behavior, where the soil surrounding a structure at a considerable horizontal distance acts as horizontal fixities [96]. After inputting all parameters, the Plaxis 3D program generated a mesh, as shown in Figure 13. A coarse mesh was utilized, with refinement concentrated around the piles. The analysis employed approximately 30,850 elements and 48,176 nodes.

In this study, an initial water depth of 150 m was assumed. The initial stresses were then calculated using Jacky's formula: $K_0 = 1 - \sin\varphi$.

4.5. Results and Discussion

This study investigated the impact of load inclination (*i*) variations on the pullout load behavior of helical piles. Four different load inclinations (*i*)—0, 20, 40, and 60 degrees—were examined. For each load inclination (*i*), the location of the top helical plate (*Zh*) varied from 0.5 to 13 m along the pile, starting from the seabed level.

4.5.1. Small-Shaft-Diameter Helical Piles

Impact of Load Inclination (*i*) on Pullout Behavior

Figure 16 presents the load–displacement curves that depict the pullout behavior of different load inclinations (*i*). These curves offer a visual representation of how the piles react to upward movement and illustrate the variations in pullout loads corresponding to different load inclinations.

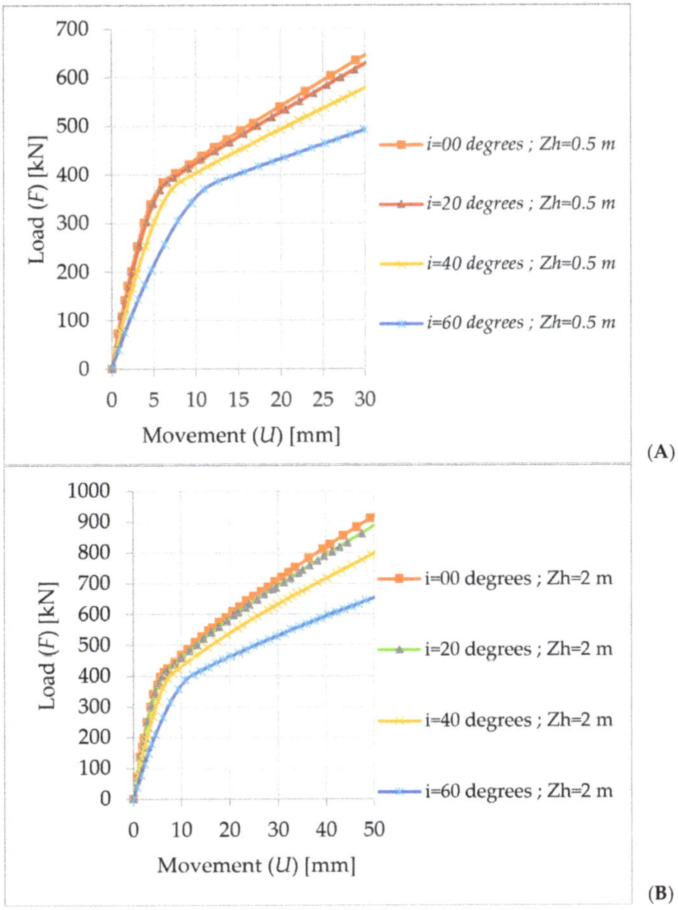

Figure 16. *Cont.*

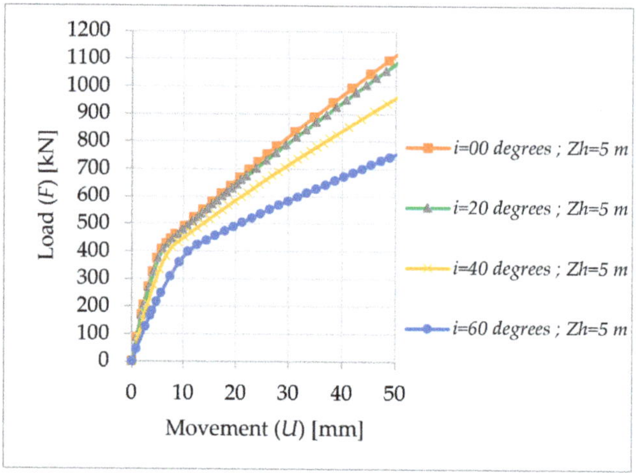

(C)

Figure 16. Pullout behavior of small-shaft-diameter helical piles at different inclination loads: (**A**) $Zh/Z = 0.034$, (**B**) $Zh/Z = 0.136$, and (**C**) $Zh/Z = 0.34$.

The investigation was aimed at assessing how varying the load inclination affects the pullout load required to resist movements of 10, 25, and 50 mm. The findings, illustrated in Figure 16, reveal that increasing the load inclination results in a decrease in the pullout load, irrespective of the helical plate's position. This suggests that piles subjected to axial forces are more effective in resisting movement. However, it is crucial to note that, beyond a certain angle of load inclination corresponding to the movement value, there was a significant decrease in load capacity. This critical angle diminished as the allowable movement and the ratio of Zh to Z increased. Here, Z represents the distance from the seabed to the helical pile at the toe, which in this study is 14.7 m, as depicted in Figure 17. Table 8 presents, based on movement and the Zh/Z ratio, the critical inclination angles that were present after a substantial decrease in load capacity occurred. Helical piles are particularly useful for tension leg mooring line types, but they can also benefit taut (or semi-taut) mooring line types since their bearing capacity can be optimized at specific inclination degrees. Helical piles are especially advantageous for mooring line types with tension legs, but because their bearing capacity may be optimized at particular inclination degrees, they can also be advantageous for taut or semi-taut mooring line types.

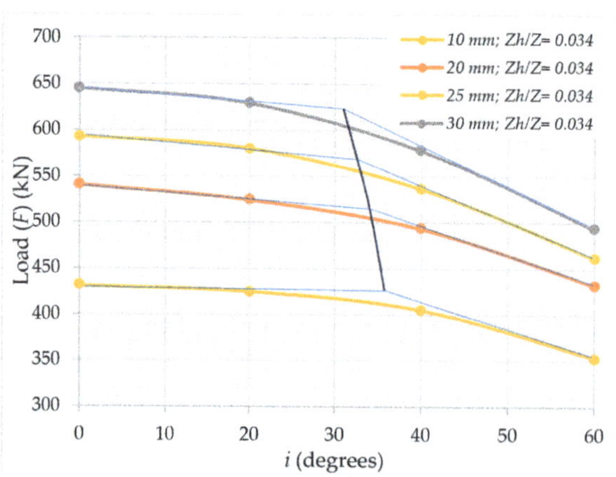

(A)

Figure 17. *Cont.*

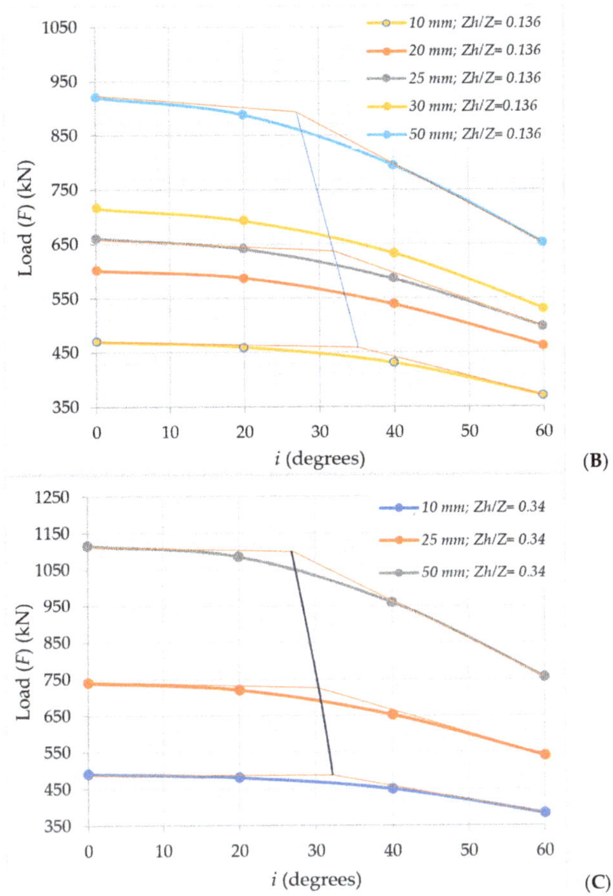

Figure 17. The relations between load capacity and load inclination angle of small-shaft-diameter helical piles at different allowable movements: (**A**) $Zh/Z = 0.034$, (**B**) $Zh/Z = 0.136$, and (**C**) $Zh/Z = 0.34$.

Table 8. The critical inclination angles of small-shaft-diameter helical piles that were present following a substantial decrease in load capacity based on movement and Zh/Z.

	Movement (mm)		
Zh*/*h	**10**	**25**	**50**
0.034	35.5	32.5	
0.136	35	32	27
0.34	32.1	30.2	26.9

Figure 18 displays the iso-surface displacements along the helical piles. The decrease in capacity with increasing load inclination was due to two primary reasons: (1) the effectiveness of the bottom helical plate decreased as the inclination angle increased, and (2) the helical plates were not designed to resist lateral loads effectively, especially given the relatively small diameter of the helical shaft. As a result, the passive load was insufficient to significantly enhance the pile's capacity. Figure 17 illustrates that the effectiveness of the helical plates diminished as the load inclination angle increased.

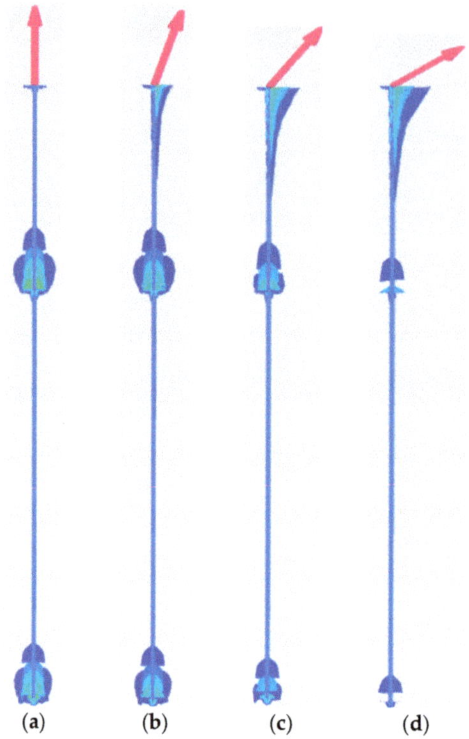

Figure 18. The iso surface displacements along the small-shaft-diameter helical piles: (**a**) $i = 0°$, (**b**) $i = 20°$, (**c**) $i = 40°$, and (**d**) $i = 60°$.

Based on these findings, it is advisable to limit the inclination angle of the mooring line attached to the small-diameter helical pile to the values shown in Table 8. This restriction ensures sufficient load-bearing capacity and stability for the piles. Adhering to this inclination threshold optimizes the balance between frictional resistance, contact area, and pullout load, thereby enhancing the overall performance and reliability of the pile foundation system.

Impact of Top Helical Plate Location (*Zh*) on the Pullout Load (*F*) Behavior

The investigation in this section is aimed at assessing the impact of the top helical plate's position (*Zh*) on its capacity to withstand pullout loads and resist movement. A detailed examination of the recorded loads is presented in Table 9, while Figure 19 visually illustrates the load behavior across various helical plate locations (*Zh*). This offers valuable insights into their response under pullout loading conditions and underscores the variations in load resistance linked to different load inclination angles.

Table 9. Load capacity at 10 and 25 mm movements of small-shaft-diameter helical piles for different Zh/Z and load inclination angles.

	U = 10 mm				U = 25 mm			
Zh/Z \ i (°)	0	20	40	60	0	20	40	60
0.034014	430	423	405	350	591	580	538	464
0.068027	440	432	412	360	605	590	542	468
0.102041	458	450	425	365	628	610	560	484
0.136054	469	460	431	370	660	642	590	496

Table 9. *Cont.*

Zh/Z \ *i* (°)	*U* = 10 mm 0	20	40	60	*U* = 25 mm 0	20	40	60
0.170068	473	464	436	373.2	685	664	610	508
0.204082	477	469	440	375.6	701	681	622	518
0.272109	485	475	445.5	380	727	708	640	532
0.340136	490	480	450	381.6	740	720	652	540
0.408163	492	485	452	382.4	752	728	662	545
0.47619	497	487	454	382.8	761	738	670	549
0.544218	500	490	457	383	770	750	678	553.2
0.612245	502	493	459	383.4	781	756	684	557
0.680272	509	496	460	384	789	762	688	561
0.748299	510	499	461	384.8	793	770	692	564
0.884354	511	500.5	464	386	785	760	692	569

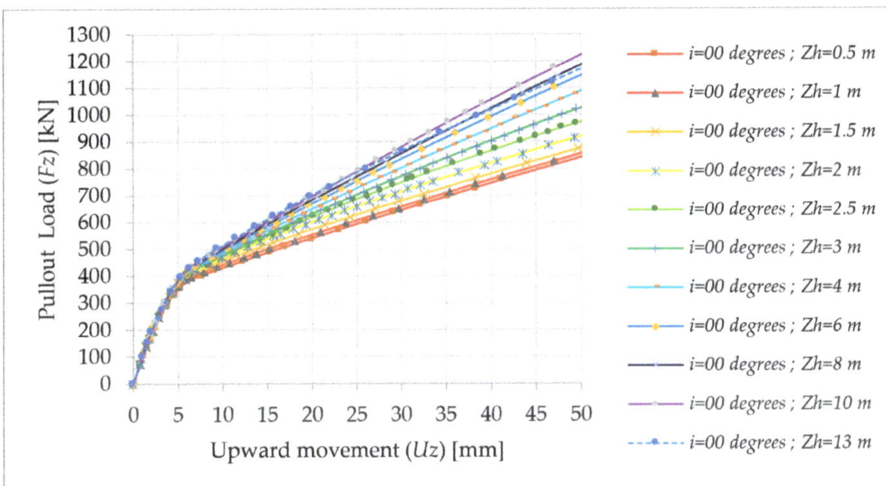

(**a**)

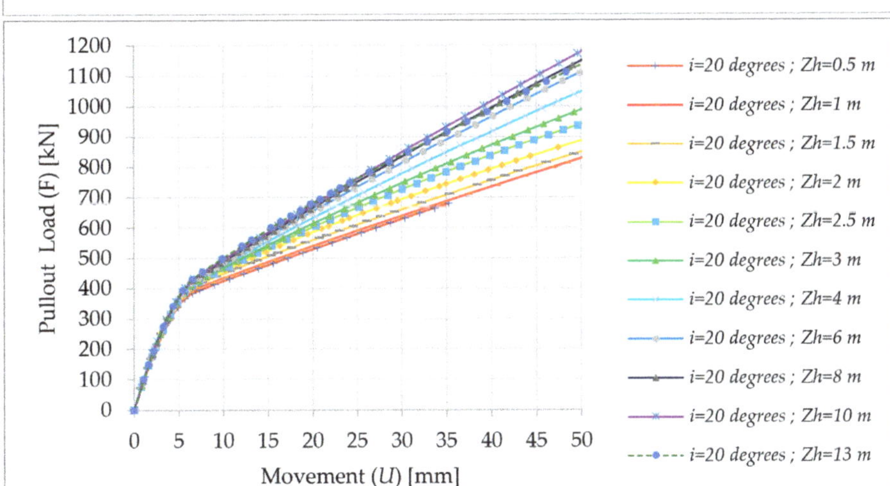

(**b**)

Figure 19. *Cont.*

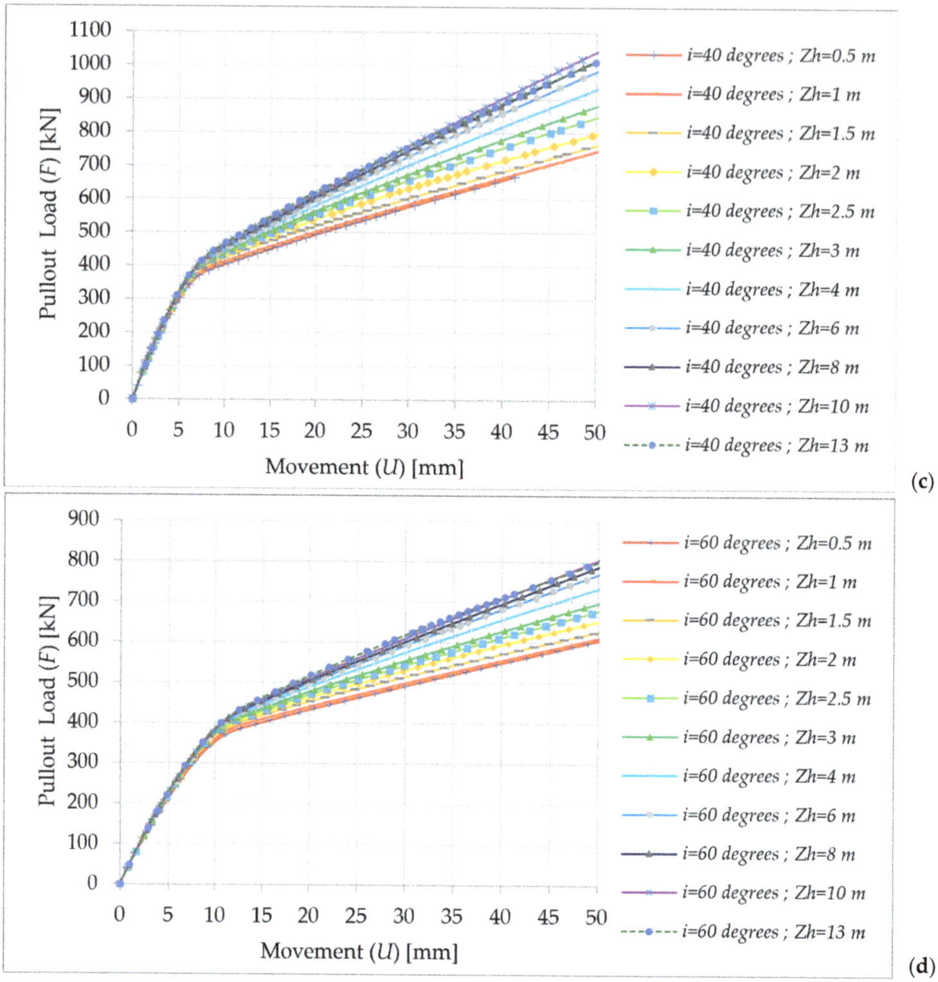

Figure 19. Load response of small-shaft-diameter helical piles at various top helical plate locations (Zh); (**a**) $i = 0°$, (**b**) $i = 20°$, (**c**) $i = 40°$, and (**d**) $i = 60°$.

The results from Table 9 suggest that increasing Zh enhances the load resistance capabilities irrespective of the load inclination, thus indicating that a deeper top helical plate is more effective in withstanding pullout loads and resisting movement. However, it was observed that the load capacity sharply increased up to a specific Zh/Z ratio, beyond which the rate of increase diminished or became more horizontal, as depicted in Figure 20. It is important to note that, after reaching a Zh/Z ratio of 0.75, there was a decrease in the load capacity, particularly noticeable for high movements, as illustrated in Figure 20. This phenomenon occurred because the helical plates came too close to one another, resulting in stress interactions that lead to a reduction in load capacity, as shown in Figure 21.

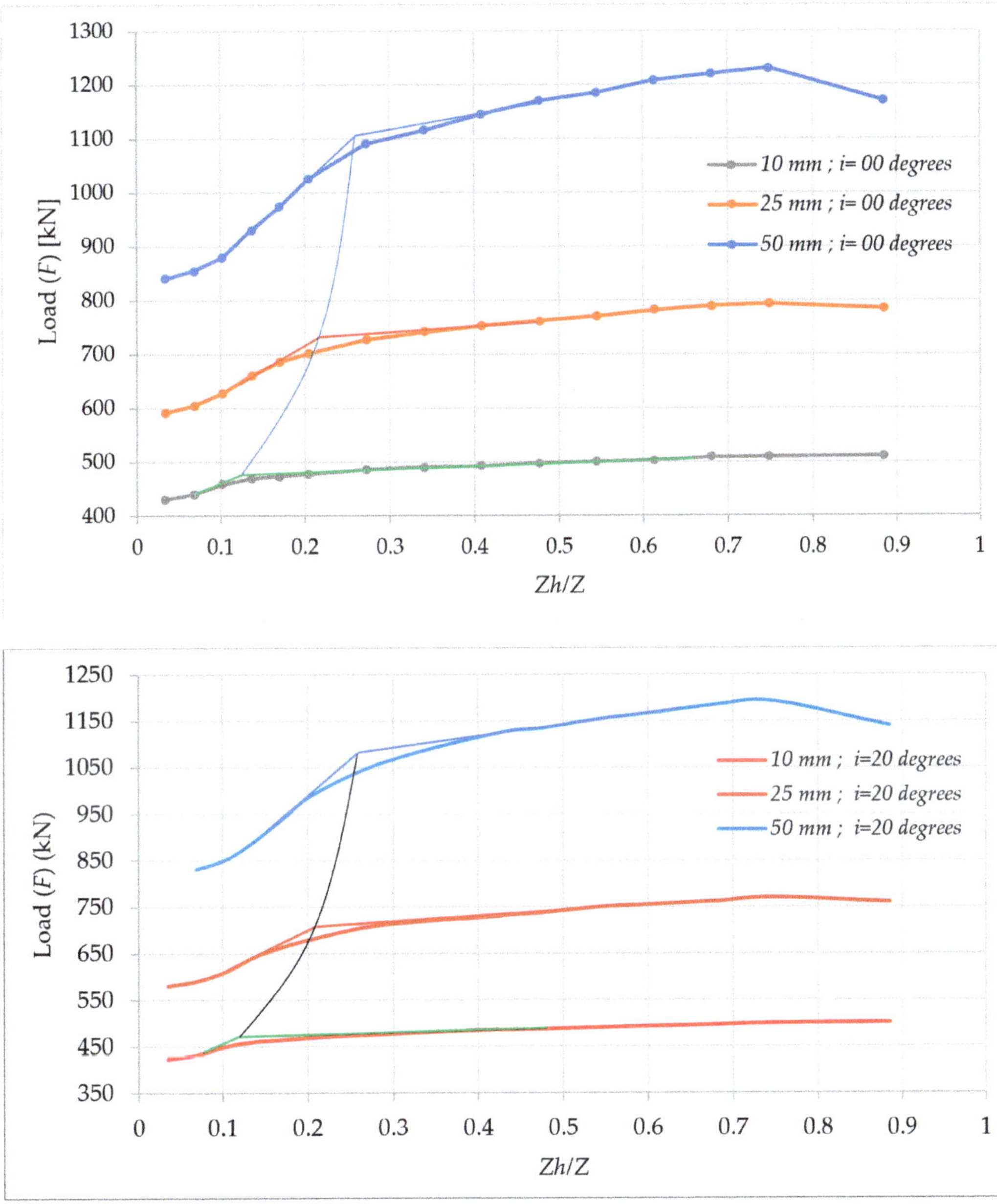

(A)

(B)

Figure 20. *Cont.*

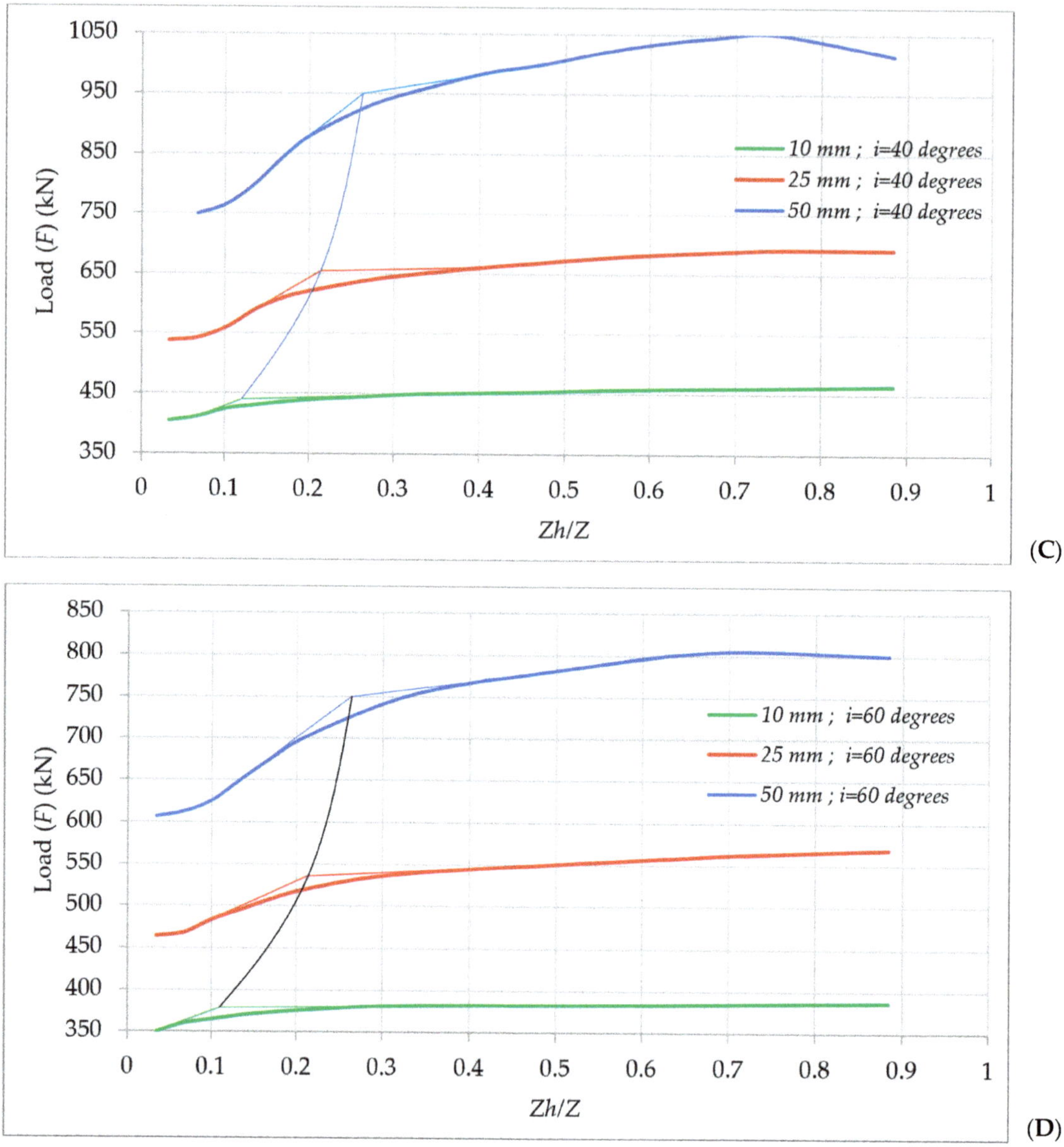

Figure 20. Relation between the load capacity and Zh/Z of small-shaft-diameter helical piles at different allowable movements: (**A**) $i = 0°$, (**B**) $i = 20°$, (**C**) $i = 40°$, and (**D**) $i = 60°$.

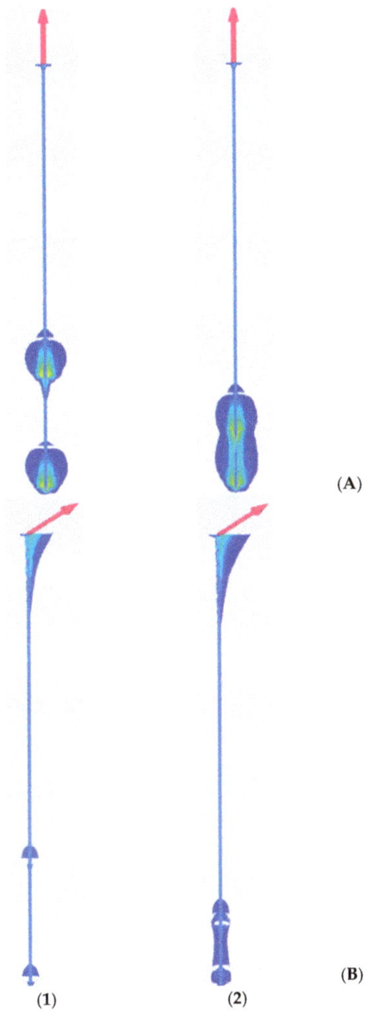

Figure 21. The iso surface displacements along the small-shaft-diameter helical piles: (**A**) $i = 0°$, (**B**) $i = 60°$, (**1**) $Zh/Z = 0.075$, and (**2**) $Zh/Z = 0.884$.

Table 10 displays the optimal Zh/Z ratios, which should surpass 0.12 for movements of 10 mm, 0.22 for movements of 25 mm, and 0.26 for movements of 50 mm.

Table 10. Critical Zh/Z values of small-shaft-diameter helical piles where the rate of increase diminishes or becomes more horizontal based on movement and load inclination angles.

	Movement (mm)		
$i°$	**10**	**25**	**50**
0	0.12	0.22	0.26
20	0.12	0.21	0.26
40	0.12	0.215	0.26
60	0.11	0.215	0.26

4.5.2. Large-Shaft-Diameter Helical Piles

Impact of Load Inclination (i) on the Pullout Behavior of Large Diameter

Figure 22 presents load–displacement curves depicting the pullout behavior of different load inclinations (i). These curves offer a visual representation of how the piles react to upward movement and illustrate the variations in pullout loads corresponding to different load inclinations.

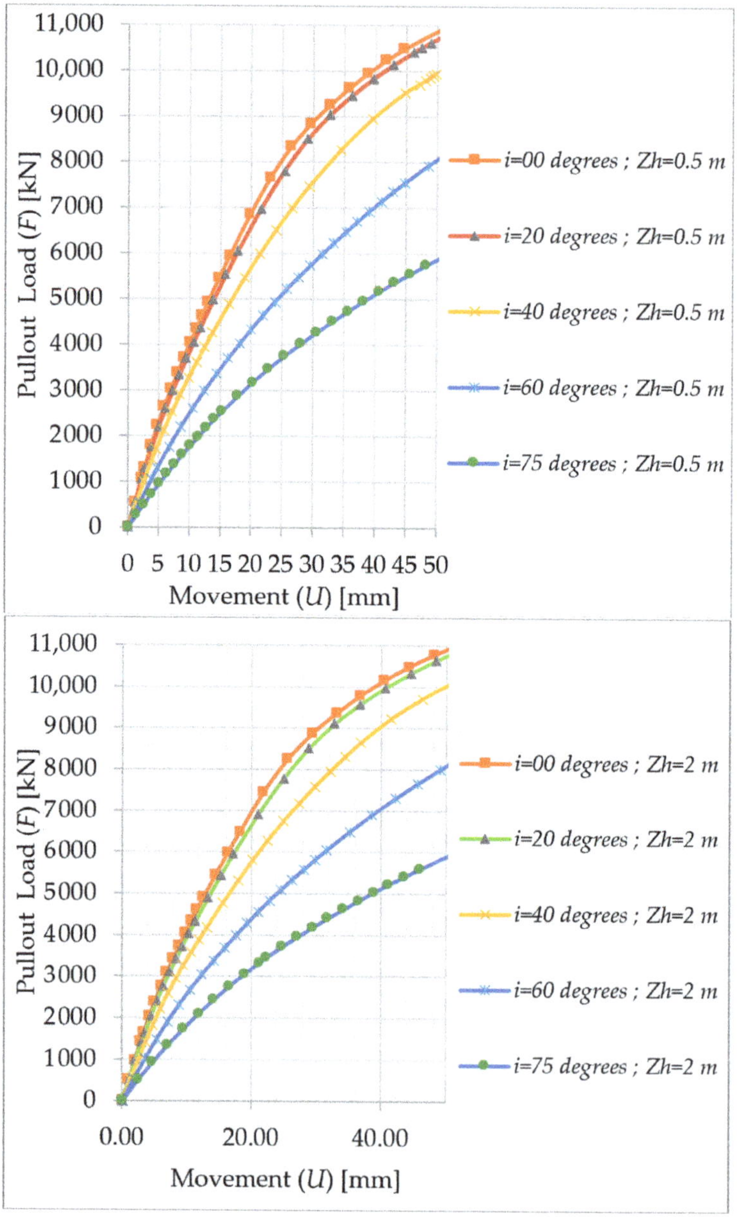

(A)

(B)

Figure 22. *Cont.*

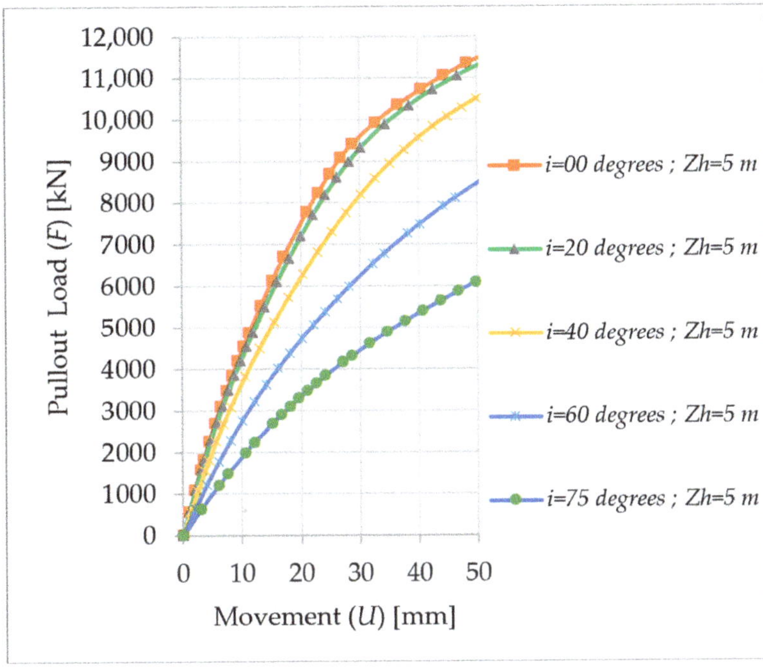

(C)

Figure 22. Pullout behavior of large-shaft-diameter helical piles at different inclination loads: (**A**) $Zh/Z = 0.034$, (**B**) $Zh/Z = 0.136$, and (**C**) $Zh/Z = 0.34$.

The following investigation was aimed at assessing how varying the load inclination affects the pullout load required to resist movements of 10, 25, and 50 mm for a large-shaft-diameter helical pile. The findings, illustrated in Figure 22, reveal that increasing the load inclination results in a decrease in the pullout load, irrespective of the helical plate's position. This suggests that piles subjected to axial forces are more effective in resisting movement, and these findings are also similar to helical piles with a small shaft diameter. However, it is crucial to note that, beyond a certain angle of load inclination corresponding to the movement value, there was a significant decrease in the load capacity. This critical angle diminishes as the ratio of Zh to Z increases, while it increases as allowable movement increases, as depicted in Figure 23 (where the Z for a large shaft diameter is 14.5 m). Table 11 presents the critical inclination angles, based on movement and the Zh/Z ratio, after which a substantial decrease in load capacity had occurred. Due to their optimized bearing capacity at specific inclination angles, helical piles are especially beneficial for tension leg mooring line types, and they can also be beneficial for taut or semi-taut mooring line types.

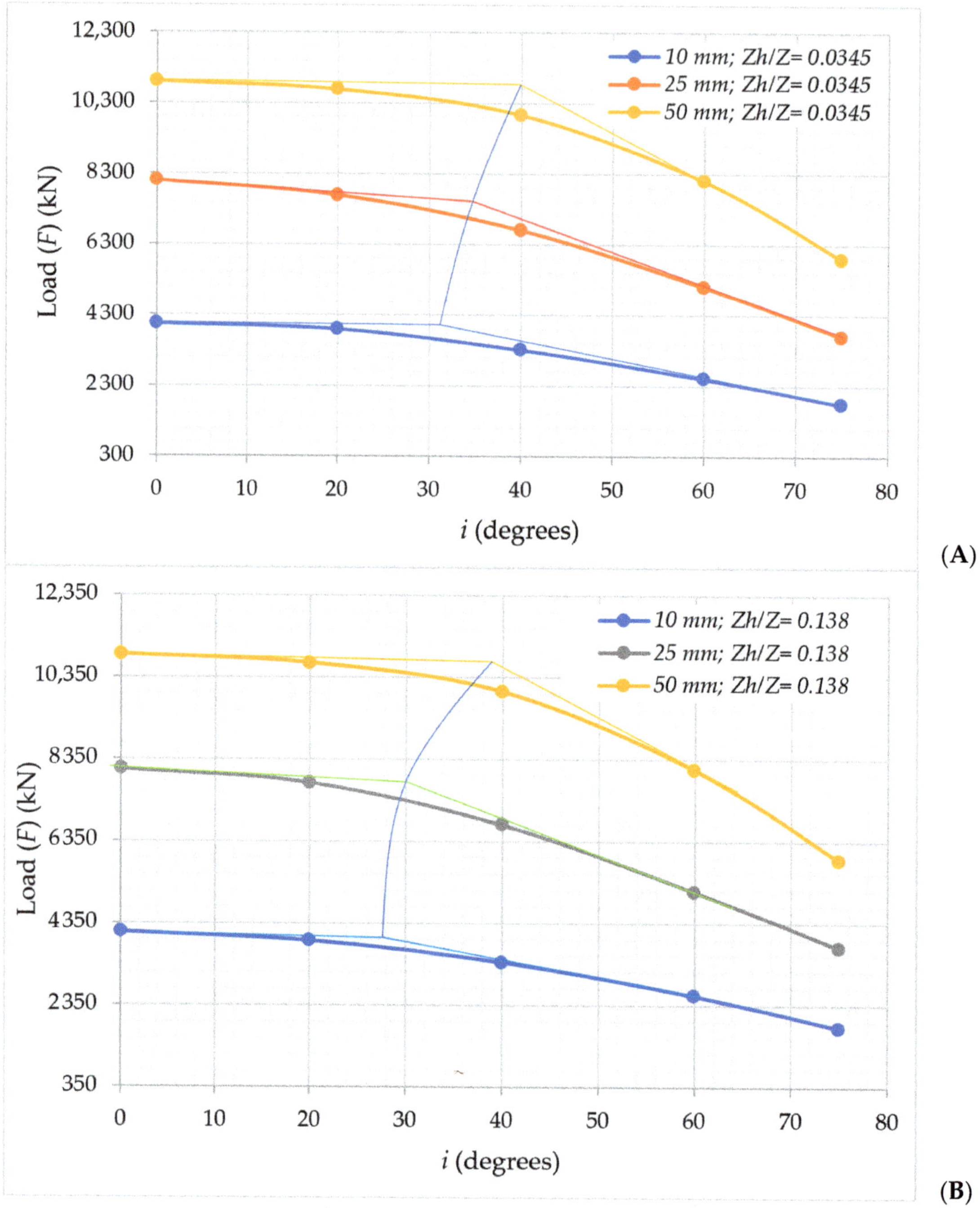

Figure 23. *Cont.*

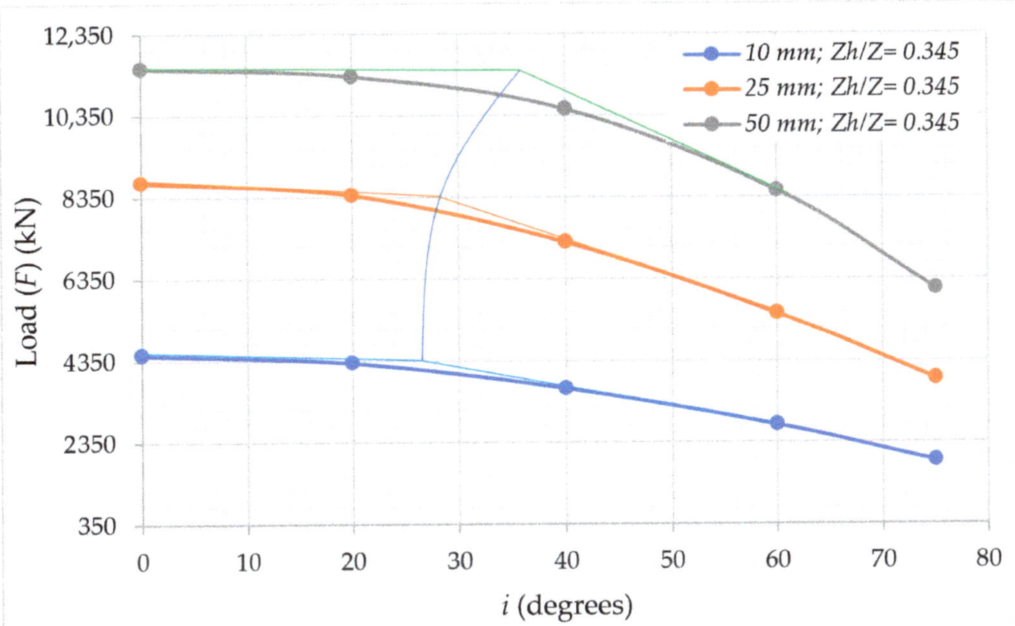

(C)

Figure 23. The relations between the load capacity and load inclination angle of large-shaft-diameter helical piles at different allowable movements: (**A**) $Zh/Z = 0.034$, (**B**) $Zh/Z = 0.136$, and (**C**) $Zh/Z = 0.34$.

Table 11. The critical inclination angles of large-shaft-diameter helical piles following a substantial decrease in load capacity based on movement and Zh/Z.

Zh/*h*	Movement (mm)		
	10	**25**	**50**
0.034	31.5	35	40
0.136	28	30	38.5
0.34	26.5	28	36

Figure 24 displays the iso-surface displacements along the helical piles. The reasons for the decrease in capacity with increasing load inclination were the same reasons as in the case of the small shaft diameter. However, the relatively large diameter of the helical shaft made the passive load sufficient to significantly enhance the capacity of the pile when compared with the small diameter of the helical shaft. As depicted in Figure 23, the effectiveness of the helical plates diminished as the load inclination angle increased.

Based on these findings, it is advisable to limit the inclination angle from the vertical line of the load or the mooring line attached to the large-diameter helical pile to no more than the values depicted in Table 11 to achieve the best bearing capacity. This restriction ensures sufficient load-bearing capacity and stability for the piles. By adhering to this inclination threshold, an optimized balance between frictional resistance, contact area, and pullout load is achieved, thereby enhancing the overall performance and reliability of the pile foundation system.

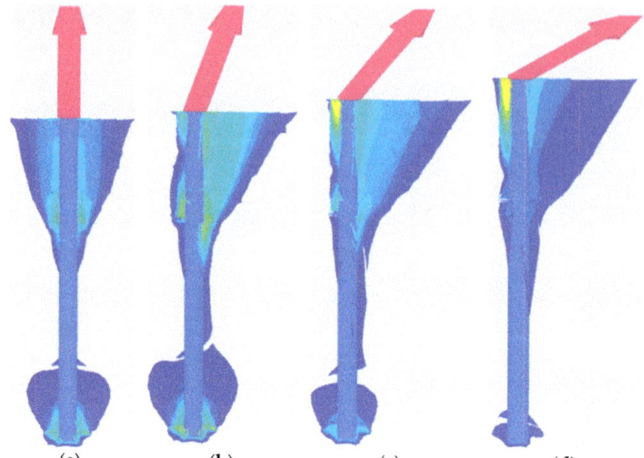

Figure 24. The iso surface displacements along the large-shaft-diameter helical piles: (**a**) $i = 0°$, (**b**) $i = 20°$, (**c**) $i = 40°$, and (**d**) $i = 60°$.

Impact of the Top Helical Plate Location (*Zh*) on the Pullout Load (*F*) Behavior

The investigation in this section is aimed at assessing the impact of the top helical plate's position (*Zh*) on a large-shaft-diameter helical pile's capacity to withstand pullout loads and resist movement. A detailed examination of the recorded loads is presented in Table 12, while Figure 25 visually illustrates the load behavior across various helical plate locations (*Zh*). This offers valuable insights into their response under pullout loading conditions, and it also underscores the variations in load resistance linked to different load inclination angles.

Table 12. The load capacity at 10 and 25 mm movements of large-shaft-diameter helical piles for different Zh/Z and load inclination angles.

	U = 10 mm				**U = 25 mm**				**U = 50 mm**			
Zh/Z \ ***i* (°)**	**0**	**20**	**40**	**60**	**0**	**20**	**40**	**60**	**0**	**20**	**40**	**60**
0.034	4035	3860	3340	2520	8062	7730	6710	5120	10,868	10,692	9970	8080
0.069	4060	3880	3360	2530	8090	7750	6722	5121	10,866	10,715	10,002	8080
0.103	4090	3908	3380	2550	8105	7762	6740	5140	10,852	10,725	10,020	8098
0.138	4120	3940	3410	2575	8130	7780	6760	5150	10,907	10,750	10,035	8102
0.172	4160	3965	3450	2602	8160	7785	6800	5182	10,930	10,711	10,060	8122
0.207	4220	4042	3505	2640	8230	7873	6860	5240	10,968	10,830	10,090	8140
0.276	4360	4170	3605	2705	8395	8058	7055	5402	11,130	10,970	10,230	8270
0.345	4470	4270	3685	2750	8720	8365	7265	5520	11,463	11,280	10,510	8470
0.414	4530	4330	3740	2781	8925	8530	7390	5582	12,070	11,797	10,885	8650
0.552	4650	4440	3835	2842	9122	8835	7580	5730	12,682	12,355	11,322	8902
0.690	4745	4528	3910	2883	9280	8895	7745	5860	12,862	12,540	11,530	9110
0.759	4770	4553	3920	2885	9335	8960	7800	5900	12,810	12,485	11,520	9200
0.828	4748	4530	3890	2860	9320	8953	7800	5880	12,588	12,280	11,402	9202
0.897	4610	4345	3770	2770	9180	8810	7650	5750	12,160	11,900	11,160	9080

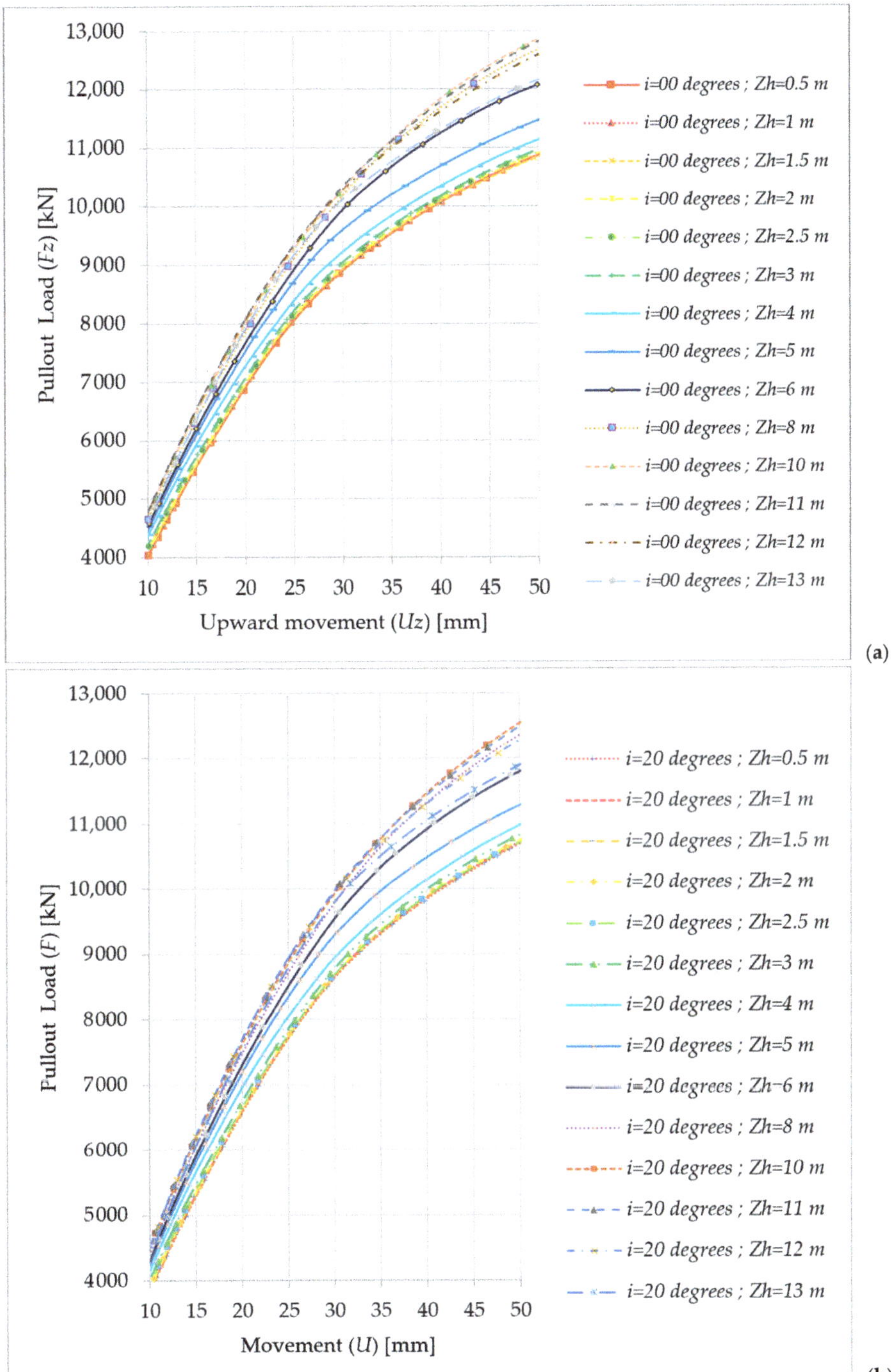

Figure 25. *Cont.*

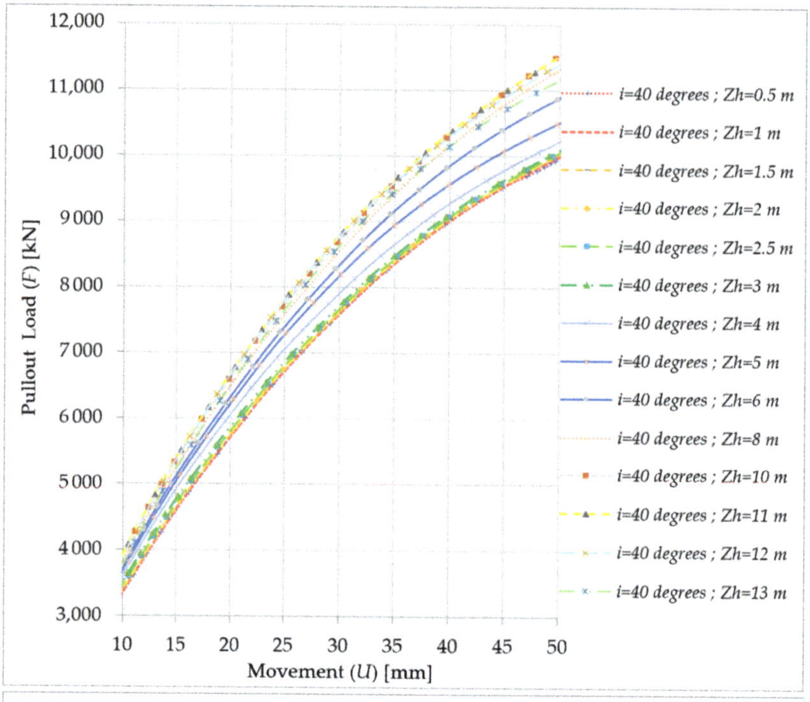

(c)

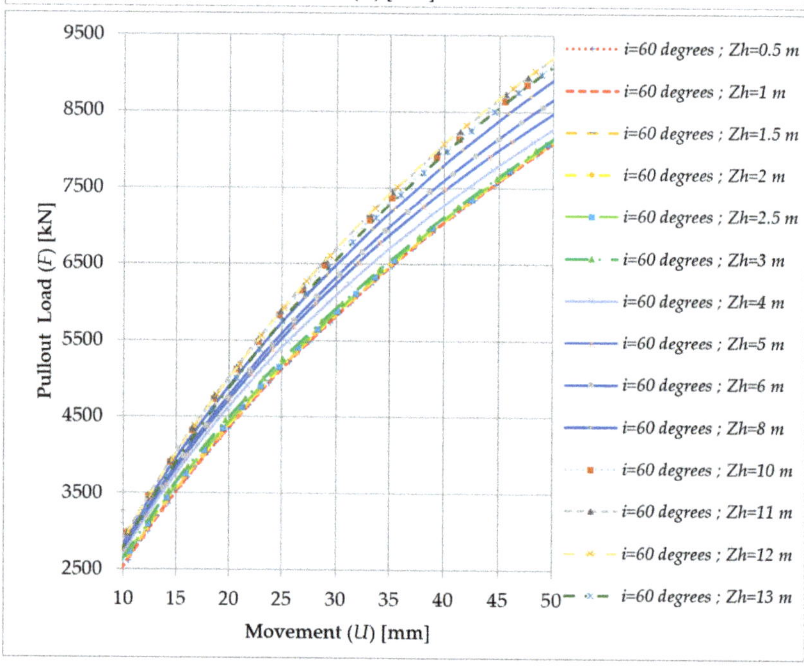

(d)

Figure 25. Load response of large-shaft-diameter helical piles at various top helical plate locations (*Zh*); (**a**) $i = 0°$, (**b**) $i = 20°$, (**c**) $i = 40°$, and (**d**) $i = 60°$.

The results from Table 12 suggest that increasing *Zh* enhances the load resistance capabilities irrespective of the load inclination, thus indicating that a deeper top helical plate is more effective in withstanding pullout loads and resisting movement. However, it was observed that the load capacity sharply increased up to a specific Zh/Z ratio, beyond which the rate of increase diminished or became more horizontal, as depicted in Figure 26. It is important to note that, after reaching a Zh/Z ratio of 0.78, there was a decrease in the load capacity, particularly noticeable for high movements, as illustrated in Figure 26. This phenomenon occurred because the helical plates came too close to one another, resulting in stress interactions that lead to a reduction in load capacity, as shown in Figure 27. These findings are almost similar to those of the small-shaft-diameter helical piles. However, the top helical plate in the large shaft diameter should be deeper than the small shaft diameter to achieve the best bearing capacity.

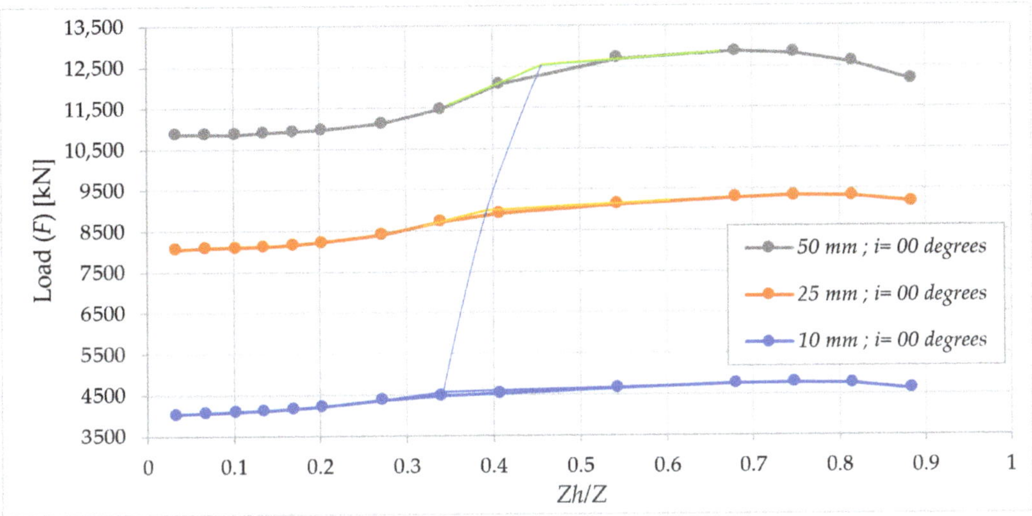

(A)

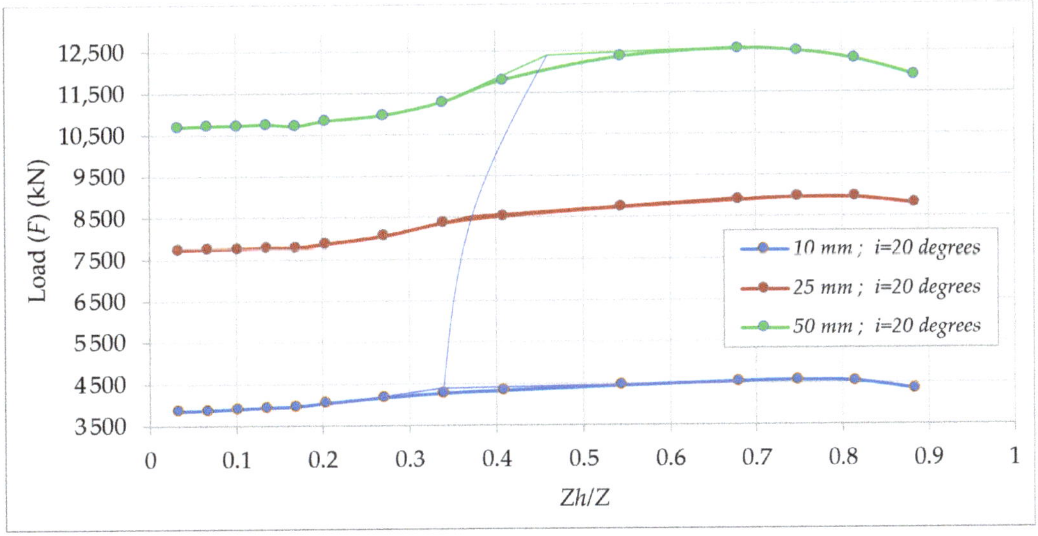

(B)

Figure 26. *Cont.*

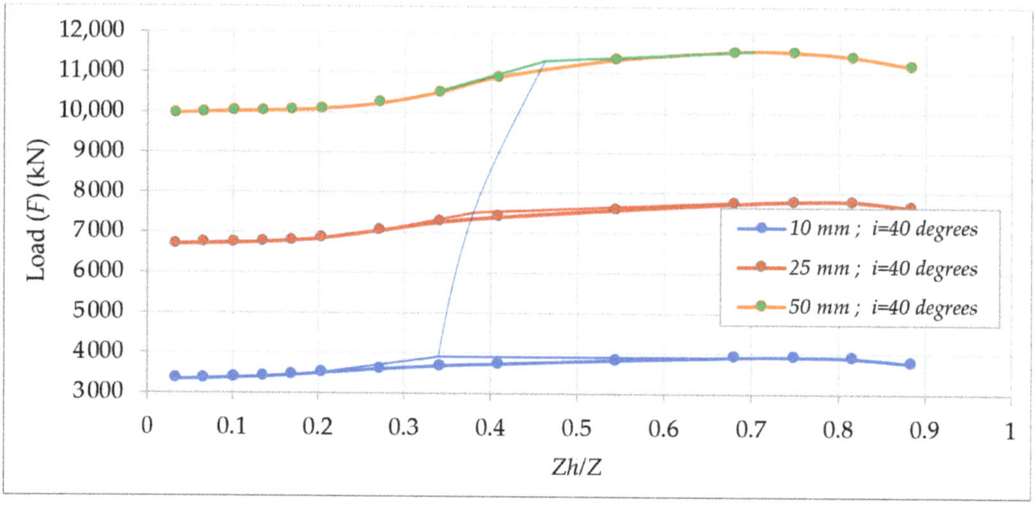

(C)

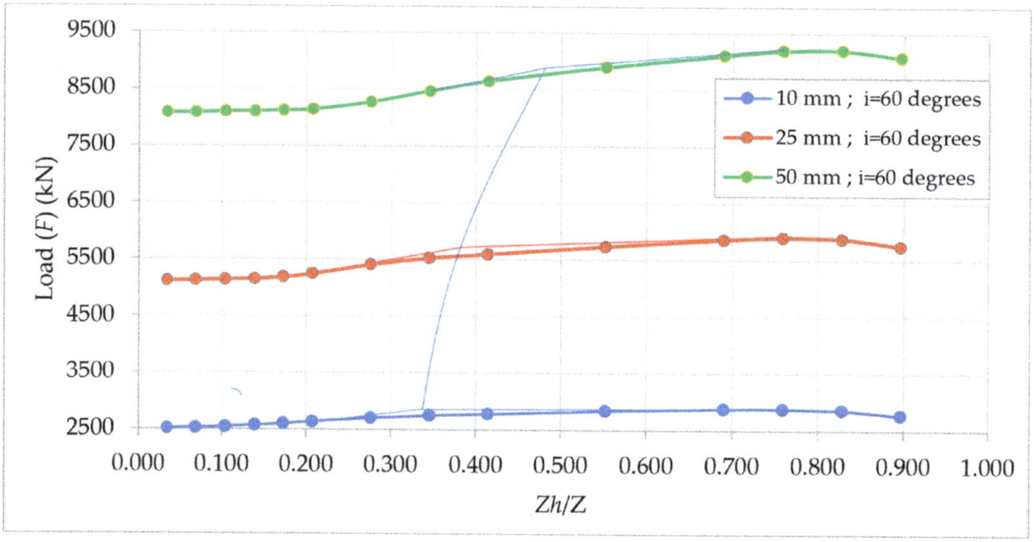

(D)

Figure 26. The relations between load capacity and Zh/Z of large-shaft-diameter helical piles at different allowable movements: (**A**) $i = 0°$, (**B**) $i = 20°$, (**C**) $i = 40°$, and (**D**) $i = 60°$.

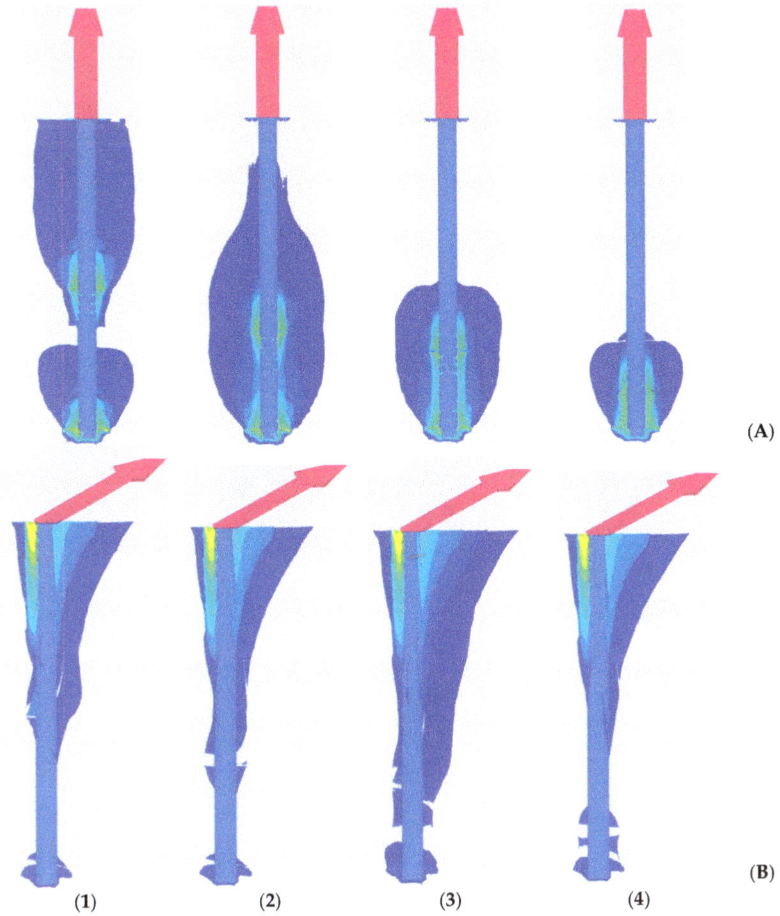

Figure 27. The iso surface displacements along the large-shaft-diameter helical piles: (**A**) $i = 0°$, (**B**) $i = 60°$, (**1**) $Zh/Z = 0.55$, (**2**) $Zh/Z = 0.69$, (**3**) $Zh/Z = 0.76$, and (**4**) $Zh/Z = 0.9$.

Table 13 displays the optimal Zh/Z ratios, which should surpass 0.34 for movements of 10 mm, 0.38 for movements of 25 mm, and 0.46 for movements of 50 mm. Therefore, in large-shaft-diameter helical piles, the top helical plates should be deeper than the small helical plate to achieve a better bearing capacity.

Table 13. Critical Zh/Z values of large-shaft-diameter helical piles where the rate of increase diminishes or becomes more horizontal based on movement and load inclination angles.

	Movement (mm)		
$i°$	**10**	**25**	**50**
0	0.34	0.38	0.46
20	0.34	0.38	0.46
40	0.34	0.38	0.46
60	0.34	0.38	0.46

5. Conclusions

The urgent need to combat climate change has spurred a shift toward renewable energy sources, notably offshore wind power. Europe leads in offshore wind development as it can capitalize on abundant wind resources. Coupled with Power-to-X technologies, offshore wind offers solutions beyond electricity generation, such as green hydrogen production. Despite initial cost barriers, long-term forecasts suggest significant cost reductions, thus paving the way for a sustainable energy future. The rapid progress in floating offshore wind technology, coupled with favorable market trends and cost reductions, positions it as a promising contributor to the global transition toward clean and sustainable energy. The optimization of offshore wind turbine designs involves a diverse array of optimization algorithms, each with its own merits and challenges. Continued research and development in this field are crucial for enhancing the efficiency, reliability, and cost-effectiveness of offshore wind energy systems.

This study has provided valuable insights into the performance of helical piles in supporting mooring lines for floating offshore wind applications. Through a comprehensive investigation of load resistance capabilities and the movement response associated with varying helical plate positions and load inclinations, several important findings have emerged. It was observed that deeper top helical plates generally enhance load resistance, although there exists a critical Zh/Z ratio beyond which the rate of load capacity increase diminishes. Moreover, beyond a Zh/Z ratio of 0.75, there is a notable decrease in load capacity, which is attributed to the stress interactions that are caused by helical plates coming too close. Additionally, optimal Zh/Z ratios were identified for different movement scenarios, providing practical guidelines for design considerations. These findings underscore the importance of the careful positioning of helical plates and load inclination management to ensure optimal performance and reliability in the pile foundation systems in floating offshore wind projects. Helical piles are particularly useful for tension leg mooring line types, but they can also benefit taut (or semi-taut) mooring line types since their bearing capacity can be optimized at specific inclination degrees. For catenary mooring line types, it is critical to optimize the shaft of the helical pile by increasing the diameter of the upper shaft section while decreasing the diameter of the lower shaft. However, more research is needed based on the inclination of the mooring line and the location of the helical plates. By adhering to these recommendations, designers and engineers can enhance the effectiveness and longevity of offshore wind structures, thus contributing to the sustainable development of renewable energy resources. Future research should look into the use of multiple helical plates and pile groups to increase load-bearing capacity and stability. Multiple plates can better distribute loads, while pile groups add support and redundancy, especially in deeper waters and harsher conditions. These configurations will improve helical pile performance, resulting in more reliable and adaptable anchoring solutions for the offshore wind energy sector.

Author Contributions: Conceptualization, A.A.; methodology, A.A. and M.M.; modeling, A.A.; validation, A.A.; formal analysis, A.A. and M.M.; investigation, A.A.; writing—original draft preparation, A.A.; writing—review and editing, A.A. and M.M. All authors have read and agreed to the published version of the manuscript.

Funding: This research received no external funding. Funding for open access was granted by Szechenyi István University (SZE).

Institutional Review Board Statement: Not applicable.

Informed Consent Statement: Not applicable.

Data Availability Statement: All data are available within the text of this manuscript.

Conflicts of Interest: The authors declare no conflicts of interest.

References

1. Ritchie, H.; Rosado, P.; Roser, M. Energy Mix. Our World in Data. 2024. Available online: https://ourworldindata.org/energy-mix (accessed on 7 April 2024).
2. De Castro, M.; Salvador, S.; Gómez-Gesteira, M.; Costoya, X.; Carvalho, D.; Sanz-Larruga, F.J.; Gimeno, L. Europe, China and the United States: Three Different Approaches to the Development of Offshore Wind Energy. *Renew. Sustain. Energy Rev.* **2019**, *109*, 55–70. [CrossRef]
3. Díaz, H.; Guedes Soares, C. Review of the Current Status, Technology and Future Trends of Offshore Wind Farms. *Ocean Eng.* **2020**, *209*, 107381. [CrossRef]
4. Rodrigues, S.; Restrepo, C.; Kontos, E.; Teixeira Pinto, R.; Bauer, P. Trends of Offshore Wind Projects. *Renew. Sustain. Energy Rev.* **2015**, *49*, 1114–1135. [CrossRef]
5. Manwell, J.F.; McGowan, J.G.; Rogers, A.L. Wind Energy Explained: Theory, Design and Application. In *Wind Energy Explained: Theory, Design and Application*; John Wiley & Sons: Hoboken, NJ, USA, 2010. [CrossRef]
6. Poudineh, R.; Brown, C.; Foley, B. Background: Role of the Offshore Wind Industry. In *Economics of Offshore Wind Power*; Palgrave Macmillan: Cham, Switzerland, 2017; pp. 1–14. [CrossRef]
7. Kaldellis, J.K.; Kapsali, M. Shifting towards Offshore Wind Energy-Recent Activity and Future Development. *Energy Policy* **2013**, *53*, 136–148. [CrossRef]
8. Esteban, M.D.; Diez, J.J.; López, J.S.; Negro, V. Why Offshore Wind Energy? *Renew. Energy* **2011**, *36*, 444–450. [CrossRef]
9. Hevia-Koch, P.; Klinge Jacobsen, H. Comparing Offshore and Onshore Wind Development Considering Acceptance Costs. *Energy Policy* **2019**, *125*, 9–19. [CrossRef]
10. Ren, Z.; Verma, A.S.; Li, Y.; Teuwen, J.J.E.; Jiang, Z. Offshore Wind Turbine Operations and Maintenance: A State-of-the-Art Review. *Renew. Sustain. Energy Rev.* **2021**, *144*, 110886. [CrossRef]
11. Burton, T.; Jenkins, N.; Sharpe, D.; Bossanyi, E. *Wind Energy Handbook*, 2nd ed.; John Wiley & Sons, Ltd.: Chichester, UK; Hoboken, NJ, USA, 2001; p. 780.
12. Sun, X.; Huang, D.; Wu, G. The Current State of Offshore Wind Energy Technology Development. *Energy* **2012**, *41*, 298–312. [CrossRef]
13. MacKinnon, D.; Dawley, S.; Steen, M.; Menzel, M.P.; Karlsen, A.; Sommer, P.; Hansen, G.H.; Normann, H.E. Path Creation, Global Production Networks and Regional Development: A Comparative International Analysis of the Offshore Wind Sector. *Prog. Plan.* **2019**, *130*, 1–32. [CrossRef]
14. Johnston, B.; Foley, A.; Doran, J.; Littler, T. Levelised Cost of Energy, A Challenge for Offshore Wind. *Renew. Energy* **2020**, *160*, 876–885. [CrossRef]
15. Markard, J.; Petersen, R. The Offshore Trend: Structural Changes in the Wind Power Sector. *Energy Policy* **2009**, *37*, 3545–3556. [CrossRef]
16. WindEurope. *Offshore Wind in Europe—Key Trends and Statistics 2020*; WindEurope: Bilbao, Spain, 2021.
17. Commission European. Directorate-General for Energy. *Communication from the Commission to the European Parliament, the Council, the European Economic and Social Committee and the Committee of the Regions. An EU Strategy to Harness the Potential of Offshore Renewable Energy for a Climate Neutral Future*; Commission European: Brussels, Belgium, 2020.
18. WindEurope. *Wind Energy in Europe: 2022 Statistics and the Outlook for 2023–2027*; WindEurope: Bilbao, Spain, 2022; 58p.
19. IRENA. *Innovation Landscape for a Renewable-Powered Future: Solutions to Integrate Variable Renewables*; International Renewable Energy Agency: Abu Dhabi, United Arab Emirates, 2019; 164p.
20. GWEC. *Global Offshore Wind Report 2021*; Global Wind Energy Council: Brussels, Belgium, 2021; p. 136.
21. Babarit, A.; Gilloteaux, J.C.; Clodic, G.; Duchet, M.; Simoneau, A.; Platzer, M.F. Techno-Economic Feasibility of Fleets of Far Offshore Hydrogen-Producing Wind Energy Converters. *Int. J. Hydrogen Energy* **2018**, *43*, 7266–7289. [CrossRef]
22. Kovalchuk, V. Techno-Economic Review of Offshore Wind Power. Master's Thesis, Lappeenranta-Lahti University of Technology, Lappeenranta, Finland, 2021.
23. Manwell, J.F. Offshore Wind Energy Technology Trends, Challenges, and Risks. In *Power Stations Using Locally Available Energy Sources*; Springer: New York, NY, USA, 2018; pp. 399–436. [CrossRef]
24. Jiang, Z. Installation of Offshore Wind Turbines: A Technical Review. *Renew. Sustain. Energy Rev.* **2021**, *139*, 110576. [CrossRef]
25. IRENA. *Renewable Power Generation Costs in 2022*; International Renewable Energy Agency: Abu Dhabi, United Arab Emirates, 2023; 208p.
26. IRENA. *Renewable Energy Benefits Leveraging Local Capacity for Offshore Wind*; International Renewable Energy Agency: Abu Dhabi, United Arab Emirates, 2018; 44p.
27. Wang, X.; Zeng, X.; Li, J.; Yang, X.; Wang, H. A Review on Recent Advancements of Substructures for Offshore Wind Turbines. *Energy Convers. Manag.* **2018**, *158*, 103–119. [CrossRef]
28. Buljan, A. Offshore Wind Turbines in 2023: 16 MW Model Installed Offshore, 18 MW WTGs Selected for New Project, 22 MW Turbine Announced. Available online: https://www.offshorewind.biz/2024/01/02/offshore-wind-turbines-in-2023-16-mw-model-installed-offshore-18-mw-wtgs-selected-for-new-project-22-mw-turbine-announced/ (accessed on 12 March 2024).
29. Trojnar, K. Simplified Design of New Hybrid Monopile Foundations for Offshore Wind Turbines. *Ocean Eng.* **2021**, *219*, 108046. [CrossRef]

30. Soares-Ramos, E.P.P.; de Oliveira-Assis, L.; Sarrias-Mena, R.; Fernández-Ramírez, L.M. Current Status and Future Trends of Offshore Wind Power in Europe. *Energy* **2020**, *202*, 117787. [CrossRef]
31. Wu, X.; Hu, Y.; Li, Y.; Yang, J.; Duan, L.; Wang, T.; Adcock, T.; Jiang, Z.; Gao, Z.; Lin, Z.; et al. Foundations of Offshore Wind Turbines: A Review. *Renew. Sustain. Energy Rev.* **2019**, *104*, 379–393. [CrossRef]
32. Arshad, M.; O'kelly, B.C. Offshore Wind-Turbine Structures: A Review. *Proc. Inst. Civ. Eng. Energy* **2015**, *166*, 139–152. [CrossRef]
33. Kaiser, M.J.; Snyder, B.F. Offshore Wind Energy System Components. In *Offshore Wind Energy Cost Modeling*; Green Energy and Technology; Springer: London, UK, 2012; pp. 13–30. [CrossRef]
34. Igoe, D.; Gavin, K.; O'Kelly, B. An Investigation into the Use of Push-in Pile Foundations by the Offshore Wind Sector. *Int. J. Environ. Stud.* **2013**, *70*, 777–791. [CrossRef]
35. Ørsted. Our Experience with Suction Bucket Jacket Foundations. Ørsted's Experience with Suction Bucket Jacket Foundations. Available online: https://orsted.com/-/media/www/docs/corp/com/our-business/wind-power/bucket-jacket_long-version.ashx?la=en&hash=bb12170bd01a84543af54599146637e5 (accessed on 3 January 2024).
36. Oh, K.Y.; Nam, W.; Ryu, M.S.; Kim, J.Y.; Epureanu, B.I. A Review of Foundations of Offshore Wind Energy Convertors: Current Status and Future Perspectives. *Renew. Sustain. Energy Rev.* **2018**, *88*, 16–36. [CrossRef]
37. Pérez-Collazo, C.; Greaves, D.; Iglesias, G. A Review of Combined Wave and Offshore Wind Energy. *Renew. Sustain. Energy Rev.* **2015**, *42*, 141–153. [CrossRef]
38. Horwath, S.; Hassrick, J.; Grismala, R.; Diller, E.; Krebs, J.; Manhard, R. *ICF Comparison of Environmental Effects from Different Offshore Wind Turbine Foundations (2021 Revision) | Tethys*; OCS Study BOEM 2021-053; U.S. Department of the Interior, Bureau of Ocean Energy Management: Sterling, VA, USA, 2020; p. 48.
39. Fu, F. *Design and Analysis of Tall and Complex Structures*; Butterworth-Heinemann: Oxford, UK, 2018; ISBN 0081011210.
40. Rystad Energy; WindEurope. *The State of the European Wind Energy Supply Chain. A «What-Would-It-Take» Analysis of the European Supply Chain's Ability to Support Ambitious Capacity Targets towards 2030*; A Rystad Energy Report in Cooperation with, WindEurope; Rystad Energy: Oslo, Norway; WindEurope: Bilbao, Spain, 2023.
41. Esteban, M.D.; López-Gutiérrez, J.S.; Negro, V. Gravity-Based Foundations in the Offshore Wind Sector. *J. Mar. Sci. Eng.* **2019**, *7*, 64. [CrossRef]
42. Thomsen, K.E. What Is an Offshore Wind Farm? In *Offshore Wind*; Academic Press: London, UK; pp. 1–7. [CrossRef]
43. Fischer, T.; De Vries, W.E.; Cordle, A. Executive Summary (WP4: Offshore Foundations and Support Structures). 2011. Available online: http://resolver.tudelft.nl/uuid:7ff42174-70ab-459d-b709-3bab9c2f9c4b (accessed on 14 January 2024).
44. Passon, P.; Branner, K.; Larsen, S.E.; Hvenekaer Rasmussen, J. *Offshore Wind Turbine Foundation Design*; DTU Wind Energy PhD, No. 0044(EN); DTU Wind Energy: Roskilde, Denmark, 2015.
45. WindEurope. *Floating Offshore Wind Vision Statement*; WindEurope: Bilbao, Spain, 2017; 16p.
46. IRENA. *Innovation Outlook Offshore Wind*; International Renewable Energy Agency: Abu Dhabi, United Arab Emirates, 2016; 160p.
47. Xu, S.; Murai, M.; Wang, X.; Takahashi, K. A Novel Conceptual Design of a Dynamically Positioned Floating Wind Turbine. *Ocean Eng.* **2021**, *221*, 108528. [CrossRef]
48. Kopperstad, K.M.; Kumar, R.; Shoele, K. Aerodynamic Characterization of Barge and Spar Type Floating Offshore Wind Turbines at Different Sea States. *Wind Energy* **2020**, *23*, 2087–2112. [CrossRef]
49. Meng, L.; He, Y.P.; Zhao, Y.S.; Yang, J.; Yang, H.; Han, Z.L.; Yu, L.; Mao, W.G.; Du, W.K. Dynamic Response of 6MW Spar Type Floating Offshore Wind Turbine by Experiment and Numerical Analyses. *China Ocean Eng.* **2020**, *34*, 608–620. [CrossRef]
50. Liu, Y.; Xiao, Q.; Incecik, A.; Peyrard, C.; Wan, D. Establishing a Fully Coupled CFD Analysis Tool for Floating Offshore Wind Turbines. *Renew. Energy* **2017**, *112*, 280–301. [CrossRef]
51. Kasyanov, V.N.; Kasyanova, E.V.; Jonkman, J.M.; Jonkman, B.J. FAST Modularization Framework for Wind Turbine Simulation: Full-System Linearization. *J. Phys. Conf. Ser.* **2016**, *753*, 082010. [CrossRef]
52. Li, L.; Cheng, Z.; Yuan, Z.; Gao, Y. Short-Term Extreme Response and Fatigue Damage of an Integrated Offshore Renewable Energy System. *Renew. Energy* **2018**, *126*, 617–629. [CrossRef]
53. Browning, J.R.; Jonkman, J.; Robertson, A.; Goupee, A.J. Calibration and Validation of a Spar-Type Floating Offshore Wind Turbine Model Using the FAST Dynamic Simulation Tool. *J. Phys. Conf. Ser.* **2014**, *555*, 012015. [CrossRef]
54. Ruzzo, C.; Fiamma, V.; Collu, M.; Failla, G.; Nava, V.; Arena, F. On Intermediate-Scale Open-Sea Experiments on Floating Offshore Structures: Feasibility and Application on a Spar Support for Offshore Wind Turbines. *Mar. Struct.* **2018**, *61*, 220–237. [CrossRef]
55. Tomasicchio, G.R.; Avossa, A.M.; Riefolo, L.; Ricciardelli, F.; Musci, E.; D'Alessandro, F.; Vicinanza, D. Dynamic Modelling of a Spar Buoy Wind Turbine. In Proceedings of the International Conference on Offshore Mechanics and Arctic Engineering—OMAE, Trondheim, Norway, 25–30 June 2017; Volume 10. [CrossRef]
56. Bae, Y.H.; Kim, M.H.; Im, S.W.; Chang, I.H. *Aero-Elastic-Control-Floater-Mooring Coupled Dynamic Analysis of Floating Offshore Wind Turbines*; ISOPE: Mountain View, CA, USA, 2011.
57. Liu, Y.; Li, S.; Yi, Q.; Chen, D. Developments in Semi-Submersible Floating Foundations Supporting Wind Turbines: A Comprehensive Review. *Renew. Sustain. Energy Rev.* **2016**, *60*, 433–449. [CrossRef]
58. Collu, M.; Borg, M.; Shires, A.; Brennan, F.P. FloVAWT: Progress on the Development of a Coupled Model of Dynamics for Floating Offshore Vertical Axis Wind Turbines. In Proceedings of the International Conference on Offshore Mechanics and Arctic Engineering—OMAE, Nantes, France, 9–14 June 2013; Volume 8. [CrossRef]

59. Roddier, D.; Cermelli, C.; Weinstein, A. WindFloat: A Floating Foundation for Offshore Wind Turbines—Part I: Design Basis and Qualification Process. In Proceedings of the International Conference on Offshore Mechanics and Arctic Engineering—OMAE, Honolulu, HI, USA, 31 May–5 June 2010; Volume 4, pp. 845–853. [CrossRef]
60. Bae, Y.H.; Kim, M.H.; Kim, H.C. Performance Changes of a Floating Offshore Wind Turbine with Broken Mooring Line. *Renew. Energy* **2017**, *101*, 364–375. [CrossRef]
61. Kim, H.C.; Kim, M.H.; Lee, J.Y.; Kim, E.S.; Zhang, Z. Global Performance Analysis of 5MW WindFloat and OC4 Semi-Submersible Floating Offshore Wind Turbines (FOWT) by Numerical Simulations 2017. In Proceedings of the 27th International Ocean and Polar Engineering Conference, San Francisco, CA, USA, 25–30 June 2017.
62. Bae, Y.H.; Kim, M.H. Coupled Dynamic Analysis of Multiple Wind Turbines on a Large Single Floater. *Ocean Eng.* **2014**, *92*, 175–187. [CrossRef]
63. Jang, H.K.; Park, S.; Kim, M.H.; Kim, K.H.; Hong, K. Effects of Heave Plates on the Global Performance of a Multi-Unit Floating Offshore Wind Turbine. *Renew. Energy* **2019**, *134*, 526–537. [CrossRef]
64. Zhao, Y.; Yang, J.; He, Y. Preliminary Design of a Multi-Column TLP Foundation for a 5-MW Offshore Wind Turbine. *Energies* **2012**, *5*, 3874–3891. [CrossRef]
65. Bachynski, E.E.; Moan, T. Design Considerations for Tension Leg Platform Wind Turbines. *Mar. Struct.* **2012**, *29*, 89–114. [CrossRef]
66. Nihei, Y.; Fujioka, H. Motion Characteristics of TLP Type Offshore Wind Turbine in Waves and Wind. In Proceedings of the International Conference on Offshore Mechanics and Arctic Engineering—OMAE, Shanghai, China, 6–11 June 2010; Volume 3, pp. 283–292. [CrossRef]
67. Bae, Y.H.; Kim, M.H.; Shin, Y.S. Rotor-Floater-Mooring Coupled Dynamic Analysis of Mini TLP-Type Offshore Floating Wind Turbines. In Proceedings of the International Conference on Offshore Mechanics and Arctic Engineering—OMAE, Shanghai, China, 6–11 June 2010; Volume 3, pp. 491–498. [CrossRef]
68. Olondriz, J.; Elorza, I.; Jugo, J.; Alonso-Quesada, S.; Pujana-Arrese, A. An Advanced Control Technique for Floating Offshore Wind Turbines Based on More Compact Barge Platforms. *Energies* **2018**, *11*, 1187. [CrossRef]
69. *Floating Offshore Wind Farms*; Green Energy and Technology; Springer International Publishing: Cham, Switzerland, 2016. [CrossRef]
70. GWEC. *Global Offshore Wind Report 2023*; Global Wind Energy Council: Brussels, Belgium, 2023.
71. IRENA. *Renewable Power Generation Costs in 2019*; International Renewable Energy Agency: Abu Dhabi, United Arab Emirates, 2020; 144p.
72. Spagnoli, G.; de Hollanda Cavalcanti Tsuha, C. A Review on the Behavior of Helical Piles as a Potential Offshore Foundation System. *Mar. Georesources Geotechnol.* **2020**, *38*, 1013–1036. [CrossRef]
73. Cerfontaine, B.; White, D.; Kwa, K.; Gourvenec, S.; Knappett, J.; Brown, M. Anchor Geotechnics for Floating Offshore Wind: Current Technologies and Future Innovations. *Ocean Eng.* **2023**, *279*, 114327. [CrossRef]
74. Hao, D.; Wang, D.; O'loughlin, C.D.; Gaudin, C. Tensile Monotonic Capacity of Helical Anchors in Sand: Interaction between Helices. *Can. Geotech. J.* **2018**, *56*, 1534–1543. [CrossRef]
75. Cerfontaine, B.; Knappett, J.A.; Brown, M.J.; Davidson, C.S.; Al-Baghdadi, T.; Sharif, Y.U.; Brennan, A.; Augarde, C.; Coombs, W.M.; Wang, L.; et al. A Finite Element Approach for Determining the Full Load–Displacement Relationship of Axially Loaded Shallow Screw Anchors, Incorporating Installation Effects. *Can. Geotech. J.* **2020**, *58*, 565–582. [CrossRef]
76. Ding, H.; Wang, L.; Zhang, P.; Le, C. Study on the Lateral Bearing Capacity of Single-Helix Pile for Offshore Wind Power. In Proceedings of the International Conference on Offshore Mechanics and Arctic Engineering—OMAE, Madrid, Spain, 17–22 June 2018; Volume 9. [CrossRef]
77. Sharif, Y.U.; Brown, M.J.; Cerfontaine, B.; Davidson, C.; Ciantia, M.O.; Knappett, J.A.; Ball, J.D.; Brennan, A.; Augarde, C.; Coombs, W.; et al. Effects of Screw Pile Installation on Installation Requirements and In-Service Performance Using the Discrete Element Method. *Can. Geotech. J.* **2020**, *58*, 1334–1350. [CrossRef]
78. Davidson, C.; Brown, M.J.; Cerfontaine, B.; Al-Baghdadi, T.; Knappett, J.; Brennan, A.; Augarde, C.; Coombs, W.; Wang, L.; Blake, A.; et al. Physical Modelling to Demonstrate the Feasibility of Screw Piles for Offshore Jacket-Supported Wind Energy Structures. *Geotechnique* **2022**, *72*, 108–126. [CrossRef]
79. Bradshaw, A.S.; Cullen, L.; Miller, Z. Field Study of Group Effects on the Pullout Capacity of "Deep" Helical Piles in Sand. *Can. Geotech. J.* **2021**, *59*, 538–545. [CrossRef]
80. Alsirawan, R.; Alnmr, A. Dynamic Behavior of Gravity Segmental Retaining Walls. *Pollack Period.* **2022**, *18*, 94–99. [CrossRef]
81. Brinkgreve, R.B.J.; Engin, E.; Engin, H.K. Validation of Empirical Formulas to Derive Model Parameters for Sands. In *Numerical Methods in Geotechnical Engineering—Proceedings of the 7th European Conference on Numerical Methods in Geotechnical Engineering, Trondheim, Norway, 6 September 2006*; 2010; pp. 137–142. Available online: https://www.researchgate.net/publication/267638739_Validation_of_empirical_formulas_to_derive_model_parameters_for_sands (accessed on 17 April 2024).
82. Salem, T.N.; Hussein, M. Axial Tensile Capacity of Helical Piles from Field Tests and Numerical Study. *Port-Said Eng. Res. J.* **2017**, *21*, 111–119. [CrossRef]
83. Brown, M.; Davidson, C.; Brennan, A.; Knappett, J.; Cerfontaine, B.; Sharif, Y. Physical Modelling of Screw Piles for Offshore Wind Energy Foundations. In Proceedings of the 1st International Symposium on Screw Piles for Energy Applications, Dundee, UK, 27–28 May 2019; pp. 31–38.

84. Law, K.H.; Geotechnical, K.H.; Bhd, S. 3D Finite Element Analysis of a Deep Excavation Considering the Effect of Anisotropic Wall Stiffness Impact. In Proceedings of the 19th Southeast Asian Geotechnical Conference & 2nd AGSSEA Conference (19SEAGC & 2AGSSEA), Kuala Lumpur, Malaysia, 31 May–3 June 2016; p. 6.
85. Al-Ani, W.; Wanatowski, D.; Chan, S.H. Numerical Analysis of Piled Embankments on Soft Soils. In Proceedings of the Geo-Shanghai 2014 International Conference, Shanghai, China, 26–28 May 2014; American Society of Civil Engineers (ASCE): Reston, VA, USA, 2014; pp. 30–39.
86. Hsiung, B.C.B.; Yang, K.H.; Aila, W.; Ge, L. Evaluation of the Wall Deflections of a Deep Excavation in Central Jakarta Using Three-Dimensional Modeling. *Tunn. Undergr. Space Technol.* **2018**, *72*, 84–96. [CrossRef]
87. Alnmr, A. Material Models to Study the Effect of Fines in Sandy Soils Based on Experimental and Numerical Results. *Acta Tech. Jaurinensis* **2021**, *14*, 651–680. [CrossRef]
88. Alsirawan, R.; Alnmr, A.; Koch, E. Experimental and Numerical Investigation of Geosynthetic-Reinforced Pile-Supported Embankments for Loose Sandy Soils. *Buildings* **2023**, *13*, 2179. [CrossRef]
89. Salgado, R.; Mitchell, J.K.; Jamiolkowski, M. Cavity Expansion and Penetration Resistance in Sand. *J. Geotech. Geoenvironmental Eng.* **1997**, *123*, 344–354. [CrossRef]
90. Krasiński, A. Numerical Simulation of Screw Displacement Pile Interaction with Non-Cohesive Soil. *Arch. Civ. Mech. Eng.* **2014**, *14*, 122–133. [CrossRef]
91. Thiyyakkandi, S.; McVay, M.; Bloomquist, D.; Lai, P. Experimental Study, Numerical Modeling of and Axial Prediction Approach to Base Grouted Drilled Shafts in Cohesionless Soils. *Acta Geotech.* **2014**, *9*, 439–454. [CrossRef]
92. Broere, W.; Van Tol, A.F. Modelling the Bearing Capacity of Displacement Piles in Sand. In *Proceedings of the Institution of Civil Engineers-Geotechnical Engineering*; Thomas Telford Ltd.: London, UK, 2015; Volume 159, pp. 195–206. [CrossRef]
93. Li, Z.; Haigh, S.K.; Bolton, M.D. Centrifuge Modelling of Mono-Pile under Cyclic Lateral Loads. In *Physical Modelling in Geotechnics, Two Volume Set*; CRC Press: London, UK, 2010; Volume 2, pp. 965–970.
94. Alnmr, A.; Ray, R.P.; Alsirawan, R. A State-of-the-Art Review and Numerical Study of Reinforced Expansive Soil with Granular Anchor Piles and Helical Piles. *Sustainability* **2023**, *15*, 2802. [CrossRef]
95. Alnmr, A.; Ray, R.P.; Alsirawan, R. Comparative Analysis of Helical Piles and Granular Anchor Piles for Foundation Stabilization in Expansive Soil: A 3D Numerical Study. *Sustainability* **2023**, *15*, 11975. [CrossRef]
96. Kaufmann, K.L.; Nielsen, B.N.; Augustesen, A.H. *Finite Element Investigations on the Interaction between a Pile and Swelling Clay*; DCE Technical Reports No. 104; Department of Civil Engineering, Aalborg University: Aalborg, Denmark, 2010.

Journal of
Marine Science and Engineering

MDPI

Review

Marine Geotechnical Research in Greece: A Review of the Current Knowledge, Challenges and Prospects

Nikolaos-Kimon Chtouris and Thomas Hasiotis *

Department of Marine Sciences, University of the Aegean, 81100 Mytilene, Greece; mard20008@aegean.gr
* Correspondence: hasiotis@aegean.gr

Abstract: Greece is expanding its energy grid system with submarine power and fiber optic cables between the mainland and the Aegean Sea islands. Additionally, pipelines have been installed to support natural gas facilities, and sites are being demarcated for the development of offshore wind parks. The above developments have necessitated extensive geotechnical surveying of the seabed; however, the survey data cannot be accessed for academic inspection or for desktop studies of future developments. This is further hindered by the limited geotechnical information in the Aegean and Ionian Seas. This review examines the existing information concerning the geotechnical behavior of the surficial sedimentary layers, including certain challenges associated with geotechnical sampling and CPTu interpretation. Certain prospects are discussed regarding marine geotechnical research in Greece, with examples from other European countries. The marine geotechnical data in Greece include geotechnical analyses of sediments cores and slope stability estimations, which are commonly associated with the seismic profiling of unstable slope areas. Underlying mechanisms of slope failure have mainly been attributed to the interbedded presence of weak layers (e.g., sapropels, tephra and underconsolidated sediments), the presence of gas and the cyclic loading from earthquake activity. Due to the limited geotechnical information, geological studies have contributed considerably to describing the distributions of gravity-induced events and lithostratigraphy. Within this context, a geological/geotechnical database is suggested where data can be collated and utilized for future studies.

Keywords: marine geotechnics; marine geological studies; weak layers; offshore works; Greece

1. Introduction

Greece is expanding and accelerating energy cable interconnections between islands of the Aegean and Ionian Seas and mainland Greece. The purpose of this endeavor is to minimize the energy costs from fossil fuels, as well as to introduce renewable energy sources (RESs) to non-interconnected islands (NIIs) [1–3]. The project to expand the electric grid of the country has been undertaken by the Independent Power Transmission Operator (IPTO) with the goal of interconnecting most islands to the mainland grid by 2030 [4]. The advantages from the interconnections regarding energy supply and capacity have been addressed in the past, with a particular emphasis having been placed on the prospect of the islands to develop RESs [5–7]. Notable examples are the Attica–Crete (500 kV DC) and Crete–Peloponnese (150 kV AC) links [2]. In the foreseeable future, projects such as the Great Sea Interconnector (GSI—formerly known as EuroAsia) will establish a HVDC link between Greece (Crete Island), Cyprus and Israel, thus expanding the European grid within the southern Aegean Sea. The CREGY interconnection between Egypt and Greece and the GAI (Green Aegean Interconnection) between Greece and Germany through the Adriatic Sea are also considered big and strategically important planned projects, where the vision is of carrying green energy from the renewable energy plants in Egypt and Greece, respectively. The above projects will enhance Greece's position as an energy focal point in the region.

In terms of RESs, marine areas have been inspected in the Aegean and Ionian Seas for the utilization of offshore wind energy with promising results [8–12]. For this reason, there are ongoing scheduled studies to designate areas for offshore wind park installation. Additionally, uninhabited islands have also been examined in the South Aegean Sea for onshore wind farm installation [13], similar to the case of Agios Georgios in the Saronic Gulf (https://www.terna-energy.com/acivities/wind-energy/aghios-georgios-island/, accessed on 17 July 2024). Moreover, Greece's anticipated role as an energy hub for southeast Europe is corroborated by a series of projects that are related to offshore natural gas facilities (LNG FSRUs and pipelines). This is exemplified by the expansion of the Revithousa LNG terminal and the prospective construction of a second Floating Storage and Regassification Unit (FSRU) next to the existing Alexandroupoli FSRU, as well as new FSRUs in the west Saronikos Gulf next to Ag. Theodoroi, Thermaikos Gulf (near Thessaloniki) and Pagasitikos Gulf (near Volos). Based on the above offshore developments, extensive marine geotechnical surveys will be needed for (i) the safe laying and burial of projected international power cables, (ii) the demarcation of suitable sites for pile foundations or floating wind turbine anchoring, (iii) the inter-array cables and links between offshore infrastructures and nearby islands or mainland and (iv) the installation of the FSRUs and related pipelines. Moreover, ports and other coastal facilities are expanding to support natural gas and offshore wind farm projects.

Initially, the description and interpretation of the seabed morphology, prevailing sedimentary processes and marine geohazards for sites with offshore infrastructures were dependent on geophysical surveys; however, when considering structure installation, it is imperative that sampling and geotechnical testing are conducted on surficial and deeper sedimentary layers. These are performed for engineering/design purposes, as well as for the validation of geophysical records. In the case of cable/pipeline installations, surveys inspect the upper 3 to 5 m of the seabed for the purpose of burying the infrastructure to protect it from physical processes (submarine landslides, currents, etc.) and/or anthropogenic activities (fishing, dredging, anchoring, etc.) [14,15]. Most of the marine surveys that have been conducted in Greece, primarily for the laying and burial of power and fiber optic cables, have utilized gravity coring for sampling, often with limited penetration and ambiguous results. Only in the last decade have surveys started to use vibro-coring (VC) and in situ cone penetration tests (CPTs), which have been facilitated by a few private energy companies, as well as the Independent Power Transmission Operator (IPTO). The above equipment was utilized for the safe characterization of subsurface layers, which correspond to the physical and mechanical properties of sediments. The usage of the above means has minimized physical and technical restrictions during sampling; therefore, questionable geological strata are now more easily validated and defined. Nonetheless, even after geological layers have been characterized according to their geotechnical properties, uncertainty can still exist. The uncertainty is usually produced from problems associated with the physical conditions of the study area (sea state during sampling, seabed slope and topography), followed by transportation, laboratory handling and geotechnical analyses of sediment cores [16].

Unfortunately, most of the data collected from surveys are not available for academic inspection. This is also an issue for desktop studies that support, in a preliminary stage, surveys for offshore installations (e.g., offshore wind parks), which rely on data accessibility. Moreover, published geotechnical research from universities/institutions in Greece is limited and has not been thoroughly updated to include additional measurements such as longer core samples from VC and/or in situ (CPT) data. Consequently, the present status in geotechnical research, regarding survey data and bibliographic information, prevents researchers from addressing challenges in geotechnical investigation such as seismic stratigraphic validation and precise geotechnical measurements. Furthermore, establishing reliable records of topography and geotechnical conditions in the Aegean and Ionian Seas is a challenge. This is primarily attributed to the irregular bathymetry in both the Aegean and Ionian Seas, which consists of numerous basins that are mainly tectonically formed, followed by high-relief slope environments (e.g., refs. [14,17–24]). In the case of slope stability, mass wasting processes have frequently been documented (e.g., refs. [14,15,25–35]); hence, their presence may compromise seafloor installations.

Considering the increasing number of planned power interconnections and other offshore construction activities as well as the demand for precise information on the geotechnical behavior of hosting sediments, the review aims to examine the current knowledge in marine geotechnical research in the Aegean and Ionian Seas and provide a better picture of the gaps as well as opportunities in marine geotechnical research.

2. Marine Geotechnical Research in Greece and the Supplementary Role of Geological Studies

Marine geotechnical studies have been implemented in various regions in the Aegean Sea (Thermaikos shelf/slope, North Aegean Shelf, Cretan Sea), Ionian Sea (Zakynthos Canyon, Zakynthos/Kefallinia Channel) and Gulf of Corinth; however, they are limited. Their primary focus concerns slope stability and mass gravitative processes, which are examined through a geotechnical analysis of sediment cores and interpretation of seismic profiles [33,36–45]. Yet, high-resolution seismic profiles crucially contribute to delineating changes in the composition of the seabed and sections where the substrate can shift from a soft/fine-grained texture to coarse (Figure 1).

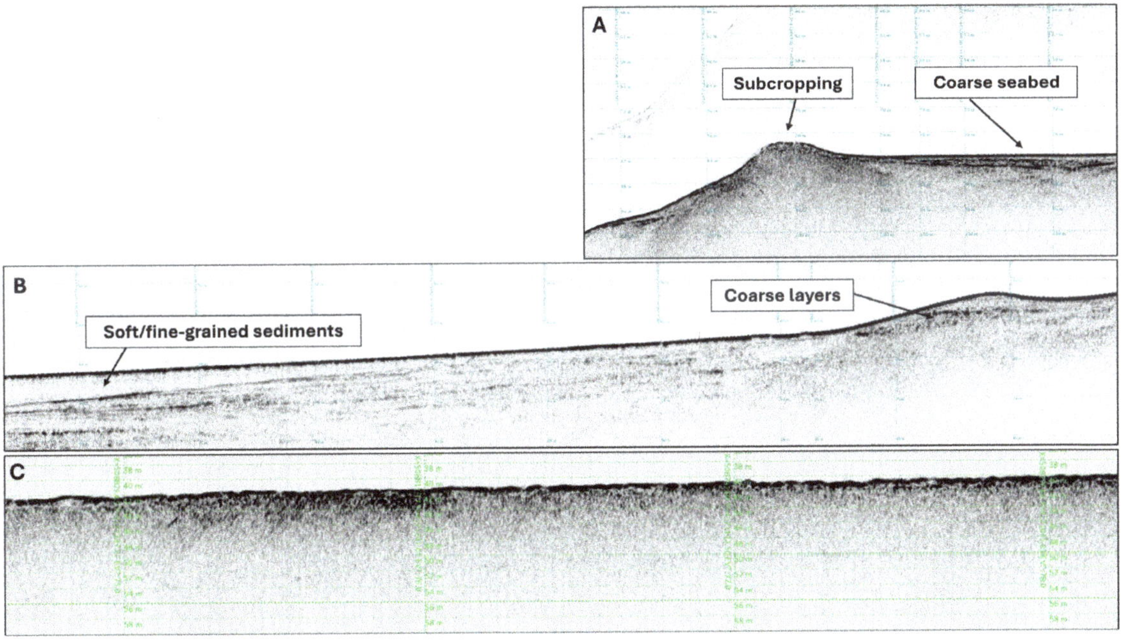

Figure 1. Examples of 3.5 kHz seismic profiles from geotechnical surveys conducted for the purposes of submarine cable installation, showing (**A**) the presence of hard sub-cropping material along a cable route followed by an interlayered coarse seabed, (**B**) a seabed section with a soft/fine-grained composition that transitions into a coarser configuration, (**C**) a generally coarse seabed based on the strong surficial acoustic reflection.

Sediment cores are typically obtained with gravity coring; hence, sediment description/analysis and seismic validation are mostly constrained at 2 to 3 m. Nonetheless, some studies [33,43,44,46–50] have achieved higher penetration. Deep geotechnical sampling has been implemented for the foundation and design of the Rio–Antirrio bridge in western Greece [51,52]. In terms of in situ measurements (CPT, SPT), applications have been found in onshore coastal sediments in the Gulf of Corinth [53], offshore slope environments in the Cretan Sea/Eastern Mediterranean [44,54], western Greece for the foundation design of the Rio–Antirrio bridge [51,52] and between the islands of Evia and Skiathos in the Aegean Sea [55].

Early geotechnical investigations have been implemented on shelf and slope environments with gravity cores and piston cores [36,46,56,57]. In the case of piston core sampling, Chassefiere and Monaco [46] achieved a 10 m penetration. An extensive geotechnical inspection was conducted by Lykousis and Pechlivanoglou [56], where geotechnical properties (porosity, plasticity, shear strength, carbonate content, organic matter and texture) were recorded at various sites in the Aegean Sea (Alexandroupoli Gulf, Kavala Gulf, South Evia Gulf, Petalion Gulf, Keratsini–Psitalia) using short piston cores. The data are in the form of ranges and hence do not provide detailed descriptions in relation to depth; therefore, they can be regarded as preliminary. Nonetheless, geotechnical variations among regions were attributed to bottom current activity and differences in sedimentation rates.

Over the decades, geological studies have provided information on gravitative processes, sediment properties (texture, carbonate content, mineralogy, etc.) and sedimentation rates [43,58–65]. In addition to sedimentary information, descriptions of eustatic sea-level changes, tectonic structure, stratigraphy (lithostratigraphy, chronostratigraphy, etc.) and oceanographic conditions (met-ocean data) provide the framework for interpreting the geological regime of a site. Important contributions of geological studies include seismic profiling of gravity-induced deposits [27,28,30,32,34,35,39,40,43,45,53,59,60,66–89] as well as gas seepage and diapirism [39,40,77–79,90–93]. All these processes/formations must be recorded and inspected since they can compromise offshore infrastructure [14].

In the context of geological investigation, paleoclimate and sedimentological studies have extracted drilled core samples and long piston cores (20 to 30 m), thus offering detailed descriptions of deep sedimentary layers. Examples can be found in the Gulf of Corinth basin area [43,49,94–96], North Aegean Shelf [97,98], Thermaikos Shelf [99–101] and Cretan Trough [102]. Deeper core sampling from basin environments offers a more comprehensive picture of the depositional history and gravitative processes (e.g., turbidites) [49,94–96,102], while drilled samples from shelf environments are mainly examined for the purposes of hydrocarbon exploration [97,101]. Additional core descriptions can be found in paleoclimate reconstructions, albeit from shallower cores [103–113].

In general, geological studies can be used for describing the lithostratigraphy (e.g., sapropels, tephra layers, organic layers, turbiditic layers, etc.), tectonic structure and geohazards of a site. In terms of lithostratigraphy, it is invaluable for recording sedimentary units that exhibit distinct physical features and by extension geotechnical behavior. In the case of sapropels, their presence represents anoxic depositional conditions due to poor water circulation; hence, they contain high organic matter, which can affect the shear strength of sediments [28,29,50,114–119]. In a similar way, the presence of interbedded tephra layers in the sedimentary column can decrease the cohesiveness of sediments and therefore their shear strength [28,117]. Tephra (volcanic) sedimentary layers are particularly prominent in the South Aegean Sea, where the Aegean Volcanic Arc is situated [37,118–121].

Studies that have conducted surficial sampling in shelf environments provide preliminary insights into the distribution of coarse/fine substrates, including sedimentological attributes (mineralogy, carbonate content, etc.). Surficial sedimentological mapping can be found in the North Aegean Shelf [88,122–130], Thermaikos Shelf [131,132], Kafireas Strait [133], South Evia Gulf [134], between Sifnos and Kimolos Islands [135] and in the South Aegean Sea [37,136], whilst Poulos [65] compiled information on the distribution and origin of the terrigenous components of the surficial sediments in the Aegean Sea seafloor. In conjunction with oceanographic data, sedimentary distributions can be used as predictors or trends of sediment mobility and erosion [131,133]. This is particularly important regarding cable interconnections, where some segments are left exposed on the seabed due to the inability to bury the infrastructure [130]. Erosional features and bedforms are also examined from seismic reflection profiles and sonar images, which can indicate the effects of local hydrodynamics (e.g., bottom currents) [86,137,138]. Comprehensive maps of sediment distribution as well as sediment thickness and geohazards (active faults, slides, gas, etc.) have been developed by IGME (e.g., ref. [139]) and have provided information for areas such as the North Aegean Shelf, Pagasitikos Gulf and Cyclades near Santorini island.

In the absence of sufficient geotechnical information on sedimentary strata, geological studies provide a preliminary framework in studying the seabed, considering the complex structure of the Aegean and Ionian Seas [21]. In that regard, changes in eustatic sea level control the distribution of lithostratigraphic units such as sapropelic layers or underconsolidated deltaic sediments that have been deposited during low sea-level conditions [29,140]. According to the above, the collation and assessment of geological studies marks the first step in laying the foundations for geotechnical investigation.

3. Geotechnical Properties of Quaternary Sedimentary Layers and Mechanisms of Sediment Instability in the Aegean and Ionian Seas

3.1. Geotechnical Study of Quaternary Sedimentary Layers and Sediment Instabilities

Geotechnical analysis of sediment cores principally encompasses texture, Atterberg limits, bulk density, carbonate content, water content, shear strength and consolidation measurements. Table 1 provides an overview of important geotechnical studies, including some notable geological studies, while Figure 2 presents the geographical location of the main marine geotechnical investigations in the Aegean and Ionian Seas. Undrained shear strength is probably the most challenging and laborious parameter in geotechnical analysis. This is due to disturbance effects inflicted on sediment cores during sampling, transportation and handing in the lab [16,141]. Moreover, different lab tests (e.g., vane shear tests, triaxial tests, direct shear, etc.) can be performed, which may produce variable estimations [55].

In Greece, shear strength measurements have been conducted with a pocket penetrometer [46], field vane test [142], vane shear apparatus [29,31,33,36–38,41,42,44,143,144], Bromhead ring shear device [44] and triaxial test [31,41]. In essence, vertical variations in shear strength provide information, in conjunction with other parameters (texture, organic matter, bulk density, Atterberg Limits, etc.), on the presence of weak layers that may be susceptible to failure; therefore, they indicate the predisposition of sediments to gravity-induced flow (e.g., slides, flows, etc.) [29].

Table 1. Sampling and analysis of sediment cores from geotechnical and geological studies in the Aegean and Ionian Seas.

Study	Location	Core Equipment and Penetration	Geotechnical Measurements
[58]	NW Aegean Sea	Gravity cores (1.9–2.4 m)	Grain size, carbonate content, SEM microscopic inspection
[56]	Aegean Sea (multiple locations)	Short piston cores (unspecified)	Grain size, mineralogy, carbonate content, organic matter, porosity, Atterberg limits, wet bulk density, shear strength
[59]	Ionian Sea (Zakynthos Channel)	Gravity cores (~1.5 m)	Grain size, organic carbon, calcium carbonate, clay mineralogy
[60]	NW Aegean Sea (Thermaikos Slope—Sporades Basin)	Gravity cores (~2.5 m)	Grain size, organic carbon, calcium carbonate, clay mineralogy
[57]	North Evia Gulf	Sediment cores (0.85–2.7 m)	Grain size, water content, carbonate content, wet bulk density, Atterberg limits, shear strength
[46]	South Aegean Sea	Piston cores (5–10 m)	Grain size, clay mineralogy, Atterberg limits, water content, wet bulk density, shear strength
[36]	NW Aegean Sea (Thermaikos Shelf/Slope)	Gravity cores (1.5–3 m)	Grain size, carbonate content, water content, Atterberg limits, shear strength

Table 1. *Cont.*

Study	Location	Core Equipment and Penetration	Geotechnical Measurements
[29]	Multiple sites (Aegean Sea)	Gravity cores	Shear strength
[116]	North Aegean Sea (Thermaikos Gulf, North Aegean Shelf)	Gravity cores (~2 m)	Visual description, organic carbon and radiocarbon dates, examination of sapropelic layers
[48]	Gulf of Corinth	Gravity cores (0.5–1 m), piston cores (7–7.5 m)	Grain size, organic carbon, calcium carbonate
[37]	South Aegean Sea	Gravity cores (0.12–2.76 m)	Grain size, Atterberg limits, water content, density
[80]	Ionian Sea (Corfu–Kefalonia Valley System)	Piston cores (3.5 m)	Grain size, organic carbon, X-ray
[38]	South Aegean Sea (Cretan Sea)	Gravity cores (2–3 m)	Grain size, carbonate content, bulk density, Atterberg limits, water content, shear strength
[41]	North Aegean Shelf/Slope	Gravity cores (~2.5 m), box cores	Bulk density, carbonate content, Atterberg limits, shear strength
[49]	Gulf of Corinth	Piston core (Calypso core—30 m)	Physical properties (core logging): magnetic susceptibility, gamma ray, resistivity, etc.
[50]	North Aegean Sea	Gravity cores (2.1–4.1 m)	Grain size, organic carbon, carbonate content, clay mineralogy, radiocarbon dating
[26]	Ionian Sea (Zakynthos Canyon/Valley)	Gravity cores (~2 m)	Sedimentological description (geotechnical analysis not presented)
[42]	NW Aegean Sea (Thermaikos Shelf and Sporades Basin)	Gravity cores (2–3 m)	Water content, wet density, shear strength
[27,28]	South Aegean Sea	Gravity cores (~2 m)	Grain size, water content, shear strength, Atterberg limits, bulk density
[44]	South Aegean Sea (Cretan Margin)	Gravity cores (4–4.6 m)	Physical properties (MSCL), shear strength
[43]	Gulf of Corinth	Gravity cores (~2.5 m), piston cores (max 30 m)	Gravity cores: physical properties (MSCL), grain size, carbonate content, organic carbon Piston cores: physical properties (MSCL), grain size
[31]	Ionian Sea, western Greece (Gulf of Corinth), NW Aegean Sea (Thermaikos Shelf/Slope)	Gravity core (2–5 m)	Grain size, organic carbon, carbonate content, Atterberg limits, water content, bulk density, overconsolidation ratio (OCR)
[94]	Gulf of Corinth	Calypso piston core (20 m)	Grain size, magnetic susceptibility and radiocarbon dates, examination of earthquake-induced layers (turbidites)
[32,33]	South Aegean Sea (Cretan Margin)	Gravity cores (1.5–4.6 m)	Grain size, shear strength, multi-sensor core logging (bulk density)
[86]	Gulf of Corinth	Gravity cores (1.1–2 m)	Grain size, mineralogy, X-ray diffraction
[138]	South Aegean Sea	Gravity cores (3.5 m)	Radiocarbon dating, visual description
[144]	Southeast Mediterranean Sea (south off Crete near Gavdos Island)	Gravity cores (1–2.4 m)	Multi-sensor core logging (magnetic susceptibility, gamma-ray density, p-wave velocity), grain size, shear strength, organic carbon, X-radiography
[96]	Gulf of Corinth	Drilled core (IODP Expedition 381)	Visual description, grain size, isotope analysis (Th/U)

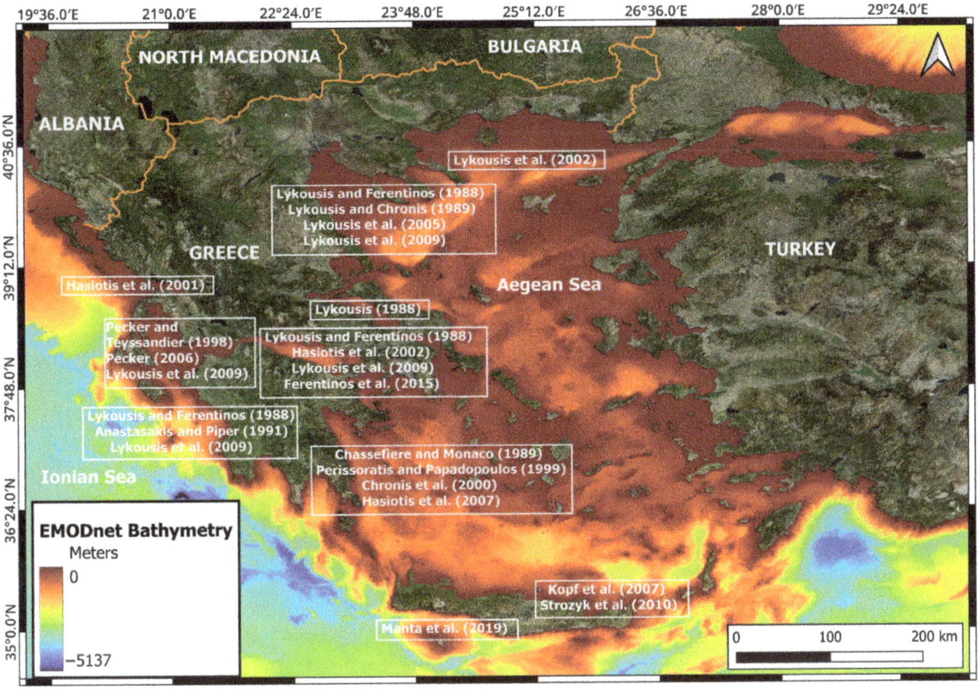

Figure 2. Map of the Aegean and Ionian Seas and locations of studies that have conducted geotechnical analyses on subsurface sediments (e.g., refs. [28,31,33,36–38,41,42,44–47,51–53,57,142,144,145]).

As mentioned in the previous section, eustatic sea-level changes, seismicity (ground accelerations) and proximity of shelf and slope environments to river outflows have primarily shaped the depositional sequences of the Aegean and Ionian Seas [25,62,100]. Eustatic sea-level changes mainly concern the last glacial period (Wurm) and the unconformities (potential failure planes) that have developed within the sedimentary column [142]. During low sea-level conditions, slope depositional environments experienced rapid sedimentation near rivers, forming underconsolidated sedimentary sequences in the process that were subsequently overlain by hemipelagic sedimentation during higher sea levels. The stacking of underconsolidated sediments between more consolidated sedimentary layers has left their internal composition susceptible to external stresses, primarily from seismic loading, and hence underlying consolidated layers can act as failure planes, initiating slides in the process [29,35,140]. Fluvial sedimentation and its effect on slope stability have been examined extensively in the Gulf of Corinth. The presence of river outflows along with their proximity to the steep slopes of the gulf have induced rapid progradation of deltas, specifically during high sedimentation rates [31,40,48,71,78]. Slope failures can be triggered within interlayered, sandy, liquefiable sedimentary sequences that are bounded by low-permeability clayey layers [53]. Liquefaction can develop under cyclic loading from earthquakes, which increases the pore stresses within sandy–silty layers, thus reducing the shear strength of sediments. This type of failure has been documented offshore for the Eratini and Tolofonas deltas [31,40,53,78,89]. The presence of shallow liquefiable horizons in the delta plains at the southern coast of the Gulf of Corinth, between the Selinountas and Kerynitis deltas, has been attributed as the main factor in the destruction and submergence of ancient Helike (372/373 B.C.), which generated a translational slide caused by an earthquake of 6 to 6.7 on the Richter scale [45]. The above studies illustrate that underlying alluvial depositional sequences may pose considerable geohazards both offshore as well as onshore, with the latter case also having the potential to generate tsunamis [45,53].

Gas seepage has been documented within deltaic sedimentary sequences in the Aegean Sea and western coast of Greece. Their presence is typically indicated on seismic reflection profiles with a characteristic acoustic blanking signal [77]. The Pockmark formation has been documented in western Greece (Gulf of Patras and Gulf of Corinth) and the Ionian Sea (offshore Killini), where gas expulsion has eroded the surficial sedimentary layers due to pore-pressure-induced stresses, forming distinct depressions in the process [26,39,77,79,91]. Gas-charged sediments have been recorded in other areas of the Ionian Sea (Corfu Shelf, Amvrakikos Gulf), western Greece (Katakolon Bay) and the North Aegean Sea (Thermaikos Gulf, North Aegean Shelf) [77,88,90,92,93]. The lateral migration of gas and subsequent concentration at subsurface sedimentary layers or seepage at the seabed are usually aided by the presence of unconformities, fault planes and salt diapirs; however, seismic activity is probably the most important factor in causing gas expulsions, which can disrupt the depositional configuration of the seabed and strength of sediments [26,39,77,79].

In the Zakynthos canyon/valley system, between Zakynthos island and the Killini Peninsula, factors affecting slope stability (gas seepage, salt diapirism, slope steepness, seismicity) are particularly pronounced, leading to frequent mass movement along the bounding slopes. The high seismicity is attributed to its proximity to the subduction zone of the Hellenic Trench [26,68]. In the NE Ionian Sea and extension of the Hellenic Arc, the Corfu–Kefalonia valley also exhibits high-inclination slopes and submarine mass movements, with oceanographic measurements also indicating erosion from currents corresponding to the deep-water formation in the Adriatic Sea [80]. Along the Hellenic Trench, south of Crete, the presence of weak layers predisposes slopes to failure, leading to frequent turbidity and mass flow [72,144,146]. Instabilities are also facilitated by alluvial deposition at the Cretan slope, which further increases the strain on slope sediments. At the northern margin of Crete, the high steepness due to tectonic uplift and seismic activity predisposes weak layers to failure [32,38]. Furthermore, subsidence of Cretan Basins induces over-steepness, thereby enhancing mass flows towards the basins [34]. It is noteworthy to mention that under an extensional tectonic regime, concurrent uplift and subsidence may not only increase slope steepness but also relocate high-inclination sections, which may reactivate mass transport processes. This indicates that gravitative deposits may not always be found at the flank of basins but may be located mid-slope, where they may become reactivated by an external force (e.g., seismic activity) [33,34]. In the North Aegean Sea, sedimentary deformations (creep) have been recorded in the Thermaikos slope (NW Aegean Sea), caused by the progressive downbending of slope sediments, which leads to slumping and sliding [25,67,69]. Sediment instabilities on slopes are also affected by the presence of growth faults within the sedimentary column [36,69].

Lithostratigraphic units that exhibit distinct physical attributes within the sedimentary column can shift the geotechnical behavior of sediments. As addressed in the previous section, the presence of sapropels in slope environments, specifically S1 (~10 to 6 Kyr B.P.), tends to leave overlying sediments susceptible to failure, depending on the external stresses induced on the seabed (seismic activity) along with other factors (gas, diapirism, sedimentation rate, etc.). The high water content and low shear strength and bulk density of this layer produce weak internal zones that can generate mass movements [15,29,36,46,115–117].

At the northern margins of the Cretan Trough (Argolikos Basin, Amorgos Basin, Christiana Basin), weak layers (sapropels, tephra, turbidites) are documented in slope environments, with local normal faulting inducing creeps and slumps along the slope [37]. The general northern region of the Cretan Trough and Cyclades Plateau exhibits frequent but not intense seismic activity; however, large seismic events do occur, such as the 1956 event (M_s = 7.5), which produced a large slump and tsunami in the surrounding vicinity [37,147]. In addition, hydrothermal activity and seismicity produced from volcanic activity are also contributing factors in inducing slope instability at island margins [27,28].

Tephra layers in the surficial sedimentary sequences can also shift the geotechnical behavior of sediments by making the sedimentary structure non-cohesive, thus leaving it prone to liquefaction [27,32,46]. Their distribution has been documented and studied primarily in cores from the South Aegean Sea [27,32,38,46]. The percentages of clay and silt are important factors in tephra layers, specifically regarding interparticle friction and granularity [46]. According to the particle shapes recorded within tephra layers, rounded silt-sized particles tend to produce less plastic behavior and a lower water content, while platelet particles increase the plasticity and water content. This illustrates the importance of particle characteristics in shaping the sedimentary fabric of sediments and by extension geotechnical behavior. Furthermore, tephra layers proximate to sapropels tend to exhibit higher water contents and lower bulk densities, while, when intermixed with clayey sediments, they can become more cohesive and thus can exhibit a higher shear strength [46]. Within this context, the geotechnical behavior of sediments may be affected by their proximity to weak layers (e.g., sapropels) within the sedimentary column. This is also corroborated by the occurrence of turbidites within sapropelic layers [37,41,47,115].

The above studies provide information on the distribution of weak zones in slope environments, along with interpretations of the underlying mechanisms of slope failure. The detection of weak layers (sapropels, tephra layers, underconsolidated layers, etc.) within the sedimentary column and seismic profile interpretation of gravity-induced deposits along the seabed can provide indications not only of existing instabilities but also of potential slope failures in the future. For this reason, it is important to provide ranges of shear strength, bulk density, water content and plasticity and, if possible, of other parameters (i.e., overconsolidation ratio, relative density, unit weight, etc.). In terms of lithostratigraphy, the physical attributes of sediments and their effect on geotechnical behavior can be examined and hence provide a link between geological and geotechnical interpretation [46]. Additionally, clay mineralogy (illite, smectite, kaolinite, etc.) also has an important role in shaping the geotechnical behavior of sediments; hence, its measurement in cores and examination of its effects on geotechnical properties is important (i.e., refs. [46,50]). When geological studies are conducted in marine environments, their approaches can enhance geotechnical assessments of the recorded lithostratigraphy. In the context of geohazards, the above studies demonstrate that there are multiple factors leading to slope instability, depending on the region; however, the most important instigating factor is seismic activity. Other reviews on geohazards in the Aegean and Ionian Seas have also highlighted seismic activity as a major factor triggering mass movements [14,25].

3.2. Geotechnical Analysis of Deep Sedimentary Strata and In Situ Testing of Sediments

Long core samples (piston cores, drilled cores) obtained from basins [49,94–96,102] and shelves [97,98,100,101] can display the structure and distribution of depositional layers. The description of intercalated turbidites from the Gulf of Corinth basin indicates the frequency of turbiditic events, which are intermittent and occur by hemipelagic sedimentation [49,94,95]. In shelf environments and near the mouths of major rivers such as Evros, drilled core samples have revealed gas present within prograding deltaic sequences, a result of the rapid sedimentation that has occurred in the area [98].

In the context of lithostratigraphic interpretation of deep sedimentary strata, geotechnical analysis is rare in the published literature. The foundation design of the Rio–Antirrio bridge in NW Peloponnese provides a rare case study, not only in terms of a geotechnical study but also for the engineering issues associated with the foundation of the structure. Specifically, the presence of underconsolidated alluvial strata (silty sands to sandy clays) at the designated site posed considerable risks in terms of the bearing capacity of the structure for seismic loading [51,52]. To examine potential failure and deformation near the foundation (gravity caissons), extensive sampling was conducted. This involved the acquisition of borehole samples, piezocone tests (CPTu), standard penetration tests (SPTs), vane tests, dilatometer tests and seismic cone tests, with sampling depths reaching 60 to 100 m below the seafloor. The geotechnical profiles obtained from the analysis showed generally weak-strength behavior, with the undrained shear strength exhibiting decreased values at certain depth intervals due to the presence of cohesionless layers. To support the structure, ground reinforcement was implemented by placing steel tubular pipes in an 8000 m^2 circular area, along with the backfilling of a gravel layer (2.8 m thick) on top, between the foundation of the caisson and the tubular pipes. The above case study shows the rigorous engineering solutions employed for the safe foundation and settlement of the Rio–Antirrio bridge in a generally unfavorable environment. Similar publications of engineering inspections and solutions for the installation of existing and/or scheduled offshore structures are missing but it is obvious that they might further improve future projects.

An important aspect that was addressed early in the review is the lack of more sophisticated or rather additional information for the interpretation of soil profiles. In the case of in situ tests (CPT), they have been utilized only over the last decade in Greece to further enhance subsurface strata. Figure 3 shows an example of a CPTu profile that registers in situ shear strength, relative density, sediment characterization (based on soil behavior charts), along with laboratory shear strength measurements from a vane test conducted on a vibro-core sample proximate to the CPTu (see Section 4.2). Figure 4 displays a CPTu profile with basic registered parameters (cone resistance, sleeve friction, pore pressure, etc.). Some studies have examined onshore coastal sedimentary layers at the northern coast of the Corinth Gulf [53] and slope sediments at the Cretan Margin [44,54]. On the coast between the Tolofonas and Eratini deltas, cone penetration tests (CPTs) as well as dynamic penetration tests (DPSH) were performed to assess the slope stability and liquefaction potential of onshore sediments [53]; however, no core samples were obtained near the in situ testing locations, and hence, soil interpretation was based on empirical information instead of field data. Conversely, CPT and gravity cores were obtained in proximity at the slope of the Cretan Margin to assess the stability of undisturbed slope sediments and slide deposits in conjunction with seismic profiling [44]. Despite some issues in CPT deployment, the registered cone resistance and shear strength were higher for undisturbed sediments and lower in the slide portion, with Multi-Sensor Core Log (MSCL) data exhibiting a low water content, bulk density and shear velocity for the slide deposits. This allowed for distinguishing the undisturbed seabed section from the landslide, which was initially not discernable from the lithostratigraphic description of the gravity cores. On the other hand, pore pressure measurements were deemed problematic due to the lack of dissipation tests. The above studies show some rare examples of geotechnical investigation and hence can offer insights into the particularities and challenges of marine environments in the Aegean and Ionian Seas (e.g., slope, topography, underconsolidated layers, etc.).

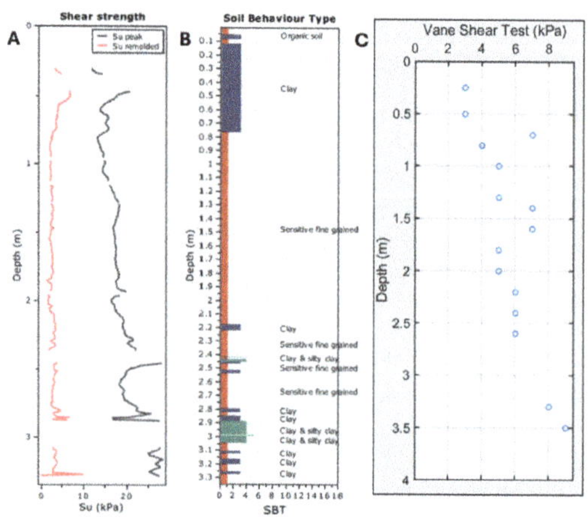

Figure 3. Example of in situ CPTu measurements from a geotechnical survey in Greece to interpret subsurface sediments for the purposes of submarine power cable installation. The interpreted CPTu profile presents in situ undrained shear strength (**A**) and soil behavior type (SBT) (**B**) when compared with a laboratory vane shear test (**C**) conducted on a core sample proximate to the CPTu.

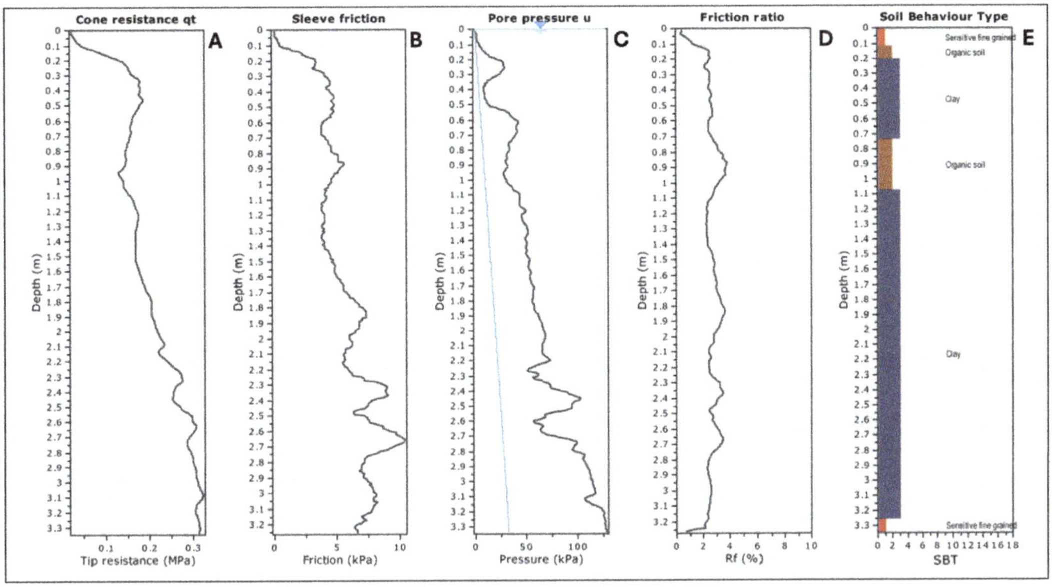

Figure 4. Example of in situ CPTu measurements from a geotechnical survey in Greece to interpret subsurface sediments for the purposes of submarine power cable installation. CPTu profile presenting the basic parameters: (**A**) cone resistance, (**B**) sleeve friction, (**C**) pore pressure (blue line: pore pressure equilibrium) (**D**) friction ratio and (**E**) soil behavior type (SBT).

3.3. Slope Stability Estimations

Slope stability estimations have been conducted in the Ionian Sea [47,142], western Greece [45,53,142,143,145], North Aegean Shelf [41], Saronic Gulf [142], Thermaikos slope [31,36,142] and South Aegean Sea [28,33,38,46]. Table 2 shows the results from slope stability assessments in the Aegean and Ionian Seas. The Infinite Slope Stability represents a simple approach in estimating slope stability; however, other relatively more intricate methods have been utilized to assess the safety factor of slopes, such as the Janbu and Bishop method [53,143]. In the case of Infinite Slope Stability, this assumes a smooth extended homogenized seabed, with important parameters being the ratio of undrained shear strength to overburden pressure, slope angle and peak ground acceleration (seismic activity) [148]. It has been implemented in both Aegean and Ionian Sea slope environments [28,33,36,38,46,47,53,142,145]. To utilize the above approach, it is also necessary to examine the available seismic reflection profiles along the sloping environments as well as assess the lithology with core samples or indirectly with CPT data [53]. The application of the Normalized-Soil Parameter (NSP) is considered a more accurate method to assess soil stability, since it compensates for the disturbance effects that are often inflicted on core samples [149]. The NSP method is usually applicable in smoother slopes; therefore, it has been implemented on prodelta depositional environments of the North Aegean Shelf [41] and other marine sites (Thermaikos slope, Gulf of Corinth and Gulf of Patra) [31]. It is noteworthy to mention that the NSP approach necessitates triaxial testing to simulate conditions under static and cyclic stresses, which is often expensive and laborious; therefore, NSP applications are rare.

In Table 2, some indicative gradient ranges and ground accelerations are provided based on the slope stability calculations. It becomes apparent that local failures can be initiated even at low inclinations with a minimum seismic disturbance. Stability is dependent primarily on the sedimentation rate, seismotectonic activity and the gradient that has developed in slope environments. The high sedimentation rate between Zakynthos, Kefalonia and Peloponnesus has formed thick underconsolidated sequences that are susceptible even at very small gradients [142]. In terms of S1 sapropelic layers in the Zakynthos slope, critical distances from epicenters of 6.5 R and 7 R earthquakes, as well as ground accelerations, were found to be less compared to overlying sedimentary sequences [47]. This further demonstrates the susceptibility of such deposits to seismic activity; however, it should be mentioned that the specific study makes some assumptions for overlying non-sapropelic strata regarding bulk density and shear strength. In the case of limited core penetration, assumptions can be made on the sedimentation conditions (sedimentation rates, composition, etc.) and shear strength behavior of subsurface sedimentary layers using theoretical (linear regression) approximations [36,143]. To further test slope stability, such assumptions can be useful in the absence of sufficient information; however, it is important that adjacent geotechnical information is available, and that seismic interpretation can provide some indications of similar sedimentation processes (e.g., prodelatic sequences). Documentation of active faults is also paramount, including potential vertical offsets that could displace sediments [41,84]. The above information shows that extensive geotechnical sampling and recording of active faults in marine areas can further enhance slope stability estimations. In that respect, the seismic activity and tectonic structure of the Aegean and Ionian Seas present the references for the calculated ground accelerations.

Table 2. Slope stability estimations in marine areas of the Aegean and Ionian Seas, along with slope gradient ranges (or averages), ground acceleration and a general assessment.

Study	Location	Slope Gradient Range (°)	Ground Acceleration (g)	General Assessment
[142]	Ionian Sea (Zakynthos–Kefalonia–Peloponnesus), Gulf of Corinth, NW Aegean Sea (Thermaikos slope), Central Aegean Sea (Saronic Gulf)	4°–7°	0.18–0.28 g	General instability for the Zakynthos–Kefalonia–Peloponnesus and Corinth Gulf slopes. Instabilities in the Saronic Gulf and some sections of the Thermaikos slope.
[36]	NW Aegean Sea (Thermaikos slope)	1°–4°	0.18–0.33 g	Slope stability for 10 m layers and instability at 20 m (theoretical approximations).
[47]	Ionian Sea (Zakynthos continental slope)	8° (average)	0.08–0.30 g	Sufficient ground acceleration for failure is 0.08 g for S1 sapropels and 0.30 g for overlying strata. Presentation of critical distances of epicenters for sufficient failure.
[38]	South Aegean Sea	1°–4°	0.07–0.13 g	Ground accelerations 0.07 to 0.13 g are sufficient to trigger failures.
[145]	Ionian Sea (Paxi and Corfu slopes)	5°–30°	0.43–1.26 g	Paxi slope exhibits instability under dynamic conditions. Corfu slope shows instability in both static and dynamic conditions.
[53]	Gulf of Corinth	2.5°–11°	0.30–0.50 g	Stable conditions of coastal sediments under cyclic loading of a M_s = 6.2 R earthquake. Failure is initiated from earthquake-induced pore pressure of subsurface liquefiable layers.

Table 2. *Cont.*

Study	Location	Slope Gradient Range (°)	Ground Acceleration (g)	General Assessment
[41]	North Aegean slope	0.5°–2.9°	0.08–0.26 g	Calculated ground accelerations for failure were less than the predicted ones, indicating high instability.
[28]	South Aegean Sea (Milos slope)	3°–26°	0.05 g	General stability of sediments under static conditions. Instability is found in shallow surficial layers (<50 cm).
[31]	NW Aegean Sea (Thermaikos slope), western Greece (Corinth Gulf, Patraikos Gulf), Ionian Sea (Kyparissiakos Gulf)	0.5°–5°	0.12–0.30 g	Instability of prodelta sediments corresponding to the low section of the High System Tract (HST), in addition to the presence of gas.
[33]	South Aegean Sea (Cretan Margin)	3°–5°	0.37–0.67 g	Critical ground accelerations of 0.37 to 0.67 g for 3° slopes and 0.40 to 0.66 g for 5° slopes.
[45]	Gulf of Corinth	2°–20°	0.30–0.55 g	Stable conditions for coastal sediments under static and cyclic loading. Failure is initiated from earthquake-induced pore pressure increase in subsurface liquefiable layers.

4. Current Challenges in Marine Geotechnical Surveying

4.1. Core Sampling

Commonly, sediment core samples are obtained at certain locations along the seismic survey lines to classify subsurface strata and subsequently ground-truth the seismic reflection character of the seabed. Additionally, in situ tests (CPTu) must also be validated, since they provide indirect information on the composition and geotechnical properties of the seabed. Both core sampling and CPTu testing are utilized to interpret the seismic stratigraphy for the purposes of burial assessments (cables/pipelines) or foundation design of offshore strictures (e.g., OWF). In the former case, the geotechnical properties of subsurface layers must be inspected to support estimations of the burial depth and method of burial. In the case of sediment coring, the type of equipment employed during sampling (gravity coring, vibro-coring, piston coring, etc.) as well as the composition of subsurface sedimentary layers (sandy or muddy texture or mixed composition) will determine the extent of ground-truthing. When considering cable/pipeline surveys, the demanding and/or limited penetration of gravity core sampling constrains lithological interpretations and by extension investigation of deeper "weak" deposits. Also, penetration is usually hindered by the presence of cohesionless sediments (sandy and/or gravelly sediments) as well as cohesive/muddy layers that display increasing consolidation with depth (e.g., stiff to hard clays). This issue becomes especially prominent when depositional environments change considerably, considering the complex and pronounced topography of the Aegean and Ionian Seas. For the above reasons, it is often justifiable to employ vibro-coring so that a deeper penetration can be achieved. Vibro-core penetration in cohesive sediments can reach up to 6 m for cable/pipeline burial and even more; however, the vibratory effects used during sampling can disturb the sediments, and hence, certain geotechnical estimations may not reflect actual conditions (e.g., undrained shear strength, consolidation). Figure 5 exhibits examples of vibro-core samples from a geotechnical survey conducted for the purposes of a power cable installation. It is noteworthy to mention that some level of disturbance, specifically concerning cohesive sediments, is expected such as changes in pore pressure. Furthermore, survey operations can disturb the internal sedimentary fabric within the cores, and thus lab measurements may be affected [16,141].

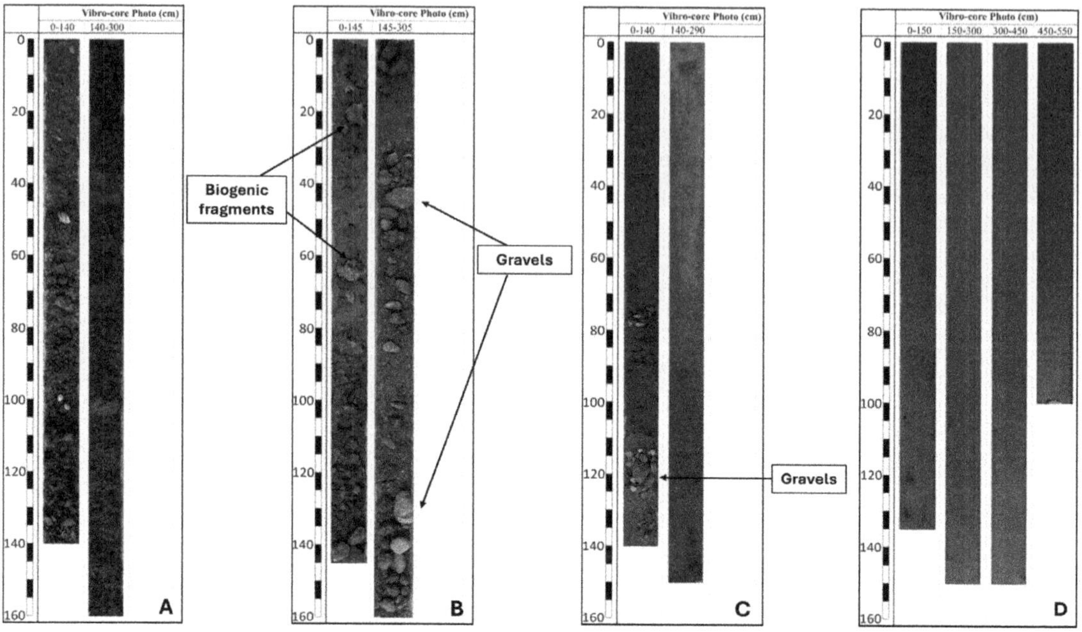

Figure 5. Examples of vibro-core samples obtained from a geotechnical survey for the purposes of power cable installation. (**A**) Core sample consisting of intermixed muddy and sandy sediments. (**B**) Transition from a muddy texture with biogenic fragments to a sandy composition with gravel. (**C**) Muddy sand texture that transitions into sand with some gravels. (**D**) Muddy composition where core penetration reaches up to 5.5 m.

4.2. CPTu Testing and Soil Property Estimation

An important opportunity in marine geotechnical research in Greece concerns piezocone (CPTu) measurement and its interpretation as well as calibration with nearby core retrieval. Over the last decade, geotechnical surveys in Greece have been systematically employing CPTu data more often since they provide continuous and supplementary information on the subsurface. The records of cone resistance (q_t), sleeve friction (f_s) and pore pressure (u_2) are measured and described in conjunction with core samples to further validate subsurface lithology. An important aspect of this process concerns the estimation of index properties (undrained shear strength, relative density, overconsolidation ratio, etc.). Specifically, CPTu index properties and undrained shear strength are derived from empirical relationships between basic CPT parameters (q_t, f_s, u_2) and lab tests that are conducted on core samples [150]. Based on these relationships, indicative cone factor values (N_{kt}, N_{ke}, $N_{\Delta u}$) have been estimated for different sediment types (stiff clays, overconsolidated clays, etc.); however, variations are observed among studies, probably due to differences in laboratory testing (triaxial tests, simple shear, vane shear test, etc.) as well as sample disturbance. In marine environments, it is typical to use the relationship with net cone resistance (N_{kt}) since it accounts for pore pressure effects.

Due to the variation when estimating cone factor values, it is often appropriate to present indicative ranges for sediment types rather than a single value; nonetheless, Robertson and Cabal [151] have suggested an average N_{kt} value of 14 for unknown sedimentary deposits. In that respect, direct estimation of undrained shear strength from CPTu can indicate trends of increase or decrease; however, it cannot provide reliable estimations. An average cone factor value or rather any value produced in a study may not reflect the regional conditions at another site; therefore, core sampling and testing will need to be continuously conducted so that correlations can be established [152]. Moreover, proper core sampling and testing becomes even more crucial in terms of obtaining consistent cone factor values for a site. The process of correlating CPTu index parameters with lab tests is also relevant for other properties such as the overconsolidation ratio, unit weight, relative density, etc. The direct application of CPTu index profiles without adequate lab testing can lead to overestimations or underestimations of soil properties; therefore, it is necessary to establish sufficient correlations for in situ readings so that reliable interpretations can be made [152,153]. In the Aegean and Ionian Seas, CPT correlations of index properties have not been published; however, existing geotechnical data from surveys that have conducted CPT tests adjacent to core sampling sites could produce a preliminary dataset of undrained shear strength measurements and indicative N_{kt} cone factor values.

5. Discussion

This review examined marine geotechnical studies in the Aegean and Ionian Sea. It is evident from Figure 2 that the central and eastern parts of the Aegean Sea lack any geotechnical study that could support information regarding the sediment composition, at least of the topmost seabed layers, or geohazards. Also, the eastern Aegean Sea islands (of the North Aegean and Dodecanese) are at the frontline of future power and communication interconnections and of other potential offshore works (i.e., locations for floating wind farms), highlighting a shortfall of geological information that could aid desktop and front-end engineering design studies. It is notable that due to the generally limited geotechnical information, supplementary interpretations from geological studies, specifically regarding lithostratigraphy, have been necessary to provide a comprehensive picture of the distribution and importance of weak layers for sediment instabilities (Table 1). The term "weak" is a general and ambiguous term; however, it reflects certain distinct attributes in relation to overlying and underlying strata, such as a low shear strength, low bulk density and high water content. The most prominent layers exhibiting weak behavior are S1 sapropels, underconsolidated deltaic layers deposited under rapid sedimentation rates, tephra (intermixed or intercalated) and loosely packed turbidites. Examination of the factors affecting slope stability in the Aegean and Ionian Seas has proven that seismic activity is the most important triggering mechanism (e.g., refs. [14,25,29]). In the context of the factors affecting the strength of slope sediments, gas-charged sediments, steep fault escarpments and liquefaction of coastal, shallow-seated sandy horizons also contribute to the initiation of mass failures. The distribution of gravitative mass events has been documented with seismic profiling mainly in slope and basin environments, but also along coastal areas fed by fluvial/deltaic sediments; however, an important parameter that may facilitate geohazards assessments is the frequency of such processes [154]. This has been demonstrated by the assessment of long core samples, followed by continuous multi-sensor core logging (MSCL) readings, where turbiditic deposition can be distinguished from hemipelagic sedimentation. Another element is the correlation of cable failures with mass movement, or any other process that may compromise seabed infrastructure, which can be used as a proxy for assessing the frequency of submarine landslides. An example of such an archive can be found in the Gulf of Corinth [14,71,155]. Based on the above, direct sediment sampling of weak layers and laboratory measurements could shed light on the detection of potential failure planes along sloping environments and on the mechanisms governing mass movements [156].

In the case of slope stability estimations, the infinite slope stability method is the most common, followed by the normalized soil parameter. The latter method is considered a more sophisticated approach in slope stability estimation; however, since it necessitates triaxial testing, it is generally rare and has been implemented only by a few studies in Greece [31,41]. To assess slope stability, shear strength profiles in slope environments are necessary as well as relatively deeper core sampling.

Regarding shear strength measurements, these are important in identifying weak zones within the sedimentary column as well as for slope stability estimation. In the case of CPTu shear strength estimation, no correlations have been established between CPTs and lab tests of shear strength, or any index property for that matter. Moreover, profiles of basic parameters also necessitate some validation from nearby core specimens, especially for establishing a reliable interpretation of soil behavior charts. This is particularly important for mixed sediments, where the CPT response may be less clear [151]. Based on the above, it should be emphasized that direct CPT index property data should be used carefully when assessing engineering conditions. The CPT can be a very useful tool; however, additional sampling is needed to establish more robust interpretations of soil strata. This also concerns the development of indicative or rather site-specific cone factor ranges, so that a priori in situ knowledge of fine-grained sediments can be established.

Another important aspect regarding shear strength is the type of laboratory test used to assess the strengths of sediments. The pocket penetrometer and the field vane test are simple, cheap and easy to use; however, other tests mentioned may produce relatively more reliable results of shear strength. This, however, is difficult to assess without some level of cross-validation. In the case of the laboratory vane apparatus, it is advised that its usage is strictly limited to soft clays; hence, application on sandy/silty clays may produce unreliable estimations. The handling of specimens also becomes an issue when estimating shear strength. This is particularly relevant for triaxial testing and/or direct shear tests.

6. Prospects and Concluding Remarks

Offshore projects are initially based on well-documented desktop studies, which rely on the availability of public or private geotechnical and geophysical datasets. In Greece, numerous marine surveys have been carried out, principally for submarine power and fiber optic links between islands and the mainland, but also for pipelines or big port construction/extension or other infrastructures, from private companies. Unfortunately, the original or interpreted data from these surveys are under a classified status; hence, they are not available to public universities/institutions for scientific inspection. Moreover, other public data are not accessible since there is no established procedure for officially requesting or even purchasing them. Addressing issues in geotechnical surveying and interpretation can be managed by developing an open-access policy regarding the dissemination of data, which can be controlled by a certain governmental authority, thus allowing for a more systematic recording of geotechnical information. The issues regarding CPTu index validation and ground-truthing can be examined thoroughly through the collation of data, where comparisons can be made on a regional and national level. This becomes even more relevant, or even essential, when considering the planned offshore projects (OWF, cables, pipelines) in the Aegean Sea [3,157].

Examples of open-access data policies can be found in the Netherlands, which has allowed for the development of geodatabases for the Dutch section of the North Sea [158]. The databases provide information on borehole data, seismic reflection profiles (2D and 3D), CPTu tests and core samples. Specifically, a large database (BRO database) has been created, where information from other databases has been collated, harmonized and processed, according to INSPIRE European Directive stipulations [159]. The BRO database has assisted in many offshore operations, such as installation of monopiles, predictions of seabed mobility and seismic integration with borehole data/in situ tests [158,160]. Furthermore, the application of neural networks and machine learning can also be tested with the utilization of integrated data from seismic and CPTu profiles or laboratory measurements, thus producing synthetic CPT records of known sedimentary strata in the process [160]. Additionally, site-specific correlations concerning CPTu index parameters can be examined more thoroughly, such as in the case of undrained shear strength [161,162]. The development of such databases has been implemented for the undrained shear strength [141,161–164]. Implementing such inventories can offer insights into the variations that are often exhibited in lab measurement and CPTu testing. Moreover, a priori knowledge can be established, thus enhancing future geotechnical investigations. Additional examples can be found in Ireland, where extensive surveying of the continental shelf has been implemented, followed by open-access documentation. Open-access data have been utilized to designate suitable sites for OWF development on the Irish continental shelf, as well as geotechnical characterization of seismic stratigraphy [165,166].

Based on the above examples, marine geotechnical research requires a more concrete approach in terms of how data are acquired, processed and interpreted. From a European perspective, the EMODnet initiative provides a prime example; however, regarding the Aegean and Ionian Seas, geological data are not extensive. In the case of geotechnical interpretation, the collation and accessibility of survey data, including published information on sedimentary strata, can provide the first step in addressing the issues concerning in situ interpretation, ground-truthing and index property estimation. For these reasons, an open-access data repository may prove instrumental, at least in terms of academic initiatives.

This review examined available published information regarding the geotechnical properties of sediments in the Aegean and Ionian Seas. Due to the limited geotechnical research, geological studies were examined for their contributory role in assessing lithostratigraphy (weak layers), gravitative mass processes and factors that trigger sediment instabilities. Yet, geotechnical analysis of cores and slope stability estimations represent important initiatives in addressing regional geohazards. Within that context, the inclusion of CPTu or other in situ measurements (e.g., SPT) can further enhance the interpretation, followed by a more extensive sampling of the seabed. A database consisting of core descriptions and physical and mechanical properties (e.g., index properties, relative density, shear strength, consolidation properties, etc.) can offer insights into the engineering behavior of sediments and establish a priori knowledge of the seabed.

According to the above, to further advance geotechnical research in the Aegean and Ionia Sea regions, it is necessary to complete the following:

(i) Gather existing data from older public surveys as well as unclassified information from private companies, to construct a marine geological (geotechnical and geophysical) inventory.
(ii) Prioritize areas where scheduled core sampling should take place to eliminate gaps in knowledge for the existing lithological units on the seabed and detect potential weak layers that could act as failure planes, as well as collate records of lithostratigraphy that may lead to weak behavior (sapropels, tephra layers, underconsolidated layers, etc.).
(iii) Adopt a systematic protocol of measurements for a minimum set of of parameters (i.e., undrained shear strength (field or laboratory), bulk density, water content, Atterberg limits, grain size) following international standards (ASTM, BS, etc.) for all the cores collected, to assess the geotechnical behavior of subsurface sediments. This is also important in the context of assessing slope stability.
(iv) Wherever feasible, provide CPTu index correlations of shear strength as well as other properties with lab measurements so that reliable estimations and interpretation of in situ data can be established. In the case of cone factor values (N_{kt}), indicative ranges can be produced and compared among studies (site-specific) so that consistency can be examined. Within that context, the testing method as well as handling of specimens are important.
(v) Finally, the development of an open-access data repository may further improve the above actions, similarly to how other countries have developed their own systems to assess the geotechnical conditions of the seabed. In the case of the Aegean and Ionian Seas, the complex geological regime and the current boom in offshore construction activities make this imperative.

Author Contributions: Conceptualization, T.H.; Methodology, N.-K.C. and T.H.; Writing—Original Draft Preparation, N.-K.C.; Writing—Review and Editing, N.-K.C. and T.H.; supervision, T.H. All authors have read and agreed to the published version of the manuscript.

Funding: This research received no external funding.

Data Availability Statement: Not applicable.

Conflicts of Interest: The authors declare no conflicts of interest.

References

1. Zafeiratou, E.; Spataru, C. Potential economic and environmental benefits from the interconnection of the Greek Islands. *Int. J. Glob. Warm.* **2017**, *13*, 426–458. [CrossRef]
2. Biza, S.; Piromalis, D.; Barkas, D.; Psomopoulos, C.S.; Tsirekis, C.D. Crete—Peloponnese 150kV AC Interconnection. Simulation Results for Transient Phenomena in Main Switches. *Energy Procedia* **2019**, *157*, 1366–1376. [CrossRef]
3. Karystianos, M.E.; Pitas, C.N.; Efstathiou, S.P.; Tsili, M.A.; Mantzaris, J.C.; Leonidaki, E.A.; Voumvoulakis, E.M.; Sakellaridis, N.G. Planning of Aegean Archipelago Interconnections to the Continental Power System of Greece. *Energies* **2021**, *14*, 3818. [CrossRef]
4. Independent Power Transmission Operator (IPTO) Sustainability Report 2022. Available online: https://www.admie.gr/sites/default/files/2023-11/Sustainability-Report-2022.pdf (accessed on 17 July 2024).
5. Papadopoulos, M.; Boulaxis, N.; Tsili, M.; Papathanssiou, S. Interconnection of the Cycladic Islands to the Mainland Grid. In Proceedings of the 5th WSEAS International Conference on Power Systems Electromagnetic Compatibility, Corfu, Greece, 23–25 August 2005.
6. Hatziargyriou, N.D.; Vrontisi, Z.; Tsikalakis, A.G.; Kilias, V. The effect of island interconnections on the increase of Wind Power penetration in the Greek system. In Proceedings of the 2007 IEEE Power Engineering Society General Meeting, Tampa, FL, USA, 24–28 June 2007.
7. Georgiou, P.N.; Mavrotas, G.; Diakoulaki, D. The effect of islands' interconnection to the mainland system on the development of renewable energy sources in the Greek power sector. *Renew. Sustain. Energy Rev.* **2011**, *15*, 2607–2620. [CrossRef]
8. Soukissian, T.H.; Denaxa, D.; Karathanasi, F.; Prospathopoulos, A.; Sarantakos, K.; Iona, A.; Georgantas, K.; Mavrakos, S. Marine Renewable Energy in the Mediterranean Sea: Status and Perspectives. *Energies* **2017**, *10*, 1512. [CrossRef]
9. Vagiona, D.G.; Kamilakis, M. Sustainable Site Selection for Offshore Wind Farms in the South Aegean—Greece. *Sustainability* **2018**, *10*, 749. [CrossRef]
10. Spyridonidou, S.; Vagiona, D.G.; Loukogeorgaki, E. Strategic Planning of Offshore Wind Farms in Greece. *Sustainability* **2020**, *12*, 905. [CrossRef]
11. Katsaprakakis, D.A.; Proka, A.; Zafirakis, D.; Damasiotis, M.; Kotsampopoulos, P.; Hatziargyriou, N.; Dakanali, E.; Arnaoutakis, G.; Xevgenos, D. Greek Islands' Energy Transition From Lighthouse Projects to the Emergence of Energy Communities. *Energies* **2022**, *15*, 5996. [CrossRef]
12. Gkeka-Serpetsidaki, P.; Tsoutsos, T. A methodological framework for optimal sitting of offshore wind farms: A case study on the island of Crete. *Energy* **2022**, *239*, 122296. [CrossRef]
13. Vagiona, D.G.; Alexiou, V. Wind Farm Deployment in Uninhabited Islets: A Case Study the Region of the South Aegean (Greece). *Wind* **2022**, *2*, 451–465. [CrossRef]
14. Ferentinos, G. Offshore geological hazards in the Hellenic arc. *Mar. Georesources Geotechnol.* **1990**, *9*, 261–277. [CrossRef]
15. Hasiotis, T.; Papatheodorou, G.; Ferentinos, G. Geological and man made hazards surveying for laying submarine cables in the Aegean and Ionian seas, Greece. In Proceedings of the International Symposium on Engineering Geology and the Environment, Athens, Greece, 23 June 1997.
16. Young, A.G.; Quiros, G.W.; Ehlers, C.J. Effects of Offshore Sampling and Testing on Undrained Soil Shear Strength. In Proceedings of the Offshore Technology Conferences, Houston TX, USA, 2–5 May 1983.
17. Mascle, J.; Martin, L. Shallow structure and recent evolution of the Aegean Sea: A synthesis based on continuous reflection profiles. *Mar. Geol.* **1990**, *94*, 271–299. [CrossRef]
18. Taymaz, T.; Jackson, J.; McKenzie, D. Active tectonics of the north and central Aegean Sea. *Geophys. J. Int.* **1991**, *106*, 433–490. [CrossRef]
19. Nomikou, P.; Papanikolaou, D. Extension of active fault zones on Nisyros volcano across the Yali-Nisyros Channel based on onshore and offshore data. *Mar. Geophys. Res.* **2011**, *32*, 181–192. [CrossRef]
20. Ocakoğlu, N.; Nomikou, P.; Işcan, Y.; Loreto, M.F.; Lampridou, D. Evidence of extensional and strike-slip deformation in the offshore Gökova-Kos area affected by the July 2017 Mw6.6 Bodrum-Kos earthquake, eastern Aegean Sea. *Geo-Mar. Lett.* **2018**, *38*, 211–225. [CrossRef]
21. Sakellariou, D.; Tsampouraki-Kraounaki, K. Plio-Quaternary Extension and Strike-Slip Tectonics in the Aegean. In *Transform Plate Boundaries and Fracture Zones*; Duarte, J.C., Ed.; Elsevier: Amsterdam, The Netherlands, 2019; Chapter 14, pp. 339–374. ISBN 9780128120644.
22. Papanikolaou, D.; Nomikou, P.; Papanikolaou, I.; Lampridou, D.; Rousakis, G.; Alexandri, M. Active tectonics and seismic Hazard in Skyros Basin, North Aegean Sea, Greece. *Mar. Geol.* **2019**, *407*, 94–110. [CrossRef]
23. Nomikou, P.; Papanikolaou, D.; Lampridou, D.; Blum, M.; Hübscher, C. The active tectonic structures along the southern margin of Lesvos Island, related to the seismic activity of July 2017, Aegean Sea, Greece. *Geo-Mar. Lett.* **2021**, *41*, 49. [CrossRef]
24. Nomikou, P.; Evangelidis, D.; Papanikolaou, D.; Lampridou, D.; Litsas, D.; Tsaparas, Y.; Koliopanos, I.; Petroulia, M. Morphotectonic Structures along the Southwestern Margin of Lesvos Island, and Their Interrelation with the Southern Strand of the North Anatolian Fault, Aegean Sea, Greece. *GeoHazards* **2021**, *2*, 415–429. [CrossRef]
25. Ferentinos, G. Recent gravitative mass movements in a highly tectonically active arc system: The Hellenic Arc. *Mar. Geol.* **1992**, *104*, 93–107. [CrossRef]

26. Hasiotis, T.; Papatheodorou, G.; Ferentinos, G. A high resolution approach in the recent sedimentation processes at the head of Zakynthos Canyon, western Greece. *Mar. Geol.* **2005**, *214*, 49–73. [CrossRef]
27. Hasiotis, T.; Papatheodorou, G.; Charalampakis, M.; Stefatos, A.; Ferentinos, G. High frequency sediment failures in a submarine volcanic environment: The Santorini (Thera) basin in the Aegean Sea. In *Submarine Mass Movements and Their Consequences*; Lykousis, V., Sakellariou, D., Locat, J., Eds.; Advances in Natural and Technological Hazard Research Series; Springer: Dordrecht, The Netherlands, 2007; Volume 27, pp. 309–316.
28. Hasiotis, T.; Papatheodorou, G.; Ferentinos, G. Sediment stability conditions west of Milos Island, west Hellenic Volcanic Arc. In *Submarine Mass Movements and Their Consequences*; Lykousis, V., Sakellariou, D., Locat, J., Eds.; Advances in Natural and Technological Hazard Research Series; Springer: Dordrecht, The Netherlands, 2007; Volume 27, pp. 317–324.
29. Lykousis, V. Submarine slope instabilities in the Hellenic arc region, northeastern Mediterranean Sea. *Mar. Georesources Geotechnol.* **1991**, *10*, 83–96. [CrossRef]
30. Lykousis, V.; Sakellariou, D.; Rousakis, G.; Alexandri, S.; Kaberi, H.; Nomikou, P.; Georgiou, P.; Balas, D. Sediment failure processes in active grabens: The western Gulf of Corinth (Greece). In *Submarine Mass Movements and Their Consequences*; Lykousis, V., Sakellariou, D., Locat, J., Eds.; Advances in Natural Hazards Series; Springer: Dordrecht, The Netherlands, 2007; Volume 27, pp. 297–305.
31. Lykousis, V.; Rousakis, G.; Sakellariou, D. Slope failures and stability analysis of shallow water prodeltas in the active margins of Western Greece, northeastern Mediterranean Sea. *Int. J. Earth Sci. (Geol. Rundsch)* **2009**, *98*, 807–822. [CrossRef]
32. Strozyk, F.; Huhn, K.; Strasser, M.; Krastel, S.; Kock, I.; Kopf, A. New evidence for massive gravitational mass-transport deposits in the southern Cretan Sea, eastern Mediterranean. *Mar. Geol.* **2009**, *263*, 97–107. [CrossRef]
33. Strozyk, F.; Strasser, M.; Förster, A.; Kopf, A.; Huhn, K. Slope failure repetition in active margin environments: Constraints from submarine landslides in the Hellenic fore arc, eastern Mediterranean. *J. Geophys. Res. Solid. Earth* **2010**, *115*, B08103. [CrossRef]
34. Strozyk, F.; Strasser, M.; Krastel, S.; Meyer, M.; Huhn, K. Reconstruction of retreating mass wasting in response to progressive slope steepening of the northeastern Cretan margin, eastern Mediterranean. *Mar. Geol.* **2010**, *271*, 44–54. [CrossRef]
35. Beckers, A.; Hubert-Ferrari, A.; Beck, C.; Papatheodorou, G.; De Batist, M.; Sakellariou, D.; Tripsanas, E.; Demoulin, A. Characteristics and frequency of large submarine landslides at the western tip of the Gulf of Corinth. *Nat. Hazards Earth Syst. Sci.* **2018**, *18*, 1411–1425. [CrossRef]
36. Lykousis, V.; Chronis, G. Mass movements, geotechnical properties and slope stability in the outer shelf—Upper slope, northwestern Aegean Sea. *Mar. Geotechnol.* **1989**, *8*, 231–247. [CrossRef]
37. Perissoratis, C.; Papadopoulos, G. Sediment instability and slumping in the southern Aegean Sea and the case history of the 1956 tsunami. *Mar. Geol.* **1999**, *161*, 287–305. [CrossRef]
38. Chronis, G.; Lykousis, V.; Anagnostou, C.; Karageorgis, A.; Stavrakakis, S.; Poulos, S. Sedimentological processes in the southern margin of the Cretan Sea (NE Mediterranean). *Prog. Oceanogr.* **2000**, *46*, 143–162. [CrossRef]
39. Hasiotis, T.; Papatheodorou, G.; Ferentinos, G. A string of large and deep gas-induced depressions (pockmarks) offshore Killini peninsula, western Greece. *Geo-Mar. Lett.* **2002**, *22*, 142–149. [CrossRef]
40. Hasiotis, T.; Charalampakis, M.; Stefatos, A.; Papatheodorou, G.; Ferentinos, G. Fan delta development and processes offshore a seasonal river in a seismically active region, NW Gulf of Corinth. *Geo-Mar. Lett.* **2006**, *26*, 199–211. [CrossRef]
41. Lykousis, V.; Roussakis, G.; Alexandri, M.; Pavlakis, P.; Papoulia, I. Sliding and regional slope stability in active margins: North Aegean Trough (Mediterranean). *Mar. Geol.* **2002**, *186*, 281–298. [CrossRef]
42. Lykousis, V.; Karageorgis, A.P.; Chronis, G.T. Delta progradation and sediment fluxes since the last glacial in the Thermaikos Gulf and the Sporades Basin, NW Aegean Sea, Greece. *Mar. Geol.* **2005**, *222–223*, 381–397. [CrossRef]
43. Lykousis, V.; Sakellariou, D.; Moretti, I.; Kaberi, H. Late Quaternary basin evolution of the Gulf of Corinth: Sequence stratigraphy, sedimentation, fault-slip and subsidence rates. *Tectonophysics* **2007**, *440*, 29–51. [CrossRef]
44. Kopf, A.; Stegmann, S.; Krastel, S.; Förster, A.; Strasser, M.; Irving, M. Marine deep-water free-fall CPT measurements for landslide characterisation off Crete, Greece (Eastern Mediterranean Sea)-PART 2: Initial data from the western Cretan Sea. In *Submarine Mass Movements and Their Consequences*; Lykousis, V., Sakellariou, D., Locat, J., Eds.; Advances in Natural Hazards Series; Springer: Dordrecht, The Netherlands, 2007; Volume 27, pp. 199–208.
45. Ferentinos, G.; Papatheodorou, G.; Geraga, M.; Christodoulou, D.; Fakiris, E.; Iatrou, M. The Disappearance of Helike-Classical Greece-New Remote Sensing and Geological Evidence. *Remote Sens.* **2015**, *7*, 1263–1278. [CrossRef]
46. Chassefiere, B.; Monaco, A. Role of Organic Matter and Particle Fabric in Mass-Physical and Geotechnical Properties: Implications for Undrained Slumping in Aegean Sea and Ionian Sea Modern Sediments. *Mar. Geol.* **1989**, *87*, 165–182. [CrossRef]
47. Anastasakis, G.C.; Piper, D.J.W. The character of seismo-turbidites in the S-1 sapropel, Zakinthos and Strofadhes basins, Greece. *Sedimentology* **1991**, *38*, 717–733. [CrossRef]
48. Poulos, S.E.; Collins, M.B.; Pattiaratchi, C.; Cramp, A.; Gull, W.; Tsimplis, M.; Papatheodorou, G. Oceanography and sedimentation in the semi-enclosed, deep-water, Gulf of Corinth (Greece). *Mar. Geol.* **1996**, *134*, 213–235. [CrossRef]
49. Moretti, I.; Lykousis, V.; Sakellariou, D.; Reynaud, J.; Benziane, B.; Prinzhoffer, A. Sedimentation and subsidence rate in the Gulf of Corinth: What we learn from the Marion Dufresne's long-piston coring. *Comptes Rendus Geosci.* **2004**, *336*, 291–299. [CrossRef]
50. Roussakis, G.; Karageorgis, A.P.; Conispoliatis, N.; Lykousis, V. Late glacial-Holocene sediment sequences in N. Aegean basins: Structure, accumulation rates and clay mineral distribution. *Geo-Mar. Lett.* **2004**, *24*, 97–111. [CrossRef]

51. Pecker, A.; Teyssandier, J.P. Seismic design for the foundations of the Rion Antirion Bridge. *Proc. Inst. Civ. Eng. Geotech. Eng.* **1998**, *131*, 4–11. [CrossRef]
52. Pecker, A. Enhanced seismic design of shallow foundations: Example of the Rion-Antirion Bridge. In Proceedings of the 4th Athenian Lecture on Geotechnical Engineering, Athens, Greece, 2006.
53. Hasiotis, T.; Papatheodorou, G.; Bouckovalas, G.; Corbau, C.; Ferentinos, G. Earthquake-induced coastal sediment instabilities in the western Gulf of Corinth, Greece. *Mar. Geol.* **2002**, *186*, 319–335. [CrossRef]
54. Stegmann, S.; Kopf, A. Marine deep-water free-fall CPT measurements for landslide characterisation off Crete, Greece (Eastern Mediterranean Sea)-PART 1: A new 4000M Cone Penetrometer. In *Submarine Mass Movements and Their Consequences*; Lykousis, V., Sakellariou, D., Locat, J., Eds.; Advances in Natural Hazards Series; Springer: Dordrecht, The Netherlands, 2007; Volume 27, pp. 199–208.
55. Chtouris, N.K.; Hasiotis, T.; Poulos, A.; Tsavliris, E. Comparison between CPT undrained shear strength and vane test measurements in surficial marine sediments. In Proceedings of the Marine and Inland Waters Research Symposium (HCMR), Porto Heli, Argolida, Greece, 16–20 September 2022.
56. Lykousis, V.; Pechlivanoglou, K. Geotechnical Properties of Shelf Sediments from Aegean Sea. *Rapp. Comm. Int. Mer. Medit.* **1985**, *29*, 2.
57. Lykousis, V. Aspects of the Geotechnical Properties and Sedimentation Mechanisms in the Shelf and Slope of the North Euboikos Gulf (Aegean Sea, Greece). *Thalassographica* **1988**, *11*, 53–63.
58. Collins, M.B.; Lykousis, V.; Ferentinos, G. Temporal variations in sedimentation patterns: NW Aegean Sea. *Mar. Geol.* **1981**, *43*, 39–48. [CrossRef]
59. Cramp, A.; Collins, M.B.; Wakefield, S.J. Sedimentation in the Zakynthos Channel—A Conduit Link to the Hellenic Trench, Eastern Mediterranean. *Mar. Geol.* **1987**, *76*, 71–87. [CrossRef]
60. Cramp, A.; Collins, M. A Late Pleistocene-Holocene Sapropelic Layer in the Northwest Aegean Sea, Eastern Mediterranean. *Geo-Mar. Lett.* **1988**, *8*, 19–23. [CrossRef]
61. Piper, D.J.W.; Perissoratis, C. Late Quaternary Sedimentation on the North Aegean Continental Margin, Greece. *Am. Assoc. Pet. Geol. Bull.* **1991**, *75*, 46–61.
62. Piper, D.J.W.; Perissoratis, C. Quaternary neotectonics of the South Aegean arc. *Mar. Geol.* **2003**, *198*, 259–288. [CrossRef]
63. Collier, R.E.L.; Leeder, M.R.; Trout, M.; Ferentinos, G.; Lyberis, E.; Papatheodorou, G. High sediment yields and cool, wet winters: Test of last glacial paleoclimates in the northern Mediterranean. *Geology* **2000**, *28*, 999–1002. [CrossRef]
64. Anastasakis, G. The anatomy and provenance of thick volcaniclastic flows in the Cretan Basin, South Aegean Sea. *Mar. Geol.* **2007**, *240*, 113–115. [CrossRef]
65. Poulos, S.E. Origin and distribution of the terrigenous component of the unconsolidated sediment of the Aegean floor: A synthesis. *Cont. Shelf Res.* **2009**, *29*, 2045–2060. [CrossRef]
66. Got, H.; Stanley, D.J.; Sorel, D. Northwestern Hellenic Arc: Concurrent Sedimentation and Deformation in a Compressive Setting. *Mar. Geol.* **1977**, *24*, 21–36. [CrossRef]
67. Brooks, M.; Ferentinos, G. Structure and Evolution of the Sporades Basin of the North Aegean Trough, Northern Aegean Sea. *Tectonophysics* **1980**, *68*, 15–30. [CrossRef]
68. Brooks, M.; Ferentinos, G. Tectonics and sedimentation in the gulf of Corinth and the Zakynthos and Kefallinia channels, western Greece. *Tectonophysics* **1984**, *101*, 25–54. [CrossRef]
69. Ferentinos, G.; Brooks, M.; Collins, M. Gravity-Induced Deformation on the North Flank and Floor of the Sporadhes Basin of the North Aegean Trough. *Mar. Geol.* **1981**, *44*, 289–302. [CrossRef]
70. Ferentinos, G.; Collins, M.B.; Pattiaratchi, C.B.; Taylor, P.G. Mechanisms of Sediment Transport and Dispersion in a Tectonically Active Submarine Valley/Canyon System: Zakynthos Straits, NW Hellenic Trench. *Mar. Geol.* **1985**, *65*, 243–269. [CrossRef]
71. Ferentinos, G.; Papatheodorou, G.; Collins, M.B. Sediment transport processes on an active submarine fault escarpment: Gulf of Corinth, Greece. *Mar. Geol.* **1988**, *83*, 43–61. [CrossRef]
72. Maldonado, A.; Kelling, G.; Anastasakis, G. Late Quaternary Sedimentation in a Zone of Continental Plate Convergence—The Central Hellenic Trench System. *Mar. Geol.* **1981**, *43*, 83–110. [CrossRef]
73. Huson, W.J.; Furton, A.R. The Lithinon Slide: A Large Submarine Slide in the south Cretan Trough, Eastern Mediterranean. *Mar. Geol.* **1985**, *65*, 103–111. [CrossRef]
74. Pavlakis, P.; Papanikolaou, D.; Chronis, G.; Lykoussis, B.; Anagnostou, C. Geological structure of inner Messiniakos Gulf. *Delt. Ell. Geol. Etair.* **1989**, *23*, 333–347.
75. Lykousis, V.; Chronis, G. Mechanisms of sediment transport and deposition: Sediment sequences and accumulation during the Holocene on the Thermaikos Plateau, the continental slope, and basin (Sporadhes Basin), Northwestern Aegean Sea, Greece. *Mar. Geol.* **1989**, *87*, 15–26. [CrossRef]
76. Piper, D.J.W.; Kontopoulos, N.; Anagnostou, C.; Chronis, G.; Panagos, A.G. Modern Fan Deltas in the Western Gulf of Corinth, Greece. *Geo-Mar. Lett.* **1990**, *10*, 5–12. [CrossRef]
77. Papatheodorou, G.; Hasiotis, T.; Ferentinos, G. Gas-charged sediments in the Aegean and Ionian Seas, Greece. *Mar. Geol.* **1993**, *112*, 171–184. [CrossRef]
78. Papatheodorou, G.; Ferentinos, G. Submarine ad coastal sediment failure triggered by the 1995, M_s = 6.1 R Aegion earthquake Gulf of Corinth, Greece. *Mar. Geol.* **1997**, *137*, 287–304. [CrossRef]

79. Hasiotis, T.; Papatheodorou, G.; Kastanos, N.; Ferentinos, G. A pockmark field in the Patras Gulf (Greece) and its activation during the 14/7/93 seismic event. *Mar. Geol.* **1996**, *130*, 333–344. [CrossRef]
80. Poulos, S.E.; Lykousis, V.; Collins, M.B.; Rohling, E.J.; Pattiaratchi, C.B. Sedimentation processes in a tectonically active environment: The Kerkyra-Kefalonia submarine valley system (NE Ionian Sea). *Mar. Geol.* **1999**, *160*, 25–44. [CrossRef]
81. Perissoratis, C.; Piper, D.J.W.; Lykousis, V. Alternating marine and lacustrine sedimentation during late Quaternary in the Gulf of Corinth rift basin, central Greece. *Mar. Geol.* **2000**, *167*, 391–411. [CrossRef]
82. Van Andel, T.; Perissoratis, C. Late Quaternary deposition history of the North Evvoikos Gulf, Aegean Sea, Greece. *Mar. Geol.* **2006**, *232*, 157–172. [CrossRef]
83. Iatrou, M.; Ferentinos, G.; Papatheodorou, G.; Piper, D.; Tripsanas, E. Anthropogenic turbidity current deposits in a seismically active graben, the Gulf of Corinth Greece: A useful tool for studying turbidity current transport processes. In *Submarine Mass Movements and Their Consequences*; Lykousis, V., Sakellariou, D., Locat, J., Eds.; Advances in Natural and Technological Hazard Research Series; Springer: Dordrecht, The Netherlands, 2007; Volume 27, pp. 149–157.
84. Papanikolaou, D.; Fountoulis, I.; Metaxas, C. Active faults, deformation rates and Quaternary paleogeography at Kyparissiakos Gulf (SW Greece) deduced from onshore and offshore data. *Quat. Int.* **2007**, *171–172*, 14–30. [CrossRef]
85. Beckers, A.; Hubert-Ferrari, A.; Beck, C.; Bodeux, S.; Tripsanas, E.; Sakellariou, D.; De Batist, M. Active faulting at the western tip of the Gulf of Corinth, Greece, from high-resolution seismic data. *Mar. Geol.* **2015**, *360*, 55–69. [CrossRef]
86. Beckers, A.; Beck, C.; Hubert-Ferrari, A.; Tripsanas, E.; Crouzet, C.; Sakellariou, D.; Papatheodorou, G.; De Batist, M. Influence of bottom currents on the sedimentary processes at the western tip of the Gulf of Corinth, Greece. *Mar. Geol.* **2016**, *378*, 312–332. [CrossRef]
87. Aksu, A.E.; Hall, J.; Yaltirak, C. Giant slope scars and mass transport deposits across the Rhodes Basin, eastern Mediterranean: Depositional and tectonic processes. *Sediment. Geol.* **2021**, *424*, 105979. [CrossRef]
88. Perissoratis, C.; Moorby, S.A.; Papavasiliou, C.; Conan, D.S.; Angelopoulos, I.; Sakellariadou, F.; Mitropoulos, D. The Geology and Geochemistry of the Surficial Sediments Off Thraki, Northern Greece. *Mar. Geol.* **1987**, *74*, 209–224. [CrossRef]
89. Papatheodorou, G.; Ferentinos, G. Sedimentation processes and basin filling depositional architecture in an active assymetric graben: Strava graben, Gulf of Corinth, Greece. *Basin Res.* **1993**, *5*, 235–253. [CrossRef]
90. Kamberis, E.; Rigakis, E.; Tsaila-Monopolis, S.; Ioakim, C.; Sotiropoulos, S. Shallow biogenic gas-accumulations in Late Cenozoic sands of Katakolon peninsula, Western Greece. *Bull. Geol. Soc. Greece* **2000**, *9*, 121–138. [CrossRef]
91. Christodoulou, D.; Papatheodorou, G.; Ferentinos, G.; Masson, M. Active seepage in two contrasting pockmark fields in the Patras and Corinth gulfs, Greece. *Geo-Mar. Lett.* **2003**, *23*, 194–199. [CrossRef]
92. Etiope, G.; Papatheodorou, G.; Christodoulou, D.P.; Ferentinos, G.; Sokos, E.; Favali, P. Methane and hydrogen sulfide seepage in the northwest Peloponnesus petroliferous basin (Greece): Origin and geohazard. *AAPG Bull.* **2006**, *90*, 701–713. [CrossRef]
93. Etiope, G.; Christodoulou, D.; Kordella, S.; Marinaro, G.; Papatheodorou, G. Offshore and onshore seepage of thermogenic gas at Katakolo Bay (Western Greece). *Chem. Geol.* **2013**, *339*, 115–126. [CrossRef]
94. Campos, C.; Beck, C.; Crouzet, C.; Carillo, E.; Van Welden, A.; Tripsanas, E. Late Quaternary paleoseismic sedimentary archive from deep central Gulf of Corinth: Time distribution of inferred earthquake-induced layers. *Ann. Geophys.* **2013**, *56*, 1–15. [CrossRef]
95. De Gelder, G.; Doan, M.L.; Beck, C.; Carlut, J.; Seibert, C.; Feuillet, N.; Carter, G.D.O.; Pechlivanidou, S.; Gawthorpe, R.L. Multi-scale and multi-parametric analysis of Late Quaternary event deposits within the active Corinth Rift (Greece). *Sedimentology* **2021**, *69*, 1573–1598. [CrossRef]
96. Gawthorpe, R.L.; Fabregas, N.; Pechlivanidou, S.; Ford, M.; Collier, R.E.L.; Carter, G.D.O.; McNeill, L.C.; Shillington, D.J. Late Quaternary mud-dominated, sedimentation of the Gulf of Corinth, Greece: Implications for deep-water depositional processes and controls on syn-rift sedimentation. *Basin Res.* **2022**, *34*, 1567–1600. [CrossRef]
97. Proedrou, P.; Papaconstantinou, C. Prinos Basin—A Model for Oil Exploration. *Bull. Geol. Soc. Greece* **2004**, *36*, 327–333. [CrossRef]
98. Karditsa, A. Recent Sedimentation Processes in the Inner Continental Shelf of Alexandroupolis Gulf (North Aegean Sea). Ph.D. Dissertation, National and Kapodistrian University of Athens, Athens, Greece, 2010.
99. Faugeres, L.; Robert, C. Etude sedimentologique et mineralogique de deux forages du golfe Thermaique (Mer Egee). *Ann. Univ. Provence. Geol. Mediter.* **1976**, *3*, 209–218. [CrossRef]
100. Lykousis, V. Sea-level changes and sedimentary evolution during the Quaternary in the northwest Aegean continental margin, Greece. *Spec. Publs. Int. Ass. Sediment.* **1991**, *12*, 123–131.
101. Makrodimitras, G.; Nikitas, A.; Ktenas, D.; Maravelis, A.G.; Rokana, N.M.; Pasadakis, N.; Tartaras, E.; Stefatos, A. Cenozoic Clastic Deposits in the Thermaikos Basin in Northern Greece and Their Reservoir Potential. *Geosciences* **2023**, *13*, 159. [CrossRef]
102. Skampa, E.; Dimiza, M.D.; Arabas, A.; Gogou, A.; Panagiotopoulos, I.P.; Tsourou, T.; Velaora, D.; Karagiorgas, M.; Baumann, K.-H.; Triantaphylou, M.V. The Cretan Basin (South Aegean Sea, NE Mediterranean) in the Early Pliocene: A paleoceanographic reconstruction. *Palaeogeogr. Palaeoclimatol. Palaecol.* **2024**, *640*, 112085. [CrossRef]
103. Aksu, A.E.; Yaşar, D.; Mudie, P.J.; Gillespie, H. Late glacial-Holocene paleoclimatic and paleoceanographic evolution of the Aegean Sea: Micropaleontological and stable isotopic evidence. *Mar. Micropaleontol.* **1995**, *25*, 1–28. [CrossRef]
104. Aksu, A.E.; Yaşar, D.; Mudie, P.J. Origin of late glacial-Holocene hemipelagic sediments in the Aegean Sea: Clay mineralogy and carbonate cementation. *Mar. Geol.* **1995**, *123*, 33–59. [CrossRef]

105. Aksu, A.E.; Yaşar, D.; Mudie, P.J. Paleoclimatic and paleoceanographic conditions leading to development of sapropel layer S 1 in the Aegean Sea. *Palaeogeogr. Palaeoclimatol. Palaeoecol.* **1995**, *116*, 71–101. [CrossRef]
106. Aksu, A.; Jenner, G.; Hiscott, R.N.; Işler, E.B. Occurrence, stratigraphy and geochemistry of Late Quaternary tephra layers in the Aegean Sea and the Marmara Sea. *Mar. Geol.* **2008**, *252*, 174–192. [CrossRef]
107. Giresse, P.; Buscail, R.; Charrière, B. Late Holocene multisource material input into the Aegean Sea: Depositional and post-depositional processes. *Oceanol. Acta* **2003**, *26*, 657–672. [CrossRef]
108. Ehrmann, W.; Schmiedl, G.; Hamann, Y.; Kuhnt, T.; Hemleben, C.; Siebel, W. Clay minerals in late glacial and Holocene sediments of the northern and southern Aegean Sea. *Palaeogeogr. Palaeoclimatol. Palaeoecol.* **2007**, *249*, 36–57. [CrossRef]
109. Ehrmann, W.; Seidel, M.; Schmiedl, G. Dynamics of Late Quaternary North African humid periods documented in the clay mineral record of central Aegean Sea sediments. *Glob. Planet. Chang.* **2013**, *107*, 186–195. [CrossRef]
110. Triantaphyllou, M.V.; Ziveri, P.; Gogou, A.; Marino, G.; Lykousis, V.; Bouloubassi, I.; Emeis, K.-C.; Kouli, K.; Dimiza, M.; Rosell-Melé, A.; et al. Late Glacial–Holocene climate variability at the south-eastern margin of the Aegean Sea. *Mar. Geol.* **2009**, *266*, 182–197. [CrossRef]
111. Geraga, M.; Ioakim, C.; Lykousis, V.; Tsaila-Monopolis, S.; Mylona, G. The high-resolution palaeoclimatic and palaeoceanographic history of the last 24,000 years in the central Aegean Sea, Greece. *Palaeogeogr. Palaeoclimatol. Palaeoecol.* **2010**, *287*, 101–115. [CrossRef]
112. Leontopoulou, G.; Christidis, G.; Geraga, M.; Papatheodorou, G.; Koutsopoulou, E. A novel mineralogical approach for provenance analysis of late Quaternary marine sediments: The case of Myrtoon Basin and Cretan Sea, Aegean, Greece. *Sediment. Geol.* **2019**, *384*, 70–84. [CrossRef]
113. Leontopoulou, G.; Christidis, G.; Rousakis, G.; Müller, N.; Papatheodorou, G.; Geraga, M. Provenance analysis of sediments in the south-east Aegean during the Upper Quaternary: A composite approach based on bulk and clay mineralogy and geochemistry. *Clay Miner.* **2021**, *56*, 229–249. [CrossRef]
114. Got, H.; Monaco, A.; Vittori, J.; Brambati, A.; Catani, G.; Masoli, M.; Pugliese, N.; Zucchi-Stolfa, M.; Belfiore, A.; Gallo, F.; et al. Sedimentation on the Ionian Active Margin (Hellenic Arc)—Provenance of Sediments and Mechanisms of Deposition. *Sediment. Geol.* **1981**, *28*, 243–272. [CrossRef]
115. Anastasakis, G.C.; Stanley, D.J.W. Sapropels and organic-rich variants in the Mediterranean: Sequence development and classification. *Geol. Soc. Lond. Spec. Publ.* **1984**, *15*, 497–510. [CrossRef]
116. Perissoratis, C.; Piper, D.J.W. Age, Regional Variation, and Shallowest Occurrence of S1 Sapropel in the Northern Aegean Sea. *Geo-Mar. Lett.* **1992**, *12*, 49–53. [CrossRef]
117. Anastasakis, G.; Piper, D. Late Neogene evolution of the western South Aegean volcanic arc: Sedimentary imprint of volcanicity around Milos. *Mar. Geol.* **2005**, *215*, 135–158. [CrossRef]
118. Perissoratis, C. The Santorini volcanic complex and its relation to the stratigraphy and structure of the Aegean Arc, Greece. *Mar. Geol.* **1995**, *128*, 37–58. [CrossRef]
119. Nomikou, P.; Carey, S.; Papanikolaou, D.; Croff Bell, K.; Sakellariou, D.; Alexandi, M.; Bejelou, K. Submarine volcanoes of the Kolumbo volcanic zone NE of Santorini Caldera, Greece. *Glob. Planet. Chang.* **2012**, *90–91*, 135–151. [CrossRef]
120. Karstens, J.; Preine, J.; Crutchley, G.J.; Kutterolf, S.; van der Bilt, W.G.M.; Hooft, E.E.E.; Druitt, T.H.; Schmid, F.; Cederstrøm, J.M.; Hübscher, C.; et al. Revised Minoan Eruption Volume as Benchmark for Large Volcanic Eruptions. *Nat. Commun.* **2023**, *14*, 2497. [CrossRef]
121. Karstens, J.; Preine, J.; Carey, S.; Bell, K.L.C.; Nomikou, P.; Hübscher, C.; Lampridou, D.; Urlaub, M. Formation of Undulating Seafloor Bedforms during the Minoan Eruption and Their Implications for Eruption Dynamics and Slope Stability at Santorini. *Earth Planet. Sci. Lett.* **2023**, *616*, 118215. [CrossRef]
122. Conispoliatis, N.; Lykousis, V. Mineralogy of the Surficial Sediments of Kavala Bay, Northern Aegean Sea. *Estuar. Coast. Shelf Sci.* **1986**, *23*, 739–749. [CrossRef]
123. Pehlivanoglou, K. Evros Delta: Evolution of Continental Shelf Sediments. *Mar. Geol.* **1989**, *87*, 27–29. [CrossRef]
124. Perissoratis, C.; Mitropoulos, D. Late Quaternary Evolution of the Northern Aegean Shelf. *Quat. Res.* **1989**, *32*, 36–50. [CrossRef]
125. Pehlivanoglou, K.; Tsirambides, A.; Trontsios, G. Origin and Distribution of Clay Minerals in the Alexandroupolis Gulf, Aegean Sea, Greece. *Estuar. Coast. Shelf Sci.* **2000**, *51*, 61–73. [CrossRef]
126. Kanellopoulos, T.; Angelidis, M.; Karageorgis, A.; Kaberi, H.; Kapsimalis, V.; Anagnostou, C. Geochemical composition of the uppermost prodelta sediments of the Evros River, northeastern Aegean Sea. *J. Mar. Syst.* **2006**, *64*, 63–78. [CrossRef]
127. Kanellopoulos, T.; Kapsimalis, V.; Poulos, S.; Angelidis, M.; Karageorgis, A.; Pavlopoulos, K. The influence of the Evros River on the recent sedimentation of the inner shelf of the NE Aegean Sea. *Environ. Geol.* **2008**, *53*, 1455–1464. [CrossRef]
128. Karditsa, A.; Poulos, S. Sedimentological investigations in ariver-influenced tideless coastal embayment: The case of inner continental shelf of the NE Aegean Sea. *Cont. Shelf Res.* **2013**, *55*, 86–96. [CrossRef]
129. Karageorgis, A.P.; Anagnostou, C.L.; Kaberi, H. Geochemistry and Mineralogy of the NW Aegean Sea Surface Sediments: Implications for River Runoff and Anthropogenic Impact. *Appl. Geochem.* **2005**, *20*, 69–88. [CrossRef]
130. Vakalas, I.; Zanarini, I. Net Transport Processes of Surficial Marine Sediments in the North Aegean Sea, Greece. *J. Mar. Sci. Eng.* **2024**, *12*, 512. [CrossRef]
131. Lykousis, V.; Collins, M.; Ferentinos, G. Modern sedimentation in the N.W. Aegean Sea. *Mar. Geol.* **1981**, *43*, 111–130. [CrossRef]

132. Lykousis, V.; Collins, M. Sedimentary environments in the Northwestern Aegean Sea, identified from sea-bed photography. *Thalassographica* **1987**, *10*, 23–35.
133. Pehlivanoglou, K. Lithology and mineralogy of surface sediments in the vicinity of the Kafireas Strait (Aegean Sea). *Geo-Mar. Lett.* **2001**, *21*, 75–85. [CrossRef]
134. Kapsimalis, V.; Panagiotopoulos, I.P.; Hatzianestis, I.; Kanellopoulos, T.D.; Tsangaris, C.; Kaberi, E.; Kontoyiannis, H.; Rousakis, G.; Kyriakidou, C.; Hatiris, H.A. A screening procedure for selecting the most suitable dredged material placement site at the sea. The case of the South Euboean Gulf, Greece. *Environ. Monit. Assess.* **2013**, *185*, 10049–10072. [CrossRef]
135. Karageorgis, A.; Ioakim, C.; Rousakis, G.; Sakellariou, D.; Vougioukalakis, G.; Panagiotopoulos, I.; Zimianitis, E.; Koutsopoulou, E.; Kanellopoulos, T.; Papatrechas, C.; et al. Geomorphology, sedimentology and geochemistry in the marine area between Sifnos and Kimolos islands, Greece. *Bull. Geol. Soc. Greece* **2016**, *50*, 334–344. [CrossRef]
136. Anagnostou, C.; Richter, D.K.; Riedel, D.; Trapp, T. Recent sediments in the South Cyclades Marine Area, Aegean Sea. *Bull. Geol. Soc. Greece* **1998**, *32*, 193–203.
137. Lykousis, V. Subaqueous bedforms on the Cyclades Plateau (NE Mediterranean)—Evidence of Cretan Deep Water Formation? *Cont. Shelf Res.* **2001**, *21*, 495–507. [CrossRef]
138. Tripsanas, E.K.; Panagiotopoulos, I.P.; Lykousis, V.; Morfis, I.; Karageorgis, A.P.; Anastasakis, A.; Kontogonis, G. Late quaternary bottom-current activity in the south Aegean Sea reflecting climate-driven dense-water production. *Mar. Geol.* **2016**, *375*, 99–119. [CrossRef]
139. IGME (Institute of Geology and Mineral Exploration). *Surficial Sediment Map of the Bottom of the Aegean Sea, Thassos-Samothraki Sheet, Scale 1:200000*; IGME: Thessaloniki, Greece, 1986.
140. Lykousis, V. Prodelta Sediments: Seismic Stratigraphy, Sedimentology, Slope Stability. Ph.D. Dissertation, University of Patras, Patras, Greece, 1990.
141. Lunne, T.; Bere, T.; Andersen, K.; Strandvik, S.; Sjursen, M. Effects of sample disturbance and consolidation procedures on measured shear strength of soft marine Norwegian clays. *Can. Geotech. J.* **2006**, *43*, 726–750. [CrossRef]
142. Lykousis, V.; Ferentinos, G. Submarine slumping and slope stability on the continental slope off Greece in relation with the seismic activity. *Bull. Geol. Soc. Greece* **1988**, *20*, 353–367.
143. Hasiotis, T. Geophysical Prospecting and Geotechnical Conditions of Submarine Slopes in Seismically Active Regions in Greece. Ph.D. Dissertation, University of Patras, Patras, Greece, 2001.
144. Manta, K.; Rousakis, G.; Anastasakis, G.; Lykousis, V.; Sakellariou, D.; Panagiotopoulos, I.P. Sediment transport mechanisms from the slopes and canyons to the deep basins south of Crete Island (southeast Mediterranean). *Geo-Mar. Lett.* **2019**, *39*, 295–312. [CrossRef]
145. Hasiotis, T.; Papatheodorou, G.; Ferentinos, G. Surficial mass movements and submarine slope stability analysis between Kerkyra and Paxi slope (Western Greece slope). *Bull. Geol. Soc. Greece* **2001**, *34*, 663–670.
146. Alves, T.; Lykousis, V.; Sakellariou, D.; Alexandri, S.; Nomikou, P. Constraining the origin and evolution of confined turbidite systems: Southern Cretan margin, Eastern Mediterranean Sea (34°30–36°N). *Geo-Mar. Lett.* **2007**, *27*, 41–61. [CrossRef]
147. Dominey-Howes, D.; Cundy, A.; Croudace, I. High energy marine flood deposits on Astypalaea Island, Greece: Possible evidence for the AD 1956 southern Aegean tsunami. *Mar. Geol.* **2000**, *163*, 303–315. [CrossRef]
148. Morgenstern, N.R. Submarine slumping and initiation of turbidity currents. In *Marine Geotechnique*; Richards, A.F., Ed.; University of Illinois Press: Urbana, IL, USA, 1967; pp. 189–220.
149. Lee, H.; Edwards, B. Regional Method to Assess Offshore Slope Stability. *J. Geotech. Eng.* **1986**, *112*, 489–509. [CrossRef]
150. Lunne, T.; Robertson, P.; Powell, J. *Cone Penetration Testing in Geotechnical Practice*; Blackie Academic: New York, NY, USA; Routledge: London, UK, 1997; pp. 981–989.
151. Robertson, P.; Cabal, K. *Guide to Cone Penetration Testing*, 7th ed.; Greg. Drilling and Testing: Signal Hill, CA, USA, 2023.
152. Been, K.; Quiñonez, A.; Sancio, R.B. Interpretation of the CPT in engineering practice. In Proceedings of the 2nd International Symposium on Cone Penetration Testing, Huntington Beach, CA, USA, 9–11 May 2010.
153. Powell, J.J.M.; Dhimitri, L. Watch out for the Use of Global Correlations and "Black Box" Interpretation of CPTU Data. In *Cone Penetration Testing 2022, Proceedings of the 5th International Symposium on Cone Penetration Testing, Bologna, Italy, 8–10 June 2022*; CRC Press: Boca Raton, FL, USA, 2022.
154. Shan, Z.; Wu, H.; Ni, W.; Sun, M.; Wang, K.; Zhao, L.; Lou, Y.; Liu, A.; Xie, W.; Zheng, X.; et al. Recent Technological and Methodological Advances for the Investigation of Submarine Landslides. *J. Mar. Sci. Eng.* **2022**, *10*, 1728. [CrossRef]
155. Heezen, B.; Ewing, M.; Johnson, G.L. The Gulf of Corinth floor. *Deep-Sea Res.* **1966**, *13*, 381–411. [CrossRef]
156. Gatter, R.; Clare, M.A.; Kuhlmann, J.; Huhn, K. Characterization of weak layers, physical controls on their global distribution and their role in submarine landslide formation. *Earth-Sci. Rev.* **2021**, *223*, 103845. [CrossRef]
157. Peloriadi, K.; Iliadis, P.; Boutikos, P.; Atsonios, K.; Grammelis, P.; Nikolopoulos, A. Technoeconomic Assessment of LNG-Fueled Solid Oxide Fuel Cells in Small Island Systems: The Patmos Isand Case Study. *Energies* **2022**, *15*, 3892. [CrossRef]
158. Peuchen, J.; Gomez Meyer, E. Geo-intelligence from datasets of offshore in-situ tests in public domain. In Proceedings of the 6th International Conference on Geotechnical and Geophysical Site Characterization (ISC2020), Budapest, Hungary, 7–11 September 2020.
159. Peuchen, J.; Meijninger, B.; Brouwer, D. North Sea as geodatabase. *AIMS Geosci.* **2019**, *5*, 66–81. [CrossRef]

160. Peuchen, J.; van Kesteren, W.; Vandeweijer, V.; Carpentier, S.; van Erp, F. Upscaling 1 500 000 synthetic CPTs to voxel XPT models of offshore sites. In Proceedings of the 5th International Conference for Cone Penetration Testing 2022, Bologna, Italy, 8–10 June 2022.
161. Mayne, P.; Peuchen, J. Evaluation of CPTU Nkt cone factor for undrained shear strength of clays. In *Cone Penetration Testing 2018 (CPT'18)*; Hicks, M.A., Pisanó, F., Peuchen, J., Eds.; Delft University of Technology: Delft, The Netherlands, 2018; pp. 423–429.
162. Mayne, P.; Peuchen, J. Undrained shear strength of clays from piezocone tests: A database approach. In Proceedings of the 5th International Conference for Cone Penetration Testing 2022, Bologna, Italy, 8–10 June 2022.
163. Karlsrud, K.; Lunne, T.; Kort, D.; Strandvik, S. CPTU correlations for clays. In Proceedings of the 16th International Conference on Soil Mechanics and Geotechnical Engineering, Osaka, Japan, 12–16 September 2005.
164. Paniagua, P.; D'Ignazio, M.; L'Heureux, J.-S.; Lunne, T.; Karlsrud, K. CPTU correlations for Norwegian clays: An update. *AIMS Geosci.* **2019**, *5*, 82–103. [CrossRef]
165. Coughlan, M.; Wheeler, A.J.; Dorschel, B.; Long, M.; Doherty, P.; Mörz, T. Stratigraphic model of the Quaternary sediments of the Western Irish Sea Mud Belt from core, geotechnical and acoustic data. *Geo-Mar. Lett.* **2019**, *39*, 223–237. [CrossRef]
166. Coughlan, M.; Long, M.; Doherty, P. Geological and geotechnical constraints in the Irish Sea for offshore renewable energy. *J. Maps* **2020**, *16*, 420–431. [CrossRef]

MDPI AG
Grosspeteranlage 5
4052 Basel
Switzerland
Tel.: +41 61 683 77 34

Journal of Marine Science and Engineering Editorial Office
E-mail: jmse@mdpi.com
www.mdpi.com/journal/jmse

www.ingramcontent.com/pod-product-compliance
Lightning Source LLC
Chambersburg PA
CBHW061845210926
51850CB00006B/976
* 9 7 8 3 7 2 5 8 6 9 2 0 6 *